Rules for Categorical Syllogisms

Rule 1: The middle term must be distributed at least once.

Fallacy: Undistributed middle

Rule 2: If a term is distributed in the conclusion, then it must be distributed in a premise.

Fallacy: Illicit major; illicit minor

Rule 3: Two negative premises are not allowed.

Fallacy: Exclusive premises

Rule 4: A negative premise requires a negative conclusion, and a negative conclusion requires a negative premise.

Fallacy: Drawing an affirmative conclusion from a negative premise; drawing a negative conclusion from affirmative premises

Rule 5: If both premises are universal, the conclusion cannot be particular.

Fallacy: Existential fallacy

NOTE: If only Rule 5 is broken, the syllogism is valid from the Aristotelian standpoint if the critical term denotes actually existing things.

Truth Tables for the Propositional Operators

p	q	$\sim p$	$p \cdot q$	$p \vee q$	$p \supset q$	$p \equiv q$
T	T	F	T	T	T	T
T	F	F	F	T	F	F
F	T	T	F	T	T	F
F	F	T	F	F	T	T

Rules for the Probability Calculus

1. $P(A \text{ or not } A) = 1$
2. $P(A \text{ and not } A) = 0$
3. $P(A \text{ and } B) = P(A) \times P(B)$ (when A and B are independent)
4. $P(A \text{ and } B) = P(A) \times P(B \text{ given } A)$
5. $P(A \text{ or } B) = P(A) + P(B)$ (when A and B are mutually exclusive)
6. $P(A \text{ or } B) = P(A) + P(B) - P(A \text{ and } B)$
7. $P(A) = 1 - P(\text{not } A)$

Tap into **engagement**

MindTap empowers you to produce your best work—consistently.

MindTap is designed to help you master the material. Interactive videos, animations, and activities create a learning path designed by your instructor to guide you through the course and focus on what's important.

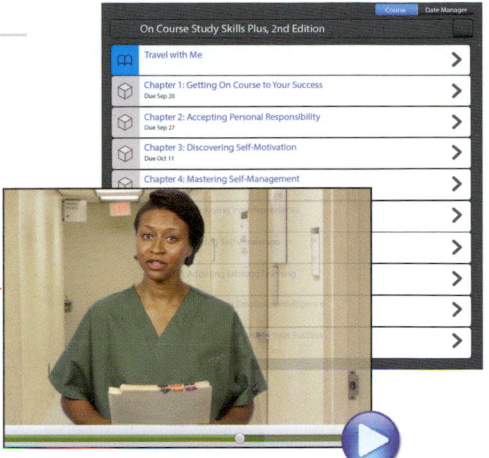

MindTap delivers real-world activities and assignments

that will help you in your academic life as well as your career.

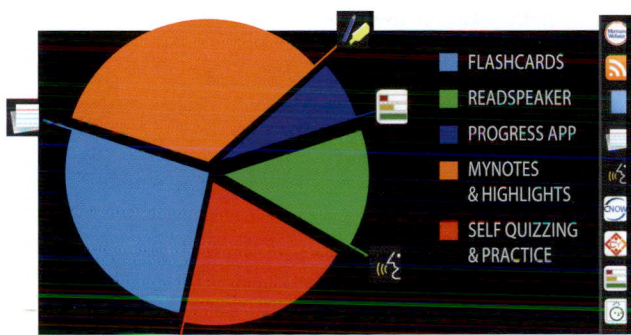

FLASHCARDS
READSPEAKER
PROGRESS APP
MYNOTES & HIGHLIGHTS
SELF QUIZZING & PRACTICE

MindTap helps you stay organized and efficient

by giving you the study tools to master the material.

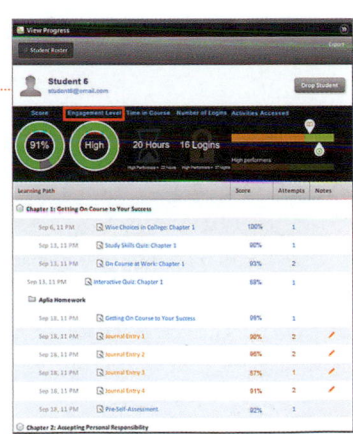

MindTap empowers and motivates

with information that shows where you stand at all times—both individually and compared to the highest performers in class.

"MindTap was very useful – it was easy to follow and everything was right there."
— Student, San Jose State University

"I'm definitely more engaged because of MindTap."
— Student, University of Central Florida

"MindTap puts practice questions in a format that works well for me."
— Student, Franciscan University of Steubenville

Tap into more info at: **www.cengage.com/mindtap**

Engaged with you.
www.cengage.com

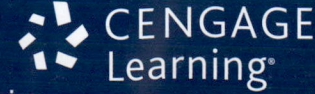

QUICK START GUIDE

1. To get started, navigate to: www.cengagebrain.com and select "Register a Product".

A new screen will appear prompting you to add a Course Key. A Course Key is a code given to you by your instructor - this is the first of two codes you will need to access MindTap. Every student in your course section should have the same Course Key.

2. Enter the Course Key and click "Register".

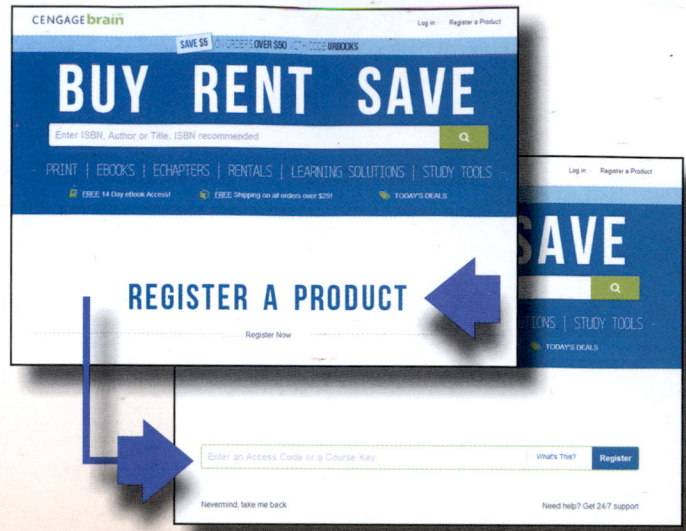

If you are accessing MindTap through your school's Learning Management System such as BlackBoard or Desire2Learn, you may be redirected to use your Course Key/Access Code there. Follow the prompts you are given and feel free to contact support if you need assistance.

3. Confirm your course information above, and proceed to the log in portion below.

If you have a CengageBrain username and password, enter it under "Returning Students" and click "Login". If you are new to the site, register under "New Students" and click "Create a New Account".

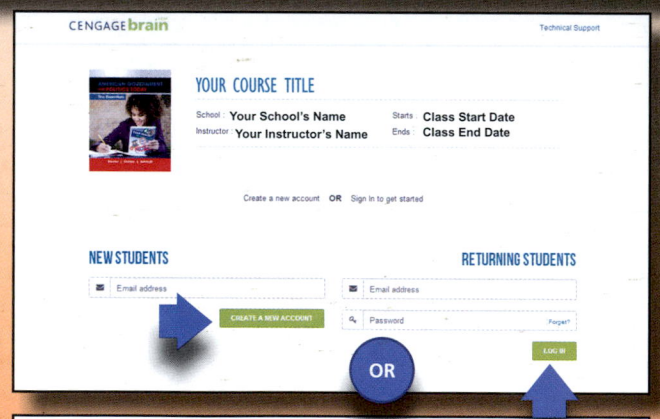

4. Now that you are logged in, you can access the course for free by selecting "Start Free Trial" for 20 days, or enter in your Access Code.

Your Access Code is unique to you and acts as payment for MindTap. You may have received it with your book or purchased it separately in the bookstore or at CengageBrain.com. Enter it and click "Register".

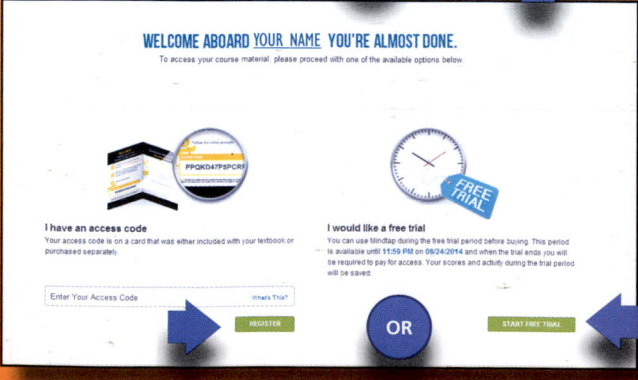

NEED HELP?

For CengageBrain Support: Login to Support.Cengage.com. Call **866-994-2427** or access our **24/7 Student Chat!** Or access the **First Day of School PowerPoint Presentation** found at cengagebrain.com.

aplia™

One million+ students,
one billion answers

In just 10 years, more than one billion answers have been submitted through Aplia, the premier online assignment solution. Millions of students use Aplia to better prepare for class and for their exams. Join them today!

Know what's important
Aplia assignments mean "no surprises"—with an at-a-glance view of current assignments organized by due date, you always know what's due, and when.

Discover real-world relevance
Aplia ties your lessons into real-world applications so you get a bigger, better picture of how you'll use your education in your future workplace.

Master the content
Automatic grading and immediate step-by-step feedback helps you master content the right way the first time.

Aplia Prepares Learners for Tests

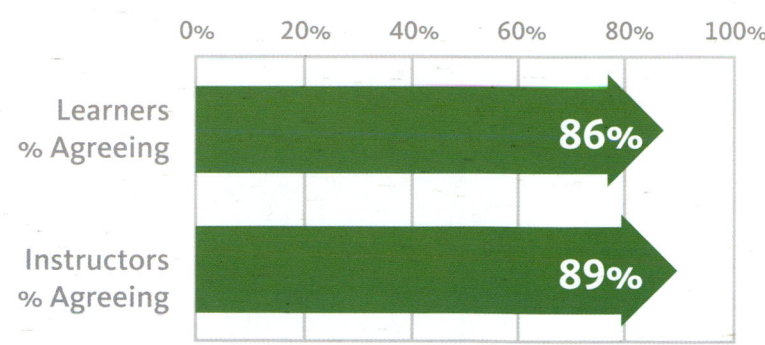

> "I was very engaged; the content in Aplia is useful. The study tools and materials in Aplia most definitely help me feel more prepared. I understood more than I would have otherwise."
>
> **Tia**
> Student, Glendale Community College

Ask your instructor about Aplia for this course.

www.cengage.com/aplia

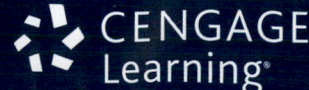
CENGAGE Learning®

LOGIC
THE ESSENTIALS

LOGIC
THE ESSENTIALS

PATRICK J. HURLEY
University of San Diego

CENGAGE
Learning

Australia • Brazil • Mexico • Singapore • United Kingdom • United States

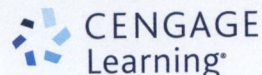

Logic: The Essentials
Patrick J. Hurley

Product Director: Suzanne Jeans

Product Manager: Debra Matteson

Content Developer: Florence Kilgo

Associate Content Developer: Joshua Duncan

Marketing Manager: Christine Sosa

Senior Content Project Manager: Cathie DiMassa

Art Director: PreMedia Global

Manufacturing Planner: Sandee Milewski

Rights Acquisition Specialist: Shalice
Shah-Caldwell

Production Service: Greg Hubit Bookworks

Copy Editor: Marne Evans

Proofreader: Debra Nichols

Text and Cover Designer: PreMedia Global

Cover Image: © fzd.it/Shutterstock

Chapter-opening and front-matter graphics:
Lock and key, © Anna Mari-West/Shutterstock.com;
striped motif, © Nik Merkulov/Shutterstock.com

Summary graphic: © Anna Mari-West/Shutterstock.com

Compositor: MPS Limited

For product information and technology assistance, contact us at
Cengage Learning Customer & Sales Support, 1-800-354-9706.

For permission to use material from this text or product,
submit all requests online at **www.cengage.com/permissions**.
Further permissions questions can be emailed to
permissionrequest@cengage.com.

Library of Congress Control Number: 2014944051

ISBN-13: 978-1-305-07092-9

ISBN-10: 1-305-07092-5

Cengage Learning
200 First Stamford Place, 4th Floor
Stamford, CT 06902
USA

Cengage Learning is a leading provider of customized learning solutions with office locations around the globe, including Singapore, the United Kingdom, Australia, Mexico, Brazil and Japan. Locate your local office at **international.cengage.com/region**.

Cengage Learning products are represented in Canada by Nelson Education, Ltd.

For your course and learning solutions, visit **www.cengage.com**.
Purchase any of our products at your local college store
or at our preferred online store **www.cengagebrain.com**.
Instructors: Please visit **login.cengage.com** and log in to access instructor-specific resources.

Printed in the United States of America
1 2 3 4 5 6 7 18 17 16 15 14

To my mother, Maggie Hurley,
in celebration of her 105th birthday

Brief Contents

Contents

Preface

The most immediate benefit derived from the study of logic is the skill needed to construct sound arguments of one's own and to evaluate the arguments of others. In accomplishing this goal, logic instills a sensitivity for the formal component in language, a thorough command of which is indispensable to clear, effective, and meaningful communication. On a broader scale, by focusing attention on the requirement for reasons or evidence to support our views, logic provides a fundamental defense against the prejudiced and uncivilized attitudes that threaten the foundations of our democratic society. Finally, through its attention to inconsistency as a fatal flaw in any theory or point of view, logic proves a useful device in disclosing ill-conceived policies in the political sphere and, ultimately, in distinguishing the rational from the irrational, the sane from the insane.

About *Logic: The Essentials*

Logic: The Essentials concentrates on the essentials of introductory logic. It is practical in orientation and content, and is loaded with class-tested, proven practice exercises. The book is tailored to address the needs of many of today's instructors who are challenged by time constraints but yet want to instill in their students a solid grasp of basic logical principles and the requisite skill to apply them in everyday life. This new text is based on the classic and best-selling textbook *A Concise Introduction to Logic*, and nearly all of the exercises in the correlative chapters, so central to the effectiveness of that text, have been retained to ensure more than enough practice for students to master the central concepts. The text focuses largely on deductive logic, but it contains sufficient treatment of induction to provide a solid footing for informal fallacies. The result is a contemporary approach—more focused, more practical, less theoretical—built on a tradition of precise, elegant, and clear presentation of the subject matter of logic, both formal and informal.

The text pedagogy is designed to make sure the main points are always presented up front so students cannot miss them, the prose is clear and uncomplicated, and excess verbiage and peripheral subject matter are avoided. To accomplish these and other related goals, the following pedagogical devices are used in the text:

- Section-opening Previews induce students to start thinking about the material that follows by connecting the section content to real-life scenarios pertinent to students' lives.

- Important terms, principles, and bits of advice are stated in marginal boxes.

- Chapters are organized so that earlier sections provide the foundation for later ones. Later sections can be skipped by instructors opting to do so.

- Relevant and up-to-date examples are used extensively.

- Key terms are introduced in boldface type and defined in the Glossary/Index.

- Central concepts are illustrated in graphic boxes.

- Numerous exercises, many drawn from real-life sources such as newspapers, textbooks, and magazines, are included to perfect student skills.

- Biographical vignettes of prominent logicians are included to give logic a human face.

- Dialogue exercises illustrate the application of logical principles to real-life situations.

- Venn diagrams for syllogisms are presented in a novel and more effective way, using color to identify the relevant areas.

- End-of-chapter summaries facilitate student review.

- Every third exercise is answered in the back of the book so students can check their work.

- Important rules and tables are printed on the inside covers for ready access, and are also presented on a tear-out card.

Digital Solutions for Students and Instructors

MindTap is a personalized digital learning platform that offers an interactive eBook, a tutorial program, and homework all in one place. Specifically, MindTap includes the MindTap Reader™ (the interactive eBook), *Learning Logic* (the tutorial program), Aplia™ (which provides robust homework assignments), and video lectures (devoted to conceptually difficult topics). For more details about this new digital solution, see the Note to the Student, Note to the Instructor, and Digital Options sections later in this preface.

On our Instructor Companion Website, instructors will find all the tools they need to teach a rich and successful introductory logic course. The protected teaching materials include an **Instructor's Manual**, which contains answers to all textbook exercises; **Lecture Slides**, customizable to fit your particular needs; and a set of image slides that contains all of the photos and art from the text. Also included is the extensive author-created **Test Bank**. The multiple-choice tests, which are machine-gradable, can be a great time saver, and they match the Practice Tests available to the students in MindTap in length and format. The Test Bank, named Cengage Learning Testing, is powered by Cognero®, an online testing system that allows you to author, edit, and manage Test-Bank content. You can create multiple test versions and instantly deliver them through your Learning Management System (LMS) from your classroom, or wherever you may be, with no special installations or downloads required.

Note to the Student

Imagine that you are interviewing for a job. The person across the desk asks about your strengths, and you reply that you are energetic, enthusiastic, and willing to work long hours. Also, you are creative and innovative, and you have good leadership skills. Then the interviewer asks about your weaknesses. You hadn't anticipated this question, but after a moment's thought you reply that your reasoning skills have never been very good.

> The interviewer quickly responds that this weakness could create big problems.
>
> "Why is that?" you ask.
>
> "Because reasoning skills are essential to good judgment. And without good judgment your creativity will lead to projects that make no sense. Your leadership skills will direct our other employees in circles. Your enthusiasm will undermine everything we have accomplished up until now. And your working long hours will make things even worse."
>
> "But don't you think there is some position in your company that is right for me?" you ask.
>
> The interviewer thinks for a moment and then replies, "We have a competitor on the other side of town. I hear they are hiring right now. Why don't you apply with them?"

The point of this brief dialogue is that good reasoning skills are essential to doing anything right. The business person uses reasoning skills in writing a report or preparing a presentation; the scientist uses them in designing an experiment or clinical trial; the department manager uses them in maximizing worker efficiency; the lawyer uses them in composing an argument to a judge or jury. And that's where logic comes in. The chief purpose of logic is to develop good reasoning skills. In fact, logic is so important that when the liberal arts program of studies was formulated fifteen hundred years ago, logic was selected as one of the original seven liberal arts. Logic remains to this day a central component of a college or university education.

From a more pragmatic angle, logic is important to earning a good score on any of the several tests required for admission to graduate professional schools—the LSAT, GMAT, MCAT, and GRE. Obviously, the designers of these tests recognize that the ability to reason logically is a prerequisite to success in these fields. Also, logic is a useful tool in relieving what has come to be called math anxiety. For whatever reason, countless students today are terrified of any form of reasoning that involves abstract symbols. If you happen to be one of these students, you should find it relatively easy to master the use of logical symbols, and your newly found comfort with these symbols will carry over into the other, more difficult fields.

Before commencing your study of logic, be sure to check out MindTap (www.cengage .com/mindtap). This highly robust Internet platform supports all of the supplements that accompany your textbook. It has the advantage of being able to play on any Internet-enabled device including desktops, laptops, and mobile devices, which allows you to learn anywhere, at any time, and on your terms. Some of the products offered on MindTap are *Learning Logic*, a set of video lectures that presents challenging subjects in logic, an eBook (MindTap Reader) containing everything in the textbook, and practice tests for every chapter. Also available is a supplement called Logic and Graduate-Level Admission Tests, which shows how the principles you will learn in studying logic can be used to answer questions on the LSAT, GMAT, MCAT, and GRE.

Among the MindTap offerings that I would especially urge you to investigate is *Learning Logic*. This is an interactive tutorial program that virtually teaches the entire course in a very user-friendly way. It tracks the textbook chapter by chapter, but your computer must be equipped with speakers or headphones, because the audio component is essential.

Because proficiency in logic involves developing a skill, it helps to work through the practice problems in *Learning Logic* and the exercises in the textbook more than once. This will help you see that good reasoning (and bad reasoning, too) follows certain patterns whose identification is crucial to success in logic. As you progress, I think you will find that learning logic can be lots of fun, and working with the online resources of MindTap should enhance your overall learning experience.

Note to the Instructor

Logic: The Essentials is in part an abridged version of *A Concise Introduction to Logic*. The approach taken in writing *Logic: The Essentials* was to cut material that, for lack of time, is often skipped over in class, but to retain material devoted to central topics and nearly all the correlative exercises. Also retained are the successful pedagogical features such as the biographical vignettes of prominent logicians and the section-opening "previews," which instructors can use as springboards for class discussion. The goal was to focus on the *essential* content most often covered in standard introductory logic courses.

For those of you familiar with my original text, topics that I have removed for the purposes of this new presentation include diagramming extended arguments, meaning and definition, the last two sections of predicate logic, and all the final chapters on induction. Also eliminated are certain redundant techniques including the two-circle Venn method for testing immediate inferences (which back up the two squares of opposition), and the Venn method for testing sorites (which backs up the far-simpler rules method). But two-circle Venn diagrams are retained for many purposes related to categorical propositions, and, of course, three-circle Venn diagrams are retained for categorical syllogisms.

A second group of materials not included in this new volume are topics of chiefly peripheral or theoretical interest. These include the use of conversion, obversion, and contraposition in multistep proofs, the use of Venn diagrams to prove the traditional square of opposition, the section related to proving the rules for categorical syllogisms, and several of the paragraphs comparing the meaning of the propositional operators with ordinary language.

As noted earlier, an important digital asset that accompanies this book is MindTap, a personalized digital learning platform that offers an interactive eBook, a tutorial program, and homework all in one place. See the Digital Options section for help in deciding which digital assets you want your students to access.

One of the more noteworthy offerings on MindTap is *Learning Logic*. This tutorial program virtually teaches the course, and it is especially helpful for students who have difficulty mastering logical principles directly from the textbook or from classroom lectures alone. *Learning Logic* contains over two thousand practice problems not contained in the textbook, and students get immediate feedback for correct and incorrect answers.

Another great product available on MindTap is Aplia™, an online homework program that improves student comprehension by increasing effort and engagement. Students get immediate feedback on their work—not only what they got right or wrong—but *why*; and they can choose to see another set of related problems if they want further practice. Aplia's simple-to-use course management interface allows instructors to post announcements, host student discussions, e-mail students, and manage the grade book. Personalized help is available from a knowledgeable and friendly support team. To learn more, ask your Cengage Learning sales representative for a demonstration, or view a specific demonstration for this book at www.aplia.com.

Another highly useful digital asset is the Instructor Companion Website, which contains the Instructor's Manual and the very substantial Test Bank (Cengage Learning Testing, powered by Cognero) composed by the author. It also includes "Existential Import: Historical Background," a paper written by the author, which provides further explanation of the Aristotelian/Boolean distinction.

While *Logic: The Essentials* is designed to be shorter than many other logic textbooks, it still offers considerable flexibility to the instructor in designing a course. Chapters are organized so that later sections can be skipped by those wishing to do so. For example, the last section of Chapter 2 (Informal Fallacies) can be skipped, those wanting to treat categorical propositions only as an introduction to predicate logic can cover just the first three sections of Chapter 3, and any of the last four sections of Chapter 4 (Categorical Syllogisms) can be skipped. The last two sections of Chapter 5 (Propositional Logic) can be skipped, and those instructors desiring only a touch of predicate logic can skip any of the last three sections of Chapter 7. The restrictions on natural deduction in predicate logic are designed to allow precisely such a treatment.

Digital Options

Logic: The Essentials is available in multiple formats and can be combined with digital solutions in a variety of ways.

1. **Textbook + MindTap.** Includes, in addition to the printed textbook, access to the MindTap course, with *Learning Logic* (the tutorial), Aplia assignments (automatically graded and featuring detailed, immediate feedback on every question), newly reworked videos (covering difficult-to-master topics in logic), chapter learning-path activities, automatically graded quizzes for almost every end-of-section problem in the book, and the full-text interactive eBook (MindTap Reader).

2. **Textbook + Aplia.** Includes, in addition to the printed textbook, access to the Aplia course (with automatically graded assignments featuring detailed, immediate feedback on every question), the course management interface (which allows instructors to post announcements, upload course materials, host student discussions, e-mail students, and manage the grade book), and the full-text interactive eBook (MindTap Reader).

3. **MindTap (alone).** Available with the interactive eBook (MindTap Reader), this option includes everything in Option 1 except the printed textbook. Available only at www.cengagebrain.com, this option can be a cost-saving choice for students.

4. **Aplia (alone).** Available with the interactive eBook (MindTap Reader), this option includes everything in Option 2 except the printed textbook. Available only at www.cengagebrain.com, this option can be a cost-saving choice for students.

5. **Instructor Companion Site.** This password-protected website for instructors features all of the Instructor's Manual, Lecture Slides, and Test Bank delivered via Cognero. Access all of your instructor resources by logging into your account at www.cengage.com/login.

6. **Custom Options.** Cengage Learning offers custom solutions for your course—whether it's making a small modification to *Logic: The Essentials* to match your syllabus or combining multiple sources to create something truly unique. You can also pair your custom text with our digital solutions such as MindTap and Aplia. For more information, visit www.cengage.com/custom.

7. **CengageBrain.** Let this be your students' online source for an à la carte offering of all of the products they need for a successful logic course. Visit www.cengagebrain.com.

Contact your personal Learning Consultant, sites.cengage.com/RepFinder/, for more information about all available options, pricing, and assistance in selecting the best solutions for your students and your course.

Acknowledgments

After several conversations with colleagues and Cengage Learning editors, I decided that the time was right for a more focused and less theoretical textbook that addresses the challenges faced by many instructors in the current teaching environment. Crafting a new book requires help on several fronts. Accordingly, I want to thank the following reviewers for their comments and suggestions:

John Abbarno, D'Youville College; Edward Abplanalp, Illinois Central College; Peter Achinstein, Johns Hopkins University; Thomas Adajian, James Madison University; Rod Adams, Front Range Community College; David Aiken, Gordon College; Torin Alter, University of Alabama, Tuscaloosa; Marcia Andrejevich, Ivy Tech; Benjamin Arah, Bowie State University; Bradley Armour-Garb, University at Albany, SUNY; Aderemi Artis, University of Michigan; Stacie Aubel, College of Southern Maryland; Emil Badici, Texas A&M University, Kingsville; Cathryn Bailey, Minnesota State University, Mankato; Robert Baird, Baylor University; Maria Balcells, Bucknell University; Ida Baltikauskas, Century College; Peter Barry, Saginaw Valley State University; Laura Bathurst, University of the Pacific; Larry Behrendt, Burlington County College; Julie Beier, Earlham College; Linda Beito, Stillman College; Michael Beltz, University of North Dakota; Lisa Bergin, Hamline University; Steve Bie, Glendale Community College, Main; Stephen Billings, Pima Community College, Downtown; David Bishop, Pima Community College, Downtown; Robert Blackburn, Roger Williams University; Jake Blair, California State

University, Hayward; Tara Blaser, Lake Land College; Stephan Blatti, University of Memphis; Macon Boczek, Kent State University, Main Campus; Paul Bohan Broderick, Bridgewater State University; Charles Booher, California State University, Fullerton; Douglas Borcoman, California State University, Dominguez Hills; Gregory Borse, University of Arkansas at Monticello; Teresa Britton, Eastern Illinois University; Paul Broderick, Framingham State University; Michelle Brown, Ohio State University; James Brudvig, Bard College; Frank Thomas Burke, University of South Carolina, Columbia; William Butchard, University of Central Florida; Aaron Butler, Warner Pacific College; Dave Bzdak, Onondaga Community College; Sandy Carden, Owensboro Community College; Chad Carmichael, Indiana University, Purdue University; James Carmine, Chatham College; John Ceballes, University of South Carolina, Columbia; Darron Chapman, Spalding University; Lynette Chen, Humboldt State University; Rick Chew, University of Central Oklahoma; Gladys Childs, Wesleyan University; Dexter Christian, Georgia Perimeter College, Clarkston Campus; Barbara Colby, Arizona State University, Tempe Campus; Julian Cole, SUNY, Buffalo State College; Louis Colombo, Bethune-Cookman University; Howard Congdon, Lock Haven University; Francis Conroy, Burlington Community College; Patricia Cook, United States Naval Academy; Jack Cooney, Ivy Tech; William Cooney, Edison State College, Lee Campus; Alberto Cordero, CUNY, Queens College; William Cornwell, Salem State University; Antonis Coumoundouros, Adrian College; Joshua Crabill, University of Southern California; William Craig, Governors State University; Philip Cronce, Chicago State University; Stephen Crowley, Boise State University; Gillian Crozier, Laurentian University; Micah Daily, Mount St. Mary's College, Doheny Campus; Richard Daims, California State University, Dominguez Hills; Drew Dalton, Florida Southern College; Stuart Dalton, Western Connecticut State University; Darian De Bolt, University of Central Oklahoma; William Desmond, Black Hawk College; William Devlin, Bridgewater State University; Joshua Dhanens, Arkansas Tech University; Jeremy Dickinson, California Polytechnic State University, San Luis Obispo; Michael Dickson, University of South Carolina, Columbia; Allan Didonato, Central Piedmont Community College; Jill Dieterle, Eastern Michigan University; Aletia Droba, Oakland Community College, Royal Oak; Jeffrey Easlick, Saginaw Valley State University; Kenny Easwaran, University of Southern California; Stacey Edgar, SUNY, Geneseo; James Elser, Arizona State University; Phillip Emerson, Binghamton University; Samantha Emswiler, John Tyler Community College; Edward Engelmann, Bridgewater State University; Joseph Farrell, Morgan State University; Maureen Feder-Marcus, SUNY College at Old Westbury; Sidney Felder, Rutgers University, New Brunswick; Robert Feleppa, Wichita State University; Keith Fennen, Miami University–Oxford; Josephy Ficarrotta, Georgetown University; Patrick Flynn, Benedictine University; Peter Fosl, Transylvania University; Nicholas G. Fotion, Emory University; Craig Fox, California University of Pennsylvania; Barbara Freres, Cardinal Stritch University; Christopher Frey, University of South Carolina, Columbia; Michael Futch, University of Tulsa; Logan Gage, Baylor University; Jonathan Gainor, Harrisburg Area Community College; Scott Galloway, Fullerton College; Paul Gass, Coppin State University; Tom Ghering, Ivy Tech; Arthur Gianelli, St. John's University, Queens Campus; Jake Gibbs, Bluegrass Community Technical College, Cooper; Randall Gibson, Ivy Tech State College, Elkhart County Campus; Edward Glowienka, Emory University; Michael Goodman, Humboldt State University; Matthew Goodwin, Northern Arizona University; Kevin Graham, Creighton University; Robert Graham,

Macomb Community College, Center; Dennis Green, City College of San Francisco, Ocean; Harold Greenstein, SUNY, Brockport; Gene Grey, Orange Coast College; Perry Grosse, Grossmont College; Stephen Grover, Queens College CUNY; Gerald Grudzen, San Jose City College; Arthur Grugan, Holy Family University; Kevin Guilfoy, Carroll University; John Gulley, Piedmont Virginia Community College; Larry Haapanen, Lewis-Clark State College; Brett Hackett, University of Colorado at Denver; Jeremiah Hackett, University of South Carolina, Columbia; Robert Hahn, Southern Illinois University at Carbondale; Matthew Hallgarth, Tarleton State University; Carl Hammer, Baruch College; Michael Hand, Texas A&M University, College Station; Erik Hanson, University of Colorado, Colorado Springs; Gary Hardcastle, Bloomsburg University; Richard Hart, Bloomfield College; Larry Harwood, Viterbo University; James Hawthorne, University of Oklahoma, Norman; Ian Michael Hegger, University of Illinois at Urbana-Champaign; Betina Henig, Lansing Community College; John Hernandez, Palo Alto College; Jacqueline Herrick, Belmont College; Travis Hicks, Merced College; Michael Hickson, Trent University; Eli Hirsch, Harvard University; Barbara Hogan, Antelope Valley College; Rachel Hollenberg, Irvine Valley College; Len Holman, College of the Desert; Matthew Homan, Christopher Newport University; Phillip Honenberger, Rowan University; Jim Hood, Kalamazoo Valley Community College; Steven Hood, University of West Florida; Alex Hooke, Stevenson University; Elizabeth Hoppe, Lewis University; William Horton, Grambling State University; Jeremy Hovda, Minneapolis Community and Technical College; Douglas Howie, North Lake College; Christopher Hudspeth, University of Wisconsin, Parkside; Jarrod Hyam, Humboldt State University; Creed Hyatt, Lehigh Carbon Community College; Daniel Imparato, Nassau Community College; Timothy Irwin, Illinois Central College; Jack Jackson, San Bernardino Valley College; William S. Jamison, University of Alaska; Anthony Jannotta, Bridgewater State University; Georgette Jaworski, University of Wisconsin, Milwaukee; Walter Jeffko, Fitchburg State University; Ralf Jenne, Valencia College, West; Bredo C. Johnsen, University of Houston; Tristan Johnson, Bridgewater State University; Michael Jones, Eastern Michigan University; John Joseph, Rowan University; Vladimir Kalugin, California State University, Northridge; Todd A. Kappelman, Dallas Baptist University; John Kearns, Rowan University; Stephen Kellert, Hamline University; Kevin Kennedy, St. John's University, Queens Campus; Patrick Kenny, Onondaga Community College; Lee Kerckhove, Palomar College; Malek Khazee, California State University, Long Beach; Andrew Khoury, Arizona State University; Robert Kimball, University of Louisville, Medical School; Christopher King, Greenville Technical College; Mary Kay Klein, Bridgewater State University; Paul Klumpe, Bridgewater State University; Gal Kober, Bridgewater State University; Daniel Koltonski, SUNY at Binghamton; Elysa Rachel Koppelman-White, Oakland University; Aaron Kostko, Saginaw Valley State University; Chris Kraatz, Indiana University, Purdue University; David Lambie, Cayuga Community College; Sean Landis, Rowan University; Hyrum Laturner, Dixie State College of Utah; Richard Legum, Kingsborough Community College; Rhona Leibel, Metropolitan State University; Alfred Lent, Ohio University, Main Campus; Edward Lenzo, Colorado State University; Jeff Leon, University of Texas; Gilbert Lepadatu, Georgia Perimeter College, Clarkston Campus; Glenn Lesses, College of Charleston, University of Charleston; Lisa Levers, Auburn University; Ronald Loeffler, Grand Valley State University, Allendale; Lavonna Lovern, Valdosta State University; Dermot Luddy, Bridgewater State University; Amanda Lusky, University of Kentucky; Mark MacDowell, Lourdes University; Ian MacKinnon,

The University of Akron; Darlene Macomber, Brookdale Community College; Kevin Maguire, University of Kentucky; Keya Maitra, University of North Carolina at Asheville; Neil Manson, University of Mississippi; Ned Markosian, Western Washington University; Kraig Martin, Baylor University; George Matthews, Pennsylvania College of Technology; Michael Matthis, Lamar University; Laura McAlinden, Bridgewater State University; Trip McCrossin, Rutgers University, New Brunswick; David McElhoes, University of Maryland, College Park; Graham McFee, California State University, Fullerton; Jon McGinnis, University of Missouri, St. Louis; Mark McIntire, Santa Barbara City College; Thomas McKenna, Concord College; Janice McLane, Morgan State University; Colin McLarty, Case Western Reserve University; Erik Meade, Southwestern Illinois College, Belleville Campus; Kevin Megill, Sauk Valley Community College; Christopher Melley, Sacred Heart University, Fairfield; Christopher Menzel, Texas A&M University, College Station; Andrew Messchaert, Porterville College; Robert Micallef, Madonna University; Orange Coast College; Michael Monge, Long Beach City College; Mathew Morgan, Bakersfield College; Jeremy Morris, Ohio University, Main Campus; Joseph Van De Mortel, Cerritos College; Colleen Moss, California State University, San Marcos; Alexis Mourenza, University of California, Santa Cruz; Robert Muhlnickel, Monroe County Community College; Cecilia Mun, Clemson University; Lori Nash, SUNY, Oswego; Paul Nnodim, Massachusetts College of Liberal Arts; Boyle Noel, Belmont University; Eoin O'Connell, Manhattan College; David O'Connor, Seton Hall University; Michael O'Malley, College of the Canyons; Nicholas Ormes, University of Denver; Charles Otwell, University of California, Irvine; Gary Owens, Harford Community College; Michael Papazian, Berry College; John Pappas, Desales University; Ross Parker, Baylor University; Wendy Parker, Ohio University, Main Campus; Jonathan Parsons, College of Dupage; Krupa Patel, San Jose State University; James Patten, Bridgewater State University; James Pearson, Bridgewater State University; Max Pensky, SUNY, Binghamton; David Pfeifer, Indiana University, Purdue University; Andrew Piker, Texas A&M University; Arthur Pindle, Spelman College; Nathan Poage, Houston Community College, Central; Anna Poetker, Bakersfield College; John Powell, Humboldt State University; Peter Prüim, East Stroudsburg University; Rick Pulling, Ivy Tech; Sebastian Purcell, SUNY, Cortland; Piers J. Rawling, Florida State University; Dwayne Raymond, Texas A&M University, College Station; Michael Reed, Eastern Michigan University; Ray Rennard, University of the Pacific; Philip Ricards, Pasadena City College; Travis Rieder, Georgetown University; David Ring, Orange Coast College; Matthew Roberts, Patrick Henry College; Bobby Robinson, Georgia Perimeter College, Clarkston Campus; Lanei Rodemeyer, Duquesne University; Guy Rohrbaugh, Auburn University; John Rollins, Northern Essex Community College; Michael Rooney, Pasadena City College; Paul Van Rooy, Bridgewater State University; James Roper, Michigan State University; Laura Rosillo, Ivy Tech; Rayka Rush, Metro Community College; Paul Rusnock, University of Ottawa; Matthew Salas, KCTCS Jefferson Community College, Downtown Campus; Rudy Saldana, Citrus College; John Santiago, College of Dupage; Raul Saucedo, Yale University; George Schedler, Southern Illinois University at Carbondale; Mark Schersten, Siena Heights University; Britt-Marie Schiller, Webster University; Jerrod Scott, Brookhaven College; Pauline Scott, Alabama State University; James Scow, Central Virginia Community College; Tal Scriven, California Polytechnic State University, San Luis Obispo; Siobhan Semmett, Wright State University; Colena Sesanker, Three Rivers Community Technical College; Jeffrey Shaw, Bristol Community College, Fall River

Campus; Brendan Shea, Winona State University; Mark Shively, Moorpark College; Allen Shotwell, Ivy Tech; Don Shull, Ivy Tech; Michael Sigman, East Los Angeles College; Matthew Silliman, Massachusetts College of Liberal Arts; Keith Simmons, University of North Carolina at Chapel Hill; Janet Simpson, Suffolk County Community College; Matthew Slater, Bucknell University; Kent Slinker, Pima Community College; Eric Snyder, Ohio State University; Jim Soto, St. Clair Community College; Tom Spademan, Mott Community College; John Spano, Baylor University; Joseph Spencer, Bridgewater State University; Barbara Stallings, Richland College; James Stam, American University, Kogod School of Business; Daniel P. Steel, Michigan State University; Claire Stegman, Wesleyan University; Jerry Steinhofer, Bridgewater State University; Matt Story, University of North Texas; Allesandra Stradella, Emory University; James Stroble, University of Hawaii, Leeward Community College; Alison Suen, Vanderbilt University; John Sullins, Sonoma State University; Weimin Sun, California State University, Northridge; Tim Sundell, University of Kentucky; Corine Sutherland, Golden West College; Jonathan Sutton, Auburn University; Mojgan Taheri, California State University, Northridge; Peter Tan, Mount St. Mary's College, Doheny Campus; R. Gregory Taylor, New Jersey City University; Ed Teall, Mt. St. Mary College; Wanda Teays, Mount St. Mary's College, Chalon Campus; Mark Thames, El Centro College; Joseph Thompson, University of Alaska Fairbanks; Michael Thompson, University of North Texas; Stephen Thompson, William Paterson University; Mark Thorsby, Lone Star College, CyFair; Michael Thune, Joliet Junior College; John J. Tilley, Indiana University, Purdue University; Garrett Timm, Aims Community College; Christopher Tollefsen, University of South Carolina, Columbia; Rene Trujillo, Bakersfield College; James Tullos, Georgia Perimeter College, Clarkston Campus; Jeffrey Turner, University of South Carolina, Columbia; Anand Vaidya, San Jose State University; William Vanderburgh, Wichita State University; Daniel Vecchio, Marquette University; Edgar Velez, Columbus State Community College; Michael Ventimiglia, Sacred Heart University; Donald Phillip Verene, Emory University; Susan Vineberg, Wayne State University; Sandra Visser, Valparaiso University; Mark Vopat, Youngstown State University; Kent Wallace, Bridgewater State University; Daniel Warren, University of California, Berkeley; Frank Waters, Mount St. Mary's College, Chalon Campus; W. Steve Watson, Bridgewater College; Judson Webb, Boston University, Boston; Eric Weber, Illinois Central College; Todd Weber, Monterey Peninsula College; Ronald Weed, University of New Brunswick; Chris Weigand, University of Central Oklahoma; Steven Weimer, Arkansas State University; John Weinberg, University of Arizona; Dennis Weiss, York College of Pennsylvania; Alistair Welchman, University of Texas at San Antonio, 1604 Campus; Clarence White, Ivy Tech Community College, Columbus; Dale Wilkerson, University of North Texas; David William Harker, East Tennessee State University; Derrick Willis, Temple College; Gordon Wilson, University of North Carolina at Asheville; Stephen Wilson, University of Cincinnati, Main Campus; Wayne Wright, University of California, Irvine; Seth Yalcin, University of California, Berkeley; Julie Yoo, California State University, Northridge; Laura Yordy, Bridgewater College; Peter Younger, Baylor University; Jinmei Yuan, Creighton University; Levis Zerpa, University of Kentucky.

Of course any errors or omissions that may remain are the result of my own oversight.

Finally, it has been a pleasure working with product manager Debra Matteson, content developer Florence Kilgo, content project managers Jill Quinn and Cathie DiMassa, production supervisor Greg Hubit, copy editor Marne Evans, proofreader Debra Nichols, and associate content developer Joshua Duncan. Most of all, I want to thank my wife, Linda Peterson, for her countless suggestions and support.

1

Basic Concepts

1.1   Arguments, Premises, and Conclusions

PREVIEW

Suppose a student with whom you are in a long-term relationship happens to see you sitting close to someone else in the library. The person you have been dating for months now accuses you of cheating and threatens to break off the relationship. You, in turn, try to prove that the event in the library was perfectly innocent and amounted to nothing. To do this, you need an argument. In this section you will learn about arguments and their basic components—premises and conclusions.

 **MindTap** *Your personal learning experience—learn anywhere, anytime.*

1

logic: The organized body of knowledge (science) that evaluates arguments.

Logic may be defined as the organized body of knowledge, or science, that evaluates arguments. All of us encounter arguments in our day-to-day experience. We read them in books and newspapers, hear them on television, and formulate them when communicating with friends and associates. The aim of logic is to develop a system of methods and principles that we may use as criteria for evaluating the arguments of others and as guides in constructing arguments of our own. Among the benefits to be expected from the study of logic is an increase in confidence that we are making sense when we criticize the arguments of others and when we advance arguments of our own.

argument: A group of statements, one or more of which (the premises) are claimed to provide support for, or reasons to believe, one of the others (the conclusion).

An argument, in its simplest form, is a group of statements, one or more of which (the premises) are claimed to provide support for, or reasons to believe, one of the others (the conclusion). Every argument may be placed in either of two basic groups: those in which the premises really do support the conclusion and those in which they do not, even though they are claimed to. The former are said to be good arguments (at least to that extent), the latter bad arguments. The purpose of logic, as the science that evaluates arguments, is thus to develop methods and techniques that allow us to distinguish good arguments from bad.

As is apparent from the given definition, the term *argument* has a very specific meaning in logic. It does not mean, for example, a mere verbal fight, as one might have with one's parent, spouse, or friend. Let us examine the features of this definition in greater detail. First of all, an argument is a group of statements. A statement is a sentence that is either true or false—in other words, typically a declarative sentence or a sentence component that could stand as a declarative sentence. The following sentences are statements:

statement: A sentence that is either true or false.

> Chocolate truffles are loaded with calories.
> Melatonin helps relieve jet lag.
> Political candidates always tell the complete truth.
> No wives ever cheat on their husbands.
> Tiger Woods plays golf and Maria Sharapova plays tennis.

truth value: The attribute by which a statement is either true or false.

The first two statements are true, the second two false. The last one expresses two statements, both of which are true. Truth and falsity are called the two possible truth values of a statement. Thus, the truth value of the first two statements is true, the truth value of the second two is false, and the truth value of the last statement, as well as that of its components, is true.

Unlike statements, many sentences cannot be said to be either true or false. Questions, proposals, suggestions, commands, and exclamations usually cannot, and so are not usually classified as statements. The following sentences are not statements:

> Where is Khartoum?   (question)
> Let's go to a movie tonight.   (proposal)
> I suggest you get contact lenses.   (suggestion)
> Turn off the TV right now.   (command)
> Fantastic!   (exclamation)

premises: The statements that set forth the reasons or evidence.

conclusion: The statement that the premises are claimed to support or imply.

The statements that make up an argument are divided into one or more premises and exactly one conclusion. The premises are the statements that set forth the reasons or evidence, and the conclusion is the statement that the evidence is claimed to support or imply. In other words, the conclusion is the statement that is claimed to follow from the premises. Here is an example of an argument:

> All film stars are celebrities.
> Halle Berry is a film star.
> Therefore, Halle Berry is a celebrity.

The first two statements are the premises; the third is the conclusion. (The claim that the premises support or imply the conclusion is indicated by the word "therefore.") In this argument the premises really do support the conclusion, and so the argument is a good one. But consider this argument:

> Some film stars are men.
> Cameron Diaz is a film star.
> Therefore, Cameron Diaz is a man.

In this argument the premises do not support the conclusion, even though they are claimed to, and so the argument is not a good one.

One of the most important tasks in the analysis of arguments is being able to distinguish premises from conclusions. If what is thought to be a conclusion is really a premise, and vice versa, the subsequent analysis cannot possibly be correct. Many arguments contain indicator words that provide clues. Some typical **conclusion indicators** are

therefore	accordingly	entails that
wherefore	we may conclude	hence
thus	it must be that	it follows that
consequently	for this reason	implies that
we may infer	so	as a result

conclusion indicator: A word or phrase that provides a clue for identifying a conclusion.

Whenever a statement follows one of these indicators, it can usually be identified as the conclusion. By process of elimination the other statements in the argument are the premises. Example:

> Tortured prisoners will say anything just to relieve the pain. Consequently, torture is not a reliable method of interrogation.

The conclusion of this argument is "Torture is not a reliable method of interrogation," and the premise is "Tortured prisoners will say anything just to relieve the pain."

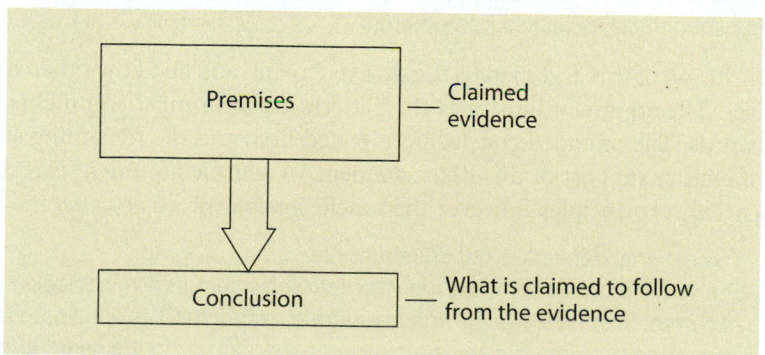

If an argument does not contain a conclusion indicator, it may contain a premise indicator. Some typical **premise indicators** are

since	in that	seeing that
as indicated by	may be inferred from	for the reason that
because	as	in as much as
for	given that	owing to

Any statement following one of these indicators can usually be identified as a premise. Example:

> Expectant mothers should never use recreational drugs, since the use of these drugs can jeopardize the development of the fetus.

The premise of this argument is "The use of these drugs can jeopardize the development of the fetus," and the conclusion is "Expectant mothers should never use recreational drugs."

In reviewing the list of indicators, note that "for this reason" is a conclusion indicator, whereas "for the reason that" is a premise indicator. "For this reason" (except when followed by a colon) means for the reason (premise) that was just given, so what follows is the conclusion. On the other hand, "for the reason that" announces that a premise is about to be stated.

Sometimes a single indicator can be used to identify more than one premise. Consider the following argument:

> It is vitally important that wilderness areas be preserved, for wilderness provides essential habitat for wildlife, including endangered species, and it is a natural retreat from the stress of daily life.

The premise indicator "for" goes with both "Wilderness provides essential habitat for wildlife, including endangered species," and "It is a natural retreat from the stress of daily life." These are the premises. By method of elimination, "It is vitally important that wilderness areas be preserved" is the conclusion.

Some arguments contain no indicators. With these, the reader/listener must ask such questions as: What single statement is claimed (implicitly) to follow from the others? What is the arguer trying to prove? What is the main point in the passage? The answers to these questions should point to the conclusion. Example:

> The space program deserves increased expenditures in the years ahead. Not only does the national defense depend on it, but the program will more than pay for itself in terms of technological spin-offs. Furthermore, at current funding levels the program cannot fulfill its anticipated potential.

The conclusion of this argument is the first statement, and all of the other statements are premises. The argument illustrates the pattern found in most arguments that lack indicator words: The intended conclusion is stated first, and the remaining statements are then offered in support of this first statement. When the argument is restructured according to logical principles, however, the conclusion is always listed *after* the premises:

P_1: The national defense is dependent on the space program.
P_2: The space program will more than pay for itself in terms of technological spin-offs.
P_3: At current funding levels the space program cannot fulfill its anticipated potential.
C: The space program deserves increased expenditures in the years ahead.

When restructuring arguments such as this, one should remain as close as possible to the original version, while at the same time attending to the requirement that premises and conclusion be complete sentences that are meaningful in the order in which they are listed.

Note that the first two premises are included within the scope of a single sentence in the original argument. For the purposes of this chapter, compound arrangements of statements in which the various components are all claimed to be true will be considered as separate statements.

Passages that contain arguments sometimes contain statements that are neither premises nor conclusions. Only statements that are actually intended to support the conclusion should be included in the list of premises. If, for example, a statement serves merely to introduce the general topic, or merely makes a passing comment, it should not be taken as part of the argument. Examples:

> The claim is often made that malpractice lawsuits drive up the cost of health care. But if such suits were outlawed or severely restricted, then patients would have no means of recovery for injuries caused by negligent doctors. Hence, the availability of malpractice litigation should be maintained intact.

> Massive federal deficits push up interest rates for everyone. Servicing the debt gobbles up a huge portion of the federal budget, which lowers our standard of living. And big deficits also weaken the value of the dollar. For these reasons, Congress must make a determined effort to cut overall spending and raise taxes. Politicians who ignore this reality imperil the future of the nation.

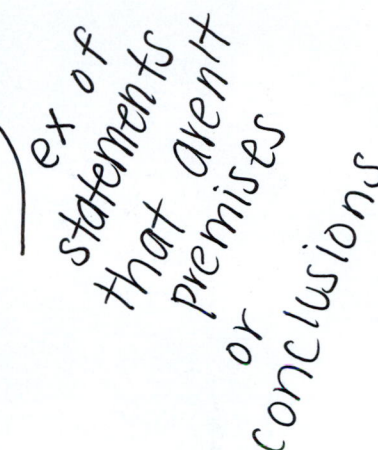 *ex of statements that aren't premises or conclusions*

In the first argument, the opening statement serves merely to introduce the topic, so it is not part of the argument. The premise is the second statement, and the conclusion is the last statement. In the second argument, the final statement merely makes a passing comment, so it is not part of the argument. The premises are the first three statements, and the statement following "for these reasons" is the conclusion.

Closely related to the concepts of argument and statement are those of inference and proposition. An **inference**, in the narrow sense of the term, is the reasoning process expressed by an argument. In the broad sense of the term, "inference" is used interchangeably with "argument." Analogously, a **proposition**, in the narrow sense, is the meaning or information content of a statement. For the purposes of this book, however, "proposition" and "statement" are used interchangeably.

Note on the History of Logic

The person who is generally credited as the father of logic is the ancient Greek philosopher Aristotle (384–322 B.C.). Aristotle's predecessors had been interested in the art of constructing persuasive arguments and in techniques for refuting the arguments of others, but it was Aristotle who first devised systematic criteria for analyzing and evaluating arguments.

Aristotle's chief accomplishment is called **syllogistic logic**, a kind of logic in which the fundamental elements are *terms,* and arguments are evaluated as good or bad depending on how the terms are arranged in the argument. Chapters 3 and 4 of this textbook are devoted mainly to syllogistic logic. But Aristotle also deserves credit for originating **modal logic**, a kind of logic that involves such concepts as possibility, necessity, belief, and doubt. In addition, Aristotle catalogued several informal fallacies, a topic treated in Chapter 2 of this book.

After Aristotle's death, another Greek philosopher, Chrysippus (280–206 B.C.), one of the founders of the Stoic school, developed a logic in which the fundamental elements were *whole propositions*. Chrysippus treated every proposition as either true or false and developed rules for determining the truth or falsity of compound propositions from the truth or falsity of their components. In the course of doing so, he laid the foundation for the truth functional interpretation of the logical connectives presented in Chapter 5 of this book and introduced the notion of natural deduction, treated in Chapter 6.

For thirteen hundred years after the death of Chrysippus, relatively little creative work was done in logic. The physician Galen (A.D. 129–ca. 199) developed the theory of the compound categorical syllogism, but for the most part philosophers confined themselves to writing commentaries on the works of Aristotle and Chrysippus. Boethius (ca. 480–524) is a noteworthy example.

The first major logician of the Middle Ages was Peter Abelard (1079–1142). Abelard reconstructed and refined the logic of Aristotle and Chrysippus as communicated by Boethius, and he originated a theory of universals that traced the universal character of general terms to concepts in the mind rather than to "natures" existing outside the mind, as Aristotle had held. In addition, Abelard distinguished arguments that are valid because of their form from those that are valid because of their content, but he held that only formal validity is the "perfect" or conclusive variety. This textbook follows Abelard on this point.

After Abelard, the study of logic during the Middle Ages flourished through the work of numerous philosophers. A logical treatise by William of Sherwood (ca. 1200–1271) contains the first expression of the "Barbara, Celarent . . ." poem quoted in Section 4.1 of this book, and the *Summulae Logicales* of Peter of Spain (ca. 1205–1277) became the standard textbook in logic for three hundred years. However, the most original contributions from this period were made by William of Ockham (ca. 1285–1347). Ockham extended the theory of modal logic, conducted an exhaustive study of the forms of valid and invalid syllogisms, and further developed the idea of a metalanguage, a higher-level language used to discuss linguistic entities such as words, terms, and propositions.

Toward the middle of the fifteenth century, a reaction set in against the logic of the Middle Ages. Rhetoric largely displaced logic as the primary focus of attention; the logic of Chrysippus, which had already begun to lose its unique identity in the Middle Ages, was ignored altogether, and the logic of Aristotle was studied only in highly simplistic presentations. A reawakening did not occur until two hundred years later through the work of Gottfried Wilhelm Leibniz (1646–1716).

Leibniz, a genius in numerous fields, attempted to develop a symbolic language or "calculus" that could be used to settle all forms of disputes, whether in theology, philosophy, or international relations. As a result of this work, Leibniz is sometimes credited with being the father of symbolic logic. Leibniz's efforts to symbolize logic were carried into the nineteenth century by Bernard Bolzano (1781–1848).

In the middle of the nineteenth century, logic commenced an extremely rapid period of development that has continued to this day. Work in symbolic logic was done by many philosophers and mathematicians, including Augustus De Morgan (1806–1871), George Boole (1815–1864), William Stanley Jevons (1835–1882), and John Venn (1834–1923). The rule bearing De Morgan's name is used in Chapter 6 of this book. Boole's interpretation of categorical propositions and Venn's method for diagramming them are covered in Chapters 3 and 4. At the same time a revival in inductive logic was initiated by the British philosopher John Stuart Mill (1806–1873), whose methods of induction have now become classic.

Across the Atlantic, the American philosopher Charles Sanders Peirce (1839–1914) developed a logic of relations, invented symbolic quantifiers, and suggested the truth-table method for formulas in propositional logic. These topics are covered in Chapters 5 and 7 of this book. The truth-table method was completed independently by Emil Post (1897–1954) and Ludwig Wittgenstein (1889–1951).

Toward the end of the nineteenth century, the foundations of modern mathematical logic were laid by Gottlob Frege (1848–1925). His *Begriffsschrift* sets forth the theory of quantification presented in Chapter 7 of this text. Frege's work was continued into the twentieth century by Alfred North Whitehead (1861–1947) and Bertrand Russell (1872–1970), whose monumental *Principia Mathematica* attempted to reduce the whole of pure mathematics to logic. The *Principia* is the source of much of the symbolism that appears in Chapters 5, 6, and 7 of this text.

During the twentieth century, much of the work in logic has focused on the formalization of logical systems and on questions dealing with the completeness and consistency of such systems. A now-famous theorem proved by Kurt Gödel (1906–1978) states that in any formal system adequate for number theory there exists an undecidable formula—that is, a formula such that neither it nor its negation is derivable from the axioms of the system. Other developments include multivalued logics and the formalization of modal logic. Most recently, logic has made a major contribution to technology by providing the conceptual foundation for the electronic circuitry of digital computers.

EXERCISE 1.1

I. Each of the following passages contains a single argument. Using the letters "P" and "C," identify the premises and conclusion of each argument, writing premises first and conclusion last. List the premises in the order in which they make the most sense (usually the order in which they occur), and write both premises and conclusion in the form of separate declarative sentences. Indicator words may be eliminated once premises and conclusion have been appropriately labeled. The exercises marked with a star are answered in the back of the book.

★1. Carbon monoxide molecules happen to be just the right size and shape, and happen to have just the right chemical properties, to fit neatly into cavities within hemoglobin molecules in blood that are normally reserved for oxygen molecules. Consequently, carbon monoxide diminishes the oxygen-carrying capacity of blood.

(Nivaldo J. Tro, *Chemistry: A Molecular Approach,* 2nd ed.)

2. Since the good, according to Plato, is that which furthers a person's real interests, it follows that in any given case when the good is known, men will seek it.

(Avrum Stroll and Richard Popkin, *Philosophy and the Human Spirit*)

3. As the denial or perversion of justice by the sentences of courts, as well as in any other manner, is with reason classed among the just causes of war, it will follow that the federal judiciary ought to have cognizance of all causes in which the citizens of other countries are concerned.

(Alexander Hamilton, *Federalist Papers,* No. 80)

★4. When individuals voluntarily abandon property, they forfeit any expectation of privacy in it that they might have had. Therefore, a warrantless search or seizure of abandoned property is not unreasonable under the Fourth Amendment.

(Judge Stephanie Kulp Seymour, *United States v. Jones*)

5. Artists and poets look at the world and seek relationships and order. But they translate their ideas to canvas, or to marble, or into poetic images. Scientists try to find relationships between different objects and events. To express the order they find, they create hypotheses and theories. Thus the great scientific theories are easily compared to great art and great literature.

(Douglas C. Giancoli, *The Ideas of Physics,* 3rd ed.)

6. The fact that there was never a land bridge between Australia and mainland Asia is evidenced by the fact that the animal species in the two areas are very different. Asian placental mammals and Australian marsupial mammals have not been in contact in the last several million years.

(T. Douglas Price and Gary M. Feinman, *Images of the Past*)

★7. It really does matter if you get enough sleep. We need sleep to think clearly, react quickly, and create memories. Studies show that people who are taught mentally challenging tasks do better after a good night's sleep. Other research suggests that sleep is needed for creative problem solving.

(U.S. National Institutes of Health, "Your Guide to Healthy Sleep")

8. The classroom teacher is crucial to the development and academic success of the average student, and administrators simply are ancillary to this effort. For this reason, classroom teachers ought to be paid at least the equivalent of administrators at all levels, including the superintendent.

(Peter F. Falstrup, letter to the editor)

9. An agreement cannot bind unless both parties to the agreement know what they are doing and freely choose to do it. This implies that the seller who intends to enter a contract with a customer has a duty to disclose exactly what the customer is buying and what the terms of the sale are.

(Manuel G. Velasquez, "The Ethics of Consumer Production")

★10. Punishment, when speedy and specific, may suppress undesirable behavior, but it cannot teach or encourage desirable alternatives. Therefore, it is crucial to use positive techniques to model and reinforce appropriate behavior that the person can use in place of the unacceptable response that has to be suppressed.

(Walter Mischel and Harriet Mischel, *Essentials of Psychology*)

11. Profit serves a very crucial function in a free-enterprise economy, such as our own. High profits are the signal that consumers want more of the output of the industry. High profits provide the incentive for firms to expand output and for more firms to enter the industry in the long run. For a firm of above-average efficiency, profits represent the reward for greater efficiency.

(Dominic Salvatore, *Managerial Economics,* 3rd ed.)

12. Cats can think circles around dogs! My cat regularly used to close and lock the door to my neighbor's doghouse, trapping their sleeping Doberman inside. Try telling a cat what to do, or putting a leash on him—he'll glare at you and say, "I don't think so. You should have gotten a dog."

(Kevin Purkiser, letter to the editor)

★13. Since private property helps people define themselves, since it frees people from mundane cares of daily subsistence, and since it is finite, no individual should accumulate so much property that others are prevented from accumulating the necessities of life.

(Leon P. Baradat, Political Ideologies, Their Origins and Impact)

14. To every existing thing God wills some good. Hence, since to love any thing is nothing else than to will good to that thing, it is manifest that God loves everything that exists.

(Thomas Aquinas, Summa Theologica)

15. Women of the working class, especially wage workers, should not have more than two children at most. The average working man can support no more and the average working woman can take care of no more in decent fashion.

(Margaret Sanger, Family Limitations)

★16. Radioactive fallout isn't the only concern in the aftermath of nuclear explosions. The nations of planet Earth have acquired nuclear weapons with an explosive power equal to more than a million Hiroshima bombs. Studies suggest that explosion of only half these weapons would produce enough soot, smoke, and dust to blanket the Earth, block out the sun, and bring on a nuclear winter that would threaten the survival of the human race.

(John W. Hill and Doris K. Kolb, Chemistry for Changing Times, 7th ed.)

17. An ant releases a chemical when it dies, and its fellows then carry it away to the compost heap. Apparently the communication is highly effective; a healthy ant painted with the death chemical will be dragged to the funeral heap again and again.

(Carol R. Ember and Melvin Ember, Cultural Anthropology, 7th ed.)

18. Every art and every inquiry, and similarly every action and pursuit, is thought to aim at some good; and for this reason the good has rightly been declared to be that at which all things aim.

(Aristotle, Nicomachean Ethics)

★19. Poverty offers numerous benefits to the nonpoor. Antipoverty programs provide jobs for middle-class professionals in social work, penology, and public health. Such workers' future advancement is tied to the continued growth of bureaucracies dependent on the existence of poverty.

(J. John Palen, Social Problems)

20. Corn is an annual crop. Butcher's meat, a crop which requires four or five years to grow. As an acre of land, therefore, will produce a much smaller quantity of the one species of food than the other, the inferiority of the quantity must be compensated by the superiority of the price.

(Adam Smith, The Wealth of Nations)

21. Neither a borrower nor lender be
For loan oft loses both itself and friend,
And borrowing dulls the edge of husbandry.

(William Shakespeare, Hamlet I, 3)

★22. The stakes in whistleblowing are high. Take the nurse who alleges that physicians enrich themselves in her hospital through unnecessary surgery; the engineer who discloses safety defects in the braking systems of a fleet of new rapid-transit vehicles; the Defense Department official who alerts Congress to military graft and overspending: all know that they pose a threat to those whom they denounce and that their own careers may be at risk.

(Sissela Bok, "Whistleblowing and Professional Responsibility")

23. If a piece of information is not "job relevant," then the employer is not entitled qua employer to know it. Consequently, since sexual practices, political beliefs, associational activities, etc., are not part of the description of most jobs, that is, since they do not directly affect one's job performance, they are not legitimate information for an employer to know in the determination of the hiring of a job applicant.

(George G. Brenkert, "Privacy, Polygraphs, and Work")

24. Many people believe that a dark tan is attractive and a sign of good health, but mounting evidence indicates that too much sun can lead to health problems. One of the most noticeable effects is premature aging of the skin. The sun also contributes to certain types of cataracts, and, what is most worrisome, it plays a role in skin cancer.

(Joseph M. Moran and Michael D. Morgan, *Meteorology,* 4th ed.)

★25. Contrary to the tales of some scuba divers, the toothy, gaping grin on the mouth of an approaching shark is not necessarily anticipatory. It is generally accepted that by constantly swimming with its mouth open, the shark is simply avoiding suffocation. This assures a continuous flow of oxygen-laden water into their mouths, over their gills, and out through the gill slits.

(Robert A. Wallace et al., *Biology: The Science of Life*)

26. Not only is the sky blue [as a result of scattering], but light coming from it is also partially polarized. You can readily observe this by placing a piece of Polaroid (for example, one lens of a pair of Polaroid sunglasses) in front of your eye and rotating it as you look at the sky on a clear day. You will notice a change in light intensity with the orientation of the Polaroid.

(Frank J. Blatt, *Principles of Physics,* 2nd ed.)

27. Since the secondary light [from the moon] does not inherently belong to the moon and is not received from any star or from the sun, and since in the whole universe there is no other body left but the earth, what must we conclude? What is to be proposed? Surely we must assert that the lunar body (or any other dark and sunless orb) is illuminated by the earth.

(Galileo Galilei, *The Starry Messenger*)

★28. Anyone familiar with our prison system knows that there are some inmates who behave little better than brute beasts. But the very fact that these prisoners exist is a telling argument against the efficacy of capital punishment as a deterrent. If the death penalty had been truly effective as a deterrent, such prisoners would long ago have vanished.

("The Injustice of the Death Penalty," *America*)

29. Though it is possible that REM sleep and dreaming are not necessary in the adult, REM deprivation studies seem to suggest otherwise. Why would REM pressure increase with deprivation if the system is unimportant in the adult?

(Herbert L. Petri, *Motivation: Theory and Research,* 2nd ed.)

30. We say that an end pursued in its own right is more complete than an end pursued because of something else, and that an end that is never choice-worthy

because of something else is more complete than ends that are choiceworthy both in their own right and because of this end. Hence, an end that is always choiceworthy in its own right, and never because of something else, is complete without qualification.

(Aristotle, *Nicomachean Ethics*)

II. The following arguments were taken from magazine and newspaper editorials and letters to the editor. In most instances the main conclusion must be rephrased to capture the full intent of the author. Write out what you interpret the main conclusion to be.

★ 1. University administrators know well the benefits that follow notable success in college sports: increased applications for admissions, increased income from licensed logo merchandise, more lucrative television deals, postseason game revenue, and more successful alumni fund drives. The idea that there is something ideal and pure about the amateur athlete is self-serving bunk.

(Michael McDonnell, letter to the editor)

2. In a nation of immigrants, people of diverse ethnic backgrounds must have a common bond through which to exchange ideas. How can this bond be accomplished if there is no common language? It is those who shelter the immigrant from learning English by encouraging the development of a multilingual society who are creating a xenophobic atmosphere. They allow the immigrant to surround himself with a cocoon of language from which he cannot escape and which others cannot penetrate.

(Rita Toften, letter to the editor)

3. The health and fitness of our children has become a problem partly because of our attitude toward athletics. The purpose of sports, especially for children, should be to make healthy people healthier. The concept of team sports has failed to do this. Rather than learning to interact and cooperate with others, youngsters are taught to compete. Team sports have only reinforced the notion that the team on top is the winner, and all others are losers. This approach does not make sports appealing to many children, and some, especially among the less fit, burn out by the time they are twelve.

(Mark I. Pitman, "Young Jocks")

★ 4. College is the time in which a young mind is supposed to mature and acquire wisdom, and one can only do this by experiencing as much diverse intellectual stimuli as possible. A business student may be a whiz at accounting, but has he or she ever experienced the beauty of a Shakespearean sonnet or the boundless events composing Hebrew history? Most likely not. While many of these neoconservatives will probably go on to be financially successful, they are robbing themselves of the true purpose of collegiate academics, a sacrifice that outweighs the future salary checks.

(Robert S. Griffith, "Conservative College Press")

5. History has shown repeatedly that you cannot legislate morality, nor does anyone have a right to. The real problem is the people who have a vested interest in sustaining the multibillion-dollar drug industry created by the laws against drugs. The legalization of drugs would remove the thrill of breaking the law; it would end the suffering caused by unmetered doses, impurities, and substandard paraphernalia. A huge segment of the underground and extralegal economy would move

into a legitimate economy, taking money away from criminals, eliminating crime and violence, and restoring many talented people to useful endeavor.

(Thomas L. Wayburn, letter to the editor)

6. Infectious disease is no longer the leading cause of death in this country, thanks to antibiotics, but there are new strains of bacteria that are resistant to—and others that grow only in the presence of—antibiotics. Yet Congress wants to cut the National Institutes of Health budget. Further cuts would leave us woefully unprepared to cope with the new microbes Mother Nature has cooking in her kitchen.

(Valina L. Dawson, letter to the editor)

★7. A person cannot reject free will and still insist on criminality and codes of moral behavior. If people are compelled by forces beyond their control (genes or environment), then their actions, no matter how vile, are excusable. That means the Nuremberg trials of Nazi murderers were invalid, and all prison gates should be flung open. The essence of our humanity is the ability to choose between right and wrong, good and evil, and act accordingly. Strip that from us and we are mere animals.

(Rabbi Gilbert S. Rosenthal, letter to the editor)

8. Ideally, decisions about health care should be based on the doctor's clinical judgment, patient preference, and scientific evidence. Patients should always be presented with options in their care. Elective cesarean section, however, is not used to treat a problem but to avoid a natural process. An elective surgery like this puts the patient at unnecessary risk, increases the risk for complications in future deliveries, and increases health-care costs.

(Anne Foster-Rosales, M.D., letter to the editor)

9. Parents who feel guilty for the little time they can (or choose to) spend with their children "pick up" after them—so the children don't learn to face the consequences of their own choices and actions. Parents who allow their children to fail are showing them greater love and respect.

(Susan J. Peters, letter to the editor)

★10. Most of the environmental problems facing us stem, at least in part, from the sheer number of Americans. The average American produces three quarters of a ton of garbage every year, consumes hundreds of gallons of gasoline, and uses large amounts of electricity (often from a nuclear power plant, coal burning, or a dam). The least painful way to protect the environment is to limit population growth.

(Craig M. Bradley, letter to the editor)

III. Define the following terms:

logic	premise	inference
argument	conclusion	proposition
statement	conclusion indicator	syllogistic logic
truth value	premise indicator	modal logic

IV. Answer "true" or "false" to the following statements:

1. The purpose of the premise or premises is to set forth the reasons or evidence given in support of the conclusion.

2. Some arguments have more than one conclusion.

3. All arguments must have more than one premise.

4. The words "therefore," "hence," "so," "since," and "thus" are all conclusion indicators.

5. The words "for," "because," "as," and "for the reason that" are all premise indicators.

6. In the strict sense of the terms, *inference* and *argument* have exactly the same meaning.

7. In most (but not all) arguments that lack indicator words, the conclusion is the first statement.

8. Any sentence that is either true or false is a statement.

9. Every statement has a truth value.

10. Aristotle is the person usually credited with being the father of logic.

aplia

Visit Aplia for section-specific problem sets.

1.2 Recognizing Arguments

PREVIEW

Suppose your instructor claims that you failed to submit an essay by the due date and that your grade will suffer as a result. In response, you might **argue** that in fact the essay was submitted on time, or **explain** why the essay was late. Explanations are different from arguments. In this section you will learn how to distinguish arguments from several forms of non-arguments, including explanations, expository passages, and illustrations.

Not all passages contain arguments. Because logic deals with arguments, it is important to be able to distinguish passages that contain arguments from those that do not. In general, a passage contains an argument if it purports to prove something; if it does not do so, it does not contain an argument.

In the previous section of this book we learned that every argument has at least one premise and exactly one conclusion. The premise or premises set forth the alleged evidence or reasons, and the conclusion asserts what is claimed to follow from the alleged evidence or reasons. This definition of an argument expresses what is needed for a passage to contain an argument:

1. At least one of the statements must claim to present evidence or reasons.

2. There must be a claim that the alleged evidence supports or implies something—that is, a claim that something follows from the alleged evidence or reasons.

It is not necessary that the premises present actual evidence or true reasons nor that the premises actually support the conclusion. But at least the premises must *claim* to present evidence or reasons, and there must be a *claim* that the evidence or reasons support or imply something. Also, you should recognize that the second claim is not equatable with the intentions of the arguer. Intentions are subjective and, as such, are

Aristotle 384–322 B.C.

Mansell/Time Life Pictures/Getty Images

Aristotle was born in Stagira, a small Greek town situated on the northern coast of the Aegean Sea. His father was a physician in the court of King Amyntas II of Macedonia, and the young Aristotle was a friend of the king's son Philip, who was later to become king himself and the father of Alexander the Great. When he was about seventeen, Aristotle was sent to Athens to further his education in Plato's Academy, the finest institution of higher learning in the Greek world. After Plato's death Aristotle left for Assos, a small town on the coast of Asia Minor, where he married the niece of the local ruler.

Six years later Aristotle accepted an invitation to return to Macedonia to serve as tutor of the young Alexander. When Alexander ascended the throne following his father's assassination, Aristotle's tutorial job was finished, and he departed for Athens where he set up a school near the temple of Apollo Lyceus. The school came to be known as the Lyceum, and Alexander supported it with contributions of money and specimens of flora and fauna derived from his far-flung conquests. After Alexander's death, an anti-Macedonian rebellion forced Aristotle to leave Athens for Chalcis, about thirty miles to the north, where he died one year later at the age of sixty-two.

Aristotle is universally recognized as the originator of logic. He defined *logic* as the study of the process by which a statement follows by necessity from one or more other statements. The most fundamental kind of statement, he thought, is the categorical proposition, and he classified the four kinds of categorical propositions in terms of their being universal, particular, affirmative, and negative. He also developed the square of opposition, which shows how one such proposition implies the truth or falsity of another, and he identified the relations of conversion, obversion, and contraposition, which provide the basis for various immediate inferences.

His crowning achievement is the theory of the categorical syllogism, a kind of argument consisting of three categorical propositions. He showed how categorical syllogisms can be catalogued in terms of mood and figure, and he developed a set of rules for determining the validity of categorical syllogisms. Also, he showed how the modal concepts of possibility and necessity apply to categorical propositions. In addition to the theory of the syllogism, Aristotle advanced the theory of definition by genus and difference, and he showed how arguments could be defective in terms of thirteen forms of informal fallacy.

Aristotle made profound contributions to many areas of human learning including biology, physics, metaphysics, epistemology, psychology, aesthetics, ethics, and politics. However, his accomplishments in logic were so extensive and enduring that two thousand years after his death, the great philosopher Immanuel Kant said that Aristotle had discovered everything that could be known about logic. His logic was not superseded until the end of the nineteenth century when Frege, Whitehead, and Russell developed modern mathematical logic.

usually not accessible to the evaluator. Rather, this claim is an objective feature of an argument grounded in its language or structure.

In deciding whether a passage contains an argument, the claim that the alleged reasons or evidence supports or implies something is usually the more important of the two. Such a claim can be either explicit or implicit. An *explicit* claim is usually asserted by premise or conclusion indicator words ("thus," "since," "because," "hence," "therefore," and so on). Example:

> Mad cow disease is spread by feeding parts of infected animals to cows, and this practice has yet to be completely eradicated. Thus, mad cow disease continues to pose a threat to people who eat beef.

The word "thus" expresses the claim that something is being inferred, so the passage is an argument.

An *implicit* claim exists if there is an inferential relationship between the statements in a passage, but the passage contains no indicator words. Example:

> The genetic modification of food is risky business. Genetic engineering can introduce unintended changes into the DNA of the food-producing organism, and these changes can be toxic to the consumer.

In this passage there is an inferential relationship between the first statement and the other two. The meaning of the last two statements is such that it naturally tends to prove the first statement. This relationship constitutes an implicit claim that evidence supports something, so we are justified in calling the passage an argument. The first statement is the conclusion, and the other two are the premises.

In deciding whether there is a claim that evidence supports or implies something, keep an eye out for (1) premise and conclusion indicator words and (2) the presence of an inferential relationship between the statements. In connection with these points, however, a word of caution is in order. First, the mere occurrence of an indicator word by no means guarantees the presence of an argument. For example, consider the following passages:

> Since Edison invented the phonograph, there have been many technological innovations.

> Since Edison invented the phonograph, he deserves credit for a major technological innovation.

In the first passage the word "since" is used in a *temporal* sense. It means "from the time that." Thus, the first passage is not an argument. In the second passage "since" is used in a *logical* sense, and so the passage *is* an argument.

The second cautionary point is that it is not always easy to detect the occurrence of an inferential relationship between the statements in a passage, and one may have to review a passage several times before making a decision. In reaching such a decision, one may find it helpful to mentally insert the word "therefore" before the various statements to see whether it makes sense to interpret one of them as following from the others. Even with this mental aid, however, the decision whether a passage contains an inferential relationship (as well as the decision about indicator words) often involves a heavy dose of interpretation. As a result, not everyone will agree about every passage. Sometimes the only answer possible is a conditional one: "*If* this passage contains an argument, then these are the premises and that is the conclusion."

To assist in distinguishing passages that contain arguments from those that do not, let us now investigate some typical kinds of nonarguments. These include simple noninferential passages, expository passages, illustrations, explanations, and conditional statements.

Simple Noninferential Passages

Simple noninferential passages are unproblematic passages that lack a claim that anything is being proved. Such passages contain statements that could be premises or conclusions (or both), but what is missing is a claim that any potential premise supports a conclusion or that any potential conclusion is supported by premises. Passages of this sort include warnings, pieces of advice, statements of belief or opinion, loosely associated statements, and reports.

> **simple noninferential passage:** A kind of nonargument that includes warnings, pieces of advice, opinions, loosely associated statements, and reports.

A **warning** is a form of expression that is intended to put someone on guard against a dangerous or detrimental situation. Examples:

> Watch out that you don't slip on the ice.

> Whatever you do, never confide personal secrets to Blabbermouth Bob.

If no evidence is given to prove that such statements are true, then there is no argument.

A **piece of advice** is a form of expression that makes a recommendation about some future decision or course of conduct. Examples:

> You should keep a few things in mind before buying a used car. Test drive the car at varying speeds and conditions, examine the oil in the crankcase, ask to see service records, and, if possible, have the engine and power train checked by a mechanic.

> Before accepting a job after class hours, I would suggest that you give careful consideration to your course load. Will you have sufficient time to prepare for classes and tests, and will the job produce an excessive drain on your energies?

As with warnings, if there is no evidence that is intended to prove anything, then there is no argument.

A **statement of belief** or **opinion** is an expression about what someone happens to believe or think about something. Examples:

> We believe that our company must develop and produce outstanding products that will perform a great service or fulfill a need for our customers. We believe that our business must be run at an adequate profit and that the services and products we offer must be better than those offered by competitors.
>
> (Robert D. Hay and Edmund R. Gray, "Introduction to Social Responsibility")

> When I can read the latte menu through the hole in my server's earlobe, something is seriously out of whack. What happened to an earring, maybe two, in each lobe? Now any surface is game. Brow, lip, tongue, cheek, nose. I've adjusted to untied shoelaces and pants that make mooning irrelevant. But when it comes to piercings, I just can't budge.
>
> (Debra Darvick, "Service with a Smile, and Plenty of Metal")

Because neither of these statements asserts any claim that a belief or opinion is supported by evidence, or that it supports some conclusion, there is no argument.

Loosely associated statements may be about the same general subject, but they lack a claim that one of them is proved by the others. Example:

> Not to honor men of worth will keep the people from contention; not to value goods that are hard to come by will keep them from theft; not to display what is desirable will keep them from being unsettled of mind.
>
> (Lao-Tzu, *Thoughts from the Tao Te Ching*)

Because there is no claim that any of these statements provides evidence or reasons for believing another, there is no argument.

A **report** consists of a group of statements that convey information about some topic or event. Example:

> The period of 1648–1789 was one of competition among the primary monarchs of Europe. Wars among the great powers were frequent but limited. France made major efforts to become paramount, but the balance of power operated to block French expansion.
>
> (Steven L. Spiegel, *World Politics in a New Era*)

These statements could serve as the premises of an argument, but because the author makes no claim that they support or imply anything, there is no argument. Another type of report is the news report:

> Witnesses said they heard a loud crack before a balcony gave way at a popular nightspot, dropping dozens of screaming people fourteen feet. At least eighty people were injured at the Diamond Horseshoe casino when they fell onto broken glass and splintered wood. Investigators are waiting for an engineer's report on the deck's occupancy load.
>
> (Newspaper clipping)

Again, because the reporter makes no claim that these statements imply anything, there is no argument.

One must be careful, though, with reports *about* arguments:

> "The Air Force faces a serious shortage of experienced pilots in the years ahead, because repeated overseas tours and the allure of high-paying jobs with commercial airlines are winning out over lucrative bonuses to stay in the service," says a prominent Air Force official.
>
> (Newspaper clipping)

Properly speaking, this passage is not an argument, because the author of the passage does not claim that anything is supported by evidence. Rather, the author reports the claim by the Air Force official that something is supported by evidence. If such passages are interpreted as "containing" arguments, it must be made clear that the argument is not the author's but one made by someone about whom the author is reporting.

Expository Passages

An **expository passage** is a kind of expression that begins with a topic sentence followed by one or more sentences that develop the topic sentence. If the objective is not to prove the topic sentence but only to expand it or elaborate on it, then there is no argument. Examples:

> There are three familiar states of matter: solid, liquid, and gas. Solid objects ordinarily maintain their shape and volume regardless of their location. A liquid occupies a definite volume, but assumes the shape of the occupied portion of its container. A gas maintains neither shape nor volume. It expands to fill completely whatever container it is in.
>
> (John W. Hill and Doris K. Kolb, *Chemistry for Changing Times,* 7th ed.)

> There is a stylized relation of artist to mass audience in the sports, especially in baseball. Each player develops a style of his own—the swagger as he steps to the plate, the unique windup a pitcher has, the clean-swinging and hard-driving hits, the precision quickness and grace of infield and outfield, the sense of surplus power behind whatever is done.
>
> (Max Lerner, *America as a Civilization*)

In each passage the topic sentence is stated first, and the remaining sentences merely develop and flesh out this topic sentence. These passages are not arguments, because they lack an inferential claim. However, expository passages differ from simple non-inferential passages (such as warnings and pieces of advice) in that many of them can also be taken as arguments. If the purpose of the subsequent sentences in the passage

expository passage: A kind of nonargument that begins with a topic sentence followed by one or more sentences that develop the topic sentence.

proves topic sentence ex.

is not only to flesh out the topic sentence but also to prove it, then the passage is an argument. Example:

> Skin and the mucous membrane lining the respiratory and digestive tracts serve as mechanical barriers to entry by microbes. Oil-gland secretions contain chemicals that weaken or kill bacteria on skin. The respiratory tract is lined by cells that sweep mucus and trapped particles up into the throat, where they can be swallowed. The stomach has an acidic pH, which inhibits the growth of many types of bacteria.
>
> (Sylvia S. Mader, Human Biology, 4th ed.)

In this passage the topic sentence is stated first, and the purpose of the remaining sentences is not only to *show how* the skin and mucous membranes serve as barriers to microbes but also to *prove* that they do this. Thus, the passage can be taken as both an expository passage and an argument.

In deciding whether an expository passage should be interpreted as an argument, try to determine whether the purpose of the subsequent sentences in the passage is merely to develop the topic sentence or also to prove that it is true. In borderline cases, ask yourself whether the topic sentence makes a claim that everyone accepts or agrees with. If it does, the passage is probably not an argument. In real-life situations authors rarely try to prove something is true when everyone already accepts it. However, if the topic sentence makes a claim that many people do not accept or have never thought about, then the purpose of the remaining sentences may be both to prove the topic sentence is true as well as to develop it. If this is so, the passage is an argument.

Finally, if even this procedure yields no definite answer, the only alternative may be to say that *if* the passage is taken as an argument, then the first statement is the conclusion and the others are the premises.

Illustrations

illustration: A kind of nonargument containing one or more examples that is intended to show what something means or how it is done.

An **illustration** is an expression involving one or more examples that is intended to show what something means or how it is done. Illustrations are often confused with arguments because many illustrations contain indicator words such as "thus." Examples:

> Chemical elements, as well as compounds, can be represented by molecular formulas. Thus, oxygen is represented by "O_2," water by "H_2O," and sodium chloride by "NaCl."

> A deciduous tree is any tree that loses its leaves during the winter. For example, maples are deciduous. And so are elms, poplars, hawthorns, and alders.

These selections are not arguments, because they make no claim that anything is being proved. In the first selection, the word "thus" indicates how something is done—namely, how chemical elements and compounds can be represented by formulas. In the second, the examples cited are intended to illustrate the meaning of the word "deciduous." It pins down the meaning by providing concrete instances.

However, as with expository passages, many illustrations can be taken as arguments. Such arguments are often called **arguments from example**. Here is an instance of one:

argument from example: An argument in which an example is cited to prove a conclusion.

> Although most forms of cancer, if untreated, can cause death, not all cancers are life-threatening. For example, basal cell carcinoma, the most common of all skin cancers, can produce disfigurement, but it almost never results in death.

In this passage the example given is intended to prove the truth of "Not all cancers are life-threatening." Thus, the passage is best interpreted as an argument.

In deciding whether an illustration should be interpreted as an argument, determine whether the passage merely shows how something is done or what something means, or whether it also purports to prove something. In borderline cases it helps to note whether the claim being illustrated is one that practically everyone accepts or agrees with. If it is, the passage is probably not an argument. As already noted, in real-life situations authors rarely attempt to prove what everyone already accepts. But if the claim being illustrated is one that many people do not accept or have never thought about, then the passage may be interpreted as an argument.

Thus, in reference to the first two examples we considered, most people are aware that elements and compounds can be expressed by formulas—practically everyone knows that water is H_2O—and most people have at least a vague idea of what a deciduous tree is. But they may not have ever considered whether some forms of cancer are not life-threatening. This is one of the reasons for evaluating the first two examples as mere illustrations and the last one as an argument.

Explanations

One of the most important kinds of nonargument is the explanation. An **explanation** is an expression that purports to shed light on some event or phenomenon. The event or phenomenon in question is usually accepted as a matter of fact. Examples:

> The sky appears blue from the earth's surface because light rays from the sun are scattered by particles in the atmosphere.

> Golf balls have a dimpled surface because the dimples reduce air drag, causing the ball to travel farther.

> Navel oranges are called by that name because they have a growth that resembles a human navel on the end opposite the stem.

Every explanation is composed of two distinct components: the explanandum and explanans. The **explanandum** is the statement that describes the event or phenomenon to be explained, and the **explanans** is the statement or group of statements that purports to do the explaining. In the first example, the explanandum is the statement "The sky appears blue from the earth's surface" and the explanans is "Light rays from the sun are scattered by particles in the atmosphere."

explanation: A kind of nonargument that purports to shed light on some event or phenomenon.

explanandum: The statement that describes the event or phenomenon to be explained.

explanans: The statement or group of statements that purports to do the explaining.

Argument		**Explanation**	
Premises	Accepted facts	Explanans	Claimed to shed light on
↓	Claimed to prove	↓	
Conclusion		Explanandum	Accepted fact

Explanations are sometimes mistaken for arguments because they often contain the indicator word "because." Yet explanations are not arguments, because in an explanation the purpose of the explanans is to shed light on, or to make sense of, the explanandum event—not to prove that it occurred. In other words, the purpose of the explanans is to show *why* something is the case, whereas in an argument, the purpose of the premises is to prove *that* something is the case.

In the first example given, the fact that the sky is blue is readily apparent to everyone. The statement that light rays from the sun are scattered by particles in the atmosphere is not intended to prove *that* the sky is blue, but rather to show *why* it is blue. In the second example, practically everyone knows that golf balls have a dimpled surface. The purpose of the passage is to explain *why* they have a dimpled surface—not to prove *that* they do. Similarly, in the third example, it is obvious that naval oranges are called naval oranges. The purpose of the passage is to shed light on why they have this name.

Thus, to distinguish explanations from arguments, identify the statement that is either the explanandum or the conclusion (usually this is the statement that precedes the word "because"). If this statement describes an accepted matter of fact, and if the remaining statements purport to shed light on this statement, then the passage is an explanation.

This method usually works to distinguish arguments from explanations. However, some passages can be interpreted as both explanations and arguments. Examples:

> Women become intoxicated by drinking a smaller amount of alcohol than men because men metabolize part of the alcohol before it reaches the bloodstream, whereas women do not.

> Household bleach should never be mixed with ammonia because the combination releases chlorine gas, which is highly poisonous.

The purpose of these passages could be to prove the first statement to those who do not accept it as fact, and to shed light on that fact to those who do accept it. Alternately, the passage could be intended to prove the first statement to a person who accepts its truth on blind faith or incomplete experience, and simultaneously to shed light on this truth. Thus, these passages can be correctly interpreted as both an explanation and an argument.

Perhaps the greatest problem confronting the effort to distinguish explanations from arguments lies in determining whether something is an accepted matter of fact. Obviously, what is accepted by one person may not be accepted by another. Thus, the effort often involves determining which person or group of people the passage is directed to—the intended audience. Sometimes the source of the passage (textbook, newspaper, technical journal, etc.) will decide the issue. But when the passage is taken totally out of context, ascertaining the source may prove impossible. In those circumstances the only possible answer may be to say that *if* the passage is an argument, then such-and-such is the conclusion and such-and-such are the premises.

Conditional Statements

conditional statement:
A kind of nonargument expressed as an "if...then..." statement.

A **conditional statement** is an "if ... then ..." statement; for example:

> If professional football games incite violence in the home, then the widespread approval given to this sport should be reconsidered.

> If Roger Federer has won more Grand Slams than any other contender, then he rightfully deserves the title of world's greatest tennis player.

Every conditional statement is made up of two component statements. The component statement immediately following the "if" is called the **antecedent**, and the one following the "then" is called the **consequent**. (Occasionally, the word "then" is left out, and occasionally the order of antecedent and consequent is reversed.) In the first example, the antecedent is "Professional football games incite violence in the home," and the consequent is "The widespread approval given to this sport should be reconsidered." In both of these examples, there is a meaningful relationship between antecedent and consequent. However, such a relationship need not exist for a statement to count as conditional. The statement "If Janet Jackson is a singer, then Denver is in Colorado" is just as much a conditional statement as those about professional football and Roger Federer.

antecedent: The part of a conditional statement that immediately follows "if."

consequent: The part of a conditional statement that immediately follows "then."

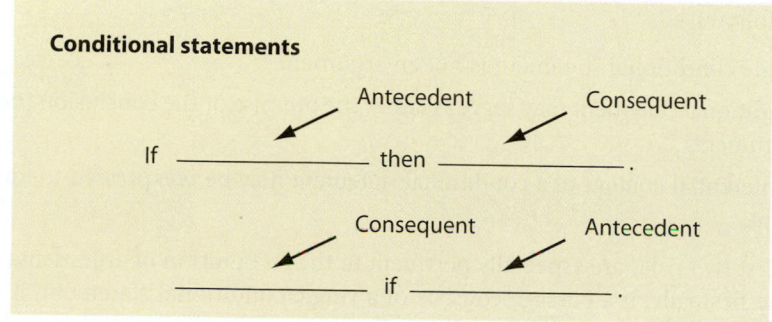

Conditional statements

Conditional statements are not arguments, because they fail to meet the criteria given earlier. In an argument, at least one statement must claim to present evidence, and there must be a claim that this evidence implies something. In a conditional statement, there is no claim that either the antecedent or the consequent presents evidence. In other words, there is no assertion that either the antecedent or the consequent is true. Rather, there is only the assertion that *if* the antecedent is true, then so is the consequent. Of course, a conditional statement as a whole may present evidence because it asserts a relationship between statements. Yet when conditional statements are taken in this sense, there is still no argument, because there is then no separate claim that this evidence implies anything.

Some conditional statements are similar to arguments, however, in that they express the outcome of a reasoning process. As such, they may be said to have a certain inferential content. Consider the following:

> If Sarah Palin loves shooting wolves from airplanes, then she has little respect for wildlife.

The link between the antecedent and consequent resembles the inferential link between the premises and conclusion of an argument. Yet there is a difference because the premises of an argument are claimed to be true, whereas no such claim is made for the antecedent of a conditional statement. Accordingly, conditional statements are not arguments.* Yet their inferential content may be reexpressed to form arguments:

> Sarah Palin loves shooting wolves from airplanes.
> Therefore, she has little respect for wildlife.

*In saying this we are temporarily ignoring the possibility of these statements being enthymemes. As we shall see in Chapter 4, an enthymeme is an argument in which a premise or conclusion (or both) is implied but not stated. If, to this example, we add the premise "Sarah Palin loves shooting wolves from airplanes" and the conclusion "Therefore Sarah Palin has little respect for wildlife," we have a complete argument. To decide whether a conditional statement is an enthymeme, we must be familiar with the context in which it occurs.

Finally, while no single conditional statement is an argument, a conditional statement may serve as either the premise or the conclusion (or both) of an argument, as the following examples illustrate:

> If Iran is developing nuclear weapons, then Iran is a threat to world peace.
> Iran is developing nuclear weapons.
> Therefore, Iran is a threat to world peace.

> If our borders are porous, then terrorists can enter the country at will.
> If terrorists can enter the country at will, then all of us are less secure.
> Therefore, if our borders are porous, then all of us are less secure.

The relation between conditional statements and arguments may now be summarized as follows:

1. A single conditional statement is not an argument.

2. A conditional statement may serve as either the premise or the conclusion (or both) of an argument.

3. The inferential content of a conditional statement may be reexpressed to form an argument.

The first two rules are especially pertinent to the recognition of arguments. According to the first rule, if a passage consists of a single conditional statement, it is not an argument. But if it consists of a conditional statement together with some other statement, then, by the second rule, it *may* be an argument, depending on such factors as the presence of indicator words and an inferential relationship between the statements.

Conditional statements are especially important in logic (and many other fields) because they express the relationship between necessary and sufficient conditions. *A* is said to be a **sufficient condition** for *B* whenever the occurrence of *A* is all that is needed for the occurrence of *B*. For example, being a dog is a sufficient condition for being an animal. On the other hand, *B* is said to be a **necessary condition** for *A* whenever *A* cannot occur without the occurrence of *B*. Thus, being an animal is a necessary condition for being a dog.

The difference between sufficient and necessary conditions is a bit tricky. So, to clarify the idea further, suppose you are given a large, closed cardboard box. Also, suppose you are told there is a dog in the box. Then you know for sure there is an animal in the box. No additional information is needed to draw this conclusion. This means that being a dog is sufficient for being an animal. However, being a dog is not necessary for being an animal, because if you are told that the box contains a cat, you can conclude with equal certainty that it contains an animal. In other words, it is not necessary for the box to contain a dog for it to contain an animal. It might equally well contain a cat, a mouse, a squirrel, or any other animal.

On the other hand, suppose you are told that whatever might be in the box, it is not an animal. Then you know for certain there is no dog in the box. The reason you can draw this conclusion is that being an animal is necessary for being a dog. If there is no animal, there is no dog. However, being an animal is not sufficient for being a dog, because if you are told that the box contains an animal, you cannot, from this information alone, conclude that it contains a dog. It might contain a cat, a mouse, a squirrel, and so on.

These ideas are expressed in the following conditional statements:

> If *X* is a dog, then *X* is an animal.
> If *X* is not an animal, then *X* is not a dog.

sufficient condition:
A is a sufficient condition for *B* whenever the occurrence of *A* is all that is needed for the occurrence of *B*.

necessary condition:
B is a necessary condition for *A* whenever *A* cannot occur without the occurrence of *B*.

The first statement says that being a dog is a sufficient condition for being an animal, and the second that being an animal is a necessary condition for being a dog. However, a little reflection reveals that these two statements say exactly the same thing. Thus, each expresses in one way a necessary condition and in another way a sufficient condition.

Section 1.2 Summary

In deciding whether a passage contains an argument, you should look for three things: (1) indicator words such as "therefore," "since," "because," and so on; (2) an inferential relationship between the statements; and (3) typical kinds of nonarguments. But remember that the mere occurrence of an indicator word does not guarantee the presence of an argument. You must check to see that the statement identified as the conclusion is claimed to be supported by one or more of the other statements. Also keep in mind that in many arguments that lack indicator words, the conclusion is the first statement. Furthermore, it helps to mentally insert the word "therefore" before the various statements before deciding that a statement should be interpreted as a conclusion. The typical kinds of nonarguments that we have surveyed are as follows:

simple noninferential passage   reports
warnings   expository passages
pieces of advice   illustrations
statements of belief   explanations
statements of opinion   conditional statements
loosely associated statements

Keep in mind that these kinds of nonarguments are not mutually exclusive, and that, for example, one and the same passage can sometimes be interpreted as both a report and a statement of opinion, or as both an expository passage and an illustration. The precise kind of nonargument a passage might be is nowhere near as important as correctly deciding whether or not it is an argument.

EXERCISE 1.2

I. Determine which of the following passages are arguments. For those that are, identify the conclusion. For those that are not, determine the kind of nonargument.

★**1.** The turkey vulture is called by that name because its red featherless head resembles the head of a wild turkey.

2. If public education fails to improve the quality of instruction in both primary and secondary schools, then it is likely that it will lose additional students to the private sector in the years ahead.

3. Freedom of the press is the most important of our constitutionally guaranteed freedoms. Without it, our other freedoms would be immediately threatened. Furthermore, it provides the fulcrum for the advancement of new freedoms.

★ 4. A mammal is a vertebrate animal that nurses its offspring. Thus, cats and dogs are mammals, as are sheep, monkeys, rabbits, and bears.

5. It is strongly recommended that you have your house inspected for termite damage at the earliest possible opportunity.

6. Mosquito bites are not always the harmless little irritations most of us take them to be. For example, some mosquitoes carry West Nile virus, and people who are infected can become very sick or even die.

★ 7. If stem-cell research is restricted, then future cures will not materialize. If future cures do not materialize, then people will die prematurely. Therefore, if stem-cell research is restricted, then people will die prematurely.

hypothetical syllogism

8. Fictional characters behave according to the same psychological probabilities as real people. But the characters of fiction are found in exotic dilemmas that real people hardly encounter. Consequently, fiction provides us with the opportunity to ponder how people react in uncommon situations, and to deduce moral lessons, psychological principles, and philosophical insights from their behavior.

(J. R. McCuen and A. C. Winkler, *Readings for Writers,* 4th ed.)

9. I believe that it must be the policy of the United States to support free peoples who are resisting attempted subjugation by armed minorities or by outside pressures. I believe that we must assist free peoples to work out their own destinies in their own way. I believe that our help should be primarily through economic and financial aid, which is essential to economic stability and orderly political processes.

(President Truman, Address to Congress, 1947)

★10. Five college students who were accused of sneaking into the Cincinnati Zoo and trying to ride the camels pleaded no contest to criminal trespass yesterday. The students scaled a fence to get into the zoo and then climbed another fence to get into the camel pit before security officials caught them, zoo officials said.

(Newspaper clipping)

11. Mortality rates for women undergoing early abortions, where the procedure is legal, appear to be as low as or lower than the rates for normal childbirth. Consequently, any interest of the state in protecting the woman from an inherently hazardous procedure, except when it would be equally dangerous for her to forgo it, has largely disappeared.

(Justice Blackmun, *Roe v. Wade*)

12. The pace of reading, clearly, depends entirely upon the reader. He may read as slowly or as rapidly as he can or wishes to read. If he does not understand something, he may stop and reread it, or go in search of elucidation before continuing. The reader can accelerate his pace when the material is easy or less than interesting, and can slow down when it is difficult or enthralling. If what he reads is moving he can put down the book for a few moments and cope with his emotions without fear of losing anything.

(Marie Winn, *The Plug-In Drug*)

★13. Any unit of length, when cubed, becomes a unit of volume. Thus, the cubic meter, cubic centimeter, and cubic millimeter are all units of volume.

(Nivaldo J. Tro, *Chemistry: A Molecular Approach,* 2nd ed.)

14. Lions at Kruger National Park in South Africa are dying of tuberculosis. "All of the lions in the park may be dead within ten years because the disease is incurable, and the lions have no natural resistance," said the deputy director of the Department of Agriculture.

(Newspaper clipping)

15. Economics is of practical value in business. An understanding of the overall operation of the economic system puts the business executive in a better position to formulate policies. The executive who understands the causes and consequences of inflation is better equipped during inflationary periods to make more-intelligent decisions than otherwise.

(Campbell R. McConnell, *Economics,* 8th ed.)

★16. Bear one thing in mind before you begin to write your paper: Famous literary works, especially works regarded as classics, have been thoroughly studied to the point where prevailing opinion on them has assumed the character of orthodoxy.

(J. R. McCuen and A. C. Winkler, *Readings for Writers,* 4th ed.)

17. Young people at universities study to achieve knowledge and not to learn a trade. We must all learn how to support ourselves, but we must also learn how to live. We need a lot of engineers in the modern world, but we do not want a world of modern engineers.

(Winston Churchill, *A Churchill Reader,* ed. Colin R. Coote)

18. No business concern wants to sell on credit to a customer who will prove unable or unwilling to pay his or her account. Consequently, most business organizations include a credit department which must reach a decision on the credit worthiness of each prospective customer.

(Walter B. Meigs and Robert F. Meigs, *Accounting*)

★19. For organisms at the sea surface, sinking into deep water usually means death. Plant cells cannot photosynthesize in the dark depths. Fishes and other animals that descend lose contact with the main surface food supply and themselves become food for strange deep-living predators.

(David H. Milne, *Marine Life and the Sea*)

20. Since the 1950s a malady called whirling disease has invaded U.S. fishing streams, frequently attacking rainbow trout. A parasite deforms young fish, which often chase their tails before dying, hence the name.

("Trout Disease—A Turn for the Worse," *National Geographic*)

21. Dachshunds are ideal dogs for small children, as they are already stretched and pulled to such a length that the child cannot do much harm one way or the other.

(Robert Benchley, quoted in *Cold Noses and Warm Hearts*)

★22. Atoms are the basic building blocks of all matter. They can combine to form molecules, whose properties are generally very different from those of the constituent atoms. Table salt, for example, a simple chemical compound formed from chlorine and sodium, resembles neither the poisonous gas nor the highly reactive metal.

(Frank J. Blatt, *Principles of Physics,* 2nd ed.)

23. The coarsest type of humor is the *practical joke*: pulling away the chair from the dignitary's lowered bottom. The victim is perceived first as a person of consequence, then suddenly as an inert body subject to the laws of physics: authority is debunked by gravity, mind by matter; man is degraded to a mechanism.

(Arthur Koestler, *Janus: A Summing Up*)

 24. If a man holding a belief which he was taught in childhood or persuaded of afterwards keeps down and pushes away any doubts which arise about it in his mind, purposely avoids the reading of books and the company of men that call in question or discuss it, and regards as impious those questions which cannot easily be asked without disturbing it—the life of that man is one long sin against mankind.

(W. K. Clifford, *The Ethics of Belief*)

★25. It is usually easy to decide whether or not something is alive. This is because living things share many common attributes, such as the capacity to extract energy from nutrients to drive their various functions, the power to actively respond to changes in their environment, and the ability to grow, to differentiate, and to reproduce.

(Donald Voet and Judith G. Voet, *Biochemistry*, 2nd ed.)

26. Words are slippery customers. The full meaning of a word does not appear until it is placed in its context.... And even then the meaning will depend upon the listener, upon the speaker, upon their entire experience of the language, upon their knowledge of one another, and upon the whole situation.

(C. Cherry, *On Human Communication*)

27. Haydn developed the string quartet from the eighteenth-century *divertimento*, giving more substance to the light, popular form and scoring it for two violins, a viola, and a cello. His eighty-three quartets, written over the course of his creative lifetime, evolved slowly into a sophisticated form. Together they constitute one of the most important bodies of chamber-music literature.

(Robert Hickok, *Exploring Music*)

★28. A person never becomes truly self-reliant. Even though he deals effectively with things, he is necessarily dependent upon those who have taught him to do so. They have selected the things he is dependent upon and determined the kinds and degrees of dependencies.

(B. F. Skinner, *Beyond Freedom and Dignity*)

29. There is no doubt that some businessmen conspire to shorten the useful life of their products in order to guarantee replacement sales. There is, similarly, no doubt that many of the annual model changes with which American (and other) consumers are increasingly familiar are not technologically substantive.

(Alvin Toffler, *Future Shock*)

30. The brain and the nervous system are composed of two types of cells—neurons and glial cells. Neurons are responsible for information transmission throughout the nervous system. Glial cells constitute the support system for the neurons. For example, glial cells take away the waste products of neurons, keep the neurons' chemical environment stable, and insulate them, allowing neurons to do their work more efficiently.

(Richard Griggs, *Psychology: A Concise Introduction*)

★31. In areas where rats are a problem, it is very difficult to exterminate them with bait poison. That's because some rats eat enough poison to die but others eat only enough to become sick and then learn to avoid that particular poison taste in the future.

(Rod Plotnik, *Introduction to Psychology*, 4th ed.)

32. Although it is customary to think of human population as increasing continuously without declines or fluctuations, population growth has not been a steady march. For example, great declines occurred during the time of the Black Death, during the fourteenth century. Entire towns were abandoned, production of food declined, and in England, one-third of the population died within a single decade.

(Daniel B. Botkin and Edward A. Keller, *Environmental Science*)

33. If someone avoids and is afraid of everything, standing firm against nothing, he becomes cowardly; if he is afraid of nothing at all and goes to face everything, he becomes rash. Similarly, if he gratifies himself with every pleasure and abstains from none, he becomes intemperate; if he avoids them all, he becomes some sort of insensible person. Temperance and bravery, then, are ruined by excess and deficiency, but preserved by the mean.

(Aristotle, *Nicomachean Ethics*)

★34. Nations are made in two ways, by the slow working of history or the galvanic force of ideas. Most nations are made the former way, emerging slowly from the mist of the past, gradually coalescing within concentric circles of shared sympathies, with an accretion of consensual institutions. But a few nations are formed and defined by the citizens' assent to a shared philosophy.

(George Will, "Lithuania and South Carolina")

35. One form of energy can be converted to another. For example, when an electric motor is connected to a battery, chemical energy is converted to electrical energy, which in turn is converted to mechanical energy.

(Raymond A. Serway, *Physics for Scientists and Engineers*, 4th ed.)

II. The following selections were originally submitted as letters to the editor of newspapers and magazines. Determine which of them can, with good reason, be considered arguments. In those that can, identify the conclusion.

★1. What this country needs is a return to the concept of swift and certain justice. If we need more courts, judges, and prisons, then so be it. And as for capital punishment, I say let the punishment fit the crime. When criminals behave more like humans, then we can start to treat them more humanely. In the meantime, I would like to see the Night Stalkers of our society swiftly executed rather than coddled by our courts and prisons.

(John Pearson)

2. Social Security is not merely a retirement program. Six and a half million children in the United States are kept out of poverty each year because of assistance from Social Security's survivors benefits program—which protects virtually all American children in the tragic event of the death of a parent. Beneficiaries include spouses and children of workers who have died or become disabled; grandparents raising grandchildren; severely disabled children; and families of fallen service members.

(Donna Butts)

3. Is there any country in the world that worries more about its kids having fun in school, making lessons exciting and relevant, and then is more disappointed with the result than the United States? We think learning is like buying a car or smoking a cigarette. Just get into the thing or draw a breath and you will be effortlessly transported to lands of pleasure and excitement.

(Charles M. Breinin)

★4. After reading your cover story, I find that cable TV has simply flooded our airwaves with more sex, violence, and teenage punk junk. Now our children can spend even less time studying and we can spend more time in blank-space stares at the idiot box. Cable would be fine with more educational channels—and fewer cheap thrills aimed at narrow-minded bubble brains.

(Jacqueline Murray)

5. Once the basic necessities have been achieved, future income is only lightly connected to well-being. Democrats generally seek to tax future income to finance programs that meet basic needs, including food, clothing shelter, retirement security, and health care. Republicans, in contrast, seek to protect future income from taxation, often at the expense of meeting the basic needs of the less fortunate. So which of our two main political parties is more concerned with achieving broad happiness, and which party is more concerned with fulfilling selfishness?

(Jonathan Carey)

6. Animal abusers are cowards who take their issues out on "easy victims"—and their targets often include their fellow humans. I cannot begin to say how many incidents I've seen involving animal abusers who commit violent acts against humans, and animal neglecters who have neglected their children or other human dependents. Treating cruelty to animals with the seriousness it deserves doesn't only protect animals, it also makes the entire community safer.

(Martin Mersereau)

★7. The creation of a third political party—the Independent Party—would allow Congressional aspirants who desire to think for themselves to claim a high ground that is currently vacant. The new party would provide a more effective forum to discuss the right course for this country and might compel the other two parties to do likewise. The pressure such a movement would put on those now stagnating in cozy sinecures would, at the least, prove entertaining for a weary, frustrated public.

(Bill Cannon)

8. I agree that when religious institutions exclude women from their hierarchies and rituals, the inevitable implication is that females are inferior. But it is important to note that when women's voices are silenced, it is not only the message that such discrimination sends that is damaging. The institutions themselves suffer. By disempowering women, religious institutions, and the broader societies in which they operate, lose the invaluable input of 51 percent of their constituents.

(Jessie Cronan)

9. It looks like India and China are going to compete for a manned landing on the moon by 2020 while America is muddling along with no real future space plan. Let's do something significant in space—say, go to Mars by 2020. We could have done it 30 years ago. Planning for a Mars mission was well along. But the nation

turned away from space after we landed on the moon, even canceling the three remaining flights to the moon. These Saturn 5 rockets now sit in museums.

(Bill Ketchum)

★10. Teenage bullying is all about power. One person has it, one person does not. Reluctant to seek help, victims feel ashamed and powerless, and they fear retaliation should they "rat out" the bully. Strong anti-bullying programs are needed to provide a means to report bullying anonymously, to train all school personnel to take reports of bullying seriously, and to offer workshops for children on how to respond to being bullied.

(Karen Schulte O'Neill)

III. The following statements represent conclusions for arguments. Each is expressed in the form of two alternatives. Select one of the alternatives for each conclusion, and then jot down several reasons that support it. Finally, incorporate your reasons into a written argument of at least 100 words that supports the conclusion. Include premise and conclusion indicators in some of your arguments, but not in all of them.

1. A constitutional amendment that outlaws flag burning should/should not be adopted.

2. Street drugs should/should not be legalized.

3. The death penalty should/should not be abolished.

4. Sanctions should/should not be imposed on students for using speech that is offensive to minorities.

5. Free health care should/should not be guaranteed to all citizens.

6. Same-sex marriages should/should not be recognized by the state.

7. The possession, ownership, and sale of handguns should/should not be outlawed.

8. Cigarettes should/should not be regulated as an addictive drug.

9. Affirmative action programs should/should not be abolished.

10. Doctors should/should not be allowed to assist terminally ill patients in committing suicide.

IV. Define the following terms:

expository passage
illustration
argument from example
explanation
explanandum
explanans

conditional statement
antecedent
consequent
sufficient condition
necessary condition

V. Answer "true" or "false" to the following statements:

1. Any passage that contains an argument must contain a claim that something is supported by evidence or reasons.

2. In an argument, the claim that something is supported by evidence or reasons is always explicit.

3. Passages that contain indicator words such as "thus," "since," and "because" are always arguments.

4. In deciding whether a passage contains an argument, we should always keep an eye out for indicator words and the presence of an inferential relationship between the statements.

5. Some expository passages can be correctly interpreted as arguments.

6. Some passages containing "for example" can be correctly interpreted as arguments.

7. In deciding whether an expository passage or an illustration should be interpreted as an argument, it helps to note whether the claim being developed or illustrated is one that is accepted by everyone.

8. Some conditional statements can be reexpressed to form arguments.

9. In an explanation, the explanandum usually describes an accepted matter of fact.

10. In an explanation, the explanans is the statement or group of statements that does the explaining.

VI. Fill in the blanks with "necessary" or "sufficient" to make the following statements true. After the blanks have been filled in, express the result in terms of conditional statements.

★1. Being a tiger is a _____ condition for being an animal.

2. Being an animal is a _____ condition for being a tiger.

3. Drinking a glass of water is a _____ condition for quenching one's thirst.

★4. Having a racket is a _____ condition for playing tennis.

5. Heating water is a _____ condition for brewing coffee.

6. Stepping on a cat's tail is a _____ condition for making the cat yowl.

★7. Burning leaves is a _____ condition for producing smoke.

8. Paying attention is a _____ condition for understanding a lecture.

9. Being exactly divisible by 4 is a _____ condition for a number being even.

★10. Uttering a falsehood is a _____ condition for telling a lie.

VII. Page through a book, magazine, or newspaper and find two arguments, one with indicator words, the other without. Copy the arguments as written, giving the appropriate reference. Then identify the premises and conclusion of each.

aplia

Visit Aplia for section-specific problem sets.

1.3 Deduction and Induction

PREVIEW

You are walking through campus on the way to class when suddenly you hear a loud pop-pop-pop. Simultaneously you see three people fall to the ground. One is screaming for help, and the other two are lying motionless. Immediately you take cover behind a nearby tree. Why do you do this? Because it appears that an assailant is shooting people and that you might be the next victim. Is it certain you will be hit? No, but there is a reasonable degree of probability. This section addresses the distinction between certain and probable reasoning.

The idea that arguments come in two forms, deductive and inductive, was first asserted by Aristotle. In the intervening centuries, deduction and induction have become a settled fixture not only in logic but in our intellectual culture. Countless books, both fiction and nonfiction, have referred to it. Einstein wrote a paper on it. And a huge number of textbooks ranging from philosophy to education, business to psychology, and chemistry to anthropology explore the subject. So what is the difference between a deductive and an inductive argument? Briefly we can say that deductive arguments are those that rest on *necessary* reasoning, while inductive arguments are those that rest on *probabilistic* reasoning.

Stated more precisely, a **deductive argument** is an argument incorporating the claim that it is *impossible* for the conclusion to be false given that the premises are true. On the other hand, an **inductive argument** is an argument incorporating the claim that it is *improbable* that the conclusion be false given that the premises are true. Two examples:

> The meerkat is closely related to the suricat.
> The suricat thrives on beetle larvae.
> Therefore, probably the meerkat thrives on beetle larvae.

> The meerkat is a member of the mongoose family.
> All members of the mongoose family are carnivores.
> Therefore, it necessarily follows that the meerkat is a carnivore.

deductive argument: An argument incorporating the claim that it is *impossible* for the conclusion to be false given that the premises are true.

inductive argument: An argument incorporating the claim that it is *improbable* for the conclusion to be false given that the premises are true.

The first of these arguments is inductive, the second deductive.

In deciding whether an argument is inductive or deductive, we look to certain objective features of the argument. These features include (1) the occurrence of special indicator words, (2) the *actual* strength of the inferential link between premises and conclusion, and (3) the form or style of argumentation. However, we must acknowledge at the outset that many arguments in ordinary language are incomplete, and because of this, deciding whether the argument should best be interpreted as deductive or inductive may be impossible.

The occurrence of special indicator words is illustrated in the examples we just considered. The word "probably" in the conclusion of the first argument suggests that the argument should be taken as inductive, and the word "necessarily" in the conclusion of the second suggests that the second argument be taken as deductive. Additional inductive indicators are "improbable," "plausible," "implausible," "likely," "unlikely," and "reasonable to conclude." Additional deductive indicators are "certainly," "absolutely," and "definitely." (Note that the phrase "it must be the case that" is simply a conclusion indicator that can occur in either deductive or inductive argments.)

Inductive and deductive indicator words often suggest the correct interpretation. However, if they conflict with one of the other criteria (discussed shortly), we should probably ignore them. Arguers often use phrases such as "it certainly follows that" for rhetorical purposes to add impact to their conclusion and not to suggest that the argument be taken as deductive. Similarly, some arguers, not knowing the distinction between inductive and deductive, will claim to "deduce" a conclusion when their argument is more correctly interpreted as inductive.

The second factor that bears on our interpretation of an argument as inductive or deductive is the *actual* strength of the inferential link between premises and conclusion. If the conclusion actually does follow with strict necessity from the premises, the argument is clearly deductive. In such an argument it is impossible for the premises to be true and the conclusion false. On the other hand, if the conclusion does not follow with strict necessity but does follow probably, it is often best to consider the argument inductive. Examples:

> All entertainers are extroverts.
> Stephen Colbert is an entertainer.
> Therefore, Stephen Colbert is an extrovert.
>
> The vast majority of entertainers are extroverts.
> Stephen Colbert is an entertainer.
> Therefore, Stephen Colbert is an extrovert.

In the first example, the conclusion follows with strict necessity from the premises. If we assume that all entertainers are extroverts and that Stephen Colbert is an entertainer, then it is impossible that Stephen Colbert not be an extrovert. Thus, we should interpret this argument as deductive. In the second example, the conclusion does not follow from the premises with strict necessity, but it does follow with some degree of probability. If we assume that the premises are true, then based on that assumption it is probable that the conclusion is true. Thus, it is best to interpret the second argument as inductive.

Occasionally, an argument contains no special indicator words, and the conclusion does not follow either necessarily or probably from the premises; in other words, it does not follow at all. This situation points to the need for the third factor to be taken into account, which is the character or form of argumentation the arguer uses.

Deductive Argument Forms

Many arguments have a distinctive character or form that indicates that the premises are supposed to provide absolute support for the conclusion. Five examples of such forms or kinds of argumentation are arguments based on mathematics, arguments from definition, and categorical, hypothetical, and disjunctive syllogisms.

An **argument based on mathematics** is an argument in which the conclusion depends on some purely arithmetic or geometric computation or measurement. For example, a shopper might place two apples and three oranges into a paper bag and then conclude that the bag contains five pieces of fruit. Or a surveyor might measure a square piece of land and, after determining that it is 100 feet on each side, conclude that it contains 10,000 square feet. Since all arguments in pure mathematics are deductive, we can usually consider arguments that depend on mathematics to be deductive as well. However, arguments that depend on statistics are a noteworthy exception. As we will see shortly, such arguments are usually best interpreted as inductive.

An **argument from definition** is an argument in which the conclusion is claimed to depend merely on the definition of some word or phrase. For example, someone might argue that because Claudia is mendacious, it follows that she tells lies, or that because a certain paragraph is prolix, it follows that it is excessively wordy. These arguments are deductive because their conclusions follow with necessity from the definitions of "mendacious" and "prolix."

A *syllogism,* in general, is an argument consisting of exactly two premises and one conclusion. Categorical syllogisms will be treated in greater depth in Chapter 4, but for now we will say that a **categorical syllogism** is a syllogism in which each statement begins with one of the words "all," "no," or "some." Example:

argument based on mathematics: A deductive argument in which the conclusion depends on some arithmetic or geometric computation or measurement.

argument from definition: A deductive argument in which the conclusion depends merely on the definition of some word or phrase.

categorical syllogism: A deductive argument having two premises and one conclusion each of which begins with "all," "no," or "some."

Ruth Barcan was born in New York City in 1921. Her mother was a homemaker, and her father a typesetter at, and contributor to, the *Jewish Daily Forward*. After completing her primary and secondary education at public schools, she enrolled in New York University, where, in addition to her academic pursuits, she won praise as an outstanding fencer. In 1941 she earned a bachelor's degree in mathematics and philosophy, and five years later she received a PhD in philosophy from Yale University. In 1942 she married Jules Alexander Marcus, a physicist, and the couple had four children, two boys and two girls.

After graduating from Yale, Barcan Marcus's early career was spent holding several postdoctoral fellowships (including a Guggenheim) and visiting professorships. In 1959 she accepted a position at Roosevelt University, followed by positions at the University of Illinois, Chicago (where she was founding department chair), and Northwestern University. In 1973 she returned to Yale as professor of philosophy.

Commencing early in her career, Barcan Marcus made pioneering contributions to the area of quantified modal logic.

Courtesy Michael Marsland

She proposed, as an axiom, the widely discussed Barcan formula, which asserts, in symbols, $(x)\Box Fx \supset \Box(x)Fx$. In English, this means that if everything is necessarily F, then it is necessary that everything is F. The formula is controversial because it implies that all objects that exist in every possible world exist in the actual world. This could be taken to imply that nothing new can be created.

Personally, Ruth Barcan Marcus was fearless, down to earth, unpretentious, and a constant supporter of others. She had a great sense of humor—and she was also endearingly absentminded. On one occasion, while in the midst of a frantic search, she received a call from the local supermarket informing her that her final exams had been found amid the frozen meats.

All ancient forests are sources of wonder.
Some ancient forests are targets of the timber industry.
Therefore, some sources of wonder are targets of the timber industry.

Arguments such as these are nearly always best treated as deductive.

A **hypothetical syllogism** is a syllogism having a conditional ("if . . . then . . .") statement for one or both of its premises. Examples:

If estate taxes are abolished, then wealth will accumulate disproportionately.
If wealth accumulates disproportionately, then democracy will be threatened.
Therefore, if estate taxes are abolished, then democracy will be threatened.

If Fox News is a propaganda machine, then it misleads its viewers.
Fox News is a propaganda machine.
Therefore, Fox News misleads its viewers.

> **hypothetical syllogism**:
> A deductive argument having two premises and one conclusion in which at least one premise is an "if . . . then . . ." statement.

Later in this book, the first of these arguments will be given the more specific name of pure hypothetical syllogism because it is composed exclusively of conditional (hypothetical) statements. The second argument is called a mixed hypothetical syllogism because only one of its component statements is a conditional. Later in this book, the second argument will be given the more specific Latin name modus ponens.

A **disjunctive syllogism** is a syllogism having a disjunctive ("either . . . or . . .")

> **disjunctive syllogism**:
> A deductive argument having two premises and one conclusion in which one premise is an "either . . . or . . ." statement.

statement as a premise. Example:

> Either global warming will be arrested, or hurricanes will become more intense.
> Global warming will not be arrested.
> Therefore, hurricanes will become more intense.

As with hypothetical syllogisms, such arguments are usually best taken as deductive. Hypothetical and disjunctive syllogisms will be treated in greater depth in Chapter 5.

Inductive Argument Forms

In general, inductive arguments are such that the content of the conclusion is in some way intended to "go beyond" the content of the premises. The premises of such an argument typically deal with some subject that is relatively familiar, and the conclusion then moves beyond this to a subject that is less familiar or that little is known about. Such an argument may take any of several forms: predictions about the future, arguments from analogy, inductive generalizations, arguments from authority, arguments based on signs, and causal inferences, to name just a few.

prediction: An inductive argument that proceeds from our knowledge of the past to a claim about the future.

A **prediction** is an argument that proceeds from our knowledge of the past to a claim about the future. For example, someone might argue that because certain meteorological phenomena have been observed to develop over a certain region of central Missouri, a storm will occur there in six hours. Or again, one might argue that because certain fluctuations occurred in the prime interest rate on Friday, the value of the dollar will decrease against foreign currencies on Monday. Nearly everyone realizes that the future cannot be known with certainty; thus, whenever an argument makes a prediction about the future, one is usually justified in considering the argument inductive.

argument from analogy: An inductive argument that depends on a similarity between two things.

An **argument from analogy** is an argument that depends on the existence of an analogy, or similarity, between two things or states of affairs. Because of the existence of this analogy, a certain condition that affects the better-known thing or situation is concluded to affect the similar, lesser-known thing or situation. For example, someone might argue that because Christina's Porsche is a great-handling car, it follows that Angela's Porsche must also be a great-handling car. The argument depends on the existence of a similarity, or analogy, between the two cars. The certitude attending such an inference is probabilistic at best.

generalization: An inductive argument that proceeds from the knowledge of a sample to a claim about the whole group.

A **generalization** is an argument that proceeds from the knowledge of a selected sample to a claim about the whole group. Because the members of the sample have a certain characteristic, it is argued that all the members of the group have that same characteristic. For example, one might argue that because three oranges selected from a certain crate were especially tasty and juicy, all the oranges from that crate are especially tasty and juicy. Or again, one might argue that because six out of a total of nine members surveyed from a certain labor union intend to vote for Johnson for union president, two-thirds of the entire membership intend to vote for Johnson. These examples illustrate the use of statistics in inductive argumentation.

argument from authority: An inductive argument that concludes something is true because a presumed expert or witness has said that it is.

An **argument from authority** is an argument that concludes something is true because a presumed expert or witness has said that it is. For example, a person might argue that earnings for Hewlett-Packard Corporation will be up in the coming quarter because of a statement to that effect by an investment counselor. Or a lawyer might argue that Mack the Knife committed the murder because an eyewitness testified to that effect under oath. Because the investment counselor and the eyewitness could be either mistaken or lying, such arguments are essentially probabilistic.

An **argument based on signs** is an argument that proceeds from the knowledge of a sign to a claim about the thing or situation that the sign symbolizes. The word "sign," as it is used here, means any kind of message (usually visual) produced by an intelligent being. For example, when driving on an unfamiliar highway one might see a sign indicating that the road makes several sharp turns one mile ahead. Based on this information, one might argue that the road does indeed make several sharp turns one mile ahead. Because the sign might be misplaced or in error about the turns, the conclusion is only probable.

A **causal inference** is an argument that proceeds from knowledge of a cause to a claim about an effect, or, conversely, from knowledge of an effect to a claim about a cause. For example, from the knowledge that a bottle of wine had been accidentally left in the freezer overnight, someone might conclude that it had frozen (cause to effect). Conversely, after tasting a piece of chicken and finding it dry and tough, one might conclude that it had been overcooked (effect to cause). Because specific instances of cause and effect can never be known with absolute certainty, one may usually interpret such arguments as inductive.

argument based on signs: An inductive argument that proceeds from knowledge of a sign to a claim about what the sign symbolizes.

1

causal inference: An inductive argument that proceeds from knowledge of a cause to a claim about an effect, or vice versa.

Further Considerations

It should be noted that the various subspecies of inductive arguments listed here are not intended to be mutually exclusive. Overlaps can and do occur. For example, many causal inferences that proceed from cause to effect also qualify as predictions. The purpose of this survey is not to demarcate in precise terms the various forms of induction but rather to provide guidelines for distinguishing induction from deduction.

Keeping this in mind, we should take care not to confuse arguments in geometry, which are always deductive, with arguments from analogy or inductive generalizations. For example, an argument concluding that a triangle has a certain attribute (such as a right angle) because another triangle, with which it is congruent, also has that attribute might be mistaken for an argument from analogy. Similarly, an argument that concludes that all triangles have a certain attribute (such as angles totaling two right angles) because any particular triangle has that attribute might be mistaken for an inductive generalization. Arguments such as these, however, are always deductive, because the conclusion follows necessarily and with complete certainty from the premises.

One broad classification of arguments not listed in this survey is scientific arguments. Arguments that occur in science can be either inductive or deductive, depending on the circumstances. In general, arguments aimed at the *discovery* of a law of nature are usually considered inductive. Suppose, for example, that we want to discover a law that governs the time required for a falling body to strike the earth. We drop bodies of various weights from various heights and measure the time it takes them to fall. Comparing our measurements, we notice that the time is approximately proportional to the square root of the distance. From this we conclude that the time required for any body to fall is proportional to the square root of the distance through which it falls. Such an argument is best interpreted as an inductive generalization.

Another type of argument that occurs in science has to do with the *application* of known laws to specific circumstances. Scientific laws are widely considered to be generalizations that hold for all times and all places. As so understood, their application to a specific situation is always deductive, even though it might relate to the future. Suppose, for example, that we want to apply Boyle's law for ideal gases to a container of gas in our laboratory. Boyle's law states that the pressure exerted by a gas on the walls of its container is inversely proportional to the volume. Applying this law, we conclude that when we reduce the volume of our laboratory sample by half, the pressure will double. This application of Boyle's law is deductive, even though it pertains to the future.

A final point needs to be made about the distinction between inductive and deductive arguments. There is a tradition extending back to the time of Aristotle that holds that inductive arguments are those that proceed from the particular to the general, while deductive arguments are those that proceed from the general to the particular. (A **particular statement** is one that makes a claim about one or more particular members of a class, while a **general statement** makes a claim about *all* the members of a class.) It is true, of course, that many inductive and deductive arguments do work in this way; but this fact should not be used as a criterion for distinguishing induction from deduction. As a matter of fact, there are deductive arguments that proceed from the general to the general, from the particular to the particular, and from the particular to the general, as well as from the general to the particular; and there are inductive arguments that do the same. For example, here is a deductive argument that proceeds from the particular to the general:

> Three is a prime number.
> Five is a prime number.
> Seven is a prime number.
> Therefore, all odd numbers between two and eight are prime numbers.

And here is one that proceeds from the particular to the particular:

> Gabriel is a wolf.
> Gabriel has a tail.
> Therefore, Gabriel's tail is the tail of a wolf.

Here is an inductive argument that proceeds from the general to the particular:

> All emeralds previously found have been green.
> Therefore, the next emerald to be found will be green.

The other varieties are easy to construct. Thus, the progression from particular to general, and vice versa, cannot be used as a criterion for distinguishing induction from deduction.

Section 1.3 Summary

To distinguish deductive arguments from inductive arguments, we attempt to evaluate the strength of the argument's inferential claim—how strongly the conclusion is claimed to follow from the premises. This claim is an objective feature of an argument, and it may or may not be related to the subjective intentions of the arguer.

To interpret an argument's inferential claim we look at three factors: special indicator words, the actual strength of the inferential link between premises and conclusion, and the form or style of argumentation. Given that we have more than one factor to look at, it is possible in a single argument for the occurrence of two of these factors to conflict with each other, leading to opposite interpretations. For example, in drawing a conclusion to a categorical syllogism (which is clearly deductive), an arguer might say "It probably follows that . . ."

particular statement:
A statement that makes a claim about *one or more* members of a class.

general statement:
A statement that makes a claim about *all* the members of a class.

(which suggests induction). To help alleviate this conflict we can list the factors in order of importance:

1. Arguments in which the premises provide absolute support for the conclusion. Such arguments are always deductive.

2. Arguments having a specific deductive character or form (e.g., categorical syllogism). This factor is often of equal importance to the first, and, when present, it provides a clear-cut indication that the argument is deductive.

3. Arguments having a specific inductive character or form (e.g., a prediction). Arguments of this sort are nearly always best interpreted as inductive.

4. Arguments containing inductive indicator language (e.g., "It probably follows that . . ."). Since arguers rarely try to make their argument appear weaker than it really is, such language can usually be trusted. But if this language conflicts with one of the first two factors, it should be ignored.

5. Arguments containing deductive indicator language (e.g., "It necessarily follows that . . ."). Arguers occasionally use such language for rhetorical purposes, to make their argument appear stronger than it really is, so such language should be evaluated carefully.

6. Arguments in which the premises provide only probable support for the conclusion. This is the least important factor, and if it conflicts with any of the earlier ones, it should probably be ignored.

Unfortunately, many arguments in ordinary language are incomplete, so it often happens that none of these factors are clearly present. Determining the inductive or deductive character of such arguments may be impossible.

EXERCISE 1.3

I. Determine whether the following arguments are best interpreted as being inductive or deductive. Also state the criteria you use in reaching your decision (i.e., the presence of indicator words, the nature of the inferential link between premises and conclusion, or the character or form of argumentation).

★1. Because triangle A is congruent with triangle B, and triangle A is isosceles, it follows that triangle B is isosceles.

2. The plaque on the leaning tower of Pisa says that Galileo performed experiments there with falling objects. It must be the case that Galileo did indeed perform those experiments there.

3. The rainfall in Seattle has been more than 15 inches every year for the past thirty years. Therefore, the rainfall next year will probably be more than 15 inches.

★4. No e-mail messages are eloquent creations. Some love letters are eloquent creations. Therefore, some love letters are not e-mail messages.

5. Amoco, Exxon, and Texaco are all listed on the New York Stock Exchange. It must be the case that all major American oil companies are listed on the New York Stock Exchange.

6. The longer a pendulum is, the longer it takes to swing. Therefore, when the pendulum of a clock is lengthened, the clock slows down.

★7. Paying off terrorists in exchange for hostages is not a wise policy, since such action will only lead them to take more hostages in the future.

8. The Matterhorn is higher than Mount Whitney, and Mount Whitney is higher than Mount Rainier. The obvious conclusion is that the Matterhorn is higher than Mount Rainier.

9. Although both front and rear doors were found open after the burglary, there were pry marks around the lock on the rear door and deposits of mud near the threshold. It must be the case that the thief entered through the rear door and left through the front.

★10. The *Wall Street Journal* has an article on the new banking regulations. The *Financial Times,* like the *Wall Street Journal,* is a highly respected business publication. Therefore, the *Financial Times* probably also has an article on the new banking regulations.

11. Cholesterol is endogenous with humans. Therefore, it is manufactured inside the human body.

12. Either classical culture originated in Greece, or it originated in Egypt. Classical culture did not originate in Egypt. Therefore, classical culture originated in Greece.

★13. World-renowned physicist Stephen Hawking says that the condition of the universe at the instant of the big bang was more highly ordered than it is today. In view of Hawking's stature in the scientific community, we should conclude that this description of the universe is correct.

14. If Alexander the Great died from typhoid fever, then he became infected in India. Alexander the Great did die from typhoid fever. Therefore, he became infected in India.

15. Crater Lake, the deepest lake in the United States, was caused by a huge volcanic eruption 7,700 years ago. Since human beings have lived around the mountain for more than 10,000 years, it is likely that people witnessed that eruption.

(National Park Service, "Crater Lake—Its History")

★16. Each element, such as hydrogen and iron, has a set of gaps—wavelengths that it absorbs rather than radiates. So if those wavelengths are missing from the spectrum, you know that that element is present in the star you are observing.

(Rick Gore, "Eyes of Science")

17. Because the apparent daily movement which is common to both the planets and the fixed stars is seen to travel from the east to the west, but the far-slower single movements of the single planets travel in the opposite direction from west to east, it is therefore certain that these movements cannot depend on the common movement of the world but should be assigned to the planets themselves.

(Johannes Kepler, *Epitomy of Copernican Astronomy*)

18. Contrary to the common notion that women tend to be chatty compared to men, little difference exists between the sexes in terms of talkativeness. Over a five-year period researchers placed unobtrusive microphones on 396 college students in various fields, at campuses in Mexico as well as in the United States. They found that both men and women spoke about 16,000 words per day.

(Richard T. Schaefer, *Sociology: A Brief Introduction,* 8th ed.)

★19. When the Romans occupied England, coal was burned. Since coal produces quite a bit of soot and sulfur dioxide, there must have been days almost 2,000 years ago when the air in the larger towns was badly polluted.

(Stanley Gedzelman, *The Science and Wonders of the Atmosphere*)

20. The graphical method for solving a system of equations is an approximation, since reading the point of intersection depends on the accuracy with which the lines are drawn and on the ability to interpret the coordinates of the point.

(Karl J. Smith and Patrick J. Boyle, *Intermediate Algebra for College Students*)

21. That [the moons of Jupiter] revolve in unequal circles is manifestly deduced from the fact that at the longest elongation from Jupiter it is never possible to see two of these moons in conjunction, whereas in the vicinity of Jupiter they are found united two, three, and sometimes all four together.

(Galileo Galilei, *The Starry Messenger*)

★22. Lenses function by refracting light at their surfaces. Consequently, their action depends not only on the shape of the lens surfaces, but also on the indices of refraction of the lens material and the surrounding medium.

(Frank J. Blatt, *Principles of Physics,* 2nd ed.)

23. Given present growth rates in underdeveloped countries, the limited practice of birth control, and the difficulty of slowing the current growth momentum, it can be said with virtual certainty that none of the people now reading this book will ever live in a world where the population is not growing.

(J. John Palen, *Social Problems*)

24. The interpretation of the laws is the proper and peculiar province of the courts. A constitution is, in fact, and must be regarded by the judges, as a fundamental law. It therefore belongs to them to ascertain its meaning, as well as the meaning of any particular act proceeding from the legislative body.

(Alexander Hamilton, *Federalist Papers,* No. 78)

★25. The Simpson incident had shown me that a dog was kept in the stables, and yet, though someone had been in and had fetched out a horse, he had not barked enough to arouse the two lads in the loft. Obviously the midnight visitor was someone whom the dog knew well.

(A. Conan Doyle, *Memoirs of Sherlock Holmes*)

26. Eternity is simultaneously whole. But time has a before and an after. Therefore time and eternity are not the same thing.

(Thomas Aquinas, *Summa Theologica*)

27. Ordinary things that we encounter every day are electrically neutral. Therefore, since negatively charged electrons are a part of everything, positively charged particles must also exist in all matter.

(James E. Brady and Gerard E. Humiston, *General Chemistry*)

★28. Animals that live on plant foods must eat large quantities of vegetation, and this consumes much of their time. Meat eaters, by contrast, have no need to eat so much or so often. Consequently, meat-eating hominines [early humans] may have had more leisure time available to explore and manipulate their environment; like lions and leopards, they would have time to spend lying around and playing.

(William A. Haviland, *Cultural Anthropology,* 8th ed.)

29. We tell people not to speed, but equip cars with air bags in case they do. So what's wrong with telling kids not to have sex, but making Plan B available in case they do?

(Susan Beck, letter to the editor)

30. Because the moon moves relative to the earth so that it returns to the same position overhead after about 25 hours, there are two high and two low tides at any point every 25 hours.

(Douglas C. Giancoli, *The Ideas of Physics,* 3rd ed.)

II. Define the following terms:

deductive argument	prediction
inductive argument	argument from analogy
argument based on	generalization
mathematics	argument from authority
argument from definition	argument based on signs
categorical syllogism	causal inference
hypothetical syllogism	particular statement
disjunctive syllogism	general statement

III. Answer "true" or "false" to the following statements:

1. In an inductive argument, it is intended that the conclusion contain more information than the premises.

2. In a deductive argument, the conclusion is not supposed to contain more information than the premises.

3. The form of argumentation the arguer uses may allow one to determine whether an argument is inductive or deductive.

4. The actual strength of the link between premises and conclusion may allow one to determine whether an argument is inductive or deductive.

5. A geometrical proof is an example of an inductive argument.

6. Most arguments based on statistical reasoning are deductive.

7. If the conclusion of an argument follows merely from the definition of a word used in a premise, the argument is deductive.

8. An argument that draws a conclusion about a thing based on that thing's similarity to something else is a deductive argument.

9. An argument that draws a conclusion that something is true because someone has said that it is, is a deductive argument.

10. An argument that presents two alternatives and eliminates one, leaving the other as the conclusion, is an inductive argument.

11. An argument that proceeds from knowledge of a cause to knowledge of an effect is an inductive argument.

12. If an argument contains the phrase "it definitely follows that," then we know for certain that the argument is deductive.

13. An argument that predicts what will happen in the future, based on what has happened in the past, is an inductive argument.

14. Inductive arguments always proceed from the particular to the general.

15. Deductive arguments always proceed from the general to the particular.

IV. Page through a book, magazine, or newspaper and find two arguments, one inductive and the other deductive. Copy the arguments as written, giving the appropriate reference. Then identify the premises and conclusion of each.

1.4 Validity, Truth, Soundness, Strength, Cogency

PREVIEW

Suppose you are undecided about your college major, and a friend tells you that you should major in criminal justice because everyone in your sorority or fraternity is majoring in that field. You know that this is a really bad argument, but what is it, exactly, that makes it bad? In this section you will learn what causes inductive and deductive arguments to be good or bad and become familiar with the language used to classify them as such.

This section introduces the central ideas and terminology needed to evaluate arguments—to distinguish good arguments from bad arguments. Regardless of the type of argument, whether deductive or inductive, the evaluation of any argument involves answering two distinct questions: (1) Do the premises support the conclusion? (2) Are all the premises true? The answer to the first question is the more important one, because if the premises fail to support the conclusion (that is, if the reasoning is bad), the argument is worthless. The material that follows first considers deductive arguments and then inductive.

Deductive Arguments

The previous section defined a deductive argument as one incorporating the claim that it is impossible for the conclusion to be false given that the premises are true. If this claim is true, the argument is said to be valid. Thus, a **valid deductive argument** is an argument in which it is impossible for the conclusion to be false given that the premises are true. In these arguments the conclusion follows with strict necessity from the premises. Conversely, an **invalid deductive argument** is a deductive argument in which it *is* possible for the conclusion to be false given that the premises are true. In these arguments the conclusion does not follow with strict necessity from the premises, even though it is claimed to.

An immediate consequence of these definitions is that there is no middle ground between valid and invalid. There are no arguments that are "almost" valid and "almost"

valid deductive argument: An argument in which it is impossible for the conclusion to be false given that the premises are true.

invalid deductive argument: A deductive argument in which it *is* possible for the conclusion to be false given that the premises are true.

invalid. If the conclusion follows with strict necessity from the premises, the argument is valid; if not, it is invalid.

To test an argument for validity we begin by assuming that all the premises are true, and then we determine if it is possible, in light of that assumption, for the conclusion to be false. Here is an example:

> All television networks are media companies.
> NBC is a television network.
> Therefore, NBC is a media company.

In this argument both premises are actually true, so it is easy to *assume* that they are true. Next we determine, in light of this assumption, if it is possible for the conclusion to be false. Clearly this is not possible. If NBC is included in the group of television networks (second premise) and if the group of television networks is included in the group of media companies (first premise), it necessarily follows that NBC is included in the group of media companies (conclusion). In other words, assuming the premises to be true and the conclusion false entails a strict *contradiction*. Thus, the argument is valid.

Here is another example:

> All automakers are computer manufacturers.
> United Airlines is an automaker.
> Therefore, United Airlines is a computer manufacturer.

In this argument, both premises are actually false, but it is easy to assume that they are true. Every automaker could have a corporate division that manufactures computers. Also, in addition to flying airplanes, United Airlines could make cars. Next, in light of these assumptions, we determine if it is possible for the conclusion to be false. Again, we see that this is not possible, by the same reasoning as the previous example. Assuming the premises to be true and the conclusion false entails a contradiction. Thus, the argument is valid.

Another example:

> All banks are financial institutions.
> Wells Fargo is a financial institution.
> Therefore, Wells Fargo is a bank.

As in the first example, both premises of this argument are true, so it is easy to assume they are true. Next we determine, in light of this assumption, if it is possible for the conclusion to be false. In this case it *is* possible. If banks were included in one part of the group of financial institutions and Wells Fargo were included in another part, then Wells Fargo would *not* be a bank. In other words, assuming the premises to be true and the conclusion false does not involve any contradiction, and so the argument is invalid.

In addition to illustrating the basic idea of validity, these examples suggest an important point about validity and truth. In general, validity is not something that is uniformly determined by the actual truth or falsity of the premises and conclusion. Both the NBC example and the Wells Fargo example have actually true premises and an actually true conclusion, yet one is valid and the other invalid. The United Airlines example has actually false premises and an actually false conclusion, yet the argument is valid. Rather, validity is something that is determined by the *relationship* between premises and conclusion. The question is not whether the premises and conclusion are true or false, but whether the premises *support* the conclusion. In the examples of valid arguments the premises do support the conclusion, and in the invalid case they do not.

In general, validity is determined not by the truth or falsity of the premises and conclusion but by the *relationship* between the premises and conclusion.

TABLE 1.1 DEDUCTIVE ARGUMENTS

	Valid	Invalid
True premises **True conclusion**	All flowers are plants. All daisies are flowers. Therefore, all daisies are plants. [sound]	All flowers are plants. All daisies are plants. Therefore, all daisies are flowers. [unsound]
True premises **False conclusion**	None exist	All roses are flowers. All daisies are flowers. Therefore, all daisies are roses. [unsound]
False premises **True conclusion**	All flowers are dogs. All poodles are flowers. Therefore, all poodles are dogs. [unsound]	All dogs are flowers. All poodles are flowers. Therefore, all poodles are dogs. [unsound]
False premises **False conclusion**	All flowers are dogs. All tigers are flowers. Therefore, all tigers are dogs. [unsound]	All roses are cats. All daisies are cats. Therefore, all daisies are roses. [unsound]

© Cengage Learning

Nevertheless, there is *one* arrangement of truth and falsity in the premises and conclusion that does determine the issue of validity. Any deductive argument having actually true premises and an actually false conclusion is invalid. The reasoning behind this fact is fairly obvious. If the premises are actually true and the conclusion is actually false, then it certainly is *possible* for the premises to be true and the conclusion false. Thus, by the definition of invalidity, the argument is invalid.

The idea that any deductive argument having actually true premises and a false conclusion is invalid may be the most important point in all of deductive logic. The entire system of deductive logic would be quite useless if it accepted as valid any inferential process by which a person could start with truth in the premises and arrive at falsity in the conclusion.

Table 1.1 presents examples of categorical syllogisms (deductive arguments) that illustrate the various combinations of truth and falsity in the premises and conclusion. In the examples having false premises, both premises are false, but it is easy to construct other examples having only one false premise. When examining this table, note that the only combination of truth and falsity that does not allow for *both* valid and invalid arguments is true premises and false conclusion. As we have just seen, any argument having this combination is necessarily invalid.

The relationship between the validity of a deductive argument and the truth or falsity of its premises and conclusion, as illustrated in Table 1.1, is summarized as follows:

Premises	Conclusion	Validity
T	T	?
T	F	Invalid
F	T	?
F	F	?

This short summary table reinforces the point that merely knowing the truth or falsity of the premises and conclusion tells us nothing about validity except in the one case of true premises and false conclusion. Any deductive argument having true premises and a false conclusion is necessarily invalid.

A **sound argument** is a deductive argument that is *valid* and has *all true premises*. Both conditions must be met for an argument to be sound; if either is missing the argument is unsound. Thus, an **unsound argument** is a deductive argument that is invalid, has one or more false premises, or both. Because a valid argument is one such that it is impossible for the premises to be true and the conclusion false, and because a sound argument does in fact have true premises, it follows that every sound argument, by definition, will have a true conclusion as well. A sound argument, therefore, is what is meant by a good, or successful, deductive argument in the fullest sense of the term.

> **sound argument**: A deductive argument that is *valid* and has *all true premises*.

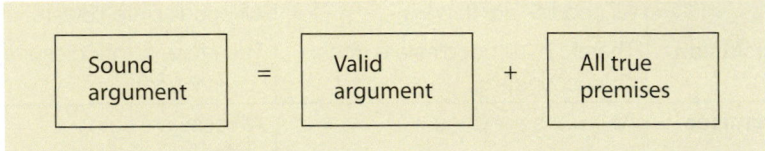

In connection with this definition of soundness, a single proviso is required: For an argument to be unsound, the false premise or premises must actually be needed to support the conclusion. An argument having a conclusion that is validly supported by true premises but having a superfluous false premise would still be sound. By similar reasoning, no addition of a false premise to an originally sound argument can make the argument unsound. Such a premise would be superfluous and should not be considered part of the argument. Analogous remarks, incidentally, extend to induction.

Since (at least from the standpoint of logic) every premise is either true or false, and every deductive argument is either valid or invalid, it follows that every deductive argument is either sound or unsound. However, given that many, if not most, premises have truth values that are unknown or impossible to determine, it is not always possible to determine the soundness of a deductive argument. But that does not mean that soundness is unimportant in logic. It is crucially important that soundness be recognized as a criterion of evaluation that is distinct from validity and that the evaluator be ever vigilant never to confuse soundness with validity.

Inductive Arguments

Section 1.3 defined an inductive argument as one incorporating the claim that it is improbable that the conclusion be false given that the premises are true. If this claim is true, the argument is said to be strong. Thus, a **strong inductive argument** is an inductive argument in which it is improbable that the conclusion be false given that the premises are true. In such arguments, the conclusion does in fact follow probably from the premises. Conversely, a **weak inductive argument** is an argument in which the conclusion does not follow probably from the premises, even though it is claimed to.

All inductive arguments depend on what philosophers call the uniformity of nature. According to this principle, the future tends to replicate the past, and regularities that prevail in one spatial region tend to prevail in other regions. For example, in the past,

> **strong inductive argument**: An inductive argument in which the conclusion follows probably from the premises.

> **weak inductive argument**: An inductive argument in which the conclusion does not follow probably from the premises.

sugar has always tasted sweet. According to the uniformity of nature, sugar will continue to taste sweet in the future. Also, just as sugar tastes sweet in Los Angeles, so does it in New York, London, and everywhere else. The uniformity of nature is the ultimate basis for our judgments about what we naturally expect to occur. Good inductive arguments are those that accord with the uniformity of nature. They have conclusions that we naturally expect to turn out true. If the conclusion of such an argument should turn out to be false, in violation of our expectations, this occurrence would cause us to react with surprise.

The procedure for testing the strength of inductive arguments runs parallel to the procedure for deduction. First we assume the premises are true, and then we determine whether, based on that assumption, the conclusion is probably true. This determination is accomplished by linking up the premises with regularities that exist in our experiential background. For example, if the argument is a causal inference, we link the information in the premises with known causal patterns. If the argument is an argument from signs, we connect the information in the premises with what we know about signs: some kinds of signs are trustworthy, others are not. If the argument is a generalization, we connect the information in the premises with what we know about a sample being representative of a population. All of these regularities are instances of the uniformity of nature. Here is an example of a prediction:

> All dinosaur bones discovered to this day have been at least 50 million years old. Therefore, probably the next dinosaur bone to be found will be at least 50 million years old.

In this argument the premise is actually true. Given that all dinosaur bones discovered to date have been over 50 million years old (and that thousands of such bones have been discovered), the uniformity of nature dictates that the next one to be discovered will also be over 50 million years old. This is what we would naturally expect, and anything to the contrary would be highly surprising. Thus, the conclusion is probably true, and so the argument is strong.

Here is another example:

> All meteorites found to this day have contained salt. Therefore, probably the next meteorite to be found will contain salt.

The premise of this argument is clearly false; but if we assume it to be true, then we would naturally expect that the next meteorite to be found would contain salt. Thus, the argument is strong.

The next example is an argument from analogy:

> Dom Pérignon champagne, which is made in France, sells for over $100 per bottle. Marquis de la Tour is also a French champagne. Therefore probably it, too, sells for over $100 per bottle.

In this argument the premises are actually true, but our background experience tells us that the mere fact that two wines come from the same country does not imply that they sell for the same price. Thus, the argument is weak. The conclusion, incidentally, happens to be false.

Another example:

> During the past fifty years, inflation has consistently reduced the value of the American dollar. Therefore, industrial productivity will probably increase in the years ahead.

In this argument, the premise is actually true and the conclusion is probably true in the actual world, but the probability of the conclusion is in no way based on the assumption that the premise is true. Because there is no direct connection between inflation and increased industrial productivity, the premise is irrelevant to the conclusion and it provides no probabilistic support for it. The conclusion is probably true independently of the premise. As a result, the argument is weak.

This last example illustrates an important distinction between strong inductive arguments and valid deductive arguments. If the conclusion of a deductive argument is necessarily true independently of the premises, the argument is still considered valid. But if the conclusion of an inductive argument is probably true independently of the premises, the argument is weak.

These four examples show that in general the strength or weakness of an inductive argument results not from the actual truth or falsity of the premises and conclusion, but from the probabilistic support the premises give to the conclusion. The dinosaur argument has a true premise and a probably true conclusion, and the meteorite argument has a false premise and a probably false conclusion; yet both are strong because the premise of each provides probabilistic support for the conclusion. The industrial productivity argument has a true premise and a probably true conclusion, but the argument is weak because the premise provides no probabilistic support for the conclusion. As in the evaluation of deductive arguments, the only arrangement of truth and falsity that establishes anything is true premises and probably false conclusion (as in the Dom Pérignon argument). Any inductive argument having true premises and a probably false conclusion is weak.

TABLE 1.2 INDUCTIVE ARGUMENTS

	Strong	Weak
True premise	Every previous U.S. president was older than 40.	A few U.S. presidents were lawyers.
Probably true conclusion	Therefore, probably the next U.S. president will be older than 40. [cogent]	Therefore, probably the next U.S. president will be older than 40. [uncogent]
True premise	None exist	A few U.S. presidents were unmarried.
Probably false conclusion		Therefore, probably the next U.S. president will be unmarried. [uncogent]
False premise	Every previous U.S. president was a TV debater.	A few U.S. presidents were dentists.
Probably true conclusion	Therefore, probably the next U.S. president will be a TV debater. [uncogent]	Therefore, probably the next U.S. president will be a TV debater. [uncogent]
False premise	Every previous U.S. president died in office.	A few U.S. presidents were dentists.
Probably false conclusion	Therefore, probably the next U.S. president will die in office. [uncogent]	Therefore, probably the next U.S. president will be a dentist. [uncogent]

© Cengage Learning

Before proceeding further, however, we must qualify and explain this last statement. When we speak of the premises being true, we mean "true" in a complete sense. The premises must not exclude or overlook some crucial piece of evidence that undermines the stated premises and requires a different conclusion. This proviso is otherwise called the *total evidence requirement*. If the total evidence requirement is not met, an argument might have literally true premises and a probably false conclusion and still be strong. Also, when we speak of the conclusion being probably false, we mean probably false in the actual world in light of all the known evidence.

Table 1.2 presents several predictions (inductive arguments) that illustrate the various combinations of truth and falsity in the premises and conclusion. Note that the only arrangement of truth and falsity that is missing for strong arguments is true premises and probably false conclusion.

The relationship between the strength of an inductive argument and the truth or falsity of its premises and conclusion, as illustrated in Table 1.2, is summarized as follows:

Premises	Conclusion	Strength
T	probably T	?
T	probably F	Weak
F	probably T	?
F	probably F	?

Like the summary table for deduction, this brief table reinforces the point that merely knowing the truth values of the premises and conclusion tells us nothing about the strength of an argument except in the one case of true premises and a probably false conclusion. Any inductive argument having true premises (in the sense just explained) and a probably false conclusion is weak.

Unlike the validity and invalidity of deductive arguments, the strength and weakness of inductive arguments allow for degrees. To be considered strong, an inductive argument must have a conclusion that is more probable than improbable. In other words, given that the premises are true, the likelihood that the conclusion is true must be more than 50 percent, and as the probability increases, the argument becomes stronger. For this purpose, consider the following pair of arguments:

> This barrel contains 100 apples.
> Three apples selected at random were found to be ripe.
> Therefore, probably all 100 apples are ripe.

> This barrel contains 100 apples.
> Eighty apples selected at random were found to be ripe.
> Therefore, probably all 100 apples are ripe.

The first argument is weak and the second is strong. However, the first is not absolutely weak nor the second absolutely strong. Both arguments would be strengthened or weakened by the random selection of a larger or smaller sample. For example, if the size of the sample in the second argument were reduced to seventy apples, the argument would be weakened. The incorporation of additional premises into an inductive argument will also generally tend to strengthen or weaken it. For example, if the premise "One unripe apple that had been found earlier was removed" were added to either argument, the argument would be weakened.

Chrysippus 280–206 B.C.

Chrysippus was born in Soli, a city located on the southeast coast of Asia Minor. Early in life he moved to Athens, where he studied under the Stoic philosopher Cleanthes, who in turn was a student of Zeno of Citium, the founder of Stoicism. Upon Cleanthes' death in 232 B.C., Chrysippus took over as leader of the school, and he produced over 700 treatises that systematized Stoic teaching. All of these works have been lost, but fragments survive in the writings of Cicero, Seneca, and others. Because of his extraordinary contribution, Chrysippus is considered to be the second founder of Stoicism.

Stoicism derives its name from the Greek word *stoa*, which means "porch"; Stoic philosophers used to gather on a porch in the Agora (public square) in Athens to discuss their views. The Stoics prized the virtue of self-sufficiency, and they emphasized the importance of not allowing oneself to be carried away by emotions or passions such as fear or love. The Stoics considered emotions to be false judgments about the goodness or badness of something. The proper therapy for those victimized by emotions is to persuade them that these judgments are indeed false because they constitute obstacles to true happiness.

Chrysippus is often considered to be the originator of propositional logic. Unlike Aristotelian logic, where the fundamental components are terms, in propositional logic the fundamental components are whole propositions or statements. Aristotle had overlooked this kind of logic, but his close friend and successor Theophrastus worked out some of the logic of the pure hypothetical syllogism (If *A*, then *B*; If *B*, then *C*; therefore, If *A*, then *C*). Also, Philo of Megara introduced the truth functional interpretation of the material conditional (If *A*, then *B*). Beginning at this point, Chrysippus advanced propositional logic to a high level of development.

Science Source

Chrysippus divided propositions into simple and compound, and he introduced a set of connectives that were used to produce compound propositions from one or more simple propositions. The compound propositions included negation, conjunction, exclusive disjunction, and implication, and Chrysippus showed how the truth value of a compound statement is a function of the truth values of its simple components. Chrysippus also introduced a set of rules of inference including what is today called *modus ponens, modus tollens,* disjunctive syllogism, and a rule similar to De Morgan's rule. Finally, he introduced the theory of natural deduction by which the conclusion of an argument can be derived from its premises through a series of discrete steps.

The broader philosophy of Chrysippus is characterized by monism and determinism. While most of us think that the universe is made up of millions of discrete entities, Chrysippus argued that in fact only one substance exists, and what appear to be individual substances are really parts of this one primary substance. Furthermore, everything that occurs is strictly governed by fate. Yet, in the face of this rigid causal determinism Chrysippus held that humans are responsible for their actions, and he tried in many ways to prove that the two viewpoints are in fact compatible with each other.

cogent argument: An inductive argument that is strong and has *all true premises.*

A **cogent argument** is an inductive argument that is *strong* and has *all true premises.* Also, the premises must be true in the sense of meeting the *total evidence requirement.* If any one of these conditions is missing, the argument is *uncogent.* Thus, an **uncogent argument** is an inductive argument that is weak, has one or more false premises, fails to meet the total evidence requirement, or any combination of these. A cogent argument is the inductive analogue of a sound deductive argument and is what is meant by a good, or successful, inductive argument without qualification. Because the conclusion of a cogent argument is genuinely supported by true premises, it follows that the conclusion of every cogent argument is probably true in the actual world in light of all the known evidence.

Cogent argument	=	Strong argument	+	All true premises

As an illustration of the need for the total evidence requirement, consider the following argument:

Swimming in the Caribbean is usually lots of fun. Today the water is warm, the surf is gentle, and on this beach there are no dangerous currents. Therefore, it would be fun to go swimming here now.

If the premises reflect all the important factors, then the argument is cogent. But if they ignore the fact that several large dorsal fins are cutting through the water (suggesting sharks), then obviously the argument is not cogent. Thus, for cogency the premises must not only be true but also not overlook some important fact that requires a different conclusion.

Finally, just as it is not always possible to determine the soundness of a deductive argument, it is not always possible to determine the cogency of an inductive argument. And this follows for two reasons. Many inductive arguments, especially those about complex real-life subjects, are not susceptible to being evaluated as clearly strong or clearly weak. And many premises have truth values that are unknown or impossible to determine. Yet, it remains important that cogency be recognized as a criterion for evaluating inductive arguments and that it not be confused with strength and weakness.

Section 1.4 Summary

For both deductive and inductive arguments, two separate questions need to be answered: (1) Do the premises support the conclusion? (2) Are all the premises true? To answer the first question we begin by *assuming* the premises to be true. Then, for deductive arguments we determine whether, in light of this *assumption*, it necessarily follows that the conclusion is true. If it does, the argument is valid; if not, it is invalid. For inductive arguments we determine whether it probably follows that the conclusion is true. If it does, the argument is strong; if not, it is weak. For inductive arguments we keep in mind the requirements that the premises actually support the conclusion and that they not ignore important evidence. Finally, if the argument is either valid or strong, we turn to the second question and determine whether the premises are actually true. If all the premises are true, the argument is sound (in the case of deduction) or cogent (in the case of induction). All invalid deductive arguments are unsound, and all weak inductive arguments are uncogent.

The various alternatives open to statements and arguments may be diagrammed as follows. Note that in logic one never speaks of an argument as being "true" or "false," and one never speaks of a statement as being "valid," "invalid," "strong," or "weak."

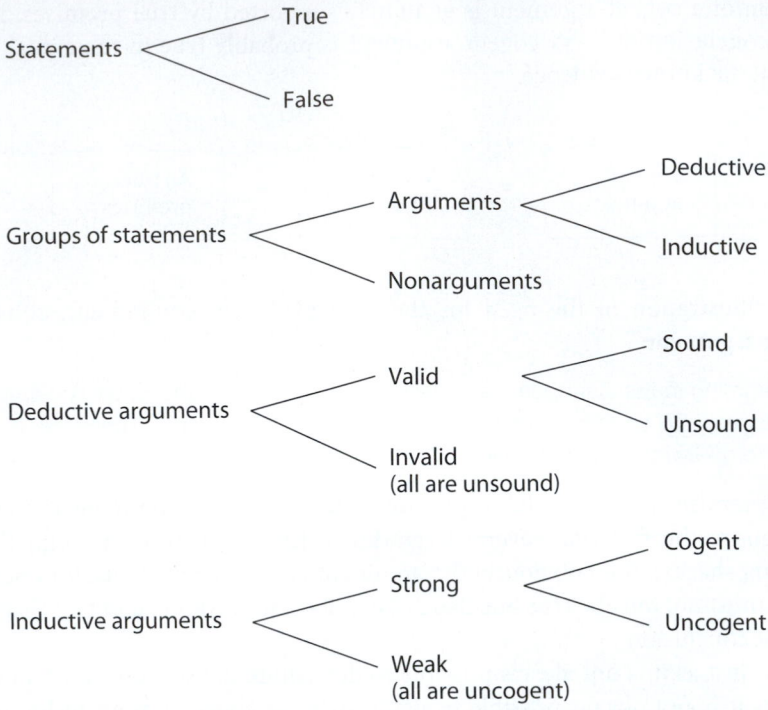

I. The following arguments are deductive. Determine whether each is valid or invalid, and note the relationship between your answer and the truth or falsity of the premises and conclusion. Finally, determine whether the argument is sound or unsound.

★1. Since *Moby Dick* was written by Shakespeare, and *Moby Dick* is a science-fiction novel, it follows that Shakespeare wrote a science-fiction novel.

2. Since London is north of Paris and south of Edinburgh, it follows that Paris is south of Edinburgh.

3. If George Washington was beheaded, then George Washington died. George Washington died. Therefore, George Washington was beheaded.

★4. The longest river in South America is the Amazon, and the Amazon flows through Brazil. Therefore, the longest river in South America flows through Brazil.

5. Since the Spanish-American War occurred before the U.S. Civil War, and the U.S. Civil War occurred after the Korean War, it follows that the Spanish-American War occurred before the Korean War.

6. The Empire State Building is taller than the Statue of Liberty, and the Statue of Liberty is taller than the Eiffel Tower. Therefore, the Empire State Building is taller than the Eiffel Tower.

★7. All leopards with lungs are carnivores. Therefore, all leopards are carnivores.

8. Chicago is a city in Michigan and Michigan is part of the United States. Therefore, Chicago is a city in the United States.

9. If President Barack Obama was born in Massachusetts, then he is a native of New England. Barack Obama is not a native of New England. Therefore, Barack Obama was not born in Massachusetts.

★10. Every province in Canada has exactly one city as its capital. Therefore, since there are thirty provinces in Canada, there are thirty provincial capitals.

11. Since the Department of Defense Building outside Washington, D.C., has the shape of a hexagon, it follows that it has seven sides.

12. Since Winston Churchill was English, and Winston Churchill was a famous statesman, we may conclude that at least one Englishman was a famous statesman.

★13. Since some fruits are green, and some fruits are apples, it follows that some fruits are green apples.

14. All physicians are individuals who have earned degrees in political science, and some lawyers are physicians. Therefore, some lawyers are persons who have earned degrees in political science.

15. The United States Congress has more members than there are days in the year. Therefore, at least two members of Congress have the same birthday.

II. The following arguments are inductive. Determine whether each is strong or weak and note the relationship between your answer and the truth or falsity of the premise(s) and conclusion. Then determine whether each argument is cogent or uncogent.

★1. The grave marker at Arlington National Cemetery says that John F. Kennedy is buried there. It must be the case that Kennedy really is buried in that cemetery.

2. The ebb and flow of the tides has been occurring every day for millions of years. But nothing lasts forever. Therefore, probably the motion of the tides will die out within a few years.

3. The vast majority of Rose Bowl games (in Pasadena, California) have been played in freezing-cold weather. Therefore, probably the next Rose Bowl game will be played in freezing-cold weather.

★4. Franklin Delano Roosevelt said that we have nothing to fear but fear itself. Therefore, women have no reason to fear serial rapists.

5. Most popular film stars are millionaires. Viola Davis is a popular film star. Therefore, probably Viola Davis is a millionaire.

6. Constructing the great pyramid at Giza required lifting massive stone blocks to great heights. Probably the ancient Egyptians had some antigravity device to accomplish this feat.

★7. People have been listening to rock and roll music for over a hundred years. Probably people will still be listening to it a year from now.

8. Paleontologists have unearthed the fossilized bones of huge reptiles, which we have named dinosaurs. Tests indicate that these bones are more than

50 million years old. Therefore, probably dinosaurs really did roam the earth 50 million years ago.

9. The Declaration of Independence says that all men are endowed by their creator with certain unalienable rights. Therefore it probably follows that a creator exists.

★10. Coca-Cola is an extremely popular soft drink. Therefore, probably someone, somewhere, is drinking a Coke right this minute.

11. Every map of the United States shows that Alabama is situated on the Pacific coast. Therefore, Alabama must be a western state.

12. When Neil Armstrong landed on the moon, he left behind a gold-plated Schwinn bicycle, which he used to ride around on the moon's surface. Probably that bicycle is still up there on the moon.

★13. The African American athlete Adrian Peterson is able to withstand tremendous impacts on the football field. However, Serena Williams, like Adrian Peterson, is a great African American athlete. Therefore, Serena Williams should be able to withstand tremendous impacts on the football field.

14. Unlike monkeys, today's humans have feet that are not suited for grasping objects. Therefore, a thousand years from now, probably humans will still have feet that are not suited for grasping objects.

15. A random sample of twenty-five famous country and western singers, which included Garth Brooks and Dolly Parton, revealed that every single one of them studied music in Tasmania. Therefore, probably the majority of famous country and western singers studied music in Tasmania.

III. Determine whether the following arguments are inductive or deductive. If an argument is inductive, determine whether it is strong or weak. If it is deductive, determine whether it is valid or invalid.

★1. Since Tom is the brother of Agatha, and Agatha is the mother of Raquel, it follows that Tom is the uncle of Raquel.

2. When a cook cannot recall the ingredients in a recipe, it is appropriate that she refresh her memory by consulting the recipe book. Similarly, when a student cannot recall the answers during a final exam, it is appropriate that she refresh her memory by consulting the textbook.

3. The Broadway Theater marquee says that *The Phantom of the Opera* is playing nightly. Therefore, it must be that case that *Phantom* is playing there tonight.

★4. Since Christmas is always on a Thursday, it follows that the day after Christmas is always a Friday.

5. Suppose figure *A* is a triangle having two equal angles. It follows that figure *A* has two equal sides.

6. By accident Karen baked her brownies two hours longer than she should have. Therefore, they have probably been ruined.

★7. After taking LSD, Alice said she saw a flying saucer land in the shopping center parking lot. Since Alice has a reputation for always telling the truth, we must conclude that a flying saucer really did land there.

8. Since Phyllis is the cousin of Denise, and Denise is the cousin of Harriet, it follows necessarily that Harriet is the cousin of Phyllis.

9. The picnic scheduled in the park for tomorrow will most likely be cancelled. It's been snowing for six days straight.

★10. Circle A has exactly twice the diameter of circle B. From this we may conclude that circle A has exactly twice the area of circle B.

11. Robert has lost consistently at blackjack every day for the past several days. Therefore, it is very likely that he will win today.

12. Since John loves Nancy and Nancy loves Peter, it follows necessarily that John loves Peter.

★13. This cash register drawer contains over 100 coins. Three coins selected at random were found to have dates earlier than 1960. Therefore, probably all of the coins in the drawer have dates earlier than 1960.

14. The Japanese attack on Pearl Harbor happened in either 1941 or 1951. But it didn't happen in 1941. Therefore, it happened in 1951.

15. Harry will never be able to solve that difficult problem in advanced calculus in the limited time allowed. He has never studied anything beyond algebra, and in that he earned only a C−.

★16. Since $x + y = 10$, and $x = 7$, it follows that $y = 4$.

17. If acupuncture is hocus pocus, then acupuncture cannot relieve chronic pain. But acupuncture can relieve chronic pain. Therefore, acupuncture is not hocus pocus.

18. If inflation heats up, then interest rates will rise. If interest rates rise, then bond prices will decline. Therefore, if inflation heats up, then bond prices will decline.

★19. Statistics reveal that 86 percent of those who receive flu shots do not get the flu. Jack received a flu shot one month ago. Therefore, he should be immune, even though the flu is going around now.

20. Since Michael is a Pisces, it necessarily follows that he was born in March.

IV. Define the following terms:

valid deductive argument	strong inductive argument
invalid deductive argument	weak inductive argument
sound argument	cogent argument
unsound argument	uncogent argument

V. Answer "true" or "false" to the following statements:

1. Some arguments, while not completely valid, are almost valid.

2. Inductive arguments allow for varying degrees of strength and weakness.

3. Invalid deductive arguments are basically the same as inductive arguments.

4. If a deductive argument has true premises and a false conclusion, it is necessarily invalid.

5. A valid argument may have a false premise and a false conclusion.

6. A valid argument may have a false premise and a true conclusion.

7. A sound argument may be invalid.

8. A sound argument may have a false conclusion.

9. A strong argument may have false premises and a probably false conclusion.

10. A strong argument may have true premises and a probably false conclusion.

11. A cogent argument may have a probably false conclusion.

12. A cogent argument must be inductively strong.

13. If an argument has true premises and a true conclusion, we know that it is a perfectly good argument.

14. A statement may legitimately be spoken of as "valid" or "invalid."

15. An argument may legitimately be spoken of as "true" or "false."

1.5 Argument Forms: Proving Invalidity

PREVIEW

While at a party you overhear someone talking about you. Disdainfully, the person observes that you don't wear designer clothing, and then comments that losers don't wear designer clothing either. The implication is that you are a loser. Hearing this infuriates you. You know the argument is clearly invalid, but how do you prove it? In this section you will learn about a simple, intuitive method to prove invalid deductive arguments invalid.

This section explores the idea that the validity of a deductive argument is determined by its form. This idea was suggested by the arguments in Table 1.1 in the previous section. All the arguments in the Valid column of that table have the same valid form, and all the arguments in the Invalid column have the same invalid form. The form of an argument illustrates the argument's internal structure or pattern of reasoning. If the pattern of reasoning is good, the argument will be valid; if not, it will be invalid.

In reference to Table 1.1, all the valid arguments have this form:

All *A* are *B*.
All *C* are *A*.
All *C* are *B*.

If *A, B,* and *C* are thought of as referring to groups of things, it is easy to see that this form is valid. Assume, by the second premise, that the *C*s (whatever they might be) are included in the *A*s, and, by the first premise, that the *A*s (whatever they might be) are included in the *B*s. Then it necessarily follows that the *C*s are included in the *B*s, which is what the conclusion asserts.

We can use this example to define what we mean by an argument form. An **argument form**, for the present purpose, is an arrangement of letters (in this case *A, B,* and *C*) and words (in this case "all" and "are") such that the uniform substitution of words or phrases in the place of the letters results in an argument. For this form, the words or phrases being substituted must refer to groups of things. Thus, if we substitute "sporting events," "engaging pastimes," and "baseball games" in the place of *A, B,* and *C,* respectively, in the argument form (left), we obtain the following argument (right):

argument form: An arrangement of letters and words such that the uniform substitution of words or phrases in place of the letters results in an argument.

All *A* are *B*.	All sporting events are engaging pastimes.
All *C* are *A*.	All baseball games are sporting events.
All *C* are *B*.	All baseball games are engaging pastimes.

This argument is called a **substitution instance** of the argument form. Any substitution instance of a valid argument form is a valid argument.

substitution instance: An argument that results from uniformly substituting words or phrases in place of the letters in an argument form.

Before proceeding to invalid arguments, we must briefly consider valid arguments in which the form is not apparent. Many of the arguments in the previous set of exercises were like this. How can we reconcile the existence of such arguments with the claim that validity is determined by form? The answer is that these arguments are incomplete, so the form is not explicit. But once such arguments are completed and correctly phrased (which we address later in this book), the form becomes apparent. For example, consider the following valid argument:

Geese are migratory waterfowl, so they fly south for the winter.

This argument is missing a premise:

Migratory waterfowl fly south for the winter.

The argument can now be rephrased to make its form apparent:

All migratory waterfowl are birds that fly south for the winter.
All geese are migratory waterfowl.
Therefore, all geese are birds that fly south for the winter.

The form of the argument is

All *A* are *B*.
All *C* are *A*.
All *C* are *B*.

This form is identical to the form we just considered and is valid. Let us now consider an invalid argument form:

All *A* are *B*.
All *C* are *B*.
All *A* are *C*.

In this argument form, if we assume that the *A*s are in the *B*s and that the *C*s are in the *B*s, it does not *necessarily* follow that the *A*s are in the *C*s. It would not follow if the *A*s were in one part of the *B*s and the *C*s were in another part, as the following diagram illustrates:

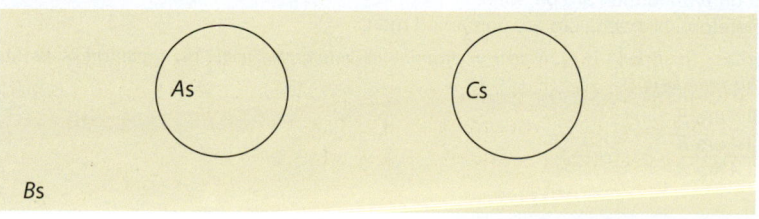

This diagram suggests that we can prove the form invalid if we can find a substitution instance having actually true premises and an actually false conclusion. In such a substitution instance the As and the Cs would be separated from each other, but they would both be included in the Bs. If we substitute "cats" for A, "animals" for B, and "dogs" for C, we have such a substitution instance:

All A are B.	All cats are animals.	True
All C are B.	All dogs are animals.	True
All A are C.	Therefore, all cats are dogs.	False

This substitution instance proves the form invalid, because it provides a concrete example of a case where the As are in the Bs, the Cs are in the Bs, but the As are *not* in the Cs.

Now, since the form is invalid, can we say that any argument that has this form is invalid? Unfortunately, the situation with invalid forms is not quite as simple as it is with valid forms. Every substitution instance of a valid form is a valid argument, but it is not the case that every substitution instance of an invalid form is an invalid argument. The reason is that some substitution instances of invalid forms are also substitution instances of valid forms.* However, we can say that any substitution instance of an invalid form is an invalid argument *provided* that it is not a substitution instance of any valid form. Thus, we will say that an argument actually *has* an invalid form if it is a substitution instance of that form and it is not a substitution instance of any valid form.

The fact that some substitution instances of invalid forms are also substitution instances of valid forms means simply that we must exercise caution in identifying the form of an argument. However, cases of ordinary language arguments that can be interpreted as substitution instances of both valid and invalid forms are so rare that this book chooses to ignore them. With this in mind, consider the following argument:

> All romantic novels are literary pieces.
> All works of fiction are literary pieces.
> Therefore, all romantic novels are works of fiction.

This argument clearly has the invalid form just discussed. This invalid form captures the reasoning process of the argument, which is obviously defective. Therefore, the argument is invalid, and it is invalid precisely because it has an invalid form.

Counterexample Method

counterexample method:
A method for proving invalidity that consists of isolating the form of an argument and then constructing a substitution instance having true premises and a false conclusion.

A substitution instance having true premises and a false conclusion (like the cats-and-dogs example just constructed) is called a counterexample, and the method we have just used to prove the romantic-novels argument invalid is called the **counterexample method**. It consists of isolating the form of an argument and then constructing a

---

*For example, the following valid argument is a substitution instance of the invalid form we have been discussing:

> All bachelors are persons.
> All unmarried men are persons.
> Therefore, all bachelors are unmarried men.

However, because "bachelors" is equivalent in meaning to "unmarried men," the argument is also a substitution instance of this valid form:

All A are B.
All A are B.
All A are A.

substitution instance having true premises and a false conclusion. This proves the form invalid, which in turn proves the argument invalid. The counterexample method can be used to prove the invalidity of any invalid argument, but it cannot prove the validity of any valid argument. Thus, before the method is applied to an argument, the argument must be known or suspected to be invalid in the first place. Let us apply the counterexample method to the following invalid categorical syllogism:

> Since some employees are not social climbers and all vice presidents are employees, we may conclude that some vice presidents are not social climbers.

This argument is invalid because the employees who are not social climbers might not be vice presidents. Accordingly, we can *prove* the argument invalid by constructing a substitution instance having true premises and a false conclusion. We begin by isolating the form of the argument:

> Some *E* are not *S*.
> All *V* are *E*.
> ――――――――――――
> Some *V* are not *S*.

Next, we select three terms to substitute in place of the letters that will make the premises true and the conclusion false. The following selection will work:

> *E* = animals
> *S* = mammals
> *V* = dogs

The resulting substitution instance is this:

> Some animals are not mammals.
> All dogs are animals.
> Therefore, some dogs are not mammals.

The substitution instance has true premises and a false conclusion and is therefore, by definition, invalid. Because the substitution instance is invalid, the form is invalid, and therefore the original argument is invalid.

In applying the counterexample method to categorical syllogisms, it is useful to keep in mind the following set of terms: "cats," "dogs," "mammals," "fish," and "animals." Most invalid syllogisms can be proven invalid by strategically selecting three of these terms and using them to construct a counterexample. Because everyone agrees about these terms, everyone will agree about the truth or falsity of the premises and conclusion of the counterexample. Also, in constructing the counterexample, it often helps to begin with the conclusion. First, select two terms that yield a false conclusion, and then select a third term that yields true premises. Another point to keep in mind is that the word "some" in logic always means "at least one." For example, the statement "Some dogs are animals" means "At least one dog is an animal"—which is true. Also note that this statement does not imply that some dogs are not animals.

Not all deductive arguments, of course, are categorical syllogisms. Consider, for example, the following hypothetical syllogism:

> If the government imposes import restrictions, the price of automobiles will rise. Therefore, since the government will not impose import restrictions, it follows that the price of automobiles will not rise.

Any deductive argument having true premises and a false conclusion is invalid.

This argument is invalid because the price of automobiles might rise even though import restrictions are not imposed. It has the following form:

If *G*, then *P*.
Not *G*.
—————
Not *P*.

This form differs from the previous one in that its letters stand for complete statements. *G*, for example, stands for "The government imposes import restrictions." If we make the substitution

G = Abraham Lincoln committed suicide.
P = Abraham Lincoln is dead.

we obtain the following substitution instance:

If Abraham Lincoln committed suicide, then Abraham Lincoln is dead.
Abraham Lincoln did not commit suicide.
Therefore, Abraham Lincoln is not dead.

Since the premises are true and the conclusion false, the substitution instance is clearly invalid. Therefore, the form is invalid, and this proves the original argument invalid.

When applying the counterexample method to an argument having a conditional statement as a premise (such as the one just discussed), it is recommended that the statement substituted in place of the conditional statement express some kind of necessary connection. In the Lincoln example, the first premise asserts the necessary connection between suicide and death. There can be no doubt about the truth of such a statement. Furthermore, if it should turn out that the conclusion is a conditional statement, note that one sure way of producing a false conditional statement is by joining a true antecedent with a false consequent. For example, the conditional statement "If Lassie is a dog, then Lassie is a cat" is clearly false.

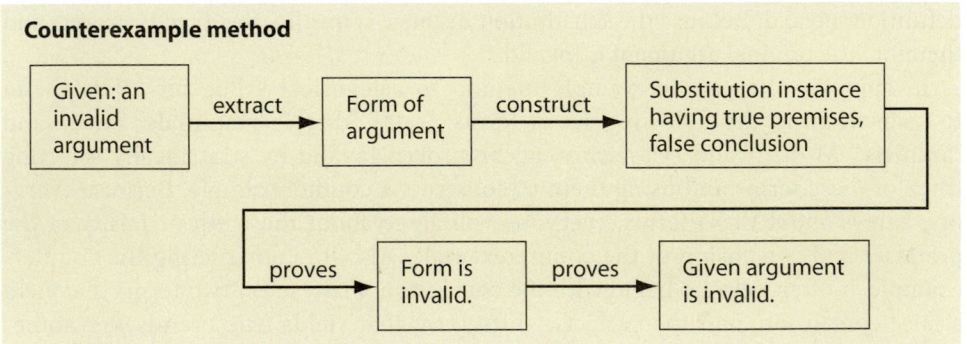

Counterexample method

Given: an invalid argument —extract→ Form of argument —construct→ Substitution instance having true premises, false conclusion —proves→ Form is invalid. —proves→ Given argument is invalid.

Being able to identify the form of an argument with ease requires a familiarity with the basic deductive argument forms. The first task consists in distinguishing the premises from the conclusion. Always write the premises first and the conclusion last. The second task involves distinguishing what we may call "form words" from "content words." To reduce an argument to its form, leave the form words as they are, and replace the content words with letters. For categorical syllogisms, the words "all," "no," "some," "are," and "not" are form words, and for hypothetical syllogisms the words "if," "then," and "not" are form words. Additional form words for other types of arguments are "either," "or," "both," and "and." For various kinds of hybrid arguments, a more intuitive approach may be needed. Here is an example:

All movie stars are actors who are famous, because all movie stars who are famous are actors.

If we replace "movie stars," "actors," and "famous" with the letters *M*, *A*, and *F*, this argument has the following form:

> All *M* who are *F* are *A*.
> ―――――――――――――――
> All *M* are *A* who are *F*.

Here is one possible substitution instance for this form:

> All humans who are fathers are men.
> Therefore, all humans are men who are fathers.

Because the premise is true and the conclusion false, the form is invalid and so is the original argument.

Using the counterexample method to prove arguments invalid requires a little ingenuity because there is no rule that will automatically produce the required term or statement to be substituted into the form. Any term or statement will work, of course, provided that it yields a substitution instance that has premises that are indisputably true and a conclusion that is indisputably false. Ideally, the truth value of these statements should be known to the average individual; otherwise, the substitution instance cannot be depended on to prove anything. If, for example, *P* in the earlier hypothetical syllogism had been replaced by the statement "George Wilson is dead," the substitution instance would be useless, because nobody knows whether this statement is true or false.

The counterexample method is useful only for proving invalidity, because the only arrangement of truth and falsity that proves anything is true premises and false conclusion. If a substitution instance is produced having true premises and a true conclusion, it does *not* prove that the argument is valid. Furthermore, the method is useful only for deductive arguments because the strength and weakness of inductive arguments is only partially dependent on the form of the argument. Accordingly, no method that relates exclusively to the form of an inductive argument can be used to prove the argument weak.

EXERCISE 1.5

I. Use the counterexample method to prove the following categorical syllogisms invalid. In doing so, follow the suggestions given in the text.

★1. All galaxies are structures that contain black holes in the center, so all galaxies are quasars, since all quasars are structures that contain black holes in the center.

2. Some evolutionists are not people who believe in the Bible, for no creationists are evolutionists, and some people who believe in the Bible are not creationists.

3. No patents are measures that discourage research and development, and all patents are regulations that protect intellectual property. Thus, no measures that discourage research and development are regulations that protect intellectual property.

★4. Some farm workers are not people who are paid decent wages, because no undocumented individuals are people who are paid decent wages, and some undocumented individuals are not farm workers.

5. Some politicians are people who will stop at nothing to win an election, and no people who will stop at nothing to win an election are true statesmen. Hence, no politicians are true statesmen.

6. All meticulously constructed timepieces are true works of art, for all Swiss watches are true works of art and all Swiss watches are meticulously constructed timepieces.

★7. No patrons of fast-food restaurants are health-food addicts. Consequently, no patrons of fast-food restaurants are connoisseurs of fine desserts, since no connoisseurs of fine desserts are health-food addicts.

8. Some toxic dumps are sites that emit hazardous wastes, and some sites that emit hazardous wastes are undesirable places to live near. Thus, some toxic dumps are undesirable places to live near.

9. All persons who assist others in suicide are people guilty of murder. Accordingly, some individuals motivated by compassion are not persons guilty of murder, inasmuch as some people who assist others in suicide are individuals motivated by compassion.

★10. Some school boards are not groups that oppose values clarification, because some school boards are not organizations with vision, and some groups that oppose values clarification are not organizations with vision.

11. All super PACs (political action committees) are unlimited spenders. For this reason, some big-time power brokers are not super PACs, inasmuch as some unlimited spenders are big-time power brokers.

12. No movie producers are uncompetitive business executives, and some Hollywood moguls are movie producers. It follows that no Hollywood moguls are uncompetitive business executives.

★13. Some improvers of humankind are not exploiters of personal information. As a result, some corporate social networks are not improvers of humankind, seeing that all corporate social networks are exploiters of personal information.

14. Some drone attacks are assaults on human life, given that some stealth operations are assaults on human life and all drone attacks are stealth operations.

15. Some near-death experiences are supernatural phenomena, and no near-death experiences are easily forgotten happenings. Consequently some easily forgotten happenings are not supernatural phenomena.

II. Use the counterexample method to prove each of the following arguments invalid.

★1. If animal species are fixed and immutable, then evolution is a myth. Therefore, evolution is not a myth, since animal species are not fixed and immutable.

2. If carbon dioxide is present in the atmosphere, then plants have a source of carbon. Hence, since plants have a source of carbon, carbon dioxide is present in the atmosphere.

1

3. If human rights are recognized, then civilization flourishes. If equality prevails, then civilization flourishes. Thus, if human rights are recognized, then equality prevails.

★4. If energy taxes are increased, then either the deficit will be reduced or conservation will be taken seriously. If the deficit is reduced, then inflation will be checked. Therefore, if energy taxes are increased, then inflation will be checked.

5. All homeless people who are panhandlers are destitute individuals. Therefore, all homeless people are destitute individuals.

6. Some wrestlers are colorful hulks, since some wrestlers are colorful and some wrestlers are hulks.

★7. All community colleges with low tuition are either schools with large enrollments or institutions supported by taxes. Therefore, all community colleges are institutions supported by taxes.

8. All merchandisers that are retailers are businesses that are inventory rotators. Therefore, all merchandisers are inventory rotators.

9. All diabetes victims are either insulin takers or glucose eliminators. Accordingly, some diabetes victims are glucose eliminators, since some diabetes victims are insulin takers.

★10. All FHA loans are living-standard enhancers for the following reasons. All reverse mortgages that are FHA loans are either living-standard enhancers or home-equity depleters, and all reverse mortgages are home-equity depleters.

III. Define the following terms:

argument form   counterexample method
substitution instance

Summary

Logic: The science that evaluates arguments.

Argument: A group of statements comprising one or more premises and one conclusion.

Premises: The statements that set forth the reasons or evidence.

Conclusion: The statement that is claimed to follow from the premises.

To distinguish premises from conclusion, look for:
- Indicator words ("hence," "therefore," "since," "because," etc.)
- An inferential relationship among the statements

Not all groups of statements are arguments. To distinguish arguments from nonarguments, look for:
- Indicator words ("hence," "since," etc.)
- An inferential relationship among the statements
- Typical kinds of nonarguments (warnings, reports, expository passages, etc.)

The most problematic kinds of nonarguments:

- Expository passages (Is the topic sentence proved by the other statements?)
- Illustrations (Could the passage be an argument from example?)
- Explanations (Could the explanandum also be a conclusion?)

Conditional statements express the relation between sufficient conditions and necessary conditions:

- *A* is a sufficient condition for *B*: The occurrence of *A* is all that is needed for the occurrence of B.
- *A* is a necessary condition for *B*: *A* cannot occur without the occurrence of *B*.

Arguments are traditionally divided into deductive and inductive:

- Deductive argument: The conclusion is claimed to follow necessarily from the premises.
- Inductive argument: The conclusion is claimed to follow probably from the premises.

To distinguish deductive arguments from inductive arguments, look for:

- Special indicator phrases ("it necessarily follows that," "it probably follows that," etc.)
- The actual strength of the inferential relationship between premises and conclusion
- Typical forms or styles of argumentation:
  - Deductive forms: Arguments based on mathematics; arguments from definition; and categorical, hypothetical, and disjunctive syllogisms
  - Inductive forms: Predictions, arguments from analogy, generalizations, arguments from authority, arguments based on signs, and causal inferences

Evaluating an argument (either deductive or inductive) involves two steps:

- Evaluating the link between premises and conclusion
- Evaluating the truth of the premises

Deductive arguments are valid, invalid, sound, or unsound.

- Valid: The conclusion actually follows from the premises.
- Sound: The argument is valid and has all true premises.

Inductive arguments are strong, weak, cogent, or uncogent.

- Strong: The conclusion actually follows from the premises.
- Cogent: The argument is strong and has all true premises.

The validity of a deductive argument is determined by the argument's form. An invalid form allows for a substitution instance having true premises and a false conclusion.

- Counterexample method:
  - Is used to prove invalidity.
  - Consists in identifying the form of a given invalid argument and producing a substitution instance having true premises and a false conclusion.
  - This proves the form invalid, which proves the given argument invalid.

2

Informal Fallacies

2.1 Fallacies in General

PREVIEW

Suppose you read this ad: "Mercury running shoes—the perfect blend of style and speed. Buy them and be the envy of your friends." You buy a pair, and you do indeed receive admiring comments. However, on a rainy day you find that the shoes literally disintegrate on your feet. Later you find that Mercury shoes are not intended for wet weather. You have been tricked by the ad. In this chapter you will learn about many ways in which arguers trick others into accepting unjustified conclusions.

 **MindTap** *Your personal learning experience—learn anywhere, anytime.*

2

A **fallacy** is a defect in an argument that arises from either a mistake in reasoning or the creation of an illusion that makes a bad argument appear good. The fallacies that appear in this chapter involve errors that occur so often that they have been given specific names. The term *non sequitur* ("it does not follow") is another name for fallacy. Both deductive and inductive arguments may contain fallacies; if they do, they are either unsound or uncogent, depending on the kind of argument. Conversely, if an argument is unsound or uncogent, it has one or more false premises or it contains a fallacy (or both).

Fallacies are usually divided into two groups: formal and informal. A **formal fallacy** is one that may be identified by merely examining the form or structure of an argument. Fallacies of this kind are found only in deductive arguments that have identifiable forms. Chapter 1 presented some of these forms: categorical syllogisms, hypothetical syllogisms, and disjunctive syllogisms. The following categorical syllogism contains a formal fallacy:

> All bullfights are grotesque rituals.
> All executions are grotesque rituals.
> Therefore, all bullfights are executions.

This argument has the following form:

> All *A* are *B*.
> All *C* are *B*.
> All *A* are *C*.

By merely examining this form, one can see that it is invalid. The fact that *A*, *B*, and *C* stand respectively for "bullfights," "grotesque rituals," and "executions" is irrelevant in detecting the fallacy. The problem may be traced to the second premise. If the letters *C* and *B* are interchanged, the form becomes valid, and the original argument, with the same change introduced, also becomes valid (but unsound).

Here is an example of a formal fallacy that occurs in a hypothetical syllogism:

> If apes are intelligent, then apes can solve puzzles.
> Apes can solve puzzles.
> Therefore, apes are intelligent.

This argument has the following form:

> If *A* then *B*.
> *B*.
> *A*.

In this case, if *A* and *B* are interchanged in the first premise, the form becomes valid, and the original argument, with the same change, also becomes valid. This fallacy and the one that precedes it will be discussed in later chapters.

In distinguishing formal from informal fallacies, remember that formal fallacies occur only in deductive arguments. Thus, if a given argument is inductive, it cannot contain a formal fallacy. Also, keep an eye out for standard deductive argument forms such as categorical syllogisms and hypothetical syllogisms. If such an argument is invalid because of an improper arrangement of terms or statements, it commits a formal fallacy. Section 1.5 investigated some of these forms and gave instruction on distinguishing the form from the content of an argument. All of the exercises at the end of that section commit formal fallacies.

Informal fallacies are those that can be detected only by examining the content of an argument. Consider the following example:

> The Brooklyn Bridge is made of atoms.
> Atoms are invisible.
> Therefore, the Brooklyn Bridge is invisible.

informal fallacy: A fallacy that can be detected only by examining the content of an argument.

To detect this fallacy one must know something about bridges—namely, that they are large visible objects, and even though their atomic components are invisible, this does not mean that the bridges themselves are invisible.

Or consider this example:

> A chess player is a person.
> Therefore, a bad chess player is a bad person.

To detect this fallacy one must know that the meaning of the word "bad" depends on what it modifies, and that being a bad chess player is quite different from being a bad person.

The various informal fallacies accomplish their purpose in so many different ways that no single umbrella theory covers them all. Some fallacies work by getting the reader or listener to feel various emotions, such as fear, pity, or camaraderie, and then attaching a certain conclusion to those emotions. Others attempt to discredit an opposing argument by associating it with certain pejorative features of its author. And then there are those that appeal to various dispositions on the part of the reader or listener, such as superstition or mental laziness, to get him or her to accept a conclusion. By studying the typical ways in which arguers apply these techniques, one is less likely to be fooled by the fallacious arguments posed by others or to stumble blindly into fallacies when constructing arguments for one's own use.

Since the time of Aristotle, logicians have attempted to classify the various informal fallacies. Aristotle himself identified thirteen and separated them into two groups. The work of subsequent logicians has produced dozens more, rendering the task of classifying them even more difficult. The presentation that follows divides twenty-two informal fallacies into five groups: fallacies of relevance, fallacies of weak induction, fallacies of presumption, fallacies of ambiguity, and fallacies of illicit transference. The final section of the chapter considers the related topics of detecting and avoiding fallacies in the context of ordinary language.

EXERCISE 2.1

Determine whether the fallacies committed by the following arguments are formal fallacies or informal fallacies.

★ 1. If Rasputin was really mad, then he deceived Czar Nicholas II. Rasputin was not really mad. Therefore, he did not deceive Czar Nicholas II.

2. Everything that runs has feet. The Columbia River runs very swiftly. Therefore, the Columbia River has feet.

3. All people who believe we create our own reality are people who lack social responsibility. All people governed by selfish motives are people who lack social responsibility. Therefore, all people who believe we create our own reality are people governed by selfish motives.

★ 4. The ship of state is like a ship at sea. No sailor is ever allowed to protest orders from the captain. For the same reason, no citizen should ever be allowed to protest presidential policies.

5. Renowned violinist Pinchas Zukerman has said, "When it comes to vodka, Smirnoff plays second fiddle to none." We must therefore conclude that Smirnoff is the best vodka available.

6. If the Chinese government systematically kills its unwanted orphans, then the Chinese government is immoral. The Chinese government is indeed immoral. Therefore, the Chinese government systematically kills its unwanted orphans.

★ 7. Sarah Jessica Parker, Ben Affleck, and Julia Roberts are Democrats. Therefore, it must be the case that all Hollywood stars are Democrats.

8. Mark Zuckerberg, CEO of Facebook, argues in favor of opening up the Arctic National Wildlife Refuge to oil drilling. But consider this: Zuckerberg is just a moneygrubbing capitalist who only cares about inflating his already bloated bank account. Clearly his arguments are ridiculous.

9. If plastic guns are sold to the public, then terrorists will carry them aboard airliners undetected. If plastic guns are sold to the public, then airline hijackings will increase. Therefore, if terrorists carry plastic guns aboard airliners undetected, then airline hijackings will increase.

★ 10. Some corporate mergers are arrangements that produce layoffs. Some arrangements that produce layoffs are social catastrophes. Therefore, some corporate mergers are social catastrophes.

aplia™

Visit Aplia for section-specific problem sets.

2.2   Fallacies of Relevance

PREVIEW

Imagine that a good friend of yours writes an editorial for the school newspaper supporting increased diversity on campus. Then another student attacks the editorial, claiming that your friend wrote it only to get attention and to compensate for the fact that he is unpopular and has a hard time getting dates. How would you respond to this argument? This section of the book explores arguments similar to the one attacking your friend's editorial.

fallacy of relevance:
A defect in an argument that occurs because the premises are logically irrelevant to the conclusion.

The **fallacies of relevance** share the common characteristic that the arguments in which they occur have premises that are *logically* irrelevant to the conclusion. Yet the premises may appear to be *psychologically* relevant, so the conclusion may *seem* to follow from the premises, even though it does not follow logically. In a good argument the premises provide genuine evidence in support of the conclusion. In an argument that commits a fallacy of relevance, on the other hand, the connection between premises and conclusion is emotional. To identify a fallacy of relevance, therefore, one must be able to distinguish genuine evidence from various forms of emotional appeal.

1. Appeal to Force
(*Argumentum ad Baculum*: Appeal to the "Stick")

The fallacy of **appeal to force** occurs whenever an arguer threatens someone to win acceptance of a conclusion. The threat may involve either physical or psychological harm, and the one threatened may be either an individual or a group of people. Obviously, such a threat is logically irrelevant to the subject matter of the conclusion, so any argument based on such a procedure is fallacious. The *ad baculum* fallacy often occurs when children argue with one another:

> *Child to playmate: Sesame Street* is the best show on TV; and if you don't believe it, I'm going to call my big brother over here and he's going to beat you up.

But it occurs among adults as well:

> *Secretary to boss:* I deserve a raise in salary for the coming year. After all, you know how friendly I am with your wife, and I'm sure you wouldn't want her to find out what's been going on between you and that sexpot client of yours.

The first example involves a physical threat, the second a psychological one. While neither threat provides any genuine evidence that the conclusion is true, both provide evidence that someone might be injured. If the two types of evidence are confused with each other, both arguer and listener may be deluded into thinking that the conclusion is supported by evidence, when in fact it is not.

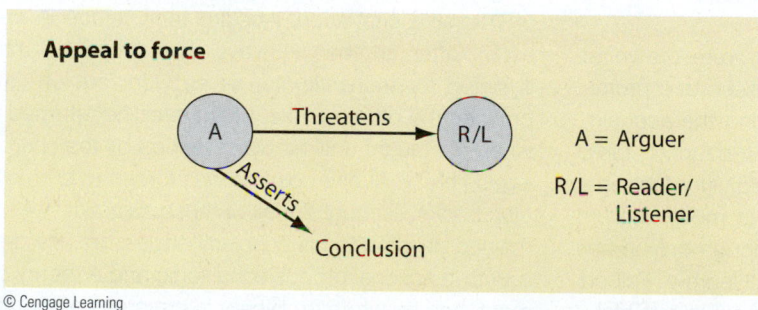

Appeal to force

A — Threatens → R/L

A — Asserts → Conclusion

A = Arguer

R/L = Reader/Listener

© Cengage Learning

The appeal to force fallacy usually accomplishes its purpose by psychologically impeding the reader or listener from acknowledging a missing premise that, if acknowledged, would be seen to be false or at least questionable. The two examples just given can be interpreted as concealing the following premises, both of which are most likely false:

> If my brother forces you to admit that *Sesame Street* is the best show on TV, then *Sesame Street* is in fact the best show.

> If I succeed in threatening you, then I deserve a raise in salary.

The conclusion of the first argument is that *Sesame Street* is the best show on TV. But just because someone is forced into saying that it is does not mean that such is the case. Similarly, the conclusion of the second argument is that the secretary deserves a raise in salary. But if the boss is threatened into raising the secretary's salary, this does not mean that the secretary deserves a raise. Many of the other informal fallacies can be interpreted as accomplishing their purpose in this way.

Peter Abelard 1079–1142

Hulton Archive/Getty Images

Generally considered the greatest logician of the Middle Ages, Peter Abelard was born in the village of Le Pallet in the Brittany region of France. His parents were members of the French nobility, and as their eldest son, Abelard was slated to inherit substantial wealth and noble standing. However, he gave up claim to this inheritance and the knighthood that went with it, choosing instead the life of a scholar.

When he was only a teenager, Abelard went off to Paris to study philosophy with William of Champeaux at the cathedral school of Notre-Dame. He proved to be a brilliant student and arrogant to a fault. He openly challenged the views of his teacher and seized on every opportunity to debate William in public. Later, he set up a rival school, describing its founder as the "only remaining philosopher in the world." Gradually, he became renowned throughout all of Europe, and he was eventually appointed to the faculty of Notre-Dame, where he attracted hundreds of students eager to learn from this illustrious master.

Around this time Abelard's attentions were drawn to Heloise, the beautiful and brilliant young niece of a prominent Parisian canon named Fulbert. Making the acquaintance of Fulbert's young protégé proved a daunting task, since her uncle kept her closely guarded. Nonetheless, Abelard persuaded Fulbert to allow him to move into his house and tutor the gifted niece, who, though only in her teens, had already mastered Greek and Hebrew. Fulbert saw this as a way of providing Heloise with a first-rate higher education, but for Abelard it provided quite a different opportunity. He later compared Fulbert's credulity in allowing him access to his charge as akin to placing a lamb in the care of a devouring wolf.

The tutoring sessions rapidly turned toward seduction, with Heloise a receptive student. Before long Heloise became pregnant and gave birth to a son whom she named Astrolabe (after the astronomical device). A public marriage might have abated the ensuing scandal, but scholars and clerics were not supposed to marry. The couple decided to marry secretly, and Heloise fled to a convent to shield herself from the scandal mongers who persecuted her for being ostensibly unwed. Meanwhile, a furious Fulbert plotted to punish Abelard, and he hired a gang of marauders to break into Abelard's lodgings in the middle of the night and castrate him.

After the castration, Abelard took refuge in one monastery after another. However his arrogance made him ill suited for monastic life, as he went out of his way to provoke the other monks. Much later, he returned to Paris where he taught until he was silenced by the church for alleged heresy. At one point he was forced to burn one of his own books. Throughout all of these calamities, Abelard remained devoted to his scholarly endeavors. He developed a truth-functional propositional logic and a theory of entailment, and he wrote prolifically in the areas of metaphysics, ethics, and philosophy of language. He is buried alongside Heloise in the Père-Lachaise Cemetery in Paris. Today, their grave site is visited by people seeking solace from the frustrations of love.

2. Appeal to Pity (*Argumentum ad Misericordiam*)

appeal to pity: An arguer evokes a feeling of pity from the reader/listener to win acceptance of a conclusion.

The appeal to pity fallacy occurs when an arguer evokes a feeling of pity from a reader or listener to win acceptance of a conclusion. This pity may be directed toward the arguer or toward some third party. Example:

Taxpayer to judge: Your Honor, I admit that I declared thirteen children as dependents on my tax return, even though I have only two. But if you find me guilty of tax evasion, my reputation will be ruined. I'll probably lose my job, my poor wife will not be able to have the operation that she desperately needs, and my kids will starve. Surely I am not guilty.

The conclusion of this argument is "Surely I am not guilty." Obviously, the conclusion is not *logically* relevant to the arguer's set of pathetic circumstances, although it is *psychologically* relevant. If the arguer succeeds in evoking pity from the listener or reader, the latter is likely to exercise his or her desire to help the arguer by accepting the argument. In this way the reader or listener may be fooled into accepting a conclusion that is not supported by any evidence. The appeal to pity is quite common and is often used by students on their instructors at exam time and by lawyers on behalf of their clients before judges and juries.

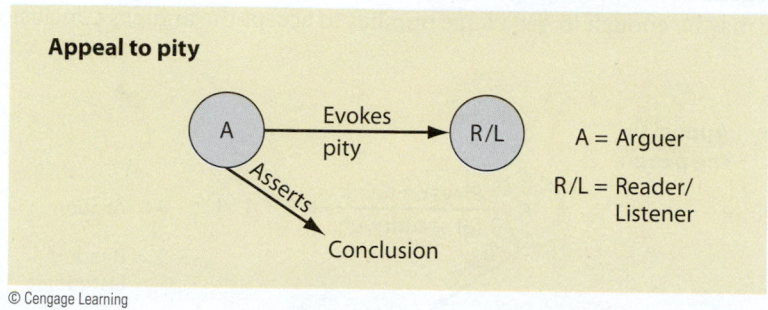

Appeal to pity

Evokes pity

A → R/L

Asserts

Conclusion

A = Arguer

R/L = Reader/Listener

© Cengage Learning

Of course, some arguments that attempt to evoke sympathetic feelings from the reader or listener are not fallacious. We might call them *arguments from compassion*. Such arguments differ from the fallacious appeal to pity in that, in addition to evoking compassion on behalf of some person, they supply information about why that person is genuinely deserving of help or special consideration. Whenever possible these nonfallacious arguments should show that the person in question is a victim of circumstances and not responsible for the dire straits he finds himself in, that the recommended help or special consideration is not illegal or inappropriate, and that it will genuinely help the person in question. In contrast to such arguments, the appeal to pity proceeds by ignoring all of these considerations and attempts to support a conclusion by merely evoking pity from the reader or listener.

3. Appeal to the People (*Argumentum ad Populum*)

Nearly everyone wants to be loved, esteemed, admired, valued, recognized, and accepted by others. The **appeal to the people** uses these desires to get the reader or listener to accept a conclusion. Two approaches are involved: one of them direct, the other indirect.

The *direct approach* occurs when an arguer, addressing a large group of people, excites the emotions and enthusiasm of the crowd to win acceptance for his or her conclusion. The objective is to arouse a kind of mob mentality. This is the strategy used by nearly every propagandist and demagogue. Adolf Hitler was a master of the technique, but speech makers at Democratic and Republican national conventions also use it with some measure of success. Waving flags and blaring music add to the overall effect. Because the individuals in the audience want to share in the camaraderie, the euphoria, and the excitement, they find themselves accepting a variety of conclusions with ever-increasing fervor.

appeal to the people: An arguer uses a person's desire to be loved, admired, and included to win acceptance of a conclusion.

An appeal to negative emotions can also generate a mob mentality. The **appeal to fear**, also known as fear mongering, is a variety of the direct form of the appeal to the people that occurs when an arguer trumps up a fear of something in the mind of the crowd and then uses that fear as a premise for some conclusion. Of course many fears that we experience in daily life are supported by solid evidence, such as the fear of getting mugged in a dark alley when several muggings have occurred there recently. In the appeal to fear fallacy, the fear is not supported by any solid evidence, and it usually rests on nothing more than irrational suspicion created by repeating a message or rumor over and over again. As the message gradually sinks in it causes the crowd to feel uneasy, and this alone may be enough to get a large number to accept the arguer's conclusion.

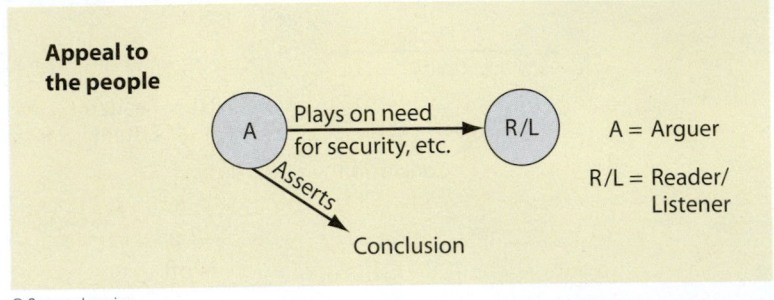

© Cengage Learning

Fear mongering has played at least a minor role in nearly every presidential election. A famous example was the so-called Daisy Commercial* used in 1964 by the Lyndon Johnson campaign to defeat Barry Goldwater. The commercial raised the specter of Goldwater's possible use of nuclear weapons in Vietnam if he were to become president. What if Goldwater were elected? Could this lead to an all-out nuclear confrontation with the Soviet Union? No one could be sure of the answer. Even though the commercial was pulled after its first airing, countless news shows picked it up and repeated it over and over again. The effect was to plant the fear of nuclear annihilation in the minds of millions of voters, and in the end it swayed many of them to side with President Johnson.

Practically any social or political change is fertile ground for appeals to fear. When Darwin's theory of evolution began to be taught in the schools, William Jennings Bryan argued that it would increase the number of wars, undermine morality, convert love into hate, and destroy civilization. His speeches were a driving force in the movement to ban the teaching of evolution. When the nation was debating whether women should be allowed to vote, Elihu Root argued that suffrage would make women "hard, harsh, unlovable, repulsive." When the Soviet Union developed the atomic bomb and became a threat to world peace, Senator Joseph McCarthy argued that Soviet spies or sympathizers had infiltrated many branches of the government including the State Department and the U.S. Army. The resulting atmosphere of fear wrecked the lives of many innocent victims.

As these examples illustrate, the direct approach of appeal to the people is often accomplished through oral communication. However, writing can also produce the same effect. By using such emotionally charged phrases as "champion of the free-enterprise system," "defender of the working man," "bleeding-heart liberal," and "profligate spender," polemicists can awaken the same kind of mob mentality in their writings as they would if they were speaking.

*This commercial, in its entirety, is readily available on the Internet.

In the *indirect approach* of appeal to the people, the arguer aims his or her appeal not at the crowd as a whole but at one or more individuals separately, focusing on some aspect of those individuals' relationship to the crowd. The indirect approach includes such specific forms as the bandwagon argument, the appeal to vanity, the appeal to snobbery, and the appeal to tradition.

The **bandwagon argument** has this general structure: Everybody believes such-and-such or does such-and-such; therefore, you should believe or do such-and-such, too. Examples:

> Everyone nowadays is on a low-carb diet. Therefore, you should go on a low-carb diet, too.

> Practically everybody believes in life after death. Therefore, you should believe in life after death, too.

The idea is that if you want to fit in with the crowd and not stick out like a sore thumb, then you, too, will go on the diet and believe in life after death. But of course the mere fact that a large group of people happen to be doing something or believe in something is not, by itself, a logical reason why you ought to do it, too.

The **appeal to vanity** is another form of the indirect approach, and it often involves linking the love, admiration, or approval of the crowd with some famous figure who is loved, admired, or approved of. This version of the fallacy is often used by advertisers, parents, and people in general.

> Of course you want to look as fresh and beautiful as Ellen DeGeneres. That means you will want to buy and use Cover Girl cosmetics.

> Daniel Craig wears an Omega wristwatch. Thus, if you want to be like him, you will buy and wear an Omega watch, too.

> *Mother to child:* You want to grow up and be just like Wonder Woman, don't you? Then eat your liver and carrots.

The idea is that if you succeed in becoming like DeGeneres, Craig, or Wonder Woman, then you will win the love and approval of the crowd; but to become like them you must buy the advertised product or, in the case of the little girl, eat the liver and carrots. Incidentally, these examples show how the appeal to vanity can overlap the false cause fallacy (presented in Section 2.3), because they might be interpreted to mean that using Cover Girl cosmetics will *cause* a person to look like Ellen DeGeneres, and so on. Of course, any such causal connection is unlikely.

In the **appeal to snobbery** the crowd that the arguer appeals to is a smaller group that is supposed to be superior in some way—more wealthy, more powerful, more culturally refined, more intelligent, and so on. As the argument goes, if the listener wants to be part of this group, then he or she will do a certain thing, think in a certain way, or buy a certain product. Example:

> The Lexus 400 series is not for everyone. Only those with considerable means and accomplishment will acquire one. To show the world that you are among the select few, you will want to purchase and drive one of these distinguished automobiles.

Even if a group of snobs might happen to think or feel something, this is not a logical reason for why you should act in conformity.

The **appeal to tradition** is yet another variety of the indirect appeal to the people. It occurs when an arguer cites the fact that something has become a tradition as

bandwagon argument: An arguer uses one's desire to feel united with the crowd to win acceptance of a conclusion.

2

grounds for some conclusion. The claim that something is a tradition is basically synonymous with the claim that a lot of people have done it that way for a long time. Examples:

> Traditionally, professional sporting events have been preceded by the national anthem. Therefore, professional sporting events should continue to be preceded by the national anthem.

> Serving turkey on Thanksgiving Day is a long-standing tradition. Therefore, we should serve turkey next Thanksgiving Day.

The mere fact that something has been done in a certain way for a long time does not by itself justify its being repeated in the future. Yet, there are some appeals to tradition that have conclusions that are true for other reasons, and this may trick a reader or listener into thinking that the argument is a good one. Example:

> Traditionally, guests have worn elegant clothing to Mrs. Channing's annual cocktail party. Therefore, it would not be a good idea for you to go naked to her party this year.

This argument is just as fallacious as the previous two. The conclusion is clearly true, but the reason why it is true is not because of any tradition but because the purpose of a cocktail party is to foster a feeling of conviviality among the guests. One of the guests showing up naked would threaten to destroy this purpose to the detriment of the host and all the other guests.

Incidentally, this final point about appeals to tradition with true conclusions applies to the other forms of *ad populum* as well. If such arguments have true conclusions, those conclusions are true for reasons other than the fact that the crowd believes something or feels something.

Both the direct and indirect approaches of the *ad populum* fallacy have the same basic structure:

> You want to be accepted/included in the group/loved/esteemed. . . . Therefore, you should accept XYZ as true.

In the direct approach the arousal of a mob mentality produces an immediate feeling of belonging, even if it relates to something feared. Each person feels united with the crowd, and this feeling evokes a sense of strength and security. When the crowd roars its approval of the conclusions that are then offered, anyone who does not accept them automatically cuts himself or herself off from the crowd and risks the loss of his or her security, strength, and acceptance. The same thing happens in the indirect approach, but the context and technique are somewhat subtler.

4. Argument Against the Person (*Argumentum ad Hominem*)

argument against the person: An arguer attacks an opposing argument by attacking the argument's author.

This fallacy always involves two arguers. One of them advances (either directly or implicitly) a certain argument, and the other then responds by directing his or her attention not to the first person's argument but to the first person *himself*. When this occurs, the second person is said to commit an **argument against the person.**

The argument against the person occurs in three forms: the *ad hominem* abusive, the *ad hominem* circumstantial, and the *tu quoque*. In the **ad hominem abusive**, the second person responds to the first person's argument by verbally abusing the first person. Example:

> Television entertainer Bill Maher argues that religion is just a lot of foolish nonsense. But Maher is an arrogant, shameless, self-righteous pig. Obviously his arguments are not worth listening to.

The author of this argument ignores the substance of Maher's argument and instead attacks Maher himself. However, because Maher's personal attributes are irrelevant to whether the premises of his religion argument support the conclusion, the argument attacking him is fallacious.

Not all cases of the *ad hominem* abusive are so blunt, but they are just as fallacious. Example:

> Dr. Phil argues that mutual self-esteem is essential to a good marriage. But Dr. Phil is not terribly well educated, and he never attended an Ivy League college. Thus, his arguments are worthless.

A very common form of the *ad hominem* abusive occurs when the responding arguer's retort is to suggest that the opposing arguer consider going somewhere else—such as out of the country ("America—Love it or leave it"), switching to a different religion or political party, or doing something ridiculous (such as jumping in a lake or flying a kite). Example:

> Billionaire investor Warren Buffet argues that wealthy people should be required to pay more taxes. I would remind Mr. Buffet that he is free to send a check to the federal treasury any time he likes.

This argument commits an *ad hominem* because instead of replying to Mr. Buffet's argument, the second arguer directs his attention to Mr. Buffet himself and suggests that if he is so concerned about the inflow of tax dollars, he can increase the amount of his own taxes. The objective is to show that Mr. Buffet's motives are misplaced.

The **ad hominem circumstantial** begins the same way as the *ad hominem* abusive, but instead of heaping verbal abuse on his or her opponent, the respondent attempts to discredit the opponent's argument by alluding to certain circumstances that affect the opponent. By doing so the respondent hopes to show that the opponent is predisposed to argue the way he or she does and should therefore not be taken seriously.

Here is an example:

> The Dalai Lama argues that China has no business in Tibet and that the West should do something about it. But the Dalai Lama just wants the Chinese to leave so he can return as leader. Naturally he argues this way. Therefore, we should reject his arguments.

The author of this argument ignores the substance of the Dalai Lama's argument and attempts to discredit it by calling attention to certain circumstances that affect the Dalai Lama—namely, that he wants to return to Tibet as its leader. But the fact that the Dalai Lama happens to be affected by these circumstances is irrelevant to whether his premises support a conclusion. The *ad hominem* circumstantial is easy to recognize because it always takes this form: "Of course Mr. X argues this way; just look at the circumstances that affect him."

ad hominem abusive: An arguer attacks an opposing arguer by verbally abusing that person.

ad hominem circumstantial: An arguer alludes to circumstances affecting an opposing arguer that predispose that person to argue in this way.

2

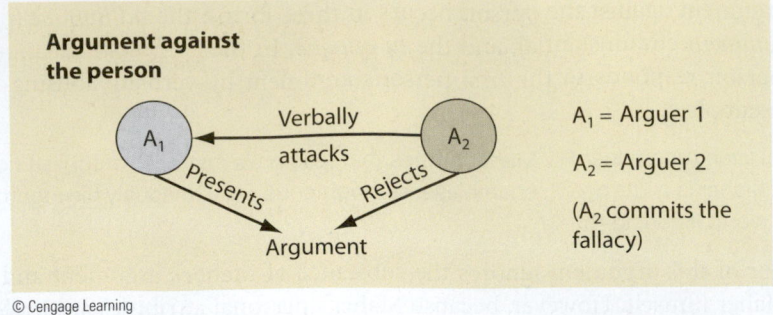

Argument against the person

Verbally attacks

Presents

Rejects

Argument

A_1 = Arguer 1

A_2 = Arguer 2

(A_2 commits the fallacy)

© Cengage Learning

tu quoque: An arguer attempts to show that an opposing arguer is a hypocrite who does not practice what he preaches.

The *tu quoque* ("you too") fallacy begins the same way as the other two varieties of the *ad hominem* argument, except that the second arguer attempts to make the first appear to be hypocritical or arguing in bad faith. The second arguer usually accomplishes this by citing features in the life or behavior of the first arguer that conflict with the latter's conclusion. The fallacy often takes the form, "How dare you argue that I should stop doing *X*; why, you do (or have done) *X* yourself." Example:

> Kim Kardashian argues that women should not have kids out of wedlock. But just look at what she did. She gave birth to her daughter North without being married. Clearly Kardashian's argument is not worth listening to.

Again, the fact that Kim Kardashian gave birth to a daughter out of wedlock is irrelevant to whether her premises support her conclusion. Thus, this argument is fallacious.

Keep in mind that the purpose of an *ad hominem* argument is to discredit another person's argument by placing its author in a bad light. Thus, for the fallacy to be committed, there must always be two arguers (at least implicitly). If it should turn out that the person being attacked is not an arguer, then the personal comments made by the attacker may well be relevant to the conclusion that is drawn. In general, personal observations are relevant to conclusions about what kind of person someone is (good, bad, stingy, trustworthy, and so forth) and whether a person has done something. Example:

> Joseph Kony, leader of the Lord's Resistance Army, has kidnapped thousands of children from villages in central Africa, murdered their parents and relatives, and forced them into military service. He has also killed thousands of elephants and sold their ivory to fund his operation. Kony is therefore a thoroughly disgusting and despicable human being.

The conclusion is not that Kony's argument is bad but that Kony himself is bad. Because the premises give relevant support to this conclusion, the argument commits no fallacy. Another example:

> Shakespeare cannot possibly have written the thirty-six plays attributed to him, because the real Shakespeare was a two-bit country businessman who barely finished the fourth grade in school and who never left the confines of his native England.

The conclusion is not that some argument of Shakespeare's is bad but that Shakespeare did not write certain plays. Again, since the premises are relevant to this conclusion, the argument commits no *ad hominem* fallacy.

Determining what kind of person someone is includes determining whether that person is trustworthy. Thus, personal comments are often relevant in evaluating whether a person's proclamations or statements, unsupported by evidence, warrant our belief. Examples of such statements include promises to do something, testimony given by a witness, and testimonials in support of a product or service. Here is an example of an argument that discredits a witness:

> Mickey has testified that he saw Freddy set fire to the building. But Mickey was recently convicted on ten counts of perjury, and he hates Freddy with a passion and would love to see him sent to jail. Therefore, you should not believe Mickey's testimony.

This argument commits no fallacy. The conclusion is not that you should reject Mickey's argument but rather that you should reject his testimony. Testimony is not argument, and the fact that the witness is a known liar and has a motive to lie now is relevant to whether we should believe him. Furthermore, note that the conclusion is not that Mickey's statement is literally false but rather that we should not *believe* the statement. It is quite possible that Mickey really did see Freddy set fire to the building and that Mickey's statement to that effect is true. But if our only reason for believing this statement is the mere fact that Mickey has made it, then given the circumstances, we are not justified in that belief. Personal factors are never relevant to truth and falsity as such, but they are relevant to believability.

Yet there is often a close connection between truth and believability, and this provides one of the reasons why *ad hominem* arguments are often effective. In evaluating any argument there are always two issues to be considered: the quality of the reasoning and the truth of the premises. As noted, both are irrelevant to the personal characteristics of the arguer. But whether we *accept* the premises as true may depend on the credibility of the arguer. Knowing that the arguer is biased or has a motive to lie may provide good grounds for distrusting the premises. Another reason why *ad hominem* arguments are effective is that they engage the emotions of readers and listeners and thereby motivate them to transfer their negative feelings about the arguer onto the argument.

5. Accident

The fallacy of **accident** is committed when a general rule is applied to a specific case it was not intended to cover. Typically, the general rule is cited (either directly or implicitly) in the premises and then wrongly applied to the specific case mentioned in the conclusion. Two examples:

> **accident**: A general rule is applied to a specific case it was not intended to cover.

> Freedom of speech is a constitutionally guaranteed right. Therefore, John Q. Radical should not be arrested for his speech that incited the riot last week.

> People are obligated to keep their promises. When Jessica married Tyler, she promised to stay with him for life. Therefore, she should stay with him now, even though he has become an abusive spouse addicted to gambling and drugs.

In the first example, the general rule is that freedom of speech is normally guaranteed, and the specific case is the speech made by John Q. Radical. Because the speech incited a riot, the rule does not apply. In the second example, the general rule is that people are obligated to keep their promises, and the specific case is that Jessica should keep her promise to stay with Tyler. The rule does not apply because Tyler is no longer the same person that Jessica made her promise to.

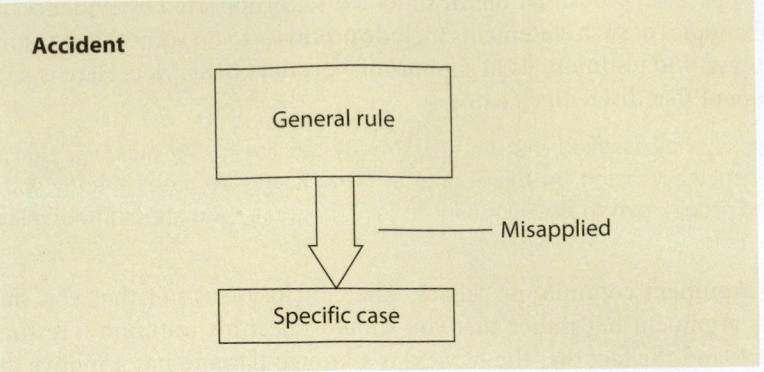

Accident

General rule

Misapplied

Specific case

The fallacy of accident gets its name from the fact that one or more accidental features of the specific case make it an exception to the rule. In the first example the accidental feature is that the speech incited a riot; in the second example the accidental features are that Tyler has become an abusive spouse and is addicted to gambling and drugs.

6. Straw Man

straw man: An arguer distorts an opponent's argument, and then attacks the distorted argument.

The **straw man** fallacy is committed when an arguer distorts an opponent's argument for the purpose of more easily attacking it, demolishes the distorted argument, and then concludes that the opponent's real argument has been demolished. By so doing, the arguer is said to have set up a straw man and knocked it down, only to conclude that the real "man" (the opposing argument) has been knocked down as well. Example:

> Mr. Goldberg has argued against prayer in the public schools. Obviously Mr. Goldberg advocates atheism. But atheism is what they used to have in Russia. Atheism leads to the suppression of all religions and the replacement of God by an omnipotent state. Is that what we want for this country? I hardly think so. Clearly Mr. Goldberg's argument is nonsense.

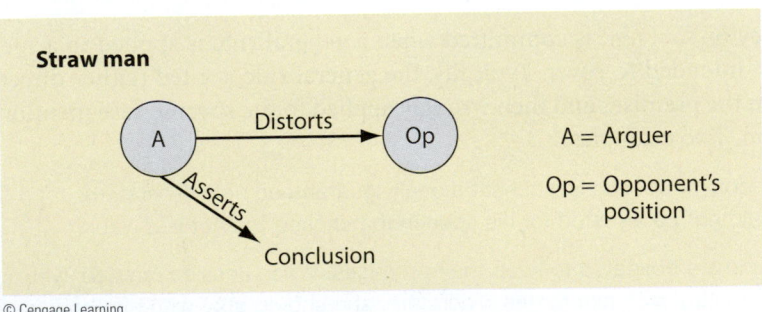

Straw man

Distorts

A → Op

Asserts

Conclusion

A = Arguer

Op = Opponent's position

© Cengage Learning

Straw man, along with argument against the person, are called refutational fallacies because they involve one arguer refuting another. These are the only fallacies presented in this chapter that always involve two arguers. In the Goldberg argument, Mr. Goldberg, who is the first arguer, has presented an argument against prayer in the public schools. The second arguer then attacks Goldberg's argument by equating it with an argument for atheism. He then attacks atheism and concludes that Goldberg's argument is nonsense. Since Goldberg's argument had nothing to do with atheism, the second argument commits the straw man fallacy.

As this example illustrates, the kind of distortion the second arguer resorts to is often an attempt to exaggerate the first person's argument or make it look more extreme than it really is. Here are two more examples:

> The garment workers have signed a petition arguing for better ventilation on the work premises. Unfortunately, air-conditioning is expensive. Air ducts would have to be run throughout the factory, and a massive heat exchange unit installed on the roof. Also, the cost of operating such a system during the summer would be astronomical. In view of these considerations the petition must be rejected.

> The student status committee has presented us with an argument favoring alcohol privileges on campus. What do the students want? Is it their intention to stay boozed up from the day they enter as freshmen until the day they graduate? Do they expect us to open a bar for them? Or maybe a chain of bars all over campus? Such a proposal is ridiculous!

In the first argument, the petition is merely for better ventilation in the factory—maybe a fan in the window during the summer. The arguer exaggerates this request to mean an elaborate air-conditioning system installed throughout the building. He then points out that this is too expensive and concludes by rejecting the petition. A similar strategy is used in the second argument. The arguer distorts the request for alcohol privileges to mean a chain of bars all over campus. Such an idea is so patently outlandish that no further argument is necessary.

7. Missing the Point (*Ignoratio Elenchi*)

All the fallacies we have discussed thus far have been instances of cases where the premises of an argument are irrelevant to the conclusion. **Missing the point** illustrates a special form of irrelevance. This fallacy occurs when the premises of an argument support one particular conclusion, but then a different conclusion, often vaguely related to the correct conclusion, is drawn. Whenever one suspects that such a fallacy is being committed, he or she should be able to identify the *correct* conclusion, the conclusion that the premises *logically* imply. This conclusion must be significantly different from the conclusion that is actually drawn. Examples:

missing the point: An arguer draws a conclusion different from the one supported by the premises.

> Crimes of theft and robbery have been increasing at an alarming rate lately. The conclusion is obvious: We must reinstate the death penalty immediately.

> Abuse of the welfare system is rampant nowadays. Our only alternative is to abolish the system altogether.

At least two correct conclusions are implied by the premise of the first argument: either "We should provide increased police protection in vulnerable neighborhoods" or "We should initiate programs to eliminate the causes of the crimes." Reinstating the death penalty is not a logical conclusion at all. Among other things, theft and robbery are not capital crimes. In the second argument the premises logically suggest some systematic effort to eliminate the cheaters rather than eliminating the system altogether.

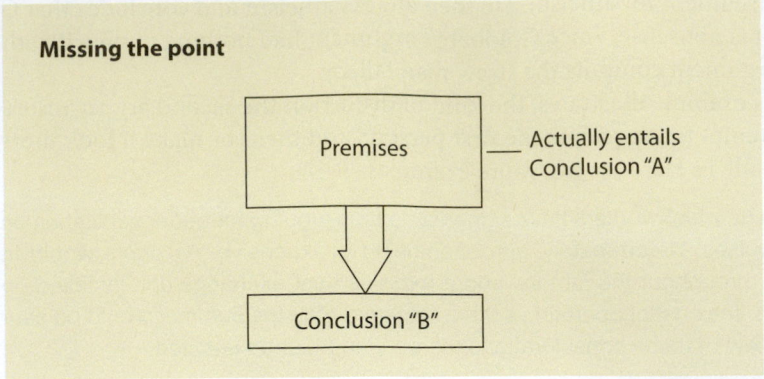

Missing the point

Premises —— Actually entails Conclusion "A"

Conclusion "B"

Ignoratio elenchi means "ignorance of the proof." The arguer is ignorant of the logical implications of his or her own premises and, as a result, draws a conclusion that misses the point entirely. The fallacy has a distinct structure all its own, but in some ways it serves as a catchall for arguments that are not clear instances of one or more of the other fallacies. An argument should not be identified as a case of missing the point, however, if one of the other fallacies fits.

8. Red Herring

This fallacy is closely associated with missing the point (*ignoratio elenchi*). The **red herring** fallacy is committed when the arguer diverts the attention of the reader or listener by changing the subject to a different but sometimes subtly related one. He or she then finishes by either drawing a conclusion about this different issue or by merely presuming that some conclusion has been established. By so doing, the arguer purports to have won the argument. The fallacy gets its name from a procedure used to train hunting dogs to follow a scent. A red herring (or bag of them) is dragged across the trail with the aim of leading the dogs astray. Since red herrings have an especially potent scent (caused in part by the smoking process used to preserve them), only the best dogs will follow the original scent.

To use the red herring fallacy effectively, the arguer must change the original subject of the argument without the reader or listener noticing it. One way of doing this is to change the subject to one that is subtly related to the original subject. Here are two examples of this technique:

> Environmentalists are continually harping about the dangers of nuclear power. Unfortunately, electricity is dangerous no matter where it comes from. Every year hundreds of people are electrocuted by accident. Since most of these accidents are caused by carelessness, they could be avoided if people would just exercise greater caution.

> There is a good deal of talk these days about the need to eliminate pesticides from our fruits and vegetables. But many of these foods are essential to our health. Carrots are an excellent source of vitamin A, broccoli is rich in iron, and oranges and grapefruit have lots of vitamin C.

Both arguments commit the red herring fallacy. In the first, the original issue is whether nuclear power is dangerous. The arguer changes this subject to the danger of

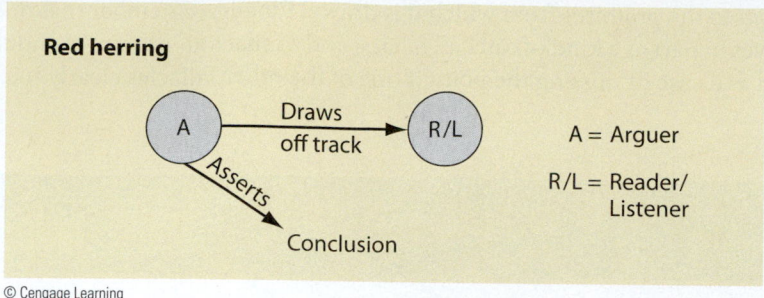

Red herring

A — Draws off track — R/L

Asserts → Conclusion

A = Arguer

R/L = Reader/Listener

© Cengage Learning

electrocution and proceeds to draw a conclusion about that. The new subject is clearly different from the possibility of nuclear explosion or meltdown, but the fact that both are related to electricity facilitates the arguer's goal of leading someone off the track. In the second argument, the original issue is pesticides, and the arguer changes it to the value of fruits and vegetables in one's diet. Again, the fact that the second topic is related to the first assists the arguer in committing the fallacy. In neither case does the arguer draw a conclusion about the original topic, but by merely diverting the attention of the reader or listener, the arguer creates the presumption of having won the argument.

A second way of using the red herring effectively is to change the subject to some flashy, eye-catching topic that is virtually guaranteed to distract the listener's attention. Topics of this sort include sex, crime, scandal, immorality, death, and any other topic that might serve as the subject of gossip. Here is an example of this technique:

> Professor Conway complains of inadequate parking on our campus. But did you know that last year Conway carried on a torrid love affair with a member of the English Department? The two used to meet every day for clandestine sex in the copier room. Apparently they didn't realize how much you can see through that fogged glass window. Even the students got an eyeful. Enough said about Conway.

The red herring fallacy can be confused with the straw man fallacy because both have the effect of drawing the reader/listener off the track. This confusion can usually be avoided by remembering the unique ways in which they accomplish this purpose. In the straw man, the arguer begins by distorting an opponent's argument and concludes by knocking down the distorted argument. In the red herring, the arguer ignores the opponent's argument (if there is one) and subtly changes the subject. Thus, to distinguish the two fallacies, one should attempt to determine whether the arguer has knocked down a distorted argument or simply changed the subject. Also keep in mind that straw man always involves two arguers, at least implicitly, whereas a red herring often does not.

Both the red herring and straw man fallacies are susceptible of being confused with missing the point, because all three involve a similar kind of irrelevancy. To avoid this confusion, one should note that both red herring and straw man proceed by generating a new set of premises, whereas missing the point does not. Straw man draws a conclusion from new premises that are obtained by distorting an earlier argument, and red herring, if it draws any conclusion at all, draws one from new premises obtained by changing the subject. Missing the point, however, draws a conclusion from the original premises. Also, in the red herring and straw man, the conclusion, if there is one, is *relevant* to the premises from which it is drawn; but in missing the point, the conclusion is *irrelevant* to the premises from which it is drawn. Finally, remember that missing the point serves in part as a kind of catchall fallacy, and a fallacious argument should not be identified as a case of missing the point if one of the other fallacies clearly fits.

EXERCISE 2.2

I. Identify the fallacies of relevance committed by the following arguments, giving a brief explanation for your answer. If no fallacy is committed, write "no fallacy."

★1. The position open in the accounting department should be given to Frank Thompson. Frank has six hungry children to feed, and his wife desperately needs an operation to save her eyesight.

2. Erica Evans, who takes orders at the local Taco Bell, argues persuasively in favor of increasing the minimum wage. But this is exactly what you would expect. Erica is paid the minimum wage, and if the minimum wage is increased, then her own salary will go up. Obviously Erica's arguments are worthless.

3. The school board argues that our schools are in desperate need of repair. But the real reason our students are falling behind is that they spend too much time on their smartphones. Becoming educated means a lot more than learning how to scroll up and down. The school board should send a letter to the parents urging them to confiscate their kids' smartphones.

★4. Whoever thrusts a knife into another person should be arrested. But surgeons do precisely this when operating. Therefore, surgeons should be arrested.

5. You should read Irving Stone's latest novel right away. It's sold over a million copies, and practically everyone in the Manhattan cocktail circuit is talking about it.

6. Friedrich Nietzsche's philosophy is not worth the paper it's printed on. Nietzsche was an immoral reprobate who went completely insane from syphilis before he died.

★7. Surely you welcome the opportunity to join our protective organization. Think of all the money you will lose from broken windows, overturned trucks, and damaged merchandise in the event of your not joining.

8. Senator Barrow advocates increased Social Security benefits for the poor. It is regrettable that the senator finds it necessary to advocate socialism. Socialism defeats initiative, takes away promised rewards, and leads directly to inefficiency and big government. It was tried for years in Eastern Europe, and it failed miserably. Clearly, socialism is no good.

9. Something is seriously wrong with high school education these days. After ten years of decline, SAT scores are still extremely low, and high school graduates are practically incapable of reading and writing. The obvious conclusion is that we should close the schools.

★10. The editors of the *Daily Register* have accused our company of being one of the city's worst water polluters. But the *Daily Register* is responsible for much more pollution than we are. After all, they own the Western Paper Company, and that company discharges tons of chemical residue into the city's river every day.

11. If 20 percent of adult Americans are functionally illiterate, then it's no wonder that morons get elected to public office. In fact, 20 percent of adult Americans *are* functionally illiterate. Therefore, it's no wonder that morons get elected to public office.

12. Ladies and gentlemen, today the lines of battle have been drawn. When the din of clashing armor has finally died away, the Republican party will emerge victorious! We are the true party of the American people! We embody the values that all real Americans hold sacred! We cherish and protect our founding fathers' vision that gave birth to the Constitution! We stand for decency and righteousness; for self-determination and the liberty to conduct our affairs as each of us freely chooses! In the coming election, victory will be ours, so help us God!

★ 13. We've all heard the argument that too much television is the reason our students can't read and write. Yet many of today's TV shows are excellent. *Grey's Anatomy* unveils the personal lives of interns at an urban hospital, *The Big Bang Theory* offers lots of laughs, and *American Idol* uncovers hidden musical talent. Today's TV is just great!

14. Surely architect Norris is not responsible for the collapse of the Central Bank Tower. Norris has had nothing but trouble lately. His daughter eloped with a child molester, his son committed suicide, and his alcoholic wife recently left for Las Vegas with his retirement savings.

15. The First Amendment to the Constitution prevents the government from interfering with the free exercise of religion. The liturgical practice of the Religion of Internal Enlightenment involves human sacrifice. Therefore, it would be wrong for the government to interfere with this religious practice.

★ 16. U.S. Senator Elizabeth Warren argues that big banks have been ripping off the American consumer for years. It's clear, however, that Warren says this only to scratch up more campaign contributions from those very consumers. Thus, you shouldn't take her arguments seriously.

17. Professor Pearson's arguments in favor of the theory of evolution should be discounted. Pearson is a cocaine-snorting sex pervert and, according to some reports, a member of the Communist Party.

18. Rudolf Höss, commandant of the Auschwitz concentration camp, confessed to having exterminated 1 million people, most of whom were Jews, in the Auschwitz gas chamber. We can only conclude that Höss was either insane or an extremely evil person.

★ 19. TV commentator Larry Kudlow argues that government should get off the back of the American businessman. Obviously, Kudlow wants to abolish government altogether. Yet without government there would be no defense, no judicial system, no Social Security, and no health and safety regulations. None of us wants to forgo these benefits. Thus, we can see that Kudlow's argument is absurd.

20. I know that some of you oppose the appointment of David Cole as the new sales manager. On further consideration, however, I am confident you will find him

well qualified for the job. If Cole is not appointed, it may become necessary to make severe personnel cutbacks in your department.

21. Animal rights activists say that animals are abused in biomedical research labs. But consider this: Pets are abused by their owners every day. Probably 25 percent of pet owners should never get near animals. Some cases of abuse are enough to make you sick.

★22. Of course you want to buy a pair of Slinky fashion jeans. Slinky jeans really show off your figure, and all the Hollywood starlets down on the Strip can be seen wearing them these days.

23. Film star Catherine Zeta-Jones says on TV that T-Mobile provides the coverage you need at the price you want. But this is exactly what you would expect given that T-Mobile pays her millions of dollars to make these ads. Thus, you shouldn't take her testimonials too seriously.

24. Dr. Morrison has argued that smoking is responsible for the majority of health problems in this country and that every smoker who has even the slightest concern for his or her health should quit. Unfortunately, however, we must consign Dr. Morrison's argument to the trash bin. Only yesterday I saw none other than Dr. Morrison himself smoking a cigar.

★25. Mr. Rhodes is suffering from amnesia and has no recollection whatever of the events of the past two weeks. We can only conclude that he did not commit the crime of murdering his wife a week ago, as he has been accused of doing.

II. Answer "true" or "false" to the following statements:

1. In the appeal to force, the arguer physically attacks the listener.

2. In the direct variety of the appeal to the people, the arguer attempts to create a kind of mob mentality.

3. If an arguer attempts to discredit courtroom testimony or a promise by pointing out that the witness or the person making the promise is a liar, then the arguer commits an *argumentum ad hominem* (argument against the person) fallacy.

4. The *argumentum ad hominem* always involves two arguers.

5. In the *argumentum ad hominem* circumstantial, the circumstances cited by the second arguer are intended precisely to malign the character of the first arguer.

6. In the *tu quoque* fallacy, the arguer threatens the reader or listener.

7. In the fallacy of accident, a general rule is applied to a specific case where it does not fit.

8. In the straw man fallacy, an arguer often distorts another person's argument by making it look more extreme than it really is.

9. Whenever one suspects that a missing the point fallacy is being committed, one should be able to state the conclusion that is logically implied by the premises.

10. In the red herring fallacy, the arguer attempts to lead the reader or listener off the track.

III. Identify the fallacies committed in the following dialogue. You should be able to find at least one case of each fallacy presented in this section.

Food for Thought

"Let's hit the produce section first," Curtis says to his fiancée Talia, as they enter Payless grocery store.

"Okay," she says.

"Oh, look," says Curtis. "The corn is on sale. Let's get some for dinner."

"I don't know," says Talia. "Did you see that sign over the display? The corn is genetically modified. I know we've never paid much attention to that sign in the past, but now I'm thinking that maybe we should."

"Why's that?" asks Curtis.

"I read an article the other day about foods containing genetically modified organisms—they call them GMO foods—and now I know what's behind this GMO business," Talia replies.

"And what is behind it?" Curtis asks.

Talia picks up an ear and sniffs it. "For starters," she says, "one of the reasons they modify corn is to make it resistant to herbicides like Roundup—you know, the stuff you spray on the weeds in the garden. So with GMO corn the farmer can spray the whole field with Roundup, the weeds will die, and the cornstalks will be unaffected."

"Sounds like a great way to grow corn," Curtis says.

"Yes," replies Talia, "but that means the corn contains a residue of Roundup. That's definitely not good. Roundup kills human cells and causes birth defects."

"Good grief," says Curtis. "If what you say is right, I think there is only one conclusion: We must ban the sale of Roundup immediately."

After pausing to scratch his head, he continues, "On the other hand, look at all the people who are buying this corn. If everyone is buying it, then I think we should, too."

"You're right that everyone is buying it," says Talia. "Nearly 90 percent of the corn sold in this country is genetically modified. But that doesn't mean that we should buy it. Look, there's a small display of organic corn over there. Let's get some of that."

"Now wait just a minute," says Curtis. "You better not be going organic on me. That would be too much. You know I like to eat out at least once a week, and most restaurants don't serve organic food. If you insist on organic, then you will stay at home cooking your own food, while I go out."

"Well, maybe I could eat conventional restaurant food once in a while," says Talia. "But organic food has become really appealing these days. That actor Christian Slater promotes it in magazine ads. And some of my friends say that he is really sexy and that you look like him! Maybe you should think about switching to organic."

"I look like Christian Slater?" asks Curtis, looking flattered. "Wow! Maybe you're right. But now that you've raised the issue, that reminds me of something. Didn't you tell me a while back that you had an uncle who grew organic food? If he makes a lot of money, you might inherit it. I bet that's what's behind this organic thing of yours."

"Not at all," says Talia. "But I'm glad you mentioned the farmers. Some of these people have invested every cent they have in growing organic food. If consumers don't buy it, these poor, hardworking farmers will all go broke. We really can't let that happen. They've put their heart and soul into growing really healthy food for people like you and me. We can't let them down."

"And here's another consideration," continues Talia. "A basic principle of morality says that we should help others in need. The owner of this grocery store needs for people to buy his organic produce. Thus, I think we have an obligation to buy it."

"Ha, ha," Curtis laughs. "According to that argument we also have a moral obligation to buy the GMO food. I don't think we have a moral obligation to buy anything. But now that I think of it, you've always been a bit resistant to anything new. When iPads came out, you didn't want one, you didn't want a flat-screen TV, and now you don't want GMO corn. You should be more open to scientific developments."

Talia smirks. "And what about you?" she asks. "You seem to think technology can solve all our problems. By that line of reasoning, we should have robots serving our every need. Robot doctors, robot lawyers, robot cooks, robot grade-school teachers. But robots will never replace human beings. Human beings have feelings. They have hopes and fears and they love each other. Robots don't love anything."

"I know nothing about robots," says Curtis, "but getting back to corn, just compare this GMO corn with the organic corn in the other bin. The GMO corn looks larger and more appetizing than the organic. In fact, we do lots of things these days to make vegetables look more appetizing and grow better. For example, we add fertilizer to the soil. Nitrogen is an important ingredient in these fertilizers, and so is phosphorus and potassium."

"I didn't realize you knew so much about fertilizer," Talia says. "I need some fertilizer for my flower garden. Could you recommend something?"

"Yes, I could. But in the meantime, shall we get some corn?" Curtis asks as he selects two ears from the GMO bin.

Talia takes one ear from his hand and puts it back. She then crosses over to the organic bin, tucks an ear under her arm, and smiles at Curtis. "One for you, one for me," she says.

Visit Aplia for section-specific problem sets.

2.3 Fallacies of Weak Induction

PREVIEW

You have your heart set on getting a little Pomeranian puppy to keep you company during long hours of study, but your roommate is dead set against it. She argues that a former roommate of hers got a pit bull to keep her company, and the dog attacked a visitor, causing serious injury. The lesson is obvious: The Pomeranian will be nothing but trouble. Is your roommate's argument a good one? Read the current section for further analysis of arguments such as this.

The **fallacies of weak induction** occur not because the premises are logically irrelevant to the conclusion, as is the case with the eight fallacies of relevance, but because the connection between premises and conclusion is not strong enough to support the conclusion. In each of the following fallacies, the premises provide at least a shred of evidence in support of the conclusion, but the evidence is not nearly good enough to cause a reasonable person to believe the conclusion. Like the fallacies of relevance, however, the fallacies of weak induction often involve emotional grounds for believing the conclusion.

fallacies of weak induction: The premises may be relevant to the conclusion, but they provide insufficient support for the conclusion.

9. Appeal to Unqualified Authority (*Argumentum ad Verecundiam*)

We saw in Chapter 1 that an argument from authority is an inductive argument in which an arguer cites the authority or testimony of another person in support of some conclusion. The **appeal to unqualified authority** fallacy is a variety of the argument from authority and occurs when the cited authority or witness lacks credibility. There are several reasons why an authority or witness might lack credibility. The person might lack the requisite expertise, might be biased or prejudiced, might have a motive to lie or disseminate "misinformation," or might lack the requisite ability to perceive or recall. The following examples illustrate these reasons:

appeal to unqualified authority: An arguer cites an untrustworthy authority in support of a conclusion.

> Dr. Bradshaw, our family physician, has stated that the creation of muonic atoms of deuterium and tritium hold the key to producing a sustained nuclear fusion reaction at room temperature. In view of Dr. Bradshaw's expertise as a physician, we must conclude that this is indeed true.

This conclusion deals with nuclear physics, and the authority is a family physician. Because it is unlikely that a physician would be an expert in nuclear physics, the argument commits an appeal to unqualified authority.

> David Duke, former Grand Wizard of the Ku Klux Klan, has stated, "Jews are not good Americans. They have no understanding of what America is." On the basis of Duke's authority, we must therefore conclude that the Jews in this country are un-American.

As an authority, David Duke is clearly biased, so his statements cannot be trusted.

> James W. Johnston, former Chairman of R. J. Reynolds Tobacco Company, testified before Congress that tobacco is not an addictive substance and that smoking cigarettes does not produce any addiction. Therefore, we should believe him and conclude that smoking does not in fact lead to any addiction.

If Mr. Johnston had admitted that tobacco is addictive, it would have opened the door to government regulation, which could put his company out of business. Thus, because Johnston had a clear motive to lie, we should not believe his statements.

> Old Mrs. Furguson (who is practically blind) has testified that she saw the defendant stab the victim with a bayonet while she was standing in the twilight shadows 100 yards from the incident. Therefore, members of the jury, you must find the defendant guilty.

Here the witness lacks the ability to perceive what she has testified to, so her testimony is untrustworthy.

Of course if an authority is credible, the resulting argument will contain no fallacy. Example:

> The county tax collector issued a press release stating that property tax revenues are higher this year than last. Therefore, we conclude that these revenues are indeed higher this year.

Normally a county tax collector would be considered a qualified expert in the area of tax revenues, so assuming the tax collector has no reason to lie, this argument is inductively strong.

In deciding whether a person is a qualified authority, one should keep two important points in mind. First, the person might be an authority in more than one field. For example, a chemist might also be an authority in biology, or an economist might also be an authority in law. The second point is that there are some areas in which practically no one can be considered an authority. Such areas include politics, morals, and religion. For example, if someone were to argue that abortion is immoral because a certain philosopher or religious leader has said so, the argument would be weak regardless of the authority's qualifications. Many questions in these areas are so hotly contested that there is no conventional wisdom an authority can depend on.

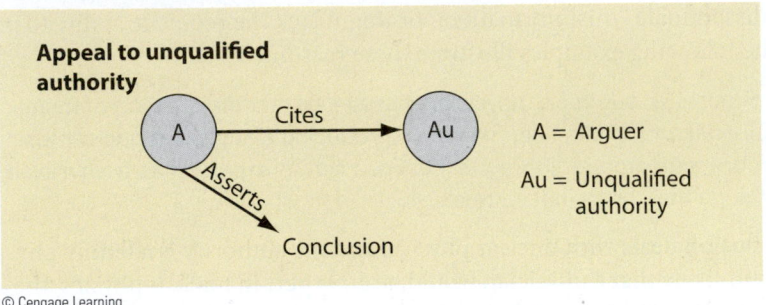

© Cengage Learning

10. Appeal to Ignorance (*Argumentum ad Ignorantiam*)

When the premises of an argument state that nothing has been proved one way or the other about something, and the conclusion then makes a definite assertion about that thing, the argument commits an **appeal to ignorance**. The issue usually involves something that is incapable of being proved or something that has not yet been proved. Example:

appeal to ignorance: The premises state that nothing has been proved about *X*, but then a conclusion is drawn about *X*.

> People have been trying for centuries to provide conclusive evidence for the claims of astrology, and no one has ever succeeded. Therefore, we must conclude that astrology is a lot of nonsense.

Conversely, the following argument commits the same fallacy.

> People have been trying for centuries to disprove the claims of astrology, and no one has ever succeeded. Therefore, we must conclude that the claims of astrology are true.

The premises of an argument are supposed to provide positive evidence for the conclusion. The premises of these arguments, however, tell us nothing about astrology; rather, they tell us about what certain unnamed and unidentified people have tried unsuccessfully to do. This evidence may provide some slight reason for believing the conclusion, but certainly not sufficient reason.

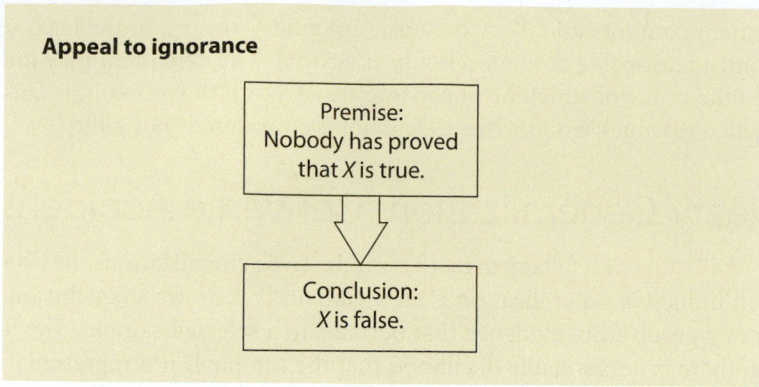

These examples do, however, lead us to the first of two important exceptions to the appeal to ignorance. The first stems from the fact that if qualified researchers investigate a certain phenomenon within their range of expertise and fail to turn up any evidence that the phenomenon exists, this fruitless search by itself constitutes positive evidence about the question. Consider, for example, the following argument:

> Teams of scientists attempted over several decades to detect the existence of the luminiferous aether, and all failed to do so. Therefore, the luminiferous aether does not exist.

The premises of this argument are true. Given the circumstances, it is likely that the scientists in question would have detected the aether if in fact it did exist. Since they did not detect it, it probably does not exist. Thus, we can say that the given argument is inductively strong (but not deductively valid).

As for the two arguments about astrology, if the attempts to prove or disprove the astrological claims had been done in a systematic way by qualified experts, the arguments would more likely be good. Exactly what is required to qualify someone to investigate astrological claims is, of course, difficult to say. But as these arguments stand, the premises state nothing about the qualifications of the investigators, and so the arguments remain fallacious.

It is not always necessary, however, that the investigators have *special* qualifications. The kinds of qualifications needed depend on the situation. Sometimes the mere ability to see and report what one sees is sufficient. Example:

> No one has ever seen Mr. Andrews drink a glass of wine, beer, or any other alcoholic beverage. Probably Mr. Andrews is a nondrinker.

Because it is highly probable that if Mr. Andrews were a drinker, somebody would have seen him drinking, this argument is inductively strong. No special qualifications are needed to be able to see someone take a drink.

The second exception to the appeal to ignorance relates to courtroom procedure. In the United States and a few other countries, a person is presumed innocent until proven guilty. If the prosecutor in a criminal trial fails to prove the guilt of the defendant beyond reasonable doubt, counsel for the defense may justifiably argue that his or her client is not guilty. Example:

This argument commits no fallacy because "not guilty" means, in the legal sense, that guilt beyond a reasonable doubt has not been proved. The defendant may indeed have committed the crime of which he or she is accused, but if the prosecutor fails to prove guilt beyond a reasonable doubt, the defendant is considered "not guilty."

11. Hasty Generalization (Converse Accident)

hasty generalization:
A general conclusion is drawn from an atypical sample.

Hasty generalization is a fallacy that affects inductive generalizations. In Chapter 1 we saw that an inductive generalization is an argument that draws a conclusion about all members of a group from evidence that pertains to a selected sample. The fallacy occurs when there is a reasonable likelihood that the sample is not representative of the group. Such a likelihood may arise if the sample is either too small or not randomly selected. Here are two examples:

> Today's money managers are a pack of thieves, every last one of them. Look at Bernie Madoff and Robert Allen Stanford. They ripped off billions of dollars from thousands of trusting clients. And Raj Rajaratnam profited to the tune of millions of dollars through illegal insider trading.

> Before the last presidential election, three residents of Harlem were quoted as saying they supported Barack Obama even though they knew nothing about his policies. Obviously the issues played no role in the outcome of that election.

In these arguments a conclusion about a whole group is drawn from premises that mention only a few instances. Because such small, atypical samples are not sufficient to support a general conclusion, each argument commits a hasty generalization.

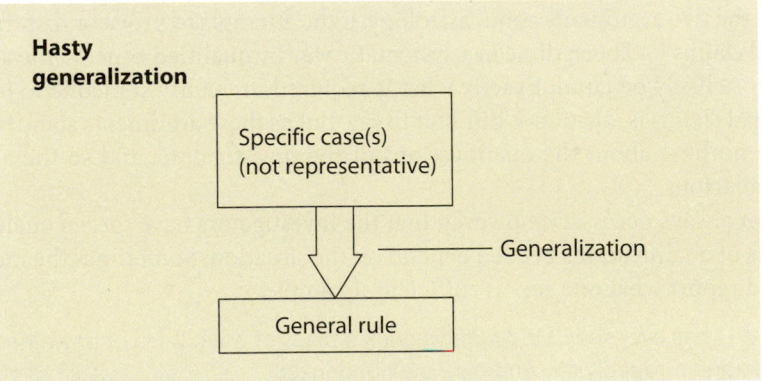

The mere fact that a sample is small, however, does not necessarily mean that it is atypical. On the other hand, the mere fact that a sample is large does not guarantee that it is typical. In the case of small samples, various factors may intervene that render such a sample typical of the larger group. Examples:

> Ten milligrams of substance Z was fed to four mice, and within two minutes all four went into shock and died. Probably substance Z, in this amount, is fatal to mice in general.

> On three separate occasions I drank a bottle of Figowitz beer and found it flat and bitter. Probably I would find every bottle of Figowitz beer flat and bitter.

Neither of these arguments commits the fallacy of hasty generalization, because in neither case is there any likelihood that the sample is atypical of the group. In the first argument the fact that the mice died in only two minutes suggests the existence of a causal connection between eating substance Z and death. If there is such a connection, it would hold for other mice as well. In the second example the fact that the taste of beer typically remains constant from bottle to bottle causes the argument to be strong, even though only three bottles were sampled.

In the case of large samples, if the sample is not random, it may not be typical of the larger group. Example:

> One hundred thousand voters from Orange County, California, were surveyed on their choice for governor, and 68 percent said they intend to vote for the Republican candidate. Clearly the Republican candidate will be elected.

Even though the sample cited in this argument is large, the argument commits a hasty generalization. The problem is that Orange County is overwhelmingly Republican, so the mere fact that 68 percent intend to vote for the Republican candidate is no indication of how others in the state intend to vote. In other words, the survey was not conducted randomly, and for this reason the sample is biased.

Hasty generalization is otherwise called "converse accident" because it proceeds in a direction opposite to that of accident. Whereas accident proceeds from the general to the particular, converse accident moves from the particular to the general. The premises cite some characteristic affecting one or more atypical instances of a certain class, and the conclusion then applies that characteristic to all members of the class.

12. False Cause

The fallacy of **false cause** occurs whenever the conclusion depends on some imagined causal connection that probably does not exist. When an argument is suspected of committing the false cause fallacy, the reader or listener should be able to say that the conclusion depends on the supposition that X causes Y, whereas X probably does not cause Y at all. Examples:

false cause: The conclusion depends on a causal connection that is weak or does not exist at all.

> During the past two months, every time that the cheerleaders have worn blue ribbons in their hair, the basketball team has been defeated. Therefore, to prevent defeats in the future, the cheerleaders should get rid of those blue ribbons.

> Successful business executives are paid salaries in excess of $100,000. Therefore, the best way to ensure that Ferguson will become a successful executive is to raise his salary to at least $100,000.

> There are more laws on the books today than ever before, and more crimes are being committed than ever before. Therefore, to reduce crime we must eliminate the laws.

The first argument depends on the supposition that the blue ribbons caused the defeats, the second on the supposition that a high salary causes success, and the third on the supposition that laws cause crime. In no case is it likely that any causal connection exists.

The first argument illustrates a variety of the false cause fallacy called *post hoc ergo propter hoc* ("after this, therefore on account of this"). This variety of the fallacy presupposes that just because one event precedes another event, the first event causes the second. Obviously, mere temporal succession is not sufficient to establish a causal connection. Nevertheless, this kind of reasoning is quite common and lies behind most forms of superstition. (Example: "A black cat crossed my path and later I tripped and sprained my ankle. It must be that black cats really are bad luck.")

The second and third arguments illustrate a variety of the false cause fallacy called **non causa pro causa** ("not the cause for the cause"). This variety is committed when what is taken to be the cause of something is not really the cause at all and the mistake is based on something other than mere temporal succession. In reference to the second argument, success as an executive causes increases in salary—not the other way around—so the argument mistakes the cause for the effect. In reference to the third argument, the increase in crime is, for the most part, only coincidental with the increase in the number of laws. Obviously, the mere fact that one event is coincidental with another is not sufficient reason to think that one caused the other.

A third variety of the false cause fallacy, and one that is probably committed more often than either of the others in their pure form, is *oversimplified cause*. This variety occurs when a multitude of causes is responsible for a certain effect but the arguer selects just one of these causes and represents it as if it were the sole cause. Here are some examples:

> The quality of education in our grade schools and high schools has been declining for years. Clearly, our teachers just aren't doing their job these days.

> Today, all of us can look forward to a longer life span than our parents and grandparents. Obviously we owe our thanks to the millions of dedicated doctors who expend every effort to ensure our health.

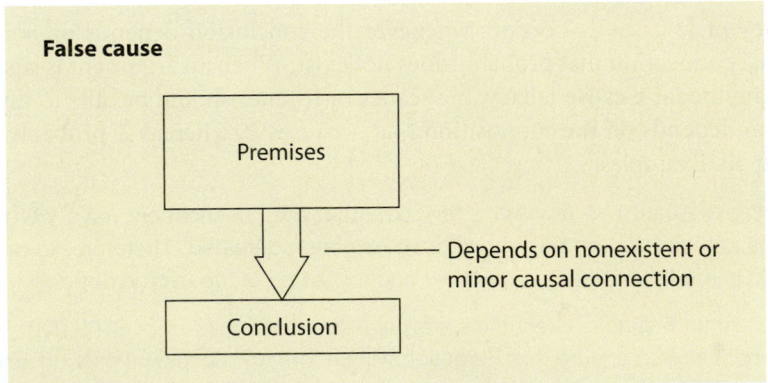

False cause

Premises

Conclusion

Depends on nonexistent or minor causal connection

In reference to the first argument, the decline in the quality of education is caused by many factors, including lack of discipline in the home, lack of parental involvement, too much television, too much time spent on video games, and drug use by students. Poor teacher performance is only one of these factors and probably a minor one at that. In the second argument, the efforts of doctors are only one among many factors responsible for our longer life span. Other, more important factors include a better diet, more exercise, reduced smoking, safer highways, and more-stringent occupational safety standards.

The oversimplified cause fallacy is usually motivated by self-serving interests. Sometimes the arguer wants to take undeserved credit for himself or herself or give undeserved credit to some movement with which he or she is affiliated. At other times, the arguer wants to heap blame on an opponent or shift blame from himself or herself onto some convenient occurrence. Instances of the fallacy can resemble either the *post hoc* or the *non causa pro causa* varieties in that the alleged cause can occur either prior to or concurrently with the effect. It differs from the other varieties of false cause fallacy in that the single factor selected for credit or blame is often partly responsible for the effect, but responsible to only a minor degree.

The last variety of false cause we will consider is called the *gambler's fallacy*. This fallacy is committed whenever the conclusion of an argument depends on the supposition that independent events in a game of chance are causally related. Here is an example:

> A fair coin was flipped five times in a row, and each time it came up heads. Therefore, it is extremely likely that it will come up tails on the next flip.

In fact, it is no more likely that the coin will come up tails on the next flip than it was on the first flip. Each flip is an independent event, so earlier flips have no causal influence on later ones. Thus, the fact that the earlier flips came up heads does not increase the likelihood that the next flip will come up tails.

For the gambler's fallacy to be committed, the events must be independent or nearly independent. Such events include rolls of a pair of fair (unloaded) dice, spins of a fair roulette wheel, and selections of lottery winning numbers. Events are not completely independent whenever the skill of the gambler affects the outcome. Thus, poker, blackjack, and horse-race betting provide less-than-perfect candidates for the gambler's fallacy.

The false cause fallacy is often convincing because it is often difficult to determine whether two phenomena are causally related. A lengthy time lapse between the operation of the cause and the occurrence of the effect can exacerbate the problem. For example, the thirty-year interval between exposure to asbestos and the onset of asbestosis impeded the recognition of a causal connection. Also, when two events are causally related, determining the degree of relatedness may be hard. Thus, there may be some connection between the electromagnetic field produced by high voltage transmission lines and leukemia, but the connection may be extremely slight. Finally, when a causal connection is recognized, it may be difficult to determine which is the cause and which is the effect. For example, an allergic reaction may be connected with an episode of anxiety, but it may be hard to tell if the reaction causes the anxiety or if the anxiety causes the reaction.

The realm of human action constitutes another area in which causal connections are notoriously difficult to establish. For example, the attorneys for accused murderer Dan White argued that Twinkies, Coke, and potato chips caused him to kill San Francisco mayor George Moscone. Other attorneys have blamed their clients' crimes on PMS, rap music, childhood abuse, mental retardation, and hallucinations. The complex nature of human motivation renders all such causal claims difficult to evaluate. The situation may become even worse when a whole nation of people are involved. Thus, the recent drop in crime rates has been attributed to "three strikes" laws, but it is difficult to say whether this or some other factor is really responsible.

One point that should be kept in mind when establishing causal connections is that statistical correlations by themselves often reveal little about what is actually going on. For example, if all that we knew about smoking and lung cancer was that the two frequently occur together, we might conclude any number of things. We might conclude that both have a common cause, such as a genetic predisposition, or we might conclude that lung cancer is a disease contracted early in life and that it manifests itself in its early stages by a strong desire for tobacco. Fortunately, in this case we have more evidence than a mere statistical correlation. This additional evidence inclines us to believe that the smoking is a cause of the cancer.

13. Slippery Slope

slippery slope: The conclusion depends on a chain reaction of causes that is not likely to occur.

The fallacy of **slippery slope** is a variety of the false cause fallacy. It occurs when the conclusion of an argument rests on an alleged chain reaction and there is not sufficient reason to think that the chain reaction will actually take place. Here is an example:

> Immediate steps should be taken to outlaw pornography once and for all. The continued manufacture and sale of pornographic material will almost certainly lead to an increase in sex-related crimes such as rape and incest. This in turn will gradually erode the moral fabric of society and result in an increase in crimes of all sorts. Eventually a complete disintegration of law and order will occur, leading in the end to the total collapse of civilization.

Because there is no good reason to think that the mere failure to outlaw pornography will result in all these dire consequences, this argument is fallacious. An equally fallacious counterargument is as follows:

> Attempts to outlaw pornography threaten basic civil rights and should be summarily abandoned. If pornography is outlawed, censorship of newspapers and news magazines is only a short step away. After that there will be censorship of textbooks, political speeches, and the content of lectures delivered by university professors. Complete mind control by the central government will be the inevitable result.

Both arguments attempt to persuade the reader or listener that the welfare of society rests on a "slippery slope" and that a single step in the wrong direction will result in an inevitable slide all the way to the bottom.

The slippery slope fallacy can involve various kinds of causality. For example, someone might argue that removing a single brick from a building would set off a chain reaction leading to the destruction of the building, or that chopping down a tall tree would set off a cascade of falling trees leading to the destruction of the forest. These arguments depend on pure physical causality. On the other hand, someone might argue that starting a rumor about the health of the economy would set off a chain reaction leading to the collapse of the stock market. Such an argument would depend on the kind of causality found in interpersonal communications.

The following example involves a chain reaction of mental causes where wanting one thing leads to wanting another.

> Professor Fallon has asked us to purchase a coffeemaker for her office. But we shouldn't do that because next she'll want a microwave, and then a convection oven. Then she'll want a full-sized refrigerator, a sink with hot and cold water, a dishwasher, and a complete set of expensive china. This will exhaust the budget of our department.

Deciding whether a slippery slope fallacy has been committed can be difficult when one is uncertain whether the alleged chain reaction will or will not occur. This question is discussed in Section 2.5. But many slippery slopes rest on a mere emotional conviction on the part of the arguer that a certain action or policy is bad, and the arguer attempts to trump up support for his or her position by citing all sorts of dire consequences that will result if the action is taken or the policy followed. In such cases there is usually little problem in identifying the argument as a slippery slope.

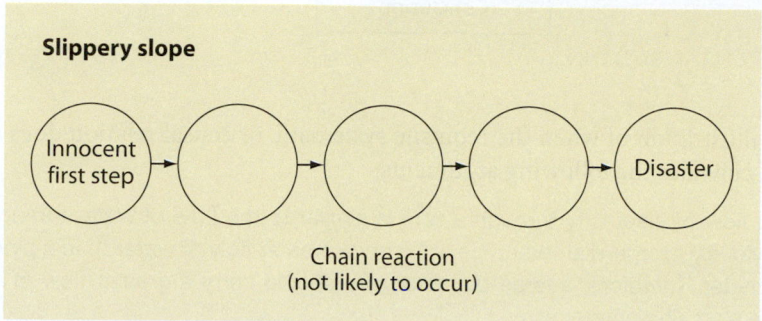

Slippery slope

Innocent first step → ○ → ○ → ○ → Disaster

Chain reaction
(not likely to occur)

14. Weak Analogy

This fallacy affects inductive arguments from analogy. As we saw in Chapter 1, an argument from analogy is an argument in which the conclusion depends on the existence of an analogy, or similarity, between two things or situations. The fallacy of **weak analogy** is committed when the analogy is not strong enough to support the conclusion that is drawn. Example:

> Amber's dog is similar in many ways to Kyle's cat. Both like being petted, they enjoy being around people, they beg for food at the dinner table, and they sleep with their owners. Amber's dog loves to romp on the beach with Amber. Therefore, Kyle's cat probably loves to romp on the beach with Kyle.

weak analogy: The conclusion depends on an analogy that is not strong enough to support it.

In this argument the similarities cited between Amber's dog and Kyle's cat probably have nothing to do with the cat's attitude toward romping on the beach. Thus, the argument is fallacious.

The basic structure of an argument from analogy is as follows:

> Entity A has attributes a, b, c, and z.
> Entity B has attributes a, b, c.
> Therefore, entity B probably has attribute z also.

Evaluating an argument having this form requires a two-step procedure: (1) Identify the attributes a, b, c, . . . that the two entities A and B share, and (2) determine how the attribute z, mentioned in the conclusion, relates to the attributes a, b, c. . . . If some causal or systematic relation exists between z and a, b, or c, the argument is strong; otherwise, it is weak. In the given example, the two entities share the attributes of liking to be petted, enjoying people, begging for food, and sleeping with their owners. Because it is highly probable that none of these attributes is systematically or causally related to romping on the beach, the argument is fallacious.

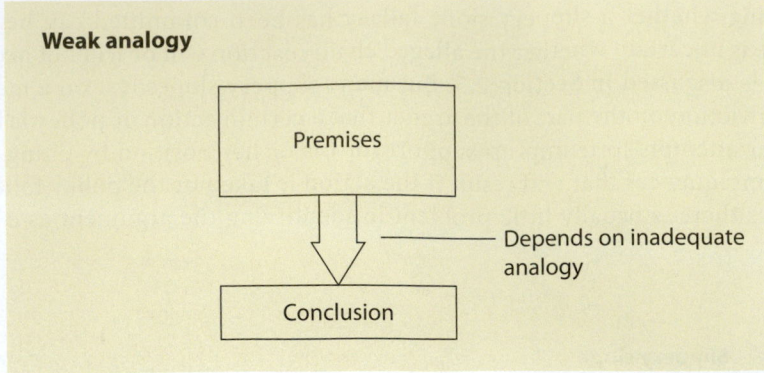

Weak analogy

Premises

Depends on inadequate analogy

Conclusion

As an illustration of when the requisite systematic or causal relation does and does not exist, consider the following arguments:

> The flow of electricity through a wire is similar to the flow of water through a pipe. Obviously a large-diameter pipe will carry a greater flow of water than a pipe of small diameter. Therefore, a large-diameter wire should carry a greater flow of electricity than a small-diameter wire.

> The flow of electricity through a wire is similar to the flow of water through a pipe. When water runs downhill through a pipe, the pressure at the bottom of the hill is greater than it is at the top. Thus, when electricity flows downhill through a wire, the voltage should be greater at the bottom of the hill than at the top.

The first argument is good and the second is fallacious. Both arguments depend on the similarity between water molecules flowing through a pipe and electrons flowing through a wire. In both cases there is a systematic relation between the diameter of the pipe/wire and the amount of flow. In the first argument this systematic relation provides a strong link between premises and conclusion, and so the argument is a good one. But in the second argument a causal connection exists between difference in elevation and increase in pressure that holds for water but not for electricity. Water molecules flowing through a pipe are significantly affected by gravity, but electrons flowing through a wire are not. Thus, the second argument is fallacious.

The theory and evaluation of arguments from analogy is one of the most complex and elusive subjects in all of logic. Additional material on arguments from analogy appears in Section 2.5 of this text.

EXERCISE 2.3

I. Identify the fallacies of weak induction committed by the following arguments, giving a brief explanation for your answer. If no fallacy is committed, write "no fallacy."

★ **1.** The *Daily News* carried an article this morning about three local teenagers who were arrested on charges of drug possession. Teenagers these days are nothing but a bunch of junkies.

2. If a car breaks down on the freeway, a passing mechanic is not obligated to render emergency road service. For similar reasons, if a person suffers a heart attack on the street, a passing physician is not obligated to render emergency medical assistance.

3. There must be something to psychical research. Three famous physicists— Oliver Lodge, James Jeans, and Arthur Stanley Eddington—took it seriously.

★4. The secretaries have asked us to provide lounge areas where they can spend their coffee breaks. This request will have to be refused. If we give them lounge areas, next they'll be asking for spas and swimming pools. Then it will be racquetball courts, tennis courts, and fitness centers. Expenditures for these facilities will drive us into bankruptcy.

5. The accumulation of pressure in a society is similar to the buildup of pressure in a boiler. If the pressure in a boiler increases beyond a critical point, the boiler will explode. Accordingly, if a government represses its people beyond a certain point, the people will rise up in revolt.

6. A few minutes after Governor Harrison finished his speech on television, a devastating earthquake struck southern Alaska. For the safety of the people up there, it is imperative that Governor Harrison make no more speeches.

★7. No one has ever been able to prove the existence of extrasensory perception. We must therefore conclude that extrasensory perception is a myth.

8. Lester Brown, universally respected author of the yearly *State of the World* report, has said that the destruction of tropical rain forests is one of the ten most serious worldwide problems. Thus, it must be the case that this is indeed a very serious problem.

9. Bill Gates and Warren Buffet give millions of dollars to charitable causes every year. It must be the case that all wealthy people give huge amounts of money to charity every year.

★10. North Korean leader Kim Jong-un says that his country's nuclear program is purely for peaceful purposes. Therefore, given Mr. Kim's familiarity with that program, we should not think for a moment that he plans to use it to develop nuclear weapons.

11. Probably no life exists on Venus. Teams of scientists have conducted exhaustive studies of the planet's surface and atmosphere, and no living organisms have been found.

12. We don't dare let the animal-rights activists get their foot in the door. If they sell us on the idea that dogs, cats, and dolphins have rights, next it will be chickens and cows. That means no more chicken Kiev or prime rib. Next it will be worms and insects. This will lead to the decimation of our agricultural industry. The starvation of the human race will follow close behind.

★13. No one would buy a pair of shoes without trying them on. Why should anyone be expected to get married without premarital sex?

14. No one has proved conclusively that America's nuclear power plants constitute a danger to people living in their immediate vicinity. Therefore, it is perfectly safe to continue to build nuclear power plants near large metropolitan centers.

15. There are more churches in New York City than in any other city in the nation, and more crimes are committed in New York City than anywhere else. So, if we are to eliminate crime, we must abolish the churches.

II. Answer "true" or "false" to the following statements:

1. If an arguer cites a statement by a recognized expert in support of a conclusion and the statement falls within the expert's range of expertise, then the arguer commits an appeal to unqualified authority.

2. If an arguer cites a statement in support of a conclusion and the statement reflects the strong bias of its author, then the arguer commits an appeal to unqualified authority.

3. In the appeal to ignorance, the arguer accuses the reader or listener of being ignorant.

4. If an attorney for the defense in an American or Canadian criminal trial argues that the prosecution has proved nothing beyond a reasonable doubt about the guilt of the defendant, then the attorney commits an appeal to ignorance.

5. Hasty generalization always proceeds from the particular to the general.

6. The *post hoc ergo propter hoc* variety of the false cause fallacy presumes that X causes Y merely because X happens before Y.

7. If an argument concludes that X causes Y simply because X and Y occur over the same time interval, then the argument commits the *non causa pro causa* variety of the false cause fallacy.

8. If the conclusion of an argument depends on the occurrence of a chain reaction of events, and there is good reason to believe that the chain reaction will actually occur, the argument commits a slippery slope fallacy.

9. The fallacy of weak analogy always depends on an alleged similarity between two things or situations.

10. If an argument from analogy depends on a causal or systematic relationship between certain attributes, and there is good reason to believe that this relationship exists, then the argument commits no fallacy.

III. Identify the fallacies of relevance and weak induction committed by the following arguments. If no fallacy is committed, write "no fallacy."

★1. On our first date, George had his hands all over me, and I found it nearly impossible to keep him in his place. A week ago Tom gave me that stupid line about how, in order to prove my love, I had to spend the night with him. Men are all alike. All any of them want is sex.

2. Tagging by graffiti artists has become a terrible problem in recent years. Obviously our schools are stifling the creative spirit of these young people.

3. According to certain reports, when Barack Obama was a youngster he attended a Muslim seminary in Indonesia for four years. Others say that when he was sworn in as a senator he placed his hand on a Koran instead of a Bible. And some say he bears a striking resemblance to the Antichrist. Moreover, countless e-mail messages speak of Muslim sleeper cells hidden away in every branch of the government. Could they all be linked to Obama? Just imagine, he gives the signal and they all spring into action. In no time our Constitution is replaced by Sharia law. We can't wait a minute longer. Obama must be impeached and removed from office.

★ 4. Todd Burpo, the best-selling author, argues in his book that heaven is real and that his son Colton met Jesus and John the Baptist in a near-death experience. But it's clear that Burpo says these things only to sell lots of books. Therefore, his arguments have no merit.

5. What the farmer sows in the spring he reaps in the fall. In the spring he sows $8-per-bushel soybeans. Therefore, in the fall he will reap $8-per-bushel soybeans.

6. World-renowned physicist Stephen Hawking claims that black holes do not gobble up everything that falls into them without leaving a trace, but that something is always left behind. Given Hawking's stature as a scientist and the many years he has worked on this problem, we should conclude that this is indeed the case.

★ 7. Emily has bought over 100 tickets on the weekly state lottery, and she has never won anything. Therefore, the likelihood increases every week that she will win something if she continues to buy tickets.

8. Johnny, of course I deserve the use of your bicycle for the afternoon. After all, I'm sure you wouldn't want your mother to find out that you played hooky today.

9. Practically everyone downloads music free of charge from the Internet these days. Therefore, you should have no qualms about doing this yourself.

★ 10. Ellen Quinn has argued that logic is not the most important thing in life. Apparently Ellen advocates irrationality. It has taken two million years for the human race to achieve the position that it has, and Ellen would throw the whole thing into the garbage. What utter nonsense!

11. When water is poured on the top of a pile of rocks, it always trickles down to the rocks on the bottom. Similarly, when rich people make lots of money, we can expect this money to trickle down to the poor.

12. Extensive laboratory tests have failed to prove any deleterious side effects of the new painkiller lexaprine. We conclude that lexaprine is safe for human consumption.

★ 13. Environmentalists accuse us of blocking the plan to convert Antarctica into a world park. In fact, nothing could be further from the truth. Antarctica is a huge continent teeming with life. It is the home of millions of penguins, seals, sea birds, and sea lions. Also, great schools of finfish and whales inhabit its coastal waters.

14. Michael Moore, the documentary filmmaker, argues that capitalist institutions are ravaging America's middle class and walking away with billions of dollars in their pockets. But Moore is just a big, fat, populist rabble-rouser, and a multimillionaire to boot. He should keep his mouth shut.

15. The operation of a camera is similar in many ways to the operation of an eye. If you are to see anything in a darkened room, the pupils of your eyes must first dilate. Accordingly, if you are to take a photograph (without flash) in a darkened room, the aperture of the camera lens must first be increased.

★ 16. Certainly Miss Malone will be a capable and efficient manager. She has a great figure, a gorgeous face, and tremendous poise, and she dresses very fashionably.

17. James Dobson, founder of Focus on the Family, says that men have the divine obligation to lead their families, and women have the divine obligation to submit

to their husband's authority. Given Dobson's apparent ability to receive messages from God, we must conclude that this statement is absolutely true.

18. Dear Internal Revenue Service: I received a notice that my taxes are being audited for last year. But you have no right to do this. The deadline for filing a return was April 15, and I filed my tax return on April 12—a full three days before the deadline.

★ 19. To prevent dangerous weapons from being carried aboard airliners, those seeking to board must pass through a magnetometer and submit to a possible pat-down search. Therefore, to prevent alcohol and drugs from being carried into rock concerts, those entering should submit to similar search procedures.

20. Mr. Flemming's arguments against the rent-control initiative on the September ballot should be taken with a grain of salt. As a landlord he would naturally be expected to oppose the initiative.

21. India is suffering a serious drought, thousands of children are dying of starvation in their mothers' arms, and homeless beggars line the streets of the major cities. Surely we must give these poor downtrodden people the chance of bettering their condition in America, the land of wealth and opportunity.

★ 22. Members of the jury, you have heard Shirley Gaines testify that the defendant did not offer to perform acts of prostitution for the undercover police officer. But Gaines is a known prostitute herself and a close friend of the defendant. Also, only a year ago she was convicted of twelve counts of perjury. Therefore, you should certainly discount Gaines's testimony.

23. It is ridiculous to hear that man from Peru complaining about America's poverty. Peru has twice as much poverty as America has ever had.

24. Angela complains that the problems on the algebra test were too hard. But have you ever seen the way Angela flirts with that good-looking quarterback on the football team? She's constantly batting those long, black eyelashes at him, and her tight-fitting sweaters leave nothing to the imagination. Angela should pay more attention to her studies.

★ 25. Nobody has ever proved that immoral behavior by elected officials erodes public morality. Therefore, we must conclude that such behavior does not erode public morality.

26. Freedom of speech is guaranteed by the First Amendment. Therefore, your friend was acting within his rights when he shouted "Fire! Fire!" in that crowded theater, even though it was only a joke.

27. No one, on encountering a wristwatch lying on a forest trail, would expect that it had simply appeared there without having been made by someone. For the same reason, no one should expect that the universe simply appeared without having been made by some being.

★ 28. On Monday I drank ten rum and Cokes, and the next morning I woke up with a headache. On Wednesday I drank eight gin and Cokes, and the next morning I woke up with a headache. On Friday I drank nine bourbon and Cokes, and the next morning I woke up with a headache. Obviously, to prevent further headaches I must give up Coke.

29. Radio entertainer Rush Limbaugh claims there is not a shred of evidence to prove that nicotine is addictive or that cigarettes cause emphysema, lung cancer, or any other disease. Given Limbaugh's apparent expertise in medical science, we can only conclude that what he says about nicotine and cigarettes is true.

30. Some of the parents in our school district have asked that we provide bilingual education in Spanish. This request will have to be denied. If we provide this service, then someone will ask for bilingual education in Greek. Then it will be German, French, and Hungarian. Polish, Russian, Chinese, Japanese, and Korean will follow close behind. We certainly can't accommodate all of them.

IV. Identify the fallacies committed in the following dialogue. You should be able to find at least one case of each fallacy presented in this section and one case of a fallacy presented in the previous section.

Gun Love

Holly and her friend Ben have just attended a panel discussion in response to a recent shooting on a college campus. As they leave the auditorium and head for the parking lot, Holly asks, "Do you agree with any of the panelists?"

"I agree with the panelist who said that guns should be banned on every campus," Ben replies. "And I would even go a step further and say that we need strict gun control throughout the U.S. The simple fact is that guns are way too available in this country."

"Sounds like you're saying that the availability of guns leads to violent crime," Holly says. "Is that what you're saying?"

"Yes, I do think guns lead to crime," Ben replies.

"Well, let me ask you this," Holly says. "Has anybody ever proved that? Has anybody ever proved that the mere availability of guns leads to violent crime? The answer is no. So until somebody proves that it does, we should conclude that gun availability does not lead to violence."

"Well, you heard what one of the panelists said about England, didn't you?" Ben asks. "England has strict limitations on gun possession, and practically no gun-related crime. I think that proves that guns do cause crime. If the U.S. would adopt the English law, crime in this country would drop like a rock."

"In fact," Holly counters, "the England example proves nothing of the sort. There's no reason to think that what works in England would also work in the U.S."

"Why do you think that?" Ben asks.

"Well," Holly responds, "you recall what the other panelist said about gun control in this country. When Evanston, Illinois, banned guns altogether a few years back, that led to no reduction at all in violent crime. That shows that gun availability does not cause crime. If every city in the country followed Evanston's example, they would get the same result."

"Sounds like you're pretty negative on gun control," Ben observes.

"Yes, I am," Holly replies. "As soon as we have gun registration, the next thing you know we'll need a license to buy a gun. And that will lead the government to impose a tax on gun ownership. Taxes always increase, and when gun owners are no longer able to pay the tax, that will lead to gun confiscation.

Finally, when guns are completely removed from the hands of the public, there will be nothing to prevent some wild-eyed fanatic from taking over the government. Complete totalitarianism will follow in no time."

"Do you really think that could happen in this country?" Ben asks.

"If it happened in Nazi Germany, it could happen here," she replies. "And, as one of the panelists said, it did happen in Nazi Germany, and Fascist Italy, too."

"So, do you think you have a right to own a gun?" Ben asks.

"Absolutely," Holly replies. "The current president of the NRA—his name escapes me at the moment—says that the right to own a gun, even an assault weapon, is guaranteed by the Constitution. Given that he knows a lot about guns, what he says about them is certainly true."

"I'll withhold judgment on that," says Ben. "But here's what I think you should do. You should take a couple deep breaths and calm down. You've turned into a gun nut. If people see what's happened to you, they won't take any of your arguments seriously."

"Think what you want about me," Holly says. "But the next time you're robbed at gunpoint, don't come crying in my direction."

Ben laughs. "Okay, I promise I won't. Well, see you around . . . if I survive!"

"See you!" she says.

2.4 Fallacies of Presumption, Ambiguity, and Illicit Transference

PREVIEW

You're out on a blind date. Initially you hit it off really well, but then your date says, "It's obvious that we're physically attracted to each other. So, either we spend the night together or it's clear that you're not interested in me." Regardless of how you might be inclined to respond to your date's proposition, do you at least feel a bit uneasy about it? If not, you should, because it amounts to a common logical fallacy. To learn more about it, and others like it, read through this section of the book.

fallacies of presumption:
The premises presume what they purport to prove.

The **fallacies of presumption** include begging the question, complex question, false dichotomy, and suppressed evidence. These fallacies arise not because the premises are irrelevant to the conclusion or provide insufficient reason for believing the conclusion but because the premises presume what they purport to prove. *Begging the question* presumes that the premises provide adequate support for the conclusion when in fact they do not, and *complex question* presumes that a question can be answered by a simple "yes," "no," or other brief answer when a more sophisticated answer is needed. *False dichotomy* presumes that an "either . . . or . . ." statement presents jointly exhaustive alternatives when in fact it does not, and *suppressed evidence* presumes that no important evidence has been overlooked by the premises when in fact it has.

William of Ockham ca. 1285–1347

The English philosopher and theologian, William of Ockham, was born in or near the village of Ockham not far from London. Little is known about his childhood, and his biographers are not even certain about the year of his birth, with estimates running from 1280 to 1290. However, they are certain that while Ockham was still a small boy, his parents delivered him to the nearest Franciscan monastery to be brought up in the monastic way of life. His parents' intentions were realized when he entered the Franciscan Order and was ordained in 1306.

Ockham studied theology at Oxford, possibly under Duns Scotus, and he lectured there. He also studied and taught at the University of Paris, where he wrote extensively on theology and philosophy. Ockham's theological views generated controversy among theologians of the day, some of whom vehemently opposed him. In 1324, he was called to Avignon, then the location of the papal court, to answer charges of heresy.

A panel of scholars had been appointed to review the charges made against Ockham, and he was obliged to remain at a Franciscan house in Avignon throughout the investigation, which lasted four years. During this time, the Franciscan minister general, Michael of Cesena, was called to Avignon, because he had become embroiled in a controversy with Pope John XXII over the issue of the poverty of Jesus and the apostles. Michael held that Jesus and the apostles did not own property but instead survived through goodwill offerings of people in the community. The Franciscans regarded themselves as emulating the model set by Jesus and the apostles, but the pope, who lived in luxury, obviously disagreed.

Though Ockham had more than enough problems of his own, the minister general asked him to research the issue to see which position was right—the pope's or the minister general's. Ockham ultimately came out on the side of the minister general, claiming that the pope was a heretic and had no business even being pope. This got the Avignon Franciscans into a great deal of trouble, and to extricate themselves they purloined several horses and rode out

© The Granger Collection, NYC

of town in the middle of the night. Ludwig of Bavaria, the Holy Roman Emperor, gave them protection, and Ockham lived out the rest of his life in Munich. While there he turned his attention to politics and political philosophy. He was a staunch advocate of the separation of church and state, claiming that the pope had no right to intervene in state affairs. The pope retaliated by excommunicating him.

Ockham is best known for endorsing a principle of parsimony that has come to be called "Ockham's razor." This principle states that, among alternative explanations, the simplest one is the best. Ockham emphasized the importance of keeping the number of entities hypothesized in an explanation to an absolute minimum. In the area of logic, he is known for his theory of truth conditions for categorical propositions, for work in the foundations of inductive reasoning, for preliminary work on a three-valued logic, and for developing a close approximation to what would later come to be known as De Morgan's rule.

The **fallacies of ambiguity** include *equivocation* and *amphiboly*. These fallacies arise from the occurrence of some form of ambiguity in either the premises or the conclusion (or both). An expression is ambiguous if it is susceptible to different interpretations in a given context. The words "light" and "bank" are ambiguous, as is the statement "Tuna are biting off the Washington coast." "Light" could mean light in weight, light in calories, or light in color. "Bank" could refer to a place where money is deposited or to the edge of a river. The statement about tuna could mean that fisherman are catching tuna off the Washington coast, or (less probably) that tuna are nibbling away at the coastline.

When the conclusion of an argument depends on a shift in meaning of an ambiguous word or phrase or on the wrong interpretation of an ambiguous statement, the argument commits a fallacy of ambiguity.

fallacies of ambiguity:
An ambiguous word, phrase, or statement leads to an incorrect conclusion.

2

The **fallacies of illicit transference** include *composition* and *division*. Arguments that commit these fallacies involve the incorrect transference of an attribute from the parts of something onto the whole, or from the whole onto the parts.

15. Begging the Question (*Petitio Principii*)

The fallacy of **begging the question** is committed whenever the arguer creates the illusion that inadequate premises provide adequate support for the conclusion by leaving out a possibly false (shaky) key premise, by restating a possibly false premise as the conclusion, or by reasoning in a circle. The Latin name for this fallacy, *petitio principii*, means "request for the source." The actual source of support for the conclusion is not apparent, and so the argument is said to beg the question. After reading or hearing the argument, the observer is inclined to ask, "But how do you know *X*?" where *X* is the needed support.

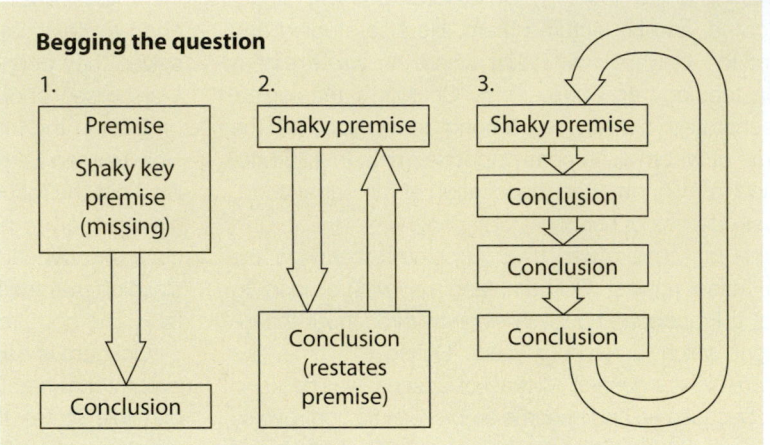

The first, and most common, way of committing this fallacy is by leaving a possibly false key premise out of the argument while creating the illusion that nothing more is needed to establish the conclusion. Examples:

> Murder is morally wrong. This being the case, it follows that abortion is morally wrong.

> We know that humans are intended to eat lots of fruit because the human hand and arm are perfectly suited for picking fruit from a tree.

> It's obvious that the poor in this country should be given handouts from the government. After all, these people earn less than the average citizen.

> Clearly, terminally ill patients have a right to doctor-assisted suicide. After all, many of these people are unable to commit suicide by themselves.

The first of these arguments begs the question "How do you know that abortion is a form of murder?" The second begs the question "Does the structure and function of the human hand and arm tell us what humans should eat?" And the third and fourth beg the questions "Just because the poor earn less than the average citizen, does this imply that the government should give them handouts?" and "Just because terminally ill patients cannot commit suicide by themselves, does it follow that they have a right to a doctor's assistance?"

These questions indicate that something has been left out of the original arguments. Thus, the first argument is missing the premise "Abortion is a form of murder"; the second is missing the premise "The structure and function of the human hand and arm tell us what humans should eat"; and so on. These premises are crucial for the soundness of the arguments. If the arguer is unable to establish the truth of these premises, then the arguments prove nothing. However, in most cases of begging the question, this is precisely the reason why such premises are left unstated. The arguer is *not* able to establish their truth, and by employing rhetorical phraseology such as "of course," "clearly," "this being the case," and "after all," the arguer hopes to create the illusion that the stated premise, by itself, provides adequate support for the conclusion when in fact it does not.

The same form of begging the question often appears in arguments concerning religious topics to justify conclusions about the existence of God, the immortality of the soul, and so on. Example:

> The world in which we live displays an amazing degree of organization. Obviously this world was created by an intelligent God.

This argument begs the question "How do you know that the organization in the world could only have come from an intelligent creator?" Of course the claim that it did come from an intelligent creator may well be true, but the burden is on the arguer to prove it. Without supporting reasons or evidence, the argument proves nothing. Yet most people who are predisposed to believe the conclusion are likely to accept the argument as a good one. The same can be said of most arguments that beg the question, and this fact suggests another reason why arguers resort to this fallacy: Such arguments tend to reinforce preexisting inclinations and beliefs.

The second form of *petitio principii* occurs when the conclusion of an argument merely restates a possibly false premise in slightly different language. In such an argument, the premise supports the conclusion, and the conclusion tends to reinforce the premise. Examples:

> Capital punishment is justified for the crimes of murder and kidnapping because it is quite legitimate and appropriate that someone be put to death for having committed such hateful and inhuman acts.

> Anyone who preaches revolution has a vision of the future for the simple reason that if a person has no vision of the future he could not possibly preach revolution.

In the first argument, saying that capital punishment is "justified" means the same thing as saying that it is "legitimate and appropriate," and in the second argument the premise and the conclusion say exactly the same thing. However, by repeating the same thing in slightly different language, the arguer creates the illusion that independent evidence is being presented in support of the conclusion, when in fact it is not. Both arguments contain rhetorical phraseology ("hateful and inhuman," "simple reason," and "could not possibly") that help effect the illusion. The first argument begs the question "How do you know that capital punishment really is legitimate and appropriate?" and the second begs the question "How do you know that people who preach revolution really do have a vision of the future?"

The third form of *petitio principii* involves circular reasoning in a chain of inferences having a first premise that is possibly false. Example:

Verizon has the best wireless service. After all, their phones have the clearest sound. And we know this is so because customers hear better on Verizon phones. And this follows from the fact that Verizon has digital technology. But this is exactly what you would expect given that Verizon has the best wireless service.

On encountering this argument, the attentive reader is inclined to ask, "Where does this reasoning begin? What is its source?" Since the argument goes in a circle, it has no beginning or source, and as a result it proves nothing. Of course, in this example the circularity is rather apparent, so the argument is not likely to convince anyone. Cases in which circular reasoning may convince involve long and complex arguments having premises that depend on one another in subtle ways and a possibly false key premise that depends on the conclusion.

In all cases of begging the question, the arguer uses some linguistic device to create the illusion that inadequate premises provide adequate support for a conclusion. Without such an illusion, the fallacy is not committed. Thus, the following arguments commit no fallacy:

> No dogs are cats.
> Therefore, no cats are dogs.

> London is in England and Paris is in France.
> Therefore, Paris is in France and London is in England.

In both of these examples, the premise amounts to little more than a restatement of the conclusion. Yet both arguments are sound because they are valid and have true premises. No fallacy is committed, because no illusion is created to make inadequate premises appear as adequate. We will study arguments of this sort in Chapters 3 and 6.

Here is another example:

> Rome is in Germany or Rome is in Germany.
> Therefore, Rome is in Germany.

This argument is valid, but it is unsound because it has a false premise. However, it commits no fallacy because, again, no illusion is created to cover anything up. Arguments having this form also appear in Chapter 6.

As with these examples, arguments that beg the question are normally valid. This is easy to see. Any argument that includes the conclusion as one of the premises is clearly valid, and those forms of the fallacy that leave a key premise out of the argument become valid when that key premise is introduced. The problem with arguments that beg the question is that they are usually unsound, or at least not clearly sound, because the premise needed to provide adequate support for the conclusion is, at best, of uncertain truth value. Because such arguments presume the truth of this premise, begging the question is called a fallacy of presumption.

16. Complex Question

complex question: Two or more questions are concealed in a single question, and a single answer is given to both.

The fallacy of **complex question** is committed when two (or more) questions are asked in the guise of a single question and a single answer is then given to both of them. Every complex question presumes the existence of a certain condition. When the respondent's answer is added to the complex question, an argument emerges that establishes the presumed condition. Thus, although not an argument as such, a complex question involves an implicit argument. This argument is usually intended to trap the respondent into acknowledging something that he or she might otherwise not want to acknowledge. Examples:

> Have you stopped cheating on exams?
>
> Where did you hide the marijuana you were smoking?

Let us suppose the respondent answers "yes" to the first question and "under the bed" to the second. The following arguments emerge:

> You were asked whether you have stopped cheating on exams. You answered, "Yes." Therefore, it follows that you have cheated in the past.
>
> You were asked where you hid the marijuana you were smoking. You replied, "Under the bed." It follows that you were in fact smoking marijuana.

On the other hand, let us suppose that the respondent answers "no" to the first question and "nowhere" to the second. We then have the following arguments:

> You were asked whether you have stopped cheating on exams. You answered, "No." Therefore, you continue to cheat.
>
> You were asked where you hid the marijuana you were smoking. You answered, "Nowhere." It follows that you must have smoked all of it.

Obviously, each of the questions is really two questions:

> Did you cheat on exams in the past? If you did cheat in the past, have you stopped now?
>
> Were you smoking marijuana? If you were smoking it, where did you hide it?

If respondents are not sophisticated enough to identify a complex question when one is put to them, they may answer quite innocently and be trapped by a conclusion that is supported by no evidence at all; or, they may be tricked into providing the evidence themselves. The correct response lies in resolving the complex question into its component questions and answering each separately.

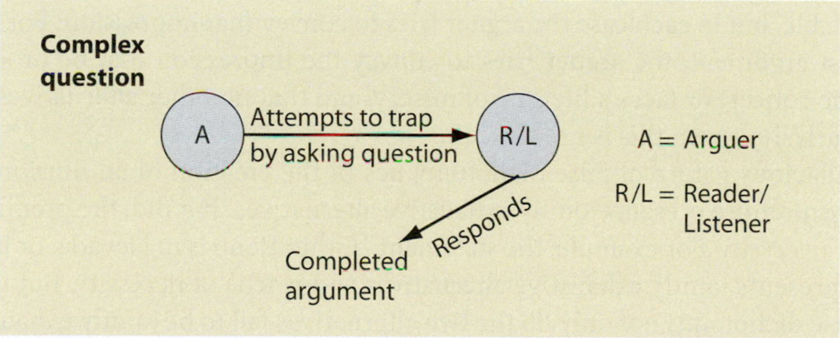

© Cengage Learning

The fallacy of complex question should be distinguished from another kind of question known in law as a leading question. A *leading question* is one in which the answer is in some way suggested in the question. Whether or not a question is a leading one is important in the direct examination of a witness by counsel. Example:

> Tell us, on April 9, did you see the defendant shoot the deceased? (leading question)
> Tell us, what did you see on April 9? (straight question)

Leading questions differ from complex questions in that they involve no logical fallacies—that is, they do not attempt to trick the respondent into admitting something he or she does not want to admit. To distinguish between the two, however, one sometimes needs to know whether prior questions have been asked. Here are some additional examples of complex questions:

Are you going to be a good little boy and eat your hamburger?
Is George Hendrix still telling lies?
How long must I put up with your snotty behavior?
When are you going to stop talking nonsense?

17. False Dichotomy

The fallacy of **false dichotomy** is committed when a disjunctive ("either . . . or . . .") premise presents two unlikely alternatives as if they were the only ones available, and the arguer then eliminates the undesirable alternative, leaving the desirable one as the conclusion. Such an argument is clearly valid, but since the disjunctive premise is false, or at least probably false, the argument is typically unsound. The fallacy is often committed by children when arguing with their parents, by advertisers, and by adults generally. Here are three examples:

Either you let me attend the Lady Gaga concert or I'll be miserable for the rest of my life. I know you don't want me to be miserable for the rest of my life, so it follows that you'll let me attend the concert.

Either you use Ultra Guard deodorant or you risk the chance of perspiration odor. Surely you don't want to risk the chance of perspiration odor. Therefore, you will want to use Ultra Guard deodorant.

Either we adopt a one-world government, or regional wars will continue forever. We certainly can't tolerate constant war. Therefore, we must adopt a one-world government.

In none of these arguments does the disjunctive premise present the only alternatives available, but in each case the arguer tries to convey that impression. For example, in the first argument, the arguer tries to convey the impression that he or she either goes to the concert or faces a lifetime of misery, and that no other alternatives are possible. Clearly, however, this is not the case.

The fallacious nature of false dichotomy lies in the creation of an illusion that the disjunctive premise presents jointly exhaustive alternatives. If it did, the premise would be true of necessity. For example, the statement "Either Reno is in Nevada, or it is not in Nevada" presents jointly exhaustive alternatives and is true of necessity. But in the fallacy of false dichotomy, not only do the two alternatives fail to be jointly exhaustive, but they are not even likely. As a result, the disjunctive premise is false, or at least probably false. Thus, the fallacy amounts to making a false or probably false premise appear true.

Also, if one of the alternatives in the disjunctive premise is factually true beyond any doubt, then the fallacy is not committed. For example, the following argument is valid and sound:

Either Seattle is in Washington, or it is in Oregon.
Seattle is not in Oregon.
Therefore, Seattle is in Washington

False dichotomy is otherwise called "false bifurcation" and the "either-or fallacy." Also, in most cases the arguer expresses only the disjunctive premise and leaves it to the reader or listener to supply the missing statements:

> Either you buy me a new mink coat, or I'll freeze to death when winter comes.

> Either I continue smoking, or I'll get fat and you'll hate to be seen with me.

The missing premise and conclusion are easily introduced.

18. Suppressed Evidence

Chapter 1 explained that a cogent argument is an inductive argument with good reasoning and true premises. The requirement of true premises includes the proviso that the premises not ignore some important piece of evidence that outweighs the presented evidence and entails a very different conclusion. If an inductive argument does indeed ignore such evidence, then the argument commits the fallacy of **suppressed evidence**. Consider, for example, the following argument:

> Most dogs are friendly and pose no threat to people who pet them. Therefore, it would be safe to pet the little dog that is approaching us now.

If the arguer ignores the fact that the little dog is excited and foaming at the mouth (which suggests rabies), then the argument commits a suppressed evidence fallacy. This fallacy is classified as a fallacy of presumption because it works by creating the presumption that the premises are both true and complete when in fact they are not.

Perhaps the most common occurrence of the suppressed evidence fallacy appears in inferences based on advertisements. Nearly every ad neglects to mention certain negative features of the product advertised. As a result, an observer who sees or hears an advertisement and then draws a conclusion from it may commit the fallacy of suppressed evidence. Example:

> The ad for Kentucky Fried Chicken says, "Buy a bucket of chicken and have a barrel of fun!" Therefore, if we buy a bucket of that chicken, we will be guaranteed to have lots of fun.

The ad fails to state that the fun does not come packaged with the chicken but must be supplied by the buyer. Also, of course, the ad fails to state that the chicken is loaded with fat and that the buyer's resultant weight gain and clogged arteries may not amount to a barrel of fun. By ignoring these facts, the argument based on the ad is fallacious.

Another rich source of the suppressed evidence fallacy is the biennial U.S. general election in which two candidates, usually a Republican and a Democrat, compete with each other for a single office. During the campaign leading up to the election countless speech makers (including the candidates themselves) tear down the policies and accomplishments of the candidate they oppose only to conclude that the candidate they favor should be elected. Example:

> Ladies and gentlemen, Mr. Smith has supported policies that will bankrupt Medicare and Social Security, his budgetary recommendations increase the federal deficit, and his approach to foreign policy will destabilize the Middle East. Therefore, you should vote to elect Jones to this office.

What the speaker fails to mention are the many undisputed successes that Smith has achieved. Also, he fails to mention that Jones is even less qualified than Smith for the

suppressed evidence: The arguer ignores important evidence that requires a different conclusion.

office, and that Jones's policies bode even worse for Medicare, Social Security, the federal deficit, and the Middle East. When these unmentioned facts are taken into account it becomes clear that it is actually Smith who should be elected.

Another way that an arguer can commit the suppressed evidence fallacy is by ignoring important events that have occurred with the passage of time that render an inductive conclusion improbable.

The following argument resembles one that Mitt Romney used in a presidential debate with Barack Obama:

> The U.S. military has fewer battleships, M1 rifles, and horse-drawn howitzers today than it did in 1940. Therefore, the U.S. military is a less effective fighting force today than it was in 1940.

The argument ignores that fact that battleships, M1 rifles, and horse-drawn howitzers became obsolete long ago and have been replaced by more-effective ships and weaponry. Thus, it is not true that the U.S. military is less effective today than it was in 1940.

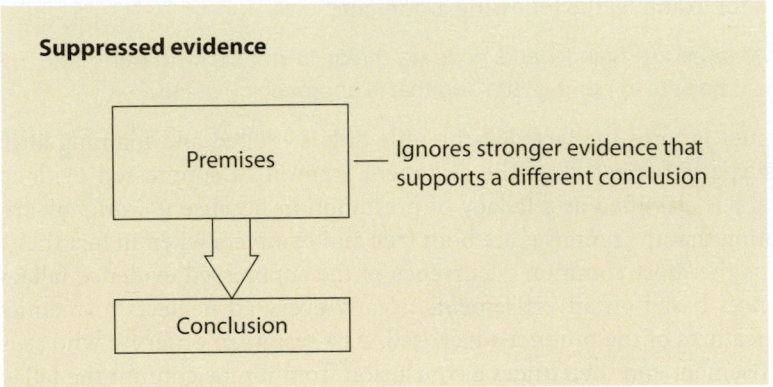

Suppressed evidence

Premises — Ignores stronger evidence that supports a different conclusion

Conclusion

Yet another form of suppressed evidence is committed by arguers who quote passages out of context from sources such as the Bible, the Constitution, and the Bill of Rights to support a conclusion that the passage was not intended to support. Consider, for example, the following argument against gun control:

> The Second Amendment to the Constitution states that the right of the people to keep and bear arms shall not be infringed. But a law controlling handguns would infringe the right to keep and bear arms. Therefore, a law controlling handguns would be unconstitutional.

In fact, the Second Amendment reads, "A well regulated militia being necessary to the security of a free state, the right of the people to keep and bear arms shall not be infringed." In other words, the constitutional right to keep and bear arms is in some way related to the preservation of a well-regulated militia. Arguably a law controlling handguns that is unrelated to the preservation of a well-regulated militia could be constitutional.

The suppressed evidence fallacy is similar to the form of begging the question in which the arguer leaves a key premise out of the argument. The difference is that suppressed evidence leaves out a premise that requires a *different* conclusion, while that form of begging the question leaves out a premise that is needed to support the *stated* conclusion. However, because both fallacies proceed by leaving a premise out of the argument, there are cases where the two fallacies overlap.

19. Equivocation

The fallacy of **equivocation** occurs when the conclusion of an argument depends on the fact that a word or phrase is used, either explicitly or implicitly, in two different senses in the argument. Such arguments are either invalid or have a false premise, and in either case they are unsound. Examples:

> Some triangles are obtuse. Whatever is obtuse is ignorant. Therefore, some triangles are ignorant.

> Any law can be repealed by the legislative authority. But the law of gravity is a law. Therefore, the law of gravity can be repealed by the legislative authority.

> We have a duty to do what is right. We have a right to speak out in defense of the innocent. Therefore, we have a duty to speak out in defense of the innocent.

> A mouse is an animal. Therefore, a large mouse is a large animal.

In the first argument "obtuse" is used in two different senses. In the first premise it describes a certain kind of angle, whereas in the second it means dull or stupid. The second argument equivocates on the word "law." In the first premise it means statutory law, and in the second it means law of nature. The third argument uses "right" in two senses. In the first premise "right" means morally correct, but in the second it means a just claim or power. The fourth argument illustrates the ambiguous use of a relative word. The word "large" means different things depending on the context. Other relative words that are susceptible to this same kind of ambiguity include "small," "good," "bad," "light," "heavy," "difficult," "easy," "tall," and "short."

To be convincing, an argument that commits an equivocation must use the equivocal word in ways that are subtly related. Of the examples just given, only the third might fulfill this requirement. Since both uses of the word "right" are related to ethics, the unalert observer may not notice the shift in meaning. Another technique is to spread the shift in meaning out over the course of a lengthy argument. Political speech makers often use phrases such as "equal opportunity," "gun control," "national security," and "environmental protection" in one way at the beginning of a speech and in quite another way at the end. A third technique consists in using such phrases one way in a speech to one group and in a different way in a speech to an opposing group. If the same people are not present at both speeches, the equivocation is not detected.

equivocation: The conclusion depends on a shift in meaning of a word or phrase.

2

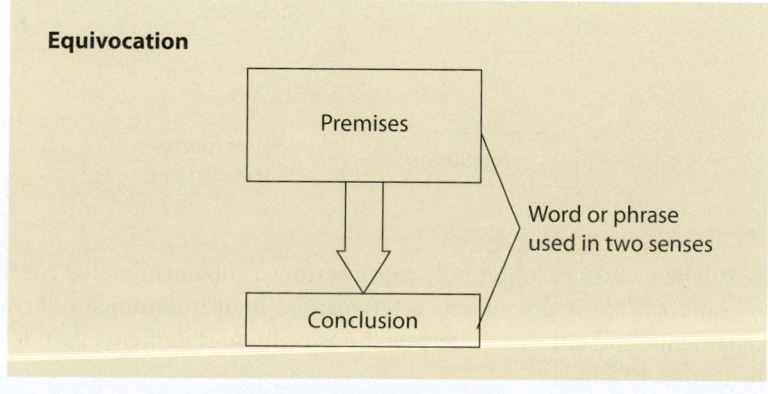

Equivocation

Premises

Word or phrase used in two senses

Conclusion

20. Amphiboly

The fallacy of **amphiboly** occurs when the arguer misinterprets an ambiguous statement and then draws a conclusion based on this faulty interpretation. The original statement is usually asserted by someone other than the arguer, and the ambiguity usually arises from a mistake in grammar or punctuation—a missing comma, a dangling modifier, an ambiguous antecedent of a pronoun, or some other careless arrangement of words. Because of this ambiguity, the statement may be understood in two clearly distinguishable ways. The arguer typically selects the unintended interpretation and proceeds to draw a conclusion based on it. Here are some examples:

> The tour guide said that standing in Greenwich Village, the Empire State Building could easily be seen. It follows that the Empire State Building is in Greenwich Village.

> John told Henry that he had made a mistake. It follows that John has at least the courage to admit his own mistakes.

> Professor Johnson said that he will give a lecture about heart failure in the biology lecture hall. It must be the case that a number of heart failures have occurred there recently.

The premise of the first argument contains a dangling modifier. Is it the observer or the Empire State Building that is supposed to be standing in Greenwich Village? The factually correct interpretation is the former. In the second argument the pronoun "he" has an ambiguous antecedent; it can refer either to John or to Henry. Perhaps John told Henry that *Henry* had made a mistake. In the third argument the ambiguity concerns what takes place in the biology lecture hall; is it the lecture or the heart failures? The correct interpretation is probably the former. The ambiguity can be eliminated by inserting commas ("Professor Johnson said that he will give a lecture, about heart failure, in the biology lecture hall") or by moving the ambiguous modifier ("Professor Johnson said that he will give a lecture in the biology lecture hall about heart failure"). Ambiguities of this sort are called *syntactical ambiguities*.

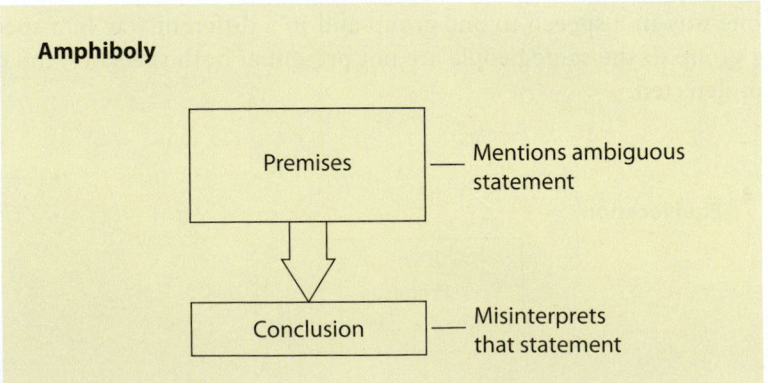

Two areas where cases of amphiboly cause serious problems involve contracts and wills. The drafters of these documents often express their intentions in terms of ambiguous statements, and alternate interpretations of these statements then lead to different conclusions. Examples:

> Mrs. Hart stated in her will, "I leave my 500-carat diamond necklace and my pet chinchilla to Alice and Theresa." Therefore, we conclude that Alice gets the necklace and Theresa gets the chinchilla.

> Mr. James signed a contract that reads, "In exchange for painting my house, I promise to pay David $5,000 and give him my new Cadillac only if he finishes the job by May 1." Therefore, since David did not finish until May 10, it follows that he gets neither the $5,000 nor the Cadillac.

In the first example the conclusion obviously favors Alice. Theresa is almost certain to argue that the gift of the necklace and chinchilla should be shared equally by her and Alice. Mrs. Hart could have avoided the dispute by adding either "respectively" or "collectively" to the end of the sentence. In the second example, the conclusion favors Mr. James. David will argue that the condition that he finish by May 1 affected only the Cadillac and that he therefore is entitled to the $5,000. The dispute could have been avoided by properly inserting a comma in the language of the promise.

Amphiboly differs from equivocation in two important ways. First, equivocation is always traced to an ambiguity in the meaning of a *word* or *phrase*, whereas amphiboly involves a syntactical ambiguity in a *statement*. The second difference is that amphiboly usually involves a mistake made by the arguer in interpreting an ambiguous statement made by someone else, whereas the ambiguity in equivocation is typically the arguer's own creation. If these distinctions are kept in mind, it is usually easy to distinguish amphiboly from equivocation. Occasionally, however, the two fallacies occur together, as the following example illustrates:

> The *Great Western Cookbook* recommends that we serve the oysters when thoroughly stewed. Apparently the delicate flavor is enhanced by the intoxicated condition of the diners.

First, it is unclear whether "stewed" refers to the oysters or to the diners, and so the argument commits an amphiboly. But if "stewed" refers to the oysters it means "cooked," and if it refers to the diners it means "intoxicated." Thus, the argument also involves an equivocation.

21. Composition

The fallacy of **composition** is committed when the conclusion of an argument depends on the erroneous transference of an attribute from the parts of something onto the whole. In other words, the fallacy occurs when it is argued that because the parts have a certain attribute, it follows that the whole has that attribute, too, and the situation is such that the attribute in question cannot be legitimately transferred from parts to whole. Examples:

composition: An attribute is incorrectly transferred from the parts of something onto the whole.

> Maria likes anchovies. She also likes chocolate ice cream. Therefore, it is certain that she would like a chocolate sundae topped with anchovies.

> Each player on this basketball team is an excellent athlete. Therefore, the team as a whole is excellent.

> Each atom in this teacup is invisible. Therefore, this teacup is invisible.

> Sodium and chlorine, the atomic components of salt, are both deadly poisons. Therefore, salt is a deadly poison.

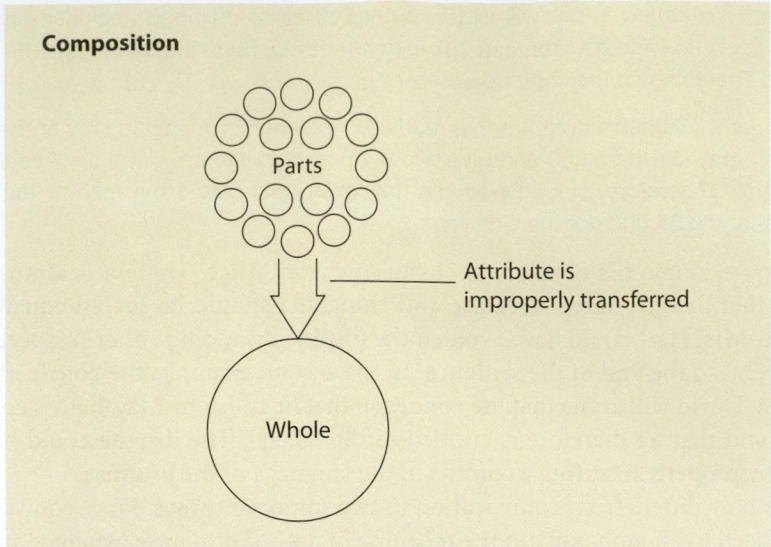

Composition

Parts

Attribute is
improperly transferred

Whole

In these arguments the attributes that are transferred from the parts onto the whole are designated by the words "Maria likes," "excellent," "invisible," and "deadly poison," respectively. In each case the transference is illegitimate, and so the argument is fallacious.

Not every such transference is illegitimate, however. Consider the following arguments:

Every atom in this teacup has mass. Therefore, this teacup has mass.

Every component in this picket fence is white. Therefore, the whole fence is white.

In each case an attribute (having mass, being white) is transferred from the parts onto the whole, but these transferences are quite legitimate. Indeed, the fact that the atoms have mass is the very reason *why* the teacup has mass. The same reasoning extends to the fence. Thus, the acceptability of these arguments is attributable, at least in part, to the *legitimate* transference of an attribute from parts onto the whole.

These examples illustrate the fact that the fallacy of composition is indeed an informal fallacy. It cannot be discovered by a mere inspection of the form of an argument—that is, by the mere observation that an attribute is being transferred from parts onto the whole. In addition, detecting this fallacy requires a general knowledge of the situation and of the nature of the attribute being transferred. The critic must be certain that, given the situation, the transference of this particular attribute is incorrect.

Further caution is required by the fact that composition is sometimes confused with hasty generalization. The only time this confusion is possible is when the "whole" is a class (such as the class of people in a city or the class of trees in a forest), and the "parts" are the members of the class. In such a case composition proceeds from the members of the class to the class itself. Hasty generalization, on the other hand, proceeds from the specific to the general. Because it is sometimes easy to mistake a statement about a class for a general statement, composition can be mistaken for hasty generalization. Such a mistake can be avoided if one is careful to keep in mind the distinction between these two kinds of statements. This distinction falls back on the difference between the **collective** and the **distributive predication** of an attribute. Consider the following statements:

Fleas are small.
Fleas are numerous.

The first statement is a general statement. The attribute of being small is predicated distributively; that is, it is assigned (or distributed) to each and every flea in the class. Each and every flea in the class is said to be small. The second statement, on the other hand, is a statement about a class as a whole, or what we will call a "class statement." The attribute of being numerous is predicated collectively; in other words, it is assigned not to the individual fleas but to the *class* of fleas. The meaning of the statement is not that each and every flea is numerous but that the class of fleas is large.

To distinguish composition from hasty generalization, therefore, the following procedure should be followed. Examine the conclusion of the argument. If the conclusion is a general statement—that is, a statement in which an attribute is predicated distributively to each and every member of a class—the fallacy committed is hasty generalization. But if the conclusion is a class statement—that is, a statement in which an attribute is predicated collectively to a class as a whole—the fallacy is composition. Example:

> Less fuel is consumed by a car than by a fire truck. Therefore, less fuel is consumed in the United States by cars than by fire trucks.

At first sight this argument might appear to proceed from the specific to the general and, consequently, to commit a hasty generalization. But in fact the conclusion is not a general statement at all but a class statement. The conclusion states that the whole class of cars uses less fuel than does the whole class of fire trucks (which is false, because there are many more cars than fire trucks). Since the attribute of using less fuel is predicated collectively, the fallacy committed is composition.

22. Division

The fallacy of **division** is the exact reverse of composition. As composition goes from parts to whole, division goes from whole to parts. The fallacy is committed when the conclusion of an argument depends on the erroneous transference of an attribute from a whole (or a class) onto its parts (or members). Examples:

> Salt is a nonpoisonous compound. Therefore, its component elements, sodium and chlorine, are nonpoisonous.

> This airplane was made in Seattle. Therefore, every component part of this airplane was made in Seattle.

> The Royal Society is over 300 years old. Professor Thompson is a member of the Royal Society. Therefore, Professor Thompson is over 300 years old.

division: An attribute is incorrectly transferred from the whole onto the parts.

In each case the attribute, designated respectively by the terms "nonpoisonous," "made in Seattle," and "over 300 years old," is illegitimately transferred from the whole or class onto the parts or members. As with the fallacy of composition, however, this kind of transference is not always illegitimate. The following arguments contain no fallacy:

> This teacup has mass. Therefore, the atoms that compose this teacup have mass.

> This field of poppies is uniformly orange. Therefore, the individual poppies are orange.

Obviously, one must be acquainted with the situation and the nature of the attribute being transferred to decide whether the fallacy of division is actually committed.

Just as composition can sometimes be confused with hasty generalization (converse accident), division can sometimes be confused with accident. As with composition, this confusion can occur only when the "whole" is a class. In such a case,

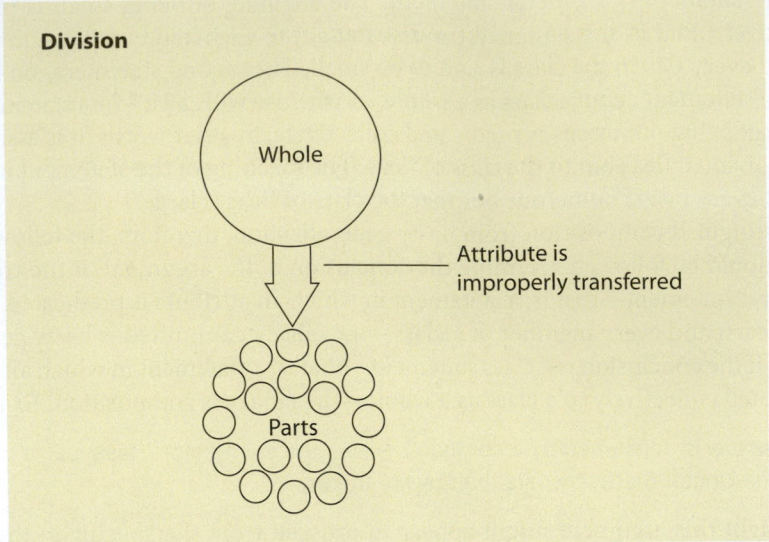

Division

Whole

Parts

Attribute is improperly transferred

division proceeds from the class to the members, whereas accident proceeds from the general to the specific. Thus, if a class statement is mistaken for a general statement, division may be mistaken for accident. To avoid such a mistake, one should analyze the premises of the argument. If the premises contain a general statement, the fallacy committed is accident; but if they contain a class statement, the fallacy is division. Example:

> Stanley Steamers have almost disappeared.
> This car is a Stanley Steamer.
> Therefore, this car has almost disappeared.

The first premise is not a general statement but a class statement. The attribute of having almost disappeared is predicated collectively. Accordingly, the fallacy committed is division, not accident.

This example also illustrates how cases of division that involve class statements can include a subtle form of equivocation. In the conclusion, the word "disappeared" means fading from vision, as when the lights are turned down; but in the first premise it means rarely seen. The equivocation is a kind of secondary fallacy that results from the primary fallacy, which is division.

The next example shows how division turns up in arguments dealing with averages.

> The average American family has 2.5 children.
> The Jones family is an average American family.
> Therefore, the Jones family has 2.5 children.

The statement "The average American family has 2.5 children" is not a general statement, but rather a class statement. The sense of the statement is not that each and every family has 2.5 children, but that the class of families having two parents is reducible to about 55 percent children and 45 percent adults. Thus, once again, the fallacy is division, and not accident.

I. Identify the fallacies of presumption, ambiguity, and illicit transference committed by the following arguments, giving a brief explanation for your answer. If no fallacy is committed, write "no fallacy."

★1. Either we require forced sterilization of Third World peoples or the world population will explode and all of us will die. We certainly don't want to die, so we must require forced sterilization.

2. Every sentence in this paragraph is well written. Therefore, the paragraph is well written.

3. An athlete is a human being. Therefore, a good athlete is a good human being.

★4. James said that he saw a picture of a beautiful girl stashed in Stephen's locker. We can only conclude that Stephen has broken the rules, because girls are not allowed in the locker room.

5. Why is it so difficult for you to reach a decision?

6. Water will quench one's thirst. Water is composed of hydrogen and oxygen. Therefore, hydrogen will quench one's thirst, and so will oxygen.

★7. People who lack humility have no sense of beauty, because everyone who has a sense of beauty also has humility.

8. Butane is combustible. Therefore, it burns.

9. Twenty years ago, Kung Fong, the great sumo wrestler, could have yanked up one of the fir trees in the new municipal arboretum with a single pull. Therefore, since Mr. Fong is as strong today as he was then, he could just as easily pull up one of those trees today.

★10. If Thomas gives Marie a ring, then Thomas and Marie will be engaged. Thomas did give Marie a ring. In fact, he phoned her just the other night. Therefore, Thomas and Marie are engaged.

11. Alex, I heard your testimony in court earlier today. Tell me, why did you lie on the witness stand?

12. Johnson is employed by the General Services Administration, and everyone knows that the GSA is the most inefficient branch of the government. Therefore, Johnson must be an inefficient worker.

★13. All men are mortal. Therefore, someday man will disappear from the earth.

14. Each and every cell in this carrot is 90 percent water. Therefore, the entire carrot is 90 percent water.

15. George said that he was interviewing for a job drilling oil wells in the supervisor's office. We can only conclude that the supervisor must have an awfully dirty office.

★16. During the fifty years that Mr. Jones worked, he contributed $90,000 to Social Security. Now that he is retired, he stands to collect $200,000 from the system. Obviously he will collect a much greater monetary value than he contributed.

17. Either you marry me right now or I'll be forced to leave you and never speak to you again. I'm sure you wouldn't want me to do that. Therefore, you'll marry me right now.

18. Either Meg Ryan or Britney Spears is a popular singer. Meg Ryan is not a popular singer. Therefore, Britney Spears is a popular singer.

★19. Switzerland is 48 percent Protestant. Heidi Gilsing is a Swiss. Therefore, Heidi Gilsing is 48 percent Protestant.

20. Picasso is the greatest artist of the twentieth century. We know that this is so because art critics have described him in these terms. These art critics are correct in their assessment because they have a more keenly developed sense of appreciation than the average person. This is true because it takes a more keenly developed sense of appreciation to realize that Picasso is the greatest artist of the twentieth century.

21. An atomic bomb causes more damage than a conventional bomb. Therefore, during World War II more damage was caused by atomic bombs than by conventional bombs.

★22. Sylvia, I saw you shopping for wine the other day. Incidentally, are you still drinking excessively?

23. The author warns about numerous computational errors in his accounting text. Therefore, he must have written it very carelessly.

24. Emeralds are seldom found in this country, so you should be careful not to misplace your emerald ring.

★25. Of course abortion is permissible. After all, a woman has a right to do as she pleases with her own body.

II. Answer "true" or "false" to the following statements:

1. Arguments that commit the fallacy of begging the question are normally valid.

2. The effect of begging the question is to hide the fact that a premise may not be true.

3. The correct way of responding to a complex question is to divide the question into its component questions and answer each separately.

4. False dichotomy always involves an "either...or..." statement, at least implicitly.

5. The fallacy of equivocation arises from a syntactical defect in a statement.

6. The fallacy of amphiboly usually involves the ambiguous use of a single word.

7. Amphiboly usually arises from the arguer's misinterpreting a statement made by someone else.

8. The fallacy of composition always proceeds from whole to parts.

9. The fallacy of division always proceeds from parts to whole.

10. A general statement makes an assertion about each and every member of a class.

11. A class statement makes an assertion about a class as a whole.

12. In the statement "Divorces are increasing," an attribute is predicated distributively.

13. In the statement "Waistlines are increasing," an attribute is predicated distributively.

14. Composition and division involve the distributive predication of an attribute.

15. Equivocation and amphiboly are classified as fallacies of ambiguity.

III. Identify the fallacies of relevance, weak induction, presumption, ambiguity, and illicit transference committed by the following arguments, giving a brief explanation for your answer. If no fallacy is committed, write "no fallacy."

★ 1. In his *History of the American Civil War*, Jeffry Noland argues that the war had little to do with slavery. However, as a historian from Alabama, Noland could not possibly present an accurate account. Therefore, his arguments should be discounted.

2. Mr. Wilson said that on July 4 he went out on the veranda and watched the fireworks go up in his pajamas. We conclude that Mr. Wilson must have had an exciting evening.

3. Oregon State Representative Dennis Richardson says that the reason the Connecticut elementary school massacre occurred is because the teachers were not armed. Thus, to prevent future shootings of this sort we must make sure that every teacher in the United States is armed with a gun.

★ 4. A crust of bread is better than nothing. Nothing is better than true love. Therefore, a crust of bread is better than true love.

5. Every member of the Delta Club is over 70 years old. Therefore, the Delta Club must be over 70 years old.

6. Of course you should eat Wheaties. Wheaties is the breakfast of champions, you know.

★ 7. Surely it's morally permissible to kill animals for food. If God didn't want us to eat animals, he wouldn't have made them out of meat.

8. The idea that black people in this country live in poverty is ridiculous. Look at Oprah Winfrey. She's a billionaire. And Denzel Washington, Morgan Freeman, and Michael Jordan are millionaires..

9. No one has ever proved that the human fetus is not a person with rights. Therefore, abortion is morally wrong.

★ 10. Giant pandas are rapidly disappearing. This animal is a giant panda. Therefore, this animal should disappear any minute now.

11. When a car breaks down so often that repairs become pointless, the car is thrown on the junk heap. Similarly, when a person becomes old and diseased, he or she should be mercifully put to death.

12. The twenty-story Carson Building is constructed of concrete blocks. Each and every concrete block in the structure can withstand an earthquake of 9.5 on the Richter scale. Therefore, the building can withstand an earthquake of 9.5 on the Richter scale.

★ 13. Childhood obesity is a major problem these days. Obviously our public health officials have not been doing their job.

14. This administration is not anti-German, as it has been alleged. Germany is a great country. It has contributed immensely to the world's artistic treasury. Goethe and Schiller made magnificent contributions to literature, and Bach, Beethoven, Wagner, and Brahms did the same in music.

15. Paul, it was great to see you at the party the other night. Everyone there was doing crack. Incidentally, how long have you been dealing that stuff?

★16. Texas oilman T. Boone Pickens says that natural-gas fracking is perfectly safe and poses no threat to the nation's drinking water. Therefore we must conclude that fracking is just as safe as he claims it is.

17. Senator Barbara Boxer's arguments for the protection of wilderness areas should be ignored. Boxer is just another one of those tree-hugging liberals who supports such legislation only to please the environmental nuts in her home state of California.

18. Professor Andrews, surely I deserve a B in logic. I know that I have gotten F's on all the tests, but if you give me an F for my final grade, I will lose my scholarship. That will force me to drop out of school, and my poor, aged parents, who yearn to see me graduate, will be grief stricken for the rest of their lives.

★19. Molecules are in constant random motion. The Statue of Liberty is composed of molecules. Therefore, the Statue of Liberty is in constant random motion.

20. Either we have prayer in our public schools or the moral fabric of society will disintegrate. The choice should be obvious.

21. White sheep eat more than black sheep (because there are more of them). Therefore, this white sheep eats more than that black sheep.

★22. If someone rents a piece of land and plants crops on it, the landlord is never permitted to come and take those crops for himself when harvest time arrives. Similarly, if couples enlist the services of a surrogate mother to provide them with a baby, the mother should never be allowed to welch on the deal and keep the baby for herself once it is born.

23. Motives and desires exert forces on people, causing them to choose one thing over another. But force is a physical quantity, governed by the laws of physics. Therefore, human choices are governed by the laws of physics.

24. Each and every brick in the completely brick-faced Wainright Building has a reddish-brown color. Therefore, the Wainright Building has a reddish-brown color.

★25. Humanitarian groups have argued in favor of housing for the poor. Unfortunately, these high-density projects have been tried in the past and have failed. In no time they turn into ghettos with astronomical rates of crime and delinquency. Clearly, these humanitarian arguments are not what they seem.

26. Pauline said that after she had removed her new mink coat from the shipping carton she threw it into the trash. We conclude that Pauline has no appreciation for fine furs.

27. We know that induction will provide dependable results in the future because it has always worked in the past. Whatever has consistently worked in the past will

continue to work in the future, and we know that this is true because it has been established by induction.

★ 28. What goes up must come down. The price of food has been going up for years. Therefore, it will surely come down soon.

29. Mr. Prime Minister, I am certain you will want to release the members of our National Liberation Group whom you currently hold in prison. After all, I'm sure you will want to avoid having car bombs go off in the centers of your most heavily populated cities.

30. Recent studies have shown that non-organic food has the same vitamins, minerals, proteins, and other nutrients as organic food. Therefore, it's just as good to eat non-organic food as organic food.

★ 31. We've all heard the complaint that millions of Americans are without adequate health care. But America's doctors, nurses, and hospitals are among the best in the world. Thousands of people come from abroad every year to be treated here. Clearly there is nothing wrong with our health-care system.

32. Real estate mogul Donald Trump argues that good management is essential to any business. But who is he to talk? Trump's own mismanagement drove Trump Entertainment Resorts into bankruptcy three times in eighteen years.

33. The farmers of our state have asked that we introduce legislation to provide subsidies for soybeans. Unfortunately, we will have to turn down their request. If we give subsidies to the soybean farmers, then the corn and wheat growers will ask for the same thing. Then it will be the cotton growers, citrus growers, truck farmers, and cattle raisers. In the end, the cost will be astronomical.

★ 34. The travel brochure states that walking up O'Connell Street, the statue of Parnell comes into view. Apparently that statue has no trouble getting around.

35. Criminals are basically stupid, because anyone who isn't basically stupid wouldn't be a criminal.

36. Professor Glazebrooks's theory about the origin of the Martian craters is undoubtedly true. Rudolph Orkin, the great concert pianist, announced his support of the theory in this morning's newspaper.

★ 37. Mr. Franklin has lost at the craps table for the last ten throws of the dice. Therefore, it is extremely likely that he will win on the next throw.

38. Raising a child is like growing a tree. Sometimes violent things, such as cutting off branches, have to be done to force the tree to grow straight. Similarly, corporal punishment must sometimes be inflicted on children to force them to develop properly.

39. Good steaks are rare these days, so don't order yours well done.

★ 40. The Book of Mormon is true because it was written by Joseph Smith. Joseph Smith wrote the truth because he was divinely inspired. We know that Joseph Smith was divinely inspired because the Book of Mormon says that he was, and the Book of Mormon is true.

41. The students attending Bradford College come from every one of the fifty states. Michelle attends Bradford College. Therefore, Michelle comes from every one of the fifty states.

42. Rhubarb pie is a dessert. Therefore, whoever eats rhubarb pie eats a dessert.

★43. The vast majority of car accidents occur within twenty miles of one's home. Apparently it is much more dangerous to drive close to home than far away from home.

44. Either you buy me a new BMW, or I won't be able to get back and forth to school. I know you want me to go to school, so the choice is clear.

45. Nobody has ever proved that using cell phones causes brain tumors. Therefore, using cell phones does not cause brain tumors.

★46. On Friday I took Virginia out to dinner. She told me that if I wasn't interested in a serious relationship, I should forget about dating her. On Saturday I took Margie to a film. When we discussed it afterward over a drink, she couldn't understand why I wasn't interested in babies. Women are all alike. All they want is a secure marriage.

47. Dozens of species of plants and animals are being wiped out every year, even though we have laws to prevent it. Clearly, we should repeal the Endangered Species Act.

48. People are driving their cars like maniacs tonight. There must be a full moon.

★49. A line is composed of points. Points have no length. Therefore, a line has no length.

50. Are you in favor of the ruinous economic policy of the Democratic Platform Committee?

IV. Identify the fallacies committed in the following dialogue. You should be able to find at least one case of each fallacy presented in this section and a few of the fallacies presented in the two previous sections.

Personal Paper Mill

Carly catches sight of Brad as the two head for their class in sociology. "Hi!" she says as she joins him. "Did you get your paper finished?"

"Yes," he replies. "And given that first-rate work deserves an A, I deserve an A for this paper."

"That's great!" she says.

"But just between you and me, I had my girlfriend write my paper."

"Don't tell me that." Carly looks disgusted. "Do you think that's moral?"

"Beats me. Why do you always insist on giving moral advice to everyone?"

"The real question is, why do you always ignore moral advice?" she asks.

"Well, the way I see it," Brad says, "there's really nothing wrong with plagiarism. After all, students who plagiarize their work usually get better grades. Anyway, I'm just following in the footsteps of most U.S. presidents. They have speechwriters who write most of their speeches. Why shouldn't I get someone to write my papers?"

"You are so stupid!" Carly replies. "Honestly, I really think everyone should stop listening to you."

"Okay, how about this?" he asks. "Either I get someone to write this paper for me, or I'll get an F in the class. I can't afford to get an F; thus, I get someone to write the paper for me."

"That's not much better," Carly replies. "But you should realize that plagiarism is really dangerous. If you get caught, it could destroy your reputation."

"I doubt many students would think badly of me," he says. "Practically everyone plagiarizes their work nowadays, and if they do it, so can I."

"It's not true that all students plagiarize their work," Carly replies. "In fact, I am quite certain that none of them do. I certainly don't, and all of the students I know don't."

"Ah, but you do plagiarize your work," Brad insists.

"What do you mean?" Carly asks.

"Well, every word of your paper appears in the dictionary, so it's clear that you plagiarized it from the dictionary."

"Very funny," Carly says. "But here's what I think. I think you should ask Professor Halvorson for an extension on your paper and write it yourself. She really takes plagiarism seriously, and she insists that all work submitted to her be original."

"But this paper is original work," Brad insists, as they enter the social sciences building. "My girlfriend has never written a paper like this before, and she didn't copy it from anyone."

Carly laughs. "I don't think that's what she means by 'original.'" Incidentally, did you remember to attach a copy of the integrity pledge to the front of your paper? The academic integrity policy says that all instructors must direct their students to sign their full name on the integrity pledge, which asserts that the work being submitted has not been plagiarized."

"Yes, I have attached a copy of the pledge document to the paper, and I signed it 'Professor Judy Halvorson,' just as the rule says."

"How dense can you get?" Carly asks. "You're not supposed to sign the professor's name! You're supposed to sign your *own* name."

"Oh," says Brad. For the first time he looks concerned. "But that means I would be lying."

"Yes, it would," Carly agrees, "but I don't see why that should bother you. Still, I can assure you of this: If you hand in the paper, you won't graduate."

"You're wrong about that," Brad counters. "Consider this. I'm a member of the senior class, and the senior class graduates in May. That means I'll graduate in May."

"I wouldn't bet on it," Carly says, as they approach their classroom. "You forget that I'm on the Academic Integrity Committee, and I've sworn to uphold the policy on plagiarism."

"Uh oh." Brad looks concerned again. "That had slipped my mind. But you won't rat on me, will you? Please, please don't. All my life I have struggled with my sense of self-esteem, and if I get an F on this paper, I will feel absolutely crushed."

"Rat on you? Well, that depends," says Carly.

They enter the classroom, and Brad gives Carly a tense smile. "On what?"

Carly smiles grimly back. "On whether you hand in the paper your girlfriend wrote."

2.5   Fallacies in Ordinary Language

PREVIEW

A friend of yours has a bad case of dandruff. He starts eating broccoli, and his dandruff clears up. Clearly the broccoli did it. But if it worked for your friend, it will work for everyone, so what we have here is a new cure for dandruff. And if you're not convinced, just think of the thousands of unfortunate dandruff sufferers who have tried every cure in the book for years and gotten no relief. This section of the book deals with passages such as this, where multiple fallacies are jumbled together.

This section addresses two topics. The first concerns the challenge of detecting the fallacies of others in ordinary language, and the second relates to the goal of avoiding fallacies in one's own arguments.

Detecting Fallacies

Most of the informal fallacies that we have seen thus far have been clear-cut, easily recognizable instances of a specific mistake. When fallacies occur in ordinary usage, however, they are often neither clear-cut nor easily recognizable. The reason is that there are innumerable ways of making mistakes in arguing, and variations inevitably occur that may not be exact instances of any specifically named fallacy. In addition, one fallacious mode of arguing may be mixed with one or more others, and the strands of reasoning may have to be disentangled before the fallacies can be named. Yet another problem arises from the fact that arguments in ordinary language are rarely presented in complete form. A premise or conclusion often is left unexpressed, which may obscure the nature of the evidence that is presented or the strength of the link between premises and conclusion.

Consider, for example, the following letter that appeared in a newspaper:

God, I am sick of "women's rights"! Every time one turns on the news we hear about some form of discrimination against some poor female who wants to be a fireman—or some "remark" that suggests or implies women are inferior to men.

I, for one, do not want to be rescued by a "woman fireman," especially if I am a 6-foot-2 male and she is a 5-foot-6 female.

Why is it that women find their "role" so degrading? What is wrong with being a wife and mother, staying home while the male goes out and "hunts for food" and brings it home to his family?

I don't think women have proven themselves to be as inventive, as capable (on the average) of world leadership, as physically capable, or as "courageous" as men. They have yet to fight a war (the average American woman) and let's face it ladies, who wants to?

Whether a person is female, black, white, handicapped—whatever—*ability* is what counts in the final analysis. Women cannot demand "equality"—no one can—unless it is earned.

When push comes to shove and a damsel is in distress, she is hard-pressed to protect herself and usually has to be rescued by a man. Until I can move a piano, beat off a potential robber or rapist, or fight a war, I am quite content to be a woman, thank you.

(Patricia Kelley)

This letter presents numerous fallacies. The phrase "poor female who wants to be a fireman" suggests a mild *ad hominem* abusive, and equating women's rights in general with the right to be a firefighter suggests a straw man. The second paragraph commits another straw man fallacy by supposing that the job of firefighter inevitably entails such activities as climbing up ladders and rescuing people. Surely there are many male firefighters who cannot do this. The same paragraph also can be interpreted as begging the question: Do women who want to be firefighters want the specific job of rescuing tall men?

The third paragraph throws out a red herring. The issue is whether women have the right to be considered for a job of their choice and whether they must be paid as much as a man in the same situation. Whether there is something wrong with being a wife and mother is quite a different issue. Also, the reference to men hunting for food suggests a possible begging of the question: Are we still locked into a "hunter-gatherer" social structure?

The paragraph about whether women have proved themselves to be as inventive, capable, and courageous as men begs yet another question: Assuming, for the sake of argument, that this is true, have women been allowed to occupy roles in society where such inventiveness, capability, and courageousness can be demonstrated? Furthermore, this paragraph commits a red herring fallacy and/or misses the point: Even if women have not proved this, what does that have to do with the issue? Most jobs do not require any high degree of inventiveness or courage or a capacity for world leadership.

The paragraph about ability begs yet another question: Is it in fact the case that women have less ability? I am not aware that anything of the sort has ever been proved. Finally, the last paragraph throws out another red herring. What does moving pianos and beating off rapists have to do with most jobs or the question of equal pay for equal work?

Probably the single most important requirement for detecting fallacies in ordinary language is alertness. The reader or listener must pay close attention to what the arguer is saying. What is the conclusion? What are the reasons given in support of the conclusion? Are the reasons relevant to the conclusion? Do the reasons support the conclusion? If the reader or listener is half asleep or lounging in that passive, drugged-out state that attends much television viewing, then none of these questions will receive answers. Under those circumstances the reader or listener will never be able to detect informal fallacies, and he or she will accept even the worst reasoning without the slightest hesitation.

Avoiding Fallacies

Why do people commit informal fallacies? Unfortunately, this question allows for no simple, straightforward answer. The reasons underlying the commission of fallacies are complex and interconnected. However, we can identify three factors that lead to most of the informal mistakes in reasoning. The first is intent. Many fallacies are committed intentionally. The arguer may know full well that his or her reasoning is defective but goes ahead with it anyway because of some benefit for himself or herself or some other person. All of the informal fallacies we have studied can be used for that purpose, but some of them are particularly well suited to it. These include the appeal to force, appeal to pity, appeal to the people, *ad hominem*, straw man, complex question, false dichotomy, and suppressed evidence. Here is such a case of appeal to force:

> I deserve a chocolate sundae for dessert, and if you don't buy me one right now, I'll start screaming and embarrass you in front of all of the people in this restaurant.

And here is a case of false dichotomy that conveys the appearance of being intentionally committed:

> Either you take me on a Caribbean cruise, or I'll have a nervous breakdown. It's up to you.

The key to avoiding fallacies that are intentionally committed probably lies in some form of moral education. The arguer must come to realize that using dishonest means in order to acquire something he or she does not deserve is just another form of cheating.

The situation becomes more complicated, however, when the sought-after goal is morally justified. Arguers sometimes use fallacious reasoning intentionally to trick a person into doing something that is really for that person's own good. Here is a false dichotomy of that sort:

> Either you control your eating and get regular exercise, or you'll have a heart attack and die. The choice is yours.

Given the beneficial consequences of controlled eating and regular exercise, some moral philosophers will find nothing wrong with this argument. Others will contend that manipulating someone into doing something violates human dignity. In either case, such arguments are logically unacceptable.

The second factor that leads to the commission of informal fallacies is a careless mental posture combined with an emotional disposition favoring or opposing some person or thing. The careless mental posture opens the door, so to speak, to fallacious reasoning, and the emotional disposition pushes the arguer through it. Even people who are thoroughly versed in the informal fallacies occasionally succumb to the deadly combination of mental carelessness and emotional impetus. For example, arguments such as the following *ad hominem* abusive can sometimes be heard in the halls of university philosophy departments:

> Professor Ballard's argument in favor of restructuring our course offering isn't worth a hoot. But what would you expect from someone who publishes in such mediocre journals? And did you hear Ballard's recent lecture on Aristotle? It was total nonsense.

When people who should know better are confronted with the fact that their argument commits a common fallacy, they often admit with embarrassment that they have not been thinking and then revise their argument according to logical principles. In contrast, people who are not familiar with the distinction between good and fallacious reasoning will likely deny that there is anything wrong with their argument. Thus, the key to avoiding fallacies that arise from mental carelessness lies in developing a thorough familiarity with the informal fallacies, combined with a habitual realization of how emotions affect people's reasoning. Everyone should realize that unchecked emotions are an open invitation to illogical reasoning, and they can lead a person to commit quite blindly every one of the fallacies we have studied thus far.

The third factor that leads to the commission of informal fallacies is far more difficult to contend with than the first two. It consists in the influence of what we might call the "worldview" of the arguer. By worldview we mean a cognitive network of beliefs, attitudes, habits, memories, values, and other elements that conditions and renders meaningful the world in which we live. Beginning in infancy, our worldview emerges quietly and unconsciously from enveloping influences—culture, language, gender, religion, politics, and social and economic status. As we grow older, it continues to develop through the shaping forces of education and experience. Once it has taken root, our worldview determines how each of us sizes up the world in which we live. Given a set of circumstances, it indicates what is reasonable to believe and what is unreasonable.

In connection with the construction and evaluation of arguments, an arguer's worldview determines the answer to questions about importance, relevance, causal connections, the qualifications of authorities, whether a sample is typical or atypical of a group, what can and cannot be taken for granted, and other factors. However, because these determinations inevitably involve unexamined presuppositions, the arguer's worldview can lead to the commission of informal fallacies. All of the fallacies we have studied so far are likely candidates, but the ones especially susceptible are appeal to pity, straw man, missing the point, appeal to unqualified authority, hasty generalization, false cause, slippery slope, weak analogy, begging the question, false dichotomy, and suppressed evidence.

Thus, a person with a victim mentality may think that his pathetic circumstances really justify some favorable treatment; an uncritical conservative may cite with complete confidence the authority of Rush Limbaugh; a person with a racist worldview may conclude that the errant behavior of a handful of Asians, African Americans, or Hispanics really is typical of the larger class; a person with a liberal worldview may quite innocently distort an opponent's argument by equating it with fascism; a pro-life arguer may consider it obvious that the fetus is a person with rights, while a pro-choice arguer may take it for granted that the fetus is not a person with rights, and so on. Consider, for example, the following argument from analogy:

> A court trial is like a professional football game. In a professional football game, the most important thing is winning. Similarly, in a trial, the most important thing is winning.

This argument is consistent with the worldview of many, if not most, lawyers. Lawyers are trained as advocates, and when they enter a courtroom they see themselves going into battle for their clients. In any battle, winning is the most important objective. But this viewpoint presupposes that truth and justice are either unattainable in the courtroom or of secondary importance. Thus, while many lawyers would evaluate this argument as nonfallacious, many nonlawyers would reject it as a weak analogy.

For another example, consider the following causal inference:

> After enslaving most of Eastern Europe for nearly fifty years, the evil Soviet empire finally collapsed. Obviously God listened to our prayers.

This argument reflects the worldview of many theists. It presupposes that there is a God, that God listens to prayers, that God is influenced by prayers, that God has the power to alter the course of history, and that God does alter the course of history. While the theist is likely to consider this argument a good one, the atheist will reject it as a blatant case of false cause.

To avoid fallacies that arise from the influence of worldviews, the arguer must acknowledge and critique his or her presuppositions. Doing so inclines the arguer to couch his or her arguments in language that takes those presuppositions into account. The result is nearly always an argument that is more intelligently crafted and, it is hoped, more persuasive. However, the task of recognizing and critiquing one's presuppositions is not easy. Presuppositions are intrinsically linked to one's worldview, and many people are not even aware that they have a worldview. The reason is that worldviews are formed through a process that is largely unconscious. Thus, the arguer must first recognize that he or she has a worldview and must then exercise constant vigilance over the presuppositions it comprises.

Even after one's presuppositions have been exposed and thoroughly critiqued, however, there is no guarantee that one's arguments will agree with the arguments of others who have critiqued their worldviews. This is because a person's worldview reflects the unique perspective that person has on the world. No two people share exactly the same perspective. Nevertheless, disclosing and critiquing the presuppositions in one's worldview lays a foundation for meaningful communication with other reasonable arguers, and it provides a context of reasonableness for working out disagreements.

In summary, the three factors that are probably responsible for most informal fallacies are intent, mental carelessness combined with emotional dispositions, and unexamined presuppositions in the arguer's worldview. However, these factors rarely occur in isolation. In the vast majority of cases, two or all three conspire to produce fallacious reasoning. This fact exacerbates the difficulty in avoiding informal fallacies in one's own arguments and in detecting fallacies in the arguments of others.

Now let us consider some cases of real-life arguments in light of the factors we have just discussed. All are taken from letters-to-the-editor columns of newspapers and magazines. The first relates to affirmative action programs:

> I'm a nonracist, nonsexist, white male born in 1969, who has never owned a slave, treated anyone as inferior because of his or her race, or sexually harassed a female co-worker. In other words, I don't owe women or minorities a thing. Since when are people required to pay for the sins of their predecessors simply because they belong to the same race or gender?
>
> (Ben Gibbons)

The author of this argument presupposes that racist and sexist patterns in society have not benefited him in any way. Among other things, he presupposes that his white ancestors in no way benefited from their being white and that none of these benefits passed down to him. On the other hand, given that he has received such benefits, he may presuppose that he is not obligated to pay any of them back. Of course, none of these things may have occurred, but the author should at least address these issues. Because he does not address them, the argument begs the question.

The next argument relates to secondhand smoke from cigarettes:

> Now, besides lung cancer and other nasty business, secondhand smoke causes deafness and impotence. Was secondhand smoke a problem when people heated their homes solely by fireplaces? How about those romantic teepees with the smoke hole at the top? And what about fireplaces in new homes? Let's have some research about the problems caused by these as well as barbecues. A little cancer with your hot dog, anyone?
>
> (Pat Sharp)

This argument seems to commit the fallacy of equivocation. The arguer begins by using "secondhand smoke" to refer to the smoke from burning tobacco, and then uses the term to refer to the smoke from fireplaces, teepee fires, and barbecues. Smoke from burning tobacco is clearly not the same thing as smoke from burning wood or charcoal. Alternately, the argument might be seen to beg the question: "But do people burn tobacco in their fireplaces and barbecues?" These fallacies probably arise either from the intentions of the author or from carelessness in failing to distinguish the two kinds of secondhand smoke. In either event, the author is probably hostile to government efforts to control secondhand tobacco smoke in confined areas.

The next argument deals with gun control:

> Detroit, the seventh largest city and one with strict gun laws, had 596 homicides last year. In the same year Phoenix, the ninth largest city and one that at the time did not require gun owners to be licensed, had 136 homicides. Criminals don't fear the toothless criminal-justice system, but they do fear armed citizens.
>
> (Paul M. Berardi)

This argument commits a false cause fallacy. The author presupposes that the availability of guns caused Phoenix to have a lower homicide rate than Detroit. The arguer also presupposes that Detroit and Phoenix are comparable as to homicide rate merely because they are roughly the same size. As a result, the argument involves a weak analogy and also begs the question. The additional factors of emotion and intent may also be present. The arguer probably hates the prospect of gun control, and he may be fully aware of the fact that Phoenix and Detroit are not comparable for his purpose, but he went ahead with the comparison anyway.

The next argument deals with religious fundamentalism:

> If we compromise God's word, we compromise the truth. To say that the fundamentalist is a loud shrill voice drowning out religious moderation implies that diluted truth is better than absolute truth.
>
> (Gerald Gleason)

This argument begs the question. The arguer presupposes that there is a God, that God has spoken, that God has revealed his intentions to fundamentalist preachers, and that those preachers accurately report the word of God. The argument also seems to reflect an emotional disposition in favor of religious fundamentalism.

The last argument we will consider relates to English as the official U.S. language:

> This great country has been held together for more than 200 years because of one simple thing: the English language. There are two things we must do: Make English the official language of the United States and do away with bilingual education.
>
> (David Moisan)

This argument misses the point. The arguer presupposes that making English the official language would guarantee that all citizens speak it and that doing away with bilingual education would accelerate the learning process of immigrant children. The argument may also reflect the fear that many feel in connection with the changes U.S. society is experiencing as a result of recent immigration.

EXERCISE 2.5

I. Most of the following selections were taken from letters-to-the-editors columns of newspapers and magazines. Identify any fallacies that may be committed, giving a brief explanation for your answer. Then, if a fallacy is identified, discuss the possible factors that led the arguer to commit the fallacy.

★ 1. Exporting cigarettes [to Asia] is good business for America; there is no reason we should be prohibited from doing so. Asians have been smoking for decades; we are only offering variety in their habit. If the Asians made tobacco smoking illegal, that would be a different situation. But as long as it is legal, the decision is up to the smokers. The Asians are just afraid of American supremacy in the tobacco industries.

(Pat Monohan)

2. When will these upper-crust intellectuals realize that the masses of working people are not in cozy, cushy, interesting, challenging, well-paying jobs, professions and businesses? My husband is now 51; for most of the last 33 years he has worked in the same factory job, and only the thought of retiring at 62 has sustained him. When he reaches that age in 11 years, who will tell him that his aging and physically wracked body must keep going another two years? My heart cries out for all the poor souls who man the assembly lines, ride the trucks or work in the fields or mines, or in the poorly ventilated, hot-in-summer, cold-in-winter factories and garages. Many cannot afford to retire at 62, 65, or even later. Never, never let them extend the retirement age. It's a matter of survival to so many.

(Isabel Fierman)

3. Women in military combat is insane. No society in its right mind would have such a policy. The military needs only young people and that means the only women who go are those in their child-bearing years. Kill them off and society will not be able to perpetuate itself.

(Jack Carman)

★ 4. Dear Ann: I've read that one aspirin taken every other day will reduce the risk of heart attack. Why not take two and double the protection?

(Boston)

5. The American Civil Liberties Union did a study that found that in the last eighty years it believes twenty-five innocent people have been executed in the United States. This is unfortunate. But, there are innocent people who die each year in highway accidents. Out of 40,000 deaths, how many deaths are related to driving while intoxicated? How many more thousands are injured and incur financial ruin or are invalids and handicapped for the remainder of their lives?

(Mahlon R. Braden)

6. Mexico's president expresses legitimate concern when he questions supplying oil to Americans who are unwilling to apply "discipline" in oil consumption. In view of the fact that his country's population is expected to double in only twenty-two years, isn't it legitimate for us to ask when Mexicans will apply the discipline necessary to control population growth and quit dumping their excess millions over our borders?

(Wayne R. Bartz)

★ 7. A parent would never give a ten-year-old the car keys, fix him or her a martini, or let him or her wander at night through a dangerous part of town. The same holds true of the Internet. Watch what children access, but leave the Net alone. Regulation is no substitute for responsibility.

(Bobby Dunning)

8. How would you feel to see your children starving and have all doors slammed in your face? Isn't it time that all of us who believe in freedom and human rights stop thinking in terms of color and national boundaries? We should open our arms and hearts to those less fortunate and remember that a time could come when we might be in a similar situation.

(Lorna Doyle)

9. A capital gains tax [reduction] benefits everyone, not just the "rich," because everyone will have more money to invest or spend in the private economy, resulting in more jobs and increasing prosperity for all. This is certainly better than paying high taxes to a corrupt, self-serving, and incompetent government that squanders our earnings on wasteful and useless programs.

(David Miller)

★ 10. After reading "Homosexuals in the Churches," I'd like to point out that I don't know any serious, capable exegetes who stumble over Saint Paul's denunciation of homosexuality. Only a fool (and there seem to be more and more these days) can fail to understand the plain words of Romans, Chapter one. God did not make anyone "gay." Paul tells us in Romans 1 that homosexuals become that way because of their own lusts.

(LeRoy J. Hopper)

11. When will they ever learn—that the Republican Party is not for the people who voted for it?

(Alton L. Stafford)

12. Before I came to the United States in July 1922, I was in Berlin where I visited the famous zoo. In one of the large cages were a lion and a tiger. Both respected each other's strength. It occurred to me that it was a good illustration of "balance of power." Each beast followed the other and watched each other's moves. When one moved, the other did. When one stopped, the other stopped.

In today's world, big powers or groups of powers are trying to maintain the status quo, trying to be as strong as or stronger than the other. They realize a conflict may result in mutual destruction. As long as the countries believe there is a balance of power we may hope for peace.

(Emilie Lackow)

★ 13. Doctors say the birth of a baby is a high point of being a doctor. Yet a medical survey shows one out of every nine obstetricians in America has stopped delivering babies.

Expectant mothers have had to find new doctors. In some rural areas, women have had to travel elsewhere to give birth.

How did this happen? It's part of the price of the lawsuit crisis.

The number of lawsuits Americans file each year is on the rise. Obstetricians are among the hardest hit—almost three out of four have faced a malpractice claim. Many have decided it isn't worth the risk.

(Magazine ad by the Insurance Information Institute)

14. The conservative diatribe found in campus journalism comes from the mouths of a handful of affluent brats who were spoon-fed through the '90s. Put them on an ethnically more diverse campus, rather than a Princeton or a Dartmouth, and then let us see how long their newspapers survive.

(David Simons)

15. I see that our courts are being asked to rule on the propriety of outlawing video games as a "waste of time and money."

It seems that we may be onto something here. A favorable ruling would open the door to new laws eliminating show business, spectator sports, cocktail lounges, the state of Nevada, public education and, of course, the entire federal bureaucracy.

(A. G. Dobrin)

★16. The death penalty is the punishment for murder. Just as we have long jail terms for armed robbery, assault and battery, fraud, contempt of court, fines for speeding, reckless driving and other numerous traffic violations, so must we have a punishment for murder. Yes, the death penalty will not deter murders any more than a speeding ticket will deter violating speed laws again, but it is the punishment for such violation!

(Lawrence J. Barstow)

17. Would you rather invest in our nation's children or Pentagon waste? The choice is yours.

(Political ad)

18. My gun has protected me, and my son's gun taught him safety and responsibility long before he got hold of a far more lethal weapon—the family car. Cigarettes kill many times more people yearly than guns and, unlike guns, have absolutely no redeeming qualities. If John Lennon had died a long, painful and expensive death from lung cancer, would you have devoted a page to a harangue against the product of some of your biggest advertisers—the cigarette companies?

(Silvia A. DeFreitas)

★19. If the advocates of prayers in public schools win on this issue, just where will it end? Perhaps next they will ask for prayers on public transportation? Prayers by government workers before they start their job each day? Or maybe, mandatory prayers in public restaurants before starting each meal might be a good idea.

(Leonard Mendelson)

20. So you want to ban smoking in all eating establishments? Well, you go right ahead and do that little thing. And when the 40 percent of smokers stop eating out, the restaurants can do one of two things: close, or raise the price of a $20 dinner 40 percent to $28.

(Karen Sawyer)

21. Pigeons are forced to leave our city to battle for life. Their struggle is an endless search for food. What manner of person would watch these hungry creatures suffer from want of food and deny them their survival? These helpless birds are too often ignored by the people of our city, with not the least bit of compassion shown to them. Pigeons are God's creatures just as the so-called human race is. They need help.

(Leslie Ann Price)

★ 22. You take half of the American population every night and set them down in front of a screen watching people getting stabbed, shot and blown away. And then you expect them to go out into the streets hugging each other?

(Mark Hustad)

23. So you think that putting the worst type of criminal out of his misery is wrong. How about the Americans who were sent to Korea, to Vietnam, to Beirut, to Central America? Thousands of good men were sacrificed supposedly for the good of our country. At the same time we were saving and protecting Charles Manson, Sirhan Sirhan [Robert Kennedy's murderer], and a whole raft of others too numerous to mention.

(George M. Purvis)

24. The fact is that the hype over "acid rain" and "global warming" is just that: hype. Take, for example, Stephen Schneider, author of *Global Warming*. In his current "study" he discusses a "greenhouse effect of catastrophic proportions," yet twenty years ago Schneider was a vocal proponent of the theory of a "new ice age."

(Urs Furrer)

★ 25. Just as our parents did for us, my husband and I rely solely on Christian Science for all the health needs of our four sons and find it invaluable for the quick cure of whatever ailments and contagions they are subject to. One particular healing that comes to mind happened several years ago when our youngest was a toddler. He had a flu-type illness that suddenly became quite serious. We called a Christian Science practitioner for treatment and he was completely well the next morning.

(Ellen Austin)

26. As somebody who has experienced the tragedy of miscarriage—or spontaneous abortion—at eight weeks, I greatly resent the position that a fetus is not a baby. I went through the grief of losing a baby, and no one should tell me otherwise.

(Ann Fons)

27. How can we pledge allegiance to the flag of the United States of America and not establish laws to punish people who burn the flag to make a statement? We are a people who punish an individual who libels another person but will not seek redress from an individual who insults every citizen of this great country by desecrating the flag.

(William D. Lankford)

★ 28. The notion of "buying American" is as misguided as the notion of buying Wisconsin, or Oshkosh, Wisconsin, or South Oshkosh, Wisconsin. For the same reasons that Wisconsin increases its standard of living by trading with the rest of the nation, America increases its standard of living by trading with the rest of the world.

(Phillip Smith)

29. We've often heard the saying, "Far better to let 100 guilty men go free than to condemn one innocent man." What happens then if we apply the logic of this argument to the question, "Is a fetus an unborn human being?" Then is it not better to let 100 fetuses be born rather than to mistakenly kill one unborn human being? This line of reasoning is a strictly humanist argument against abortion.

(James Sebastian)

30. In our society it is generally considered improper for a man to sleep, shower, and dress amid a group of women to whom he normally would be sexually attracted. It seems to me, then, to be equally unacceptable that a gay man sleep, shower, and dress in a company of men to whom, we assume, he would be no less sexually attracted.

(Mark O. Temple)

★31. I say "bravo" and "right on!" Now we have some real-life humane heroes to look up to! These brave people [a group of animal liberators] went up against the insensitive bureaucratic technology, and won, saving former pet animals from senseless torture.

If researchers want to experiment, let them use computers, or themselves—but not former pet animals! I know it's bad enough they use monkeys and rats, but if those animals are bred knowing nothing else but these Frankensteins abusing them it's different (but not better) than dogs or cats that have been loved and petted all their lives to suddenly be tortured and mutilated in the name of science. End all animal research! Free all research animals!

Right on, animal liberators!

(Linda Magee)

32. Dear Ann: Recently I was shopping downtown in 20-below-zero weather. A stranger walked up to me and said, "I wonder how many beautiful rabbits died so you could have that coat?" I noticed she was wearing a down coat, so I asked if the geese they got the down from to make her coat were still alive. She looked surprised. Obviously she had never given it a thought.

If people are so upset about cruelty to animals, why don't they go after the folks who refuse to spend the money to have their pets neutered and spayed? Thousands of dogs are put to death every year because the animal pounds can't feed and house them. Talk about cruelty to animals—that's the best example there is.

("Baby It's Cold Outside")

33. I prayed for the U.S. Senate to defeat the prayer amendment—and it did. There is a God.

(Richard Carr)

★34. People of the Philippines, I have returned! The hour of your redemption is here! Rally to me! Let the indomitable spirit of Bataan and Corregidor lead on! As the lines of battle roll forward to bring you within the zone of operations, rise and strike! For future generations of your sons and daughters, strike! Let no heart be faint! Let every arm be steeled! The guidance of divine God points the way! Follow in his name to the Holy Grail of righteous victory!

(General Douglas MacArthur)

35. As the oldest of eleven children (all married), I'd like to point out our combined family numbers more than 100 who vote only for pro-life candidates. Pro-lifers have children, pro-choicers do not.

(Mrs. Kitty Reickenback)

36. I am 12 years old. My class had a discussion on whether police used unnecessary force when arresting the people from Operation Rescue.

My teacher is an ex-cop, and he demonstrated police holds to us. They don't hurt at all unless the person is struggling or trying to pull away. If anybody was hurt when they were arrested, then they must have been struggling with the officers trying to arrest them.

(Ben Torre-Bueno)

★ 37. As corporate farms continue to gobble up smaller family farms, they control a larger percentage of the grain and produce raised in the United States. Some have already reached a point in size where, if they should decide to withhold their grain and produce from the marketplace, spot shortages could occur and higher prices would result. The choice is to pay us family farmers now or pay the corporations later.

(Delwin Yost)

38. If you buy our airline ticket now you can save 60 percent, and that means 60 percent more vacation for you.

(Radio ad)

39. Why all the flap about atomic bombs? The potential for death is always with us. Of course, if you just want something to worry about, go ahead. Franklin D. Roosevelt said it: "The only thing we have to fear is fear itself."

(Lee Flemming Reese)

★ 40. September 17 marked the anniversary of the signing of the U.S. Constitution. How well have we, the people, protected our rights? Consider what has happened to our private-property rights.

"Property has divine rights, and the moment the idea is admitted into society that property is not as sacred as the laws of God, anarchy and tyranny begin." (John Quincy Adams, 1767–1848, Sixth President of the United States).

Taxes and regulations are the two-edged sword which gravely threatens the fabric of our capitalistic republic. The tyranny of which Adams speaks is with us today in the form of government regulators and regulations which have all but destroyed the right to own property. Can anarchy be far behind?

(Timothy R. Binder)

41. Evolution would have been dealt serious setbacks if environmentalists had been around over the eons trying to save endangered species.

Species are endangered because they just do not fit the bigger picture any more as the world changes. That's not bad. It's just life.

In most cases we have seen the "endangered species" argument is just a ruse; much deeper motives usually exist, and they are almost always selfish and personal.

(Tom Gable)

42. The problem that I have with the pro-choice supporters' argument is that they make "choice" the ultimate issue. Let's face facts. No one has absolute freedom of choice sanctioned by the law. One can choose to rob a bank, but it's not lawful. Others can choose to kill their one-year-old child, but it is not legal. Why then should a woman have the legal right to take the life of her unborn child?

(Loretta S. Horn)

★43. If a car or truck kills a person, do politicians call for car control or truck control? And call in all cars/trucks?

If a child burns down a house do we have match control or child control and call in all of each?

Gun control and confiscation is equally as pathetic a thought process in an age of supposed intelligence.

(Pete Hawes)

44. I was incensed to read in your article about the return of anti-Semitism that New York City Moral Majority Leader Rev. Dan C. Fore actually said that "Jews have a God-given ability to make money, almost a supernatural ability. . . ." I find it incredibly ironic that he and other Moral Majority types conveniently overlook the fact that they, too, pack away a pretty tidy sum themselves through their fundraising efforts. It is sad that anti-Semitism exists, but to have this prejudice voiced by leaders of religious organizations is deplorable. These people are in for quite a surprise come Judgment Day.

(John R. Murks)

45. I couldn't help but compare the ducks in Fairbanks, Alaska, who refuse to fly south for the winter to our welfare system. Instead of going south, four ducks have set up housekeeping there because people keep feeding them. The biologist dealing with the ducks said that while it's nice that people are concerned, in the long run it isn't good for the ducks because it conditions them to stay when they need to get to warmer temperatures. Our welfare system, in many instances, conditions people to stay on welfare. Compassion is a wonderful virtue, and we need to help people who need help, but is it compassionate to keep people on welfare who should be developing and using their God-given abilities to do for themselves what the government is doing for them?

(Donna Symes)

★46. Why are people so shocked that Susan Smith apparently chose to kill her children because they had become an inconvenience? Doesn't this occur every day in abortion clinics across the country? We suspect Smith heard very clearly the message many feminists have been trying to deliver about the expendable nature of our children.

(Kevin and Diana Cogan)

47. What's wrong with kids today? Answer: nothing, for the majority of them. They are great.

Witness the action of two San Diego teenage boys recently, when the Normal Heights fire was at its worst. They took a garden hose to the roof of a threatened house—a house belonging to four elderly sisters, people they didn't even know. They saved the house, while neighboring houses burned to the ground.

In the Baldwin Hills fire, two teenage girls rescued a blind, retired Navy man from sure death when they braved the flames to find him, confused, outside his burning house. He would probably have perished if they hadn't run a distance to rescue him.

(Theodore H. Wickham)

48. Now that Big Brother has decided that I must wear a seatbelt when I ride in a car, how long will it take before I have to wear an inner tube when I swim in my pool, a safety harness when I climb a ladder, and shoes with steel-reinforced toecaps when I carry out the garbage?

(G. R. Turgeon)

★**49.** Dear Ann: I was disappointed in your response to the girl whose mother used the strap on her. The gym teacher noticed the bruises on her legs and backside and called it "child abuse." Why are you against strapping a child when the Bible tells us in plain language that this is what parents should do?

The Book of Proverbs mentions many times that the rod must be used. Proverbs 23:13 says: "Withhold not correction from the child for if thou beatest him with the rod he shall not die." Proverbs 23:14 says: "Thou shalt beat him with the rod and shalt deliver his soul from death."

There is no substitute for a good whipping. I have seen the results of trying to reason with kids. They are arrogant, disrespectful and mouthy. Parents may wish for a more "humane" way, but there is none. Beating children is God's way of getting parents to gain control over their children.

(Davisville, W.Va.)

50. The Fourth Amendment guarantees our right to freedom from unreasonable search and seizure. It does not prohibit *reasonable* search and seizure. The matter of sobriety roadblocks to stop drunk drivers boils down to this: Are such roadblocks reasonable or unreasonable? The majority of people answer: "Reasonable." Therefore, sobriety roadblocks should not be considered to be unconstitutional.

(Haskell Collier)

51. The Supreme Court recently ruled that a police department in Florida did not violate any rights of privacy when a police helicopter flew over the backyard of a suspected drug dealer and noticed marijuana growing on his property. Many people, including groups like the Anti-Common Logic Union, felt that the suspect's right to privacy outweighed the police department's need to protect the public at large.

The simple idea of sacrificing a right to serve a greater good should be allowed in certain cases. In this particular case the danger to the public wasn't extremely large; marijuana is probably less dangerous than regular beer. But anything could have been in that backyard—a load of cocaine, an illegal stockpile of weapons, or other major threats to society.

(Matt Cookson)

★52. I am 79 and have been smoking for 60 years. My husband is 90 and has inhaled my smoke for some 50 years with no bad effects.

I see no reason to take further steps to isolate smokers in public places, other than we now observe.

Smokers have taken punishment enough from neurotic sniffers, some of whom belong in bubbles. There are plenty of injudicious fumes on our streets and freeways.

(Helen Gans)

53. The mainstream press finds itself left behind by talk radio, so they try to minimize its importance. Americans are finding the true spirit of democracy in community and national debate. Why should we be told what to believe by a news weekly or the nightly news when we can follow public debate as it unfolds on talk radio?

(Adam Abbott)

54. The issue is not whether we should subsidize the arts, but whether anyone should be able to force someone else to subsidize the arts. You and I are free to *give* any amount of our money to any artistic endeavor we wish to support. When the government gets involved, however, a group of bureaucrats is given the power to *take* our money and give it to the arts they wish to support. We are not consulted. That is not a way to promote a responsible culture. That is tyranny.

(Jerry Harben)

55. Who are these Supreme Court justices who have the guts to OK the burning of our flag?

If the wife or daughter of these so-called justices were raped, could the rapist be exonerated because he took the First Amendment? That he was just expressing himself? How about murder in the same situation?

(Robert A. Lewis)

56. I have one question for those bleeding hearts who say we should not have used the atomic bomb: If the nation responsible for the Rape of Nanking, the Manchurian atrocities, Pearl Harbor, and the Bataan Death March had invented the bomb first, don't you think they would have used it? So do I.

(Bill Blair)

57. Since when did military service become a right, for gays or anyone else? The military has always been allowed to discriminate against people who don't meet its requirements, including those who are overweight or too tall or too short. There is an adequate supply of personnel with the characteristics they need. And there is no national need for gays in the military.

(William R. Cnossen)

★58. There is something very wrong about the custom of tipping. When we go to a store, we don't decide what a product is worth and pay what we please; we pay the price or we leave. Prices in coffee bars and restaurants should be raised, waiters should be paid a decent wage, and the words "no tipping" should be clearly visible on menus and at counters.

(George Jochnowitz)

59. Most Americans do not favor gun control. They know that their well-being depends on their own ability to protect themselves. So-called "assault rifles" are used in few crimes. They are not the weapon of choice of criminals, but they are for people trying to protect themselves from government troops.

(Larry Herron)

60. Holding a gun, a thief robs John Q. Public of thousands of dollars. Holding a baby, an unmarried mother robs taxpayers of thousands of dollars. If one behavior is considered a crime, then so should the other.

(Louis R. Ward)

II. Turn to the editorial pages of a newspaper or the letters column of a magazine and find an instance of a fallacious argument in the editorials or letters to the editor. Identify the premises and conclusion of the argument and write an analysis at least one paragraph in length identifying the fallacy or fallacies committed and the factors that may have led the arguer to commit them.

aplia

Visit Aplia for section-specific problem sets.

Summary

Fallacy: A defect in an argument that arises from a mistake in reasoning or the creation of an illusion that makes a bad argument appear good. There are two kinds of fallacy:

- Formal fallacy: Detectable by analyzing the form of an argument.
- Informal fallacy: Detectable only by analyzing the content of an argument.

Fallacies of Relevance: The premises are not relevant to the conclusion:

- Appeal to force: Arguer threatens the reader/listener.
- Appeal to pity: Arguer elicits pity from the reader/listener.
- Appeal to the people: Arguer incites a mob mentality (direct form) or appeals to our desire for security, love, or respect (indirect form). This fallacy includes appeal to fear, the bandwagon argument, appeal to vanity, appeal to snobbery, and appeal to tradition.
- Argument against the person: Arguer personally attacks an opposing arguer by verbally abusing the opponent (*ad hominem* abusive), presenting the opponent as predisposed to argue as he or she does (*ad hominen* circumstantial), or by presenting the opponent as a hypocrite (*tu quoque*).

  Note: For this fallacy to occur, there must be two arguers.

- Accident: A general rule is applied to a specific case it was not intended to cover.
- Straw man: Arguer distorts an opponent's argument and then attacks the distorted argument.

  Note: For this fallacy to occur, there must be two arguers.

- Missing the point: Arguer draws a conclusion different from the one supported by the premises.

  Note: Do not cite this fallacy if another fallacy fits.

- Red herring: Arguer leads the reader/listener off the track.

Fallacies of Weak Induction: The premises may be relevant to the conclusion, but they supply insufficient support for the conclusion:

- Appeal to unqualified authority: Arguer cites an untrustworthy authority.
- Appeal to ignorance: Premises report that nothing is known or proved about some subject, and then a conclusion is drawn about that subject.
- Hasty generalization: A general conclusion is drawn from an atypical sample.
- False cause: Conclusion depends on a nonexistent or minor causal connection. This fallacy has four forms: *post hoc ergo propter hoc, non causa pro causa,* oversimplified cause, and the gambler's fallacy.
- Slippery slope: Conclusion depends on an unlikely chain reaction of causes.
- Weak analogy: Conclusion depends on a defective analogy (similarity).

Fallacies of Presumption: The premises presume what they purport to prove:

- Begging the question: Arguer creates the illusion that inadequate premises are adequate by leaving out a key premise, restating the conclusion as a premise, or reasoning in a circle.
- Complex question: Multiple questions are concealed in a single question.
- False dichotomy: An "either . . . or . . ." premise presents two unlikely alternatives as if they were the only ones available.
- Suppressed evidence: Arguer ignores important evidence that requires a different conclusion.

Fallacies of Ambiguity: An ambiguous word, phrase, or statement leads to an incorrect conclusion:

- Equivocation: Conclusion depends on a shift in meaning of a word or phrase.
- Amphiboly: Conclusion depends on an incorrect interpretation of an ambiguous statement made by someone other than the arguer.

Fallacies of Illicit Transference: An attribute is incorrectly transferred from the parts of something onto the whole or from the whole onto the parts:

- Composition: An attribute is incorrectly transferred from the parts to the whole.
- Division: An attribute is incorrectly transferred from the whole to the parts.

Fallacies that occur in real-life argumentation may be hard to detect:

- They may not exactly fit the pattern of the named fallacies.
- They may involve two or more fallacies woven together in a single passage.

Three factors underlie the commission of fallacies in real-life argumentation:

- The intent of the arguer (the arguer may intend to mislead someone).
- Mental carelessness combined with unchecked emotions.
- Unexamined presuppositions in the arguer's worldview.

3

Categorical Propositions

3.1   The Components of Categorical Propositions

PREVIEW

Suppose you accidentally sit down with the wrong group in the airport and miss your flight. Or you are on your way to a final exam, but when you open the classroom door you are shocked to find that you don't recognize the group of students. Or you accidentally mix sleeping pills in with your morning vitamins. Groups of people and things are important to everybody. Your favorite NFL team is a group. The people you call your friends constitute a group. Chapter 3 will improve your ability to reason about groups.

 *Your personal learning experience—learn anywhere, anytime.*

In Chapter 1 we saw that a proposition (or statement—here we are ignoring the distinction) is a sentence that is either true or false. A proposition that relates two classes, or categories, is called a **categorical proposition**. The classes in question are denoted respectively by the **subject term** and the **predicate term**, and the proposition asserts that either all or part of the class denoted by the subject term is included in or excluded from the class denoted by the predicate term. Here are some examples of categorical propositions:

categorical proposition:
A proposition that relates two classes (or categories).

> *American Idol* contestants hope for recognition.
> Junk foods do not belong in school cafeterias.
> Many of today's unemployed have given up on finding work.
> Not all romances have a happy ending.
> Oprah Winfrey publishes magazines.

The first statement asserts that the entire class of *American Idol* contestants is included in the class of people who hope for recognition, the second that the entire class of junk foods is excluded from the class of things that belong in school cafeterias, and the third that part of the class of today's unemployed people is included in the class of people who have given up on finding work. The fourth statement asserts that part of the class of romances is excluded from the class of things that have a happy ending, and the last statement asserts that the class that has Oprah Winfrey as its single member is included in the class of people who publish magazines.

Since any categorical proposition asserts that either all or part of the class denoted by the subject term is included in or excluded from the class denoted by the predicate term, it follows that there are exactly four types of categorical propositions: (1) those that assert that the whole subject class is included in the predicate class, (2) those that assert that part of the subject class is included in the predicate class, (3) those that assert that the whole subject class is excluded from the predicate class, and (4) those that assert that part of the subject class is excluded from the predicate class. A categorical proposition that expresses these relations with complete clarity is called a **standard-form categorical proposition**. A categorical proposition is in standard form if and only if it is a substitution instance of one of the following four forms:

standard-form categorical proposition: A proposition that has one of four basic forms.

> All *S* are *P*.
> No *S* are *P*.
> Some *S* are *P*.
> Some *S* are not *P*.

Many categorical propositions, of course, are not in standard form because, among other things, they do not begin with the words "all," "no," or "some." In the final section of this chapter we will develop techniques for translating categorical propositions into standard form, but for now we may restrict our attention to those that are already in standard form.

The words "all," "no," and "some" are called **quantifiers** because they specify how much of the subject class is included in or excluded from the predicate class. The first form asserts that the whole subject class is included in the predicate class, the second that the whole subject class is excluded from the predicate class, and so on. (Incidentally, in formal deductive logic the word "some" always means at least one.) The letters *S* and *P* stand respectively for the subject and predicate terms, and the words "are" and "are not" are called the **copula** because they link (or "couple") the subject term with the predicate term.

Alice Ambrose 1906–2001

Alice Ambrose was born in 1906 in Lexington, Illinois. She was orphaned at age 13, but still managed to attend Millikin University in Decatur and graduate with a major in mathematics and philosophy. After earning a PhD in philosophy from the University of Wisconsin, where she worked on Whitehead and Russell's *Principia Mathematica,* she entered a postdoctoral program at Cambridge University. There she studied under, and became a close disciple of, the famous philosopher Ludwig Wittgenstein. (She received a second PhD from that university in 1938.) In 1937 she accepted a teaching position in philosophy at Smith College, where she remained until her retirement in 1972.

Within a year after arriving at Smith, Ambrose met and married the philosopher Morris Lazerowitz, with whom she coauthored several books and articles. One was a textbook in symbolic logic, commonly called "Ambrose and Lazerowitz" that was used by a generation of young philosophers. Other subjects on which Ambrose did important work include the foundations of mathematics,

finitism in mathematics, logical impossibility, the justification of induction, and Wittgenstein's theory of proof. Ambrose was a particularly lucid writer, and this, combined with her keen insight, won widespread recognition by philosophers and logicians.

From 1975 to 1976 Ambrose served as president of the American Philosophical Association (Eastern Division). Interestingly, in that office she was immediately preceded by John Rawls, and immediately succeeded by Hillary Putnam. Ambrose was also a dedicated supporter of peace and social justice, and she remained active as a speaker and writer until her death in 2001 at the age of 94. Today Smith College sponsors an annual address in her honor.

Consider the following example:

> All members of the American Medical Association are people holding degrees from recognized academic institutions.

This standard-form categorical proposition is analyzed as follows:

quantifier:	all
subject term:	members of the American Medical Association
copula:	are
predicate term:	people holding degrees from recognized academic institutions

In resolving standard-form categorical propositions into their four components, one must keep these components separate. They do not overlap. In this regard, note that "subject term" and "predicate term" do not mean the same thing in logic that "subject" and "predicate" mean in grammar. The *subject* of the example statement includes the quantifier "all," but the *subject term* does not. Similarly, the *predicate* includes the copula "are," but the *predicate term* does not.

Two additional points should be noted about standard-form categorical propositions. The first is that the form "All *S* are not *P*" is *not* a standard form. This form is ambiguous and can be rendered as either "No *S* are *P*" or "Some *S* are not *P*," depending on the content. The second point is that there are exactly three forms of quantifiers and two forms of copulas. Other texts allow the various forms of the verb "to be" (such as "is," "is not," "will," and "will not") to serve as the copula. For the sake of uniformity, this book restricts the copula to "are" and "are not." The last section of this chapter describes techniques for translating these alternate forms into the two accepted ones.

Originated by Aristotle, the theory of categorical propositions has constituted one of the core topics in logic for over 2,000 years. It remains important even today because many of the statements we make in ordinary discourse are either categorical propositions as they stand or are readily translatable into them. Standard-form categorical propositions represent an ideal of clarity in language, and a familiarity with the relationships that prevail among them provides a backdrop of precision for all kinds of linguistic usage. In Chapter 4 we will see how categorical propositions may be combined to produce *categorical syllogisms,* a kind of argumentation that is closely related to the most basic forms of human reasoning.

EXERCISE 3.1

3

In the following categorical propositions identify the quantifier, subject term, copula, and predicate term.

★1. Some executive-pay packages are insults to ordinary workers.

2. No stressful jobs are occupations conducive to a healthy lifestyle.

3. All oil-based paints are products that contribute to photochemical smog.

★4. Some preachers who are intolerant of others' beliefs are not television evangelists.

5. All trials in which a coerced confession is read to the jury are trials in which a guilty verdict can be reversed.

6. Some artificial hearts are mechanisms that are prone to failure.

★7. No sex-education courses that are taught competently are programs that are currently eroding public morals.

8. Some universities that emphasize research are not institutions that neglect undergraduate education.

aplia

Visit Aplia for section-specific problem sets.

3.2 Quality, Quantity, and Distribution

PREVIEW

How one class of things relates to another is often important to keep in mind. For example, if you tell lies, it's important to keep separate the class of people you have lied to from the class of people you have told the truth. And if the class of people you would like to date partly overlaps the class of people your best friend would like to date, ignoring this fact might lead to trouble. The relations between classes form the subject matter of this section of the book.

Quality and quantity are attributes of categorical propositions. In order to see how these attributes pertain, it is useful to rephrase the meaning of categorical propositions in class terminology:

Proposition	Meaning in class notation
All S are P.	Every member of the S class is a member of the P class; that is, the S class is included in the P class.
No S are P.	No member of the S class is a member of the P class; that is, the S class is excluded from the P class.
Some S are P.	At least one member of the S class is a member of of the P class.
Some S are not P.	At least one member of the S class is not a member of of the P class.

The **quality** of a categorical proposition is either affirmative or negative depending on whether it affirms or denies class membership. Accordingly, "All S are P" and "Some S are P" have **affirmative** quality, and "No S are P" and "Some S are not P" have **negative** quality. These are called **affirmative propositions** and **negative propositions**, respectively.

The **quantity** of a categorical proposition is either universal or particular, depending on whether the statement makes a claim about *every* member or just *some* member of the class denoted by the subject term. "All S are P" and "No S are P" each assert something about every member of the S class and thus are **universal propositions**. "Some S are P" and "Some S are not P" assert something about one or more members of the S class and hence are **particular propositions**.

Note that the quantity of a categorical proposition may be determined through mere inspection of the quantifier. "All" and "no" immediately imply universal quantity, while "some" implies particular. But categorical propositions have no "qualifier." In universal propositions the quality is determined by the quantifier, and in particular propositions it is determined by the copula.

Particular propositions mean no more and no less than the meaning assigned to them in class notation. The statement "Some S are P" does *not* imply that some S are not P, and the statement "Some S are not P" does *not* imply that some S are P. It often *happens*, of course, that substitution instances of these statement forms are both true. For example, "Some apples are red" is true, as is "Some apples are not red." But the fact that one is true does not *necessitate* that the other be true. "Some zebras are animals" is true (because at least one zebra is an animal), but "Some zebras are not animals" is false. Similarly, "Some turkeys are not fish" is true, but "Some turkeys are fish" is false. Thus, the fact that one of these statement forms is true does not *logically imply* that the other is true, as these substitution instances clearly prove.

Since the early Middle Ages the four kinds of categorical propositions have commonly been designated by letter names corresponding to the first four vowels of the Roman alphabet: **A, E, I, O**. The universal affirmative is called an **A proposition**, the universal negative an **E proposition**, the particular affirmative an **I proposition**, and the particular negative an **O proposition**. Tradition has it that these letters were derived from the first two vowels in the Latin words *affirmo* ("I affirm") and *nego* ("I deny"), thus:

> **quality** of a categorical proposition: Affirmative or negative.

> **quantity** of a categorical proposition: Universal or particular.

> **A, E, I, O**: The names of the four kinds of categorical propositions.

		n
Universal	A	E
	f	
	f	g
Particular	I	O
	r	
	m	
	o	

The material presented thus far in this section may be summarized as follows:

Proposition	Letter name	Quantity	Quality
All S are P.	A	universal	affirmative
No S are P.	E	universal	negative
Some S are P.	I	particular	affirmative
Some S are not P.	O	particular	negative

distribution: A term in a categorical proposition is *distributed* if the proposition makes an assertion about every member of the class denoted by the term.

Unlike quality and quantity, which are attributes of *propositions*, **distribution** is an attribute of the *terms* (subject and predicate) of propositions. A term is said to be distributed if the proposition makes an assertion about every member of the class denoted by the term; otherwise, it is undistributed. Stated another way, a term is distributed if and only if the statement assigns (or distributes) an attribute to every member of the class denoted by the term. Thus, if a statement asserts something about every member of the *S* class, then *S* is distributed; if it asserts something about every member of the *P* class, then *P* is distributed; otherwise *S* and *P* are undistributed.

Let us imagine that the members of the classes denoted by the subject and predicate terms of a categorical proposition are contained respectively in circles marked with the letters "*S*" and "*P*." The meaning of the statement form "All *S* are *P*" may then be represented by the following diagram:

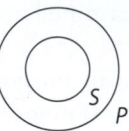

The *S* circle is contained in the *P* circle, which represents the fact that every member of *S* is a member of *P*. (Of course, should *S* and *P* represent terms denoting identical classes, the two circles would overlap exactly.) As the diagram shows, "All *S* are *P*" makes a claim about every member of the *S* class, since the statement says that every member of *S* is in the *P* class. But the statement does not make a claim about every member of the *P* class, since there may be some members of *P* that are outside of *S*. Thus, by the definition of "distributed term" already given, *S* is distributed and *P* is not. In other words, for any universal affirmative (**A**) proposition, the subject term, whatever it may be, is distributed, and the predicate term is undistributed.

Let us now consider the universal negative (**E**) proposition. "No *S* are *P*" states that the *S* and *P* classes are separate, which may be represented as follows:

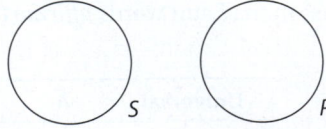

This statement makes a claim about every member of *S* and every member of *P*. It asserts that every member of *S* is separate from every member of *P*, and also that every member of *P* is separate from every member of *S*. Accordingly, by our definition, both the subject and predicate terms of universal negative (**E**) propositions are distributed.

The particular affirmative (**I**) proposition states that at least one member of *S* is a member of *P*. If we represent this one member of *S* that we are certain about by an asterisk, the resulting diagram looks like this:

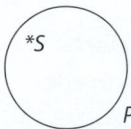

Since the asterisk is inside the *P* class, it represents something that is simultaneously an *S* and a *P*; in other words, it represents a member of the *S* class that is also a member of the *P* class. Thus, the statement "Some *S* are *P*" makes a claim about one member (at least) of *S* and also one member (at least) of *P*, but not about all members of either class. Hence, by the definition of distribution, neither *S* nor *P* is distributed.

The particular negative (**O**) proposition asserts that at least one member of *S* is not a member of *P*. If we once again represent this one member of *S* by an asterisk, the resulting diagram is as follows:

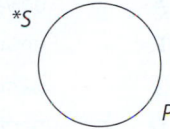

Since the other members of *S* may or may not be outside of *P*, it is clear that the statement "Some *S* are not *P*" does not make a claim about every member of *S*, so *S* is not distributed. But, as may be seen from the diagram, the statement does assert that every member of *P* is separate and distinct from this one member of *S* that is outside the *P* circle. Thus, in the particular negative (**O**) proposition, *P* is distributed and *S* is undistributed.

At this point the notion of distribution may be somewhat vague and elusive. Unfortunately, there is no simple and easy way to make the idea graphically clear. The best that can be done is to repeat some of the things that have already been said. First of all, distribution is an attribute or quality that the subject and predicate terms of a categorical proposition may or may not possess, depending on the kind of proposition. If the proposition in question is an **A** type, then the subject term, whatever it may be, is distributed. If it is an **E** type, then both terms are distributed; if an **I** type, then neither; and if an **O** type, then the predicate term. If a certain term is *distributed* in a proposition, this simply means that the proposition says something about every member of the class that the term denotes. If a term is *undistributed*, the proposition does not say something about every member of the class.

An easy way to remember the rule for distribution is to keep in mind that universal (**A** and **E**) statements distribute their subject terms and negative (**E** and **O**) statements distribute their predicate terms. As an aid to remembering this arrangement, the following mnemonic may be useful: "Unprepared Students Never Pass." Attending to the first letter in these words may help one recall that Universals distribute Subjects, and Negatives distribute Predicates. Another mnemonic that accomplishes the same purpose is "Any Student Earning B's Is Not On Probation." In this mnemonic the first letters may help one recall that **A** statements distribute the Subject, **E** statements distribute Both terms, **I** statements distribute Neither term, and **O** statements distribute the Predicate.

Finally, note that the attribute of distribution, while not particularly important to subsequent developments in this chapter, is essential to the evaluation of syllogisms in the next chapter.

The material of this section may now be summarized as follows:

Proposition	Letter name	Quantity	Quality	Terms distributed
All S are P.	A	universal	affirmative	S
No S are P.	E	universal	negative	S and P
Some S are P.	I	particular	affirmative	none
Some S are not P.	O	particular	negative	P

EXERCISE 3.2

I. For each of the following categorical propositions identify the letter name, quantity, and quality. Then state whether the subject and predicate terms are distributed or undistributed.

★1. No vampire movies are films without blood.

2. All governments that bargain with terrorists are governments that encourage terrorism.

3. Some symphony orchestras are organizations on the brink of bankruptcy.

★4. Some Chinese leaders are not thoroughgoing opponents of capitalist economics.

5. All human contacts with benzene are potential causes of cancer.

6. No labor strikes are events welcomed by management.

★7. Some hospitals are organizations that overcharge the Medicare program.

8. Some affirmative action plans are not programs that result in reverse discrimination.

II. Change the quality but not the quantity of the following statements:

★1. All drunk drivers are threats to others on the highway.

2. No wildlife refuges are locations suitable for condominium developments.

3. Some slumlords are people who eventually wind up in jail.

★4. Some CIA operatives are not champions of human rights.

III. Change the quantity but not the quality of the following statements:

★1. All owners of pit bull terriers are people who can expect expensive lawsuits.

2. No tax proposals that favor the rich are fair proposals.

3. Some grade-school administrators are people who choke the educational process.

★4. Some residents of Manhattan are not people who can afford to live there.

IV. Change both the quality and the quantity of the following statements:

★1. All oil spills are events catastrophic to the environment.

2. No alcoholics are people with a healthy diet.

3. Some Mexican vacations are episodes that end with gastrointestinal distress.

★4. Some corporate lawyers are not people with a social conscience.

3

3.3 Venn Diagrams and the Modern Square of Opposition

PREVIEW

Think of a football game. At kickoff time, all the members of one team are at one end of the field, and all the members of the other team are at the other end. This idea of assigning distinct spatial regions to two classes (the two teams) is the basic idea behind Venn diagrams for categorical propositions. Two circles identify the two regions, and you are supposed to imagine all the members of one class as occupying one circle and all the members of the other class as occupying the other circle.

Existential Import

The primary goal of our inquiry into categorical propositions is to disclose the role that such propositions play in the formation of arguments. However, it turns out that we can interpret universal (**A** and **E**) propositions in two different ways, and according to one of these interpretations an argument might be valid, while according to the other it might be invalid. Thus, before turning to the evaluation of arguments, we must explore the two possible interpretations of universal propositions. Our investigation will focus on what is called **existential import**. To illustrate this concept, consider the following pair of propositions:

> All Tom Cruise's movies are hits.
>
> All unicorns are one-horned animals.

existential import: A proposition has *existential import* if it implies that the things talked about actually exist.

The first proposition implies that Tom Cruise has indeed made some movies. In other words, the statement has existential import. It implies that one or more things denoted by the subject term actually exist. On the other hand, no such implication is made by the statement about unicorns. The statement might be said to be true, because unicorns, by definition, have a single horn. But the statement does not imply that unicorns actually exist.

Thus, the question arises: Should universal propositions be interpreted as implying that the things talked about actually exist? Or should they be interpreted as implying no such thing? In response to this question, logicians have taken two different approaches. Aristotle held that universal propositions about existing things have existential import. In other words, such statements imply the existence of the things talked about:

Aristotelian standpoint

All pheasants are birds.	Implies the existence of pheasants.
No pine trees are maples.	Implies the existence of pine trees.
All satyrs are vile creatures.	Does not imply the existence of satyrs.

The first two statements have existential import because their subject terms denote actually existing things. The third statement has no existential import, because satyrs do not exist.

On the other hand, according to the theory developed by the nineteenth-century logician George Boole (as perfected by John Venn), no universal propositions have existential import. Such statements never imply the existence of the things talked about:

Boolean standpoint

All trucks are vehicles.	Does not imply the existence of trucks.
No roses are daisies.	Does not imply the existence of roses.
All werewolves are monsters.	Does not imply the existence of werewolves.

We might summarize these results by saying that the Aristotelian standpoint is "open" (or receptive) to existence.* When things exist, the Aristotelian standpoint recognizes their existence, and universal statements about those things have existential import. In other words, existence counts for something. On the other hand, the Boolean standpoint is "closed" (unreceptive) to existence. When things exist, the Boolean standpoint does not recognize their existence, and universal statements about those things have no existential import. Conversely, when things do not exist, neither the Aristotelian nor the Boolean standpoint recognizes any existence. Under these circumstances, the Aristotelian standpoint merges with the Boolean.†

The Aristotelian standpoint differs from the Boolean standpoint only with regard to universal (**A** and **E**) propositions. The two standpoints are identical with regard to particular (**I** and **O**) propositions. Both the Aristotelian and the Boolean standpoints recognize that particular propositions make a positive assertion about existence. For

---

*In general, we interpret this openness to existence as extending to the subject class, the predicate class, and the complements of these classes. However, in the present account we confine our attention to the subject class. The concept of class complement is discussed in Section 3.4 (Obversion).

†For a more complete account of the relation between the Aristotelian and the Boolean standpoints, see "Existential Import: Historical Background," by Patrick J. Hurley. This paper is available on MindTap and on the Instructor Companion Site.

George Boole 1815–1864

The English mathematician and philosopher George Boole is known primarily for the development of Boolean algebra—a type of logic based on the three fundamental operations of *and, or,* and *not.* The American philosopher and logician Charles Sanders Peirce was captivated by Boole's ideas, and he saw a possible application in the area of electrical circuitry. Fifty years later, the American mathematician and engineer Claude Shannon put theory to practice by showing how Boole's system could be used in designing telephone routing switches. This innovation subsequently led to the development of electronic digital computers.

Boole's early years were marked by struggle. His father, John, was a cobbler, and his mother, Mary Ann, a lady's maid. They could afford only the most basic education for their son, which John supplemented by teaching mathematics and science to young George and by hiring a Latin tutor for him. Boole taught himself Greek, French, and German. His father, a leading member of the Mechanics Institute, was intrigued by the application of mathematics in making instruments, and he passed this interest to his son. Though poverty limited the resources available to him, Boole used mathematics journals borrowed from the institute to further his mathematics education on his own.

When George was only sixteen, his father's shoemaking business folded, and it fell to him to support the family by working as an assistant teacher. When he was twenty-two, he took over the operation of a boarding school after its former director had died, and his whole family assisted him in running it. Throughout this period, Boole continued his study of mathematics, and at age twenty-nine he published a paper on the use of algebraic methods in solving differential equations. In recognition of this work he

received the Royal Society Medal, which brought him considerable fame in the mathematical world.

Three years later Boole published *The Mathematical Analysis of Logic*, which brought to fruition some of Leibniz's earlier speculations on the relationship between mathematics and logic. It also showed how the symbolism of mathematics could be imported into logic. This work won him a professorship at Queens College, in Cork, Ireland, where he remained for the rest of his life. Seven years later he published a much larger and more mature work on the same subject, *An Investigation of the Laws of Thought, on Which Are Founded the Mathematical Theories of Logic and Probabilities*. This later work presented a complete system of symbolic reasoning.

Boole married Mary Everest (the niece of Sir George Everest, after whom Mt. Everest is named). He met her when she came to visit her famous uncle in Cork, and the relationship developed through his giving her lessons on differential equations. The couple had five daughters, but when Boole was only forty-nine his life was cut short from what was probably pneumonia. Boole had walked two miles in the pouring rain to lecture at Queens, and he delivered the lecture in wet clothing. After he developed a high fever and became desperately ill, his wife, thinking that a good cure always mirrors the cause, poured cold water on him as he lay in bed. He died shortly thereafter.

example, from both standpoints, the statement "Some cats are animals" asserts that at least one cat exists that is an animal. Also, from both standpoints, "Some fish are not mammals" asserts that at least one fish exists that is not a mammal. Thus, from both standpoints, the word "some" implies existence.*

Adopting either the Aristotelian or the Boolean standpoint amounts to accepting a set of ground rules for interpreting the meaning of universal propositions. Either

---

*In ordinary language, the word "some" occasionally implies something less than actual existence. For example, the statement "Some unicorns are tenderhearted" does not seem to suggest that unicorns actually exist, but merely that among the group of imaginary things called "unicorns," there is a subclass of tenderhearted ones. In the vast majority of cases, however, "some" in ordinary language implies existence. The logical "some" conforms to these latter uses.

standpoint can be adopted for any categorical proposition or any argument composed of categorical propositions. Taking the Aristotelian standpoint amounts to recognizing that universal statements about existing things convey evidence about existence. Conversely, for a statement to convey such evidence, the Aristotelian standpoint must be taken and the subject of the statement must denote actually existing things. Taking the Boolean standpoint, on the other hand, amounts to ignoring any evidence about existence that universal statements might convey.

Because the Boolean standpoint is closed to existence, it is simpler than the Aristotelian standpoint, which recognizes existential implications. For this reason, we will direct our attention first to arguments considered from the Boolean standpoint. Later, in Section 3.5, we will extend our treatment to the Aristotelian standpoint.

Venn Diagrams

From the Boolean standpoint, the four kinds of categorical propositions have the following meaning. Notice that the first two (universal) propositions imply nothing about the existence of the things denoted by S:

>All S are P. = No members of S are outside P.
>No S are P. = No members of S are inside P.
>Some S are P. = At least one S exists that is a P.
>Some S are not P. = At least one S exists that is not a P.

Adopting this interpretation of categorical propositions, the nineteenth-century logician John Venn developed a system of diagrams to represent the information they express. These diagrams have come to be known as **Venn diagrams**.

Venn diagram: An arrangement of overlapping circles in which each circle represents the class denoted by a term in a categorical proposition.

A Venn diagram is an arrangement of overlapping circles in which each circle represents the class denoted by a term in a categorical proposition. Because every categorical proposition has exactly two terms, the Venn diagram for a single categorical proposition consists of two overlapping circles. Each circle is labeled so that it represents one of the terms in the proposition. Unless otherwise required, we adopt the convention that the left-hand circle represents the subject term, and the right-hand circle the predicate term. Such a diagram looks like this:

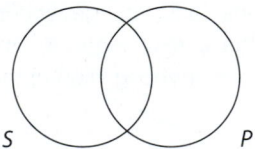

The members of the class denoted by each term should be thought of as situated inside the corresponding circle. Thus, the members of the S class (if any such members exist) are situated inside the S circle, and the members of the P class (if any such members exist) are situated inside the P circle. If any members are situated inside the area where the two circles overlap, then such members belong to both the S class and the P class. Finally, if any members are situated outside both circles, they are members of neither S nor P.

Suppose, for example, that the S class is the class of Americans and the P class is the class of farmers. Then, if we use numerals to identify the four possible areas, the diagram looks like this:

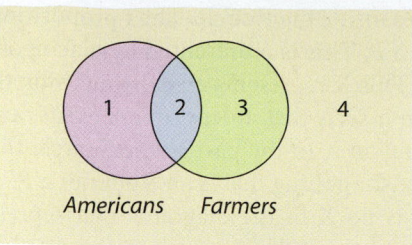

Anything in the area marked "1" is an American but not a farmer, anything in the area marked "2" is both an American and a farmer, and anything in the area marked "3" is a farmer but not an American. The area marked "4" is the area outside both circles; thus, anything in this area is neither a farmer nor an American.

We can now use Venn diagrams to represent the information expressed by the four kinds of categorical proposition. To do this we make a certain kind of mark in a diagram. Two kinds of marks are used: shading an area and placing an X in an area. Shading an area means that the shaded area is empty,* and placing an X in an area means that at least one thing exists in that area. The X may be thought of as representing that one thing. If no mark appears in an area, this means that nothing is known about that area; it may contain members or it may be empty. Shading is always used to represent the content of universal (**A** and **E**) propositions, and placing an X in an area is always used to represent the content of particular (**I** and **O**) propositions. The content of the four kinds of categorical propositions is represented as follows:

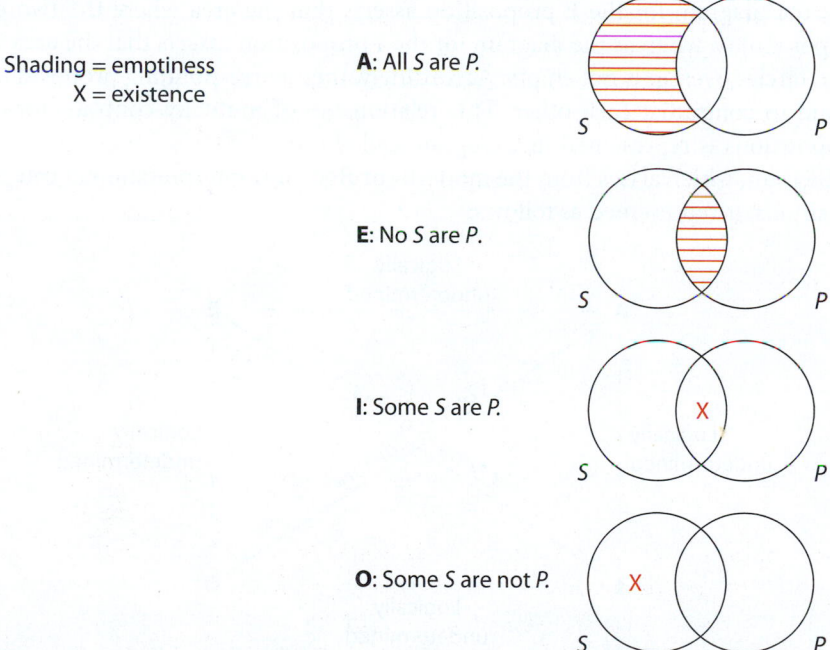

Shading = emptiness
X = existence

A: All S are P.

E: No S are P.

I: Some S are P.

O: Some S are not P.

Recall that the **A** proposition asserts that no members of S are outside P. This is represented by shading the part of the S circle that lies outside the P circle. The **E** proposition asserts that no members of S are inside P. This is represented by shading the part of

*In many mathematics texts, shading an area of a Venn diagram indicates that the area is not empty. The significance of shading in logic is exactly the opposite.

the *S* circle that lies inside the *P* circle. The **I** proposition asserts that at least one *S* exists and that *S* is also a *P*. This is represented by placing an X in the area where the *S* and *P* circles overlap. This X represents an existing thing that is both an *S* and a *P*. Finally, the **O** proposition asserts that at least one *S* exists, and that *S* is not a *P*. This is represented by placing an X in the part of the *S* circle that lies outside the *P* circle. This X represents an existing thing that is an *S* but not a *P*.

Because there is no X in the diagrams that represent the universal propositions, these diagrams say nothing about existence. For example, the diagram for the **A** proposition merely asserts that nothing exists in the part of the *S* circle that lies outside the *P* circle. The area where the two circles overlap and the part of the *P* circle that lies outside the *S* circle contain no marks at all. This means that something might exist in these areas, or they might be completely empty. Similarly, in the diagram for the **E** proposition, no marks appear in the left-hand part of the *S* circle and the right-hand part of the *P* circle. This means that these two areas might contain something or, on the other hand, they might not.

The Modern Square of Opposition

Let us compare the diagram for the **A** proposition with the diagram for the **O** proposition. The diagram for the **A** proposition asserts that the left-hand part of the *S* circle is empty, whereas the diagram for the **O** proposition asserts that this same area is not empty. These two diagrams make assertions that are the exact opposite of each other. As a result, their corresponding statements are said to contradict each other. Analogously, the diagram for the **E** proposition asserts that the area where the two circles overlap is empty, whereas the diagram for the **I** proposition asserts that the area where the two circles overlap is not empty. Accordingly, their corresponding propositions are also said to contradict each other. This relationship of mutually contradictory pairs of propositions is represented in a diagram called the **modern square of opposition**. This diagram, which arises from the modern (or Boolean) interpretation of categorical propositions, is represented as follows:

modern square of opposition: A diagram that represents mutually contradictory pairs of propositions.

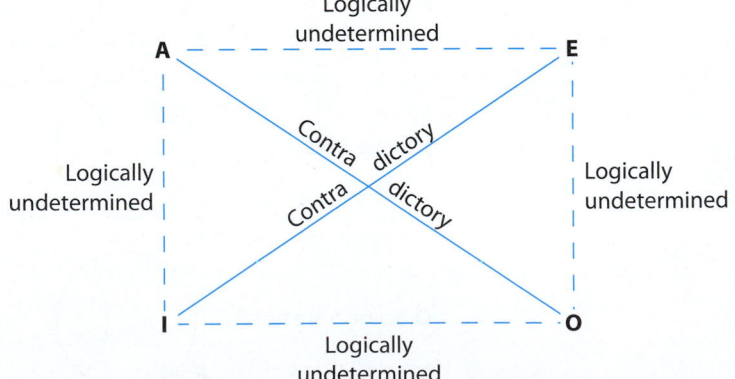

If two propositions are related by the **contradictory relation**, they necessarily have opposite truth value. Thus, if a certain **A** proposition is given as true, the corresponding **O** proposition must be false. Similarly, if a certain **I** proposition is given as false, the corresponding **E** proposition must be true. But no other inferences are possible. In particular, given the truth value of an **A** or **O** proposition, nothing can be determined about the truth value of the corresponding **E** or **I** propositions. These propositions are said to have **logically undetermined truth value**. Like all propositions, they do have a truth value, but logic alone cannot determine what it is. Similarly, given the truth value of an **E** or **I** proposition, nothing can be determined about the truth value of the corresponding **A** or **O** propositions. They, too, are said to have logically undetermined truth value.

Testing Immediate Inferences

Since the modern square of opposition provides logically necessary results, we can use it to test certain arguments for validity. We begin by assuming the premise is true, and we enter the pertinent truth value in the square. We then use the square to compute the truth value of the conclusion. If the square indicates that the conclusion is true, the argument is valid; if not, the argument is invalid. Here is an example:

> Some trade spies are not masters at bribery.
> Therefore, it is false that all trade spies are masters at bribery.

Arguments of this sort are called immediate inferences because they have only one premise. Instead of reasoning from one premise to the next, and then to the conclusion, we proceed immediately from the single premise to the conclusion. To test this argument for validity, we begin by assuming that the premise, which is an **O** proposition, is true, and we enter this truth value in the square of opposition. We then use the square to compute the truth value of the corresponding **A** proposition. By the contradictory relation, the **A** proposition is false. Since the conclusion claims that the **A** proposition is false, the conclusion is true, and therefore the argument is valid. Arguments that are valid from the Boolean standpoint are said to be unconditionally valid because they are valid regardless of whether their terms refer to existing things.

Note that the conclusion of this argument has the form "It is false that all *S* are *P*." Technically, statements of this type are not standard-form categorical propositions because, among other things, they do not begin with a quantifier. To remedy this difficulty we adopt the convention that statements having this form are equivalent to "'All *S* are *P*' is false." Analogous remarks apply to the negations of the **E**, **I**, and **O** statements.

Here is another example:

> It is false that all meteor showers are common spectacles.
> Therefore, no meteor showers are common spectacles.

We begin by assuming that the premise is true. Since the premise claims that an **A** proposition is false, we enter "false" into the square of opposition. We then use the square to compute the truth value of the corresponding **E** proposition. Since there is no relation that links the **A** and **E** propositions, the **E** proposition has undetermined truth value. Thus, the conclusion of the argument has undetermined truth value, and the argument is invalid.

We conclude with a special kind of inference:

> All nurses are health-care professionals.
> Therefore, some nurses are health-care professionals.

The premise is an **A** proposition and the conclusion is an **I** proposition. Since the relation between the **A** and the **I** on the modern square is logically undetermined,

immediate inference:
An argument having only one premise.

unconditionally valid:
Valid regardless of whether an argument's terms refer to actually existing things.

3

the inference is invalid. However, if we were to assume that the premise had existential import, the premise would imply the existence of nurses, and this would imply the truth of the conclusion. So, the only thing that makes this inference invalid is the fact that the Boolean standpoint does not interpret universal statements as having existential import. Inferences of this sort are said to commit the *existential fallacy*.

From the Boolean standpoint, the existential fallacy is a formal fallacy that occurs whenever an argument is invalid merely because the premise or premises lack existential import. Such arguments always have a universal premise or premises and a particular conclusion. The fallacy consists in attempting to derive a conclusion having existential import from a premise that lacks it.

Any inference that proceeds from an **A** proposition (assumed to be true) to an **I** proposition, or from an **E** proposition (assumed to be true) to an **O** proposition commits the existential fallacy from the Boolean standpoint. Furthermore, these are the only inferences that commit the existential fallacy. However, these rules require further explanation.

A statement asserting that any categorical proposition is false is logically equivalent to a statement asserting that the contradictory of that proposition is true. Two statements are said to be logically equivalent when they necessarily have the same truth value. Accordingly, consider the following inference form:

> It is false that some *A* are *B*.
> Therefore, some *A* are not *B*.

The premise is logically equivalent to "No *A* are *B*." Hence, this inference form is logically equivalent to:

> No *A* are *B*.
> Therefore, some *A* are not *B*.

This inference form proceeds from an **E** proposition to an **O** proposition. As a result, it is invalid and commits the existential fallacy.

There are exactly eight inference forms that commit the existential fallacy. Four of them are as follows. (The other four are to be found in Exercise III at the end of this section.)

Existential fallacy

> All *A* are *B*.
> Therefore, some *A* are *B*.
>
> It is false that some *A* are not *B*.
> Therefore, it is false that no *A* are *B*.
>
> No *A* are *B*.
> Therefore, it is false that all *A* are *B*.
>
> It is false that some *A* are *B*.
> Therefore, some *A* are not *B*.

After the propositions beginning with "It is false that . . ." are replaced with their true contradictories, you will see that each inference proceeds from either an **A** proposition to an **I** proposition or from an **E** proposition to an **O** proposition.

---

existential fallacy: A formal fallacy that occurs whenever an argument is invalid merely because the premises lack existential import.

logically equivalent statements: Statements that necessarily have the same truth value.

3

I. Draw Venn diagrams for the following propositions.

★1.　No life decisions are happenings based solely on logic.

2.　All electric motors are machines that depend on magnetism.

3.　Some political campaigns are mere attempts to discredit opponents.

★4.　Some rock-music lovers are not fans of Madonna.

5.　All redistricting plans are sources of controversy.

6.　No tax audits are pleasant experiences for cheaters.

★7.　Some housing developments are complexes that exclude children.

8.　Some cruise ships are not steam-driven vessels.

II. Use the modern square of opposition to determine whether the following immediate inferences are valid or invalid from the Boolean standpoint.

★1.　No sculptures by Rodin are boring creations.
　　 Therefore, all sculptures by Rodin are boring creations.

2.　It is false that some lunar craters are volcanic formations.
　　 Therefore, no lunar craters are volcanic formations.

3.　All trial lawyers are people with stressful jobs.
　　 Therefore, some trial lawyers are people with stressful jobs.

★4.　All dry martinis are dangerous concoctions.
　　 Therefore, it is false that some dry martinis are not dangerous concoctions.

5.　It is false that no jazz musicians are natives of New Orleans.
　　 Therefore, some jazz musicians are not natives of New Orleans.

6.　Some country doctors are altruistic healers.
　　 Therefore, some country doctors are not altruistic healers.

★7.　No fertility drugs are solutions to every problem.
　　 Therefore, it is false that all fertility drugs are solutions to every problem.

8.　It is false that no credit cards are things that contain holograms.
　　 Therefore, some credit cards are things that contain holograms.

9.　It is false that some stunt pilots are not colorful daredevils.
　　 Therefore, it is false that some stunt pilots are colorful daredevils.

★10.　No vampires are avid connoisseurs of garlic bread.
　　 Therefore, it is false that some vampires are avid connoisseurs of garlic bread.

11.　No talk radio shows are accurate sources of information.
　　 Therefore, some talk radio shows are not accurate sources of information.

12.　Some stellar constellations are spiral-shaped objects.
　　 Therefore, no stellar constellations are spiral-shaped objects.

★13. It is false that some soap bubbles are not occasions of glee.
   Therefore, some soap bubbles are occasions of glee.

14. It is false that all weddings are light-hearted celebrations.
   Therefore, some weddings are not light-hearted celebrations.

15. It is false that some chocolate soufflés are desserts containing olives.
   Therefore, it is false that all chocolate soufflés are desserts containing olives.

III. This section of Chapter 3 identified four forms of the existential fallacy. Use the modern square of opposition to identify the other four. In doing so, keep in mind that all forms of this fallacy have a universal premise and a particular conclusion, that "It is false that some *A* are *B*" and "It is false that some *A* are not *B*" are universal propositions, and "It is false that all *A* are *B*" and "It is false that no *A* are *B*" are particular.

3.4 Conversion, Obversion, and Contraposition

PREVIEW

After watching a vampire flick on TV, you discuss the movie with some friends. One insists that every vampire movie is a horror film, while another says that every movie that is not a horror film is also not about vampires. A third says that these two statements are the same, while a fourth says they are not. How would you settle this disagreement? Could you prove that what you say is correct? This section of the book is all about relations between statements such as these.

For a preliminary glimpse into the content of this section, consider the statement "No dogs are cats." This statement claims that the class of dogs is separated from the class of cats. But the statement "No cats are dogs" claims the same thing. Thus, the two statements have the same meaning and the same truth value. For another example, consider the statement "Some dogs are not retrievers." This statement claims there is at least one dog outside the class of retrievers. But the statement "Some dogs are non-retrievers" claims the same thing, so again, the two statements have the same meaning and the same truth value.

Conversion, obversion, and contraposition are operations that can be performed on a categorical proposition, resulting in a new statement that may or may not have the same meaning and truth value as the original statement. Venn diagrams are used to determine how the two statements relate to each other.

Conversion

conversion: Switching the subject term with the predicate term.

The simplest of the three operations is **conversion**, and it consists of switching the subject term with the predicate term. For example, if the statement "No foxes are hedgehogs" is converted, the resulting statement is "No hedgehogs are foxes." This new statement is called the *converse* of the given statement. To see how the four types of categorical propositions relate to their converse, compare the following sets of Venn diagrams:

Given statement form		Converse	

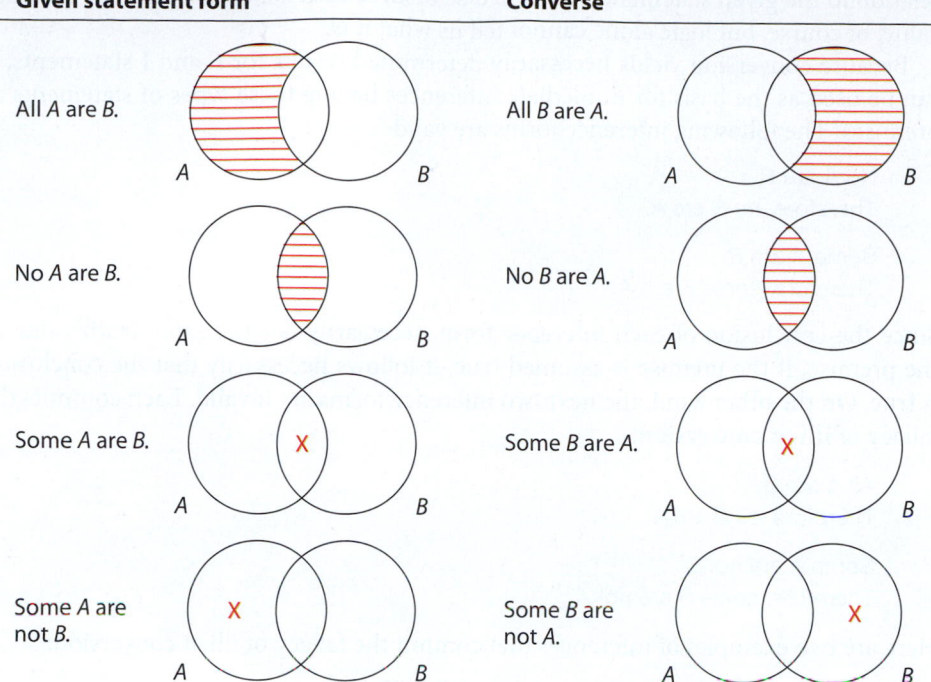

All *A* are *B*.

A   *B*

All *B* are *A*.

A   *B*

No *A* are *B*.

A   *B*

No *B* are *A*.

A   *B*

Some *A* are *B*.

X

A   *B*

Some *B* are *A*.

X

A   *B*

Some *A* are
not *B*.

X

A   *B*

Some *B* are
not *A*.

X

A   *B*

If we examine the diagram for the **E** statement, we see that it is identical to that of its converse. Also, the diagram for the **I** statement is identical to that of its converse. This means that the **E** statement and its converse are logically equivalent, and the **I** statement and its converse are logically equivalent. Recall from Section 3.3 that two statements are said to be logically equivalent when they necessarily have the same truth value. Thus, converting an **E** or **I** statement gives a new statement that always has the same truth value (and the same meaning) as the given statement. These equivalences are strictly proved by the Venn diagrams for the **E** and **I** statements.

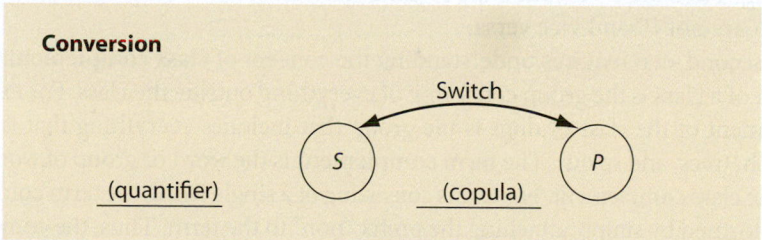

Conversion

Switch

(quantifier)   S   (copula)   P

On the other hand, the diagram for the **A** statement is clearly not identical to the diagram for its converse, and the diagram for the **O** statement is not identical to the diagram for its converse. Also, these pairs of diagrams are not the exact opposite of each other, as is the case with contradictory statements. This means that an **A** statement and its converse are logically unrelated as to truth value, and an **O** statement and its converse are logically unrelated as to truth value. In other words, converting an **A** or **O** statement gives a new statement whose truth value is logically undetermined in relation to the given statement. The converse of an **A** or **O** statement does have a truth value, of course, but logic alone cannot tell us what it is.

Because conversion yields necessarily determined results for **E** and **I** statements, it can be used as the basis for immediate inferences having these types of statements as premises. The following inference forms are valid:

No *A* are *B*.
Therefore, no *B* are *A*.

Some *A* are *B*.
Therefore, some *B* are *A*.

Since the conclusion of each inference form necessarily has the same truth value as the premise, if the premise is assumed true, it follows necessarily that the conclusion is true. On the other hand, the next two inference forms are invalid. Each commits the fallacy of **illicit conversion**:

All *A* are *B*.
Therefore, all *B* are *A*.

Some *A* are not *B*.
Therefore, some *B* are not *A*.

Here are two examples of inferences that commit the fallacy of illicit conversion:

All cats are animals.   (True)
Therefore, all animals are cats.   (False)

Some animals are not dogs.   (True)
Therefore, some dogs are not animals.   (False)

Obversion

obversion: Changing the quality and replacing the predicate with its term complement.

More complicated than conversion, obversion requires two steps: (1) changing the quality (without changing the quantity), and (2) replacing the predicate with its term complement. The first part of this operation was treated in Exercise 3.2. It consists in changing "No *S* are *P*" to "All *S* are *P*" and vice versa, and changing "Some *S* are *P*" to "Some *S* are not *P*" and vice versa.

The second step requires understanding the concept of **class complement**. The complement of a class is the group consisting of everything outside the class. For example, the complement of the class of dogs is the group that includes everything that is not a dog (cats, fish, trees, and so on). The **term complement** is the word or group of words that denotes the class complement. For terms consisting of a single word, the term complement is usually formed by simply attaching the prefix "non" to the term. Thus, the complement of the term "dog" is "non-dog," the complement of the term "book" is "non-book," and so on.

The relationship between a term and its complement can be illustrated by a Venn diagram. For example, if a single circle is allowed to represent the class of dogs, then everything outside the circle represents the class of non-dogs:

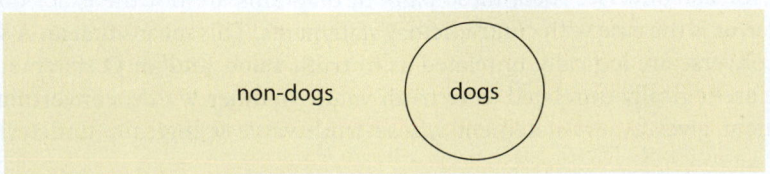

We now have everything we need to form the *obverse* of categorical propositions. First we change the quality (without changing the quantity), and then we replace the predicate term with its term complement. For example, if we are given the statement "All horses are animals," then the obverse is "No horses are non-animals"; and if we are given the statement "Some trees are maples," then the obverse is "Some trees are not non-maples." To see how the four types of categorical propositions relate to their obverse, compare the following sets of Venn diagrams:

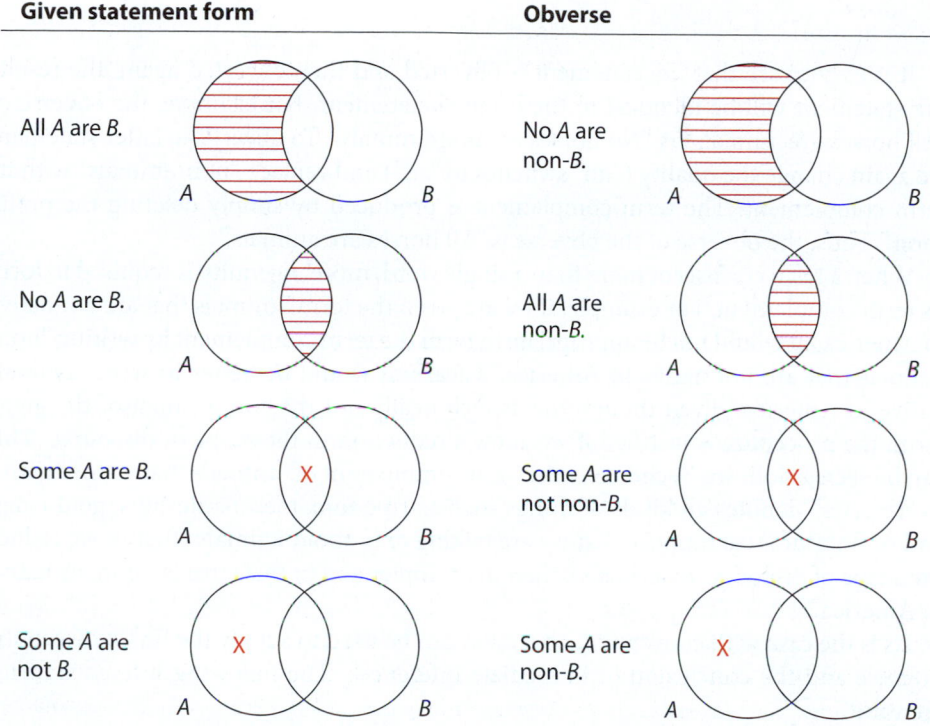

Given statement form	Obverse
All *A* are *B*.	No *A* are non-*B*.
No *A* are *B*.	All *A* are non-*B*.
Some *A* are *B*.	Some *A* are not non-*B*.
Some *A* are not *B*.	Some *A* are non-*B*.

To see how the obverse diagrams are drawn, keep in mind that "non-*B*" designates the area outside the *B* circle. Thus, "No *A* are non-*B*" asserts that the area where *A* overlaps non-*B* is empty. This is represented by shading the left-hand part of the *A* circle. "All *A* are non-*B*" asserts that all members of *A* are outside *B*. This means that no members of *A* are inside *B*, so the area where *A* overlaps *B* is shaded. "Some *A* are not non-*B*" asserts that at least one member of *A* is not outside *B*. This means that at least one member of *A* is inside *B*, so an X is placed in the area where *A* and *B* overlap. Finally, "Some *A* are non-*B*" asserts that at least one member of *A* is outside *B*, so an X is placed in the left-hand part of the *A* circle.

If we examine these pairs of diagrams, we see that the diagram for each given statement form is identical to the diagram for its obverse. This means that each of the four types of categorical proposition is logically equivalent to (and has the same meaning as) its obverse. Thus, if we obvert an **A** statement that happens to be true, the resulting statement will be true; if we obvert an **O** statement that happens to be false, the resulting statement will be false, and so on.

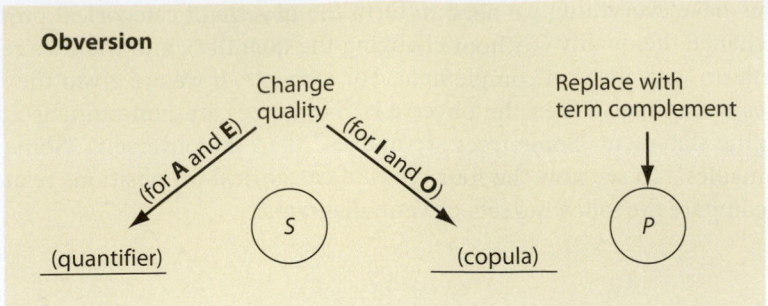

Obversion

Change quality

(for **A** and **E**) (for **I** and **O**)

Replace with term complement

S

(quantifier) (copula)

P

It is easy to see that if a statement is obverted and then obverted again, the resulting statement will be identical to the original statement. For example, the obverse of "All horses are animals" is "No horses are non-animals." To obvert the latter statement we again change the quality ("no" switches to "all") and replace "non-animals" with its term complement. The term complement is produced by simply deleting the prefix "non." Thus, the obverse of the obverse is "All horses are animals."

When a term consists of more than a single word, more ingenuity is required to form its term complement. For example, if we are given the term "animals that are not native to America," it would not be appropriate to form the term complement by writing "non-animals that are not native to America." Clearly it would be better to write "animals native to America." Even though this is technically not the complement of the given term, the procedure is justified if we allow a reduction in the scope of discourse. This can be seen as follows. Technically the term complement of "animals that are not native to America" denotes all kinds of things such as ripe tomatoes, battleships, gold rings, and so on. But if we suppose that we are talking *only* about animals (that is, we reduce the scope of discourse to animals), then the complement of this term is "animals native to America."

As is the case with conversion, obversion can be used to supply the link between the premise and the conclusion of immediate inferences. The following inference forms are valid:

All *A* are *B*.
Therefore, no *A* are non-*B*.

Some *A* are *B*.
Therefore, some *A* are not non-*B*.

No *A* are *B*.
Therefore, all *A* are non-*B*.

Some *A* are not *B*.
Therefore, some *A* are non-*B*.

Because the conclusion of each inference form necessarily has the same truth value as its premise, if the premise is assumed true, it follows necessarily that the conclusion is true.

Contraposition

contraposition: Switching the subject and predicate terms and replacing them with their term complements.

Like obversion, **contraposition** requires two steps: (1) switching the subject and predicate terms and (2) replacing the subject and predicate terms with their term complements. For example, if the statement "All goats are animals" is contraposed, the resulting statement is "All non-animals are non-goats." This new statement is called the contrapositive of the given statement. To see how all four types of categorical propositions relate to their contrapositive, compare the following sets of diagrams:

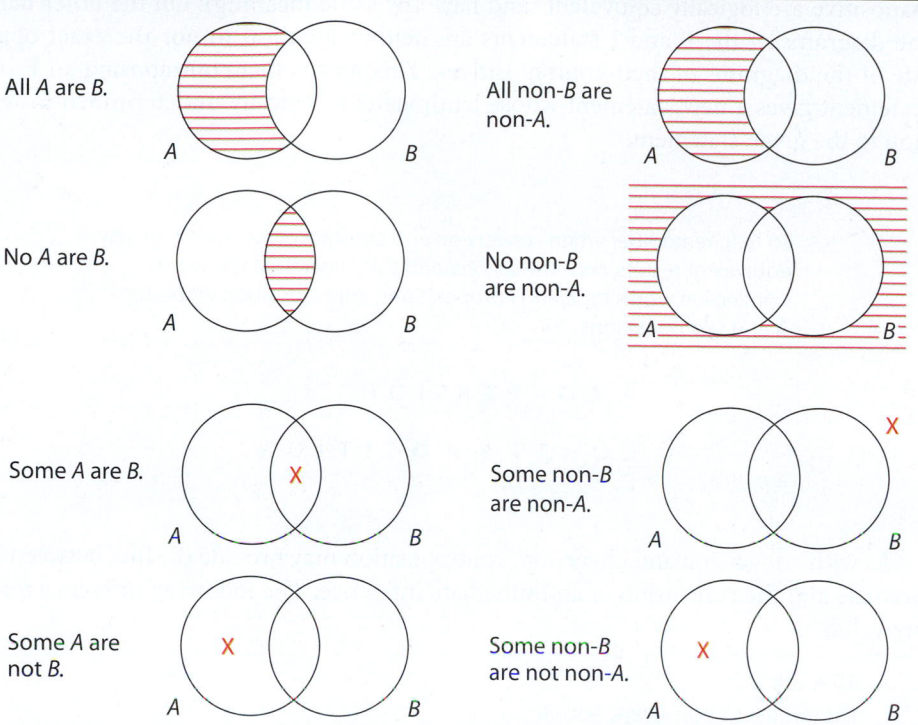

Given statement form	Contrapositive
All *A* are *B*.	All non-*B* are non-*A*.
No *A* are *B*.	No non-*B* are non-*A*.
Some *A* are *B*.	Some non-*B* are non-*A*.
Some *A* are not *B*.	Some non-*B* are not non-*A*.

To see how the first diagram on the right is drawn, remember that "non-*A*" designates the area outside *A*. Thus, "All non-*B* are non-*A*" asserts that all members of non-*B* are outside *A*. This means that no members of non-*B* are inside *A*. Thus, we shade the area where non-*B* overlaps *A*. "No non-*B* are non-*A*" asserts that the area where non-*B* overlaps non-*A* is empty. Since non-*B* is the area outside the *B* circle and non-*A* is the area outside the *A* circle, the place where these two areas overlap is the area outside both circles. Thus, we shade this area. "Some non-*B* are non-*A*" asserts that something exists in the area where non-*B* overlaps non-*A*. Again, this is the area outside both circles, so we place an X in this area. Finally, "Some non-*B* are not non-*A*" asserts that at least one member of non-*B* is outside non-*A*. This means that at least one member of non-*B* is inside *A*, so we place an X in the area where non-*B* overlaps *A*.

Now, inspection of the diagrams for the **A** and **O** statements reveals that they are identical to the diagrams of their contrapositive. Thus, the **A** statement and its contrapositive

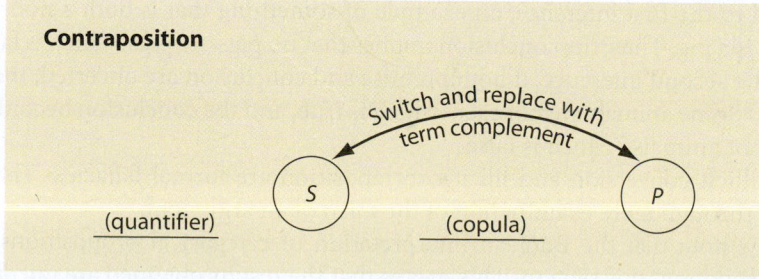

Contraposition

Switch and replace with term complement

(quantifier)   S   (copula)   P

are logically equivalent (and have the same meaning), and the **O** statement and its contrapositive are logically equivalent (and have the same meaning). On the other hand, the diagrams of the **E** and **I** statements are neither identical to nor the exact opposite of the diagrams of their contrapositives. This means that contraposing an **E** or **I** statement gives a new statement whose truth value is logically undetermined in relation to the given statement.

Logically equivalent results:
Conversion: **E** and **I**.
Obversion: All.
Contraposition: **A** and **O**.

To help remember when conversion and contraposition yield logically equivalent results, note the second and third vowels in the words. Conversion works for **E** and **I** propositions, contraposition works for **A** and **O** propositions.

CONVERSION

CONTRAPOSITION

As with conversion and obversion, contraposition may provide the link between the premise and the conclusion of an immediate inference. The following inference forms are valid:

All *A* are *B*.
Therefore, all non-*B* are non-*A*.

Some *A* are not *B*.
Therefore, some non-*B* are not non-*A*.

On the other hand, the following inference forms are invalid. Each commits the fallacy of **illicit contraposition**:

Some *A* are *B*.
Therefore, some non-*B* are non-*A*.

No *A* are *B*.
Therefore, no non-*B* are non-*A*.

Here are two examples of inferences that commit the fallacy of illicit contraposition:

No dogs are cats.   (True)
Therefore, no non-cats are non-dogs.   (False)

Some animals are non-cats.   (True)
Therefore, some cats are non-animals.   (False)

In regard to the first inference, an example of something that is both a non-cat and a non-dog is a pig. Thus, the conclusion implies that no pigs are pigs, which is false. In regard to the second inference, if both premise and conclusion are obverted, the premise becomes "Some animals are not cats," which is true, and the conclusion becomes "Some cats are not animals," which is false.

Both illicit conversion and illicit contraposition are formal fallacies: They can be detected through mere examination of the form of an argument.

Finally, note that the Boolean interpretation of categorical propositions has prevailed throughout this section. This means that the results obtained are unconditional, and they hold true regardless of whether the terms in the propositions denote actually existing things. Thus, they hold for propositions about unicorns and leprechauns just as they do for propositions about dogs and animals. These results are summarized in the following table.

CONVERSION: SWITCH SUBJECT AND PREDICATE TERMS

Given Statement	Converse	Truth Value
E: No A are B.	No B are A.	Same truth value as given statement
I: Some A are B.	Some B are A.	
A: All A are B.	All B are A.	Undetermined truth value
O: Some A are not B.	Some B are not A.	

OBVERSION: CHANGE QUALITY; REPLACE PREDICATE WITH TERM COMPLEMENT

Given Statement	Obverse	Truth Value
A: All A are B.	No A are non-B.	Same truth value as given statement
E: No A are B.	All A are non-B.	
I: Some A are B.	Some A are not non-B.	
O: Some A are not B.	Some A are non-B.	

CONTRAPOSITION: SWITCH SUBJECT AND PREDICATE TERMS; REPLACE EACH WITH ITS TERM COMPLEMENT

Given Statement	Contrapositive	Truth Value
A: All A are B.	All non-B are non-A.	Same truth value as given statement
O: Some A are not B.	Some non-B are not non-A.	
E: No A are B.	No non-B are non-A.	Undetermined truth value
I: Some A are B.	Some non-B are non-A.	

EXERCISE 3.4

I. Exercises 1 through 6 provide a statement, its truth value in parentheses, and an operation to be performed on that statement. Supply the new statement and the truth value of the new statement. (*Hint*: For number 1, first obtain the converse of "No A are non-B"; then, since the given statement is a true **E** proposition, use this information to calculate the truth value of the converse.)

Exercises 7 through 12 provide a statement, its truth value in parentheses, and a new statement. Determine how the new statement was derived from the given statement and supply the truth value of the new statement. (*Hint*: For number 7, first compare the terms in the given statement with the terms in the new statement. This will tell you the operation. Then, since the given statement is a false **E** proposition, use this information together with the operation to calculate the truth value of the new statement.)

Given statement	Operation	New statement	Truth value
★1. No *A* are non-*B*. (T)	conv.	_____	_____
2. Some *A* are *B*. (T)	contrap.	_____	_____
3. All *A* are non-*B*. (F)	obv.	_____	_____
★4. All non-*A* are *B*. (F)	contrap.	_____	_____
5. Some non-*A* are not *B*. (T)	conv.	_____	_____
6. Some non-*A* are non-*B*. (T)	obv.	_____	_____
★7. No non-*A* are non-*B*. (F)	_____	No *B* are *A*.	_____
8. Some *A* are not non-*B*. (T)	_____	Some *A* are *B*.	_____
9. All *A* are non-*B*. (F)	_____	All non-*B* are *A*.	_____
★10. No non-*A* are *B*. (F)	_____	All non-*A* are non-*B*.	_____
11. Some non-*A* are not *B*. (T)	_____	Some non-*B* are not *A*.	_____
12. Some *A* are non-*B*. (F)	_____	Some non-*B* are *A*.	_____

II. Perform the operations of conversion, obversion, and contraposition as indicated.

1. Convert the following propositions and state whether the converse is logically equivalent or not logically equivalent to the given proposition.

   ★a. All hurricanes are storms intensified by global warming.

   b. No sex-change operations are completely successful procedures.

   c. Some murals by Diego Rivera are works that celebrate the revolutionary spirit.

   d. Some forms of carbon are not substances with a crystalline structure.

2. Obvert the following propositions and state whether the obverse is logically equivalent or not logically equivalent to the given proposition.

   ★a. All radically egalitarian societies are societies that do not preserve individual liberties.

   b. No cult leaders are people who fail to brainwash their followers.

   c. Some college football coaches are people who do not slip money to their players.

   d. Some budgetary cutbacks are not actions fair to the poor.

3. Contrapose the following propositions and state whether the contrapositive is logically equivalent or not logically equivalent to the given proposition.

   ★a. All physicians whose licenses have been revoked are physicians ineligible to practice.

   b. No unpersecuted migrants are migrants granted asylum.

   c. Some politicians who do not defend Social Security are politicans who do not want to increase taxes.

   d. Some opponents of gay marriage are not opponents of civil unions.

III. Use conversion, obversion, and contraposition to determine whether the following arguments are valid or invalid. For those that are invalid, name the fallacy committed.

★1. All commodity traders are gamblers who risk sudden disaster.
  Therefore, all gamblers who risk sudden disaster are commodity traders.

2. No child abusers are people who belong in day-care centers.
  Therefore, all child abusers are people who do not belong in day-care centers.

3. Some states having limited powers are not slave states.
  Therefore, some free states are not states having unlimited powers.

★4. Some insane people are illogical people.
  Therefore, some logical people are sane people.

5. Some organ transplants are not sensible operations.
  Therefore, some organ transplants are senseless operations.

6. No individuals who laugh all the time are people with a true sense of humor.
  Therefore, no people with a true sense of humor are individuals who laugh all the time.

★7. All periods when interest rates are high are times when businesses tend not to expand.
  Therefore, all times when businesses tend to expand are periods when interest rates are low.

8. Some swimsuits are not garments intended for the water.
  Therefore, some garments intended for the water are not swimsuits.

9. No promises made under duress are enforceable contracts.
  Therefore, no unenforceable contracts are promises made in the absence of duress.

★10. All ladies of the night are individuals with low self-esteem.
  Therefore, no ladies of the night are individuals with high self-esteem.

11. Some graffiti writers are artists relieving pent-up frustrations.
  Therefore, some artists relieving pent-up frustrations are graffiti writers.

12. Some peaceful revolutions are episodes that erupt in violence.
  Therefore, some episodes that do not erupt in violence are non-peaceful revolutions.

★13. Some insurance companies are not humanitarian organizations.
  Therefore, some humanitarian organizations are not insurance companies.

14. Some fossil fuels are unrenewable energy sources.
  Therefore, some fossil fuels are not renewable energy sources.

15. All hired killers are criminals who deserve the death penalty.
  Therefore, all criminals who deserve the death penalty are hired killers.

★16. No nonprescription drugs are medicines without adverse effects.
  Therefore, no medicines with adverse effects are prescription drugs.

17. All fire-breathing dragons are lizards that languish in soggy climates.
  Therefore, no fire-breathing dragons are lizards that flourish in soggy climates.

18. Some distant galaxies are not structures visible to the naked eye.
  Therefore, some structures visible to the naked eye are not distant galaxies.

★ 19.   All unpleasant experiences are things we do not like to remember.
         Therefore, all things we like to remember are pleasant experiences.

   20.   Some pro-lifers are not people concerned with child welfare.
          Therefore, some pro-lifers are people unconcerned with child welfare.

3.5   The Traditional Square of Opposition

PREVIEW

A friend of yours argues that it is morally wrong to buy any product made in a sweatshop. So when that same friend buys a new iPhone, you point out that the iPhone was made in a sweatshop in China. Still, your friend insists that he did nothing wrong in buying it. You are quick to observe that your friend is contradicting himself. But your friend then denies he is contradicting himself. Just what does it mean for two statements to contradict each other? That, and more, is the subject of this section of the book.

In Section 3.3 we adopted the Boolean standpoint, and we saw how the modern square of opposition applies regardless of whether the propositions refer to actually existing things. In this section, we adopt the Aristotelian standpoint, which recognizes that universal propositions about existing things have existential import. For such propositions the traditional square of opposition becomes applicable. Like the modern square, the **traditional square of opposition** is a diagram that illustrates logically necessary relations among the four kinds of categorical propositions. However, because the Aristotelian standpoint recognizes the additional factor of existential import, the traditional square supports more inferences than does the modern square. It is represented as follows:

traditional square of opposition: A diagram that illustrates logically necessary relations between the four kinds of categorical propositions.

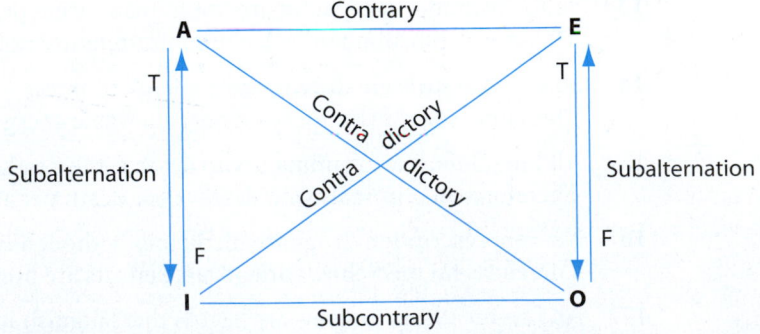

The four relations in the traditional square of opposition may be characterized as follows:

Contradictory	=	opposite truth value
Contrary	=	at least one is false (not both true)
Subcontrary	=	at least one is true (not both false)
Subalternation	=	truth flows downward, falsity flows upward

The **contradictory relation** is the same as that found in the modern square. Thus, if a certain **A** proposition is given as true, the corresponding **O** proposition is false, and vice versa, and if a certain **A** proposition is given as false, the corresponding **O** proposition is true, and vice versa. The same relation holds between the **E** and **I** propositions. The contradictory relation thus expresses complete opposition between propositions.

The **contrary relation** differs from the contradictory in that it expresses only partial opposition. Thus, if a certain **A** proposition is given as true, the corresponding **E** proposition is false (because at least one must be false), and if an **E** proposition is given as true, the corresponding **A** proposition is false. But if an **A** proposition is given as false, the corresponding **E** proposition could be *either* true or false without violating the "at least one is false" rule. In this case, the **E** proposition has logically undetermined truth value. Similarly, if an **E** proposition is given as false, the corresponding **A** proposition has logically undetermined truth value.

These results are borne out in ordinary language. Thus, if we are given the actually true **A** proposition "All cats are animals," the corresponding **E** proposition "No cats are animals" is false, and if we are given the actually true **E** proposition "No cats are dogs," the corresponding **A** proposition "All cats are dogs" is false. Thus, the **A** and **E** propositions cannot both be true. However, they can both be false. "All animals are cats" and "No animals are cats" are both false.

The **subcontrary relation** also expresses a kind of partial opposition. If a certain **I** proposition is given as false, the corresponding **O** proposition is true (because at least one must be true), and if an **O** proposition is given as false, the corresponding **I** proposition is true. But if either an **I** or an **O** proposition is given as true, then the corresponding proposition could be either true or false without violating the "at least one is true" rule. Thus, in this case the corresponding proposition would have logically undetermined truth value.

Again, these results are borne out in ordinary language. If we are given the actually false **I** proposition "Some cats are dogs," the corresponding **O** proposition "Some cats are not dogs" is true, and if we are given the actually false **O** proposition "Some cats are not animals," the corresponding **I** proposition "Some cats are animals" is true. Thus, the **I** and **O** propositions cannot both be false, but they can both be true. "Some animals are cats" and "Some animals are not cats" are both true.

The **subalternation relation** is represented by two arrows: a downward arrow marked with the letter T (true), and an upward arrow marked with an F (false). These arrows can be thought of as pipelines through which truth values "flow." The downward arrow "transmits" only truth, and the upward arrow only falsity. Thus, if an **A** proposition is given as true, the corresponding **I** proposition is true also, and if an **I** proposition is given as false, the corresponding **A** proposition is false. But if an **A** proposition is given as false, this truth value cannot be transmitted downward, so the corresponding **I** proposition will have logically undetermined truth value. Conversely, if an **I** proposition is given as true, this truth value cannot be transmitted upward, so the corresponding **A** proposition will have logically undetermined truth value. Analogous reasoning prevails for the subalternation relation between the **E** and **O** propositions. To remember the direction of the arrows for subalternation, imagine that truth "trickles down," and falsity "floats" up.

Now that we have examined these four relations individually, let us see how they can be used together to determine the truth values of corresponding propositions. The first rule of thumb that we should keep in mind when using the square to compute more than one truth value is always to use contradiction first. Now, let us suppose that we are told that the nonsensical proposition "All adlers are bobkins" is true. Suppose further that adlers actually exist, so we are justified in using the traditional square of opposition. By the contradictory relation, "Some adlers are not bobkins" is false. Then, by either the contrary or the subalternation relation, "No adlers are bobkins" is false. Finally, by either contradictory, subalternation, or subcontrary, "Some adlers are bobkins" is true.

Next, let us see what happens if we assume that "All adlers are bobkins" is false. By the contradictory relation, "Some adlers are not bobkins" is true, but nothing more can be determined. In other words, given a false **A** proposition, both contrary and sub-alternation yield undetermined results, and given a true **O** proposition (the one whose truth value we just determined), subcontrary and subalternation yield undetermined results. Thus, the corresponding **E** and **I** propositions have logically undetermined truth value. This result illustrates two more rules of thumb. Assuming that we always use the contradictory relation first, if one of the remaining relations yields a logically undetermined truth value, the others will as well. The other rule is that whenever one statement turns out to have logically undetermined truth value, its contradictory will also. Thus, statements having logically undetermined truth value will always occur in pairs, at opposite ends of diagonals on the square.

Testing Immediate Inferences

Next, let us see how we can use the traditional square of opposition to test immediate inferences for validity. Here is an example:

> All Swiss watches are works of art.
> Therefore, it is false that no Swiss watches are works of art.

We begin, as usual, by assuming the premise is true. Since the premise is an **A** proposition, by the contrary relation the corresponding **E** proposition is false. But this is exactly what the conclusion says, so the argument is valid.

Here is another example:

> Some viruses are structures that attack T cells.
> Therefore, some viruses are not structures that attack T cells.

Here the premise and conclusion are linked by the subcontrary relation. According to that relation, if the premise is assumed true, the conclusion has logically undetermined truth value, and so the inference is invalid. It commits the formal fallacy of **illicit subcontrary**. Analogously, inferences that depend on an incorrect application of the contrary relation commit the formal fallacy of **illicit contrary**, and inferences that depend on an illicit application of subalternation commit the formal fallacy of **illicit subalternation**. Some forms of these fallacies are as follows:

Illicit contrary

> It is false that all *A* are *B*.
> Therefore, no *A* are *B*.

> It is false that no *A* are *B*.
> Therefore, all *A* are *B*.

Illicit subcontrary

> Some *A* are *B*.
> Therefore, it is false that some *A* are not *B*.

> Some *A* are not *B*.
> Therefore, some *A* are *B*.

Illicit subalternation

> Some *A* are not *B*.
> Therefore, no *A* are *B*.

> It is false that all *A* are *B*.
> Therefore, it is false that some *A* are *B*.

Cases of the incorrect application of the contradictory relation are so infrequent that an "illicit contradictory" fallacy is not usually recognized.

As we saw at the beginning of this section, for the traditional square of opposition to apply, the Aristotelian standpoint must be adopted, and the propositions to which it is applied must assert something about actually existing things. The question may now be asked, What happens when the Aristotelian standpoint is adopted but the propositions are about things that do not exist? The answer is that under these conditions the traditional square reverts to the modern square (see Section 3.3). Inferences that are based on a correct application of the contradictory relation are valid, but inferences that are based on an otherwise correct application of the other three relations are invalid and commit the existential fallacy.

The reason for this result is easy to see. The modern square of opposition rests on the Boolean standpoint, and the traditional square rests on the Aristotelian standpoint. But the Aristotelian standpoint differs from the Boolean only with respect to universal propositions about existing things. The Aristotelian standpoint interprets these propositions as having existential import, while the Boolean standpoint does not. But universal propositions about things that do not exist have no existential import from the Aristotelian standpoint. In other words, the Aristotelian standpoint interprets these propositions in exactly the same way as does the Boolean. Thus, for universal propositions about things that do not exist, the traditional square reverts to the modern square.

Accordingly, the **existential fallacy** is committed from the Aristotelian standpoint when and only when contrary, subcontrary, and subalternation are used (in an otherwise correct way) to draw a conclusion from a premise about things that do not exist. All such inferences begin with a universal proposition, which has no existential import, and they conclude with a particular proposition, which has existential import. The existential fallacy is never committed in connection with the contradictory relation, nor is it committed in connection with conversion, obversion, or contraposition, all of which hold regardless of existence. The following inferences commit the existential fallacy from the Aristotelian standpoint:

> All witches who fly on broomsticks are fearless women.
> Therefore, some witches who fly on broomsticks are fearless women.

> No wizards with magical powers are malevolent beings.
> Therefore, it is false that all wizards with magical powers are malevolent beings.

The first depends on an otherwise correct use of the subalternation relation, and the second on an otherwise correct use of the contrary relation. If flying witches and magical wizards actually existed, both arguments would be valid. But since they do not exist, both arguments are invalid and commit the existential fallacy. In regard to the second example, recall that the conclusion, which asserts that an **A** proposition is false, is actually a particular proposition. Thus, this example, like the first one, proceeds from the universal to the particular.

> ### Existential fallacy examples: Two standpoints
>
> All cats are animals.
> Some cats are animals. } Boolean: Invalid, existential fallacy
> Aristotelian: Valid
>
> All unicorns are animals.
> Some unicorns are animals. } Boolean: Invalid, existential fallacy
> Aristotelian: Invalid, existential fallacy

conditionally valid: Valid on condition that the subject term of the premise denotes actually existing things.

The phrase **conditionally valid** applies to an inference after the Aristotelian standpoint has been adopted and we are not certain if the subject term of the premise denotes actually existing things. For example, the following inference is conditionally valid:

> All students who failed the exam are students on probation.
> Therefore, some students who failed the exam are students on probation.

The validity of this inference rests on whether there were in fact any students who failed the exam. The inference is either valid or invalid, but we lack sufficient information about the meaning of the premise to tell which is the case. Once it becomes known that there are indeed some students who failed the exam, we can assert that the inference is valid from the Aristotelian standpoint. But if there are no students who failed the exam, the inference is invalid because it commits the existential fallacy.

Similarly, all inference *forms* that depend on valid applications of contrary, subcontrary, and subalternation are conditionally valid because we do not know if the letters in the propositions denote actually existing things. For example, the following inference form, which depends on the contrary relation, is conditionally valid:

> All *A* are *B*.
> Therefore, it is false that no *A* are *B*.

If "dogs" and "animals" are substituted in place of *A* and *B,* respectively, the resulting inference is valid. But if "unicorns" and "animals" are substituted, the resulting inference is invalid because it commits the existential fallacy. In Section 3.3, we noted that all inferences (and inference forms) that are valid from the Boolean standpoint are *unconditionally valid.* They are valid regardless of whether their terms denote actually existing things.

In testing an inference for validity, we are never concerned with the actual truth of the premise. Regardless of whether the premise is actually true or false, we always begin by assuming it to be true, and then we determine how this assumption bears on the truth or falsity of the conclusion. The actual truth of the premise affects only the soundness of the argument. So let us now turn to the question of soundness. Recall from Section 1.4 that a sound argument is one that is valid and has all true premises, and consider the following example:

> All cats are dogs.
> Therefore, some cats are dogs.

The premise is obviously false; but if we assume it to be true, then it follows necessarily by subalternation that the conclusion is true. Thus, the inference is valid. However, because the premise is false, the inference is unsound.

Here is another example:

> No rabbits are toads.
> Therefore, it is false that all rabbits are toads.

This inference is sound. By the contrary relation it is valid, and it also has a true premise.

Here is a final example:

> Some unicorns are not gazelles.
> Therefore, it is false that all unicorns are gazelles.

This inference differs from the others in that the premise asserts the existence of something that does not actually exist (namely, unicorns). In other words, the premise seems to be self-contradictory. Nevertheless, the inference can be evaluated in the usual way. If the premise is assumed true, then it necessarily follows that the conclusion is true by the contradictory relation. Thus, the inference is valid. But the inference is unsound because it has a false premise. The premise asserts the existence of something that does not actually exist.

EXERCISE 3.5

I. Use the traditional square of opposition to find the answers to these problems. When a statement is given as false, simply enter an "F" into the square of opposition and compute (if possible) the other truth values.

★1. If "All fashion fads are products of commercial brainwashing" is true, what is the truth value of the following statements?

   a. No fashion fads are products of commercial brainwashing.

   b. Some fashion fads are products of commercial brainwashing.

   c. Some fashion fads are not products of commercial brainwashing.

2. If "All fashion fads are products of commercial brainwashing" is false, what is the truth value of the following statements?

   a. No fashion fads are products of commercial brainwashing.

   b. Some fashion fads are products of commercial brainwashing.

   c. Some fashion fads are not products of commercial brainwashing.

3. If "No sting operations are cases of entrapment" is true, what is the truth value of the following statements?

   a. All sting operations are cases of entrapment.

   b. Some sting operations are cases of entrapment.

   c. Some sting operations are not cases of entrapment.

★4. If "No sting operations are cases of entrapment" is false, what is the truth value of the following statements?

    a. All sting operations are cases of entrapment.

    b. Some sting operations are cases of entrapment.

    c. Some sting operations are not cases of entrapment.

5. If "Some assassinations are morally justifiable actions" is true, what is the truth value of the following statements?

    a. All assassinations are morally justifiable actions.

    b. No assassinations are morally justifiable actions.

    c. Some assassinations are not morally justifiable actions.

6. If "Some assassinations are morally justifiable actions" is false, what is the truth value of the following statements?

    a. All assassinations are morally justifiable actions.

    b. No assassinations are morally justifiable actions.

    c. Some assassinations are not morally justifiable actions.

★7. If "Some obsessive-compulsive behaviors are not curable diseases" is true, what is the truth value of the following statements?

    a. All obsessive-compulsive behaviors are curable diseases.

    b. No obsessive-compulsive behaviors are curable diseases.

    c. Some obsessive-compulsive behaviors are curable diseases.

8. If "Some obsessive-compulsive behaviors are not curable diseases" is false, what is the truth value of the following statements?

    a. All obsessive-compulsive behaviors are curable diseases.

    b. No obsessive-compulsive behaviors are curable diseases.

    c. Some obsessive-compulsive behaviors are curable diseases.

II. Use the traditional square of opposition to determine whether the following immediate inferences are valid or invalid. Name any fallacies that are committed.

★1. All advocates of school prayer are individuals who insist on imposing their views on others.
Therefore, some advocates of school prayer are individuals who insist on imposing their views on others.

2. It is false that no jailhouse informants are people who can be trusted.
Therefore, some jailhouse informants are not people who can be trusted.

3. All homemakers are people with real jobs.
Therefore, it is false that no homemakers are people with real jobs.

★4. It is false that some trolls are not creatures who live under bridges.
Therefore, it is false that no trolls are creatures who live under bridges.

5. Some campus romances are episodes plagued by violence.
Therefore, some campus romances are not episodes plagued by violence.

6. Some pornographic publications are materials protected by the First Amendment.
Therefore, it is false that no pornographic publications are materials protected by the First Amendment.

★**7.** It is false that all mainstream conservatives are people who support free legal services for the poor.
Therefore, no mainstream conservatives are people who support free legal services for the poor.

8. It is false that some forms of human creativity are activities amenable to mathematical analysis.
Therefore, it is false that all forms of human creativity are activities amenable to mathematical analysis.

9. It is false that some tooth fairies are daytime visitors.
Therefore, some tooth fairies are not daytime visitors.

★**10.** It is false that some orthodox psychoanalysts are not individuals driven by a religious fervor.
Therefore, it is false that some orthodox psychoanalysts are individuals driven by a religious fervor.

11. Some school busses manufactured on the moon are not plasma-powered vehicles.
Therefore, it is false that all school busses manufactured on the moon are plasma-powered vehicles.

12. It is false that some network news programs are exercises in mediocrity.
Therefore, it is false that no network news programs are exercises in mediocrity.

★**13.** No flying reindeer are animals who get lost in the fog.
Therefore, it is false that all flying reindeer are animals who get lost in the fog.

14. It is false that no leveraged buyouts are deals unfair to workers.
Therefore, all leveraged buyouts are deals unfair to workers.

15. It is false that some wood ticks are not carriers of Lyme disease.
Therefore, some wood ticks are carriers of Lyme disease.

III. Use the traditional square of opposition to determine whether the following immediate inferences are valid or invalid and sound or unsound. Name any fallacies that are committed.

★**1.** All dolphins are polar bears.
Therefore, it is false that no dolphins are polar bears.

2. It is false that some recessions are not periods of economic decline.
Therefore, it is false that no recessions are periods of economic decline.

3. It is false that some suicide survivors are comeback kids.
Therefore, some suicide survivors are not comeback kids.

★**4.** It is false that some ruby earrings are not pieces of jewelry.
Therefore, some ruby earrings are pieces of jewelry.

5. It is false that all visitors to Rio are Carnival addicts.
   Therefore, no visitors to Rio are Carnival addicts.

6. Some tax cheats are not honest citizens.
   Therefore, no tax cheats are honest citizens.

★7. All truthful lies are curious assertions.
   Therefore, some truthful lies are curious assertions.

8. It is false that no bankrupt hair salons are thriving enterprises.
   Therefore, all bankrupt hair salons are thriving enterprises.

9. It is false that some functional skateboards are not devices equipped with wheels.
   Therefore, all functional skateboards are devices equipped with wheels.

★10. Some film directors are artistic visionaries.
   Therefore, some film directors are not artistic visionaries.

IV. Exercises 1 through 10 provide a statement, its truth value in parentheses, and an operation to be performed on that statement. Supply the new statement and the truth value of the new statement. Exercises 11 through 20 provide a statement, its truth value in parentheses, and a new statement. Determine how the new statement was derived from the given statement and supply the truth value of the new statement. Take the Aristotelian standpoint in working these exercises and assume that the terms refer to actually existing things.

Given statement	Operation/ relation	New statement	Truth value
★1. All non-A are B. (T)	contrap.	_____	_____
2. Some A are non-B. (F)	subalt.	_____	_____
3. No A are non-B. (T)	obv.	_____	_____
★4. Some non-A are not B. (T)	subcon.	_____	_____
5. No A are non-B. (F)	contradic.	_____	_____
6. No A are B. (T)	contrap.	_____	_____
★7. All non-A are B. (T)	contrary	_____	_____
8. Some A are not non-B. (F)	obv.	_____	_____
9. No A are non-B. (F)	conv.	_____	_____
★10. Some non-A are non-B. (F)	subcon.	_____	_____
11. Some non-A are not B. (T)	_____	All non-A are B.	_____
12. Some A are non-B. (T)	_____	Some non-B are A.	_____
★13. All non-A are B. (F)	_____	No non-A are non-B.	_____
14. Some non-A are not B. (T)	_____	No non-A are B.	_____
15. All A are non-B. (F)	_____	All non-B are A.	_____
★16. Some non-A are non-B. (F)	_____	No non-A are non-B.	_____
17. Some A are not non-B. (T)	_____	Some B are not non-A.	_____

18. No non-*A* are *B*. (T)   —————   Some non-*A* are not *B*. ——

★19. No *A* are non-*B*. (F)   —————   All *A* are non-*B*.   ——

20. Some non-*A* are *B*. (F)   —————   Some non-*A* are not *B*. ——

V. Use either the traditional square of opposition or conversion, obversion, or contraposition to determine whether the following immediate inferences are valid or invalid. For those that are invalid, name the fallacy committed.

★1. It is false that some jogging events are not aerobic activities.
     Therefore, it is false that no jogging events are aerobic activities.

2. No meat-eating vegetarians are individuals with a high-protein diet.
     Therefore, no individuals with a high-protein diet are meat-eating vegetarians.

3. Some jobs in health care are not glamorous occupations.
     Therefore, some jobs in health care are glamorous occupations.

★4. Some terminally ill patients are patients who do not want to live.
     Therefore, some patients who want to live are recovering patients.

5. All Barbie dolls are toys that engender a false sense of values.
     Therefore, no Barbie dolls are toys that engender a true sense of values.

6. All flying elephants are jolly pachyderms.
     Therefore, some flying elephants are jolly pachyderms.

★7. It is false that some international terrorists are political moderates.
     Therefore, some international terrorists are not political moderates.

8. No pet hamsters are animals that need much attention.
     Therefore, it is false that all pet hamsters are animals that need much attention.

9. Some hedge-fund managers are not responsible investors.
     Therefore, some responsible investors are not hedge-fund managers.

★10. It is false that all substances that control cell growth are hormones.
     Therefore, no substances that control cell growth are hormones.

11. Some cases of whistle-blowing are actions disloyal to employers.
     Therefore, some cases of whistle-blowing are not actions loyal to employers.

12. No stolen computer chips are easy items to trace.
     Therefore, no difficult items to trace are computer chips that are not stolen.

★13. Some economists are followers of Ayn Rand.
     Therefore, some economists are not followers of Ayn Rand.

14. All porcelain figurines are fragile artifacts.
     Therefore, it is false that some porcelain figurines are not fragile artifacts.

15. Some pleasant recollections are not missed opportunities.
     Therefore, some availed opportunities are not unpleasant recollections.

aplia
Visit Aplia for section-specific problem sets.

3.6 Translating Ordinary Language Statements into Categorical Form

PREVIEW

You are engaged in a discussion with a friend about why some students have an easier time getting dates than other students. Your friend makes this observation: "Only people who laugh a lot get dates. This implies that a few people who get dates laugh a lot." Is your friend's argument valid? If so, how would you prove that it is? What is the meaning of the words "only" and "a few"? In the current section of the book you will learn how to deal with statements containing words such as these.

Although few statements that occur in ordinary written and oral expression are categorical propositions in standard form, many of them can be translated into standard-form propositions. Such translation has two chief benefits. The first is that the operations and inferences pertinent to standard-form categorical propositions (contrary, subcontrary, etc.) become applicable to these statements. The second is that such statements, once translated, are completely clear and unambiguous as to their meaning. Many statements in ordinary language are susceptible to multiple interpretations, and each interpretation represents one possible mode of translation. The effort to translate such statements discloses the various interpretations and thus helps prevent misunderstanding and confusion.

Translating statements into categorical form is like any other kind of translation in that no set of specific rules will cover every possible form of phraseology. Yet, one general rule always applies: Understand the *meaning* of the given statement, and then reexpress it in a new statement that has a proper quantifier, subject term, copula, and predicate term. Some of the forms of phraseology that are typically encountered are terms without nouns, nonstandard verbs, singular propositions, adverbs and pronouns, unexpressed and nonstandard quantifiers, conditional statements, exclusive propositions, "the only," and exceptive propositions.

> Rule for translating: Understand the *meaning* of the given statement and then reexpress it in a new statement that has a proper quantifier, subject term, copula, and predicate term.

1. Terms Without Nouns

The subject and predicate terms of a categorical proposition must contain either a plural noun or a pronoun that serves to denote the class indicated by the term. Nouns and pronouns denote classes, while adjectives (and participles) connote attributes. If a term consists of only an adjective, a plural noun or pronoun should be introduced to make the term genuinely denotative. Examples:

Some roses are red.   Some roses are red *flowers*.

All tigers are carnivorous.   All tigers are carnivorous *animals*.

2. Nonstandard Verbs

According to the position adopted earlier in this chapter, the only copulas that are allowed in standard-form categorical propositions are "are" and "are not." Statements in ordinary usage, however, often incorporate other forms of the verb "to be." Such statements may be translated as the following examples illustrate:

| Some college students will become educated. | Some college students *are people who* will become educated. |
| Some dogs would rather bark than bite. | Some dogs *are animals that* would rather bark than bite. |

In other statements no form of the verb "to be" occurs at all. These may be translated as the following examples indicate:

| Some birds fly south during the winter. | Some birds *are animals that* fly south during the winter. |
| All ducks swim. | All ducks *are swimmers*.
 or
 All ducks *are animals that* swim. |

3. Singular Propositions

A **singular proposition (statement)** is a proposition that makes an assertion about a specific person, place, thing, or time. Singular propositions are typically translated into universals by means of a parameter. A **parameter** is a phrase that, when introduced into a statement, affects the form but not the meaning. Some parameters that may be used to translate singular propositions are these:

> people identical to
> places identical to
> things identical to
> cases identical to
> times identical to

For example, the statement "Socrates is mortal" may be translated as "All people identical to Socrates are people who are mortal." Because only one person is identical to Socrates, namely Socrates himself, the term "people identical to Socrates" denotes the class that has Socrates as its only member. In other words, it simply denotes Socrates. Such a translation admittedly leaves some of the original information behind, because singular statements usually have existential import, whereas universal statements do not—at least from the Boolean standpoint. But if such translations are interpreted from the Aristotelian standpoint, the existential import is preserved. Here are some examples:

George went home.	All *people identical to* George are *people who* went home.
Sandra did not go shopping.	No *people identical to* Sandra are *people who* went shopping.
There is a radio in the bedroom.	All *places identical to* the bedroom are *places* there is a radio. or *Some* radios are *things* in the bedroom.
The moon is full tonight.	All *things identical to* the moon are *things that* are full tonight. or All *times identical to* tonight are *times* the moon is full.

I hate gin.	All *people identical to* me are *people who* hate gin.
	or
	All *things identical to* gin are *things that* I hate.

In translating singular statements, note that the parameter "people identical to" is *not* the same as "people similar to" or "people like." There may be many people *like* Socrates, but there is only one person *identical to* Socrates. Also note that parameters should *not* be used when the term in question already has a plural noun (or pronoun) that denotes the intended class. Such use is not wrong, technically, but it is redundant. Example:

Diamonds are carbon allotropes.	*Correct:*	All diamonds are carbon allotropes.
	Redundant:	All things identical to diamonds are things identical to carbon allotropes.

4. Adverbs and Pronouns

When a statement contains a spatial adverb such as "where," "wherever," "anywhere," "everywhere," or "nowhere," or a temporal adverb such as "when," "whenever," "anytime," "always," or "never," it may be translated in terms of "places" or "times," respectively. Statements containing pronouns such as "who," "whoever," "anyone," "what," "whatever," or "anything" may be translated in terms of "people" or "things," respectively. Examples:

He always wears a suit to work.	All *times* he goes to work are *times* he wears a suit.
He is always clean shaven.	All *times* are *times* he is clean shaven.
She never brings her lunch to school.	No *times* she goes to school are *times* she brings her lunch.
Nowhere on earth are there any unicorns.	No *places* on earth are *places* there are unicorns.
Whoever works hard will succeed.	All *people* who work hard are *people* who will succeed.
Whenever he wins he celebrates.	All *times* he wins are *times* he celebrates.
She goes where she chooses.	All *places* she chooses to go are *places* she goes.
She does what she wants.	All *things* she wants to do are *things* she does.

Notice the order of the subject and predicate terms in the last four examples. When translating statements such as these it is often easy to confuse the subject term with the predicate term. However, since these statements are all translated as **A** type categorical propositions, such a mix-up amounts to committing the fallacy of illicit conversion. To prevent it from happening, keep this rule in mind: For "W" words ("who," "what,"

John Stuart Mill 1806–1873

John Stuart Mill, who would become the most important English-speaking philosopher of the nineteenth century, was born in London to the philosopher and historian James Mill and his wife, Harriet Barrow. From a very early age the father took charge of his son's education, imposing on him an unusually strict course of studies. The boy began studying Greek at age three; he began Latin, geometry, and algebra at eight; and by fourteen he had read most of the Latin and Greek classics. Also, by that time he had developed a thorough knowledge of history, scholastic and Aristotelian logic, and higher-level mathematics. At seventeen he accepted a position with the East India Company, a private corporation that virtually ruled all of India. He remained there for twenty-five years, eventually becoming chief examiner, which put him largely in charge of the company.

When he was twenty, Mill suffered an acute attack of depression that lasted for several months. Although he managed to continue his work, everything seemed worthless to him at that time. This condition was most likely brought on by the severity of his educational upbringing, which had attended to his intellect but left his emotional life a desert. Gradually he pulled himself out by reading the poetry of William Wordsworth. Four years later Mill met Harriet Taylor, with whom he became emotionally but not sexually intimate (she was married at that time). Taylor would exert a profound influence on him for the rest of his life. After the death of her husband, nineteen years after she and Mill first met, they were married.

Today John Stuart Mill is widely known for his essay "On Liberty" and his book *Utilitarianism*. The essay is a sustained argument in favor of freedom of speech and

the maximization of individual liberty against the strictures of government. *Utilitarianism* further develops the ethical theory promoted by James Mill and Jeremy Bentham. As perfected by John Stuart Mill, this theory holds that we should always perform the action that produces the greatest happiness for the greatest number of people. This work was important, among other reasons, for creating an ethical theory that was not based on any theology or religion. Mill also wrote extensively on women's rights, and when he was later elected to a three-year term in Parliament, he became the first member to urge that women receive the right to vote.

Mill's greatest work was his *System of Logic*, which went through eight editions during his lifetime. In that book Mill argues that deductive argumentation, far from being the paradigmatic form of reasoning most philosophers take it to be, is largely bereft of value because it never yields any new knowledge. Also, it is essentially dependent on induction. Thus, it is really induction that should be studied as the primary engine of scientific discovery.

In 1858 Harriet Taylor died from a lung infection while the couple were visiting Avignon, France. Nearly inconsolable, Mill bought a house there so he could be near her grave. He died in Avignon fifteen years later, and his body was buried alongside hers.

"when," "where," "whoever," "whatever," "whenever," "wherever"), the language following the "W" word goes into the subject term of the categorical proposition.

5. Unexpressed Quantifiers

Many statements in ordinary usage have quantifiers that are implied but not expressed. In introducing the quantifiers one must be guided by the most probable meaning of the statement. Examples:

Emeralds are green gems.	*All* emeralds are green gems.
There are lions in the zoo.	*Some* lions are animals in the zoo.
A tiger is a mammal.	*All* tigers are mammals.
A fish is not a mammal.	*No* fish are mammals.
A tiger roared.	*Some* tigers are animals that roared.
Children are human beings.	*All* children are human beings.
Children live next door.	*Some* children are people who live next door.

6. Nonstandard Quantifiers

In some ordinary language statements, the quantity is indicated by words other than the three standard-form quantifiers. Such words include "few," "a few," "not every," "anyone," and various other forms. Another problem occurs when the quantifier "all" is combined with the copula "are not." As we have already seen, statements of the form "All *S* are not *P*" are *not* standard-form categorical propositions. Depending on their meaning, they should be translated as either "No *S* are *P*" or "Some *S* are not *P*." When the intended meaning is "Some *S* are not *P*," the meaning may be indicated by placing oral emphasis on the word "all." For example, "*All* athletes are not superstars" means "Some athletes are not superstars." Here are some additional examples:

A few soldiers are heroes.	*Some* soldiers are heroes.
Anyone who votes is a citizen.	*All* voters are citizens.
Not everyone who votes is a Democrat.	*Some* voters are not Democrats.
Not a single dog is a cat.	*No* dogs are cats.
All newborns are not able to talk.	*No* newborns are people able to talk.
All prisoners are not violent.	*Some* prisoners are not violent people.
Many entertainers are comedians	*Some* entertainers are comedians.
Several demonstrators were arrested.	*Some* demonstrators are people who were arrested.
Few sailors entered the regatta.	*Some* sailors are people who entered the regatta *and some* sailors are not people who entered the regatta.

Notice that this last statement beginning with "few" cannot be translated as a single categorical proposition. Such statements (and some beginning with "a few") must be translated as a compound arrangement of an **I** proposition and an **O** proposition. Statements beginning with "almost all" and "not quite all" must be handled in the same way. When these statements occur in arguments, the arguments must be treated in the same way as those containing exceptive propositions, which will be discussed shortly.

7. Conditional Statements

When the antecedent and consequent of a conditional statement refer to the same class of things, the statement can usually be translated into categorical form. Such statements are always translated as universals. Language following the word "if" goes in the subject term of the categorical proposition, and language following "only if" goes in the predicate term. Examples:

If it's a mouse, then it's a mammal.	All mice are mammals.
If a bear is hungry, then it is dangerous.	All hungry bears are dangerous animals.
Jewelry is expensive if it is made of gold.	All pieces of jewelry made of gold are expensive things.
A car is a Camry only if it's a Toyota.	All Camrys are Toyotas.

Conditional statements having a negated consequent are usually best translated as **E** propositions. Examples:

If it's a turkey, then it's not a mammal.	No turkeys are mammals.
If an animal has four legs, then it is not a bird.	No four-legged animals are birds.
A knife will cut only if it isn't dull.	No knives that cut are dull knives.

The word "unless" means "if not." Since language following the word "if" goes in the subject, statements containing "unless" are translated as categorical propositions having negated subject terms. Examples:

Tomatoes are edible unless they are spoiled.	All unspoiled tomatoes are edible tomatoes.
Unless a boy misbehaves he will be treated decently.	All boys who do not misbehave are boys who will be treated decently.

8. Exclusive Propositions

Many propositions that involve the words "only," "none but," "none except," and "no . . . except" are exclusive propositions. Efforts to translate them into categorical propositions often lead to confusing the subject term with the predicate term. To avoid such confusion keep in mind that language following "only," "none but," "none except," and "no . . . except" goes in the predicate term of the categorical proposition. For example, the statement "Only executives can use the silver elevator" is translated "All people who can use the silver elevator are executives." If it were translated "All executives are people who can use the silver elevator," the translation would be incorrect. Examples:

Only elected officials will attend the convention.	All people who will attend the convention are elected officials.
None but the brave deserve the fair.	All people who deserve the fair are brave people.
No birds except peacocks are proud of their tails.	All birds proud of their tails are peacocks.

| He owns only blue-chip stocks. | All stocks he owns are blue-chip stocks. |
| She invited only wealthy socialites. | All people she invited are wealthy socialites. |

For a statement involving "only," "none but," "none except," and "no . . . except" to be a genuinely exclusive proposition, the word that follows these words must be a *plural* noun or pronoun. If the word that follows "only," "none but," or the like designates an *individual*, the statement really asserts two things. For example, the statement "Only Megan painted a picture" asserts that Megan painted a picture *and* that no other person painted a picture. Thus it would be translated as two statements: "All people identical to Megan are people who painted a picture, *and* all people who painted a picture are people identical to Megan." This section of the book will ignore cases where the word following "only," "none but," or the like designates an individual.

Also note that many English statements containing "only" are ambiguous because "only" can be interpreted as modifying alternate words in the statement. Consider, for example, the statement "He only jogs after sunset." Does this mean "He is the only person who jogs after sunset" or "He jogs and does not walk after sunset" or "The only time he jogs is after sunset"? If the statement's context does not provide an answer, the translator is free to pick any of these senses for translation. This same ambiguity, incidentally, affects the last two examples in the earlier list. Accordingly, they might also be translated "All things he owns are blue-chip stocks" and "All socialites she invited are wealthy people."

9. "The Only"

Statements beginning with the words "the only" are translated differently from those beginning with "only." For example, the statement "The only cars that are available are Chevrolets" means "If a car is available, then it is a Chevrolet." This in turn is translated as "All cars that are available are Chevrolets." In other words, language following "the only" goes in the subject term of the categorical proposition. Examples:

| The only animals that live in this canyon are skunks. | All animals that live in this canyon are skunks. |
| Accountants are the only ones who will be hired. | All those who will be hired are accountants. |

Statements involving "the only" are similar to those involving "only" in this one respect: When the statement is about an *individual*, two statements are needed to translate it. For example, "The only person who painted a picture is Megan" means that Megan painted a picture, *and* no other person painted a picture. The statement is equivalent in meaning to "Only Megan painted a picture." Thus, it is translated "All people identical to Megan are people who painted a picture, *and* all people who painted a picture are people identical to Megan." Statements involving "the only" that refer to individuals are ignored throughout the remainder of this chapter.

3

10. Exceptive Propositions

Propositions of the form "All except *S* are *P*" and "All but *S* are *P*" are exceptive propositions. They must be translated not as single categorical propositions but as pairs of conjoined categorical propositions. Statements that include the phrase "none except," on the other hand, are exclusive (not exceptive) propositions. "None except" is synonymous with "none but." Here are some examples of exceptive propositions:

All except students are invited.	No students are invited people, and all nonstudents are invited people.
All but managers must report to the president.	No managers are people who must report to the president, and all nonmanagers are people who must report to the president.

Because exceptive propositions cannot be translated into single categorical propositions, many of the simple inferences and operations pertinent to categorical propositions cannot be applied to them. Arguments that contain exceptive propositions as premises or conclusion can be evaluated only through the application of extended techniques. This topic is taken up in the next chapter.

3

Key word (to be eliminated)	Translation hint
whoever, wherever, always, anyone, never, etc.	use "all" together with people, places, times
a few, several, many	use "some"
if … then	use "all" or "no"
unless	use "if not"
only, none but, none except, no … except	use "all"
the only	use "all"
all but, all except, few	two statements required
not every, not all	use "some … are not"
there is, there are	use "some"

Rule for A propositions

Language following these words goes in the subject term: "if," "the only," and "W" words ("who," "what," "when," "where," "whoever," "whatever," "whenever," "wherever").

Language following these words goes in the predicate term: "only if," "only," "none but," "none except," and "no … except."

I. Translate the following into standard-form categorical propositions.

★1. Any bank that makes too many risky loans will fail.

2. Temporary workers are not eligible for fringe benefits.

3. Terrorist attacks succeed whenever security measures are lax.

★4. Bromine is extractable from seawater.

5. Not all guilt feelings are psychological aberrations.

6. Every jazz fan admires Duke Ellington.

★7. If it's a halogen, then it isn't chemically inert.

8. A television show that depicts violence incites violence.

9. Manipulators do not make good marriage partners.

★10. None but pirate ships fly the Jolly Roger.

11. She gains weight whenever she's depressed.

12. She's depressed whenever she gains weight.

★13. A man is a bachelor only if he is unmarried.

14. Warmth always relieves pain.

15. Joseph J. Thomson discovered the electron.

★16. A few organic silicones are used as lubricants.

17. Only nuclear-powered vehicles are suitable for deep-space exploration.

18. Comets are the only heavenly bodies with tails.

★19. There is a giant star in the Tarantula Nebula.

20. If a pregnant woman drinks alcohol, she risks giving birth to a deformed child.

21. No shellfish except oysters make pearls.

★22. Only diabetics require insulin treatments.

23. The electroscope is a device for detecting static electricity.

24. Occasionally there are concerts in Central Park.

★25. Berlin was the setting for the 1936 Olympic Games.

26. The Kentucky Derby is never run in January.

27. The only way to get rid of a temptation is to yield to it.

★28. Where there's smoke, there's fire.

29. Lunar eclipses do not occur unless the moon is full.

30. Radio transmissions are disrupted whenever sunspot activity increases.

★31. If an ore isn't radioactive, then it isn't pitchblende.

32. All but the rats left the sinking ship.

33. A pesticide is dangerous if it contains DDT.

★34. John Grisham writes only novels about lawyers.

35. He who hesitates is lost.

36. Modern corporations are all run in the interest of their managers.

★37. Unless the sun is shining, a rainbow cannot occur.

38. Whoever suffers allergic reactions has a weakened immune system.

39. All fruits except pineapples ripen after they are picked.

★40. Few corporate raiders are known for their integrity.

41. Monkeys are found in the jungles of Guatemala.

42. Monkeys are mammals.

★43. I like strawberries.

44. All passengers are not allowed to smoke on board the aircraft.

45. All flowers are not fragrant.

★46. Cynthia travels where she wants.

47. Bats are the only true flying mammals.

48. Not every river runs to the sea.

★49. Physicists do not understand the operation of superconductors.

50. Many apartment dwellers are victimized by noise.

51. There are forced labor camps in China.

★52. Whatever increases efficiency improves profitability.

53. Dolphins are swimming between the breakers.

54. Feathers are not heavy.

★55. Few picnics are entirely free of ants.

56. A civil right is unalienable if it is a human right.

57. She says what she pleases.

★58. Several contestants won prizes.

59. An animal is a feline only if it is a cat.

60. Renee does whatever she is told to do.

II. The following exercises contain typical mistakes that students make in attempting to translate statements into standard form. Correct the errors and redundancies in these attempted translations.

★1. Some of the figure-skating finalists are performers who are athletes that may win medals.

2. All cars identical to BMWs are the only cars that young lawyers drive.

3. All vertebrates except cartilaginous fishes are animals with a bony skeleton.

★4. No downhill skiers are effective competitors if they suffer from altitude sickness.

5. All substances like cobalt are things that are substances identical to ferromagnetic metals.

6. No people identical to nuclear pacifists are people who believe a just war is possible.

★7. All people identical to matadors are not performers who succumb easily to fear.

8. All companies identical to Google are looking forward to a bright future.

9. No toxic dumps are ecological catastrophes unless they leak.

★10. All crocodiles are things identical to dangerous animals when they are hungry.

III. Translate the premise and conclusion of the following immediate inferences into standard-form categorical propositions. Then use conversion, obversion, contraposition, or the traditional square of opposition to determine whether each is valid or invalid. For those that are invalid, name the fallacy committed.

★1. Flu vaccines are never completely effective.
   Therefore, not every flu vaccine is completely effective.

2. Only diamonds are a girl's best friend.
   Therefore, every diamond is a girl's best friend.

3. A child destined to succeed in life has high self-esteem.
   Therefore, a child with low self-esteem is not destined to succeed in life.

★4. If a date is a good dinner companion, then she does not spend every minute texting.
   Therefore, if a date does not spend every minute texting, then she is not a bad dinner companion.

5. There are banks that engage in money laundering.
   Therefore, there are banks that do not engage in money laundering.

6. Not a single major storm fails to cause flight cancellations.
   Therefore, every major storm causes flight cancellations.

★7. Tax cuts never please everyone.
   Therefore, every tax cut pleases everyone.

8. Military exercises are sometimes condemned by opponents.
   Therefore, any military exercise is condemned by opponents.

9. It is false that not a single charter school is an academic underperformer.
   Therefore, several charter schools are academic underperformers.

★10. Fake artworks are sold on eBay.
   Therefore, a few items sold on eBay are fake artworks.

aplia™

Visit Aplia for section-specific problem sets.

Summary

Categorical Proposition: A proposition that relates two classes (or categories). Standard-form categorical propositions occur in four forms and are identified by letter names:

- **A**: All *S* are *P*.
- **E**: No *S* are *P*.
- **I** : Some *S* are *P*.
- **O**: Some *S* are not *P*.

Every standard-form categorical proposition has four components:
- Quantifier ("all," "no," "some")
- Subject term
- Copula ("are," "are not")
- Predicate term

The *quality* of a categorical proposition:
- Affirmative (All *S* are *P*, Some *S* are *P*.)
- Negative (No *S* are *P*, Some *S* are not *P*.)

The *quantity* of a categorical proposition:
- Universal (All *S* are *P*, No *S* are *P*.)
- Particular (Some *S* are *P*, Some *P* are not *P*.)

The subject and predicate terms are distributed if the proposition makes an assertion about every member of the class denoted by the term; otherwise, undistributed:
- **A**: Subject term is distributed.
- **E**: Subject and predicate terms are distributed.
- **I** : Neither term is distributed.
- **O**: Predicate term is distributed.

Universal (**A** and **E**) propositions allow for two different interpretations:
- Aristotelian: Universal propositions about existing things have existential import.
- Boolean: Universal propositions have no existential import.

The modern square of opposition is a diagram that represents necessary inferences from the Boolean standpoint:
- **A** and **O** propositions contradict each other.
- **E** and **I** propositions contradict each other.

The content of categorical propositions may be represented by two-circle Venn diagrams:
- Shading an area indicates that the area is empty.
- Entering an X in an area means that the area is not empty.

Using Venn diagrams to test an immediate inference:
- Enter the content of the premise and conclusion in separate Venn diagrams.
- See if the content of the conclusion diagram is contained in the premise diagram.

Three operations that sometimes yield logically equivalent results:
- Conversion: Switch *S* and *P*. Logically equivalent results for **E, I**.
- Obversion: Change the quality, replace *P* with its term complement. Logically equivalent results for **A, E, I, O**.
- Contraposition: Switch *S* and *P*, replace *S* and *P* with term complements. Logically equivalent results for **A, O**.

Two formal fallacies may occur when these operations are used to derive conclusions:

- Illicit conversion: Performing conversion on an **A** or **O** premise.
- Illicit contraposition: Performing contraposition on an **E** or **I** premise.

The traditional square of opposition applies to categorical propositions when the Aristotelian standpoint is adopted and the subject term refers to existing things:

- Contrary: Holds between **A** and **E**. At least one is false.
- Subcontrary: Holds between **I** and **O**. At least one is true.
- Subalternation: Holds between **A** and **I** and between **E** and **O**. Truth flows downward and falsity flows upward.
- Contradiction: Holds as in the modern square.

Three formal fallacies may occur when the traditional square is used to derive conclusions:

- Illicit contrary: Results from an incorrect application of Contrary.
- Illicit subcontrary: Results from an incorrect application of Subcontrary.
- Illicit subalternation: Results from an incorrect application of Subalternation.

Existential Fallacy: Occurs when Contrary, Subcontrary, or Subalternation are used on premises whose subject terms refer to nonexistent things.

Translation: Propositions not in standard from may be put into standard form.

- Translation must have a proper quantifier, subject term, copula, predicate term.
- Translate singular propositions by using a parameter.
- Translate adverbs and pronouns by using "persons," "places," "things," "times."
- For **A** propositions:
  - Language following "if," "the only," and "W" words goes in the subject term.
  - Language following "only if," "only," "none but," "none except," and "no . . . except" goes in the predicate term.

4

Categorical Syllogisms

4.1   Standard Form, Mood, and Figure

PREVIEW

While walking across a bridge you feel a sudden jolt, and then the bridge starts swaying like crazy. Fortunately, it remains standing, but later you hear that another bridge in the area collapsed. Why didn't the bridge you were on collapse? The strength of a bridge is largely determined by its structure, and the bridge you crossed may have had greater structural integrity than the one that did collapse. In this section you will learn that the validity of an argument, like the strength of a bridge, depends on its form, or structure.

 **MindTap** *Your personal learning experience—learn anywhere, anytime.*

In the general sense of the term, a **syllogism** is a deductive argument consisting of two premises and one conclusion. Provisionally we will define a *categorical syllogism* as a syllogism consisting of three categorical propositions and containing a total of three different terms, each of which appears twice in distinct propositions. (We will give a more precise definition shortly.) The following argument is a categorical syllogism:

> All soldiers are patriots.
> No traitors are patriots.
> Therefore, no traitors are soldiers.

Each of the three terms in a categorical syllogism has its own name depending on its position in the argument. The **major term**, by definition, is the predicate of the conclusion, and the **minor term** is the subject of the conclusion. The **middle term**, which provides the middle ground between the two premises, is the one that occurs once in each premise and does not occur in the conclusion. Thus, for the argument just given, the major term is "soldiers," the minor term is "traitors," and the middle term is "patriots."

The premises of a categorical syllogism also have their own names. The **major premise**, by definition, is the one that contains the major term, and the **minor premise** is the one that contains the minor term. Thus, in the syllogism just given the major premise is "All soldiers are patriots," and the minor premise is "No traitors are patriots." Now that we are supplied with these definitions, we may proceed to the idea of standard form. A **standard-form categorical syllogism** is one that meets the following four conditions:

1. All three statements are standard-form categorical propositions.

2. The two occurrences of each term are identical.

3. Each term is used in the same sense throughout the argument.

4. The major premise is listed first, the minor premise second, and the conclusion last.

The first condition requires that each statement have a proper quantifier, subject term, copula, and predicate term. The second condition is clear. The third rules out the possibility of equivocation. For example, if a syllogism containing the word "men" used that term in the sense of human beings in one statement and in the sense of male human beings in another statement, the syllogism would really contain more than three terms and would therefore not be in standard form. Finally, the fourth condition merely requires that the three statements be listed in the right order.

The syllogism about soldiers is in standard form because all four conditions are fulfilled. However, the following syllogism is not in standard form, because the fourth condition is violated:

> All watercolors are paintings.
> Some watercolors are masterpieces.
> Therefore, some paintings are masterpieces.

To put this syllogism into standard form the order of the premises must be reversed. The major premise (the one containing "masterpieces," which is the predicate term in the conclusion) must be listed first, and the minor premise (the one containing "paintings," which is the subject term in the conclusion) must be listed second.

Now that we have a definition of standard-form categorical syllogism, we can give a more precise definition of categorical syllogism. A **categorical syllogism** is a deductive argument consisting of three categorical propositions that is capable of being translated into standard form. For an argument to qualify as a categorical syllogism, all three

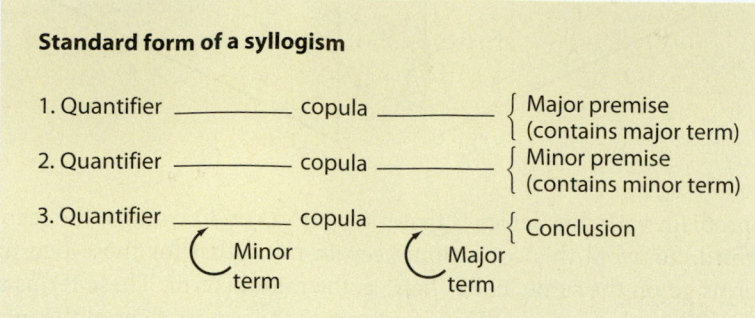

Standard form of a syllogism

1. Quantifier _____ copula _____ { Major premise (contains major term)
2. Quantifier _____ copula _____ { Minor premise (contains minor term)
3. Quantifier _____ copula _____ { Conclusion

Minor term ⌣   Major term ⌣

statements need not be standard-form categorical propositions; but if they are, the analysis is greatly simplified. For this reason, all of the syllogisms presented in the first four sections of this chapter will consist of statements that are in standard form. In later sections, techniques will be developed for translating non-standard-form syllogisms into equivalent arguments that are in standard form.

After a categorical syllogism has been put into standard form, its validity or invalidity may be determined through mere inspection of the form. The individual form of a syllogism consists of two factors: mood and figure. The **mood** of a categorical syllogism consists of the letter names of the propositions that make it up. For example, if the major premise is an **A** proposition, the minor premise an **O** proposition, and the conclusion an **E** proposition, the mood is **AOE**. To determine the mood of a categorical syllogism, one must first put the syllogism into standard form; the letter name of the statements may then be noted to the side of each. The mood of the syllogism is then designated by the order of these letters, reading the letter for the major premise first, the letter for the minor premise second, and the letter for the conclusion last.

The **figure** of a categorical syllogism is determined by the location of the two occurrences of the middle term in the premises. Four different arrangements are possible. If we let *S* represent the subject of the conclusion (minor term), *P* the predicate of the conclusion (major term), and *M* the middle term, and leave out the quantifiers and copulas, the four possible arrangements may be illustrated as follows:

Figure 1	Figure 2	Figure 3	Figure 4
Ⓜ P	P Ⓜ	Ⓜ P	P Ⓜ
S Ⓜ	S Ⓜ	Ⓜ S	Ⓜ S
S P	S P	S P	S P

In the first figure the middle term is top left, bottom right; in the second, top right, bottom right, and so on. Example:

No painters are sculptors.
Some sculptors are artists.
Therefore, some artists are not painters.

This syllogism is in standard form. The mood is **EIO** and the figure is four. The form of the syllogism is therefore designated as **EIO**-4.

To remember how the four figures are defined, imagine the four possible arrangements of the middle term as depicting the outline of a shirt collar:

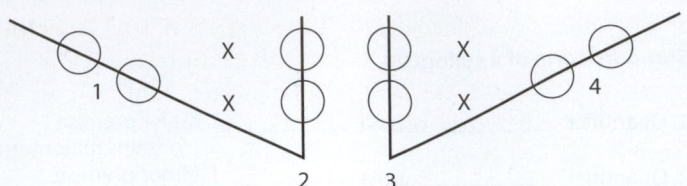

The only problem with this device is that it may lead you to confuse the second figure with the third. To avoid this confusion, keep in mind that for these two figures the *S* and *P* terms go on the same "collar flap" as the middle term. These terms are represented by the *X*'s in the diagram. Thus, for figure 2 the occurrences of the middle term are on the right side of the syllogism, and for figure 3 they are on the left side.

Since there are four kinds of categorical propositions and there are three categorical propositions in a categorical syllogism, there are 64 possible moods (4 × 4 × 4 = 64). And since there are four different figures, there are 256 different forms of categorical syllogisms (4 × 64 = 256).

Once the mood and figure of a syllogism is known, the validity of the syllogism can be determined by checking the mood and figure against a list of valid syllogistic forms. To do this, first adopt the Boolean standpoint and see if the syllogism's form appears in the following table of unconditionally valid forms. If it does, the syllogism is valid from the Boolean standpoint. In other words, it is valid regardless of whether its terms denote actually existing things.

UNCONDITIONALLY VALID FORMS

Figure 1	Figure 2	Figure 3	Figure 4
AAA	EAE	IAI	AEE
EAE	AEE	AII	IAI
AII	EIO	OAO	EIO
EIO	AOO	EIO	

If the syllogism does not appear on the list of unconditionally valid forms, then adopt the Aristotelian standpoint and see if the syllogism's form appears in the following table of conditionally valid forms. If it does, the syllogism is valid from the Aristotelian standpoint on condition that a certain term (the "critical" term) denotes actually existing things. The required condition is stated in the last column.

CONDITIONALLY VALID FORMS

Figure 1	Figure 2	Figure 3	Figure 4	Required condition
AAI	AEO		AEO	S exists
EAO	EAO			
		AAI	EAO	M exists
		EAO		
			AAI	P exists

For example, the **AAI**-1 is valid from the Aristotelian standpoint if the subject of the conclusion (the minor term) denotes actually existing things. The **EAO**-3 is valid if the middle term denotes actually existing things. Thus, if we are given an **AAI**-1 syllogism and the minor term is "cats," then the syllogism is valid from the Aristotelian standpoint. But if the minor term is "unicorns," then the syllogism is invalid. On the other hand, if the minor term is "students who failed the exam" and we are not certain if there are any such students, then the syllogism is conditionally valid.

The relationship between the Aristotelian standpoint and the Boolean standpoint is illustrated in the following bar graph:

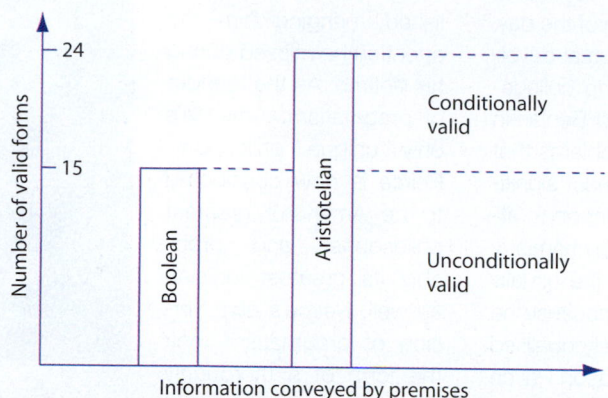

The graph shows that when the premises of a syllogistic form are recognized as conveying information about existence, an additional nine forms become valid.

Interestingly, during the Middle Ages logic students used to memorize a little poem that served as a rule of thumb for distinguishing valid from invalid syllogisms. The vowels in the words identified the mood, and the words "prioris," "secundae," and so on the figure.

> Barbara, Celarent, Darii, Ferioque prioris;
> Cesare, Camestres, Festino, Baroco secundae;
> Tertia, Darapti, Disamis, Datisi, Felapton,
> Bocardo, Ferison habet: quarta insuper addit
> Bramantip, Camenes, Dimaris, Fesapo, Fresison.

For example, the "Barbara" syllogism (this designation is still encountered today) is **AAA**-1, "Celarent" is **EAE**-1, and so on. This poem conforms substantially to the two tables given earlier, except that five forms have been left out. The reason these forms were left out is that the logicians of that time considered them weak: They draw a particular conclusion from premises that would support a (stronger) universal conclusion. For example, the weaker **AAI**-1 is left out in favor of the stronger **AAA**-1. Needless to say, few students today depend on this poem to distinguish valid from invalid syllogisms.

We have seen how, given the syllogism, we can obtain the mood and figure. But sometimes we need to go in the reverse direction: from the mood and figure to the syllogistic form. Suppose we are given the form **EIO**-4. To reconstruct the syllogistic form is easy. First use the mood to determine the skeleton of the form:

E	No _____ are _____.
I	Some _____ are _____.
O	Some _____ are not _____.

Then use the figure to determine the arrangement of the middle terms:

E	No _____ are *M*.
I	Some *M* are _____.
O	Some _____ are not _____.

Charles Sanders Peirce 1839–1914

Charles Sanders Peirce (pronounced "purse") was born in Cambridge, Massachusetts. His father, Benjamin, was the leading mathematician of the day, and he took a special interest in his son's intellectual development. Under his direction Charles was reading college-level material, including logic, at age twelve, and Benjamin would challenge the boy with highly complex problems that Charles would solve on his own. Although his most significant education came from his father, Charles went on to attend Harvard University, where he received a BS in chemistry in 1863. Yet, he was not a successful student (he usually placed in the lower quarter of his class), partly because he showed disdain for his professors as inadequately qualified to teach him. This arrogance is likely the main reason Peirce lived a difficult life. He died in poverty at age seventy-four in the then-isolated town of Milford, Pennsylvania.

NOAA's People Collection

Throughout his life Peirce suffered a painful and debilitating neurological condition that may have been responsible for his detached, depressed, and sometimes violent behavior. It may also have been the reason he could not obtain a tenured university position. In 1879 he did secure a position as a lecturer at Johns Hopkins University, and in some ways, he proved himself a remarkable teacher—a collection of his students' essays is considered a key work in the development of logic. Yet, despite his teaching, Peirce was discharged from his faculty position. He had recently separated from his wife and had lived with another woman before his divorce was finalized. This "immoral" behavior and other supposed transgressions were probably the chief factors leading to his dismissal. After that he never held another academic position.

Without an academic base, Peirce continued to write copiously, producing some 80,000 pages of material; yet he did not complete a single book in logic or philosophy, which limited his influence while alive. Beginning in the late 1930s, his writings were collected and published, bringing him the attention he missed during his lifetime. As the founder of pragmatism, America's only unique philosophy, Peirce is now considered to be America's greatest philosopher and probably its greatest logician as well. Peirce's own version of pragmatism took the form of a thoroughly scientific enterprise according to which the meaning of a concept depends on the practical effect it has on how we lead our lives and conduct our inquiries.

In logic Peirce is best known for his work in the logic of relations and quantification theory. The theory of quantification that Peirce developed is the one that led ultimately to the writing of *Principia Mathematica* by Whitehead and Russell, and it closely resembles the system used today in most logic courses. In the logic of relations, Peirce extended the work done by De Morgan by applying the concepts of Boolean algebra to relative terms such as "friend of " or "enemy of." This work has also significantly impacted the way we treat this subject today. In addition, Peirce was a leader in exploring the use of truth values, and he was the first to develop a three-valued logic incorporating true, false, and an intermediate or unknown value. In propositional logic Peirce succeeded in reducing all the connectives to one, and in inductive logic he rejected the subjectivist theory of probability in favor of an objectivist theory based on observed regularities.

Finally, supply the major and minor terms, using the letters *S* and *P* to designate the subject and predicate of the conclusion. The predicate of the conclusion is always repeated in the first premise, and the subject of the conclusion is repeated in the second premise:

E	No *P* are *M*.
I	Some *M* are *S*.
O	Some *S* are not *P*.

I. The following syllogisms are in standard form. Identify the major, minor, and middle terms, as well as the mood and figure of each. Then use the two lists of valid syllogistic forms to determine whether each is valid from the Boolean standpoint, valid from the Aristotelian standpoint, or invalid.

★ 1. All neutron stars are things that produce intense gravity.
All neutron stars are extremely dense objects.
Therefore, all extremely dense objects are things that produce intense gravity.

2. No insects that eat mosquitoes are insects that should be killed.
All dragonflies are insects that eat mosquitoes.
Therefore, no dragonflies are insects that should be killed.

3. No environmentally produced diseases are inherited afflictions.
Some psychological disorders are not inherited afflictions.
Therefore, some psychological disorders are environmentally produced diseases.

★ 4. No people who mix fact with fantasy are good witnesses.
Some hypnotized people are people who mix fact with fantasy.
Therefore, some hypnotized people are not good witnesses.

5. All ozone molecules are good absorbers of ultraviolet rays.
All ozone molecules are things destroyed by chlorine.
Therefore, some things destroyed by chlorine are good absorbers of ultraviolet rays.

II. Put the following syllogisms into standard form, using letters to represent the terms, and name the mood and figure. Then use the two lists of valid syllogistic forms to determine whether each is valid from the Boolean standpoint, valid from the Aristotelian standpoint, or invalid.

★ 1. No Republicans are Democrats, so no Republicans are big spenders, since all big spenders are Democrats.

2. Some latchkey children are not kids who can stay out of trouble, for some youngsters prone to boredom are latchkey children, and no kids who can stay out of trouble are youngsters prone to boredom.

3. No rent-control proposals are regulations welcomed by landlords, and all regulations welcomed by landlords are measures that allow a free hand in raising rents. Therefore, some rent-control proposals are measures that allow a free hand in raising rents.

★ 4. Some insects that feed on milkweed are not foods suitable for birds, inasmuch as no monarch butterflies are foods suitable for birds and all monarch butterflies are insects that feed on milkweed.

5. No undocumented individuals are people who have a right to welfare payments, and some migrant workers are undocumented individuals. Thus, some people who have a right to welfare payments are migrant workers.

4

6. Some African nations are not countries deserving military aid, because some African nations are not upholders of human rights, and all countries deserving military aid are upholders of human rights.

★7. All pranksters are exasperating individuals, consequently some leprechauns are exasperating individuals, since all leprechauns are pranksters.

8. Some racists are not people suited to be immigration officials, given that some humanitarians are not people suited to be immigration officials, and no humanitarians are racists.

9. No people who respect human life are terrorists, and all airline hijackers are terrorists. Hence, no airline hijackers are people who respect human life.

★10. Some silicates are crystalline substances, because all silicates are oxygen compounds, and some oxygen compounds are not crystalline substances.

III. Reconstruct the syllogistic forms from the following combinations of mood and figure:

★1. **OAE**-3

2. **EIA**-4

3. **AII**-3

★4. **IAE**-1

5. **AOO**-2

6. **EAO**-4

★7. **AAA**-1

8. **EAO**-2

9. **OEI**-3

★10. **OEA**-4

IV. Construct the following syllogisms.

★1. An **EIO**-2 syllogism with these terms—*major*—dogmatists; *minor*—theologians; *middle*—scholars who encourage freethinking.

2. An unconditionally valid syllogism in the first figure with a particular affirmative conclusion and these terms: *major*—people incapable of objectivity; *minor*—Supreme Court justices; *middle*—lockstep ideologues.

3. An unconditionally valid syllogism in the fourth figure having two universal premises and these terms: *major*—teenage suicides; *minor*—heroic episodes; *middle*—tragic occurrences.

★4. A valid syllogism having mood **OAO** and these terms: *major*—things capable of replicating by themselves; *minor*—structures that invade cells; *middle*—viruses.

5. A valid syllogism in the first figure having a universal negative conclusion and these terms: *major*—guarantees of marital happiness; *minor*—prenuptial agreements; *middle*—legally enforceable documents.

V. Answer "true" or "false" to the following statements:

1. Every syllogism is a categorical syllogism.

2. Some categorical syllogisms cannot be put into standard form.

3. The statements in a categorical syllogism need not be expressed in standard form.

4. The statements in a standard-form categorical syllogism need not be expressed in standard form.

5. In a standard-form categorical syllogism the two occurrences of each term must be identical.

6. The major premise of a standard-form categorical syllogism contains the subject of the conclusion.

7. To determine its mood and figure, a categorical syllogism must first be put into standard form.

8. In a standard-form syllogism having Figure 2, the two occurrences of the middle term are on the right.

9. The unconditionally valid syllogistic forms are valid from both the Boolean and the Aristotelian standpoints.

10. The conditionally valid syllogistic forms are invalid if the requisite condition is not fulfilled.

4

4.2 Venn Diagrams

PREVIEW

You hear on TV that a robbery is in progress at a local bank. The bank employees are being held as hostages in the vault, while the customers are hiding from the robbers in a meeting room. You then discover that a friend of yours was in the bank when the robbery began. You reason that since your friend was a customer, he is in the meeting room—which means that he is not being held hostage. This reasoning process, which assigns classes to three spatial areas, underlies the application of Venn diagrams to syllogisms.

Venn diagrams provide the most intuitively evident and, in the long run, easiest to remember technique for testing the validity of categorical syllogisms. The technique is basically an extension of the one developed in Chapter 3 to represent the informational content of categorical propositions. Because syllogisms contain three terms, whereas propositions contain only two, the application of Venn diagrams to syllogisms requires three overlapping circles.

These circles should be drawn so that seven areas are clearly distinguishable within the diagram. The second step is to label the circles, one for each term. The precise order of the labeling is not critical, but we will adopt the convention of always assigning the lower-left circle to the subject of the conclusion, the lower-right circle to the predicate of the conclusion, and the top circle to the middle term. This convention is easy to remember because it conforms to the arrangement of the terms in a standard-form syllogism: The subject of the conclusion is on the lower left, the predicate of the conclusion is on the lower right, and the middle term is in the premises, above the conclusion.*

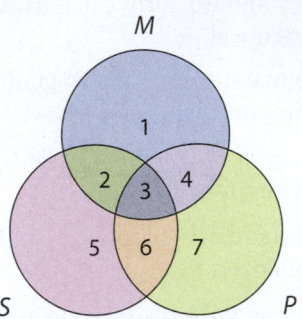

Anything in the area marked "1" is an *M* but neither an *S* nor a *P*, anything in the area marked "2" is both an *S* and an *M* but not a *P*, anything in the area marked "3" is a member of all three classes, and so on.

The test procedure consists of transferring the information content of the premises to the diagram and then inspecting the diagram to see whether it necessarily implies the truth of the conclusion. If the information in the diagram does do this, the argument is valid; otherwise it is invalid.

The use of Venn diagrams to evaluate syllogisms usually requires a little practice at first. Perhaps the best way of learning the technique is through illustrative examples, but a few pointers are needed first:

1. Marks (shading or placing an X) are entered only for the premises. No marks are made for the conclusion.

2. If the argument contains one universal premise, this premise should be entered first in the diagram. If there are two universal premises, either one can be done first.

3. When entering the information contained in a premise, one should concentrate on the circles corresponding to the two terms in the statement. While the third circle cannot be ignored altogether, it should be given only minimal attention.

4. When inspecting a completed diagram to see whether it supports a particular conclusion, one should remember that particular statements assert two things. "Some *S* are *P*" means "At least one *S* exists *and* that *S* is a *P*"; "Some *S* are not *P*" means "At least one *S* exists *and* that *S* is not a *P*."

*Some textbooks present three-circle Venn diagrams with two circles on the top and one on the bottom. This textbook presents them the way John Venn himself drew them, with two circles on the bottom and one on the top. See his Symbolic Logic (London: Macmillan, 1881), 105, 114, 116.

5. When shading an area, one must be careful to shade *all* of the area in question. Examples:

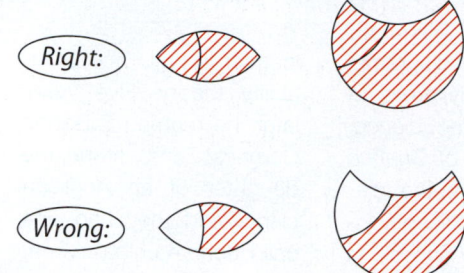

6. The area where an X goes is always initially divided into two parts. If one of these parts has already been shaded, the X goes in the unshaded part. Examples:

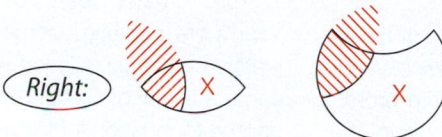

If one of the two parts is not shaded, the X goes on the line separating the two parts. Examples:

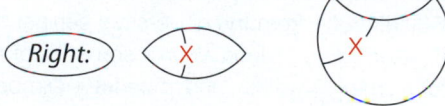

This means that the X may be in either (or both) of the two areas—but it is not known which one.

7. An X should never be placed in such a way that it dangles outside of the diagram, and it should never be placed on the intersection of two lines.

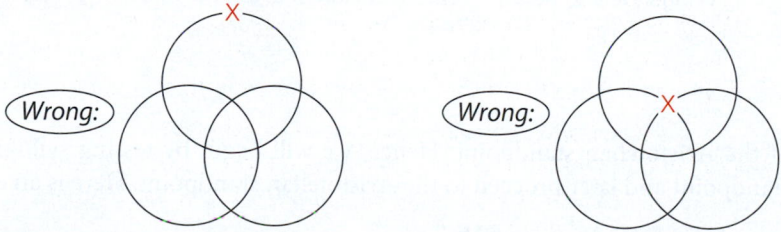

Boolean Standpoint

Because the Boolean standpoint does not recognize universal premises as having existential import, its approach to testing syllogisms is simpler and more general than that

> Boolean standpoint: No existential import for **A** and **E** propositions.

John Venn 1834–1923

John Venn is known mainly for his circle diagrams, which have contributed to work in many areas of mathematics and logic, including computer science, set theory, and statistics. His book *The Logic of Chance* (1866) advanced probability theory by introducing the relative frequency interpretation of probability; it significantly influenced later developments in statistical theory as well. In *Symbolic Logic* (1881) he defended George Boole against various critics and rendered the new logic intelligible to non-mathematical thinkers. Finally, in *The Principles of Empirical and Inductive Logic* (1889) he criticized Mill's methods of induction as being of limited application as an engine of discovery in science.

John Venn was born in Hull, England, the son of Henry Venn, the Drypool parish rector, and Martha Sykes Venn, who died when John was a child. The Venns were prominent members of the evangelical movement within the Church of England. John Venn's grandfather had been an evangelical leader, as was his father, whom his contemporaries regarded as the head of the evangelical movement. His father served for many years in an administrative capacity for the Church Missionary Society, and John was expected to follow in the family tradition. In 1858, after graduating from Gonville and Caius (pronounced "keys") College, Cambridge, he was ordained and served for a time as a curate in parishes near London.

Perhaps owing to his contact with Henry Sidgwick and other Cambridge agnostics, Venn's confidence in the Thirty-Nine Articles of the Church of England began to erode. Also, as a result of his reading the works of De Morgan, Boole, and Mill, his interest shifted almost totally from theological matters to issues related to logic. At age twenty-eight, Venn returned to Cambridge to become a

lecturer in logic and probability theory. Five years later, he married Susanna Carnegie Edmonstone, the daughter of an Anglican cleric, and they had one child, John Archibald Venn. In 1883, at age forty-nine, Venn became a fellow of the Royal Society and received the degree of Doctor of Science.

The greater part of Venn's life centered completely on his association with Cambridge. In 1857 he became a fellow of Caius, and he remained a member of the college foundation for sixty-six years, until his death. During the last twenty years of his life he served as college president, during which time he wrote a history of the college. Also, in collaboration with his son, he completed Part I of the massive *Alumni Cantabrigienses*, which contains short biographies of 76,000 graduates and office holders ranging from the university's earliest days through 1751.

John Venn's son said of his father that he was a "fine walker and mountain climber." Also, in keeping with his view that abstract subjects such as logic and mathematics ought to serve practical utility, Venn loved to use this knowledge to build machines. He invented a cricket bowling machine that was used against the best batsman of an Australian team. The machine "clean bowled" this batsman four times. Today Venn is memorialized by a stained-glass window in the dining hall of Caius College that contains a representation of a Venn diagram.

of the Aristotelian standpoint. Hence, we will begin by testing syllogisms from that standpoint and later proceed to the Aristotelian standpoint. Here is an example:

1. No *P* are *M*.   **EAE**-2
   All *S* are *M*.
   No *S* are *P*.

Since both premises are universal, it makes no difference which premise we enter first in the diagram. To enter the major premise, we concentrate our attention on the *M* and *P* circles, which are highlighted with color:

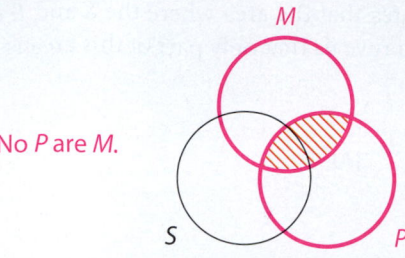

No *P* are *M*.

We now complete the diagram by entering the minor premise. In doing so, we concentrate our attention on the *S* and *M* circles, which are highlighted with color:

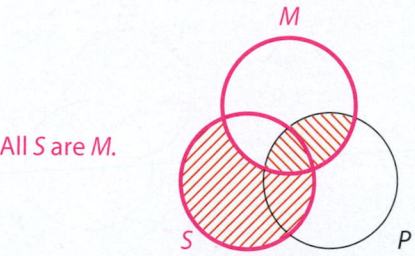

All *S* are *M*.

The conclusion states that the area where the *S* and *P* circles overlap is shaded. Inspection of the diagram reveals that this area is indeed shaded, so the syllogistic form is valid. Because the form is valid from the Boolean standpoint, it is *unconditionally valid*. In other words, it is valid regardless of whether its premises are recognized as having existential import.

Here is another example:

> 2. All *M* are *P*.　　**AEE**-1
>   No *S* are *M*.
>   No *S* are *P*.

Again, both premises are universal, so it makes no difference which premise we enter first in the diagram. To enter the major premise, we concentrate our attention on the *M* and *P* circles:

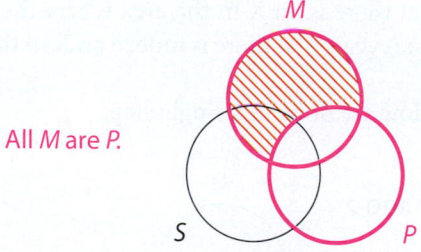

All *M* are *P*.

To enter the minor premise, we concentrate our attention on the *M* and *S* circles:

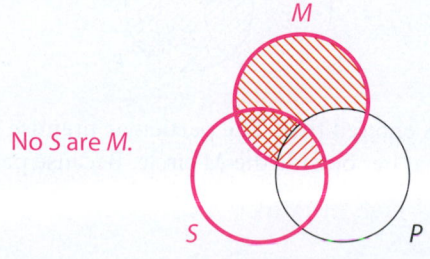

No *S* are *M*.

4

Again, the conclusion states that the area where the S and P circles overlap is shaded. Inspection of the diagram reveals that only part of this area is shaded, so the syllogistic form is invalid.

Another example:

3. Some P are M.   **IAI**-4
   All M are S.
   Some S are P.

We enter the universal premise first. To do so, we concentrate our attention on the M and S circles:

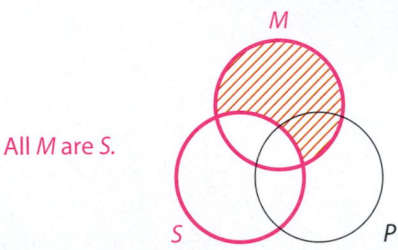

All M are S.

To enter the particular premise, we concentrate our attention on the M and P circles. This premise tells us to place an X in the area where the M and P circles overlap. Because part of this area is shaded, we place the X in the remaining area:

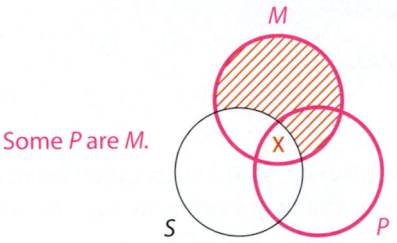

Some P are M.

The conclusion states that there is an X in the area where the S and P circles overlap. Inspection of the diagram reveals that there is indeed an X in this area, so the syllogistic form is valid.

The examples that follow are done in a single step.

4. All P are M.   **AOO**-2
   Some S are not M.
   Some S are not P.

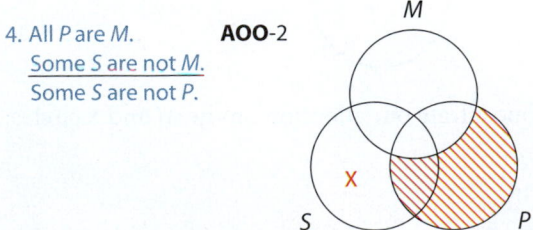

The universal premise is entered first. The particular premise tells us to place an X in the part of the S circle that lies outside the M circle. Because part of this area is shaded, we place the X in the remaining area. The conclusion states that there is an X that is inside the *S* circle but outside the *P* circle. Inspection of the diagram reveals that there is indeed an X in this area, so the syllogistic form is valid.

5. Some *M* are *P.*   **IAI**-1
    All *S* are *M.*
    Some *S* are *P.*

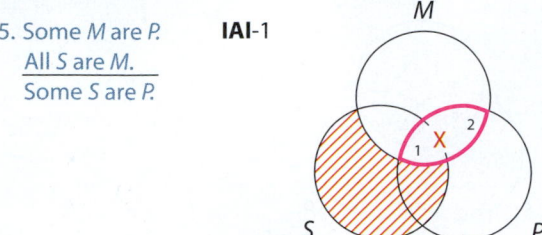

As usual, we enter the universal premise first. In entering the particular premise, we concentrate on the area where the *M* and *P* circles overlap. (For emphasis, this area is colored in the diagram.) Because this overlap area is divided into two parts (the areas marked "1" and "2"), we place the X on the line (arc of the *S* circle) that separates the two parts. The conclusion states that there is an X in the area where the *S* and *P* circles overlap. Inspection of the diagram reveals that the single X is dangling outside of this overlap area. We do not know if it is in or out. Thus, the syllogistic form is invalid.

6. All *M* are *P.*   **AOO**-1
   Some *S* are not *M.*
   Some *S* are not *P.*

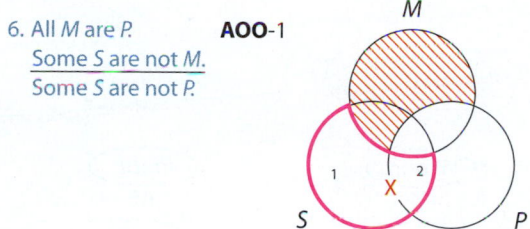

In entering the particular premise, we concentrate our attention on the part of the *S* circle that lies outside the *M* circle (colored area). Because this area is divided into two parts (the areas marked "1" and "2"), we place the X on the line (arc of the *P* circle) separating the two areas. The conclusion states that there is an X that is inside the *S* circle but outside the *P* circle. There *is* an X in the *S* circle, but we do not know whether it is inside or outside the *P* circle. Hence, the syllogistic form is invalid.

7. All *M* are *P.*   **AAA**-1
   All *S* are *M.*
   All *S* are *P.*

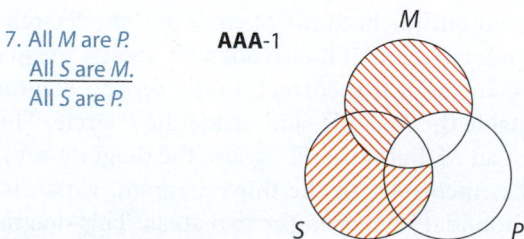

This is the "Barbara" syllogism. The conclusion states that the part of the S circle that is outside the P circle is empty. Inspection of the diagram reveals that this area is indeed empty. Thus, the syllogistic form is valid.

8. Some *M* are not *P*.   **OIO**-1
   Some *S* are *M*.
   Some *S* are not *P*.

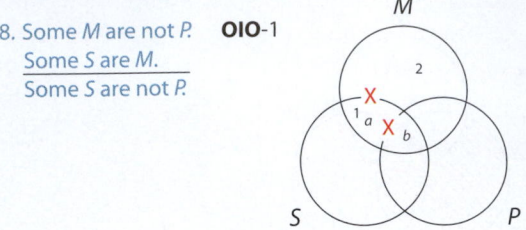

In this diagram no areas have been shaded, so there are two possible areas for each of the two X's. The X from the first premise goes on the line (arc of the S circle) separating areas 1 and 2, and the X from the second premise goes on the line (arc of the P circle) separating areas *a* and *b*. The conclusion states that there is an X that is inside the S circle but outside the P circle. We have no certainty that the X from the first premise is inside the S circle, and while the X from the second premise is inside the S circle, we have no certainty that it is outside the P circle. Hence, the syllogistic form is invalid.

We have yet to explain the rationale for placing the X on the boundary separating two areas when neither of the areas is shaded. Consider this syllogistic form:

No *P* are *M*.
Some *S* are not *M*.
Some *S* are *P*.

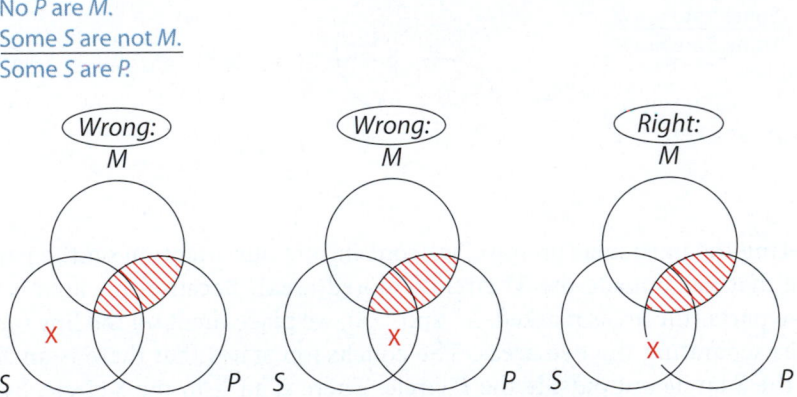

In each of the three diagrams the content of the first premise is represented correctly. The problem concerns placing the X from the second premise. In the first diagram the X is placed inside the S circle but outside both the M circle and the P circle. This diagram asserts: "At least one S is not an M and it is also not a P." Clearly the diagram says more than the premise does, and so it is incorrect. In the second diagram the X is placed inside the S circle, outside the M circle, and inside the P circle. This diagram asserts: "At least one S is not an M, but it is a P." Again, the diagram says more than the premise says, and so it is incorrect. In the third diagram, which is done correctly, the X is placed on the boundary between the two areas. This diagram asserts: "At least one S is not an M, and it may or may not be a P." In other words, nothing at all is said about P, and so the diagram represents exactly the content of the second premise.

Aristotelian Standpoint

For the syllogistic forms tested thus far, we have adopted the Boolean standpoint, which does not recognize universal premises as having existential import. We now shift to the Aristotelian standpoint, where existential import can make a difference to validity. The table of conditionally valid syllogistic forms presented in Section 4.1 names nine forms that are valid from the Aristotelian standpoint if a certain condition is fulfilled. The following syllogism has one of those forms:

9. No fighter pilots are tank commanders.
    All fighter pilots are courageous individuals.
    Therefore, some courageous individuals are not tank commanders.

First, we replace the terms with letters and test the syllogism from the Boolean standpoint:

No *F* are *T*.   **EAO**-3
All *F* are *C*.
Some *C* are not *T*.

The conclusion asserts that there is an X that is inside the *C* circle but outside the *T* circle. Inspection of the diagram reveals no X's at all, so the syllogism is invalid from the Boolean standpoint. But if we take another look at the diagram, we notice something special about it. There is one circle (the *F* circle) that is all shaded except for one area. This means that if we assume that the *F* circle has something in it, then we know exactly where that something is. In other words, if we assume that the premises have existential import, then we know exactly where those existing things are in the diagram. They lie in the one open area of the *F* circle.

The next step is to adopt the Aristotelian standpoint and assume that the premises have existential import. To represent this assumption of existence, we enter an X in the open area of the *F* circle. But this cannot be an ordinary X, which represents the positive claim of existence made by **I** and **O** propositions. It must be a special kind of X representing the assumption that **A** and **E** propositions imply the existence of something. For this special kind of X, we take an ordinary X and surround it with a small circle. We now enter such an X in the open area of the *F* circle:

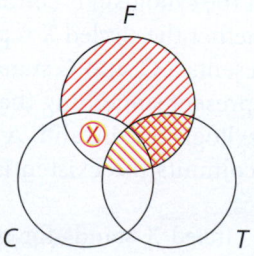

The diagram now indicates that the syllogism is conditionally valid; in other words, it is valid on condition that there really is something in the *F* circle. Thus, we proceed

> Aristotelian standpoint: Interpre... **A** and **E** propositions as having existential import.

> Keep an eye out for syllogisms having a particular conclusion where one circle is all shaded except for one area.

4

to the final step and determine whether the circled X represents something that actually exists. Since the circled X represents an *F*, and since *F* stands for fighter pilots, the circled X does represent something that exists. Thus, the condition is fulfilled, and the syllogism is valid from the Aristotelian standpoint.

The *F* circle in this diagram represents the critical term, first mentioned in connection with the table of conditionally valid forms in Section 4.1. The critical term is the term listed in the farthest right-hand column of that table. As the diagram shows, if the circle for the critical term has at least one member, then this member is necessarily also in the circle representing the subject of the conclusion (in this case *C*).

Here is another example:

10. All reptiles are scaly animals.
    All currently living tyrannosaurs are reptiles.
    Therefore, some currently living tyrannosaurs are scaly animals.

First we test the syllogism from the Boolean standpoint:

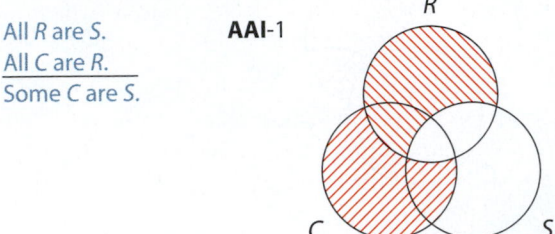

All *R* are *S*.   **AAI**-1
All *C* are *R*.
Some *C* are *S*.

The conclusion asserts that there is an X in the area where the *C* and *S* circles overlap. Since the diagram contains no X's at all, the syllogism is invalid from the Boolean standpoint. But then we notice that there is one circle (the *C* circle) that is all shaded except for one area. Thus, we adopt the Aristotelian standpoint, and we enter a circled X in that area:

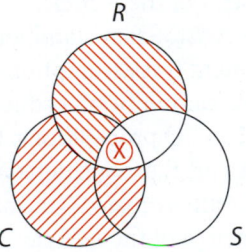

The diagram now indicates that the syllogism is conditionally valid, so we proceed to the final step and determine whether the circled X represents something that actually exists. Since the circled X represents a *C*, and *C* stands for currently living tyrannosaurs, the circled X does not represent something that actually exists. Thus, the condition is not fulfilled, and the syllogism is invalid. As we will see in the next section of this chapter, the syllogism commits the existential fallacy from the Aristotelian standpoint.

In determining whether the circled X stands for something that exists, we always look to the Venn circle that is all shaded except for one area. If the term corresponding to that circle denotes existing things, then the circled X represents one of those things.

In some diagrams, however, there may be two Venn circles that are all shaded except for one area, and each may contain a circled X in the unshaded area. In these cases we direct our attention only to the circled X needed to draw the conclusion. If that circled X stands for something that exists, the argument is valid; if not, it is invalid.

EXERCISE 4.2

I. Use Venn diagrams to determine whether the following standard-form categorical syllogisms are valid from the Boolean standpoint, valid from the Aristotelian standpoint, or invalid. Then, identify the mood and figure, and cross-check your answers with the tables of valid syllogisms found in Section 4.1.

★ 1. All corporations that overcharge their customers are unethical businesses.
Some unethical businesses are investor-owned utilities.
Therefore, some investor-owned utilities are corporations that overcharge their customers.

2. No AIDS victims are people who pose an immediate threat to the lives of others.
Some kindergarten children are AIDS victims.
Therefore, some kindergarten children are not people who pose an immediate threat to the lives of others.

3. No individuals truly concerned with the plight of suffering humanity are people motivated primarily by self-interest.
All television evangelists are people motivated primarily by self-interest.
Therefore, some television evangelists are not individuals truly concerned with the plight of suffering humanity.

★ 4. All high-fat diets are diets high in cholesterol.
Some diets high in cholesterol are not healthy food programs.
Therefore, some healthy food programs are not high-fat diets.

5. No engineering majors are candidates for nightly hookups.
No candidates for nightly hookups are deeply emotional individuals.
Therefore, no deeply emotional individuals are engineering majors.

6. All impulse buyers are consumers with credit cards.
All shopaholics are impulse buyers.
Therefore, all shopaholics are consumers with credit cards.

★ 7. No pediatricians are individuals who jeopardize the health of children.
All faith healers are individuals who jeopardize the health of children.
Therefore, no faith healers are pediatricians.

8. Some individuals prone to violence are not men who treat others humanely.
Some police officers are individuals prone to violence.
Therefore, some police officers are not men who treat others humanely.

9. Some ATM locations are places criminals lurk.
All places criminals lurk are places to avoid at night.
Therefore, some places to avoid at night are ATM locations.

★ 10. No corporations that defraud the government are organizations the government should deal with.
Some defense contractors are not organizations the government should deal with.
Therefore, some defense contractors are not corporations that defraud the government.

11. All circular triangles are plane figures.
All circular triangles are three-sided figures.
Therefore, some three-sided figures are plane figures.

12. All supernovas are objects that emit massive amounts of energy.
All quasars are objects that emit massive amounts of energy.
Therefore, all quasars are supernovas.

★ 13. No people who profit from the illegality of their activities are people who want their activities legalized.
All drug dealers are people who profit from the illegality of their activities.
Therefore, no drug dealers are people who want their activities legalized.

14. Some individuals who risk heart disease are people who will die young.
Some smokers are individuals who risk heart disease.
Therefore, some smokers are people who will die young.

15. Some communications satellites are rocket-launched failures.
All communications satellites are devices with antennas.
Therefore, some devices with antennas are rocket-launched failures.

★ 16. All currently living dinosaurs are giant reptiles.
All giant reptiles are ectothermic animals.
Therefore, some ectothermic animals are currently living dinosaurs.

17. All survivalists are people who enjoy simulated war games.
No people who enjoy simulated war games are soldiers who have tasted the agony of real war.
Therefore, all soldiers who have tasted the agony of real war are survivalists.

18. No spurned lovers are Valentine's Day fanatics.
Some moonstruck romantics are Valentine's Day fanatics.
Therefore, some moonstruck romantics are not spurned lovers.

★ 19. No theocracies are regimes open to change.
All theocracies are governments that rule by force.
Therefore, some governments that rule by force are not regimes open to change.

20. Some snowflakes are not uniform solids.
All snowflakes are six-pointed crystals.
Therefore, some six-pointed crystals are not uniform solids.

II. Use Venn diagrams to obtain the conclusion that is validly implied by each of the following sets of premises. If no conclusion can be validly drawn, write "no conclusion."

★ 1. No P are M.
All S are M.
_____

2. Some P are not M.
Some M are S.
_____

3. Some M are P.
All S are M.
_____

★ 4. Some M are not P.
All M are S.
_____

5.	Some *P* are *M*.	**8.**	All *P* are *M*.
	All *M* are *S*.		All *S* are *M*.
6.	No *M* are *P*.	**9.**	No *P* are *M*.
	Some *S* are not *M*.		Some *M* are *S*.
★ **7.**	All *M* are *P*.	★ **10.**	No *P* are *M*.
	All *S* are *M*.		No *M* are *S*.

III. Answer "true" or "false" to the following statements:

1. In the use of Venn diagrams to test the validity of syllogisms, marks are sometimes entered in the diagram for the conclusion.

2. When an X is placed on the arc of a circle, it means that the X could be in either (or both) of the two areas that the arc separates.

3. If an X lies on the arc of a circle, the argument cannot be valid.

4. When representing a universal statement in a Venn diagram, one always shades two of the seven areas in the diagram (unless one of these areas is already shaded).

5. If a completed diagram contains two X's, the argument cannot be valid.

6. If the conclusion asserts that a certain area is shaded, and inspection of the diagram reveals that only half that area is shaded, the argument is valid.

7. If the conclusion asserts that a certain area contains an X and inspection of the diagram reveals that only half an X appears in that area, the argument is valid.

8. If the conclusion is in the form "All *S* are *P*," and inspection of the diagram reveals that the part of the *S* circle that is outside the *P* circle is shaded, then the argument is valid.

9. If, in a completed diagram, three areas of a single circle are shaded, and placing a circled X in the one remaining area would make the conclusion true, then the argument is valid from the Aristotelian standpoint but not from the Boolean standpoint.

10. If, in a completed diagram, three areas of a single circle are shaded, but the argument is not valid from the Boolean standpoint, then it must be valid from the Aristotelian standpoint.

Visit Aplia for section-specific problem sets.

4.3   Rules and Fallacies

PREVIEW

Your college or university probably specifies rules that a student must satisfy in order to graduate. You must earn a certain number of course units, the courses must be in designated subject areas, you must maintain a certain GPA, and so on. If you follow all of the rules, you will reach your goal—which is graduation. Likewise, there are rules that determine whether the premises of a categorical syllogism support the conclusion. If all the rules are followed, the syllogism is valid.

The idea that valid syllogisms conform to certain rules was first expressed by Aristotle. Many such rules are discussed in Aristotle's own account, but logicians of today generally settle on five or six.* If any one of these rules is violated, a specific formal fallacy is committed and, accordingly, the syllogism is invalid. Conversely, if none of the rules is broken, the syllogism is valid. These rules may be used as a convenient cross-check against the method of Venn diagrams. We will first consider the rules as they apply from the Boolean standpoint, and then shift to the Aristotelian standpoint.

Boolean Standpoint

If a syllogism obeys all five rules, then it is unconditionally valid.

Of the five rules presented in this section, the first two depend on the concept of distribution, the second two on the concept of quality, and the last on the concept of quantity. In applying the first two rules, you may want to recall either of the two mnemonic devices presented in Chapter 3: "Unprepared Students Never Pass" and "Any Student Earning B's Is Not On Probation." These mnemonics help one remember that the four categorical propositions distribute their terms as follows:

Statement type	Terms distributed
A	subject
E	subject, predicate
I	none
O	predicate

Here is the first rule.

Rule 1: The Middle Term Must Be Distributed at Least Once.

Fallacy: **Undistributed middle**

Example: All sharks are fish.
            All salmon are fish.
            All salmon are sharks.

In this standard-form categorical syllogism the middle term is "fish." In both premises "fish" occurs as the predicate of an **A** proposition and therefore it is not distributed in either premise. Thus, the syllogism commits the fallacy of undistributed middle and is invalid. If the major premise were rewritten to read "All fish are sharks," then "fish" would be distributed in that premise and the syllogism would be valid. But, of course, it would still be unsound because the rewritten premise would be false.

The logic behind Rule 1 may be explained by recounting how the middle term accomplishes its intended purpose, which is to provide a common ground between the subject and predicate terms of the conclusion. Let us designate the minor, major, and middle terms by the letters S, P, and M, respectively, and let us suppose that M is distributed in the major premise. By definition, P is related to the *whole* of the M class.

*Some texts include a rule stating that the three terms of a categorical syllogism must be used in the same sense throughout the argument. In this text this requirement is included as part of the definition of standard-form categorical syllogism and is subsequently incorporated into the definition of categorical syllogism. See Section 4.1.

Then, when the *M* class is related either in whole or in part to *S*, *S* and *P* necessarily become related. Analogous reasoning prevails if we suppose that *M* is distributed in the minor premise. But if *M* is undistributed in both premises, *S* and *P* may be related to *different parts* of the *M* class, in which case there is no common ground for relating *S* and *P*. This is exactly what happens in our fish example. The terms "salmon" and "sharks" are related to different parts of the fish class, so no common ground exists for relating them.

Rule 2: If a Term Is Distributed in the Conclusion, Then It Must Be Distributed in a Premise.

Fallacies: **Illicit major; illicit minor**

Examples: All horses are animals.
Some dogs are not horses.
Some dogs are not animals.

All tigers are mammals.
All mammals are animals.
All animals are tigers.

In the first example the major term, "animals," is distributed in the conclusion but not in the major premise, so the syllogism commits the fallacy of illicit major, or, more precisely, "illicit process of the major term." In the second example the minor term, "animals," is distributed in the conclusion but not in the minor premise. The second example therefore commits the fallacy of illicit minor, or "illicit process of the minor term."

In applying this rule, one must always examine the conclusion first. If no terms are distributed in the conclusion, Rule 2 cannot be violated. If one or both terms in the conclusion are distributed, then the appropriate premise must be examined. If the term distributed in the conclusion is also distributed in the premise, then the rule is not violated. But, if the term is not distributed in the premise, the rule is violated and the syllogism is invalid. In applying Rule 2 (and also Rule 1), you may find it helpful to begin by marking all the distributed terms in the syllogism—either by circling them or by labeling them with a superscript letter "d."

The logic behind Rule 2 is easy to understand. Let us once again designate the minor, major, and middle terms by the letters *S*, *P*, and *M*, respectively, and let us suppose that a certain syllogism commits the fallacy of illicit major. The conclusion of that syllogism then makes an assertion about every member of the *P* class, but the major premise makes an assertion about only some members of the *P* class. Because the minor premise, by itself, says nothing at all about the *P* class, the conclusion clearly contains information not contained in the premises, and the syllogism is therefore invalid. Analogous reasoning applies to the fallacy of illicit minor.

Rule 2 becomes intuitively plausible when it is recognized that distribution is a positive attribute. Granting this, an argument that has a term distributed in the conclusion but not in the premises has *more* in the conclusion than it does in the premises and is therefore invalid. Of course, it is always permissible to have more in a premise than appears in the conclusion, so it is perfectly all right for a term to be distributed in a premise but not in the conclusion.

Rule 3: Two Negative Premises Are Not Allowed.

Fallacy: **Exclusive premises**

Example: No fish are mammals.
Some dogs are not fish.
Some dogs are not mammals.

This syllogism may be seen as invalid because it has true premises and a false conclusion. The defect stems from the fact that it has two negative premises.

On reflection, Rule 3 should be fairly obvious. Let S, P, and M once again designate the minor, major, and middle terms. Now, if the P class and the M class are separate either wholly or partially, and the S class and the M class are separate either wholly or partially, nothing is said about the relation between the S class and the P class. These two classes may be either distinct or identical in whole or in part. Venn diagrams may be used effectively to illustrate the fact that no conclusion can be validly drawn from two negative premises.

Rule 4: A Negative Premise Requires a Negative Conclusion, and a Negative Conclusion Requires a Negative Premise.

Fallacy: **Drawing an affirmative conclusion from a negative premise**

or

Drawing a negative conclusion from affirmative premises

Examples: All crows are birds.
Some wolves are not crows.
Some wolves are birds.

All triangles are three-angled polygons.
All three-angled polygons are three-sided polygons.
Some three-sided polygons are not triangles.

These arguments may be seen as invalid because each has true premises and a false conclusion. The first draws an affirmative conclusion from a negative premise, and the second draws a negative conclusion from affirmative premises.

The logic behind Rule 4 may be seen as follows. If S, P, and M once again designate the minor, major, and middle terms, an affirmative conclusion always states that the S class is contained either wholly or partially in the P class. The only way that such a conclusion can follow is if the S class is contained either wholly or partially in the M class, and the M class wholly in the P class. In other words, it follows only when both premises are affirmative. But if, for example, the S class is contained either wholly or partially in the M class, and the M class is separate either wholly or partially from the P class, such a conclusion will never follow. Thus, an affirmative conclusion cannot be drawn from negative premises.

Conversely, a negative conclusion asserts that the S class is separate either wholly or partially from the P class. But if both premises are affirmative, they assert class inclusion rather than separation. Thus, a negative conclusion cannot be drawn from affirmative premises.

As a result of the interaction of these first four rules, it turns out that no valid syllogism can have two particular premises. This result is convenient to keep in mind, because it allows us to identify as invalid any standard-form syllogism in which both

4

premises start with "some." Because it is logically derivable from the first four rules, a separate rule to this effect is not given here.

Rule 5: If Both Premises Are Universal, the Conclusion Cannot Be Particular.

Fallacy: **Existential fallacy**

Example: All mammals are animals.
All tigers are mammals.
Some tigers are animals.

The example has two universal premises and a particular conclusion, so it violates Rule 5. It commits the existential fallacy from the Boolean standpoint. The reason the syllogism is invalid from the Boolean standpoint is that the conclusion asserts that tigers exist, whereas the premises make no such assertion. From the Boolean standpoint, universal premises have no existential import.

In applying Rule 5, keep in mind that the existential fallacy is a fallacy that occurs when a syllogism is invalid merely because the premises lack existential import. Thus, if a syllogism is invalid for some other reason (that is, if it commits some other fallacy), it does not commit the existential fallacy. Hence, before deciding that a syllogism breaks Rule 5, make certain that no other rule is violated. If a syllogism does break one of the other four rules, Rule 5 does not apply.

Aristotelian Standpoint

Any categorical syllogism that breaks one of the first four rules is invalid from the Aristotelian standpoint. However, if a syllogism breaks only Rule 5, it is valid from the Aristotelian standpoint on condition that the critical term denotes at least one existing thing. (The critical term is the term listed in the farthest right-hand column of the table of conditionally valid syllogistic forms presented in Section 4.1.) In the example given in connection with Rule 5, the critical term is "tigers," and the syllogism breaks no other rules, so it is valid from the Aristotelian standpoint. The conclusion asserts that tigers exist, and from the Aristotelian standpoint the premises imply their existence. On the other hand, consider the following example:

All mammals are animals.
All unicorns are mammals.
Some unicorns are animals.

In this example, the critical term is "unicorns." Since unicorns do not exist, the premises have no existential import from the Aristotelian standpoint. Thus, the syllogism is invalid from the Aristotelian standpoint, and it commits the existential fallacy from that standpoint. Of course, it also commits the existential fallacy from the Boolean standpoint.

In addition to consulting the table of conditionally valid forms, one way of identifying the critical term is to draw a Venn diagram. The critical term is the one that corresponds to the circle that is all shaded except for one area. In the case of two such circles, it is the one that corresponds to the Venn circle containing the circled X on which the conclusion depends. Another way of identifying the critical term is through

4

If a syllogism breaks only Rule 5, then it is conditionally valid.

examination of the distributed terms in the syllogism. The critical term is the one that is *superfluously distributed*. In other words, it is the term that, in the premises, is distributed in more occurrences than is necessary for the syllogism to obey the first two rules. Here are three examples:

All M^d are P.	No M^d are P^d.	All P^d are M.
All S^d are M.	All M^d are S.	All M^d are S.
Some S are P.	Some S are not P^d.	Some S are P.

The distributed terms are tagged with a superscript "d." In the first syllogism, *M* must be distributed to satisfy Rule 1, but *S*, in the second premise, need not be distributed to satisfy any rule. Thus, by the *superfluous distribution rule*, *S* is the term that must denote actually existing things for the syllogism to be valid from the Aristotelian standpoint. In the second syllogism, *P* must be distributed in the first premise to satisfy Rule 2, and *M* must be distributed once to satisfy Rule 1; but *M* is distributed twice. Thus, *M* is the term that must denote existing things for the syllogism to be valid from the Aristotelian standpoint. In the third syllogism, *M* must be distributed to satisfy Rule 1, but *P* need not be distributed to satisfy any rule. Thus, in this syllogism, *P* is the critical term.

You may recall that the existential fallacy from the Boolean standpoint first appeared in Section 3.3, where it arose in connection with the modern square of opposition. Also, the existential fallacy from the Aristotelian standpoint first appeared in Section 3.5, where it arose in connection with the traditional square of opposition. The two versions of the existential fallacy that appear in connection with Rule 5 stem from the same mistake as it relates to categorical syllogisms.

Finally, if you turn to the table of conditionally valid forms in Section 4.1, you will see that all of the forms listed there break Rule 5. All of them have universal premises and a particular conclusion, and they break no other rule. Thus, all of them commit the existential fallacy from the Boolean standpoint. But if the Aristotelian standpoint is adopted and the critical term refers to something that does not exist, the Aristotelian standpoint gives exactly the same results as the Boolean. (See Section 3.3.) Thus, under these conditions, all of the syllogistic forms in the conditionally valid table commit the existential fallacy from the Aristotelian standpoint as well.

EXERCISE 4.3

I. Reconstruct the following syllogistic forms and use the five rules for syllogisms to determine if they are valid from the Boolean standpoint, conditionally valid from the Aristotelian standpoint, or invalid. For those that are conditionally valid, identify the condition that must be fulfilled. For those that are invalid from either the Boolean or Aristotelian standpoint, name the fallacy or fallacies committed. Check your answers by constructing a Venn diagram for each.

★1. AAA-3
  2. IAI-2
  3. EIO-1

★4. AAI-2
  5. IEO-1
  6. EOO-4

★7. EAA-1

8. AII-3

9. AAI-4

★10. IAO-3

11. AII-2

12. AIO-3

★13. AEE-4

14. EAE-4

15. EAO-3

★16. EEE-1

17. EAE-1

18. OAI-3

★19. AOO-2

20. EAO-1

II. Use the five rules to determine whether the following standard-form syllogisms are valid from the Boolean standpoint, valid from the Aristotelian standpoint, or invalid. For those that are invalid from either the Boolean or Aristotelian standpoint, name the fallacy or fallacies committed. Check your answer by constructing a Venn diagram for each.

★1. Some nebulas are clouds of gas.
Some clouds of gas are objects invisible to the naked eye.
Therefore, some objects invisible to the naked eye are nebulas.

2. No individuals sensitive to the difference between right and wrong are people who measure talent and success in terms of wealth.
All corporate takeover experts are people who measure talent and success in terms of wealth.
Therefore, no corporate takeover experts are individuals sensitive to the difference between right and wrong.

3. No endangered species are creatures loved by the timber industry.
All spotted owls are endangered species.
Therefore, some spotted owls are not creatures loved by the timber industry.

★4. Some cases of affirmative action are not measures justified by past discrimination.
No cases of affirmative action are illegal practices.
Therefore, some illegal practices are not measures justified by past discrimination.

5. All transparent metals are good conductors of heat.
All transparent metals are good conductors of electricity.
Therefore, some good conductors of electricity are good conductors of heat.

6. All members of the National Rifle Association are people opposed to gun control.
All members of the National Rifle Association are law-abiding citizens.
Therefore, all law-abiding citizens are people opposed to gun control.

★7. No searches based on probable cause are violations of Fourth Amendment rights.
Some warrantless searches are violations of Fourth Amendment rights.
Therefore, some warrantless searches are not searches based on probable cause.

8. All war zones are places where abuse of discretion is rampant.
Some places where abuse of discretion is rampant are international borders.
Therefore, some international borders are war zones.

9. All inside traders are people subject to prosecution.
Some executives with privileged information are not people subject to prosecution.
Therefore, some executives with privileged information are inside traders.

★10. All successful flirts are masters at eye contact.
All masters at eye contact are people genuinely interested in others.
Therefore, some people genuinely interested in others are successful flirts.

III. Answer "true" or "false" to the following statements:

1. If a standard-form categorical syllogism violates one of the first four rules, it may still be valid.

2. If a valid standard-form syllogism has an **E** statement as its conclusion, then both the major and minor terms must be distributed in the premises.

3. If a standard-form syllogism has two **I** statements as premises, then it is invalid.

4. If a standard-form syllogism has an **E** and an **O** statement as premises, then no conclusion follows validly.

5. If a standard-form syllogism has an **I** statement as its conclusion, then Rule 2 cannot be violated.

6. If a valid standard-form syllogism has an **O** statement as its conclusion, then its premises can be an **A** and an **I** statement.

7. If a valid standard-form syllogism has an **E** statement as a premise, then its conclusion can be an **A** statement.

8. If a standard-form syllogism breaks only Rule 5 and its three terms are "dogs," "cats," and "animals," then the syllogism is valid from the Boolean standpoint.

9. If a standard-form syllogism breaks only Rule 5 and its three terms are "dogs," "cats," and "animals," then the syllogism is valid from the Aristotelian standpoint.

10. If a standard-form syllogism breaks only Rule 5 and its three terms are "elves," "trolls," and "gnomes," then the syllogism is valid from the Aristotelian standpoint.

aplia™

Visit Aplia for section-specific problem sets.

4.4   Reducing the Number of Terms

PREVIEW

As a favor to a friend, you offer to do her laundry. After you remove the clothing from the dryer, you begin to match her socks. But you are dismayed to find that six individual socks seem to have no exact match. But then you discover that if you turn three of those six socks inside out, they match the other three. Reducing the terms in a syllogism is a bit like turning socks inside out to create a match. The goal is to end up with three pairs of terms that are exact matches.

Categorical syllogisms, as they occur in ordinary spoken and written expression, are seldom phrased according to the precise norms of the standard-form syllogism. Sometimes quantifiers, premises, or conclusions are left unexpressed, chains of syllogisms are strung together into single arguments, and terms are mixed together with their negations in a single argument. The final four sections of this chapter are concerned with

Saul Kripke b. 1940

Steve Pyke/Premium Archive/Getty Images

As a child, Saul Kripke demonstrated prodigious intellectual abilities. By the age of ten he had read all the plays of Shakespeare, and he discovered algebra, which he said he could have invented on his own. By fourteen he had mastered geometry and calculus and became deeply involved in philosophy. At seventeen he wrote a paper, published in the prestigious *Journal of Symbolic Logic*, that introduced a completeness theorem for modal logic. Legend has it that when this paper reached the attention of the Harvard mathematics department, someone there invited him to apply for a teaching position. He replied, "My mother said that I should finish high school and go to college first." Today Kripke is considered by many to be the world's greatest living philosopher and logician.

Saul Kripke was born the son of a rabbi in Bay Shore, New York, in 1940. He attended public grade school and high school in Omaha, Nebraska, and then Harvard University where, during his sophomore year, he taught a graduate-level course at MIT. In 1962 he graduated *summa cum laude* with a bachelor's degree in mathematics. After that, instead of going to graduate school, he simply began teaching—first at Harvard, then Rockefeller University, then Princeton University, and finally CUNY Graduate Center. He has received honorary degrees from several universities, and in 2001 he received the Schock Prize (comparable to the Nobel Prize) in Logic and Philosophy.

Kripke is universally hailed for his work in modal logic where, in addition to proving its formal completeness, he created a semantics, now called Kripke semantics, in which a proposition is said to be necessarily true when it holds in all possible worlds and possibly true when it holds in some possible world. Also, his book *Naming and Necessity* made ground-breaking contributions to the philosophy of language by introducing a new theory of reference for proper names.

4

developing techniques for reworking such arguments in order to render them testable by Venn diagrams or by the rules for syllogisms.

In this section we consider arguments that contain more than three terms but that can be modified to reduce the number of terms to three. Consider the following:

> All photographers are non-writers.
> Some editors are writers.
> Therefore, some non-photographers are not non-editors.

Goal: Each term must have a perfect match.

This syllogism is clearly not in standard form because it has six terms: "photographers," "editors," "writers," "non-photographers," "non-editors," and "non-writers." But because three of the terms are complements of the other three, the number of terms can be reduced to a total of three, each used twice in distinct propositions. To accomplish the reduction, we can use the three operations of conversion, obversion, and contraposition discussed in Chapter 3. But, of course, since the reworked syllogism must be equivalent in meaning to the original one, we must use these operations only on the kinds of statements for which they yield logically equivalent results. That is, we must use conversion only on **E** and **I** statements and contraposition only on **A** and **O** statements. Obversion yields logically equivalent results for all four kinds of categorical statements.

Let us rewrite our six-term argument using letters to represent the terms, and then obvert the first premise and contrapose the conclusion in order to eliminate the negated letters:

Symbolized argument	Reduced argument
All *P* are non-*W*.	No *P* are *W*.
Some *E* are *W*.	Some *E* are *W*.
Some non-*P* are not non-*E*.	Some *E* are not *P*.

Because the first premise of the original argument is an **A** statement and the conclusion an **O** statement, and because the operations performed on these statements yield logically equivalent results, the reduced argument is equivalent in meaning to the original argument. The reduced argument is in standard syllogistic form and may be evaluated either with a Venn diagram or by the five rules for syllogisms. The application of these methods indicates that the reduced argument is valid. We conclude, therefore, that the original argument is also valid.

It is not necessary to eliminate the negated terms in order to reduce the number of terms. It is equally effective to convert certain non-negated terms into negated ones. Thus, instead of obverting the first premise of the example argument and contraposing the conclusion, we could have contraposed the first premise and converted and then obverted the second premise. The operation is performed as follows:

Symbolized argument	Reduced argument
All *P* are non-*W*.	All *W* are non-*P*.
Some *E* are *W*.	Some *W* are not non-*E*.
Some non-*P* are not non-*E*.	Some non-*P* are not non-*E*.

The reduced argument is once again equivalent to the original one, but now we must reverse the order of the premises to put the syllogism into standard form:

Some *W* are not non-*E*.
All *W* are non-*P*.
Some non-*P* are not non-*E*.

When tested with a Venn diagram or by means of the five rules, this argument will, of course, also be found valid, and so the original argument is valid. When using a Venn diagram, no unusual method is needed; the diagram is simply lettered with the three terms "*W*," "non-*E*," and "non-*P*."

The most important point to remember in reducing the number of terms is that conversion and contraposition must never be used on statements for which they yield undetermined results. That is, conversion must never be used on **A** and **O** statements, and contraposition must never be used on **E** and **I** statements. The operations that are allowed are summarized as follows:

Conversion:	No *A* are *B*.	No *B* are *A*.
	Some *A* are *B*.	Some *B* are *A*.
Obversion:	All *A* are *B*.	No *A* are non-*B*.
	No *A* are *B*.	All *A* are non-*B*.
	Some *A* are *B*.	Some *A* are not non-*B*.
	Some *A* are not *B*.	Some *A* are non-*B*.
Contraposition:	All *A* are *B*.	All non-*B* are non-*A*.
	Some *A* are not *B*.	Some non-*B* are not non-*A*.

Rewrite the following arguments using letters to represent the terms, reduce the number of terms, and put the arguments into standard form. Then test the new forms with Venn diagrams or by means of the five rules for syllogisms to determine the validity or invalidity of the original arguments.

★1. Some intelligible statements are true statements, because all unintelligible statements are meaningless statements and some false statements are meaningful statements.

2. Some people who do not regret their crimes are convicted murderers, so some convicted murderers are people insusceptible of being reformed, since all people susceptible of being reformed are people who regret their crimes.

3. All Peace Corps volunteers are people who have witnessed poverty and desolation, and all people insensitive to human need are people who have failed to witness poverty and desolation. Thus, all Peace Corps volunteers are people sensitive to human need.

★4. Some unintentional killings are not punishable offenses, inasmuch as all cases of self-defense are unpunishable offenses, and some intentional killings are cases of self-defense.

5. All aircraft that disintegrate in flight are unsafe planes. Therefore, no poorly maintained aircraft are safe planes, because all well-maintained aircraft are aircraft that remain intact in flight.

6. No objects that sink in water are chunks of ice, and no objects that float in water are things at least as dense as water. Accordingly, all chunks of ice are things less dense than water.

★7. Some proposed flights to Mars are inexpensive ventures, because all unmanned space missions are inexpensive ventures, and some proposed flights to Mars are not manned space missions.

8. All schools driven by careerism are institutions that do not emphasize liberal arts. It follows that some universities are not institutions that emphasize liberal arts, for some schools that are not driven by careerism are universities.

9. No cases of AIDS are infections easily curable by drugs, since all diseases that infect the brain are infections not easily curable by drugs, and all diseases that do not infect the brain are cases other than AIDS.

★10. Some foreign emissaries are people without diplomatic immunity, so some people invulnerable to arrest and prosecution are foreign emissaries, because no people with diplomatic immunity are people vulnerable to arrest and prosecution.

aplia™

Visit Aplia for section-specific problem sets.

4.5   Ordinary Language Arguments

PREVIEW

Suppose you are struggling in your biology class and you are afraid you might not pass. You decide to speak to the instructor, who tells you: "You won't pass the course unless you pass the final exam—but surely you will pass the final exam; it's relatively easy. Thus, you will pass the course." Should this response cause you to rest more easily? In this section you will learn how to test the validity of arguments such as the one given by your instructor.*

Many arguments that are not standard-form categorical syllogisms as written can be translated into standard-form syllogisms. In doing so we often use techniques developed in the last section of Chapter 3—namely, inserting quantifiers, modifying subject and predicate terms, and introducing copulas. The goal, of course, is to produce an argument consisting of three standard-form categorical propositions that contain a total of three different terms, each of which occurs twice in distinct propositions. Once translated, the argument can be tested by means of a Venn diagram or the rules for syllogisms.

Since the task of translating arguments into standard-form syllogisms involves not only converting the component statements into standard form but adjusting these statements one to another so that their terms occur in matched pairs, a certain amount of practice may be required before it can be done with facility. In reducing the terms to three matched pairs it is often helpful to identify some factor common to two or all three propositions and to express this common factor through the strategic use of parameters. For example, if all three statements are about people, the term "people" or "people identical to" might be used; or if they are about times or places, the term "times" or "times identical to" or the term "places" or "places identical to" might be used. Here is an example:

> Whenever people put off marriage until they are older, the divorce rate decreases. Today, people are putting off marriage until they are older. Therefore, the divorce rate is decreasing today.

The temporal adverbs "whenever" and "today" suggest that "times" should be used as the common factor. Following this suggestion, we have this:

> All times people put off marriage until they are older are times the divorce rate decreases. All present times are times people put off marriage until they are older. Therefore, all present times are times the divorce rate decreases.

This is a standard-form categorical syllogism. Notice that each of the three terms is matched with an exact duplicate in a different proposition. To obtain such a match, it is sometimes necessary to alter the wording of the original statement just slightly. Now if we adopt the convention

M = times people put off marriage until they are older
D = times the divorce rate decreases
P = present times

the syllogism may be symbolized as follows:

> All *M* are *D*.
> All *P* are *M*.
> All *P* are *D*.

Goal: The terms must occur in matched pairs.

Look for: A "common denominator" for at least two terms.

This is the so-called "Barbara" syllogism and is, of course, valid. Here is another example:

> Boeing must be a manufacturer because it hires riveters, and any company that hires riveters is a manufacturer.

For this argument the parameter "companies" suggests itself:

> All companies identical to Boeing are manufacturers, because all companies identical to Boeing are companies that hire riveters, and all companies that hire riveters are manufacturers.

The first statement, of course, is the conclusion. When the syllogism is written in standard form, it will be seen that it has, like the previous syllogism, the form **AAA**-1.

Here is another example:

> If a piece of evidence is trustworthy, then it should be admissible in court. Polygraph tests are not trustworthy. Therefore, they should not be admissible in court.

To translate this argument, using a single common factor is not necessary:

> All trustworthy pieces of evidence are pieces of evidence that should be admissible in court. No polygraph tests are trustworthy pieces of evidence. Therefore, no polygraph tests are pieces of evidence that should be admissible in court.

This syllogism commits the fallacy of illicit major and is therefore invalid.

As was mentioned in Section 3.6, arguments containing an exceptive proposition must be handled in a special way. Let us consider one that contains an exceptive proposition as a premise:

> All of the jeans except the Levi's are on sale. Therefore, since the Calvin Klein jeans are not Levi's, they must be on sale.

The first premise is translated as two conjoined categorical propositions: "No Levi's are jeans on sale," and "All jeans that are not Levi's are jeans on sale." These give rise to two syllogisms:

> No Levi's are jeans on sale.
> No Calvin Klein jeans are Levi's.
> Therefore, all Calvin Klein jeans are jeans on sale.
>
> All jeans that are not Levi's are jeans on sale.
> No Calvin Klein jeans are Levi's.
> Therefore, all Calvin Klein jeans are jeans on sale.

The first syllogism, which is in standard form, is invalid because it has two negative premises. The second one, on the other hand, is not in standard form, because it has four terms. If the second premise is obverted, so that it reads "All Calvin Klein jeans are jeans that are not Levi's," the syllogism becomes an **AAA**-1 standard-form syllogism, which is valid.

Each of these two syllogisms may be viewed as a pathway in which the conclusion of the original argument might follow necessarily from the premises. Since it does follow via the second syllogism, the original argument is valid. If both of the resulting syllogisms turned out to be invalid, the original argument would be invalid.

Translate the following arguments into standard-form categorical syllogisms, then use Venn diagrams or the rules for syllogisms to determine whether each is valid or invalid. See Section 3.6 for help with the translation.

★1. Physicists are the only scientists who theorize about the nature of time, and Stephen Hawking certainly does that. Therefore, Stephen Hawking must be a physicist.

2. Whenever suicide rates decline, we can infer that people's lives are better adjusted. Accordingly, since suicide rates have been declining in recent years, we can infer that people's lives have been better adjusted in recent years.

3. Environmentalists purchase only fuel-efficient cars. Hence, Jeep Wranglers must not be fuel efficient, since environmentalists do not purchase them.

★4. Whoever wrote the Declaration of Independence had a big impact on civilization, and Thomas Jefferson certainly had that. Therefore, Thomas Jefferson wrote the Declaration of Independence.

5. There are public schools that teach secular humanism. Therefore, since secular humanism is a religion, there are public schools that teach religion.

6. Any city that has excellent art museums is a tourist destination. Therefore, Paris is a tourist destination, because it has excellent art museums.

★7. Shania Twain sings what she wants. Hence, since Shania sings country songs, it follows that she must want to sing country songs.

8. Not all interest expenses are tax deductible. Home-mortgage payments are interest expenses. Thus, they are not tax deductible.

9. If a marriage is based on a meshing of neuroses, it allows little room for growth. If a marriage allows little room for growth, it is bound to fail. Therefore, if a marriage is based on a meshing of neuroses, it is bound to fail.

★10. TV viewers cannot receive scrambled signals unless they have a decoder. Whoever receives digital satellite signals receives scrambled signals. Therefore, whoever receives digital satellite signals has a decoder.

11. Wherever icebergs are present, threats to shipping exist. Icebergs are not present in the South Pacific. Hence, there are no threats to shipping in the South Pacific.

12. According to surveys, there are college students who think that Africa is in North America. But anyone who thinks that has no knowledge of geography. It follows that there are college students who have no knowledge of geography.

★13. Diseases carried by recessive genes can be inherited by offspring of two carriers. Thus, since cystic fibrosis is a disease carried by recessive genes, it can be inherited by offspring of two carriers.

14. All of the movies except the chick flicks were exciting. Hence, the action films were exciting, because none of them is a chick flick.

15. Autistic children are occasionally helped by aversion therapy. But aversion therapy is sometimes inhumane. Thus, autistic children are sometimes helped by inhumane therapy.

aplia™

Visit Aplia for section-specific problem sets.

4.6 Enthymemes

PREVIEW

Suppose, while driving your car, you notice the flashing light of a police cruiser in your rearview mirror. When the officer pulls you over, he says that you were speeding in a school zone and that he's going to issue you a traffic citation. When you ask how much the fine is for speeding in a school zone, he tells you it is two hundred dollars. Immediately you draw the conclusion that your ticket is going to cost you two hundred dollars. The reasoning process you used is typical of what is involved in enthymemes, which we now take up.

An **enthymeme** is an argument that is expressible as a categorical syllogism but that is missing a premise or a conclusion. Examples:

> The corporate income tax should be abolished; it encourages waste and high prices.

> Animals that are loved by someone should not be sold to a medical laboratory, and lost pets are certainly loved by someone.

The first enthymeme is missing the premise "Whatever encourages waste and high prices should be abolished," and the second is missing the conclusion "Lost pets should not be sold to a medical laboratory."

Enthymemes occur frequently in ordinary spoken and written English for several reasons. Sometimes it is simply boring to express every statement in an argument. The listener or reader's intelligence is called into play when he or she is required to supply a missing statement, thereby sustaining his or her interest. On other occasions the arguer may want to slip an invalid or unsound argument past an unwary listener or reader, and this aim may be facilitated by leaving a premise or conclusion out of the picture.

Many enthymemes are easy to convert into syllogisms. The reader or listener must first determine what is missing, whether it is a premise or conclusion, and then introduce the missing statement with the aim of converting the enthymeme into a good argument. Attention to indicator words will often provide the clue as to the nature of the missing statement, but a little practice can render this task virtually automatic. The missing statement need not be expressed in categorical form; expressing it in the general context of the other statements is sufficient and is often the easier alternative. Once this is done, the entire argument may be translated into categorical form and then tested with a Venn diagram or by the rules for syllogisms. Example:

> Venus completes its orbit in less time than the Earth, because Venus is closer to the sun.

> *Missing premise:* Any planet closer to the sun completes its orbit in less time than the Earth.

Translating this argument into categorical form, we have

> All planets closer to the sun are planets that complete their orbit in less time than the Earth.
> All planets identical to Venus are planets closer to the sun.
> All planets identical to Venus are planets that complete their orbit in less time than the Earth.

This syllogism is valid (and sound).

enthymeme: A categorical syllogism missing a premise or conclusion.

4

Goal: Supply the missing statement.

Any enthymeme (such as the one about Venus) that contains an indicator word is missing a premise. This may be seen as follows. If an enthymeme contains a conclusion indicator, then the conclusion follows it, which means that the missing statement is a premise. On the other hand, if the enthymeme contains a premise indicator, then the conclusion precedes it, which means, again, that the missing statement is a premise.

If, however, an enthymeme contains no indicator words at all (such as the two enthymemes at the beginning of this section), then the missing statement could be either a premise or a conclusion. If the two given statements are joined by a word such as "and," "but," "moreover," or some similar conjunction, the missing statement is usually a conclusion. If not, the first statement is usually the conclusion, and the missing statement is a premise. To test this latter alternative, it may help to mentally insert the word "because" between the two statements. If this insertion makes sense, the missing statement is a premise.

After the nature of the missing statement has been determined, the next task is to write it out. To do so, one must first identify its terms. This can be done by taking account of the terms that are given. Two of the terms in the given statements will match up with each other. Once this pair of terms is found, attention should be focused on the other two terms. These are the ones that will be used to form the missing statement. In constructing the missing statement, attention to the rules for syllogisms may be helpful (if the resulting syllogism is to be valid). For example, if the missing statement is a conclusion and one of the given premises is negative, the missing conclusion must be negative. Or if the missing statement is a premise and the stated conclusion is universal, the missing premise must be universal.

The enthymemes that we have considered thus far have been fairly straightforward. The kinds of enthymemes that occur in letters-to-the-editor columns of magazines and newspapers often require a bit more creativity to convert into syllogisms. Consider the following:

> The motorcycle has served as basic transportation for the poor for decades. It deserves to be celebrated.
>
> (William B. Fankboner)

The conclusion is the last statement, and the missing premise is that any vehicle that has served as basic transportation for the poor for decades deserves to be celebrated. The enthymeme may be written as a standard-form syllogism as follows:

> All vehicles that have served as basic transportation for the poor for decades are vehicles that deserve to be celebrated.
> All vehicles identical to the motorcycle are vehicles that have served as basic transportation for the poor for decades.
> Therefore, all vehicles identical to the motorcycle are vehicles that deserve to be celebrated.

The syllogism is valid and arguably sound. Here is another example:

> I know several doctors who smoke. In a step toward my own health, I will no longer be their patient. It has occurred to me that if they care so little about their own health, how can they possibly care about mine?
>
> (Joan Boyer)

In this argument the author draws three connections: the connection between doctors' smoking and doctors' caring about their own health, between doctors' caring about

4

their own health and doctors' caring about the author's health, and between doctors' caring about the author's health and doctors who will have the author as a patient. Two arguments are needed to express these connections:

> All doctors who smoke are doctors who do not care about their own health.
> All doctors who do not care about their own health are doctors who do not care about my health.
> Therefore, all doctors who smoke are doctors who do not care about my health.

And,

> All doctors who smoke are doctors who do not care about my health.
> All doctors who do not care about my health are doctors who will not have me as a patient.
> Therefore, all doctors who smoke are doctors who will not have me as a patient.

Notice that the conclusion of the first argument becomes a premise in the second argument. To put these arguments into final standard form, the order of the premises must be reversed. Both arguments are valid, but probably not sound.

EXERCISE 4.6

I. In the following enthymemes, determine whether the missing statement is a premise or a conclusion. Then supply the missing statement, attempting whenever possible to convert the enthymeme, into a valid argument. The missing statement need not be expressed as a standard-form categorical proposition.

★1. Some police chiefs undermine the evenhanded enforcement of the law, because anyone who fixes parking tickets does that.

2. Any form of cheating deserves to be punished, and plagiarism is a form of cheating.

3. Carrie Underwood is a talented singer. After all, she's won several Grammy awards.

★4. A few fraternities have dangerous initiation rites, and those that do have no legitimate role in campus life.

5. Only nonprofit organizations are exempt from paying taxes, so churches must be exempt.

6. All of the operas except Mozart's were well performed, and *Carmen* was not written by Mozart.

★7. Not all phone calls are welcome, but those from friends are.

8. Higher life-forms could not have evolved through merely random processes, because no organized beings could have evolved that way.

9. None but great novels are timeless, and *The Brothers Karamazov* is a great novel.

★10. Antiwar protests have been feeble in recent years because there is no military draft.

11. Wherever water exists, human life can be sustained, and water exists on the moon.

12. If a symphony orchestra has effective fund-raisers, it will survive; and the Cleveland Symphony Orchestra has survived for years.

★13. Mechanistic materialists do not believe in free will, because they think that everything is governed by deterministic laws.

14. A contract to buy land is not enforceable unless it's in writing, but our client's contract to buy land *is* in writing.

15. The only telescopes that are unaffected by the atmosphere are orbiting telescopes, and the Hubble telescope is in orbit.

II. Translate the enthymemes in Part I of this exercise into standard-form categorical syllogisms and test them for validity.

III. The following enthymemes were originally submitted in letters to the editors of various magazines and newspapers. Convert them into valid standard-form syllogisms. In some cases two syllogisms may be required.

★1. If the Defense Department is so intent on fighting alcohol abuse, why does it make alcohol so readily available and acceptable? Alcohol is tax free at post liquor stores, and enlisted men's and officers' clubs make drinking almost a mandatory facet of military life.

(Diane Lynch)

2. All aid to Israel should be stopped at once. Why should the American taxpayer be asked to send billions of dollars to Israel when every city in the United States is practically broke and millions of people are out of work?

(Bertha Grace)

3. Suicide is not immoral. If a person decides that life is impossible, it is his or her right to end it.

(Donald S. Farrar)

★4. The best way to get people to read a book is to ban it. The fundamentalist families in Church Hill, Tennessee, have just guaranteed sales of *Macbeth*, *The Diary of Anne Frank*, *The Wizard of Oz*, and other stories.

(Paula Fleischer)

5. The budget deficit will not be brought under control because to do so would require our elected leaders in Washington to do the unthinkable—act courageously and responsibly.

(Bruce Crutcher)

6. The Constitution bans any law that is so vague that "men of common intelligence must necessarily guess at its meaning." Sexual harassment laws, however, are so vague that no one knows what they mean.

(Hans Bader)

★7. College students of today are the higher-income taxpayers of tomorrow. Congress should consider financial aid as an investment in the financial future of our country.

(Carol A. Steimel)

8. Our genes and our environment control our destinies. The idea of conscious choice is ridiculous. Yes, prisons should be designed to protect society, but they should not punish the poor slobs who were headed for jail from birth.

(Paul R. Andrews)

9. Encouraging toy-gun play gives children a clear message that the best way to deal with frustration and conflict is with a gun. Is this the message that we want to be sending our kids?

(Patricia Owen)

★ 10. The U.S. surgeon general's latest report on cigarettes and cancer is an interesting example of natural selection in the late twentieth century. The intelligent members of our species will quit smoking, and survive. The dummies will continue to puff away.

(Kelly Kinnon)

IV. Page through a magazine or newspaper and identify five topics of current interest. Construct an enthymeme involving each topic.

V. Translate the arguments in the following dialogue into standard-form categorical syllogisms. The dialogue contains more than twenty arguments, and most are expressed in the form of enthymemes. The first translated syllogism may be found in the answer key in the back of the book.

Do Kids Make Parents Happy?

Tad and Lara, his fiancée, are walking in the park. Tad pauses a moment to look at some children playing in the grass. Lara stops beside him.

"I know we've talked about this before," she says, "but I wish you'd get over this idea about us having a bunch of kids."

"I'll think about it," Tad says. "But could you tell me once again about why you don't want any?"

"I think most couples believe that kids automatically bring happiness," Lara says. "But that's simply not the case. I've read some recent studies about this. They show that childless couples experience higher levels of emotional well-being than couples with kids. Thus, childless couples are happier than couples with kids."

"I've read those studies of yours," Tad says, "but I don't know what to make of them. Consider this. Kids make you laugh, and laughter is essential to happiness. So kids do make you happy. Plus, in a way, having kids makes you immortal."

"How do you figure *that*?"

"Okay, not immortal exactly, but I mean that they make you participate in a kind of immortality. Your children grow up and have children, and those children have children, and on it goes. This feeling of contributing to the perpetuation of the human race makes you happy, don't you think?"

"Frankly," Lara replies, "that's all a bit too removed from the 'now' to suit me. Maybe at the beginning when a couple is expecting their first child, they tend to be happy. But once the baby arrives, the honeymoon ends. The newborn has to be fed every couple of hours, the parents aren't getting any sleep, and those parents aren't happy."

"Well, very tired, yes, but unhappy?" says Tad. "Plus, it's temporary and only lasts for the first few months."

"And after the first few months, you have toys and food all over the house and sticky stuff on all the furniture. How happy is living in a constant mess going to make you?"

"Not very, I guess. But there's more to life than a neat house. Having kids will force us not to be selfish, and no one who's selfish is truly happy. Also, kids promote an atmosphere of growth. Watching kids learn, change, and grow makes parents happy. Don't you think that's true?"

"Sure," Lara says, "in theory. In reality, growing means infants become toddlers who scream, whine, and throw tantrums. Having to listen to all that racket makes no one happy. And then, life just gets more hectic. Kids constantly have to be driven to and from school, dancing lessons, Little League, the mall—all detracting from the happiness of the parents. Right?"

"Right," Tad says, "but kids are fun. They're constantly playing; and having playful children around you brings happiness. Plus some kids grow up to accomplish extraordinary things. How could one not be happy at witnessing the success of one's child?"

"Okay," says Lara, "but kids take up a tremendous amount of time. Couples who have kids often have no time for vacations—I know that wouldn't make you happy. And some couples with kids don't even have time for sex. How would you like that?"

"I wouldn't," Tad admits. "But maybe we could learn to manage our time better than those other couples. Which leads me to something else: Having kids will force us to work together as a couple. That will deepen our relationship, and deeper relationships are happier relationships. And don't forget unconditional love. Kids love you for who you are. They don't care what you look like, whether you're overweight, or what kind of car you drive. Being loved like that makes you happy."

"Well, of course it does," says Lara. "But what about money? Kids cost a fortune. Food, clothing, medical bills, and a college education will leave us constantly broke. Can we be happy like that? And what about my career? I have goals, just like you. If I'm constantly pregnant or taking care of little kids, I'll never achieve them. I can't possibly be happy if that happens."

"No," Tad says. "We'd have to work that out. As we grow older, though, think about what our lives will be like without any children. We'll be lonely and cut off, with no one to call us and no grandchildren to visit us. Does that sound like happiness to you?"

"Ha!" Lara says. "You assume that the kids will eventually leave the house. You forget that we live in the age of boomerang offspring. After they finish school, they come back home to live, and you never get rid of them. How does that grab you?"

"Well, we didn't stay around long after college. I think when we decided to leave the nest and get married, we made our parents truly happy."

"Yeah," Lara replies. "I think we did. So maybe we've proved your case. Some kids, at least, end up making their parents happy."

4.7 Sorites

PREVIEW

Suppose an instructor bans the use of all electronic devices in the classroom. This measure might generate a thread of arguments on a message board. One student might argue that she needs her laptop to compose class notes. Another needs his iPad to retrieve information from the Internet for class discussion. Yet another needs his Droid to check e-mails. Each argument adds to the original one and alters its direction. This string of arguments containing many premises is similar to a sorites.

A **sorites** is a chain of categorical syllogisms in which the intermediate conclusions have been left out. The name is derived from the Greek word *soros*, meaning "heap," and is pronounced "sōrītëz," with the accent on the second syllable. The plural form is also "sorites." Here is an example:

> All bloodhounds are dogs.
> All dogs are mammals.
> No fish are mammals.
> Therefore, no fish are bloodhounds.

sorites: A chain of categorical syllogisms without the intermediate conclusions.

The first two premises validly imply the intermediate conclusion "All bloodhounds are mammals." If this intermediate conclusion is then treated as a premise and put together with the third premise, the final conclusion follows validly. The sorites is thus composed of two valid categorical syllogisms and is therefore valid. The rule in evaluating a sorites is based on the idea that a chain is only as strong as its weakest link. If any of the component syllogisms in a sorites is invalid, the entire sorites is invalid.

A **standard-form sorites** is one in which each of the component propositions is in standard form, each term occurs twice, the predicate of the conclusion is in the first premise, and each successive premise has a term in common with the preceding one.* The sorites in the example is in standard form. Each of the propositions is in standard form, each term occurs twice; the predicate of the conclusion, "bloodhounds," is in the first premise; the other term in the first premise, "dogs," is in the second premise, and so on.

Although a sorites can be tested using Venn diagrams, the easiest technique consists in applying five rules that closely resemble the rules for syllogisms. The rules are as follows:

If a sorites obeys all five rules, then it is unconditionally valid.

> **Rule 1**: Each of the middle terms must be distributed at least once.
> **Rule 2**: If a term is distributed in the conclusion, then it must be distributed in a premise.
> **Rule 3**: Two negative premises are not allowed.
> **Rule 4**: A negative premise requires a negative conclusion, and a negative conclusion requires a negative premise.
> **Rule 5**: If all the premises are universal, the conclusion cannot be particular.

Rule 1 refers to the "middle terms" in the sorites. These are the terms that occur in matched pairs in the premises. The conclusion referred to in Rules 2, 4, and 5 is the

---

*Actually, there are two definitions of standard-form sorites: the Goclenian and the Aristotelian. The one given here is the Goclenian. In the Aristotelian version, the premises are arranged so that the subject of the conclusion occurs in the first premise.

final conclusion of the sorites. Also, as with categorical syllogisms, if a sorites breaks only Rule 5, it is valid from the Aristotelian standpoint on condition that its critical term refers to at least one existing thing.

If a sorites breaks only Rule 5, then it is conditionally valid.

The critical term can be identified in the same way as it is for categorical syllogisms. There are three possible approaches. By entering the mood and figure of the last component syllogism of the sorites into the table of conditionally valid forms in Section 4.1, the critical term is given in the farthest right-hand column. Applying the superfluous distribution rule, the critical term is the term in the premises that is distributed in more occurrences than is necessary for the sorites to obey the first two rules. And in the Venn diagram for the final component syllogism of the sorites, the critical term is the one that corresponds to the circle that is all shaded except for one area. In the case of two such circles, it is the one that corresponds to the Venn circle containing the circled X on which the conclusion depends.

Before applying the rules, it helps to put the sorites into standard form; in either event the sorites must be written so that the terms occur in matched pairs. The following sorites is in standard form, and the distributed terms are marked with a superscript "d." As is apparent, there are three middle terms: M, K, and R.

All S^d are M.
All K^d are M.
No K^d are R^d.
Some F are R.
Some F are not S^d.

This sorites breaks Rule 1 because neither occurrence of M in the first two premises is distributed. Thus, the sorites is invalid. Note that no other rule is broken. Both of the K's in lines 2 and 3 are distributed, one of the R's in lines 3 and 4 is distributed, S is distributed in the conclusion and also in the first premise, there is a negative conclusion and only one negative premise, and while the conclusion is particular so is one of the premises.

The logic behind the five rules is as follows. For Rule 1, each of the middle terms in the sorites is also a middle term in one of the component syllogisms. Thus, if Rule 1 is broken, one of the component syllogisms has an undistributed middle, making the entire sorites invalid.

For Rule 2, when the sorites is in standard form, the predicate of the conclusion must appear in each of the intermediate conclusions. Thus, if the predicate of the conclusion is distributed, it must also be distributed in each of the intermediate conclusions, and also in the first premise. Otherwise, one of the component syllogisms would have either an illicit major or an illicit minor, making the entire sorites invalid. Analogously, if the subject of the conclusion is distributed, it must also be distributed in the last premise. Otherwise, the last component syllogism would have an illicit minor, making the entire sorites invalid.

For Rule 3, when a negative premise appears in the list of premises, the conclusion derived from that premise must be negative, as must all subsequent conclusions. Otherwise, one of the component syllogisms would break Rule 4 for syllogisms. If a second negative premise should appear, the syllogism consisting of that premise and the prior intermediate conclusion would commit the fallacy of exclusive premises, making the entire sorites invalid.

Similarly, for Rule 4, when a negative premise appears in the list of premises, all subsequent conclusions must be negative. Otherwise, one of the component syllogisms would break Rule 4 for syllogisms. Conversely, if the conclusion of the sorites is negative, either the last premise or the last intermediate conclusion must be negative. Otherwise, the last component syllogism would break Rule 4 for syllogisms. If the last intermediate conclusion is negative, then either the prior premise or the prior intermediate conclusion must be negative. If we continue this reasoning, we see that some prior premise must be negative.

For Rule 5, a particular conclusion has existential import, while universal premises (from the Boolean standpoint) do not. Thus, if all the premises are universal and the conclusion is particular, the sorites as a whole commits the existential fallacy.

One of the advantages of the rules method for testing a sorites is that invalidity can often be detected through immediate inspection. Once a sorites has been put into standard form, any sorites having more than one negative premise is invalid, and any sorites having a negative premise and an affirmative conclusion (or vice versa) is invalid. Also, as with syllogisms, any sorites having more than one particular premise is invalid. This last requirement is implied by the other rules.

EXERCISE **4.7**

I. Rewrite the following sorites in standard form, reducing the number of terms when necessary. Then use the five rules for sorites to test each one for validity.

★**1.**　No *B* are *C*.
　　　Some *D* are *C*.
　　　All *A* are *B*.
　　　Some *D* are not *A*.

2.　No *C* are *D*.
　　　All *A* are *B*.
　　　Some *C* are not *B*.
　　　Some *D* are not *A*.

3.　No *S* are *M*.
　　　All *F* are *S*.
　　　Some *M* are *H*.
　　　All *E* are *F*.
　　　Some *H* are not *E*.

★**4.**　Some *T* are *K*.
　　　No *K* are *N*.
　　　Some *C* are *Q*.
　　　All *T* are *C*.
　　　Some *Q* are not *N*.

5.　All *B* are *C*.
　　　No *C* are *D*.
　　　All *E* are *A*.
　　　All *A* are *B*.
　　　Some *E* are not *D*.

6.　All *M* are non-*P*.
　　　Some *M* are *S*.
　　　All *K* are *P*.
　　　Some non-*K* are not non-*S*.

★**7.**　All non-*U* are non-*V*.
　　　No *U* are non-*W*.
　　　All *V* are *Y*.
　　　No *X* are *W*.
　　　All *Y* are non-*X*.

8.　All *D* are non-*C*.
　　　All non-*B* are non-*A*.
　　　Some *E* are *D*.
　　　All *B* are *C*.
　　　Some non-*A* are not non-*E*.

9. All non-*L* are non-*K*.
Some *K* are *M*.
All *P* are non-*L*.
No non-*N* are *M*.
No *Q* are non-*P*.
Some *N* are not *Q*.

★10. All *R* are *S*.
No non-*V* are *T*.
No *Q* are non-*R*.
No non-*Q* are *P*.
All *T* are non-*S*.
All *V* are non-*P*.

II. The following sorites are valid. Rewrite each sorites in standard form, using letters to represent the terms and reducing the number of terms whenever necessary. Then use the rules method to prove each one valid.

★1. Whatever produces oxygen supports human life.
Rain forests produce oxygen.
Nothing that supports human life should be destroyed.

Rain forests should not be destroyed.

2. No restrictive trade policies fail to invite retaliation.
Trade wars threaten our standard of living.
Some Chinese trade policies are restrictive.
Policies that invite retaliation lead to a trade war.

Some Chinese trade policies threaten our standard of living.

3. Anything that poisons drinking water causes disease and death.
Chemicals percolating through the soil contaminate aquifers.
Dumped chemicals percolate through the soil.
Whatever contaminates aquifers poisons drinking water.

Dumped chemicals cause disease and death.

★4. Nothing that is brittle is ductile.
Superconductors are all ceramics.
Only ductile things can be pulled into wires.
Ceramics are brittle.

Superconductors cannot be pulled into wires.

5. Some college students purchase their term papers.
Any cheat is expelled from college.
No one will achieve his career goals who is expelled.
No one who purchases term papers is other than a cheat.

Some college students will not achieve their career goals.

6. Creation science does not favor the teaching of evolution.
Nothing should be taught that frustrates the understanding of life.
Whatever opposes the teaching of evolution impedes the learning of biology.
Anything that enhances the understanding of life fosters the learning of biology.

Creation science should not be taught.

★7. Whoever gives birth to crack babies increases future crime rates.
Some pregnant women use crack.
None but criminals increase future crime rates.
Pregnant crack users never give birth to anything but crack babies.

Some pregnant women are criminals.

8. Whatever retards population growth increases food availability.
Anything that prevents starvation enhances life.
Birth-control measures never accelerate population growth.
Anything that enhances life should be encouraged.
Whatever increases food availability prevents starvation.

Birth-control measures should not be discouraged.

9. A few countries allow ivory trading.
Whatever country resists elephant killing discourages poachers.
Any country that allows ivory trading encourages poachers.
No country that promotes the extinction of elephants should escape the condemnation of the civilized world.
Any country that supports elephant killing promotes the extinction of elephants.

A few countries should be condemned by the civilized world.

★10. Anything that promotes skin cancer causes death.
Whatever preserves the ozone layer prevents the release of CFCs.
Nothing that resists skin cancer increases UV radiation.
Anything that destroys the ozone layer increases UV radiation.
There are packaging materials that release CFCs.
Nothing that causes death should be legal.

Some packaging materials should be illegal.

III. The following sorites are taken from Lewis Carroll's *Symbolic Logic*. All are valid. Rewrite each sorites in standard form, using letters to represent the terms and reducing the number of terms whenever necessary. Then use the rules method to prove each one valid.

★1. No ducks waltz.
No officers ever decline to waltz.
All my poultry are ducks.

My poultry are not officers.

2. No experienced person is incompetent.
Jenkins is always blundering.
No competent person is always blundering.

Jenkins is inexperienced.

3. No terriers wander among the signs of the zodiac.
Nothing that does not wander among the signs of the zodiac is a comet.
Nothing but a terrier has a curly tail.

No comet has a curly tail.

★ 4. All hummingbirds are richly colored.
No large birds live on honey.
Birds that do not live on honey are dull in color.

All hummingbirds are small.

5. All unripe fruit is unwholesome.
All these apples are wholesome.
No fruit grown in the shade is ripe.

These apples were grown in the sun.

6. All my sons are slim.
No child of mine is healthy who takes no exercise.
All gluttons who are children of mine are fat.
No daughter of mine takes any exercise.

All gluttons who are children of mine are unhealthy.

★ 7. The only books in this library that I do not recommend for reading are unhealthy in tone.
The bound books are all well-written.
All the romances are healthy in tone.
I do not recommend you to read any of the unbound books.

All the romances in this library are well-written.

8. No interesting poems are unpopular among people of real taste.
No modern poetry is free from affectation.
All your poems are on the subject of soap bubbles.
No affected poetry is popular among people of real taste.
No ancient poem is on the subject of soap bubbles.

All your poems are uninteresting.

9. All writers who understand human nature are clever.
No one is a true poet unless he can stir the hearts of men.
Shakespeare wrote *Hamlet*.
No writer who does not understand human nature can stir the hearts of men.
None but a true poet could have written *Hamlet*.

Shakespeare was clever.

★ 10. I trust every animal that belongs to me.
Dogs gnaw bones.
I admit no animals into my study unless they beg when told to do so.
All the animals in the yard are mine.
I admit every animal that I trust into my study.
The only animals that are really willing to beg when told to do so are dogs.

All the animals in the yard gnaw bones.

aplia
Visit Aplia for
section-specific
problem sets.

Summary

Categorical Syllogism:
- A deductive argument consisting of three categorical propositions.
- Containing three different terms.
- Each term occurs twice in distinct propositions.

Terms in a Categorical Syllogism:
- Major term: The term that occurs in the predicate of the conclusion.
- Minor term: The term that occurs in the subject of the conclusion.
- Middle term: The term that occurs twice in the premises.

Premises of a Categorical Syllogism:
- Major premise: The premise that contains the major term.
- Minor premise: The premise that contains the minor term.

Standard-Form Categorical Syllogism:
- All three propositions are in standard form.
- The two occurrences of each term are identical.
- Each term is used in the same sense throughout the argument.
- The major premise is listed first, minor premise second, conclusion last.

The validity of a categorical syllogism is determined by its mood and figure:
- Mood: Consists of the letter names of the propositions in the syllogism.
- Figure: Is determined by how the occurrences of the middle term are arranged.

Tables for Categorical Syllogisms:
- Unconditionally valid: Lists all forms valid from the Boolean standpoint.
- Conditionally valid: Lists additional forms valid from the Aristotelian standpoint.
- Critical term: The term listed in the farthest right-hand column of the conditionally valid table.

Venn Diagrams: To test a syllogism:
- Enter the information from the premises into the diagram.
- Look at the completed diagram to see if it supports the conclusion.
- If a syllogism having universal premises and a particular conclusion is not valid from the Boolean standpoint, test it from the Aristotelian standpoint.

Rules for Syllogisms: For a syllogism to be valid from the Boolean standpoint:
- The middle term must be distributed in at least one premise;
- A term distributed in the conclusion must also be distributed in a premise;
- At least one premise must be affirmative;
- A negative conclusion requires a negative premise, and vice versa;
- A particular conclusion requires a particular premise.

If only the last rule is broken, a syllogism is valid from the Aristotelian standpoint on condition that the critical term refers to at least one existing thing.

Some syllogisms having more than three terms can be reduced to standard form:
- Each additional term must be a complement of one of the others.
- Conversion, obversion, and contraposition must be applied only when they yield logically equivalent results.

4

Ordinary Language Syllogisms: The component propositions are not in standard form.
- Can be converted into standard-form syllogisms by applying the techniques presented in Section 3.6.

Enthymemes: Syllogisms that are missing a premise or conclusion.
- Can be converted into standard-form syllogisms by supplying the missing statement.

Sorites: A chain of syllogisms in which the intermediate conclusions are missing.
- Using the five rules to test a sorites:
  - Put the sorites into standard form.
  - Apply the rules.
  - If only the last rule is broken, a sorites is valid from the Aristotelian standpoint on condition that the critical term refers to at least one existing thing.

5

Propositional Logic

5.1   Symbols and Translation

PREVIEW

If you have contributed to Internet chat boards or sent text messages you may have used abbreviations. Some common ones are LOL (laughing out loud), IMO (in my opinion), BTW (by the way), CUL8R (see you later), B4 (before), and D8 (date). The idea is that simpler expressions are often more manageable, especially on hand-held devices. The same idea holds in logic. Simplifying the components of an argument paves the way for a speedy evaluation of the argument's validity.

Your personal learning experience—learn anywhere, anytime.

Earlier chapters showed that the validity of a deductive argument is purely a function of its form. By knowing the form of an argument, we can often tell immediately whether it is valid or invalid. Unfortunately, however, ordinary linguistic usage often obscures the form of an argument. To dispel this obscurity, logic introduces various simplifying procedures. In Chapter 4, letters were used to represent the terms in a syllogism, and techniques were developed to reduce syllogisms to what is called standard form. In this chapter, form recognition is facilitated through the introduction of special symbols called **operators**, or **connectives**. When arguments are expressed in terms of these symbols, determining validity often becomes a matter of mere visual inspection.

In the two previous chapters, the fundamental elements were terms. In **propositional logic**, however, the fundamental elements are whole statements (or propositions). Statements are represented by letters, and these letters are then combined by means of the operators to form more-complex symbolic representations.

To understand the symbolic representation used in propositional logic, we must distinguish simple statements from compound statements. A **simple statement** is one that does not contain any other statement as a component. Here are some examples:

> Fast foods tend to be unhealthy.
> James Joyce wrote *Ulysses*.
> Parakeets are colorful birds.
> The bluefin tuna is threatened with extinction.

Any convenient uppercase letter may be selected to represent each statement. Thus, *F* might be selected to represent the first, *J* the second, *P* the third, and *B* the fourth. As will be explained shortly, lowercase letters are reserved for use as statement variables.

A **compound statement** is one that contains at least one simple statement as a component. Here are some examples:

> ~A It is not the case that Al Qaeda is a humanitarian organization.
> D • C Dianne Reeves sings jazz, and Christina Aguilera sings pop.
> P ∨ E Either people get serious about conservation or energy prices will skyrocket.
> N ⊃ F If nations spurn international law, then future wars are guaranteed.
> B ≡ R The Broncos will win if and only if they run the ball.

Using uppercase letters to stand for the simple statements, these compound statements may be represented as follows:

> It is not the case that *A*.
> *D* and *C*.
> Either *P* or *E*.
> If *N* then *F*.
> *B* if and only if *R*.

In the first example, note that the statement is compound even though it contains only a single component (*A*). In general, negative statements are interpreted as compound units consisting of an affirmative statement and the phrase "it is not the case that."

The expressions "it is not the case that," "and," "or," "if . . . then . . . ," and "if and only if" are translated by logical operators. The five logical operators* are as follows:

---

*Some textbooks use the ampersand, &, in place of the dot; the arrow, →, in place of the horseshoe; and the double arrow, ↔, in place of the triple bar.

Operator	Name	Logical function	Used to translate
~	tilde	negation	not, it is not the case that
•	dot	conjunction	and, also, moreover
∨	wedge	disjunction	or, unless
⊃	horseshoe	implication	if . . . then . . . , only if
≡	triple bar	equivalence	if and only if

Saying that logical operators are used to "translate" these English expressions does not mean that the expressions and the operators are identical. As in any translation (from English to French, for example), a certain distortion of meaning occurs. The meaning of such English expressions as "and," "or," and "if and only if" is often vague and may vary with context, whereas the meaning of the logical operators is clear, precise, and invariable. Thus, when we say that the logical operators may be used to translate expressions in ordinary language, we mean that the operators capture a certain aspect of their correlative English expressions. The precise character of this aspect is spelled out in the next section of this chapter. The purpose of the current section is to develop a familiarity with the logical operators through practice in translation.

When we use the operators to translate the previous examples of compound statements, the results are as follows:

It is not the case that A.	~A
D and C.	D • C
Either P or E.	P ∨ E
If N then F.	N ⊃ F
B if and only if R.	B ≡ R

The statement ~A is called a **negation**. The statement D • C is called a **conjunctive statement** (or a **conjunction**), and the statement P ∨ E is called a **disjunctive statement** (or a **disjunction**); in the conjunctive statement, the components D and C are called **conjuncts**, and in the disjunctive statement the components P and E are called **disjuncts**. The statement N ⊃ F is called a **conditional statement** (or a **conditional**), and it expresses the relation of **material implication**. Its components are called **antecedent** (N) and **consequent** (F). Lastly, B ≡ R is called a **biconditional statement** (or a **biconditional**), and it expresses the relation of **material equivalence**.

Let us now use the logical operators to translate additional English statements. The tilde symbol is used to translate any negated simple proposition:

Rolex does not make computers.	~R
It is not the case that Rolex makes computers.	~R
It is false that Rolex makes computers.	~R

As these examples show, the tilde is always placed *in front* of the proposition it negates. All of the other operators are placed *between* two propositions. Also, unlike the other operators, the tilde cannot be used to connect two propositions. Thus, G ~ H is not a proper expression. But the tilde is the only operator that can immediately follow another operator. Thus, it would be proper to write G • ~H. In the Rolex examples, the tilde is used to negate a simple proposition, but it can also be used to negate a compound proposition—for example ~(G • F). In this case the tilde negates the entire expression inside the parentheses.

negation: A statement such as ~A.

conjunction: A statement such as A • B.

disjunction: A statement such as A ∨ B.

conditional: A statement such as A ⊃ B.

biconditional: A statement such as A ≡ B.

5

> These statements are all **negations**. The main operator is a tilde.
>
> $\sim B$
> $\sim(G \supset H)$
> $\sim[(A \equiv F) \bullet (C \equiv G)]$

At this point we should define what is called the main operator in a compound statement. The **main operator** is the operator that has as its scope everything else in the statement. If there are no parentheses in the statement, the main operator will either be the only operator or, if there is more than one, it will be the operator that is not a tilde. If there are parentheses, brackets, or braces in the statement, the main operator will be the operator that lies outside all parentheses, brackets, and braces; if there is more than one such operator, the main operator will be the one that is not a tilde.

For example, in the statement $H \bullet (J \vee K)$, the main operator is the dot, because its scope extends to everything else in the statement, whereas the scope of the wedge extends only to the J and K. In the statement $\sim(K \bullet M)$, the main operator is the tilde because its scope extends to everything else. In the statement $K \supset \sim(L \bullet M)$, the main operator is the horseshoe, because, once again, its scope extends to everything else in the statement. Excluding the tilde, it is the only operator outside the parentheses.

The dot symbol is used to translate such conjunctions as "and," "also," "but," "however," "yet," "still," "moreover," "although," and "nevertheless":

Tiffany sells jewelry, and Gucci sells cologne.	$T \bullet G$
Tiffany sells jewelry, but Gucci sells cologne.	$T \bullet G$
Tiffany sells jewelry; however, Gucci sells cologne.	$T \bullet G$
Tiffany and Ben Bridge sell jewelry.	$T \bullet B$

Note that the last example is equivalent in meaning to "Tiffany sells jewelry, and Ben Bridge sells jewelry." To translate such a statement as a conjunction of two simple statements, the original statement must be equivalent to a compound statement in English. For example, the statement "Mary and Louise are friends" is *not* equivalent in meaning to "Mary is a friend, and Louise is a friend," so this statement cannot be translated as $M \bullet L$.

> These statements are all **conjunctions**. The main operator is a dot.
>
> $K \bullet \sim L$
> $(E \vee F) \bullet \sim(G \vee H)$
> $[(R \supset T) \vee (S \supset U)] \bullet [(W \equiv X) \vee (Y \equiv Z)]$

The wedge symbol is used to translate "or" and "unless." A previous chapter explained that "unless" is equivalent in meaning to "if not." This equivalence holds in propositional logic as well, but in propositional logic it is usually simpler to equate "unless" with "or." For example, the statement "You won't graduate unless you pass freshman English" is equivalent to "Either you pass freshman English or you won't graduate" and also to "If you don't pass freshman English, then you won't graduate." As the next section demonstrates, the wedge symbol has the meaning of "and/or"—that is, "or"

5

in the inclusive sense. Although "or" and "unless" are sometimes used in an exclusive sense, the wedge is usually used to translate them as well.

The word "either," which is often used to introduce disjunctive statements, has primarily a punctuational meaning. The placement of this word often tells us where parentheses and brackets must be introduced in the symbolic expression. If parentheses or brackets are not needed, "either" does not affect the translation. A similar point applies to the word "both," which is often used to introduce conjunctive statements. Here are some disjunctive statements:

Aspen allows snowboards or Telluride does.	$A \vee T$
Either Aspen allows snowboards or Telluride does.	$A \vee T$
Aspen allows snowboards unless Telluride does.	$A \vee T$
Unless Aspen allows snowboards, Telluride does.	$A \vee T$

From the English sense of these statements, it should be clear that $A \vee T$ is logically equivalent to $T \vee A$. Also $T \cdot G$ is logically equivalent to $G \cdot T$. Logically equivalent propositions necessarily have the same truth value.

> These statements are all **disjunctions**. The main operator is a wedge.
>
> $\sim C \vee \sim D$
> $(F \cdot H) \vee (\sim K \cdot \sim L)$
> $\sim[S \cdot (T \supset U)] \vee \sim[X \cdot (Y \equiv Z)]$

The horseshoe symbol is used to translate "if . . . then . . . ," "only if," and similar expressions that indicate a conditional statement. The expressions "in case," "provided that," "given that," and "on condition that" are usually translated in the same way as "if." By customary usage, the horseshoe symbol is also used to translate "implies." Although "implies" is used most properly to describe the relationship between the premises and conclusion of an argument, we may accept this translation as an alternate meaning for "implies."

The function of "only if" is, in a sense, just the reverse of "if." For example, the statement "You will catch a fish only if your hook is baited" does not mean "If your hook is baited, then you will catch a fish." If it meant this, then everyone with a baited hook would catch a fish. Rather, the statement means "If your hook is not baited, then you will not catch a fish," which is logically equivalent to "If you catch a fish, then your hook was baited." To avoid mistakes in translating "if" and "only if" remember this rule: The statement that follows "if" is always the antecedent, and the statement that follows "only if" is always the consequent. Thus, "C only if H" is translated $C \supset H$, whereas "C if H" is translated $H \supset C$. Additional examples:

If Purdue raises tuition, then so does Notre Dame.	$P \supset N$
Notre Dame raises tuition if Purdue does.	$P \supset N$
Purdue raises tuition only if Notre Dame does.	$P \supset N$
Cornell cuts enrollment provided that Brown does.	$B \supset C$
Cornell cuts enrollment on condition that Brown does.	$B \supset C$
Brown's cutting enrollment implies that Cornell does.	$B \supset C$

In translating conditional statements, it is essential not to confuse antecedent with consequent. Just as $6 \div 3$ is not equal to $3 \div 6$, the statement $A \supset B$ is not logically equivalent to $B \supset A$.

> These statements are all **conditionals** (material implications). The main operator is a horseshoe.
>
> $H \supset \sim J$
> $(A \lor C) \supset \sim(D \bullet E)$
> $[K \lor (S \bullet \sim T)] \supset [\sim F \lor (M \bullet O)]$

sufficient condition: The statement to the left of the horseshoe.

The horseshoe symbol is also used to translate statements phrased in terms of sufficient conditions and necessary conditions. Event A is said to be a **sufficient condition** for event B whenever the occurrence of A is all that is required for the occurrence of B. On the other hand, event A is said to be a **necessary condition** for event B whenever B cannot occur without the occurrence of A. For example, having the flu is a sufficient condition for feeling miserable, whereas having air to breathe is a necessary condition for survival. Other things besides having the flu might cause a person to feel miserable, but that by itself is sufficient; other things besides having air to breathe are required for survival, but without air, survival is impossible. In other words, air is necessary.

necessary condition: The statement to the right of the horseshoe.

To translate statements involving sufficient and necessary conditions into symbolic form, place the statement that names the sufficient condition in the antecedent of the conditional and the statement that names the necessary condition in the consequent. The mnemonic device "SUN" may be conveniently used to keep this rule in mind. Turning the U sideways creates $S \supset N$, wherein S and N designate sufficient and necessary conditions, respectively. Whatever is given as a sufficient condition goes in the place of the S, and whatever is given as a necessary condition goes in the place of the N:

Hilton's opening a new hotel is a sufficient condition for Marriott's doing so. $H \supset M$

Hilton's opening a new hotel is a necessary condition for Marriott's doing so. $M \supset H$

The triple-bar symbol is used to translate the expressions "if and only if" and "is a sufficient and necessary condition for":

JFK tightens security if and only if O'Hare does. $J \equiv O$

JFK's tightening security is a sufficient and necessary condition for O'Hare's doing so. $J \equiv O$

Analysis of the first statement reveals that $J \equiv O$ is logically equivalent to $(J \supset O) \bullet (O \supset J)$. The statement "JFK tightens security only if O'Hare does" is translated $J \supset O$, and "JFK tightens security if O'Hare does" is translated $O \supset J$. Combining the two English statements, we have $(J \supset O) \bullet (O \supset J)$, which is just a longer way of writing $J \equiv O$. A similar analysis applies to the second statement. Because the order of the two conjuncts can be reversed, $J \equiv O$ is logically equivalent to $O \equiv J$. However, when translating such statements, we adopt the convention that the letter representing the first English statement is written to the left of the triple bar, and the letter representing the second English statement is written to the right of the triple bar. Thus, the examples given are translated $J \equiv O$, and not $O \equiv J$.

These statements are all **biconditionals** (material equivalences). The main operator is a triple bar.

$M \equiv \sim T$

$\sim (B \lor D) \equiv \sim (A \cdot C)$

$[K \lor (F \supset I)] \equiv [\sim L \cdot (G \lor H)]$

Whenever more than two letters appear in a translated statement, we must use parentheses, brackets, or braces to indicate the proper range of the operators. The statement $A \cdot B \lor C$, for example, is ambiguous. When parentheses are introduced, this statement becomes either $(A \cdot B) \lor C$ or $A \cdot (B \lor C)$. These two statements are not logically equivalent. Thus, with statements such as these, some clue must be found in the English statement that indicates the correct placement of the parentheses in the symbolic statement. Such clues are usually given by commas and semicolons, by such words as "either" and "both," and by the use of a single predicate in conjunction with two or more subjects. The following examples illustrate the correct placement of parentheses and brackets:

Prozac relieves depression and Allegra combats allergies, or Zocor lowers cholesterol.	$(P \cdot A) \lor Z$
Prozac relieves depression, and Allegra combats allergies or Zocor lowers cholesterol.	$P \cdot (A \lor Z)$
Either Prozac relieves depression and Allegra combats allergies or Zocor lowers cholesterol.	$(P \cdot A) \lor Z$
Prozac relieves depression and either Allegra combats allergies or Zocor lowers cholesterol.	$P \cdot (A \lor Z)$
Prozac relieves depression or both Allegra combats allergies and Zocor lowers cholesterol.	$P \lor (A \cdot Z)$
Prozac relieves depression and Allegra or Zocor lowers cholesterol.	$P \cdot (A \lor Z)$
If Merck changes its logo, then if Pfizer increases sales, then Lilly will reorganize.	$M \supset (P \supset L)$
If Merck's changing its logo implies that Pfizer increases sales, then Lilly will reorganize.	$(M \supset P) \supset L$
If Schering and Pfizer lower prices or Novartis downsizes, then Warner will expand production.	$[(S \cdot P) \lor N] \supset W$

correct parentheses & Brackets (handwritten annotation)

Do not confuse these three statement forms:

A if B	$B \supset A$
A only if B	$A \supset B$
A if and only if B	$A \equiv B$

When a tilde appears in a symbolic expression, by convention it is considered to affect only the unit that immediately follows it. For example, in the expression $\sim K \lor M$

Gottfried Wilhelm Leibniz 1646–1716

Gottfried Wilhelm Leibniz was a polymath who knew virtually everything that could be known at the time about nearly every area of intellectual endeavor. He also made important contributions to many of them, including physics, engineering, philosophy, theology, history, law, politics, and philology. In mathematics Leibniz invented differential and integral calculus (independently of Newton) and the theory of differential equations. He also discovered the binary number system (used by all of today's digital computers), and he created the first calculating machine that could add, subtract, multiply, and divide. In metaphysics he created the famous theory of monads which, among other things, explained the relation between the soul and the body.

Leibniz was born in Leipzig to prominent parents. His father (who died when Leibniz was six) was a professor of moral philosophy at the city's university, and his mother was the daughter of a famous lawyer. As a child Leibniz proved himself a prodigy. By age twelve he was fluent in Latin and had a passing knowledge of Greek, both of which he had learned by himself. By thirteen he was deep into the works of Aristotle and scholastic philosophy, and at fourteen he entered the University of Leipzig, where he studied philosophy, mathematics, and law. After completing that program he began a doctoral program in law; however, when he applied for the degree at age twenty, he was refused because of his youth. Not to be outdone, Leibniz presented his thesis to the University of Altdorf, and the professors there were so impressed that they immediately awarded him the degree of Doctor of Laws and offered him a professorship.

Quite early in life Leibniz developed a taste for the finer things in life, including expensive clothing; long, flowing wigs; fancy carriages; and luxurious accommodations. However, following the death of his mother when he was eighteen, an uncle received what should have been Leibniz's inheritance. When this happened Leibniz figured that the best way of satisfying his expensive tastes was to attach himself to the wealthy and the powerful, which he did with great success. He entered the employment of the elector of Mainz, and by the age of twenty-four he held the rank of privy counselor of justice, one of the highest positions in the government. His work as a diplomat allowed him the opportunity to travel widely and meet most of the prominent figures in Europe. Later he worked for the Duke of Hanover, a position that also allowed much time for travel and independent study.

Leibniz is sometimes called the father of symbolic logic for his work in developing the *universal characteristic,* a symbolic language in which any item of information can be represented in a natural and systematic way, together with the *calculus ratiocinator,* a deductive system for manipulating the symbols and deriving consequences. Given the dispassionate nature of this enterprise, Leibniz thought that it would serve to resolve differences of opinion in religion, theology, and philosophy. However, at age seventy he died in Hanover before completing the project.

the tilde affects only the *K;* in the expression $\sim(K \vee M)$ it affects the entire expression inside the parentheses. In English, the expression "It is not the case that *K* or *M*" is ambiguous, because the range of the negating words is indefinite. To eliminate this ambiguity, we now adopt the convention that the negating words are considered to affect only the unit that follows them. Thus, "It is not the case that *K* or *M*" is translated $\sim K \vee M$.

The statement "Not both *S* and *T*" is translated $\sim(S \cdot T)$. By an important rule called *De Morgan's rule,* this statement is logically equivalent to $\sim S \vee \sim T$. For example, the statement "Not both Steven and Thomas were fired" is equivalent in meaning to "Either Stephen was not fired or Thomas was not fired." Because the former statement is *not* equivalent in meaning to "Stephen was not fired and Thomas was not fired," $\sim(S \cdot T)$ is *not* logically equivalent to $\sim S \cdot \sim T$. Analogously, the statement "Not either S or T" is translated $\sim(S \vee T)$, which by De Morgan's rule is logically equivalent to $\sim S \cdot \sim T$. For example, "Not either Steven or Thomas was fired" is equivalent in meaning to "Steven was not fired and Thomas was not fired." Thus, $\sim(S \vee T)$ is *not* logically equivalent to $\sim S \vee \sim T$. The following examples illustrate these points:

Megan is not a winner, but Kathy is.	$\sim M \cdot K$
Not both Megan and Kathy are winners.	$\sim(M \cdot K)$
Either Megan or Kathy is not a winner.	$\sim M \vee \sim K$
Both Megan and Kathy are not winners.	$\sim M \cdot \sim K$
Not either Megan or Kathy is a winner.	$\sim(M \vee K)$
Neither Megan nor Kathy is a winner.	$\sim(M \vee K)$

(Handwritten margin notes: "(Not both / neither)", "ex: of non-logically equivalent", "either ~")

> **Notice the function of "either" and "both":**
>
> | | |
> |---|---|
> | Not either *A* or *B*. | $\sim(A \vee B)$ |
> | Either not *A* or not *B*. | $\sim A \vee \sim B$ |
> | Not both *A* and *B*. | $\sim(A \cdot B)$ |
> | Both not *A* and not *B*. | $\sim A \cdot \sim B$ |

The symbolic expressions that we have used throughout this section to translate meaningful, unambiguous English statements are called **well-formed formulas (WFFs)**. "WFFs" is usually pronounced "woofs." A well-formed formula is a *syntactically* correct arrangement of symbols. In English, for example, the expression "there is a cat on the porch" is syntactically correct, but "Porch on the is cat a there" is not syntactically correct. Some examples of symbolic arrangements that are *not* well-formed formulas are "$A \supset \vee B$," "$A \cdot B (\vee C)$," and "$\sim \vee B \equiv \supset C$."

A few informal cues for constructing well-formed formulas follow. In these cues, the term *statements* includes simple statements and compound statements. Remember, $\sim A$ is a compound statement.

Statements cannot be combined without an operator occurring between them.

Not WFFs:	AB, $A(B \supset C)$, $(A \supset B)(B \vee C)$
WFFs:	$A \supset B$, $A \vee \sim B$, $A \cdot (B \equiv C)$

A tilde cannot immediately follow a statement, but it can immediately precede any statement (except when it immediately follows a statement).

Not WFFs:	$A\sim$, $A\sim B$, $(A \cdot B)\sim$
WFFs:	$\sim A$, $\sim(A \cdot B)$, $\sim\sim A$

A tilde cannot immediately precede any other operator.

Not WFFs:	$\sim \cdot A$, $A\sim \vee B$

A dot, wedge, horseshoe, or triple bar must go immediately between statements.

Not WFFs:	$\cdot A$, $A \vee$, $A \cdot \supset B$
WFFs:	$A \cdot B$, $A \supset \sim B$, $A \vee (B \cdot C)$

well-formed formula (WFF): A syntactically correct arrangement of symbols.

5

SECTION 5.1 SYMBOLS AND TRANSLATION **245**

Parentheses, brackets, and braces must be inserted to prevent ambiguity.

Not WFFs: $A \supset B \vee C$, $A \cdot B \equiv C$

WFFs: $A \supset (B \vee C)$, $(A \cdot B) \supset C$

Summary	Operator
not, it is not the case that, it is false that	~
and, yet, but, however, moreover, nevertheless, still, also, although, both, additionally, furthermore	•
or, unless	∨
if . . . then, only if, implies, given that, in case, provided that, on condition that, sufficient condition for, necessary condition for (Note: Do not confuse antecedent with consequent!)	⊃
if and only if, is equivalent to, sufficient and necessary condition for	≡

EXERCISE 5.1

I. Translate the following statements into symbolic form using capital letters to represent affirmative English statements.

★1. Cartier does not make cheap watches.

2. Arizona has a national park but Nebraska does not.

3. Either Stanford or Tulane has an architecture school.

★4. Both Harvard and Baylor have medical schools.

5. If Chanel has a rosewood fragrance, then so does Lanvin.

6. Chanel has a rosewood fragrance if Lanvin does.

★7. Maureen Dowd writes incisive editorials if and only if Paul Krugman does.

8. Reese Witherspoon wins best actress only if Martin Scorsese wins best director.

9. Armani will launch a leather collection given that Gucci rejects skinny models.

★10. The Packers' winning most of their games implies that Aaron Rodgers is a great quarterback.

11. Bill Gates does not support malaria research unless Warren Buffet does.

12. Mercedes will introduce a hybrid model only if Lexus and BMW do.

★13. Mariah Carey sings pop and either Elton John sings rock or Diana Krall sings jazz.

14. Either Mariah Carey sings pop and Elton John sings rock or Diana Krall sings jazz.

15. Not both Jaguar and Porsche make motorcycles.

★16. Both Jaguar and Porsche do not make motorcycles.

17. Either Nokia or Seiko makes cell phones.

18. Not either Ferrari or Maserati makes economy cars.

★19. Neither Ferrari nor Maserati makes economy cars.

20. Either Ferrari or Maserati does not make economy cars.

21. If Bill O'Reilly spins the news, then if Chris Matthews fights back, then Rachel Maddow tells it straight.

★22. If Bill O'Reilly's spinning the news implies that Chris Matthews fights back, then Rachel Maddow tells it straight.

23. Tommy Hilfiger celebrates casual if and only if neither Ralph Lauren nor Calvin Klein offers street chic.

24. If Saks promotes gift cards, then either Macy's or Bloomingdale's puts on a fashion show.

★25. Either Rado does not make a sapphire watch or if Movado makes one then so does Pulsar.

26. If either Lockheed Martin or Raytheon floods the world with weapons of war, then neither General Dynamics nor Boeing reduces the likelihood of armed conflict.

27. If Electronic Arts and Activision Blizzard sell extremely violent video games, then either Colt or Smith & Wesson can expect increased profits.

★28. Mercury is a planet given that both Pluto and Ceres are not.

29. Saturn has rings, and Neptune is windy or Jupiter is massive.

30. Saturn has rings and Neptune is windy, or Jupiter is massive.

★31. Tiffany and Ben Bridge will release an emerald collection unless Zales and Kay do not.

32. Chevron continues to pollute provided that British Petroleum does, but Koch Industries and Exxon Mobil deny climate change.

33. Either Sonia Sotomayor or Antonin Scalia have a modern approach to the Constitution, but it is not the case that both do.

★34. Barack Obama emphasizes peaceful negotiation; but if North Korea starts a war, then either China or Japan will be involved.

35. It is not the case that both Iran gives up its nuclear program and Sudan or Pakistan combats terrorism.

36. It is not the case that either Hezbollah will renounce violence or Al Qaeda and the Taliban will be defeated.

★37. If Monsanto poisons the entire human race, then if Nestlé buries us in bottles, then Smithfield and Tyson load us up with antibiotics.

38. If Maria Cantwell promotes alternative energy, then if Patty Murray supports wilderness areas, then Dianne Feinstein's advocating gun control implies that Susan Collins does so, too.

39. It is not the case that either Tiger Woods and Maria Sharapova play professional football or Drew Brees and Serena Williams play professional baseball.

★40. It is not the case that both Kobe Bryant or Shaquille O'Neal plays professional tennis and Calvin Johnson or Matt Ryan plays professional basketball.

41. Israel's abandoning its settlements is a sufficient condition for the Palestinians' declaring an end to hostilities.

42. Israel's abandoning its settlements is a necessary condition for the Palestinians' declaring an end to hostilities.

★43. Israel's abandoning its settlements is a sufficient and necessary condition for the Palestinians' declaring an end to hostilities.

44. The Taliban's being defeated is a sufficient condition for Pakistan's winning the war on terror only if Afghanistan's securing its borders is a necessary condition for the UN's stopping the opium trade.

45. Katie Couric and Diane Sawyer report international news if and only if Erica Hill and Norah O'Donnell cover political developments.

★46. It is not the case that both Walmart's jeopardizing worker safety implies that Target does and Costco's treating workers decently implies that Kmart does.

47. Cameron Diaz promotes environmental causes if Ben Affleck supports civil liberties, provided that Sean Penn opposes the death penalty.

48. JP Morgan's getting another bailout implies that Goldman Sachs cheats its clients, given that Bank of America's foreclosing on more homes implies that neither Morgan Stanley nor Citigroup curtails obscene bonuses.

★49. If Christina Aguilera's singing soul and Justin Timberlake's singing pop are sufficient and necessary conditions for Kelly Clarkson's singing rock, then neither Beyoncé nor Shakira will sing rap.

50. Nassau's advertising sizzling night clubs is a necessary condition for Puerto Vallarta's offering luxury hotels; moreover, Cancun's having turquoise waters and Acapulco's promising powder-white beaches is a sufficient condition for Jamaica's offering reggae music.

II. Translate the following statements into symbolic form using capital letters to represent affirmative English statements.

★1. Unless we reduce the incidence of child abuse, future crime rates will increase.

2. If pharmaceutical makers conceal test results, they are subject to substantial fines.

3. African safaris are amazing, but they are also expensive.

★4. Cigarette manufacturers are neither honest nor socially responsible.

5. Psychologists and psychiatrists do not both prescribe antidepressant drugs.

6. If health maintenance organizations cut costs, then either preventive medicine is emphasized or the quality of care deteriorates.

★7. A necessary condition for a successful business venture is good planning.

8. If cocaine is legalized, then its use may increase but criminal activity will decline.

9. Ozone depletion in the atmosphere is a sufficient condition for increased cancer rates.

★10. If affirmative action programs are dropped, then if new programs are not created, then minority applicants will suffer.

11. If Internet use continues to grow, then more people will become cyberaddicts and normal human relations will deteriorate.

12. Human life will not perish unless either we poison ourselves with pollution or a large asteroid collides with the Earth.

★13. Cooling a group of atoms to absolute zero and keeping them bunched together is a necessary and sufficient condition for producing a Bose–Einstein condensate.

14. If motion pictures contain subliminal sex messages or if they challenge the traditional family, then conservative politicians call for censorship.

15. Either clear-cutting in national forests is halted and old-growth trees are allowed to stand, or salmon runs will be destroyed and bird habitats obliterated.

★16. Three-strikes laws will be enforced and longer sentences imposed only if hundreds of new prisons are built, and that will happen only if taxes are increased.

17. The Ebola virus is deadly, but it will become a major threat to humanity if and only if it becomes airborne and a vaccine is not developed.

18. If evolutionary biology is correct, then higher life-forms arose by chance, and if that is so, then it is not the case that there is any design in nature and divine providence is a myth.

★19. If banks charge fees for teller-assisted transactions, then more people will use ATMs; and if that happens and ATM fees increase, then banks will close branches and profits will skyrocket.

20. If corporate welfare continues, then taxpayer interests will be ignored and billions of tax dollars will go to giant corporations; and if the latter occurs, then there will not be anything left for the poor and the budget will not be balanced.

III. Determine which of the following are *not* well-formed formulas.

1. $(S \cdot \sim T) \vee (\sim U \cdot W)$

2. $\sim(K \vee L) \cdot (\supset G \vee H)$

3. $(E \sim F) \vee (W \equiv X)$

4. $(B \supset \sim T) \equiv \sim(\sim C \supset U)$

5. $(F \equiv \sim Q) \cdot (A \supset E \vee T)$

6. $\sim D \vee \sim[(P \supset Q) \cdot (T \supset R)]$

7. $[(D \cdot \vee Q) \supset (P \vee E)] \vee [A \supset (\cdot H)]$

8. $M(N \supset Q) \vee (\sim C \cdot D)$

9. $\sim(F \vee \sim G) \supset [(A \equiv E) \cdot \sim H]$

10. $(R \equiv S \cdot T) \supset \sim(\sim W \cdot \sim X)$

aplia™

Visit Aplia for section-specific problem sets.

5.2 Truth Functions

PREVIEW

Suppose you have an assignment to write a paper on the design of the Taj Mahal. You begin your research by pulling up Google Earth and typing in the name of the building. You are then afforded views of the Taj from all possible directions. This gives you an excellent idea of what the building looks like. In this section we show how truth tables accomplish something similar with the five logical operators. A truth table gives you a "complete view" of an operator by showing how it functions under all possible conditions.

The truth value of a compound proposition expressed in terms of one or more logical operators is said to be a function of the truth values of its components. This means that the truth value of the compound proposition is completely determined by the truth values of its components. If the truth values of the components are known, then the truth value of the compound proposition can be calculated from the definitions of the logical operators. Accordingly, a **truth function** is any compound proposition whose truth value is completely determined by the truth values of its components.

truth function: A compound proposition whose truth value is completely determined by the truth values of its components.

Many compound propositions in ordinary language are not truth functions. For example, the statement "Mary believes that Paul is dishonest" is compound because it contains the statement "Paul is dishonest" as a component. Yet the truth value of the compound statement is not determined by the truth value of the component, because Mary's beliefs about Paul are not compelled by any attribute that Paul may or may not possess.

The first part of this section presents the definitions of the five logical operators, the second part shows how they are used to compute the truth values of more-complicated propositions, and the third examines further the degree to which symbolized expressions match the meaning of expressions in ordinary language.

Definitions of the Logical Operators

The definitions of the logical operators are presented in terms of **statement variables**, which are lowercase letters (p, q, r, s) that can stand for any statement. For example, the statement variable p could stand for the statements A, $A \supset B$, $B \lor C$, and so on.

Statement variables are used to construct statement forms. A **statement form** is an arrangement of statement variables and operators such that the uniform substitution of statements in place of the variables results in a statement. For example, $\sim p$ and $p \supset q$ are statement forms because substituting the statements A and B in place of p and q, respectively, results in the statements $\sim A$ and $A \supset B$. A compound statement is said to have a certain form if it can be produced by substituting statements in place of the letters in that form. Thus, $\sim A$, $\sim(A \lor B)$, and $\sim[A \bullet (B \lor C)]$ are negations because they can be produced by substituting statements in place of p in the form $\sim p$.

truth table: An arrangement of truth values that shows in every possible case how the truth value of a compound proposition is determined by the truth values of its simple components.

Now let us consider the definition of the tilde operator (negation). This definition is given by a **truth table**, an arrangement of truth values that shows in every possible case how the truth value of a compound proposition is determined by the truth values of its simple components. The truth table for negation shows how any statement having the form of a negation ($\sim p$) is determined by the truth value of the statement that is negated (p):

Negation	p	$\sim p$
	T	F
	F	T

A **negation** has a truth value opposite that of the statement negated.

The truth table shows that $\sim p$ is false when p is true and that $\sim p$ is true when p is false. This is exactly what we would expect, because it perfectly matches ordinary English usage. Examples: *It is not true that*

It is not the case that McDonald's makes hamburgers. $\qquad\qquad \sim M$

It is not the case that Starbucks makes hamburgers. $\qquad\qquad \sim S$

The first statement is false because M is true, and the second is true because S is false.

Let us now consider the definition of the dot operator (conjunction). The truth table that follows shows how any statement having the form of a conjunction ($p \bullet q$) is determined by the truth values of its conjuncts (p, q):

Conjunction	p	q	$p \bullet q$
	T	T	T
	T	F	F
	F	T	F
	F	F	F

A **conjunction** is true only when both conjuncts are true.

This truth table shows that a conjunction is true when its two conjuncts are true and is false in all other cases. This definition reflects ordinary language usage almost as perfectly as negation. Consider the following conjunctive statements:

Ferrari and Maserati make sports cars. $\qquad\qquad F \bullet M$

Ferrari and GMC make sports cars. $\qquad\qquad F \bullet G$

GMC and Jeep make sports cars. $\qquad\qquad G \bullet J$

The first statement is true, because both conjuncts are true; but the second and third statements are false, because at least one of their conjuncts is false.

Turning now to the definition of the wedge operator (disjunction), the truth table is as follows:

Disjunction	p	q	$p \vee q$
	T	T	T
	T	F	T
	F	T	T
	F	F	F

A **disjunction** is false only when both disjuncts are false.

The truth table indicates that the disjunction is true when at least one of the disjuncts is true and that otherwise it is false. The truth-functional interpretation of "or" is that of *inclusive* disjunction: Cases in which the disjunction is true include the case when both disjuncts are true. This inclusive sense of "or" corresponds to many instances of ordinary usage, as the following examples illustrate:

Either Steven King or Cate Blanchett is a novelist. $\qquad\qquad S \vee C$

Either Steven King or Danielle Steel is a novelist. $\qquad\qquad S \vee D$

Either Kobe Bryant or Tiger Woods is a novelist. $\qquad\qquad K \vee T$

The first two statements are true, because in each case at least one of the disjuncts is true. The third is false, because both disjuncts are false.

The match between the truth-functional definition of disjunction and ordinary usage is not perfect, however. Sometimes the sense of a statement in ordinary language is that of *exclusive* disjunction. Examples:

> The Orient Express is on either track A or track B.
>
> You can have either soup or salad with this meal.
>
> Tammy is either ten or eleven years old.

The sense of these statements excludes the possibility of both alternatives being true. Thus, if these statements were translated using the wedge, a portion of their ordinary meaning would be lost. If the exclusive aspect of these "either . . . or . . ." statements is essential, the symbolic equivalent of "but not both" can be attached to their translations. Thus the first statement could be translated $(A \lor B) \cdot \sim(A \cdot B)$.

Let us now consider the horseshoe operator (material implication, or conditional). Its truth table is as follows:

A **conditional** is false only when the antecedent is true and the consequent is false.

Conditional
(material implication)

p	q	$p \supset q$
T	T	T
T	F	F
F	T	T
F	F	T

The truth table shows that a conditional statement is false when the antecedent is true and the consequent false and is true in all other cases. This truth-functional interpretation of conditional statements conforms in part with the ordinary meaning of "if . . . then . . ." and in part it diverges. Consider the following examples:

If Nicole Kidman is an actor, then so is Meryl Streep.	$N \supset M$
If Nicole Kidman is an actor, then so is Wolf Blitzer.	$N \supset W$
If Wolf Blitzer is an actor, then so is Helen Hunt.	$W \supset H$
If Wolf Blitzer is an actor, then so is Piers Morgan.	$W \supset P$

In these statements *N, M,* and *H* are true and *W* and *P* are false. Thus, according to the truth-functional interpretation, the first statement is true and the second false. This result conforms in large measure to our expectations. But the truth-functional interpretation of the last two statements is true. Although this result may not conflict with our expectations, it is not at all clear why these statements should be considered true.

For an intuitive approach to this problem, imagine that your logic instructor made the following statement: "If you get an A on the final exam, then you will get an A for the course." Under what conditions would you say that your instructor had lied to you? Clearly, if you got an A on the final exam but did not get an A for the course, you would say that she had lied. This outcome corresponds to a true antecedent and a false consequent. On the other hand, if you got an A on the final exam and also got an A for the course, you would say that she had told the truth (true antecedent, true consequent). But what if you failed to get an A on the final exam? Two alternatives are then possible: Either you got an A for the course anyway (false antecedent, true consequent) or you did not get an A for the course (false antecedent, false consequent). In neither case, though, would you say that your instructor had lied to you. Giving her the benefit of the doubt, you would say that she had told the truth.

Lastly, let us consider the definition of the triple-bar operator (material equivalence, or biconditional). Its truth table is as follows:

Biconditional
(material equivalence)

p	q	$p \equiv q$
T	T	T
T	F	F
F	T	F
F	F	T

> A **biconditional** is true only when the two statements have the same truth value.

The truth table shows that the biconditional is true when its two components have the same truth value and that otherwise it is false. These results are required by the fact that $p \equiv q$ is simply a shorter way of writing $(p \supset q) \cdot (q \supset p)$. If p and q are either both true or both false, then $p \supset q$ and $q \supset p$ are both true, making their conjunction true. But if p is true and q is false, then $p \supset q$ is false, making the conjunction false. Similarly, if p is false and q is true, then $q \supset p$ is false, again making the conjunction false. Thus, $p \equiv q$ is true when p and q have the same truth value and false when they have opposite truth values.

The truth-table definition of the triple-bar symbol conforms quite closely with ordinary usage, as the following examples illustrate:

Bill Maher is a show host if and only if Jimmy Fallon is.　　$B \equiv J$

Bill Maher is a show host if and only if Emma Watson is.　　$B \equiv E$

Emma Watson is a show host if and only if Matt Damon is.　　$E \equiv M$

In these statements, B and J are true and E and M false. Thus, from the truth-functional standpoint, the first is true and the second false. This is what we would ordinarily expect. The third statement, however, turns out to be true because both of its components are false. While this result may not be what we would expect, it does not violate our expectations either. Other biconditional statements having false components are more obviously true. Example:

Mitt Romney was elected president if and only if he received a majority vote from the electoral college.

This statement asserts what is required for any candidate to be elected or not elected, and so it is clearly true.

In summary, the definitions of the five logical operators conform reasonably well with ordinary linguistic usage. However, as the last part of this section shows, the match is less than perfect. Before considering this question, though, let us use the operator definitions to compute the truth values of more-complicated statements.

Computing the Truth Value of Longer Propositions

To compute the truth value of a more complicated expression, use this procedure: Enter the truth values of the simple components directly beneath the letters. Then use these truth values to compute the truth values of the compound components. The truth value of a compound statement is written beneath the operator representing it. Let us suppose, for example, that we are told in advance that the simple propositions A, B, and C are true and D, E, and F are false. We may then compute the truth value of the following compound proposition:

$$(A \lor D) \supset E$$

First, we write the truth values of the simple propositions immediately below the respective letters and bring the operators and parentheses down:

$$(A \lor D) \supset E$$

$$(T \lor F) \supset F$$

Next, we compute the truth value of the proposition in parentheses and write it beneath the operator to which it pertains:

$$(A \lor D) \supset E$$

$$(T \lor F) \supset F$$

$$T \quad \supset F$$

Finally, we use the last-completed line to obtain the truth value of the conditional, which is the main operator in the proposition:

$$(A \lor D) \supset E$$

$$(T \lor F) \supset F$$

$$T \quad \supset F$$

$$Ⓕ$$

The final answer is circled. This is the truth value of the compound proposition given that A is true and D and E are false.

The general strategy is to build the truth values of the larger components from the truth values of the smaller ones. In general, the order to be followed in entering truth values is this:

1. Individual letters representing simple propositions

2. Tildes immediately preceding individual letters

3. Operators joining letters or negated letters

4. Tildes immediately preceding parentheses

5. And so on

In entering truth values, begin with the individual letters and work outward.

Here are some additional examples. As before, let A, B, and C be true, D, E, and F false. Note that the computed truth values are written beneath the operators to which they pertain. The final answers, which are written beneath the main operators, are circled.

1. $(B \bullet C) \supset (E \supset A)$
   $(T \bullet T) \supset (F \supset T)$
   $\quad T \quad \supset \quad T$
   $\quad\quad Ⓣ$

2. $\sim (C \lor \sim A) \supset \sim B$
   $\sim (T \lor \sim T) \supset \sim T$
   $\sim (T \lor F) \quad \supset F$
   $\sim \quad T \quad \quad \supset F$
   $F \quad \quad \quad \supset F$
   $ \quad \quad (T)$

3. $[\sim (D \lor F) \bullet (B \lor \sim A)] \supset \sim (F \supset \sim C)$
   $[\sim (F \lor F) \bullet (T \lor \sim T)] \supset \sim (F \supset \sim T)$
   $[\sim (F \lor F) \bullet (T \lor F) \;] \supset \sim (F \supset F \;)$
   $[\sim \quad F \quad \bullet \quad T \quad \;] \supset \sim \quad T$
   $[T \quad \quad \bullet \quad T \quad \;] \supset F$
   $\quad \quad T \quad \quad \quad \quad \supset F$
   $\quad \quad \quad \quad (F)$

If preferred, the truth values of the compound components may be entered directly beneath the operators, without using the line-by-line approach illustrated in these examples. The following examples illustrate this second approach, which is used in the next section:

1. $[(D \equiv \sim A) \bullet \sim (C \bullet \sim B)] \equiv \sim [(A \supset \sim D) \lor (C \equiv E)]$

   F T F T T T T F F T (F) F T T T F T T F F

2. $\sim \{[(C \bullet \sim E) \supset \sim (A \bullet \sim B)] \supset [\sim (B \lor D) \equiv (\sim C \lor E)]\}$

   (F) T T T F T T T F F T T F T T F T F T F F

Truth Functions and Ordinary Language

The first part of this section showed that the definitions of the five logical operators conform reasonably well with ordinary linguistic usage. However, the match is less than perfect.

In regard to the dot operator, which is used to translate "and" and "but," the match fails, at least in part, when the meaning of a conjunctive statement depends on the order of the conjuncts. Consider the following statements:

She got married and had a baby. $M \bullet B$

She had a baby and got married. $B \bullet M$

The first statement implies that the marriage occurred first, and the baby came later, while the second statement implies that the baby came first. This implied meaning is lost in the truth-functional interpretation, because $M \bullet B$ is logically equivalent to $B \bullet M$.

In regard to the wedge operator, which is used to translate "or" and "unless," we saw that the wedge is defined as inclusive disjunction, but we observed that the English word "or" sometimes has the sense of exclusive disjunction. In the following statements, "unless" is used in the exclusive sense.

Pork is not properly cooked unless the meat is white.

These logs will make a nice campfire unless they are wet.

The first statement suggests that the meat cannot be white and at the same time not be properly cooked, and the second suggests that the logs cannot be wet and at the same time be used to make a nice campfire. Thus, if these statements are translated using the wedge operator, part of the meaning will be left out. If this additional part is essential, it can be included by adding the symbolic equivalent of "but not both" to the translation.

In connection with the horseshoe operator, the fact that a conditional statement is true when the antecedent is false can lead to a conflict with the ordinary language meaning. Consider the following statements:

> If Barbara Boxer advocates the use of cocaine, then she is a good senator.

> If Chicago is in Michigan, then Chicago is very close to Miami.

According to their ordinary language interpretation, both of these statements are false. Good senators do not advocate the use of cocaine, and Michigan is far from Miami. Yet, when these statements are interpreted as material conditionals, both turn out to be true, because their antecedents are false. In cases like these, when the truth-functional interpretation of a conditional statement conflicts with the ordinary language interpretation, using the horseshoe operator to translate it may not be appropriate.

EXERCISE 5.2

I. Identify the main operator in the following propositions.

★1. $\sim(A \vee M) \cdot \sim(C \supset E)$

2. $(G \cdot \sim P) \supset \sim(H \vee \sim W)$

3. $\sim[P \cdot (S \equiv K)]$

★4. $\sim(K \cdot \sim O) \equiv \sim(R \vee \sim B)$

5. $(M \cdot B) \vee \sim[E \equiv \sim(C \vee I)]$

6. $\sim[(P \cdot \sim R) \supset (\sim E \vee F)]$

★7. $\sim[(S \vee L) \cdot M] \supset (C \vee N)$

8. $[\sim F \vee (N \cdot U)] \equiv \sim H$

9. $E \cdot [(F \supset A) \equiv (\sim G \vee H)]$

★10. $\sim[(X \vee T) \cdot (N \vee F)] \vee (K \supset L)$

II. Write the following compound statements in symbolic form, then use your knowledge of the historical events referred to by the simple statements to determine the truth value of the compound statements.

★1. It is not the case that Hitler ran the Third Reich.

2. Nixon resigned the presidency and Lincoln wrote the Gettysburg Address.

3. France bombed Pearl Harbor, or Lindbergh crossed the Atlantic.

★4. Hitler ran the Third Reich and Nixon did not resign the presidency.

5. Edison invented the telephone, or Custer was killed by the Indians.

6. Alexander the Great civilized America if Napoleon ruled France.

★7. Washington was assassinated only if Edison invented the telephone.

8. Lincoln wrote the Gettysburg Address if and only if France bombed Pearl Harbor.

9. It is not the case that either Alexander the Great civilized America or Washington was assassinated.

★10. If Hitler ran the Third Reich, then either Custer was killed by the Indians or Einstein discovered aspirin.

11. Either Lindbergh crossed the Atlantic and Edison invented the telephone or both Nixon resigned the presidency and it is false that Edison invented the telephone.

12. Lincoln's having written the Gettysburg Address is a sufficient condition for Alexander the Great's having civilized America if and only if Washington's being assassinated is a necessary condition for Custer's having been killed by the Indians.

★13. Both Hitler ran the Third Reich and Lindbergh crossed the Atlantic if neither Einstein discovered aspirin nor France bombed Pearl Harbor.

14. It is not the case that Custer was killed by the Indians unless both Nixon resigned the presidency and Edison invented the telephone.

15. Custer was killed by the Indians, and Lincoln wrote the Gettysburg Address only if either Washington was assassinated or Alexander the Great civilized America.

III. Determine the truth values of the following symbolized statements. Let A, B, and C be true and X, Y, and Z be false. Circle your answer.

★1. $A \cdot X$

2. $B \cdot \sim Y$

3. $X \vee \sim Y$

★4. $\sim C \vee Z$

5. $B \supset \sim Z$

6. $Y \supset \sim A$

★7. $\sim X \supset Z$

8. $B \equiv Y$

9. $\sim C \equiv Z$

★10. $\sim(A \cdot \sim Z)$

11. $\sim B \vee (Y \supset A)$

12. $A \supset \sim(Z \vee \sim Y)$

★13. $(A \cdot Y) \vee (\sim Z \cdot C)$

14. $\sim(X \vee \sim B) \cdot (\sim Y \vee A)$

15. $(Y \supset C) \cdot \sim(B \supset \sim X)$

★16. $(C \equiv \sim A) \vee (Y \equiv Z)$

17. $\sim(A \cdot \sim C) \supset (\sim X \supset B)$

18. $\sim[(B \vee \sim C) \cdot \sim(X \vee \sim Z)]$

★19. $\sim[\sim(X \supset C) \equiv \sim(B \supset Z)]$

20. $(X \supset Z) \supset [(B \equiv \sim X) \cdot \sim(C \vee \sim A)]$

21. $[(\sim X \vee Z) \supset (\sim C \vee B)] \cdot [(\sim X \cdot A) \supset (\sim Y \cdot Z)]$

★22. $\sim[(A \equiv X) \vee (Z \equiv Y)] \vee [(\sim Y \supset B) \cdot (Z \supset C)]$

23. $[(B \cdot \sim C) \vee (X \cdot \sim Y)] \supset \sim[(Y \cdot \sim X) \vee (A \cdot \sim Z)]$

24. $\sim\{\sim[(C \vee \sim B) \cdot (Z \vee \sim A)] \cdot \sim[\sim(B \vee Y) \cdot (\sim X \vee Z)]\}$

★25. $(Z \supset C) \supset \{[(\sim X \supset B) \supset (C \supset Y)] \equiv [(Z \supset X) \supset (\sim Y \supset Z)]\}$

IV. When possible, determine the truth values of the following symbolized statements. Let A and B be true, Y and Z false. P and Q have unknown truth value. If the truth value of the statement cannot be determined, write "undetermined."

★1. $A \vee P$

2. $Q \vee Z$

3. $Q \cdot Y$

★4. $Q \cdot A$

5. $P \supset B$

6. $Z \supset Q$

★7. $A \supset P$

8. $P \equiv \sim P$

9. $(P \supset A) \supset Z$

★10. $(P \supset A) \equiv (Q \supset B)$

11. $(Q \supset B) \supset (A \supset Y)$

12. $\sim(P \supset Y) \vee (Z \supset Q)$

★13. $\sim(Q \cdot Y) \equiv \sim(Q \vee A)$

14. $[(Z \supset P) \supset P] \supset P$

15. $[Q \supset (A \vee P)] \equiv [(Q \supset B) \supset Y]$

5

5.3 Truth Tables for Propositions

PREVIEW

In the previous section you saw how a truth table gives you a complete view of a proposition similar to how Google Earth gives you a complete view of a building. If it should turn out that every side of a building is white, then you would call the whole building white. If every side should be black, then the whole building would be black. Similarly, if the final column of a truth table should be all true, then the proposition is called one thing. If all false, then it is called something else.

The previous section showed how the truth value of a compound proposition could be determined, given a *designated* truth value for each simple component. A truth table gives the truth value of a compound proposition for *every possible* truth value of its simple components. Each line in the truth table represents one such possible arrangement of truth values.

In constructing a truth table the first step is to determine the number of lines (or rows). Because each line represents one possible arrangement of truth values, the total number of lines is equal to the number of possible combinations of truth values for the simple propositions. As we saw in Section 5.2, if there is only one simple proposition, p, the number of lines in the truth table is two, because there are only two possible truth values for p: true, and false. If there are two simple propositions, p and q, there are four lines, because there are four combinations of truth values: p true and q true, p true and q false, p false and q true, and p false and q false. The relationship between the number of different simple propositions and the number of lines in the truth table is expressed as follows:

Number of different simple propositions	Number of lines in truth table
1	2
2	4
3	8
4	16
5	32
6	64

The number of lines in a truth table is 2^n, where n is the number of different simple propositions.

The relationship between these two columns of numbers is expressed by the formula,

$$L = 2^n$$

where L designates the number of lines in the truth table, and n the number of *different* simple propositions.

Let us now construct a truth table for a compound proposition. We may begin with a fairly simple one:

$(A \lor \sim B) \supset B$

The number of different simple propositions is two. Thus the number of lines in the truth table is four. We draw these lines beneath the proposition as follows:

$(A \lor \sim B) \supset B$

_____

_____

_____

_____

The next step is to divide the number of lines in half. The result is 2. Then we go to the first letter on the left (A) and enter T on the first two lines and F on the remaining two lines.

$(A \lor \sim B) \supset B$

T _____

T _____

F _____

F _____

In entering truth values, begin
with the columns for the
individual letters and work
outward.

Next we divide that number (two) in half and, since the result is one, write one T, one F, one F, one T, and one F beneath the next letter (B):

```
(A ∨ ~ B) ⊃ B
   T      T
   T      F
   F      T
   F      F
```

Inspection of the truth table at this stage reveals that every possible combination of truth and falsity has now been assigned to A and B. In other words, the truth table exhausts the entire range of possibilities. The next step is to duplicate the B column under the second B.

```
(A ∨ ~ B) ⊃ B
   T     T   T
   T     F   F
   F     T   T
   F     F   F
```

This much has been automatic.

Now, using the principles developed in the previous section, we compute the remaining columns. First, the column under the tilde is computed from the column under B:

```
(A ∨ ~ B) ⊃ B
   T   F T   T
   T   T F   F
   F   F T   T
   F   T F   F
```

Next, the column under the wedge is computed from the column under A and the column under the tilde:

```
(A ∨ ~ B) ⊃ B
   T T F T   T
   T T T F   F
   F F F T   T
   F T T F   F
```

Outline the column under the
main operator.

Last, the column under the horseshoe is computed from the column under the wedge and the column under B:

```
(A ∨ ~ B) ⊃ B
   T T F T  T  T
   T T T F  F  F
   F F F T  T  T
   F T T F  F  F
```

The column under the main operator is outlined to indicate that it represents the entire compound proposition. Inspecting the completed truth table, we see that the truth value of the compound proposition is true when B is true and false when B is false, regardless of the truth value of A.

Let us consider another example: $(C \cdot \sim D) \supset E$. The number of different letters is three, so the number of lines is eight. Under C we make half this number true, half false (that is, four true, four false). Then, under D we make half *this* number true, half false, and so on (two true, two false, two true, two false). Finally, under E the truth value alternates on every line. The truth table thus exhausts every possible arrangement of truth values:

(C	•	~	D)	⊃	E
T			T		T
T			T		F
T			F		T
T			F		F
F			T		T
F			T		F
F			F		T
F			F		F

Now we compute the truth values for the remaining columns—first for the tilde, then for the dot, and finally for the horseshoe:

(C	•	~	D)	⊃	E
T	F	F	T	**T**	T
T	F	F	T	**T**	F
T	T	T	F	**T**	T
T	T	T	F	**F**	F
F	F	F	T	**T**	T
F	F	F	T	**T**	F
F	F	T	F	**T**	T
F	F	T	F	**T**	F

Inspecting the completed truth table, we see that the compound proposition is false only when C is true and D and E are false.

An alternate method for constructing truth tables, which turns out to be faster for certain compound propositions, replicates the type of truth table used to define the meaning of the five logical operators in Section 5.2. Suppose, for example, that we are given this proposition: $[(A \lor B) \cdot (B \supset A)] \supset B$. We would begin by constructing columns for the simple propositions A and B, writing them to the left of the given proposition:

A	B	[(A ∨ B) • (B ⊃ A)] ⊃ B
T	T	
T	F	
F	T	
F	F	

We would then use the columns on the left to derive the truth values of the compound propositions. We would compute first the truth values of the expressions in parentheses, then the dot, and finally the right-hand horseshoe:

A	B	[(A	∨	B)	•	(B	⊃	A)]	⊃	B
T	T		T		T		T		**T**	
T	F		T		T		T		**F**	
F	T		T		F		F		**T**	
F	F		F		F		T		**T**	

Classifying Statements

Truth tables may be used to determine whether the truth value of a compound statement depends solely on its form or whether it also depends on the specific truth values of its components. A compound statement is said to be a **logically true** or tautologous statement if it is true regardless of the truth values of its components. It is said to be a **logically false** or self-contradictory statement if it is false regardless of the truth values of its components. And it is said to be a contingent statement if its truth value varies depending on the truth values of its components. By inspecting the column of truth values under the main operator, we can determine how the compound proposition should be classified:

tautologous: All true under main operator.

self-contradictory: All false under main operator.

contingent: At least one true, at least one false under main operator.

Column under main operator	Statement classification
All true	tautologous (logically true)
All false	self-contradictory (logically false)
At least one true, at least one false	contingent

As the truth table we developed earlier indicates, $(C \bullet {\sim}D) \supset E$ is a contingent proposition. The column under the main operator contains at least one T and at least one F. In other words, the truth value of the compound proposition is "contingent" on the truth values of its components. Sometimes it is true, sometimes false, depending on the truth values of the components.

On the other hand, consider the following truth tables:

```
[(G ⊃ H) • G] ⊃ H          (G ∨ H) ≡ (~ G • ~ H)
 T T T  T T  |T| T           T T T  |F|  F T F F T
 T F F  F T  |T| F           T T F  |F|  F T F T F
 F T T  F F  |T| T           F T T  |F|  T F F F T
 F T F  F F  |T| F           F F F  |F|  T F T T F
```

The proposition on the left is tautologous (logically true or a **tautology**) because the column under the main operator is all true. The one on the right is self-contradictory (logically false) because the main operator column is all false. In neither case is the truth value of the compound proposition contingent on the truth values of the components. The one on the left is true regardless of the truth values of its components—in other words, *necessarily* true. The one on the right is *necessarily* false.

If a proposition is either logically true or logically false, its truth value depends merely on its form and has nothing to do with its content. As a result, such statements do not make any genuine assertions about things in the world. For example, the tautologous statement "It is either raining or it is not raining" provides no information about the weather. Similarly, the self-contradictory statement "It is raining and it is not raining" provides no information about the weather. On the other hand, the contingent statement "It is raining in the mountains" does provide information about the weather.

Note the difference between evaluating a single statement and comparing two statements.

Comparing Statements

Truth tables may also be used to determine how two propositions are related to each other. Two propositions are said to be **logically equivalent statements** if they have the same truth value on each line under their main operators, and they are **contradictory**

statements if they have opposite truth values on each line under their main operators. If neither of these relations hold, the propositions are either consistent or inconsistent. Two (or more) propositions are **consistent statements** if there is at least one line on which both (or all) of them turn out to be true, and they are **inconsistent statements** if there is no line on which both (or all) of them turn out to be true. By comparing the main operator columns, one can determine which is the case. However, because the first two relations are stronger than (and may overlap) the second two, the first two relations should be considered first.

Columns under main operators	Relation
Same truth value on each line	logically equivalent
Opposite truth value on each line	contradictory
There is at least one line on which the truth values are both true	consistent
There is no line on which the truth values are both true	inconsistent

For example, the following two propositions are logically equivalent. The main operator columns of their respective truth tables are identical. Note that for proper comparison the columns under K must be identical and the columns under L must be identical.

```
K ⊃ L              ~ L  ⊃  ~ K
T T T              F T  T  F T         Logically equivalent
T F F              T F  F  F T
F T T              F T  T  T F
F T F              T F  T  T F
```

Logically equivalent: Same truth value on each line.

For any two propositions that are logically equivalent, the biconditional statement formed by joining them with a triple bar is tautologous. Thus $(K \supset L) \equiv (\sim L \supset \sim K)$ is tautologous. This is easy to see because the columns under the main operators of $K \supset L$ and $\sim L \supset \sim K$ are identical.

The next two propositions are contradictory:

```
K ⊃ L              K •  ~ L
T T T              T F  F T          Contradictory
T F F              T T  T F
F T T              F F  F T
F T F              F F  T F
```

Contradictory: Opposite truth value on each line.

The next two propositions are consistent. On the first line of each truth table the column under the main operator turns out true. This means that it is possible for both propositions to be true, which is the meaning of consistency:

```
K ∨ L              K • L
T T T              T T T            Consistent
T T F              T F F
F T T              F F T
F F F              F F F
```

Consistent: There is at least one line on which the truth values are both true.

Finally, the next two propositions are inconsistent. There is no line in the columns under the main operators where the truth values are both true:

```
K ≡ L            K • ~ L
T T T            T F  F T
T F F            T T  T F        Inconsistent
F F T            F F  F T
F T F            F F  T F
```

Any pair of propositions is either consistent or inconsistent. Furthermore, some consistent propositions are also logically equivalent, and some inconsistent propositions are either contradictory or logically equivalent. Because of this partial overlap, pairs of propositions are usually first classified in terms of the stronger of these relations, which are logical equivalence and contradiction. If neither of these stronger relations applies, then the pair of propositions is classified in terms of the weaker relations, consistency and inconsistency.

Unlike logical equivalence and contradiction, which usually relate exactly two propositions, consistency and inconsistency often apply to larger groups of propositions. For consistency, the only requirement is that there be at least one line in the group of truth tables where all of the propositions are true, and for inconsistency the only requirement is that there be no such line. As a result of these requirements, the statement consisting of the conjunction of a group of inconsistent propositions will always be self-contradictory, whereas the statement consisting of the conjunction of a group of consistent propositions will never be self-contradictory.

Consistency and inconsistency are important because, among other things, they can be used to evaluate the overall rationality of a person's stated position on something. If the statements expressing such a position are consistent, then there is at least a possibility that the position makes sense. This is so because there will be at least one line in the group of truth tables where all of the person's statements are true. On the other hand, if the statements are inconsistent, then there is no possibility that the position makes sense. In this case there is no line in the truth tables where all of the statements are true. The group of statements, conjoined together, amounts to a self-contradiction.

The truth tables for consistency and logical equivalence also illustrate the important difference between two propositions being factually true and their being logically equivalent. For example, the statements "Water boils at 100°C" and "The current population of the United States is over 300 million" are both true in the present actual world. This real-world situation conforms to the one truth-table line on which both statements are true. As a result of this line, the two statements are consistent. However, they are not logically equivalent, because their truth values are not *necessarily* the same. The truth value of the second proposition might change in the future, while that of the first would remain the same. An analogous distinction, incidentally, holds between two statements having actually opposite truth values and their being contradictory.

I. Use truth tables to determine whether the following symbolized statements are tautologous, self-contradictory, or contingent.

★1. $N \supset (N \supset N)$

2. $(G \supset G) \supset G$

3. $(S \supset R) \cdot (S \cdot \sim R)$

★4. $[(E \supset F) \supset F] \supset E$

5. $(\sim K \supset H) \equiv \sim(H \lor K)$

6. $(M \supset P) \lor (P \supset M)$

★7. $[(Z \supset X) \cdot (X \lor Z)] \supset X$

8. $[(C \supset D) \cdot \sim C] \supset \sim D$

9. $[X \supset (R \supset F)] \equiv [(X \supset R) \supset F]$

★10. $[G \supset (N \supset \sim G)] \cdot [(N \equiv G) \cdot (N \lor G)]$

11. $[(Q \supset P) \cdot (\sim Q \supset R)] \cdot \sim(P \lor R)$

12. $[(H \supset N) \cdot (T \supset N)] \supset [(H \lor T) \supset N]$

★13. $[U \cdot (T \lor S)] \equiv [(\sim T \lor \sim U) \cdot (\sim S \lor \sim U)]$

14. $\{[(G \cdot N) \supset H] \cdot [(G \supset H) \supset P]\} \supset (N \supset P)$

15. $[(F \lor E) \cdot (G \lor H)] \equiv [(G \cdot E) \lor (F \cdot H)]$

II. Use truth tables to determine whether the following pairs of symbolized statements are logically equivalent, contradictory, consistent, or inconsistent. First, determine whether the pairs of propositions are logically equivalent or contradictory; then, if these relations do not apply, determine if they are consistent or inconsistent.

★1. $\sim D \lor B$ $\sim(D \cdot \sim B)$

2. $F \cdot M$ $\sim(F \lor M)$

3. $\sim K \supset L$ $K \supset \sim L$

★4. $R \lor \sim S$ $S \cdot \sim R$

5. $\sim A \equiv X$ $(X \cdot \sim A) \lor (A \cdot \sim X)$

6. $H \equiv \sim G$ $(G \cdot H) \lor (\sim G \cdot \sim H)$

★7. $(E \supset C) \supset L$ $E \supset (C \supset L)$

8. $N \cdot (A \lor \sim E)$ $\sim A \cdot (E \lor \sim N)$

9. $M \supset (K \supset P)$ $(K \cdot M) \supset P$

★10. $W \equiv (B \cdot T)$ $W \cdot (T \supset \sim B)$

11. $G \cdot (E \lor P)$ $\sim(G \cdot E) \cdot \sim(G \cdot P)$

12. $R \cdot (Q \lor S)$ $(S \lor R) \cdot (Q \lor R)$

★13. $H \bullet (K \lor J)$ $(J \bullet H) \lor (H \bullet K)$

14. $Z \bullet (C \equiv P)$ $C \equiv (Z \bullet \sim P)$

15. $Q \supset \sim(K \lor F)$ $(K \bullet Q) \lor (F \bullet Q)$

III. Use truth tables to obtain the answers to the following exercises:

★1. Renowned economist Harold Carlson makes the following prediction: "The balance of payments will decrease if and only if interest rates remain steady; however, it is not the case that either interest rates will not remain steady or the balance of payments will decrease." What can we say about Carlson's prediction?

2. A high school principal made this statement to the school board: "Either music is not dropped from the curriculum or the students will become cultural philistines; furthermore, the students will not become cultural philistines if and only if music is dropped from the curriculum." Assuming the principal is correct, what has she told us about music and the students? (*Hint*: Construct a truth table for the principal's statement and examine the line on which the statement turns out true.)

3. Christina and Thomas are having a discussion about their plans for the evening. Christina: "If you don't love me, then I'm certainly not going to have sex with you." Thomas: "Well, that means that if I do love you, then you will have sex with me, right?" Is Thomas correct? (*Hint*: Construct a truth table for each statement and compare them.)

★4. Two astronomers are discussing supernovas. Dr. Frank says, "Research has established that if a supernova occurs within ten light-years of the Earth, then life on Earth will be destroyed." Dr. Harris says, "Research has also established that either a supernova will not occur within ten light-years of the Earth or life on Earth will not be destroyed." Is it possible that both astronomers are correct? If so, what can we determine about the occurrence of a supernova?

5. Antonia Martinez, who is running for the state senate, makes this statement: "Either a tax reduction is feasible only if both educational costs do not increase and the welfare program is abolished, or a tax reduction is feasible and either the welfare program will not be abolished or educational costs will increase." What has Martinez told us about taxes, educational costs, and welfare?

6. Automotive expert Frank Goodbody has this to say about Japanese imports: "If Mitsubishi is the sportiest, then both Toyota is the most trouble-free and Isuzu is not the lowest priced. If Isuzu is the lowest priced, then both Toyota is not the most trouble-free and Mitsubishi is the sportiest." Is it possible that Goodbody is correct in his assessment? If so, what may we conclude about Mitsubishi, Toyota, and Isuzu?

★7. Two stockbrokers are having a discussion. One claims that Netmark will introduce a new product if and only if both Datapro cuts its workforce and Compucel expands production. The other claims that Datapro will cut its workforce, and Compucel will expand production if and only if Netmark introduces a new product. Is it possible that both stockbrokers are right? If so, what have they told us about these companies?

8. Eric Carson sums up his beliefs about God as follows: "God exists if and only if either life is meaningful or the soul is not immortal. God exists and the soul is immortal. If God exists, then life is not meaningful." Is it possible that Eric's beliefs make sense?

9. Cindy, Jane, and Amanda witnessed a bank robbery. At trial, Cindy testified that Lefty did not enter the bank, and if Howard pulled a gun, then Conrad collected the money. Jane testified that if Howard did not pull a gun, then Lefty entered the bank. Amanda testified that if Conrad collected the money, then Howard pulled a gun. Is it possible that all three witnesses told the truth? If so, what can we conclude about Lefty, Howard, and Conrad?

★10. Nicole Evans expresses her philosophy as follows: "If the mind is identical to the brain, then personal freedom does not exist and humans are not responsible for their actions. If personal freedom does not exist, then the mind is identical to the brain. Either humans are responsible for their actions or the mind is not identical to the brain. If personal freedom exists, then humans are responsible for their actions." Is it possible that Nicole's philosophy makes sense? If so, what does it say about the mind, personal freedom, and responsibility?

Visit Aplia for section-specific problem sets.

5.4 Truth Tables for Arguments

PREVIEW

Have you ever seen a demonstration or stage show involving ultraviolet light (black light)? When the light is turned on, certain objects, including white paper, chlorophyll, tonic water, and twenty-dollar bills, fluoresce or glow. Their color pops out against the darkened background. Using truth tables to test arguments is similar, in a way, and almost as simple as turning on a light switch. To a trained eye, the line that shows an invalid argument to be invalid pops out against the other lines.

Truth tables provide the standard technique for testing the validity of arguments in propositional logic. To construct a truth table for an argument, follow these steps:

1. Symbolize the arguments using letters to represent the simple propositions.

2. Write out the symbolized argument, placing a single slash between the premises and a double slash between the last premise and the conclusion.

3. Draw a truth table for the symbolized argument as if it were a proposition broken into parts, outlining the columns representing the premises and conclusion.

4. Look for a line in which all of the premises are true and the conclusion is false. If such a line exists, the argument is invalid; if not, it is valid.

For example, let us test the following argument for validity:

If juvenile killers are as responsible for their crimes as adults are, then execution is a justifiable punishment.
Juvenile killers are not as responsible for their crimes as adults are.
Therefore, execution is not a justifiable punishment.

The first step is to symbolize the argument:

$$J \supset E$$
$$\frac{\sim J}{\sim E}$$

Now a truth table may be constructed. Since the symbolized argument contains two different letters, the truth table has four lines. Make sure that identical letters have identical columns beneath them. Here are the columns for the individual letters:

```
J ⊃ E  /  ~ J  //  ~ E
T   T        T        T
T   F        T        F
F   T        F        T
F   F        F        F
```

invalid: All the premises are true and the conclusion is false.

The truth table is now completed, and the columns representing the premises and conclusion are outlined:

```
J ⊃ E  /  ~ J  //  ~ E
T [T] T   [F] T   [F] T
T [F] F   [F] T   [T] F
F (T) T   (T) F   (F) T
F [T] F   [T] F   [T] F
```

Inspection of the third line reveals that both of the premises are true and the conclusion is false. The argument is therefore invalid.

Another example:

If insider trading occurs, then investors will not trust the securities markets. If investors do not trust the securities markets, then business in general will suffer. Therefore, if insider trading occurs, then business in general will suffer.

The completed truth table is this:

```
O ⊃ ~ T  /  ~ T ⊃ B  //  O ⊃ B
T [F] F T    F T [T] T    T [T] T
T [F] F T    F T [T] F    T [F] F
T [T] T F    T F [T] T    T [T] T
T [T] T F    T F [F] F    T [F] F
F [T] F T    F T [T] T    F [T] T
F [T] F T    F T [T] F    F [T] F
F [T] T F    T F [T] T    F [T] T
F [T] T F    T F [F] F    F [T] F
```

Inspection of the truth table reveals that there is no line on which both premises are true and the conclusion is false. The argument is therefore valid.

The logic behind the method of truth tables is easy to understand. By definition, a valid argument is one in which it is not possible for the premises to be true and the

Ada Byron, Countess of Lovelace 1815–1852

Ada Byron, born in 1815, was the only child of the English poet George Gordon (Lord Byron) and Annabella Milbanke. By the time Ada was born, Lady Byron had grown to detest her husband, and she did everything in her power to ensure that Ada would grow up to be as much unlike him as possible. Lady Byron had a talent for mathematics, which her husband did not share in the least, so she hired a series of tutors to instruct young Ada in that discipline. One of those tutors was the famous mathematician and logician Augustus De Morgan, with whom Ada became a close friend.

In 1835 Ada Byron married William King, and when King was elevated to Earl of Lovelace three years later, Ada became Countess of Lovelace. The couple had three children, but the duties of wife and mother did not interrupt Ada's study of mathematics and logic. Two years prior to her marriage Ada met Charles Babbage, an early inventor of mechanical computers, and when she was first shown Babbage's

Difference Engine, she immediately grasped all the intricacies of its operation. A few years later, when Babbage proposed a design for the Analytic Engine, Ada wrote a lengthy program for the new machine, and she envisioned how it could be used not only to solve problems in mathematics, but to produce music and graphics as well. Because of this work, Ada Byron is usually credited with being the first computer programmer.

Ada had suffered problems with her health ever since childhood, and as she grew older, these problems were aggravated by alcohol abuse. In 1852 she died from cancer at the young age of thirty-six.

---

conclusion false. A truth table presents every possible combination of truth values that the components of an argument may have. Therefore, if no line exists on which the premises are true and the conclusion false, then it is not possible for the premises to be true and the conclusion false, in which case the argument is valid. Conversely, if there *is* a line on which the premises are true and the conclusion false, then it *is* possible for the premises to be true and the conclusion false, and the argument is invalid. Accordingly, to test the validity of an argument, use this procedure:

> **Look for a line that has all true premises and a false conclusion. If you find such a line, the argument is invalid. If not, the argument is valid.**

Truth tables provide a convenient illustration of the fact that any argument having inconsistent premises is valid regardless of what its conclusion may be, and any argument having a tautologous conclusion is valid regardless of what its premises may be. Example:

The sky is blue.
The sky is not blue.
Therefore, Paris is the capital of France.

$S \ / \ \sim S \ / / \ P$

S	~	S	P
T	F	T	T
T	F	T	T
F	T	F	F
F	T	F	F

Since the premises of this argument are inconsistent, there is no line on which the premises are both true. Accordingly, there is no line on which the premises are both

> Any argument having inconsistent premises is valid.

true and the conclusion false, so the argument is valid. Of course, the argument is unsound, because it has a false premise. Another example:

Bern is the capital of Switzerland. Therefore, it is either raining or it is not raining.

$$B \, // \, R \lor \sim R$$

T	T	T	F	T
T	F	T	T	F
F	T	T	F	T
F	F	T	T	F

Any argument having a tautologous conclusion is valid.

The conclusion of this argument is a tautology. Accordingly, there is no line on which the premise is true and the conclusion false, and so the argument is valid. Incidentally, it is also sound, because the premise is true.

The conditional statement having the conjunction of an argument's premises as its antecedent and the conclusion as its consequent is called the argument's **corresponding conditional**. For example, the corresponding conditional of the second argument tested in this section is $[(O \supset \sim T) \bullet (\sim T \supset B)] \supset (O \supset B)$. For any valid argument (such as this one), the corresponding conditional is a tautology. This is easy to see. In any valid argument, there is no line on which the premises are all true and the conclusion false. Thus, in the corresponding conditional, there is no line on which the antecedent is true and the consequent false, so the corresponding conditional is true on every line.

EXERCISE 5.4

I. Translate the following arguments into symbolic form. Then determine whether each is valid or invalid by constructing a truth table for each.

★1. If national elections deteriorate into TV popularity contests, then smooth-talking morons will get elected. Therefore, if national elections do not deteriorate into TV popularity contests, then smooth-talking morons will not get elected.

2. Brazil has a huge foreign debt. Therefore, either Brazil or Argentina has a huge foreign debt.

3. If fossil fuel combustion continues at its present rate, then a greenhouse effect will occur. If a greenhouse effect occurs, then world temperatures will rise. Therefore, if fossil fuel combustion continues at its present rate, then world temperatures will rise.

★4. If there are dried-up riverbeds on Mars, then water once flowed on the Martian surface. There are dried-up riverbeds on Mars. Therefore, water once flowed on the Martian surface.

5. If high school graduates are deficient in reading, they will not be able to compete in the modern world. If high school graduates are deficient in writing, they will not be able to compete in the modern world. Therefore, if high school graduates are deficient in reading, then they are deficient in writing.

6. The disparity between rich and poor is increasing. Therefore, political control over economic equality will be achieved only if restructuring the economic system along socialist lines implies that political control over economic equality will be achieved.

★7. Einstein won the Nobel Prize either for explaining the photoelectric effect or for the special theory of relativity. But he did win the Nobel Prize for explaining the photoelectric effect. Therefore, Einstein did not win the Nobel Prize for the special theory of relativity.

8. If microchips are made from diamond wafers, then computers will generate less heat. Computers will not generate less heat and microchips will be made from diamond wafers. Therefore, synthetic diamonds will be used for jewelry.

9. Either the USS *Arizona* or the USS *Missouri* was not sunk in the attack on Pearl Harbor. Therefore, it is not the case that either the USS *Arizona* or the USS *Missouri* was sunk in the attack on Pearl Harbor.

★10. If racial quotas are adopted for promoting employees, then qualified employees will be passed over; but if racial quotas are not adopted, then prior discrimination will go unaddressed. Either racial quotas will or will not be adopted for promoting employees. Therefore, either qualified employees will be passed over or prior discrimination will go unaddressed.

II. Determine whether the following symbolized arguments are valid or invalid by constructing a truth table for each.

★1. $K \supset \sim K$
$\underline{}$
$\sim K$

2. $R \supset R$
$\underline{}$
R

3. $P \equiv \sim N$
$\underline{}$
$N \vee P$

★4. $\sim(G \bullet M)$
$\underline{M \vee \sim G}$
$\sim G$

5. $K \equiv \sim L$
$\underline{\sim(L \bullet \sim K)}$
$K \supset L$

6. Z
$\underline{}$
$E \supset (Z \supset E)$

★7. $\sim(W \bullet \sim X)$
$\underline{\sim(X \bullet \sim W)}$
$X \vee W$

8. $C \equiv D$
$\underline{E \vee \sim D}$
$E \supset C$

9. $A \equiv (B \vee C)$
$\underline{\sim C \vee B}$
$A \supset B$

★10. $J \supset (K \supset L)$
$\underline{K \supset (J \supset L)}$
$(J \vee K) \supset L$

11. $\sim(K \equiv S)$
$\underline{S \supset \sim(R \vee K)}$
$R \vee \sim S$

12. $E \supset (F \bullet G)$
$\underline{F \supset (G \supset H)}$
$E \supset H$

★13. $A \supset (N \vee Q)$
$\underline{\sim(N \vee \sim A)}$
$A \supset Q$

14. $G \supset H$
$R \equiv G$
$\underline{\sim H \vee G}$
$R \equiv H$

5

15. $L \supset M$
    $M \supset N$
    $N \supset L$
    $\underline{}$
    $L \vee N$

★16. $S \supset T$
    $S \supset \sim T$
    $\underline{\sim T \supset S}$
    $S \vee \sim T$

17. $W \supset X$
    $X \supset W$
    $X \supset Y$
    $\underline{Y \supset X}$
    $W \equiv Y$

18. $K \equiv (L \vee M)$
    $L \supset M$
    $M \supset K$
    $\underline{K \vee L}$
    $K \supset L$

★19. $A \supset B$
    $(A \cdot B) \supset C$
    $\underline{A \supset (C \supset D)}$
    $A \supset D$

20. $\sim A \vee R$
    $\sim(N \cdot \sim C)$
    $R \supset C$
    $\underline{C \supset \sim N}$
    $A \vee C$

III. The following dialogue contains eleven arguments. Translate each into symbolic form, and then use truth tables to determine whether each is valid or invalid.

Romance with an Android

"I just came from Professor Shaw's class on the philosophy of human nature," Nick says to his friend Erin, as he meets her in the hallway. "We discussed the question of whether an android could be a person and whether we would ever consider going out on a date with an android—assuming it looked just like an attractive human."

"Sounds like an interesting class," Erin replies, "but an android could never be a person."

"Why is that?" Nick asks.

"It's really quite simple," she says. "If an android is a person, then it's rational. But no android is rational, so it's not a person."

"But wait," Nick says. "Androids can solve problems, and they can also deliberate. And if they can either deliberate or solve problems, then they're rational. Right? So androids are rational, after all."

"No they're not," Erin says. "If an android is rational, then it's conscious, and if it's conscious, then it has reflective mental activity—it can reflect on its own act of thinking. But no android can do that, so it's not rational."

"How do you know that no android has reflective mental activity?" he asks.

"Because an android has reflective mental activity only if it has a soul," Erin says. "And it's ridiculous to think that an android could have a soul. Hence it has no reflective mental activity."

"But consider this," Nick says. "Either a soul is a material entity or it's a non-material entity. You would agree with that, wouldn't you?"

"Of course," Erin replies. "Your statement is a tautology."

"Okay," says Nick. "Now let me finish the argument. If a soul is a material entity, then if an android is material, it could easily have a soul. But if a soul is a nonmaterial entity, then if God could infuse a soul into it, then it could have a soul. Now an android is material and God could infuse a soul into an android—after all, God can do anything. Thus, an android could have a soul."

"Well, I know that Descartes considered humans to be machines with souls, but to me it's crazy to think that God would infuse a soul into a computer. He might as well infuse a soul into a pile of rocks. Anyway, let me try another approach," Erin says. "If an android is a person, then it has free will. But if androids are programmed, then they have no free will. Androids are just computers made to appear like humans, and every computer is programmed. Hence, once again, an android is not a person. What do you think of that?"

"By your reasoning," Nick replies, "even humans may not be free."

"How is that?" Erin asks.

"Well," he says, "whatever we do is caused by our biological makeup or by our social conditioning. If it's caused by our biological makeup, then it's determined. If it's caused by our social conditioning, then it's determined, too. And if it's determined, then it's not free. Thus, whatever we do is not free."

"Not so," Erin objects. "Our actions may be influenced by our biological makeup and our social conditioning, but they're not caused by them. Not strictly. And if they're not strictly caused by them, they're not determined by them, and if they're not determined by them, then they're free. Thus, our actions are free."

"Well, I don't know what it means for our actions to be influenced by something yet not be determined," Nick replies. "If X is influenced by Y, then X is caused by Y, and if X is caused by Y, then X is determined by Y. Thus, if X is influenced by Y, then X is determined by Y."

"I think you're equivocating on the meaning of cause," Erin replies. "But if you're unconvinced, how about this: If an android is a person, then it has feelings. And if it has feelings, then it can feel love or compassion. But no android loves anything. Just imagine two computers in love. The very thought is absurd. So is one android feeling compassion for another. Thus, an android cannot be a person."

"Well, look at it this way," Nick replies. "Feelings are either mental or they're physical. If they're mental, then they're brain states, and if they're brain states then androids could have them—because all brain states are just arrangements of atoms. If feelings are physical, then androids could have them—because, once again, all physical things are just arrangements of atoms. Thus, androids can have feelings."

Erin laughs. "That's the worst reasoning I've ever heard in my life. Sure, feelings may be accompanied by physical states, but they're not identical with them. Anyway, before I have to head off to class, tell me this: Do you really think that androids could be persons?"

"I think it's possible," Nick replies.

"So, would you go out on a date with an android?"

"That depends," he says.

"On what?" Erin asks.

"On whether I think she'd be good in bed," he replies.

"Uh-huh." She sighs. "Well, I'm off to class. Bye."

5

5.5   Indirect Truth Tables

PREVIEW

You hear a knock on the door. When you open it, nobody is there. But then you glance down and see a little blond puppy with a ribbon tied around its neck. You assume this is a gift from your friend Alex. But if that's so, then Alex's dog must have recently had puppies. But if Alex's dog had pup- *pies, then at least one must be blond. When you find that none were blond, you conclude that the gift is not from Alex. This reasoning process, which begins with an assumption and proceeds backward, is similar to what you will use for indirect truth tables.*

Indirect truth tables provide a shorter and faster method for testing the validity of arguments than do ordinary truth tables. This method is especially applicable to arguments that contain a large number of different simple propositions. For example, an argument containing five different simple propositions would require an ordinary truth table having thirty-two lines. The indirect truth table for such an argument, on the other hand, would usually require only a single line and could be constructed in a fraction of the time required for the ordinary truth table.

Indirect truth tables can also be used to test a series of statements for consistency. In Section 5.3 we showed how ordinary truth tables are used to test pairs of statements for consistency and we noted that consistency was a relation that applied to any group of propositions. In this section we use indirect truth tables to test groups of three, four, five, and six propositions for consistency. Given the abbreviated nature of indirect truth tables, this evaluation can usually be done much more quickly than it can with ordinary truth tables.

Preliminary Skills

> For indirect truth tables, you must be able to reason backward from the truth value of the main operator to the truth values of the simple statements.

Using indirect truth tables requires developing the skill to work backward from the truth value of the main operator of a compound statement to the truth values of its simple components. Suppose, for example, that you are given a conjunctive statement that is true:

$$A \bullet B$$
$$T$$

Because a conjunctive statement can be true in only one way, you know immediately that both A and B are true:

$$A \bullet B$$
$$T \ T \ T$$

Suppose, on the other hand, that you are given a conditional statement that is false:

$$A \supset B$$
$$F$$

Since a conditional statement can be false in only one way, you know that A is true and B is false:

$$A \supset B$$
$$T \ F \ F$$

But suppose you are given a conditional statement that is true:

$A \supset B$
    T

Since a conditional statement can be true in three ways, you cannot compute the truth values of A and B. It could be the case that A is true and B is true, or A is false and B is true, or A is false and B is false. But let us suppose, in relation to this example, that you have one more piece of information. Suppose you know that B is false:

$A \supset B$
  T F

Then you know immediately that A is false. If A were true, then the truth value under the horseshoe would have to be false. But since this truth value is given as true, A must be false:

$A \supset B$
 F T F

Similarly, suppose you are given a disjunctive statement with these truth values:

$A \lor B$
 F T

Then you know immediately that B is true, because if a disjunctive statement is true, at least one of the disjuncts must be true:

$A \lor B$
 F T T

Computing the truth values for the simple components of a compound proposition, as we have just done, requires a thorough knowledge of the truth-table definitions of the five operators given in Section 5.2. But after a little practice with examples such as these, this skill becomes almost automatic.

Testing Arguments for Validity

To construct an indirect truth table for an argument, we begin by assuming that the argument is invalid. That is, we assume that it is possible for the premises to be true and the conclusion false. Truth values corresponding to true premises and false conclusion are entered beneath the main operators for the premises and conclusion. Then, working backward, the truth values of the separate components are derived. If no contradiction is obtained in the process, this means that it is indeed possible for the premises to be true and the conclusion false, as originally assumed, so the argument is therefore invalid. If, however, the attempt to make the premises true and the conclusion false necessarily leads to a contradiction, it is not possible for the premises to be true and the conclusion false, in which case the argument is valid. Consider the following symbolized argument:

$\sim A \supset (B \lor C)$
$\sim B$
$\overline{C \supset A}$

We begin as before by writing the symbolized argument on a single line, placing a single slash between the premises and a double slash between the last premise and the conclusion. Then we assign T to the premises and F to the conclusion:

$\sim A \supset (B \lor C) \ / \sim B \ // \ C \supset A$

~~~
        T              T            F
~~~

We can now derive the truth values of *B*, *C*, and *A*, as follows:

$\sim A \supset (B \lor C) / \sim B \ // \ C \supset A$

~~~
        T             T F    T F F
~~~

These truth values are now transferred to the first premise:

$\sim A \ \supset (B \lor C) \ / \sim B \ // \ C \supset A$

~~~
 T F   T F T T        T F      T F F
~~~

We thus have a perfectly consistent assignment of truth values, which makes the premises true and the conclusion false. The argument is therefore invalid. If an ordinary truth table were constructed for this argument, it would be seen that the argument fails on the line on which *A* is false, *B* is false, and *C* is true. This is the exact arrangement found in the indirect truth table we just finished.

Here is another example. As always, we begin by assigning T to the premises and F to the conclusion:

$A \supset (B \lor C) / B \supset D / A \ // \sim C \supset D$

~~~
    T              T        T        F
~~~

From the conclusion we can now derive the truth values of *C* and *D*, which are then transferred to the first two premises:

$A \supset (B \lor C) / B \supset D / A \ // \sim C \supset D$

~~~
   T        F        T F   T    T F F F
~~~

The truth value of *B* is now derived from the second premise and transferred, together with the truth value of *A*, to the first premise:

$A \supset (B \lor C) / B \supset D / A \ // \sim C \supset D$

~~~
 (T T F F) F    F T F   T    T F F F
~~~

A contradiction now appears in the truth values assigned to the first premise, since T ⊃ F is F. The inconsistent truth values are circled. Because every step was strictly necessitated by some prior step, we have shown that it is impossible for the premises to be true and the conclusion false. The argument is therefore valid.

Sometimes a single row of truth values is not sufficient to prove an argument valid. Example:

$\sim A \supset B / B \supset A / A \supset \sim B \ // \ A \bullet \sim B$

~~~
        T          T           T              F
~~~

Since a conditional statement can be true in any one of three ways, and a conjunctive statement can be false in any one of three ways, merely assigning truth to the premises and falsity to the conclusion of this argument is not sufficient to obtain the truth values of any of the component statements. When faced with a situation such as this, the best way of proceeding is either to list all of the possible ways that one of the premises can be true or all of the possible ways that the conclusion can be false, and to proceed from there. For this argument, let us select the conclusion. Since the conclusion is a false conjunctive statement, the first conjunct can be true and the other false, the first can be

5

A derived contradiction means the argument is valid.

false and the other true, or they can both be false. Thus, we obtain the following:

~ A ⊃ B / B ⊃ A / A ⊃ ~ B // A • ~ B
  T   T   T   T F F T
  T   T   T   F F T F
  T   T   T   F F F T

Extending the truth values of *A* and *B* to the premises, we obtain the following result:

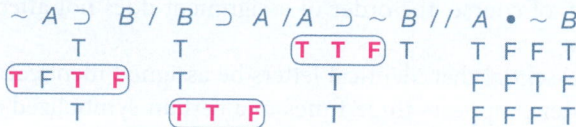

Since each line necessarily leads to a contradiction, the argument is valid. If a contradiction had been avoided on some line, the argument would, of course, be invalid, because it would be possible for the premises to be true and the conclusion false. Note that in this argument it is not necessary to fill out all the truth values on any one line to be forced into a contradiction. On each line the contradiction is necessarily derived within the context of a single premise.

If an indirect truth table requires more than one line, the method to be followed is this: Either select one of the premises and compute all of the ways it can be made true, or select the conclusion and compute all of the ways it can be made false. This selection should be dictated by the requirement of simplicity. For example, if the conclusion can be made false in only two ways, while each of the premises can be made true in three ways, then select the conclusion. On the other hand, if one of the premises can be made true in only two ways while the conclusion can be made false in three ways, then select that premise. If neither of these situations prevails, then select the conclusion.

Having made your selection, proceed to compute the truth values of each line, beginning with the first. If no contradiction is derived on this line, stop! The argument has been proved invalid. If a contradiction *is* derived on the first line, proceed to the second line. If no contradiction is derived on this line, then, again, the argument has been proved invalid. If a contradiction *is* derived, proceed to the third line, and so on. Remember, the objective is to produce a line having no contradiction. Once such a line is produced, the argument has been proved invalid, and no further work need be done. If, on the other hand, each line necessarily leads to a contradiction, the argument is valid.

Three final points need to be made about indirect truth tables for arguments. First, if a contradiction is obtained in the assignment of truth values, every step leading to it must be logically implied by some prior step. In other words, the contradiction must be unavoidable. If a contradiction is obtained after truth values are assigned haphazardly or by guessing, then nothing has been proved. The objective is not to produce a contradiction but to *avoid* one (if possible).

For example, in the following indirect truth table a contradiction is apparent in the first premise:

A ⊃ B / C ⊃ B // A ⊃ C
T T F   F T F   T F F

Yet the argument is invalid. The contradiction that appears is not *required* by the assignment of truth to the premises and falsity to the conclusion. The following indirect truth table, which is done correctly, proves the argument invalid:

$$A \supset B \, / \, C \supset B \, // \, A \supset C$$
$$\text{T T T} \quad \text{F T T} \quad \text{T F F}$$

The second point is that for valid arguments the order in which the truth values are assigned may affect where the contradiction is obtained. That is, depending on the order of assignment, the contradiction may appear in the first premise, second premise, third premise, and so on. But, of course, the order of assignment does not affect the final determination of validity.

The last point is that it is essential that identical letters be assigned identical truth values. For example, if the letter A appears three times in a certain symbolized argument and the truth value T is assigned to it in one occurrence, then the same truth value must be assigned to it in the other occurrences as well. After the truth table has been completed, each letter should be rechecked to ensure that one and the same truth value has been assigned to its various occurrences.

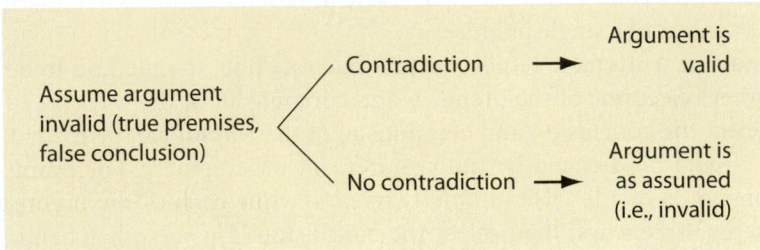

Testing Statements for Consistency

The method for testing a series of statements for consistency is similar to the method for testing arguments. We begin by writing the statements on a line, separating each with a single slash mark. (Since we have no conclusion, we use no double slash marks.) Then we assume that the statements are consistent. We assign a T to the main operator of each, and we then compute the truth values of the components. If this computation leads necessarily to a contradiction, the statements are not as we assumed them to be. That is, they are inconsistent. But if no contradiction is reached, the statements are consistent. Here is an example:

$$A \lor B$$
$$B \supset (C \lor A)$$
$$C \supset \sim B$$
$$\sim A$$

First, we write the statements on a single line separated by a single slash mark; we then assign T to each of the main operators:

$$A \lor B \, / \, B \supset (C \lor A) \, / \, C \supset \sim B \, / \, \sim A$$
$$\quad \text{T} \qquad \text{T} \qquad\qquad \text{T} \qquad\quad \text{T}$$

Next, we compute the truth values of the components. First we compute the truth value of A. Next, we enter this truth value in the first statement and compute the truth value of B. Next, we enter the truth value of B in the second statement and compute the truth value of C. Finally, the truth values of C and B are carried to the third statement:

$$A \lor B \, / \, B \supset (C \lor A) \, / \, C \supset \sim B \, / \, \sim A$$
$$\text{F T T} \quad \text{T T} \;\; \text{T T F} \quad \boxed{\text{T T F}} \;\; \text{T} \quad \text{T F}$$

Deriving a contradiction means statements are inconsistent.

5

Augustus De Morgan 1806–1871

Hulton Archive/Getty Images

The English logician and mathematician Augustus De Morgan is famous for the development of predicate quantification and the invention of relational algebra—an algebra fundamental to the work of Russell and Whitehead in their *Principia Mathematica.* He is known to all students of symbolic logic owing to his formulation of what came to be known as De Morgan's rule of inference.

De Morgan was born in Madura, India, where his father was employed by the East India Company. He became blind in one eye not long after birth, and after his family returned to England his fellow students often taunted him and played cruel tricks on him because of his disability. When he was ten, his father died coming home from another trip to India. This left the boy under the influence of his mother, a devout Anglican who wanted her son to become an Anglican priest.

De Morgan obtained a BA from Trinity College, Cambridge, and might have received a master's degree but for the fact that Cambridge then required all candidates to take a theological test. Because of his commitment to the ideal of religious neutrality, De Morgan refused to take this test. Perhaps in rebellion against his mother's influence, he developed a lifelong habit of avoiding churches, claiming that he could not bear hearing sermons. Following his refusal to take the exam, he continued his studies at University College London, a new institution founded on the principle of religious neutrality. At age twenty-two, he became the first professor of mathematics there.

Three years into his professorship, De Morgan became involved in a disagreement with the administration regarding its treatment of a colleague. De Morgan led a faculty protest, and in the end he resigned his position on the faculty. Five years later, he returned to his former position after

his replacement accidentally drowned. He remained there for thirty years, until, at age sixty, he became involved in another administrative dispute—this time over a decision that De Morgan considered to be in violation of the university's stated policy of religious neutrality. He again resigned in protest, bringing his academic career to an end. Though active in academic politics, he curiously abstained from all involvement in national politics. An acquaintance once remarked that "he never voted in an election, and never visited the House of Commons."

De Morgan was proud of his son, George, who became a distinguished mathematician in his own right, and he was disconsolate at his son's untimely death, which occurred when De Morgan was sixty-two. The death of a daughter, during that same period, compounded his grief, and De Morgan died three years later, possibly owing to grief and stress.

De Morgan was known for his sense of humor and his interest in odd facts. He produced an almanac of full moons spanning a 4,000-year period. A lunar crater is named after him. He liked to point out that he was x years old in the year x^2 (43 in 1849). He also enjoyed composing bits of verse in imitation of famous poets—for example, "Great fleas have little fleas upon their backs to bite 'em, and little fleas have lesser fleas, and so *ad infinitum*" (after Jonathan Swift).

5

Since this computation leads necessarily to a contradiction (third statement), the group of statements is inconsistent.

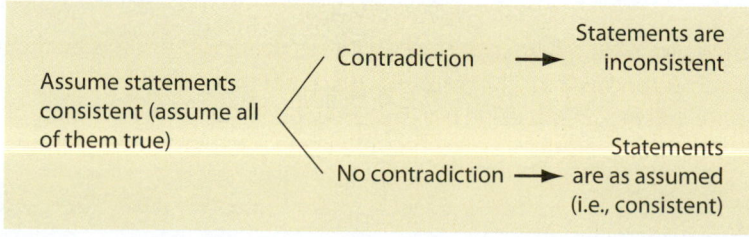

Here is another example. The statements are written on a single line, and a T is assigned to each of the main operators:

$$A \supset (B \bullet C) / C \supset \sim A / B \vee A / B \supset C$$
$$ T T T T$$

Since all of the statements can be true in three ways, we select one of them (the fourth) and figure all of the ways it can be true:

$$A \supset (B \bullet C) / C \supset \sim A / B \vee A / B \supset C$$
$$ T T T T \; T \; T$$
$$ F \; T \; T$$
$$ F \; T \; F$$

Filling out the first line leads to no contradiction, so the statements are consistent:

$$A \supset (B \bullet C) / C \supset \sim A / B \vee A / B \supset C$$
$$F \; T \; \; T \; T \; T T \; T \; T \; F T \; T \; F T \; T \; T$$
$$ F \; T \; T$$
$$ F \; T \; F$$

As with testing arguments, the objective is to *avoid* a contradiction. As soon as no contradiction is reached, we stop. The statements are consistent. Only if all three lines had led to a contradiction would these statements be inconsistent.

Rule for all multiline indirect truth tables

Contradiction is derived ⟶ Go to next line (if there is one).

No contradiction is derived ⟶ Stop. Argument is invalid/
Statements are consistent.

5

EXERCISE 5.5

I. When possible, compute the truth values of the simple components in the following compound propositions. If no truth value can be computed, write a question mark (?) under the letter or letters with unknown truth value.

★1. $K \vee D$
   F T

2. $Q \supset N$
   T

3. $B \equiv D$
   T F

★4. $N \supset G$
   T T

5. $S \supset B$
   T F

6. $K \bullet B$
   T

★7. $C \vee A$
   T F

8. $S \equiv E$
   T

9. $M \supset R$
   T T

★10. $H \lor J$
   T T

11. $E \equiv P$
   T F

12. $H \lor S$
   T

★13. $C \supset P$
   F

14. $G \cdot B$
   F

15. $S \equiv Q$
   T F

★16. $G \lor K$
   F

17. $N \supset \sim P$
   T T

18. $\sim A \equiv D$
   F T

★19. $\sim L \supset M$
   T F

20. $E \supset \sim M$
   T   F

21. $\sim N \equiv R$
   F F

★22. $\sim (H \lor B)$
   T

23. $Q \supset (R \cdot S)$
   T F

24. $K \supset \sim (S \equiv M)$
   T F   F

★25. $A \lor \sim (C \cdot \sim R)$
   F T

II. Use indirect truth tables to determine whether the following arguments are valid or invalid.

★1. $B \supset C$
   $\underline{\sim C}$
   $\sim B$

2. $\sim E \lor F$
   $\underline{\sim E}$
   $\sim F$

3. $P \supset (Q \cdot R)$
   $\underline{R \supset S}$
   $P \supset S$

★4. $\underline{\sim (I \equiv J)}$
   $\sim (I \supset J)$

5. $W \supset (X \supset Y)$
   $\underline{X \supset (Y \supset Z)}$
   $W \supset (X \supset Z)$

6. $A \supset (B \lor C)$
   $C \supset (D \cdot E)$
   $\underline{\sim B}$
   $A \supset \sim E$

★7. $G \supset H$
   $H \supset I$
   $\sim J \supset G$
   $\underline{\sim I}$
   J

8. $J \supset (\sim L \supset \sim K)$
   $K \supset (\sim L \supset M)$
   $\underline{(L \lor M) \supset N}$
   $J \supset N$

9. $P \cdot (Q \lor R)$
   $(P \cdot R) \supset \sim (S \lor T)$
   $\underline{(\sim S \lor \sim T) \supset \sim (P \cdot Q)}$
   $S \equiv T$

★10. $(M \lor N) \supset O$
   $O \supset (N \lor P)$
   $M \supset (\sim Q \supset N)$
   $\underline{(Q \supset M) \supset \sim P}$
   $N \equiv O$

5

11. $(A \lor B) \supset (C \bullet D)$
$\dfrac{(\sim A \lor \sim B) \supset E}{(\sim C \lor \sim D) \supset E}$

12. $F \supset G$
$\sim H \lor I$
$(G \lor I) \supset J$
$\dfrac{\sim J}{\sim (F \lor H)}$

★13. $(A \lor B) \supset (C \bullet D)$
$(X \lor \sim Y) \supset (\sim C \bullet \sim W)$
$\dfrac{(X \lor Z) \supset (A \bullet E)}{\sim X}$

14. $\sim G \supset (\sim H \bullet \sim I)$
$J \supset H$
$K \supset (L \bullet M)$
$\dfrac{K \lor J}{L \bullet G}$

15. $N \lor \sim O$
$P \lor O$
$P \supset Q$
$(N \lor Q) \supset (R \bullet S)$
$S \supset (R \supset T)$
$\dfrac{O \supset (T \supset U)}{U}$

III. Use indirect truth tables to determine whether the following groups of statements are consistent or inconsistent.

★1. $K \equiv (R \lor M)$
$K \bullet \sim R$
$M \supset \sim K$

2. $F \equiv (A \bullet \sim P)$
$A \supset (P \bullet S)$
$S \supset \sim F$
$A \bullet \sim F$

3. $(G \lor \sim Q) \supset (F \lor B)$
$\sim (F \lor Q)$
$B \supset N$
$(F \lor N) \supset Q$

★4. $(N \lor C) \equiv E$
$N \supset \sim (C \lor H)$
$H \supset E$
$C \supset H$

5. $P \lor \sim S$
$S \lor \sim T$
$T \lor \sim X$
$X \lor \sim J$
$J \lor \sim P$

6. $(Q \lor K) \supset C$
$(C \bullet F) \supset (N \lor L)$
$C \supset (F \bullet \sim L)$
$Q \bullet \sim N$

★7. $S \supset (R \equiv A)$
$A \supset (W \bullet \sim R)$
$R \equiv (W \lor T)$
$S \bullet U$
$U \supset T$

8. $(E \lor H) \supset (K \bullet D)$
$D \supset (M \bullet B)$
$B \supset \sim E$
$\sim (H \lor K)$
$D \supset B$

9. $G \supset P$
$P \supset (A \bullet \sim G)$
$(R \lor T) \supset G$
$Y \supset R$
$B \supset T$
$Y \lor B$

★10. $A \lor Z$
$A \supset (T \bullet F)$
$Z \supset (M \bullet Q)$
$Q \supset \sim F$
$T \supset \sim M$
$M \supset A$

5

5.6 Argument Forms and Fallacies

PREVIEW

If you have ever played a board game such as checkers or chess, you know that the motion of the pieces must conform to certain patterns. For example, in checkers a piece must always move diagonally. In chess a knight must always move in an "L" configuration.

If you violate these patterns, the opposing player will accuse you of cheating. Similarly, simple arguments must conform to certain patterns to be valid. If such an argument breaks the pattern, anyone familiar with logic will recognize the argument as a fallacy.

Many of the arguments that occur in propositional logic have forms that bear specific names and can be immediately recognized as either valid or invalid. The first part of this section presents some of the more common ones and explains how they are recognized. The second part discusses ways of refuting two of these forms, constructive and destructive dilemmas. The third part presents a word of caution relating to invalid forms. Finally, the fourth part applies to real-life arguments some of the principles developed in the first part.

Common Argument Forms

In Section 5.2 we defined a statement form as an arrangement of statement variables and operators such that the uniform substitution of statements in place of the variables results in a statement. An example of a statement form is $p \bullet q$, where p and q are statement variables. Analogously, an **argument form** is an arrangement of statement variables and operators such that the uniform substitution of statements in place of the variables results in an *argument*. The resulting argument is said to be a **substitution instance** of its related argument form. For example, the following arrangement of statement variables and an operator is an argument form:

> All substitution instances of a valid argument form are valid arguments.

$$\frac{p \bullet q}{p}$$

If the statements A and B are uniformly substituted in place of the p and q of the argument form, we obtain the following substitution instance, which is an argument:

$$\frac{A \bullet B}{A}$$

We can think of the relationship between an argument and its form as analogous to the relationship between an animal and its skeleton. Just as a skeleton can carry a lot of flesh, so can an argument form, so to speak. The following argument has the form we just considered.

$$\frac{[G \supset (J \vee K)] \bullet [(H \vee N) \supset L]}{[G \supset (J \vee K)]}$$

A *valid* argument form is an argument form that satisfies the truth-table test.

The first valid argument form we consider is **disjunctive syllogism**, which is defined as follows:

Disjunctive syllogism (DS):

$$p \lor q$$
$$\underline{\sim p}$$
$$q$$

The validity of this form can be easily checked by a truth table. Now, given that validity is purely a function of the form of an argument, any argument produced by uniformly substituting statements in place of the variables in this argument form is a valid argument. Such an argument is said to *have* the form of a disjunctive syllogism. The following argument was produced in this way and is therefore valid:

Either Harvard or Princeton is in New Jersey.	$H \lor P$
Harvard is not in New Jersey.	$\underline{\sim H}$
Therefore, Princeton is in New Jersey.	P

The validity of a disjunctive syllogism arises from the fact that one of the premises presents two alternatives and the other premise eliminates one of those alternatives, leaving the other as the conclusion. This so-called "method of elimination" is essential to the validity of a disjunctive syllogism. If one premise should present two alternatives and the other premise should *affirm* one of those alternatives, the argument is invalid (unless the conclusion is a tautology). Example:

Either Harvard or Amherst is in Massachusetts.	$H \lor A$
Harvard is in Massachusetts.	H
Therefore, Amherst is not in Massachusetts.	$\sim A$

Since both Harvard and Amherst are in Massachusetts, the premises are true and the conclusion is false. Thus, the argument is invalid. Because the wedge symbol designates inclusive disjunction, the disjunctive premise includes the possibility of both disjuncts being true. Thus, for the argument to be valid, the other premise must eliminate one of the disjuncts.

The next valid argument form we consider is **pure hypothetical syllogism**. It consists of two premises and one conclusion, all of which are hypothetical (conditional) statements, and is defined as follows:

Pure hypothetical syllogism (HS):

$$p \supset q$$
$$\underline{q \supset r}$$
$$p \supset r$$

Any argument that has the form of a pure hypothetical syllogism (that is, any argument that can be produced by uniformly substituting statements in place of the variables in the form) is a valid argument. Example:

If world population continues to grow, then cities will become hopelessly overcrowded.	$W \supset C$
If cities become hopelessly overcrowded, then pollution will become intolerable.	$C \supset P$
Therefore, if world population continues to grow, then pollution will become intolerable.	$W \supset P$

The validity of a pure hypothetical syllogism is grounded in the fact that the premises link together like a chain. In the population argument, the consequent of the first

5

premise is identical to the antecedent of the second. If the premises fail to link together in this way, the argument may be invalid. Example:

> If Kevin Bacon is a man, then Kevin Bacon is a human being. $\quad M \supset H$
> If Kevin Bacon is a woman, then Kevin Bacon is a human being. $\quad W \supset H$
> Therefore, if Kevin Bacon is a man, then Kevin Bacon is a woman. $\quad \overline{M \supset W}$

The premises of this argument are true, and the conclusion is false. Thus, the argument is invalid.

Another important valid argument form is called **modus ponens** ("asserting mode"). It consists of a conditional premise, a second premise that asserts the antecedent of the conditional premise, and a conclusion that asserts the consequent:

Modus ponens (MP):

$$p \supset q$$
$$\underline{p}$$
$$q$$

Any argument having the form of modus ponens is a valid argument. Example:

> If twelve million children die yearly from starvation, then
> something is wrong with food distribution. $\qquad T \supset S$
> Twelve million children die yearly from starvation. $\qquad \underline{T}$
> Therefore, something is wrong with food distribution. $\qquad S$

Closely associated with modus ponens is **modus tollens** ("denying mode"). Modus tollens is a valid argument form consisting of one conditional premise, a second premise that denies the consequent of the conditional premise, and a conclusion that denies the antecedent. It is defined as follows:

Modus tollens (MT):

$$p \supset q$$
$$\underline{\sim q}$$
$$\sim p$$

Although a little harder to understand than modus ponens, modus tollens can be understood by the following reasoning process: The conclusion states that we do not have p, because if we did have p, then (by the first premise) we would have q, and we do not have q (by the second premise). Any argument that has the form of modus tollens is a valid argument. Example:

> If Japan cares about endangered species, then it has
> stopped killing whales. $\qquad C \supset S$
> Japan has not stopped killing whales. $\qquad \underline{\sim S}$
> Therefore, Japan does not care about endangered species. $\qquad \sim C$

Two invalid forms are closely associated with modus ponens and modus tollens. These are **affirming the consequent** and **denying the antecedent**. Affirming the consequent consists of one conditional premise, a second premise that asserts the consequent of the conditional, and a conclusion that asserts the antecedent:

Affirming the consequent (AC):

$$p \supset q$$
$$\frac{q}{p}$$

Any argument that has the form of affirming the consequent is an invalid argument.*
The following argument has this form and is therefore invalid:

If Napoleon was killed in a plane crash, then Napoleon is dead.	$K \supset D$
Napoleon is dead.	D
Therefore, Napoleon was killed in a plane crash.	K

Given that this argument has true premises and a false conclusion, it is clearly invalid.
Denying the antecedent consists of a conditional premise, a second premise that denies the antecedent of the conditional, and a conclusion that denies the consequent:

Do not confuse MP and MT (which are valid) with AC and DA (which are invalid).

Denying the antecedent (DA):

$$p \supset q$$
$$\frac{\sim p}{\sim q}$$

Any argument that has the form of denying the antecedent is an invalid argument. Example:

If Napoleon was killed in a plane crash, then Napoleon is dead.	$K \supset D$
Napoleon was not killed in a plane crash.	$\sim K$
Therefore, Napoleon is not dead.	$\sim D$

Again, this argument has true premises and a false conclusion, so it is clearly invalid.
A **constructive dilemma** is a valid argument form that consists of a conjunctive premise made up of two conditional statements, a disjunctive premise that asserts the antecedents in the conjunctive premise (like modus ponens), and a disjunctive conclusion that asserts the consequents of the conjunctive premise. It is defined as follows:

Constructive dilemma (CD):

$$(p \supset q) \bullet (r \supset s)$$
$$\frac{p \vee r}{q \vee s}$$

Any argument that has the form of a constructive dilemma is a valid argument. Example:

If we choose nuclear power, then we increase the risk of a nuclear accident; but if we choose conventional power, then we add to the greenhouse effect.	$(N \supset I) \bullet (C \supset A)$
We must choose either nuclear power or conventional power.	$N \vee C$
Therefore, we either increase the risk of a nuclear accident or add to the greenhouse effect.	$I \vee A$

* See "Note on Invalid Forms" later in this section.

5

The **destructive dilemma** is also a valid argument form. It is similar to the constructive dilemma in that it includes a conjunctive premise made up of two conditional statements and a disjunctive premise. However, the disjunctive premise denies the consequents of the conditionals (like modus tollens), and the conclusion denies the antecedents:

Destructive dilemma (DD):

$(p \supset q) \bullet (r \supset s)$
$\dfrac{\sim q \vee \sim s}{\sim p \vee \sim r}$

Any argument that has the form of a destructive dilemma is a valid argument. Example:

If we are to reverse the greenhouse effect, then we must choose nuclear power; but if we are to lower the risk of a nuclear accident, then we must choose conventional power.	$(R \supset N) \bullet (L \supset C)$
We will either not choose nuclear power or not choose conventional power.	$\sim N \vee \sim C$
Therefore, we will either not reverse the greenhouse effect or not lower the risk of a nuclear accident.	$\sim R \vee \sim L$

Refuting Constructive and Destructive Dilemmas

Now that we are familiar with several argument forms in propositional logic, we may return for a closer look at two of them, constructive and destructive dilemmas. Arguments having these forms occur frequently in public debate, where an arguer may use them to trap an opponent. Since both forms are valid, the only direct mode of defense available to the opponent is to prove the dilemma unsound. This can be done by proving at least one of the premises false. If the conjunctive premise (otherwise called the

Grasping by the horns:
Prove the conjunctive
premise false by proving   e.g.: $(p \supset q) \bullet (r \supset s)$
either conjunct false   T F   F Ⓕ

Escaping between the horns:
Prove the disjunctive   e.g.: $p \vee r$
premise false   F Ⓕ F

"horns of the dilemma") is proven false, the opponent is said to have "grasped the dilemma by the horns." This, of course, may be done by proving either one of the conditional statements false. If, on the other hand, the disjunctive premise is proven false, the opponent is said to have "escaped between the horns of the dilemma." The latter strategy often involves finding a third alternative that excludes the two that are given in the disjunctive premise. If such a third alternative can be found, both of the given disjuncts will be proved false. Consider the following constructive dilemma:

> If taxes increase, the economy will suffer, and if taxes decrease, needed government services will be curtailed. Since taxes must either increase or decrease, it follows that the economy will suffer or that needed government services will be curtailed.

It is easy to escape between the horns of this dilemma by arguing that taxes could be kept as they are, in which case they would neither increase nor decrease.

Some dilemmas, however, do not allow for the possibility of escaping between the horns. Consider the following constructive dilemma:

> If we encourage competition, we will have no peace, and if we do not encourage competition, we will make no progress. Since we must either encourage competition or not encourage it, we will either have no peace or make no progress.

Since the disjunctive premise of this dilemma is a tautology, it cannot be proven false. This leaves the strategy of grasping the dilemma by the horns, which may be done by proving either of the conditional statements in the conjunctive premise false. One debater might want to attack the first conditional and argue that competition and peace can coexist, while another might want to attack the second and argue that progress can be achieved through some means other than encouraging competition.

The strategy to be followed in refuting a dilemma is therefore this: Examine the disjunctive premise. If this premise is a tautology, attempt to grasp the dilemma by the horns by attacking one or the other of the conditional statements in the conjunctive premise. If the disjunctive premise is not a tautology, then either escape between the horns by, perhaps, finding a third alternative, or grasp the dilemma by the horns—whichever is easier.

A third, indirect strategy for refuting a dilemma involves constructing a counterdilemma. This is typically done by changing either the antecedents or the consequents of the conjunctive premise while leaving the disjunctive premise as it is, so as to obtain a different conclusion. If the dilemma in question is a constructive dilemma, the consequents of the conjunctive premise are changed. Here are possible counterdilemmas for the two dilemmas just presented:

> If taxes increase, needed government services will be extended, and if taxes decrease, the economy will improve. Since taxes must either increase or decrease, it follows that needed government services will be extended or the economy will improve.

> If we encourage competition, we will make progress, and if we do not encourage competition, we will have peace. Since we must either encourage competition or not encourage it, we will either make progress or have peace.

Constructing a counterdilemma falls short of a refutation of a given dilemma because it merely shows that a different approach can be taken to a certain problem. It does not cast any doubt on the soundness of the original dilemma. Yet the strategy is often effective because it testifies to the cleverness of the debater who can accomplish it successfully. In the heat of debate the attending audience is often persuaded that the original argument has been thoroughly demolished.

Note on Invalid Forms

Throughout this book we have seen that any substitution instance of a valid argument form is a valid argument. For example, consider modus ponens:

$$p \supset q$$
$$\underline{p}$$
$$q$$

Literally any two statements uniformly substituted in the place of p and q will result in a valid argument. Thus, the following symbolized arguments both have the form of modus ponens, and are accordingly valid:

$$S \supset T$$
$$\underline{S}$$
$$T$$

$$(K \vee B) \supset (N \cdot R)$$
$$\underline{K \vee B}$$
$$N \cdot R$$

In the first argument S and T are uniformly substituted in the place of p and q, and in the second argument $K \vee B$ and $N \cdot R$ are uniformly substituted in the place of p and q.

However, this result does not extend to invalid argument forms. Consider, for example, affirming the consequent:

$$p \supset q$$
$$\underline{q}$$
$$p$$

Sometimes the uniform substitution of statements in the place of p and q results in an invalid argument, and sometimes it does not. Both of the following symbolized arguments are substitution instances of affirming the consequent, but the one on the left is invalid while the one on the right is valid:

> Not every substitution instance of an invalid form is invalid.

$$G \supset N$$
$$\underline{N}$$
$$G$$

$$(F \vee D) \supset (F \cdot D)$$
$$\underline{F \cdot D}$$
$$F \vee D$$

To deal with this problem we adopt a convention about when an argument will be said to *have* an invalid form. We will say that an argument has an invalid form if it is a substitution instance of that form *and* it is not a substitution instance of any valid form. According to this convention only the argument on the left has the form of affirming the consequent. The argument on the right does not have this form because it is a substitution instance of the following valid form:

$$(p \vee q) \supset (p \cdot q)$$
$$\underline{p \cdot q}$$
$$p \vee q$$

The validity of this form results from the fact that the conclusion follows from the second premise alone, without any involvement of the first premise. This fact may be easily checked with a truth table.

Here is another invalid form:

$$p \supset q$$
$$\underline{r \supset q}$$
$$p \supset r$$

Both of the following symbolized arguments are substitution instances of this form, but only the one on the left is invalid:

$$K \supset L$$
$$\underline{R \supset L}$$
$$K \supset R$$

$$\sim C \supset A$$
$$\underline{(C \supset E) \supset A}$$
$$\sim C \supset (C \supset E)$$

The argument on the right is valid because its conclusion is a tautology. Accordingly, only the argument on the left will be said to have the invalid form in question.

The point of this discussion is that when we attempt to determine the validity of arguments through mere inspection, we have to exert caution with invalid forms. The mere fact that an argument is a substitution instance of an invalid form does not guarantee that it is invalid. Before judging it invalid we must make sure that it is not valid for some other reason, such as its conclusion being a tautology. However, as concerns the exercises at the end of this section, all of the arguments that are substitution instances of invalid forms are invalid. In other words, none of them is like either of the right-hand examples considered in these paragraphs.

Summary and Application

Any argument having one of the following forms is valid:

$p \lor q$ $\underline{\sim p}$ q	disjunctive syllogism (DS)	$p \supset q$ $\underline{q \supset r}$ $p \supset r$	pure hypothetical syllogism (HS)
$p \supset q$ $\underline{p}$ q	modus ponens (MP)	$p \supset q$ $\underline{\sim q}$ $\sim p$	modus tollens (MT)
$(p \supset q) \cdot (r \supset s)$ $\underline{p \lor r}$ $q \lor s$	constructive dilemma (CD)	$(p \supset q) \cdot (r \supset s)$ $\underline{\sim q \lor \sim s}$ $\sim p \lor \sim r$	destructive dilemma (DD)

Any argument having either of the following forms is invalid:

$p \supset q$ $\underline{q}$ p	affirming the consequent (AC)	$p \supset q$ $\underline{\sim p}$ $\sim q$	denying the antecedent (DA)

In identifying arguments as having these argument forms, use the following procedure. First symbolize the argument, using uppercase letters for the simple propositions. Then see whether the symbolized argument fits the pattern of one of these forms. For example, the following symbolized argument has the form of modus ponens, and is therefore valid:

$K \supset R$
$\underline{K}$
R

The order of the premises never affects an argument's form.

If K and R are substituted respectively in place of p and q in the modus ponens form, we obtain the symbolized argument in question.

However, not every attempt at argument recognition is as simple as this. For more-complicated cases it helps to keep two points in mind:

The order of the premises never affects the argument's form.

Negated letters can be substituted in place of the p, q, r, and s of an argument form just as can non-negated letters.

In regard to the first point, consider these symbolized arguments:

N $\sim S$
$\underline{N \supset B}$ $\underline{S \lor F}$
B F

The argument on the left is modus ponens, and the one on the right is a disjunctive syllogism. To see this more clearly, simply switch the order of the premises.

In regard to the second point (involving negated letters), consider these examples:

$$\begin{array}{ll} \sim G \supset \sim H & \quad \sim K \supset \sim M \\ \underline{\sim G} & \quad \underline{\sim \sim M} \\ \sim H & \quad \sim \sim K \end{array}$$

The argument on the left is modus ponens, and the one on the right is modus tollens. To produce the argument on the left, substitute $\sim G$ in the place of p in the modus ponens form, and $\sim H$ in the place of q. For the argument on the right, substitute $\sim K$ in the place of p in the modus tollens form, and $\sim M$ in the place of q.

Another problem that complicates the task of argument recognition arises from the fact that many arguments can be translated in alternate ways. Consider, for example, this argument:

Either the witness lied or Bob is guilty.
The witness told the truth.
Therefore, Bob is guilty.

If we select L to represent "The witness lied," then the argument can be translated into symbols as follows:

$$\begin{array}{l} L \vee B \\ \underline{\sim L} \\ B \end{array}$$

This symbolized argument is clearly an instance of disjunctive syllogism.

On the other hand, if we select T to represent "The witness told the truth," then we have this translation:

$$\begin{array}{l} \sim T \vee B \\ \underline{T} \\ B \end{array}$$

Technically this is not an instance of disjunctive syllogism, because the second premise, T, is not preceded by a tilde. To avoid this kind of difficulty in connection with alternative translations, we introduce two rules. They should be obvious, but if there is any doubt about them they can be proved using truth tables. The rules are as follows:

Sometimes how an argument is translated can affect form recognition.

p is logically equivalent to $\sim\sim p$.   (double negation)
$p \vee q$ is logically equivalent to $q \vee p$.   (commutativity)

According to the first rule, double tildes may be either inserted or deleted prior to any statement, and according to the second rule the order of the components in a disjunctive statement may be reversed. Applying the double negation rule to the second premise of the symbolized argument above, we have

Double negation allows us to insert and remove double tildes.

$$\begin{array}{l} \sim T \vee B \\ \underline{\sim\sim T} \\ B \end{array}$$

After this change, the argument is now an instance of disjunctive syllogism.

For examples of how the commutativity rule is applied, consider these symbolized arguments:

$M \lor E$
$\underline{\sim E}$
M

$(R \supset L) \bullet (T \supset K)$
$\underline{T \lor R}$
$L \lor K$

Technically the argument on the left is not an instance of disjunctive syllogism because the letters in the first premise are in the wrong order, and the argument on the right is not an instance of constructive dilemma because the letters in the second premise are in the wrong order. We can reverse the order of these letters by applying the commutativity rule:

Commutativity allows us to switch the order of disjuncts.

$E \lor M$
$\underline{\sim E}$
M

$(R \supset L) \bullet (T \supset K)$
$\underline{R \lor T}$
$L \lor K$

After these changes, the argument on the left is now clearly an instance of disjunctive syllogism, and the one on the right is an instance of constructive dilemma.

Here are some additional examples. In some cases the symbolized argument must be rewritten using double negation or commutativity before it fits the pattern of the argument form indicated.

$\sim A \supset \sim B$		$A \supset \sim B$	
$\underline{\sim B \supset C}$	HS—valid	$\underline{B \supset \sim C}$	invalid
$\sim A \supset C$		$A \supset \sim C$	
$\sim A \supset \sim B$		$\sim A \supset B$	
$\underline{B}$	MT—valid	$\underline{A}$	DA—invalid
A		$\sim B$	
$\sim A \lor \sim B$		$\sim A \lor B$	
$\underline{A}$	DS—valid	$\underline{\sim A}$	invalid
$\sim B$		B	
$(A \supset \sim B) \bullet (\sim C \supset D)$		$(\sim A \supset B) \bullet (C \supset \sim D)$	
$\underline{A \lor \sim C}$	CD—valid	$\underline{B \lor \sim D}$	invalid
$\sim B \lor D$		$A \lor \sim C$	
$A \lor \sim B$		$A \supset \sim B$	
$\underline{B}$	DS—valid	$\underline{\sim B}$	AC—invalid
A		A	
A		$A \lor C$	
$\underline{A \supset B}$	MP—valid	$\underline{(A \supset B) \bullet (C \supset D)}$	CD—valid
B		$B \lor D$	

Let us now see how the argument forms presented in this section can be used to interpret the structure of some real-life arguments. Consider the following letter to the editor of a newspaper:

If U.S. servicemen are indeed being held in Southeast Asia, what is the motivation of their captors? No government there has asked for anything in return, as might be expected if they were deliberately holding Americans.

(Norm Oshrin)

This argument is enthymematic; in other words, it is missing certain parts. The author intends to prove that U.S. servicemen are not being held in Southeast Asia—because if they were, their captors would be demanding something for their return. The argument can thus be structured as a modus tollens:

> If U.S. servicemen are being held in Southeast Asia, then their captors have demanded something for their return.
>
> Their captors have not demanded something for their return.
>
> Therefore, U.S. servicemen are not being held in Southeast Asia.

Here is another example:

> In a time when an entire nation believes in Murphy's law (that if anything can go wrong, it surely will) and has witnessed serious accidents in the highly regulated, supposedly fail-safe nuclear industry, it's fascinating that people can persist in the fantasy that an error will not occur in the area of nuclear weaponry.
>
> (Burk Gossom, *Newsweek*)

Although this argument allows for more than one analysis, clearly the arguer presents two main reasons why we can expect an accident in the area of nuclear weaponry: "Murphy's law" (which everyone believes to be true) dictates it, and accidents have occurred in the area of nuclear power (which is presumed fail-safe). Thus, at the very least, we can extract two modus ponens arguments from this selection:

> If everyone believes Murphy's law, then we can expect accidents in nuclear weaponry.
>
> Everyone believes Murphy's law.
>
> Therefore, we can expect accidents in nuclear weaponry.

> If accidents have occurred in nuclear power, then we can expect accidents in nuclear weaponry.
>
> Accidents have occurred in nuclear power.
>
> Therefore, we can expect accidents in nuclear weaponry.

Many arguments that we encounter in ordinary life can be interpreted as instances of valid argument forms. After being so interpreted, however, not all will turn out sound. The invalid forms (denying the antecedent and affirming the consequent) should be reserved for the relatively few arguments that are clearly invalid as originally expressed.

5

EXERCISE 5.6

I. Interpret the following symbolized arguments in light of the eight argument forms presented in this section. In some cases a symbolized argument must be rewritten using commutativity or double negation before it becomes an instance of one of these forms. Those not having a named form are invalid.

★1. $N \supset C$
   $\sim C$
   $\overline{\sim N}$

2. $S \supset F$
   $F \supset \sim L$
   $\overline{S \supset \sim L}$

3. $A \lor \sim Z$
$\dfrac{\sim Z}{A}$

4. $(S \supset \sim P) \bullet (\sim S \supset D)$
$\dfrac{S \lor \sim S}{\sim P \lor D}$
★

5. $\sim N$
$\dfrac{\sim N \supset T}{T}$

6. $M \lor \sim B$
$\dfrac{\sim M}{\sim B}$

7. $(E \supset N) \bullet (\sim L \supset \sim K)$
$\dfrac{\sim N \lor K}{\sim E \lor L}$
★

8. $W \supset \sim M$
$\dfrac{\sim M}{W}$

9. $\sim B \supset \sim L$
$\dfrac{G \supset \sim B}{G \supset \sim L}$

10. $F \supset O$
$\dfrac{\sim F}{\sim O}$
★

11. $(K \lor B) \bullet (N \lor Q)$
$\dfrac{K \lor N}{B \lor Q}$

12. X
$\dfrac{X \supset \sim E}{\sim E}$

13. $P \lor \sim S$
$\dfrac{S}{P}$
★

14. $B \bullet T$
$\dfrac{T}{\sim B}$

15. $\sim R \lor \sim Q$
$\dfrac{(G \supset Q) \bullet (H \supset R)}{\sim G \lor \sim H}$

16. $\sim G \supset H$
$\dfrac{H}{\sim G}$
★

17. $K \supset \sim C$
$\dfrac{C}{\sim K}$

18. $(I \supset M) \bullet (\sim O \supset A)$
$\dfrac{\sim O \lor I}{M \lor A}$

19. $X \supset \sim F$
$\dfrac{W \supset \sim F}{W \supset X}$
★

20. $\sim L \supset U$
$\dfrac{L}{\sim U}$

II. Translate the following arguments into symbolic notation and then interpret them in light of the eight argument forms presented in this section. In some cases a symbolized argument must be rewritten using commutativity or double negation before it becomes an instance of one of these forms. Those not having a named form are invalid.

★1. A Boeing 757 crashed into the Pentagon on 9/11 only if two giant engines were found outside the building. It is not the case that two giant engines were found outside the building. Therefore, a Boeing 757 did not crash into the Pentagon on 9/11.

2. If Michelangelo painted the ceiling of the Sistine Chapel, then he was familiar with stories from the Old Testament. Michelangelo was familiar with stories from the Old Testament. Therefore, Michelangelo painted the ceiling of the Sistine Chapel.

3. If you enter the teaching profession, you will have no money for vacations; and if you do not enter the teaching profession, you will have no time for vacations. Since you must either enter or not enter the teaching profession, it follows that either you will have no money or no time for vacations.

★4. Either the wealthiest people are the happiest, or it is not the case that money can buy everything. The wealthiest people are not the happiest. Therefore, money cannot buy everything.

5. Either drivers are forbidden to send text messages, or the highways will not become safer. Drivers are forbidden to send text messages. Therefore, the highways will become safer.

6. If the sun is a variable star, then its energy will drop drastically at some point in the future. If the sun's energy drops drastically at some point in the future, then the Earth will become a giant ice ball. Therefore, if the sun is a variable star, then the Earth will become a giant ice ball.

★7. Nano-thermite is present in the debris from the World Trade Center. But if that is so, then the buildings were brought down by controlled demolition. Therefore, the buildings were brought down by controlled demolition.

8. If TV viewing provides genuine relaxation, then TV enhances the quality of life. But TV viewing does not provide genuine relaxation. Therefore, TV does not enhance the quality of life.

9. If high school clinics are to stem the tide of teenage pregnancy, then they must dispense birth-control devices; but if they want to discourage illicit sex, then they must not dispense these devices. Since high school clinics must either dispense or not dispense birth-control devices, either they will not stem the tide of teenage pregnancy, or they will not discourage illicit sex.

★10. If limits are imposed on medical-malpractice suits, then patients will not be adequately compensated for their injuries; but if the cost of malpractice insurance continues to rise, then physicians will be forced out of business. Limits will not be imposed, and the cost of malpractice insurance will not continue to rise. Therefore, patients will be adequately compensated and physicians will not be forced out of business.

11. If Prohibition succeeded in the 1920s, then the war on drugs will succeed today. But Prohibition did not succeed in the 1920s. Therefore, the war on drugs will not succeed today.

12. If life is always better than death, then people do not commit suicide. People do commit suicide. Therefore, life is not always better than death.

★13. If we want to arrest criminals, then police must engage in high-speed chases; but if we want to protect motorists, then police must not engage in high-speed chases. Since police must either engage or not engage in high-speed chases, either we will not arrest criminals or not protect motorists.

14. Either industrial pollutants will be more stringently controlled, or acid rain will continue to fall. Industrial pollutants will be more stringently controlled. Therefore, acid rain will not continue to fall.

15. Insurance companies contribute millions of dollars to political campaigns. But if that is so, then meaningful insurance reform is impossible. Therefore, meaningful insurance reform is impossible.

★ 16. If Mexico does not get its population growth under control, then its unemployment problem will never be solved. Mexico's unemployment problem will never be solved. Therefore, Mexico will not get its population growth under control.

17. Either the dinosaurs were not cold blooded or they were not the ancestors of modern birds. The dinosaurs were the ancestors of modern birds. Therefore, the dinosaurs were not cold blooded.

18. If coal burning continues, then heavy metals will be released into the atmosphere. If heavy metals are not released into the atmosphere, then nervous-system damage will decrease. Therefore, if coal burning does not continue, then nervous-system damage will decrease.

★ 19. If sea levels rise twenty feet worldwide, then coastal cities from New York to Sydney will be inundated. If the ice sheets on Antarctica slip into the sea, then sea levels will rise twenty feet worldwide. Therefore, if the ice sheets on Antarctica slip into the sea, then coastal cities from New York to Sydney will be inundated.

20. If tax credits are given for private education, then the government will be supporting religion; but if tax credits are not given for private education, then some parents will end up paying double tuition. Either tax credits will or will not be given for private education. Therefore, either the government will be supporting religion, or some parents will end up paying double tuition.

III. Identify the following dilemmas as either constructive or destructive. Then suggest a refutation for each by escaping between the horns, grasping by the horns, or constructing a counterdilemma.

★ 1. If Melinda spends the night studying, she will miss the party; but if she does not spend the night studying, she will fail the test tomorrow. Melinda must either spend the night studying or not studying. Therefore, she will either miss the party or fail the test.

2. If we build our home in the valley, it will be struck by floods; and if we build it on the hilltop, it will be hit by lightning. Since we must either build it in the valley or on the hilltop, our home will either be struck by floods or hit by lightning.

3. If psychotherapists respect their clients' right to confidentiality, then they will not report child abusers to the authorities; but if they have any concern for the welfare of children, then they will report them. Psychotherapists must either report or not report child abusers to the authorities. Therefore, psychotherapists either have no respect for their clients' right to confidentiality or no concern for the welfare of children.

★ 4. If corporations are to remain competitive, then they must not spend money to neutralize their toxic waste; but if the environment is to be preserved, then corporations must spend money to neutralize their toxic waste. Corporations either will or will not spend money to neutralize their toxic waste. Therefore, either they will not remain competitive, or the environment will be destroyed.

5. If physicians pull the plug on terminally ill patients, then they risk being charged with murder; but if they do not pull the plug, they prolong their patients' pain and

suffering. Since physicians with terminally ill patients must do one or the other, either they risk being charged with murder or they prolong their patients' pain and suffering.

6. If the Mitchells get a divorce, they will live separately in poverty; but if they stay married, they will live together in misery. Since they must either get a divorce or stay married, they will either live separately in poverty or together in misery.

★7. If college students want courses that are interesting and rewarding, then they must major in liberal arts; but if they want a job when they graduate, then they must major in business. College students will either not major in liberal arts, or they will not major in business. Therefore, either they will not take courses that are interesting and rewarding, or they will not have a job when they graduate.

8. If merchants arrest suspected shoplifters, then they risk false imprisonment; but if they do not arrest them, they risk loss of merchandise. Merchants must either arrest or not arrest suspected shoplifters. Therefore, they will either risk false imprisonment or loss of merchandise.

9. If women threatened with rape want to avoid being maimed or killed, then they must not resist their assaulter; but if they want to ensure successful prosecution of the assailant, they must resist him. Since women threatened with rape must do one or the other, either they will risk being maimed or killed or they will jeopardize successful prosecution of the assailant.

★10. If we prosecute suspected terrorists, then we risk retaliation by other terrorists; but if we release them, then we encourage terrorism. Since we must either prosecute or release suspected terrorists, we either risk retaliation by other terrorists or we encourage terrorism.

IV. The following dialogue contains at least fifteen arguments. Translate each into symbolic notation, and then interpret them in light of the eight argument forms presented in this section.

A Little Help from a Friend

"I can only talk for a minute," Liz says to her friend Amy. "I have this bio midterm tomorrow, and I'm afraid I'm going to fail it."

"Okay," Amy replies. "I'll cut out after a minute or two. But why are you so afraid?"

"Because I really haven't studied at all. I figure if I don't pull an all-nighter, I'll fail the test. But I can't fail the test, so I must pull the all-nighter."

"I don't envy you," says Amy, digging in her purse. "But I have this little tablet of Adderall that might get you through. As I see it, either you take the tab or you'll fall asleep by midnight. But you can't fall asleep, so you must take the tab."

Liz stares at the little orange pill. "Adderall is for attention deficit disorder. You don't have that, do you?"

"No," says Amy. "I got the tab from my boyfriend, Zach, who talked the health clinic out of a whole bottle by faking ADD."

"Wow," says Liz. "Do you think it's safe for me to take it?"

"Of course," replies Amy. "Zach takes it all the time when he needs an extra spurt of energy, and he's had no adverse reactions. I've even tried it once or twice. If it's safe for Zach, then it's safe for me, and if it's safe for me, then it's safe for you. The conclusion is obvious."

"And do you really think the Adderall will help me pass the test?" asks Liz.

"Absolutely," says Amy. "If you take it, you'll be totally focused for the test, and you must be focused. Hence, you take it, girl."

"I don't know," Liz says as she takes a closer look at the little pill. "If I take it, then I'll feel like an athlete who takes performance-enhancing drugs. I'll feel like I'm putting myself at an unfair advantage over the other students. I don't want to do that, so maybe I shouldn't take it."

She thinks for a moment and sighs. "Either I take the Adderall or I don't. If I take it, I'll feel like I cheated, but if I don't take it, I'll fail the test. Thus, I'll feel like I cheated, or I'll fail the test. Either way, I lose."

Amy smiles. "There's another way of looking at it. Either you take the Adderall or you don't. If you take it, you'll pass the test, and if you don't take it, you'll have a clear conscience. Thus, you'll either pass the test or you'll have a clear conscience. Either way, you win."

"Very clever," says Liz, "but that really doesn't solve my problem."

"Okay," says Amy. "But maybe your problem isn't as bad as you think. Consider this: Older people take drugs all the time to help their memory and their sex lives. If it's okay for them to take those drugs—and it is—then it's okay for you to take the Adderall. You shouldn't sweat it."

"That's true," says Liz, "but those older people suffer from a medical condition. If I had ADD, I'd be justified in taking the Adderall, but I don't. So I'm not justified."

"Let's look at it another way," says Amy. "You could get through the night with lots of coffee and Red Bull. If it's okay to drink coffee and Red Bull—and it is—then it's okay to take the Adderall. The conclusion is clear."

"Not quite," says Liz. "Coffee and Red Bull aren't really comparable to Adderall—at least not if it's as good as you say it is. Suppose that I'm faced with this option: Either I drink lots of coffee and Red Bull, or I take the Adderall. I would say no to the coffee and Red Bull because it's less effective, and it leaves me frazzled. Thus, I would take the Adderall. See, the two are not the same."

"Maybe not," says Amy, "but think about it this way. We take advantage of new technology every day without giving it a second thought. We use cell phones instead of landlines because they're more convenient. We use light-bulbs instead of candles because we see better with them. And we use Adderall instead of coffee because it makes us sharper. If it's ethically okay to use cell phones, then it's okay to use Adderall; and it's certainly okay to use cell phones—just as it's okay to use lightbulbs. Hence, it's okay to use Adderall."

"The problem with that line of reasoning," Liz observes, "is that using light-bulbs and cell phones doesn't put anyone at a competitive advantage. Everyone uses them, so we're all on an equal footing. But not every student uses Adderall to pass a test. If everyone used it, I would have no problem with it. But not everyone uses it, so I do have a problem."

"I can see your point," Amy says. "At fifteen or twenty bucks a pop on the underground market, not every student can afford Adderall. If it were cheap, then everyone would use it. But it's not cheap, so many students don't."

Amy smiles again at her friend. "Messy stuff," she says. "So, what do you think you'll do?"

"I don't know." Liz groans and puts her face in her hands. "But leave that tab on my desk. I'll see how it goes. . . . I'll give myself until midnight."

V. The following selections were taken from letters-to-the-editor columns of newspapers. Each contains one or more arguments, but the exact form of the argument may be hidden or ambiguous. Use the argument forms presented in this section to structure the selections as specifically named arguments.

★**1.** There is a simple way to put a big dent in the national human-organ shortage: Allocate organs first to the people who have agreed to donate their own. Giving organs first to registered donors would persuade more people to register, and that would make the allocation system fairer. People who aren't willing to share the gift of life should go to the end of the waiting list.

(David J. Undis)

2. Okay, I've tried it for a week again this year, but I still don't like daylight saving time. My grass is brown enough already—it doesn't need another hour of daylight each day. Let's turn the clocks back to the way God intended—standard time.

(Jim Orr)

3. The religious right, in its impassioned fervor to correct our alleged moral wrongs and protect the rights of our unborn "children," may one day realize its ultimate goal of a constitutional amendment banning abortion. And what will the punishment be for those caught performing or receiving an abortion? The death penalty, of course.

(David Fisher)

★**4.** Most educators believe math instructors ought to emphasize group problem solving. If *group* problem solving is so important (and I think it is), why do we place such emphasis on individual testing? The national math test is a mistake.

(Frederick C. Thayer)

5. If voluntary school prayer for our children is going to make them more moral, then just think what mandatory church attendance on Sunday could do for the rest of us.

(Roderick M. Boyes)

6. A country that replaces the diseased hearts of old white men but refuses to feed schoolchildren, pay women adequately, educate adolescents, or care for the elderly—that country is doomed. We are acting as if there is no tomorrow. Where is our shame?

(Robert Birch)

★**7.** We cannot afford to close the library at Central Juvenile Hall. These young people, in particular, need to have access to ideas, dreams, and alternative ways of living. It can make the difference for many students who might become interested in reading for the first time in their lives while in Juvenile Hall.

(Natalie S. Field)

8. If the death penalty deters one person from becoming a murderer, it is effective. There are also some other important reasons for having the death penalty. First, the families and friends of innocent victims have the right to see effective retribution. Second, terminating the life of a killer is more economical than keeping him in jail at the taxpayer's expense. Third, everyone will have greater respect for the judicial system when justice is carried out.

(Doug Kroker)

9. Regarding the bill to require parental consent for a minor's abortion, I would like to point out that the pious platitudes about parental authority quickly fall by the wayside when the minor wants to keep the baby and the parents say, "Don't be silly! You have an abortion and finish your education." If the parents can veto a minor's abortion, shouldn't they also be able to require one? Better the choice, either pro or con, be left to the girl/woman herself.

(Jane Roberts)

★10. More than a million adult videos are rented each week. Nor, as the propagandists would have you believe, does viewing such material lead to violent sex crimes. If it did, there would be over one million such crimes per week.

(Lybrand P. Smith)

aplia

Visit Aplia for section-specific problem sets.

Summary

Propositional Logic:
- The fundamental units are whole statements (propositions).
- Simple statements are represented by capital letters (A, B, C, etc.):
- These are combined via logical operators to form compound statements.

The logical operators:
  - Tilde ($\sim$) forms negations ("not," "it is not the case that").
  - Dot ($\bullet$) forms conjunctions ("and," "also," "moreover," etc.).
  - Wedge ($\vee$) forms disjunctions ("or," "unless").
  - Horseshoe ($\supset$) forms conditionals ("if . . . then," "only if," etc.).
  - Triple bar ($\equiv$) forms biconditionals ("if and only if," etc.).

Truth Table:
- An arrangement of truth values that shows in every possible case how the truth value of a compound statement is determined by the truth values of its components.
- Used to define the meaning of the five logical operators:
  - $\sim p$ is true only when p is false.
  - $p \bullet q$ is true only when both p and q are true.
  - $p \vee q$ is false only when both p and q are false.
  - $p \supset q$ is false only when p is true and q is false.
  - $p \equiv q$ is true only when p and q have the same truth value.

- Used to classify individual compound statements:
  - Tautologous: Truth values under main operator are all true.
  - Self-contradictory: Truth values under main operator are all false.
  - Contingent: Under main operator: at least one true, at least one false.

- Used to compare one compound statement with another:
  - Logically equivalent: Truth values under main operators are the same on each line.
  - Contradictory: Truth values under main operators are opposite on each line.
  - Consistent: There is at least one line under main operators where all of the truth values are true.
  - Inconsistent: There is no line under main operators where all of the truth values are true.

- Used to test arguments for validity:
  - Invalid: There is a line on which all the premises are true and the conclusion false.
  - Valid: There is no such line.

Indirect Truth Table: A usually shorter truth table constructed by first assigning truth values to the main operators and then working backward to the simple components.

- Used to test arguments for validity:
  - Begin by assuming the premises true and the conclusion false.
  - Valid: Assumption necessarily leads to a contradiction.
  - Invalid: Assumption does not necessarily lead to a contradiction.

- Used to test a series of statements for consistency:
  - Begin by assuming all of the statements true.
  - Inconsistent: Assumption necessarily leads to a contradiction.
  - Consistent: Assumption does not necessarily lead to a contradiction.

Argument Forms and Fallacies:

- Valid forms:
  - Disjunctive syllogism: $p \lor q \,/ \sim p \,// q$
  - Pure hypothetical syllogism: $p \supset q \,/ q \supset r \,// p \supset r$
  - Modus ponens: $p \supset q \,/ p \,// q$
  - Modus tollens: $p \supset q \,/ \sim q \,// \sim p$
  - Constructive dilemma: $(p \supset q) \bullet (r \supset s) \,/ p \lor r \,// q \lor s$
  - Destructive dilemma $(p \supset q) \bullet (r \supset s) \,/ \sim q \lor \sim s \,// \sim p \lor \sim r$

- Invalid forms (fallacies):
  - Affirming the consequent: $p \supset q \,/ q \,// p$
  - Denying the antecedent: $p \supset q \,/ \sim p \,// \sim q$

- Logical equivalencies:
  - p is logically equivalent to $\sim\sim p$
  - $p \lor q$ is logically equivalent to $q \lor p$

5

6

Natural Deduction in Propositional Logic

6.1 Rules of Implication I

PREVIEW

Suppose you are going on a hike. The departure point and the ending point have been predetermined, as have the supplies you will take. You have been given a trail map with several alternate routes. Such a hike is similar to solving the problems in this section of the book. The departure point and supplies are like premises, the ending point is like the conclusion, and the alternate routes are like the intermediate steps linking the premises to the conclusion. In most cases the choice of routes allows for creativity.

 MindTap™ Your personal learning experience—learn anywhere, anytime.

Natural deduction is a method for deriving the conclusion of valid arguments expressed in the symbolism of propositional logic. The method consists in using **rules of inference** (valid argument forms) to derive either a conclusion directly, or a series of intermediate conclusions that links the premises of an argument with the stated conclusion. Natural deduction gets its name from the fact that it resembles the ordinary step-by-step reasoning process people use in daily life. It also resembles the method used in geometry to derive theorems relating to lines and figures; but whereas each step in a geometrical proof depends on some mathematical principle, each step in a logical proof depends on a rule of inference.

Natural deduction is similar in some respects to the truth table method for testing arguments. Both methods can be used to prove a valid argument valid; but natural deduction is largely useless for invalid arguments, so we still need truth tables. However, the method of natural deduction is more illuminating than truth tables are. Natural deduction shows how a conclusion "comes out" of the premises, whereas truth tables show nothing of the sort. Also, while truth tables are relatively automatic and mechanical, natural deduction requires insight and creativity. As a result, most students find that natural deduction is challenging and fun, while truth tables can be tedious, especially for long arguments.

The first eight rules of inference are called **rules of implication** because they consist of simple, valid argument forms whose premises *imply* their conclusions. The first four rules of implication should be familiar from Section 5.6. They are listed together with an illustration of their use as follows.

> **natural deduction**: A method for deriving the conclusion of a valid argument in which each step is justified by a rule of inference.

> **rule of inference**: A valid argument form used to justify steps in a proof.

> **rule of implication**: A kind of rule of inference in which the first line (or lines) implies the last line.

1. Modus ponens (MP)

$$p \supset q$$
$$\underline{p \qquad}$$
$$q$$

If Su Lin is a panda, then Su Lin is cute.
Su Lin is a panda.
Su Lin is cute.

2. Modus tollens (MT)

$$p \supset q$$
$$\underline{\sim q}$$
$$\sim p$$

If Koko is a koala, then Koko is cuddly.
Koko is not cuddly.
Koko is not a koala.

3. Pure hypothetical syllogism (HS)

$$p \supset q$$
$$\underline{q \supset r}$$
$$p \supset r$$

If Leo is a lion, then Leo roars.
If Leo roars, then Leo is fierce.
If Leo is a lion, then Leo is fierce.

4. Disjunctive syllogism (DS)

$$p \lor q$$
$$\underline{\sim p}$$
$$q$$

Scooter is either a mouse or a rat.
Scooter is not a mouse.
Scooter is a rat.

Modus ponens says that given a conditional statement and its antecedent on lines by themselves, we can assert its consequent on a line by itself. **Modus tollens** says that given a conditional statement and the negation of its consequent on lines by themselves, we can assert the negation of its antecedent on a line by itself. **Pure hypothetical syllogism** ("hypothetical syllogism" for short) says that given two conditional statements on lines by themselves such that the consequent of one is identical with the antecedent of the other, we can assert on a line by itself a conditional statement whose antecedent is the antecedent of the first conditional and whose consequent is the consequent of the second conditional. Note in the rule that the two premises hook together like links of a chain.

Disjunctive syllogism says that given a disjunctive statement and the negation of the left-hand disjunct on lines by themselves, we can assert the right-hand disjunct on a line by itself. Because of the way this rule is written, only the right-hand disjunct can be asserted as the conclusion. However, once we are supplied with the commutativity rule (see Section 6.3), we will be able to switch the order of the disjuncts in the first line, and this will allow us to assert what was originally the left-hand disjunct as the conclusion. Disjunctive syllogism is otherwise called the method of elimination. The short premise eliminates one of the alternatives in the disjunctive premise, leaving the other as the conclusion.

These four rules will be sufficient to derive the conclusion of many simple arguments in propositional logic. Further, once we are supplied with all eighteen rules together with conditional proof, the resulting system will be sufficient to derive the conclusion of any valid argument in propositional logic. Conversely, since each rule is a valid argument form unto itself, any conclusion derived from their correct use results in a valid argument.

Applying the rules of inference rests on the ability to visualize more- or less-complex arrangements of simple propositions as substitution instances of the rules. For a fairly simple substitution instance of modus ponens, consider the following:

Strategy: Try to visualize the lines in a proof as substitution instances of the rules.

1. $\sim A \supset B$	$p \supset q$
2. $\sim A$	p
3. B	q

When $\sim A$ and B are mentally substituted, respectively, in place of the p and q of the modus ponens rule, then you should be able to see that the argument on the left is an instance of the rule. The fact that A is preceded by a tilde is irrelevant.

Here is a more complex example:

1. $(A \bullet B) \supset (C \vee D)$	$p \supset q$
2. $A \bullet B$	p
3. $C \vee D$	q

In this case, if you mentally substitute $A \bullet B$ and $C \vee D$, respectively, in place of p and q in the rule, you can see that the argument on the left is an instance of modus ponens. This example illustrates the fact that any pair of compound statements can be uniformly substituted in place of p and q to produce a substitution instance of the rule.

Finally, the order of the premises never makes a difference:

1. A	p
2. $A \supset (B \supset C)$	$p \supset q$
3. $B \supset C$	q

In this case, if you mentally substitute A and $B \supset C$ in place of p and q, you can see, once again, that the argument on the left is an instance of modus ponens. The fact that the order of the premises is reversed makes no difference.

These arguments are all instances of **modus ponens** (MP):

$\sim F \supset (G \equiv H)$	$(A \vee B) \supset \sim(C \bullet D)$	$K \bullet L$
$\sim F$	$A \vee B$	$(K \bullet L) \supset [(R \supset S) \bullet (T \supset U)]$
$G \equiv H$	$\sim(C \bullet D)$	$(R \supset S) \bullet (T \supset U)$

Now let us use the rules of inference to construct a proof. Such a proof consists of a sequence of propositions, each of which is either a premise or is derived from preceding propositions by application of a rule of inference and the last of which is the conclusion of the original argument. Let us begin with the following example:

> If the Astros switch leagues, then the Braves will not win the pennant.
> If the Cubs retain their manager, then the Braves will win the pennant.
> The Astros will switch leagues. Therefore, the Cubs will not retain their manager.

The first step is to symbolize the argument, numbering the premises and writing the intended conclusion to the right of the last premise, separated by a slash mark:

1. $A \supset \sim B$
2. $C \supset B$
3. A / $\sim C$

The next step is to derive the conclusion through a series of inferences. For this step, always begin by trying to "find" the conclusion in the premises. The conclusion to be derived is $\sim C$, and we see that C appears in the antecedent of line 2. We could derive $\sim C$ from line 2 by modus tollens if we had $\sim B$, so now we look for $\sim B$. Turning our attention to line 1, we see that we could derive $\sim B$ by modus ponens if we had A, and we do have A on line 3. Thus, we have now thought through the entire proof, and we can begin to write it out. First, we derive $\sim B$ by modus ponens from lines 1 and 3:

Begin by "finding" the conclusion in the premises.

1. $A \supset \sim B$
2. $C \supset B$
3. A / $\sim C$
4. $\sim B$ 1, 3, MP

The justification for line 4 is written to the right, directly beneath the slash mark. If you have trouble understanding how line 4 was derived, imagine substituting A and $\sim B$ in place of p and q in the modus ponens rule. Then you can see that lines 1, 3, and 4 constitute a substitution instance of that rule.

The final step is to derive $\sim C$ from lines 2 and 4 by modus tollens:

1. $A \supset \sim B$
2. $C \supset B$
3. A / $\sim C$
4. $\sim B$ 1, 3, MP
5. $\sim C$ 2, 4, MT

The proof is now complete. The justification for line 5 is written directly beneath the justification for line 4.

These arguments are all instances of **modus tollens** (MT):

$$\frac{\begin{array}{l}(D \lor F) \supset K \\ \sim K\end{array}}{\sim(D \lor F)} \qquad \frac{\begin{array}{l}\sim G \supset \sim(M \lor N) \\ \sim\sim(M \lor N)\end{array}}{\sim\sim G} \qquad \frac{\begin{array}{l}\sim T \\ [(H \lor K) \bullet (L \lor N)] \supset T\end{array}}{\sim[(H \lor K) \bullet (L \lor N)]}$$

The next example is already translated into symbols:

1. $A \supset B$
2. $\sim A \supset (C \lor D)$
3. $\sim B$
4. $\sim C$ / D

Once again, to derive the conclusion, always begin by trying to "find" it in the premises. The intended conclusion is D, and after inspecting the premises we find D in line 2. If we had the consequent of that line, $C \lor D$, on a line by itself, we could derive D by disjunctive syllogism if we had $\sim C$. And we do have $\sim C$ on line 4. Also, we could derive $C \lor D$ by modus ponens if we had $\sim A$, so now we look for $\sim A$. Turning our attention to line 1, we see that we could derive $\sim A$ by modus tollens if we had $\sim B$, and we do have $\sim B$ on line 3. Thus, we have now thought through the entire proof, and we can write it out:

1. $A \supset B$
2. $\sim A \supset (C \lor D)$
3. $\sim B$
4. $\sim C$ / D
5. $\sim A$ 1, 3, MT
6. $C \lor D$ 2, 5, MP
7. D 4, 6, DS

As usual, the justification for each line is written directly beneath the slash mark preceding the intended conclusion. If you have trouble understanding line 6, imagine substituting $\sim A$ and $C \lor D$ in place of p and q in the modus ponens rule. Then you can see that lines 2, 5, and 6 constitute a substitution instance of that rule.

These arguments are all instances of **pure hypothetical syllogism** (HS):

$A \supset (D \bullet F)$	$\sim M \supset (R \supset S)$	$(L \supset N) \supset [(S \lor T) \bullet K]$
$(D \bullet F) \supset \sim H$	$(C \lor K) \supset \sim M$	$(C \equiv F) \supset (L \supset N)$
$A \supset \sim H$	$(C \lor K) \supset (R \supset S)$	$(C \equiv F) \supset [(S \lor T) \bullet K]$

Here is another example.

1. $F \supset G$
2. $F \lor H$
3. $\sim G$
4. $H \supset (G \supset I)$ / $F \supset I$

The intended conclusion is $F \supset I$. When we attempt to find it in the premises, we see no such statement. This tells us that we should adopt "plan B" and look at the main operator of the conclusion, a strategy that often gives us a clue as to how the conclusion can be built up. In this case the main operator is a horseshoe, so we ask: What rule gives us a horseshoe—that is, a conditional statement? The answer is: pure hypothetical syllogism.

Having tentatively settled on pure hypothetical syllogism for deriving the conclusion, we now look for two conditional statements, which, when combined, will yield $F \supset I$. In line 1 we find $F \supset G$ and in line 4 we find $G \supset I$, but before we can apply pure hypothetical syllogism, we must obtain $G \supset I$ on a line by itself. Examining line 4, we see that $G \supset I$ could be derived by modus ponens, if we had H on a line by itself,

Alternately, begin by looking at the main operator of the conclusion for a clue.

6

and examining line 2, we see that *H* could be derived by disjunctive syllogism if we had ~*F* on a line by itself. Turning to line 1, we see that ~*F* could be derived by modus tollens if we had ~*G* on a line by itself, and we do have ~*G* on line 3. Thus, we have now thought through the entire proof, and we can write it out:

1. *F* ⊃ *G*
2. *F* ∨ *H*
3. ~*G*
4. *H* ⊃ (*G* ⊃ *I*)   / *F* ⊃ *I*
5. ~*F*   1, 3, MT
6. *H*   2, 5, DS
7. *G* ⊃ *I*   4, 6, MP
8. *F* ⊃ *I*   1, 7, HS

In addition to adopting plan B, which involves looking at the conclusion's main operator for a clue about deriving the conclusion, this proof teaches another important lesson about every proof. Every line in a proof can be used multiple times. In line 5, we used line 1 in conjunction with the modus tollens rule, and in line 8 we used that same line again in conjunction with pure hypothetical syllogism. Any line can be used as many times as we need it.

These arguments are all instances of **disjunctive syllogism** (DS):

U ∨ ~(*W* • *X*)	~(*E* ∨ *F*)	~*B* ∨ [(*H* ⊃ *M*) • (*S* ⊃ *T*)]
~*U*	(*E* ∨ *F*) ∨ (*N* ⊃ *K*)	~~*B*
~(*W* • *X*)	*N* ⊃ *K*	(*H* ⊃ *M*) • (*S* ⊃ *T*)

The next example is more complex:

1. ~(*A* • *B*) ∨ [~(*E* • *F*) ⊃ (*C* ⊃ *D*)]
2. ~~(*A* • *B*)
3. ~(*E* • *F*)
4. *D* ⊃ *G*   / *C* ⊃ *G*

Again, when we attempt to find the intended conclusion in the premises, we see no such statement. But then we notice that the main operator of the conclusion is a horseshoe, and we find *C* ⊃ *D* on line 1 and *D* ⊃ *G* on line 4. We could derive the conclusion by pure hypothetical syllogism if we could obtain *C* ⊃ *D* on a line by itself. Examining line 1, we see that we could derive *C* ⊃ *D* by modus ponens if we could obtain both ~(*E* • *F*) ⊃ (*C* ⊃ *D*) and ~(*E* • *F*) on lines by themselves, and we see that ~(*E* • *F*) appears on line 3. Also, examining line 1, we see that we could derive ~(*E* • *F*) ⊃ (*C* ⊃ *D*) by disjunctive syllogism if we had ~~(*A* • *B*) on a line by itself, and we do have it on line 2. Thus, we can now write out the proof:

1. ~(*A* • *B*) ∨ [~(*E* • *F*) ⊃ (*C* ⊃ *D*)]
2. ~~(*A* • *B*)
3. ~(*E* • *F*)
4. *D* ⊃ *G*   / *C* ⊃ *G*
5. ~(*E* • *F*) ⊃ (*C* ⊃ *D*)   1, 2, DS
6. *C* ⊃ *D*   3, 5, MP
7. *C* ⊃ *G*   4, 6, HS

6

If you have trouble seeing how lines 5 and 6 are derived, for line 5 imagine substituting $\sim(A \bullet B)$ and $\sim(E \bullet F) \supset (C \supset D)$, in place of the p and q of the disjunctive syllogism rule. Then you can see that lines 1, 2, and 5 constitute a substitution instance of that rule. For line 6, imagine substituting $\sim(E \bullet F)$ and $(C \supset D)$ in place of p and q in the modus ponens rule. Then you can see that lines 5, 3, and 6 constitute a substitution instance of that rule.

In applying the four rules of inference introduced in this section, we have noted that various expressions first had to be obtained on lines by themselves. If this procedure is not followed, the resulting proof will likely be invalid. For an example of an invalid application of modus ponens, consider the following:

1. $A \supset (B \supset C)$
2. B
3. C 1, 2, MP (invalid)

This inference is invalid because $B \supset C$ must first be obtained on a line by itself. In deriving the conclusion of an argument we always assume the premises are true. But if we assume line 1 of this proof is true, this does not entail that $B \supset C$ is true. What line 1 says is that *if* A is true, then $B \supset C$ is true. Thus, $B \supset C$ cannot be treated as a premise. We do not know if it is true or false.

Here are some additional examples of invalid inferences:

1. $A \lor B$
2. A
3. $\sim B$ 1, 2, HS (invalid—line 2 must negate A in line 1, not assert it)

1. $A \supset B$
2. B
3. A 1, 2, MP (invalid—line 2 must assert the antecedent of line 1, not the consequent)

1. $A \supset B$
2. $A \supset C$
3. $B \supset C$ 1, 2, HS (invalid—the consequent of one conditional must be identical with the antecedent of the other)

1. $A \supset B$
2. $\sim A$
3. $\sim B$ 1, 2, MT (invalid—line 2 must negate the consequent of line 1, not the antecedent)

1. $(A \supset B) \supset C$
2. $\sim B$
3. $\sim A$ 1, 2, MT (invalid—$A \supset B$ must first be obtained on a line by itself)

1. $A \supset (B \supset C)$
2. $C \supset D$
3. $B \supset D$ 1, 2, HS (invalid—$B \supset C$ must first be obtained on a line by itself)

1. $(A \lor B) \supset C$
2. $\sim A$
3. B 1, 2, DS (invalid—$A \lor B$ must first be obtained on a line by itself)

We conclude this section with some strategies for applying the first four rules of inference.

Strategy 1: Always begin by attempting to "find" the conclusion in the premises. If the conclusion is not present in its entirety in the premises, look at the main operator of the conclusion. This will provide a clue as to how the conclusion should be derived.

Strategy 2: If the conclusion contains a letter that appears in the consequent of a conditional statement in the premises, consider obtaining that letter via modus ponens:

1. $A \supset B$
2. $C \vee A$
3. A / B
4. B 1, 3, MP

Strategy 3: If the conclusion contains a negated letter and that letter appears in the antecedent of a conditional statement in the premises, consider obtaining the negated letter via modus tollens:

1. $C \supset B$
2. $A \supset B$
3. $\sim B$ / $\sim A$
4. $\sim A$ 2, 3, MT

Strategy 4: If the conclusion is a conditional statement, consider obtaining it via pure hypothetical syllogism:

1. $B \supset C$
2. $C \supset A$
3. $A \supset B$ / $A \supset C$
4. $A \supset C$ 1, 3, HS

Strategy 5: If the conclusion contains a letter that appears in a disjunctive statement in the premises, consider obtaining that letter via disjunctive syllogism:

1. $A \supset B$
2. $A \vee C$
3. $\sim A$ / C
4. C 2, 3, DS

Of course, these strategies apply to deriving any line prior to the conclusion, just as they apply to deriving the conclusion.

EXERCISE 6.1

I. For each of the following lists of premises, derive the conclusion and supply the justification for it. There is only one possible answer for each problem.

★(1) 1. $G \supset F$
     2. $\sim F$
     3. _____ ____

(2) 1. S
     2. $S \supset M$
     3. _____ ____

(3) 1. $R \supset D$
     2. $E \supset R$
     3. _____ ____

★(4) 1. $B \vee C$
     2. $\sim B$
     3. _____ ____

(5) 1. N
2. $N \lor F$
3. $N \supset K$
4. _____ ____

(6) 1. $\sim J \lor P$
2. $\sim J$
3. $S \supset J$
4. _____ ____

★(7) 1. $H \supset D$
2. $F \supset T$
3. $F \supset H$
4. _____ ____

(8) 1. $S \supset W$
2. $\sim S$
3. $S \lor N$
4. _____ ____

(9) 1. $F \supset \sim A$
2. $N \supset A$
3. $\sim F$
4. $\sim A$
5. _____ ____

★(10) 1. $H \supset A$
2. A
3. $A \lor M$
4. $G \supset H$
5. _____ ____

(11) 1. $W \lor B$
2. W
3. $B \supset T$
4. $W \supset A$
5. _____ ____

(12) 1. $K \supset \sim R$
2. $\sim R$
3. $R \lor S$
4. $R \supset T$
5. _____ ____

★(13) 1. $\sim C \supset \sim F$
2. $L \supset F$
3. $\sim \sim F$
4. $F \lor \sim L$
5. _____ ____

(14) 1. $N \supset \sim E$
2. $\sim \sim S$
3. $\sim E \lor \sim S$
4. $\sim S \lor N$
5. _____ ____

(15) 1. $\sim R \supset \sim T$
2. $\sim T \lor B$
3. $C \supset \sim R$
4. $\sim C$
5. _____ ____

★(16) 1. $\sim K$
2. $\sim K \supset \sim P$
3. $\sim K \lor G$
4. $G \supset Q$
5. _____ ____

(17) 1. $F \lor (A \supset C)$
2. $A \lor (C \supset F)$
3. A
4. $\sim F$
5. _____ ____

(18) 1. $(R \supset M) \supset D$
2. $M \supset C$
3. $D \supset (M \lor E)$
4. $\sim M$
5. _____ ____

★(19) 1. $(S \lor C) \supset L$
2. $\sim S$
3. $\sim L$
4. $S \supset (K \supset L)$
5. _____ ____

(20) 1. $(A \lor W) \supset (N \supset Q)$
2. $Q \supset G$
3. $\sim A$
4. $(Q \supset G) \supset (A \lor N)$
5. _____ ____

II. The following symbolized arguments are missing a premise. Write the premise needed to derive the conclusion (last line), and supply the justification for the conclusion. Try to construct the simplest premise needed to derive the conclusion.

★(1) 1. $B \lor K$
2. _____
3. K _____

(2) 1. $N \supset S$
2. _____
3. S _____

(3) 1. $K \supset T$
2. _____
3. $\sim K$ _____

★(4) 1. $C \supset H$
2. _____
3. $R \supset H$ _____

(5) 1. $F \supset N$
2. $N \supset T$
3. _____
4. $\sim F$ _____

(6) 1. $W \lor T$
2. $A \supset W$
3. _____
4. $A \supset T$ _____

★(7) 1. $M \supset B$
2. $Q \supset M$
3. _____
4. M _____

(8) 1. $C \lor L$
2. $L \supset T$
3. _____
4. L _____

(9) 1. $E \supset N$
2. $T \lor \sim E$
3. $S \supset E$
4. _____
5. E _____

★(10) 1. $H \supset A$
2. $S \supset H$
3. $\sim M \lor H$
4. _____
5. $\sim H$ _____

(11) 1. $T \supset N$
2. $G \supset T$
3. $H \lor T$
4. _____
5. $F \supset T$ _____

(12) 1. $G \supset C$
2. $M \lor G$
3. $T \lor \sim G$
4. _____
5. G _____

★(13) 1. $\sim S \supset \sim B$
2. $R \lor \sim B$
3. $\sim B \supset \sim S$
4. _____
5. $\sim \sim B$ _____

(14) 1. $\sim R \supset D$
2. $\sim J \supset \sim R$
3. $N \lor \sim R$
4. _____
5. $\sim F \supset \sim R$ _____

(15) 1. $\sim S \lor \sim P$
2. $\sim K \supset P$
3. $\sim P \supset F$
4. _____
5. $\sim P$ _____

★(16) 1. $J \supset E$
2. $B \lor \sim J$
3. $\sim Z \supset J$
4. _____
5. J _____

(17) 1. $(H \supset C) \supset A$
2. $N \supset (F \supset K)$
3. $(E \cdot R) \supset K$
4. _____
5. $H \supset K$ _____

(18) 1. $(S \supset M) \supset G$
2. $S \supset (M \cdot G)$
3. $G \supset (R \supset \sim S)$
4. _____
5. $\sim S$ _____

★(19) 1. $(W \lor \sim F) \supset H$
2. $(H \lor G) \supset \sim F$
3. $T \supset (F \supset G)$
4. _____
5. $\sim F$ _____

(20) 1. $(H \cdot A) \lor T$
2. $\sim S \supset (P \supset T)$
3. $(N \lor T) \supset P$
4. _____
5. T _____

III. Use the first four rules of inference to derive the conclusions of the following symbolized arguments.

★(1) 1. ~C ⊃ (A ⊃ C)
  2. ~C / ~A

(2) 1. F ∨ (D ⊃ T)
  2. ~F
  3. D / T

(3) 1. (K • B) ∨ (L ⊃ E)
  2. ~(K • B)
  3. ~E / ~L

★(4) 1. P ⊃ (G ⊃ T)
  2. Q ⊃ (T ⊃ E)
  3. P
  4. Q / G ⊃ E

(5) 1. ~W ⊃ [~W ⊃ (X ⊃ W)]
  2. ~W / ~X

(6) 1. J ⊃ (K ⊃ L)
  2. L ∨ J
  3. ~L / ~K

★(7) 1. ~S ⊃ D
  2. ~S ∨ (~D ⊃ K)
  3. ~D / K

(8) 1. A ⊃ (E ⊃ ~F)
  2. H ∨ (~F ⊃ M)
  3. A
  4. ~H / E ⊃ M

(9) 1. ~G ⊃ (G ∨ ~A)
  2. ~A ⊃ (C ⊃ A)
  3. ~G / ~C

★(10) 1. N ⊃ (J ⊃ P)
   2. (J ⊃ P) ⊃ (N ⊃ J)
   3. N / P

(11) 1. G ⊃ [~O ⊃ (G ⊃ D)]
   2. O ∨ G
   3. ~O / D

(12) 1. ~M ∨ (B ∨ ~T)
   2. B ⊃ W
   3. ~ ~M
   4. ~W / ~T

★(13) 1. R ⊃ (G ∨ ~A)
   2. (G ∨ ~A) ⊃ ~S
   3. G ⊃ S
   4. R / ~A

(14) 1. (L ≡ N) ⊃ C
   2. (L ≡ N) ∨ (P ⊃ ~E)
   3. ~E ⊃ C
   4. ~C / ~P

(15) 1. ~J ⊃ [~A ⊃ (D ⊃ A)]
   2. J ∨ ~A
   3. ~J / ~D

★(16) 1. (B ⊃ ~M) ⊃ (T ⊃ ~S)
   2. B ⊃ K
   3. K ⊃ ~M
   4. ~S ⊃ N / T ⊃ N

(17) 1. H ∨ (Q ∨ F)
   2. R ∨ (Q ⊃ R)
   3. R ∨ ~H
   4. ~R / F

(18) 1. ~A ⊃ (B ⊃ ~C)
   2. ~D ⊃ (~C ⊃ A)
   3. D ∨ ~A
   4. ~D / ~B

★(19) 1. ~G ⊃ [G ∨ (S ⊃ G)]
   2. (S ∨ L) ⊃ ~G
   3. S ∨ L / L

(20) 1. H ⊃ [~E ⊃ (C ⊃ ~D)]
   2. ~D ⊃ E
   3. E ∨ H
   4. ~E / ~C

(21) 1. ~B ⊃ [(A ⊃ K) ⊃ (B ∨ ~K)]
   2. ~J ⊃ K
   3. A ⊃ ~J
   4. ~B / ~A

★(22) 1. (C ⊃ M) ⊃ (N ⊃ P)
   2. (C ⊃ N) ⊃ (N ⊃ M)
   3. (C ⊃ P) ⊃ ~M
   4. C ⊃ N / ~C

(23) 1. (R ⊃ F) ⊃ [(R ⊃ ~G) ⊃ (S ⊃ Q)]
   2. (Q ⊃ F) ⊃ (R ⊃ Q)
   3. ~G ⊃ F
   4. Q ⊃ ~G / S ⊃ F

(24) 1. ~A ⊃ [A ∨ (T ⊃ R)]
   2. ~R ⊃ [R ∨ (A ⊃ R)]
   3. (T ∨ D) ⊃ ~R
   4. T ∨ D / D

★ (25) 1. $\sim N \supset [(B \supset D) \supset (N \vee \sim E)]$
　　　 2. $(B \supset E) \supset \sim N$
　　　 3. $B \supset D$
　　　 4. $D \supset E \qquad / \sim D$

IV. Translate the following arguments into symbolic form and use the first four rules of inference to derive the conclusion of each. The letters to be used for the simple statements are given in parentheses after each exercise. Use these letters in the order in which they are listed.

★ 1. If the average child watches more than five hours of television per day, then either his power of imagination is improved or he becomes conditioned to expect constant excitement. The average child's power of imagination is not improved by watching television. Also, the average child does watch more than five hours of television per day. Therefore, the average child is conditioned to expect constant excitement. (W, P, C)

2. If a ninth planet exists, then its orbit is perpendicular to that of the other planets. Either a ninth planet is responsible for the death of the dinosaurs, or its orbit is not perpendicular to that of the other planets. A ninth planet is not responsible for the death of the dinosaurs. Therefore, a ninth planet does not exist. (E, O, R)

3. If quotas are imposed on textile imports only if jobs are not lost, then the domestic textile industry will modernize only if the domestic textile industry is not destroyed. If quotas are imposed on textile imports, the domestic textile industry will modernize. The domestic textile industry will modernize only if jobs are not lost. Therefore, if quotas are imposed on textile imports, the domestic textile industry will not be destroyed. (Q, J, M, D)

★ 4. If teachers are allowed to conduct random drug searches on students only if teachers are acting in loco parentis, then if teachers are acting in loco parentis, then students have no Fourth Amendment protections. Either students have no Fourth Amendment protections or if teachers are allowed to conduct random drug searches on students, then teachers are acting in loco parentis. It is not the case that students have no Fourth Amendment protections. Therefore, teachers are not allowed to conduct random drug searches on students. (R, L, F)

5. Either funding for nuclear fusion will be cut or if sufficiently high temperatures are achieved in the laboratory, nuclear fusion will become a reality. Either the supply of hydrogen fuel is limited, or if nuclear fusion becomes a reality, the world's energy problems will be solved. Funding for nuclear fusion will not be cut. Furthermore, the supply of hydrogen fuel is not limited. Therefore, if sufficiently high temperatures are achieved in the laboratory, the world's energy problems will be solved. (C, H, R, S, E)

6. Either the continents are not subject to drift or if Antarctica was always located in the polar region, then it contains no fossils of plants from a temperate climate. If the continents are not subject to drift, then Antarctica contains no fossils of plants from a temperate climate. But it is not the case that Antarctica contains no fossils of plants from a temperate climate. Therefore, Antarctica was not always located in the polar region. (D, L, F)

★ 7. If terrorists take more hostages, then terrorist demands will be met if and only if the media give full coverage to terrorist acts. Either the media will voluntarily limit

6

the flow of information or if the media will recognize they are being exploited by terrorists, they will voluntarily limit the flow of information. Either the media will recognize they are being exploited by terrorists or terrorists will take more hostages. The media will not voluntarily limit the flow of information. Therefore, terrorist demands will be met if and only if the media give full coverage to terrorist acts. (*H, D, A, V, R*)

8. Either we take recycling seriously or we will be buried in garbage. If we incinerate our garbage only if our health is jeopardized, then we do not take recycling seriously. If our landfills are becoming exhausted, then if we incinerate our garbage, then toxic ash will be produced. If toxic ash is produced, then our health is jeopardized. Our landfills are becoming exhausted. Therefore, we will be buried in garbage. (*R, B, I, H, L, T*)

9. If the drug interdiction program is strengthened only if cocaine becomes more readily available, then either the number of addicts is decreasing or the war on drugs is failing. If the drug interdiction program is strengthened, then smugglers will shift to more easily concealable drugs. If smugglers shift to more easily concealable drugs, then cocaine will become more readily available. Furthermore, the number of addicts is not decreasing. Therefore, the war on drugs is failing. (*D, C, N, W, S*)

★10. If the death penalty is not cruel and unusual punishment, then either it is cruel and unusual punishment or if society is justified in using it, then it will deter other criminals. If the death penalty is cruel and unusual punishment, then it is both cruel and unusual and its use degrades society as a whole. It is not the case that both the death penalty is cruel and unusual and its use degrades society as a whole. Furthermore, the death penalty will not deter other criminals. Therefore, society is not justified in using the death penalty. (*C, J, D, U*)

Visit Aplia for section-specific problem sets.

6.2 Rules of Implication II

PREVIEW

While on your hike, you encounter a stream, about 20 feet wide, that you must cross. The stream has several rocks protruding above the surface for 100 feet or so. To get across you must select a series of stepping-stones, placed fairly close together, starting near one bank and ending near the other. Crossing the stream illustrates the kind of strategic thinking you must use in constructing proofs. Continued practice with these proofs is guaranteed to improve your capacity for strategic thinking in many areas of life.

6

Four additional rules of implication are listed here. Constructive dilemma should be familiar from Chapter 5. The other three are new. They are listed together with an illustration of their use as follows.*

Some textbooks include a rule called absorption *by which the statement form p ⊃ (q • p) is deduced from p ⊃ q. This rule is necessary only if conditional proof is not presented. This textbook opts in favor of conditional proof, to be introduced shortly.*

5. Constructive dilemma (CD)

$(p \supset q) \bullet (r \supset s)$ If Oscar is a dog, then you'll have fleas, and
                                        if Oscar is a cat, then you'll have fur balls.

$p \lor r$ Oscar is either a dog or a cat.

$q \lor s$ You'll have either fleas or fur balls.

6. Simplification (Simp)

$p \bullet q$ Eliza has long legs and runs fast.

p Eliza has long legs.

7. Conjunction (Conj)

p Roxy has big eyes.

q Roxy has a tail.

$p \bullet q$ Roxy has big eyes and a tail.

8. Addition (Add)

p Theo has spots.

$p \lor q$ Theo has either spots or stripes.

Like the previous four rules, these are fairly easy to understand, but if there is any doubt about them their validity may be proven by means of a truth table.

Constructive dilemma can be understood as involving two modus ponens steps. The first premise states that if we have p then we have q, and if we have r then we have s. But since, by the second premise, we do have either p or r, it follows by modus ponens that we have either q or s. Constructive dilemma is the only form of dilemma that will be included as a rule of inference. By the rule of transposition, which will be presented in Section 6.4, any argument that is a substitution instance of the destructive dilemma form can be easily converted into a substitution instance of constructive dilemma. Destructive dilemma, therefore, is not needed as a rule of inference.

These arguments are both instances of **constructive dilemma** (CD):

$\sim M \lor N$	$[(K \supset T) \supset (A \bullet B)] \bullet [(H \supset P) \supset (A \bullet C)]$
$(\sim M \supset S) \bullet (N \supset \sim T)$	$(K \supset T) \lor (H \supset P)$
$S \lor \sim T$	$(A \bullet B) \lor (A \bullet C)$

Simplification states that if two propositions are given as true on a single line, then each of them is true separately. According to the strict interpretation of the simplification rule, only the left-hand conjunct may be stated in the conclusion. Once the commutativity rule for conjunction has been presented, however (see Section 6.3), we will be justified in replacing a statement such as $H \bullet K$ with $K \bullet H$. Once we do this, the K will appear on the left, and the appropriate conclusion is K.

These arguments are all instances of **simplification** (Simp):

$\sim F \bullet (U \equiv E)$	$(M \lor T) \bullet (S \supset R)$	$[(X \supset Z) \bullet M] \bullet (G \supset H)$
$\sim F$	$M \lor T$	$(X \supset Z) \bullet M$

6

Conjunction states that two propositions—for example, H and K—asserted separately on different lines may be conjoined on a single line. The two propositions may be conjoined in whatever order we choose (either $H \cdot K$ or $K \cdot H$) without appeal to the commutativity rule for conjunction.

> These arguments are all instances of **conjunction** (Conj):
>
> | $\sim E$ | $C \supset M$ | $R \supset (H \cdot T)$ |
> |---|---|---|
> | $\sim G$ | $D \supset N$ | $K \supset (H \cdot O)$ |
> | $\sim E \cdot \sim G$ | $(C \supset M) \cdot (D \supset N)$ | $[R \supset (H \cdot T)] \cdot [K \supset (H \cdot O)]$ |

Addition states that whenever a proposition is asserted on a line by itself it may be joined disjunctively with any proposition we choose. In other words, if G is asserted to be true by itself, it follows that $G \vee H$ is true. This may appear somewhat puzzling at first, but once one realizes that $G \vee H$ is a much weaker statement than G by itself, the puzzlement should disappear. The new proposition must, of course, always be joined disjunctively (not conjunctively) to the given proposition. If G is stated on a line by itself, we are *not* justified in writing $G \cdot H$ as a consequence of addition.

> These arguments are all instances of **addition** (Add):
>
> | S | $(C \cdot D)$ | $W \equiv Z$ |
> |---|---|---|
> | $S \vee \sim T$ | $(C \cdot D) \vee (K \cdot \sim P)$ | $(W \equiv Z) \vee [A \supset (M \supset O)]$ |

The use of these four rules may now be illustrated. Consider the following argument:

1. $A \supset B$
2. $(B \vee C) \supset (D \cdot E)$
3. A / D

As usual, we begin by looking for the conclusion in the premises. D appears in the consequent of the second premise, which we can derive via simplification if we first obtain $B \vee C$. This expression as such does not appear in the premises, but from lines 1 and 3 we see that we can derive B by itself via modus ponens. Having obtained B, we can derive $B \vee C$ via addition. The proof has now been thought through and can be written out as follows:

1. $A \supset B$
2. $(B \vee C) \supset (D \cdot E)$
3. A / D
4. B 1, 3, MP
5. $B \vee C$ 4, Add
6. $D \cdot E$ 2, 5, MP
7. D 6, Simp

Another example:

1. $K \supset L$
2. $(M \supset N) \cdot S$
3. $N \supset T$
4. $K \vee M$ / $L \vee T$

6

Seeing that $L \vee T$ does not appear as such in the premises, we look for the separate components. Finding L and T as the consequents of two distinct conditional statements causes us to think that the conclusion can be derived via constructive dilemma. If a constructive dilemma can be set up, it will need a disjunctive statement as its second premise, and such a statement appears on line 4. Furthermore, each of the components of this statement, K and M, appears as the antecedent of a conditional statement, exactly as they both should for a dilemma. The only statement that is missing now is $M \supset T$. Inspecting line 2 we see that we can obtain $M \supset N$ via simplification, and putting this together with line 3 gives us $M \supset T$ via hypothetical syllogism. The completed proof may now be written out:

1. $K \supset L$
2. $(M \supset N) \cdot S$
3. $N \supset T$
4. $K \vee M$ / $L \vee T$
5. $M \supset N$ 2, Simp
6. $M \supset T$ 3, 5, HS
7. $(K \supset L) \cdot (M \supset T)$ 1, 6, Conj
8. $L \vee T$ 4, 7, CD

Another example:

1. $\sim M \cdot N$
2. $P \supset M$
3. $Q \cdot R$
4. $(\sim P \cdot Q) \supset S$ / $S \vee T$

When we look for $S \vee T$ in the premises we find S in the consequent of line 4 but no T at all. This signals an important principle: Whenever the conclusion of an argument contains a letter not found in the premises, addition must be used to introduce the missing letter. Addition is the *only* rule of inference that can introduce new letters. To introduce T by addition, however, we must first obtain S on a line by itself. S can be derived from line 4 via modus ponens if we first obtain $\sim P \cdot Q$. This, in turn, can be derived via conjunction, but first $\sim P$ and Q must be obtained individually on separate lines. Q can be derived from line 3 via simplification and $\sim P$ from line 2 via modus tollens, but the latter step requires that we first obtain $\sim M$ on a line by itself. Since this can be derived from line 1 via simplification, the proof is now complete. It may be written out as follows:

> Whenever the conclusion contains a letter not found in the premises, use Addition to introduce it.

1. $\sim M \cdot N$
2. $P \supset M$
3. $Q \cdot R$
4. $(\sim P \cdot Q) \supset S$ / $S \vee T$
5. $\sim M$ 1, Simp
6. $\sim P$ 2, 5, MT
7. Q 3, Simp
8. $\sim P \cdot Q$ 6, 7, Conj
9. S 4, 8, MP
10. $S \vee T$ 9, Add

Addition is used together with disjunctive syllogism to derive the conclusion of arguments having inconsistent premises. As we saw in Chapter 5, such arguments are always valid. The procedure is illustrated as follows:

1. *S*
2. ~*S*   / *T*
3. *S* ∨ *T*   1, Add
4. *T*   2, 3, DS

With arguments of this sort the conclusion is always introduced via addition and then separated via disjunctive syllogism. Since addition can be used to introduce any letter or arrangement of letters we choose, it should be clear from this example that inconsistent premises validly entail any conclusion whatever.

To complete this presentation of the eight rules of implication, let us consider some of the typical ways in which they are *misapplied*. Examples are as follows:

1. *P* ∨ (*S* • *T*)
2. *S*   1, Simp (invalid—*S* • *T* must first be obtained on a line by itself)

1. *K*
2. *K* • *L*   1, Add (invalid—the conclusion must be a disjunctive statement)

1. *M* ∨ *N*
2. *M*   1, Simp (invalid—simplification is possible only with a conjunctive premise; line 1 is a disjunction)

1. *G* ⊃ *H*
2. *G* ⊃ (*H* ∨ *J*)   1, Add (improper—*J* must be added to the whole line, not just to the consequent of line 1)

1. *L* ⊃ *M*
2. *L* ⊃ *N*
3. *M* • *N*   1, 2, Conj (invalid—*M* and *N* must first be obtained on lines by themselves)

1. ~(*P* • *Q*)
2. ~*P*   1, Simp (invalid—parentheses must be removed first)

1. ~(*P* ∨ *Q*)
2. ~*P*
3. *Q*   1, 2, DS (invalid—parentheses must be removed first)

The use of addition in the *G* ⊃ *H* example is called "improper" because the letter that is added is not added to the whole line. It turns out, however, that even though the addition rule is not correctly applied here, the inference is still valid. Hence, this inference is not called "invalid," as the others are. As for the last two examples, a rule will be presented in the next section (De Morgan's rule) that will allow us to remove parentheses preceded by negation signs. But even after the parentheses have been removed from these examples, the inferences remain invalid.

Like the previous section, this one ends with a few strategies for applying the last four rules of implication:

Strategy 6: If the conclusion contains a letter that appears in a conjunctive statement in the premises, consider obtaining that letter via simplification:

1. *A* ⊃ *B*
2. *C* • *B*
3. *C* ⊃ *A*   / *C*
4. *C*   2, Simp

Strategy 7: If the conclusion is a conjunctive statement, consider obtaining it via conjunction by first obtaining the individual conjuncts:

1. $A \supset C$
2. B
3. $\sim C$ / $B \cdot \sim C$
4. $B \cdot \sim C$ 2, 3, Conj

Strategy 8: If the conclusion is a disjunctive statement, consider obtaining it via constructive dilemma or addition:

1. $(A \supset B) \cdot (C \supset D)$
2. $B \supset C$
3. $A \vee C$ / $B \vee D$
4. $B \vee D$ 1, 3, CD

1. $A \vee C$
2. B
3. $C \supset D$ / $B \vee D$
4. $B \vee D$ 2, Add

Strategy 9: If the conclusion contains a letter not found in the premises, addition *must* be used to introduce that letter.

Strategy 10: Conjunction can be used to set up constructive dilemma:

1. $A \supset B$
2. $C \supset D$
3. $A \vee C$ / $B \vee D$
4. $(A \supset B) \cdot (C \supset D)$ 1, 2, Conj
5. $B \vee D$ 3, 4, CD

EXERCISE 6.2

I. For each of the following lists of premises, derive the indicated conclusion and complete the justification. In problems 4 and 8 you can add any statement you choose.

★(1) 1. $S \vee H$
     2. $B \cdot E$
     3. $R \supset G$
     4. _____ ____, Simp

(2) 1. $(N \supset T) \cdot (F \supset Q)$
     2. $(N \supset R) \vee (F \supset M)$
     3. $N \vee F$
     4. _____ ____, CD

(3) 1. D
     2. W
     3. ____ ____, Conj

★(4) 1. H
     2. ____ ____, Add

(5) 1. $R \cdot (N \vee K)$
     2. $(G \cdot T) \vee S$
     3. $(Q \cdot C) \supset (J \cdot L)$
     4. _____ ____, Simp

(6) 1. $\sim R \vee P$
     2. $(P \supset \sim D) \cdot (\sim R \supset S)$
     3. $(\sim R \supset A) \cdot (P \supset \sim N)$
     4. _____ ____, CD

6

★(7) 1. $(Q \lor K) \bullet \sim B$
    2. $(M \bullet R) \supset D$
    3. $(W \bullet S) \lor (G \bullet F)$
    4. _____ _____, Simp

(8) 1. $E \bullet G$
    2. _____ _____, Add

(9) 1. $\sim B$
    2. $F \lor N$
    3. _____ _____, Conj

★(10) 1. $S \lor \sim C$
    2. $(S \supset \sim L) \bullet (\sim C \supset M)$
    3. $(\sim N \supset S) \bullet (F \supset \sim C)$
    4. _____ _____, CD

II. In the following symbolized arguments, derive the line needed to obtain the conclusion (last line), and supply the justification for both lines.

★(1) 1. $G \supset N$
    2. $G \bullet K$
    3. _____ _____
    4. $G \lor T$ _____

(2) 1. $\sim A$
    2. $A \lor E$
    3. _____ _____
    4. $\sim A \bullet E$ _____

(3) 1. $B \supset N$
    2. $B \lor K$
    3. $K \supset R$
    4. _____ _____
    5. $N \lor R$ _____

★(4) 1. T
    2. $T \supset G$
    3. $(T \lor U) \supset H$
    4. _____ _____
    5. H _____

(5) 1. $S \supset E$
    2. $E \lor (S \bullet P)$
    3. $\sim E$
    4. _____ _____
    5. S _____

(6) 1. N
    2. $N \supset F$
    3. $(N \supset A) \bullet (F \supset C)$
    4. _____ _____
    5. $A \lor C$ _____

★(7) 1. J
    2. $\sim L$
    3. $F \supset L$
    4. _____ _____
    5. $\sim F \bullet J$ _____

(8) 1. $(E \supset B) \bullet (Q \supset N)$
    2. $K \supset E$
    3. $B \supset K$
    4. _____ _____
    5. $E \supset K$ _____

(9) 1. $G \lor N$
    2. $\sim G$
    3. $\sim G \supset (H \bullet R)$
    4. _____ _____
    5. H _____

★(10) 1. M
    2. $(M \bullet E) \supset D$
    3. E
    4. _____ _____
    5. D _____

III. Use the first eight rules of inference to derive the conclusions of the following symbolized arguments:

★(1) 1. $\sim M \supset Q$
    2. $R \supset \sim T$
    3. $\sim M \lor R$ / $Q \lor \sim T$

(2) 1. $N \supset (D \bullet W)$
    2. $D \supset K$
    3. N / $N \bullet K$

(3) 1. $E \supset (A \bullet C)$
    2. $A \supset (F \bullet E)$
    3. E / F

★(4) 1. $(H \lor \sim B) \supset R$
    2. $(H \lor \sim M) \supset P$
    3. H / $R \bullet P$

6

(5) 1. $G \supset (S \cdot T)$
   2. $(S \vee T) \supset J$
   3. G / J

(6) 1. $(L \vee T) \supset (B \cdot G)$
   2. $L \cdot (K \equiv R)$ / $L \cdot B$

★(7) 1. $(\sim F \vee X) \supset (P \vee T)$
   2. $F \supset P$
   3. $\sim P$ / T

(8) 1. $(N \supset B) \cdot (O \supset C)$
   2. $Q \supset (N \vee O)$
   3. Q / $B \vee C$

(9) 1. $(U \vee W) \supset (T \supset R)$
   2. $U \cdot H$
   3. $\sim R \cdot \sim J$ / $U \cdot \sim T$

★(10) 1. $(D \vee E) \supset (G \cdot H)$
   2. $G \supset \sim D$
   3. $D \cdot F$ / M

(11) 1. $(B \vee F) \supset (A \supset G)$
   2. $(B \vee E) \supset (G \supset K)$
   3. $B \cdot \sim H$ / $A \supset K$

(12) 1. $(P \supset R) \supset (M \supset P)$
   2. $(P \vee M) \supset (P \supset R)$
   3. $P \vee M$ / $R \vee P$

★(13) 1. $(C \supset N) \cdot E$
   2. $D \vee (N \supset D)$
   3. $\sim D$ / $\sim C \vee P$

(14) 1. $F \supset (\sim T \cdot A)$
   2. $(\sim T \vee G) \supset (H \supset T)$
   3. $F \cdot O$ / $\sim H \cdot \sim T$

(15) 1. $(\sim S \vee B) \supset (S \vee K)$
   2. $(K \vee \sim D) \supset (H \supset S)$
   3. $\sim S \cdot W$ / $\sim H$

★(16) 1. $(C \vee \sim G) \supset (\sim P \cdot L)$
   2. $(\sim P \cdot C) \supset (C \supset D)$
   3. $C \cdot \sim R$ / $D \vee R$

(17) 1. $[A \vee (K \cdot J)] \supset (\sim E \cdot \sim F)$
   2. $M \supset [A \cdot (P \vee R)]$
   3. $M \cdot U$ / $\sim E \cdot A$

(18) 1. $\sim H \supset (\sim T \supset R)$
   2. $H \vee (E \supset F)$

3. $\sim T \vee E$
4. $\sim H \cdot D$ / $R \vee F$

★(19) 1. $(U \cdot \sim \sim P) \supset Q$
   2. $\sim O \supset U$
   3. $\sim P \supset O$
   4. $\sim O \cdot T$ / Q

(20) 1. $(M \vee N) \supset (F \supset G)$
   2. $D \supset \sim C$
   3. $\sim C \supset B$
   4. $M \cdot H$
   5. $D \vee F$ / $B \vee G$

(21) 1. $(F \cdot M) \supset (S \vee T)$
   2. $(\sim S \vee A) \supset F$
   3. $(\sim S \vee B) \supset M$
   4. $\sim S \cdot G$ / T

★(22) 1. $(\sim K \cdot \sim N) \supset$
         $[(\sim P \supset K) \cdot (\sim R \supset G)]$
   2. $K \supset N$
   3. $\sim N \cdot B$
   4. $\sim P \vee \sim R$ / G

(23) 1. $(\sim A \vee D) \supset (B \supset F)$
   2. $(B \vee C) \supset (A \supset E)$
   3. $A \vee B$
   4. $\sim A$ / $E \vee F$

(24) 1. $(J \supset K) \cdot (\sim O \supset \sim P)$
   2. $(L \supset J) \cdot (\sim M \supset \sim O)$
   3. $\sim K \supset (L \vee \sim M)$
   4. $\sim K \cdot G$ / $\sim P$

★(25) 1. $(\sim M \cdot \sim N) \supset [(\sim M \vee H) \supset (K \cdot L)]$
   2. $\sim M \cdot (C \supset D)$
   3. $\sim N \cdot (F \equiv G)$ / $K \cdot \sim N$

(26) 1. $(P \vee S) \supset (E \supset F)$
   2. $(P \vee T) \supset (G \supset H)$
   3. $(P \vee U) \supset (E \vee G)$
   4. P / $F \vee H$

(27) 1. $(S \supset Q) \cdot (Q \supset \sim S)$
   2. $S \vee Q$
   3. $\sim Q$ / $P \cdot R$

★(28) 1. $(D \supset B) \cdot (C \supset D)$
   2. $(B \supset D) \cdot (E \supset C)$
   3. $B \vee E$ / $D \vee B$

6

(29) 1. $(R \supset H) \cdot (S \supset I)$
2. $(\sim H \cdot \sim L) \supset (R \lor S)$
3. $\sim H \cdot (K \supset T)$
4. $H \lor \sim L$ / $I \lor M$

(30) 1. $(W \cdot X) \supset (Q \lor R)$
2. $(S \lor F) \supset (Q \lor W)$
3. $(S \lor G) \supset (\sim Q \supset X)$
4. $Q \lor S$
5. $\sim Q \cdot H$ / R

IV. Translate the following arguments into symbolic form and use the first eight rules of inference to derive the conclusion of each. Use the letters in the order in which they are listed.

★1. If topaz is harder than quartz, then it will scratch quartz and also feldspar. Topaz is harder than quartz and it is also harder than calcite. Therefore, either topaz will scratch quartz or it will scratch corundum. (T, Q, F, C, O)

2. If clear-cutting continues in primary forests and the Endangered Species Act is not repealed, then either the Endangered Species Act will be repealed or thousands of animal species will become extinct. Clear-cutting continues in primary forests. The Endangered Species Act will not be repealed. Therefore, thousands of animal species will become extinct. (C, E, T)

3. If either executive salaries are out of control or exorbitant bonuses are paid, then either shareholders will be cheated or ordinary workers will be paid less. Executive salaries are out of control and the rich are getting richer. If shareholders are cheated, then future investors will stay away; also, if ordinary workers are paid less, then consumer spending will decline. If either future investors stay away or consumer spending declines, then the economy will suffer. Therefore, the economy will suffer. (S, B, C, P, R, F, D, E)

★4. Either animals are mere mechanisms or they feel pain. If either animals feel pain or they have souls, then they have a right not to be subjected to needless pain and humans have a duty not to inflict needless pain on them. It is not the case that animals are mere mechanisms. Therefore, animals have a right not to be subjected to needless pain. (M, P, S, R, D)

5. If half the nation suffers from depression, then if either the insurance companies have their way or the psychiatrists have their way, then everyone will be taking antidepressant drugs. If either half the nation suffers from depression or sufferers want a real cure, then it is not the case that everyone will be taking antidepressant drugs. Half the nation suffers from depression. Therefore, it is not the case that either the insurance companies or the psychiatrists will have their way. (H, I, P, E, W)

6. If either parents get involved in their children's education or the school year is lengthened, then if the children learn phonics, their reading will improve and if they are introduced to abstract concepts earlier, their math will improve. If either parents get involved in their children's education or nebulous subjects are dropped from the curriculum, then either the children will learn phonics or they will be introduced to abstract concepts earlier. Parents will get involved in their children's education, and writing lessons will be integrated with other subjects. Therefore, either the children's reading or their math will improve. (P, S, L, R, I, M, N, W)

★7. If either manufacturers will not concentrate on producing a superior product or they will not market their product abroad, then if they will not concentrate on producing a superior product, then the trade deficit will worsen. Either manufacturers will concentrate on producing a superior product or the trade deficit will not worsen. Manufacturers will not concentrate on producing a superior product. Therefore, today's business managers lack imagination. (*C, M, T, B*)

8. If either medical fees or malpractice awards escape restrictions, then health-care costs will soar and millions of poor will go uninsured. If the lawyers get their way, then malpractice awards will escape restrictions. If the doctors get their way, then medical fees will escape restrictions. Either the doctors or the lawyers will get their way, and insurance companies will resist reform. Therefore, health-care costs will soar. (*F, A, H, P, L, D, I*)

9. If we are less than certain the human fetus is a person, then we must give it the benefit of the doubt. If we are certain the human fetus is a person, then we must accord it the right to live. If either we must give the fetus the benefit of the doubt or accord it the right to live, then we are not less than certain the fetus is human and it is not merely a part of the mother's body. Either we are less than certain the human fetus is a person or we are certain about it. If we are certain the human fetus is a person, then abortion is immoral. Therefore, abortion is immoral. (*L, G, C, A, M, I*)

★10. If the assassination of terrorist leaders violates civilized values and also is not effective in the long run, then if it prevents terrorist atrocities, then it is effective in the long run. If the assassination of terrorist leaders violates civilized values, then it is not effective in the long run. The assassination of terrorist leaders violates civilized values and is also illegal. If the assassination of terrorist leaders is not effective in the long run, then either it prevents terrorist atrocities or it justifies acts of revenge by terrorists. Therefore, the assassination of terrorist leaders justifies acts of revenge by terrorists and also is not effective in the long run. (*V, E, P, I, J*)

aplia™
Visit Aplia for section-specific problem sets.

6.3   Rules of Replacement I

PREVIEW

After crossing the stream, you encounter a rocky cliff about 25 feet high that you must scale. You can now practice some of your rock-climbing skills. As you climb, you must find a series of crevices in the rock for your hands, and little ledges for your feet. The *crevices and ledges must not be too far apart, and they must lead continuously upward. This involves a higher level of strategic thinking than crossing the stream required. The following section of the book will give you great practice for this kind of thinking.*

6

Unlike the rules of implication, which are basic argument forms, the ten **rules of replacement** are expressed in terms of pairs of logically equivalent statement forms, either of which can replace the other in a proof sequence. To express these rules, a new symbol, called a **double colon** (::), is used to designate logical equivalence. This symbol is a *metalogical* symbol in that it makes an assertion not about things but about symbolized statements: It asserts that the expressions on either side of it have the same truth

rule of replacement: A rule of inference expressed as a logical equivalence.

value regardless of the truth values of their components. Underlying the use of the rules of replacement is an **axiom of replacement**, which asserts that within the context of a proof, logically equivalent expressions may replace each other. The first five rules of replacement are as follows:

9. De Morgan's rule (DM):

$\sim(p \cdot q) :: (\sim p \vee \sim q)$

$\sim(p \vee q) :: (\sim p \cdot \sim q)$

10. Commutativity (Com):

$(p \vee q) :: (q \vee p)$

$(p \cdot q) :: (q \cdot p)$

11. Associativity (Assoc):

$[p \vee (q \vee r)] :: [(p \vee q) \vee r]$

$[p \cdot (q \cdot r)] :: [(p \cdot q) \cdot r]$

12. Distribution (Dist):

$[p \cdot (q \vee r)] :: [(p \cdot q) \vee (p \cdot r)]$

$[p \vee (q \cdot r)] :: [(p \vee q) \cdot (p \vee r)]$

13. Double negation (DN):

$p :: \sim\sim p$

De Morgan's rule (named after the nineteenth-century logician Augustus De Morgan) was discussed in Section 5.1 in connection with translation. There it was pointed out that "Not both *p* and *q*" is logically equivalent to "Not *p* or not *q*," and that "Not either *p* or *q*" is logically equivalent to "Not *p* and not *q*." When applying De Morgan's rule, one should keep in mind that it holds only for conjunctive and disjunctive statements (not for conditionals or biconditionals). The rule may be summarized as follows: When moving a tilde inside or outside a set of parentheses, a dot switches with a wedge and vice versa.

Commutativity asserts that the truth value of a conjunction or disjunction is unaffected by the order in which the components are listed. In other words, the component statements may be commuted, or switched for one another, without affecting the truth value. The validity of this rule should be immediately apparent. You may recall from arithmetic that the commutativity rule also applies to addition and multiplication and asserts, for example, that $3 + 5$ equals $5 + 3$, and that 2×3 equals 3×2. However, it does *not* apply to division; $2 \div 4$ does not equal $4 \div 2$. A similar lesson applies in logic: The commutativity rule applies only to conjunction and disjunction; it does *not* apply to implication.

Associativity states that the truth value of a conjunctive or disjunctive statement is unaffected by the placement of parentheses when the same operator is used throughout. In other words, the way in which the component propositions are grouped, or associated with one another, can be changed without affecting the truth value. The validity of this rule is quite easy to see, but if there is any doubt about it, it may be readily checked by means of a truth table. You may recall that the associativity rule also applies to addition and multiplication and asserts, for example, that $3 + (5 + 7)$ equals $(3 + 5) + 7$, and that $2 \times (3 \times 4)$ equals $(2 \times 3) \times 4$. But it does *not* apply to division: $(8 \div 4) \div 2$ does not equal $8 \div (4 \div 2)$. Analogously, in logic, the associativity rule applies only to conjunctive and disjunctive statements; it does *not* apply to conditional statements. Also note, when applying this rule, that the order of the letters remains unchanged; only the placement of the parentheses changes.

Distribution, like De Morgan's rule, applies only to conjunctive and disjunctive statements. When a proposition is conjoined to a disjunctive statement in parentheses or disjoined to a conjunctive statement in parentheses, the rule allows us to put that proposition together with each of the components inside the parentheses, and also to go in the reverse direction. In the first form of the rule, a statement is distributed through a disjunction, and in the second form, through a conjunction. While the rule may not be immediately obvious, it is easy to remember: The operator that is at first outside the parentheses goes inside, and the operator that is at first inside the parentheses goes outside. Note also how distribution differs from commutativity and associativity. The latter two rules apply only when the *same* operator (either a dot or a wedge) is used throughout a statement. Distribution applies when a dot and a wedge appear *together* in a statement.

Double negation is fairly obvious and needs little explanation. The rule states simply that pairs of tildes immediately adjacent to one another may be either deleted or introduced without affecting the truth value of the statement.

There is an important difference between the rules of implication, treated in the first two sections of this chapter, and the rules of replacement. The rules of implication derive their name from the fact that each is a simple argument form in which the premises imply the conclusion. To be applicable in natural deduction, certain lines in a proof must be interpreted as substitution instances of the argument form in question. Stated another way, the rules of implication are applicable only to *whole lines* in a proof. For example, step 3 in the following proof is not a legitimate application of modus ponens, because the first premise in the modus ponens rule is applied to only a *part* of line 1.

1. $A \supset (B \supset C)$
2. B
3. C 1, 2, MP (invalid)

The rules of replacement, on the other hand, are not rules of implication but rules of logical equivalence. Since, by the axiom of replacement, logically equivalent statement forms can always replace one another in a proof sequence, the rules of replacement can be applied either to a whole line or to any part of a line. Step 2 in the following proof is a quite legitimate application of De Morgan's rule, even though the rule is applied only to the consequent of line 1:

> The rules of replacement can be applied either to whole lines or to parts of lines.

1. $S \supset \sim(T \cdot U)$
2. $S \supset (\sim T \vee \sim U)$ 1, DM (valid)

Another way of viewing this distinction is that the rules of implication are "one-way" rules, whereas the rules of replacement are "two-way" rules. The rules of implication allow us to proceed only from the premise lines of a rule to the conclusion line, but the rules of replacement allow us to replace either side of an equivalence expression with the other side.

Application of the first five rules of replacement may now be illustrated. Consider the following argument:

1. $A \supset \sim(B \cdot C)$
2. $A \cdot C$ / $\sim B$

Examining the premises, we find *B* in the consequent of line 1. This leads us to suspect that the conclusion can be derived via modus ponens. If this is correct, the tilde would then have to be taken inside the parentheses via De Morgan's rule and the resulting ~*C* eliminated by disjunctive syllogism. The following completed proof indicates that this strategy yields the anticipated result:

    1. *A* ⊃ ~(*B* • *C*)
    2. *A* • *C*   / ~*B*
    3. *A*   2, Simp
    4. ~(*B* • *C*)   1, 3, MP
    5. ~*B* ∨ ~*C*   4, DM
    6. *C* • *A*   2, Com
    7. *C*   6, Simp
    8. ~ ~*C*   7, DN
    9. ~*C* ∨ ~*B*   5, Com
    10. ~*B*   8, 9, DS

The rationale for line 6 is to get *C* on the left side so that it can be separated via simplification. Similarly, the rationale for line 9 is to get ~*C* on the left side so that it can be eliminated via disjunctive syllogism. Line 8 is required because, strictly speaking, the negation of ~*C* is ~ ~*C*—not simply *C*. Thus, *C* must be replaced with ~ ~*C* to set up the disjunctive syllogism. If your instructor permits it, you can combine commutativity and double negation with other inferences on a single line, as the following shortened proof illustrates. However, we will avoid this practice throughout the remainder of the book.

    1. *A* ⊃ ~(*B* • *C*)
    2. *A* • *C*   / ~*B*
    3. *A*   2, Simp
    4. ~(*B* • *C*)   1, 3, MP
    5. ~*B* ∨ ~*C*   4, DM
    6. *C*   2, Com, Simp
    7. ~*B*   5, 6, Com, DN, DS

Another example:

    1. *D* • (*E* ∨ *F*)
    2. ~*D* ∨ ~*F*   / *D* • *E*

The conclusion requires that we get *D* and *E* together. Inspection of the first premise suggests distribution as the first step in achieving this. The completed proof is as follows:

    1. *D* • (*E* ∨ *F*)
    2. ~*D* ∨ ~*F*   / *D* • *E*
    3. (*D* • *E*) ∨ (*D* • *F*) 1, Dist
    4. (*D* • *F*) ∨ (*D* • *E*) 3, Com
    5. ~(*D* • *F*)   2, DM
    6. *D* • *E*   4, 5, DS

Some proofs require that we use distribution in the reverse manner. Consider this argument:

1. $(G \cdot H) \vee (G \cdot J)$
2. $(G \vee K) \supset L$ / L

The conclusion can be obtained from line 2 via modus ponens if we first obtain $G \vee K$ on a line by itself. Since K does not occur in the first premise at all, it must be introduced by addition. Doing this requires in turn that we obtain G on a line by itself. Distribution applied to line 1 provides the solution:

1. $(G \cdot H) \vee (G \cdot J)$
2. $(G \vee K) \supset L$ / L
3. $G \cdot (H \vee J)$ 1, Dist
4. G 3, Simp
5. $G \vee K$ 4, Add
6. L 2, 5, MP

Application of the associativity rule is illustrated in the next proof:

1. $M \vee (N \vee O)$
2. $\sim O$ / $M \vee N$
3. $(M \vee N) \vee O$ 1, Assoc
4. $O \vee (M \vee N)$ 3, Com
5. $M \vee N$ 2, 4, DS

Before O can be eliminated via disjunctive syllogism from line 1, it must be moved over to the left side. Associativity and commutativity together accomplish this objective.

In some arguments the attempt to "find" the conclusion in the premises is not immediately successful. When confronted with such an argument, one should often begin by "deconstructing" the conclusion using the rules of replacement. In other words, one should first apply the rules of replacement to the conclusion to see how it is put together. After this is done, how the premises entail the conclusion may be evident. This procedure is justified by the fact that the rules of replacement are two-way rules. As a result, after the conclusion is deconstructed, it can be derived by using the same rules in reverse order. Here is an example of such an argument:

> The rules of replacement allow us to "deconstruct" the conclusion.

1. $K \supset (F \vee B)$
2. $G \cdot K$ / $(F \cdot G) \vee (B \cdot G)$

If immediate inspection does not reveal how the conclusion should be derived, we may begin by applying the rules of replacement to the conclusion. The form of the conclusion suggests the distribution rule, but first we must use commutativity to move the G's to the left-hand side. The deconstruction proceeds as follows:

$(F \cdot G) \vee (B \cdot G)$
$(G \cdot F) \vee (B \cdot G)$ Com
$(G \cdot F) \vee (G \cdot B)$ Com
$G \cdot (F \vee B)$ Dist

Now we see that if we can obtain G on a line by itself, and $F \vee B$ on a line by itself, we can combine them on a single line via the conjunction rule. We can then derive the

Willard Van Orman Quine 1908–2000

Prior to his death in the year 2000, Willard Van Orman Quine was widely considered to be, as Stuart Hampshire put it, "the most distinguished and influential of living philosophers." At that time, over 2,000 scholarly articles had been written about his work.

Quine was born in Akron, Ohio, in 1908 to a father who founded a heavy-equipment company and a mother who taught elementary school. He earned his bachelor's degree in mathematics from Oberlin College, where he graduated *summa cum laude* in 1930. He then entered Harvard University, where he switched to philosophy so he could study under Alfred North Whitehead. He earned his PhD in a record two years. Except for four years during World War II, when he served in the Navy decoding messages from German submarines, Quine remained affiliated with Harvard for the remainder of his life.

Quine wrote twenty-two books, the first five of which dealt with mathematical logic. One of the goals of the earlier books was to show how the foundations of mathematics could be laid out in less than a fourth of the space taken by Whitehead and Russell's *Principia Mathematica*. One of his most famous publications was "Two Dogmas of Empiricism," which shook the pillars of analytic philosophy by undermining the sacrosanct distinction between analytic and synthetic statements. As a result of this work, even the truths of logic and mathematics became subject to the dictates of empirical experience.

As a boy, Quine had a fascination with collecting stamps and drawing maps, which, as an adult, he translated into a zest for world travel. He visited 118 countries, became fluent in six different languages, delivered lectures all over the world, and was awarded the first Schock Prize (Stockholm, 1993) and the Kyoto Prize (Tokyo, 1996). He was married twice, raised two children from each marriage, loved Dixieland jazz, and played the banjo, mandolin, and piano. He was singularly unpretentious, had an unfailing curiosity about a vast range of topics, and delighted in teaching freshman logic as well as advanced courses in philosophy. He died in Boston at the age of ninety-two.

conclusion via distribution and commutativity. Inspection of the premises reveals that *G* can be derived from line 2 of the premises by simplification, and *F* ∨ *B* can be derived from line 1 by modus ponens. The completed proof is as follows:

1. $K \supset (F \lor B)$
2. $G \cdot K$ / $(F \cdot G) \lor (B \cdot G)$
3. G 2, Simp
4. $K \cdot G$ 2, Com
5. K 4, Simp
6. $F \lor B$ 1, 5, MP
7. $G \cdot (F \lor B)$ 3, 6, Conj
8. $(G \cdot F) \lor (G \cdot B)$ 7, Dist
9. $(F \cdot G) \lor (G \cdot B)$ 8, Com
10. $(F \cdot G) \lor (B \cdot G)$ 9, Com

Here are some strategies for applying the first five rules of replacement. Most of them show how these rules may be used together with other rules.

Strategy 11: Conjunction can be used to set up De Morgan's rule:

1. $\sim A$
2. $\sim B$
3. $\sim A \cdot \sim B$ 1, 2, Conj
4. $\sim (A \lor B)$ 3, DM

Strategy 12: Constructive dilemma can be used to set up De Morgan's rule:

1. $(A \supset \sim B) \cdot (C \supset \sim D)$
2. $A \vee C$
3. $\sim B \vee \sim D$ 1, 2, CD
4. $\sim(B \cdot D)$ 3, DM

Strategy 13: Addition can be used to set up De Morgan's rule:

1. $\sim A$
2. $\sim A \vee \sim B$ 1, Add
3. $\sim(A \cdot B)$ 2, DM

Strategy 14: Distribution can be used in two ways to set up disjunctive syllogism:

1. $(A \vee B) \cdot (A \vee C)$
2. $\sim A$
3. $A \vee (B \cdot C)$ 1, Dist
4. $B \cdot C$ 2, 3, DS

1. $A \cdot (B \vee C)$
2. $\sim(A \cdot B)$
3. $(A \cdot B) \vee (A \cdot C)$ 1, Dist
4. $A \cdot C$ 2, 3, DS

Strategy 15: Distribution can be used in two ways to set up simplification:

1. $A \vee (B \cdot C)$
2. $(A \vee B) \cdot (A \vee C)$ 1, Dist
3. $A \vee B$ 2, Simp

1. $(A \cdot B) \vee (A \cdot C)$
2. $A \cdot (B \vee C)$ 1, Dist
3. A 2, Simp

Strategy 16: If inspection of the premises does not reveal how the conclusion should be derived, consider using the rules of replacement to deconstruct the conclusion. (See the final example in this section.)

EXERCISE 6.3

I. For each of the following lists of premises, derive the indicated conclusion and complete the justification. For double negation, avoid the occurrence of triple tildes. Exercise 6 has two possible answers.

★(1) 1. $\sim(E \supset H)$
     2. $\sim(N \vee G)$
     3. $\sim A \vee D$
     4. _____ ____, DM

(2) 1. $G \supset (N \supset K)$
 2. $R \vee (D \supset F)$
 3. $S \cdot (T \vee U)$
 4. _____ ____, Dist

(3) 1. $M \vee (G \vee T)$
 2. $P \cdot (S \supset N)$
 3. $D \cdot (R \vee K)$
 4. _____ ____, Assoc

★(4) 1. $B \supset W$
 2. $G \equiv F$
 3. $S \cdot A$
 4. _____ ____, Com

(5) 1. $\sim\sim R \vee T$
 2. $\sim N \vee \sim B$
 3. $\sim A \supset \sim H$
 4. _____ ____, DN

(6) 1. $(F \vee N) \supset (K \cdot D)$
 2. $(H \cdot Z) \vee (H \cdot W)$
 3. $(P \supset H) \vee (P \supset N)$
 4. _____ ____, Dist

★(7) 1. $\sim(G \cdot \sim Q)$
 2. $\sim(K \equiv \sim B)$
 3. $\sim T \supset \sim F$
 4. _____ ____, DM

(8) 1. $G \supset (\sim L \supset T)$
 2. $L \equiv (\sim R \supset \sim C)$
 3. $J \supset (S \vee \sim N)$
 4. _____ ____, Com

(9) 1. $S \supset (M \supset D)$
 2. $(K \cdot G) \vee B$
 3. $(E \cdot H) \cdot Q$
 4. _____ ____, Assoc

★(10) 1. $\sim R \vee \sim P$
 2. $\sim F \supset \sim W$
 3. $G \cdot \sim A$
 4. _____ ____, DM

(11) 1. $\sim B \vee E$
 2. $\sim E \cdot \sim A$
 3. $\sim C \supset \sim R$
 4. _____ ____, DN

(12) 1. $\sim G \cdot (S \supset A)$
 2. $\sim S \supset (B \cdot K)$
 3. $\sim Q \vee (T \cdot R)$
 4. _____ ____, Dist

★(13) 1. $F \supset (\sim S \vee M)$
     2. $H \supset (\sim L \cdot \sim D)$
     3. $N \supset (\sim G \supset \sim C)$
     4. _____ ____, DM

(14) 1. $F \supset (P \supset \sim E)$
     2. $C \vee (S \cdot \sim B)$
     3. $M \cdot (R \cdot \sim T)$
     4. _____ ____, Assoc

(15) 1. $(D \vee \sim K) \cdot (D \vee \sim W)$
     2. $(S \vee \sim Z) \vee (P \vee \sim T)$
     3. $(Q \supset \sim N) \cdot (Q \supset \sim F)$
     4. _____ ____, Dist

II. In the following symbolized arguments, derive the line needed to obtain the conclusion (last line), and supply the justification for both lines.

★(1) 1. $K \vee C$
    2. $\sim C$
    3. _____ ____
    4. K ____

(2) 1. $G \supset (R \vee N)$
    2. $\sim R \cdot \sim N$
    3. _____ ____
    4. $\sim G$ ____

(3) 1. $H \cdot T$
    2. _____ ____
    3. T ____

★(4) 1. $(L \cdot S) \cdot F$
    2. _____ ____
    3. L ____

(5) 1. $\sim B \vee K$
    2. _____ ____
    3. $\sim(B \cdot \sim K)$ ____

(6) 1. $C \supset \sim A$
    2. A
    3. _____ ____
    4. $\sim C$ ____

★(7) 1. $(D \cdot M) \vee (D \cdot N)$
    2. _____ ____
    3. D ____

(8) 1. $(U \vee T) \supset R$
    2. $T \vee U$
    3. _____ ____
    4. R ____

(9) 1. $\sim L \vee M$
    2. L
    3. _____ ____
    4. M ____

★(10) 1. $D \vee (N \cdot H)$
     2. _____ ____
     3. $D \vee N$ ____

(11) 1. $(K \vee E) \cdot (K \vee G)$
     2. $\sim K$
     3. _____ ____
     4. $E \cdot G$ ____

(12) 1. $(N \supset T) \cdot (F \supset Q)$
     2. $F \vee N$
     3. _____ ____
     4. $T \vee Q$ ____

★(13) 1. $(M \vee G) \vee T$
     2. $\sim M$
     3. _____ ____
     4. $G \vee T$ ____

(14) 1. $(\sim A \supset T) \cdot (\sim S \supset K)$
     2. $\sim(A \cdot S)$
     3. _____ ____
     4. $T \vee K$ ____

(15) 1. $\sim R$
     2. _____ ____
     3. $\sim(R \cdot T)$ ____

6

III. Use the first thirteen rules of inference to derive the conclusions of the following symbolized arguments:

★ (1) 1. $(\sim M \supset P) \cdot (\sim N \supset Q)$
      2. $\sim(M \cdot N)$ / $P \vee Q$

(2) 1. $\sim S$ / $\sim(F \cdot S)$

(3) 1. $J \vee (K \cdot L)$
      2. $\sim K$ / J

★ (4) 1. $\sim(N \cdot T)$
      2. T / $\sim N$

(5) 1. $H \supset \sim A$
      2. A / $\sim(H \vee \sim A)$

(6) 1. $R \supset \sim B$
      2. $D \vee R$
      3. B / D

★ (7) 1. $T \supset (B \vee E)$
      2. $\sim E \cdot T$ / B

(8) 1. $(O \vee M) \supset S$
      2. $\sim S$ / $\sim M$

(9) 1. $Q \vee (L \vee C)$
      2. $\sim C$ / $L \vee Q$

★ (10) 1. $(K \cdot H) \vee (K \cdot L)$
      2. $\sim L$ / H

(11) 1. $\sim(\sim E \cdot \sim N) \supset T$
      2. $G \supset (N \vee E)$ / $G \supset T$

(12) 1. $H \cdot (C \cdot T)$
      2. $\sim(\sim F \cdot T)$ / F

★ (13) 1. $(E \cdot I) \vee (M \cdot U)$
      2. $\sim E$ / $\sim(E \vee \sim M)$

(14) 1. $\sim(J \vee K)$
      2. $B \supset K$
      3. $S \supset B$ / $\sim S \cdot \sim J$

(15) 1. $(G \cdot H) \vee (M \cdot G)$
      2. $G \supset (T \cdot A)$ / A

★ (16) 1. $(Q \cdot N) \vee (N \cdot T)$
      2. $(Q \vee C) \supset \sim N$ / T

(17) 1. $\sim(U \vee R)$
      2. $(\sim R \vee N) \supset (P \cdot H)$
      3. $Q \supset \sim H$ / $\sim Q$

(18) 1. $\sim(F \cdot A)$
      2. $\sim(L \vee \sim A)$
      3. $D \supset (F \vee L)$ / $\sim D$

★ (19) 1. $[(I \vee M) \vee G] \supset \sim G$
      2. $M \vee G$ / M

(20) 1. $E \supset \sim B$
      2. $U \supset \sim C$
      3. $\sim(\sim E \cdot \sim U)$ / $\sim(B \cdot C)$

(21) 1. $\sim(K \vee F)$
      2. $\sim F \supset (K \vee C)$
      3. $(G \vee C) \supset \sim H$ / $\sim(K \vee H)$

★ (22) 1. $S \vee (I \cdot \sim J)$
      2. $S \supset \sim R$
      3. $\sim J \supset \sim Q$ / $\sim(R \cdot Q)$

(23) 1. $(J \vee F) \vee M$
      2. $(J \vee M) \supset \sim P$
      3. $\sim F$ / $\sim(F \vee P)$

(24) 1. $(K \cdot P) \vee (K \cdot Q)$
      2. $P \supset \sim K$ / $Q \vee T$

★ (25) 1. $E \vee \sim(D \vee C)$
      2. $(E \vee \sim D) \supset C$ / E

(26) 1. $A \cdot (F \cdot L)$
      2. $A \supset (U \vee W)$
      3. $F \supset (U \vee X)$ / $U \vee (W \cdot X)$

(27) 1. $(T \cdot R) \supset P$
      2. $(\sim P \cdot R) \cdot G$
      3. $(\sim T \vee N) \supset H$ / H

★ (28) 1. $P \vee (I \cdot L)$
      2. $(P \vee I) \supset \sim(L \vee C)$
      3. $(P \cdot \sim C) \supset (E \cdot F)$ / $F \vee D$

(29) 1. $B \vee (S \cdot N)$
      2. $B \supset \sim S$
      3. $S \supset \sim N$ / $B \vee W$

(30) 1. $(\sim M \vee E) \supset (S \supset U)$
      2. $(\sim Q \vee E) \supset (U \supset H)$
      3. $\sim(M \vee Q)$ / $S \supset H$

★ (31) 1. $(\sim R \vee D) \supset \sim(F \cdot G)$
      2. $(F \cdot R) \supset S$
      3. $F \cdot \sim S$ / $\sim(S \vee G)$

(32) 1. $\sim Q \supset (C \cdot B)$
      2. $\sim T \supset (B \cdot H)$
      3. $\sim(Q \cdot T)$ / B

(33) 1. $\sim(A \cdot G)$
2. $\sim(A \cdot E)$
3. $G \vee E$ $/ \sim(A \cdot F)$

(35) 1. $(T \cdot K) \vee (C \cdot E)$
2. $K \supset \sim E$
3. $E \supset \sim C$ $/ T \cdot K$

★ **(34)** 1. $(M \cdot N) \vee (O \cdot P)$
2. $(N \vee O) \supset \sim P$ $/ N$

IV. Translate the following arguments into symbolic form and then use the first thirteen rules of inference to derive the conclusion of each. Use the translation letters in the order in which they are listed.

★**1.** Either health-care costs are skyrocketing and they are attributable to greedy doctors, or health-care costs are skyrocketing and they are attributable to greedy hospitals. If health-care costs are skyrocketing, then both the government should intercede and health care may have to be rationed. Therefore, health-care costs are skyrocketing and health care may have to be rationed. (*S, D, H, I, R*)

2. Either the ancient Etruscans were experienced city planners and they invented the art of writing or they were highly skilled engineers and they invented the art of writing. If the ancient Etruscans were bloodthirsty numskulls (as scholars once thought), they did not invent the art of writing. Therefore, the ancient Etruscans were not bloodthirsty numskulls (as scholars once thought). (*C, I, H, B*)

3. It is not the case that either the Earth's molten core is stationary or that it contains no iron. If it is not the case that both the Earth's molten core is stationary and has a regular topography, then either the Earth's core contains no iron or the direction of the Earth's magnetic field is subject to change. Therefore, the direction of the Earth's magnetic field is subject to change. (*S, C, R, D*)

★**4.** Either mosquito genes can be cloned or mosquitoes will become resistant to all insecticides and the incidence of encephalitis will increase. If either mosquito genes can be cloned or the incidence of encephalitis increases, then mosquitoes will not become resistant to all insecticides. Therefore, either mosquito genes can be cloned or mosquitoes will multiply out of control. (*G, R, E, M*)

5. Protein engineering will prove to be as successful as genetic engineering, and new enzymes will be developed for producing food and breaking down industrial wastes. If protein engineering proves to be as successful as genetic engineering and new enzymes are developed for breaking down industrial wastes, then it is not the case that new enzymes will be developed for producing food but not medicines. Therefore, protein engineering will prove to be as successful as genetic engineering and new enzymes will be developed for producing medicines. (*E, P, B, M*)

6. If workers have a fundamental right to a job, then unemployment will be virtually nonexistent but job redundancy will become a problem. If workers have no fundamental right to a job, then production efficiency will be maximized but job security will be jeopardized. Workers either have or do not have a fundamental right to a job. Therefore, either unemployment will be virtually nonexistent or production efficiency will be maximized. (*F, U, R, P, S*)

★**7.** If China is to reduce its huge trade surplus, then it must either convince its citizens to spend more or it must move its manufacturing facilities to other countries. It is not the case that China will either increase its imports or convince its citizens to spend more. Furthermore, it is not the case that China will either allow foreign construction companies to compete on an equal footing or move its manufacturing facilities to other countries. Therefore, China will not reduce its huge trade surplus. (*R, C, M, I, A*)

8. If women are by nature either passive or uncompetitive, then it is not the case that there are lawyers who are women. If men are by nature either insensitive or without the ability to nurture, then it is not the case that there are kindergarten teachers who are men. There are lawyers who are women and kindergarten teachers who are men. Therefore, it is not the case that either women by nature are uncompetitive or men by nature are without the ability to nurture. (*P, U, L, I, W, K*)

9. It is not the case that either the sun's interior rotates faster than its surface or Einstein's general theory of relativity is wrong. If the sun's interior does not rotate faster than its surface and eccentricities in the orbit of Mercury can be explained by solar gravitation, then Einstein's general theory of relativity is wrong. Therefore, eccentricities in the orbit of Mercury cannot be explained by solar gravitation. (*S, E, M*)

★10. Either school dropout programs are not as effective as they could be, or they provide basic thinking skills and psychological counseling to their students. Either school dropout programs are not as effective as they could be, or they adequately prepare their students for getting a job and working effectively with others. Either school dropout programs do not provide psychological counseling to their students or they do not provide adequate preparation for working effectively with others. Therefore, school dropout programs are not as effective as they could be. (*E, B, P, G, W*)

V. The following dialogue contains eight arguments. Translate each into symbolic form and then use the first thirteen rules of inference to derive the conclusion of each.

With This Ring

"Hi. I didn't expect to see you here," says Ken as he catches sight of Gina on the steps of the church. "You must be friends with the bride."

"I am," she says, "and are you a friend of the groom?"

"A friend of a friend of the groom," he replies. "So I don't know too many people here."

"Well, I'll be happy to keep you company until the ceremony starts," Gina says. "And it looks like things are running late, so we'll have a few minutes."

She looks around and sighs. "Every time I attend a wedding," she says, "I feel sad for a lesbian couple I know who would give just about anything to get married. Unfortunately this state doesn't allow same-sex marriage."

"Well, I don't think that's unfortunate," says Ken. "If marriage is sacred, then we shouldn't tamper with it; and if that's the case, then we shouldn't allow same-sex marriage. And I do think marriage is sacred, so we shouldn't allow same-sex marriage."

Gina looks shocked. Ken continues. "Look," he says, "the Bible condemns homosexuality. If either Leviticus or Romans is true, then homosexuality is an abomination and it must be avoided. And if it must be avoided or it's contrary to nature, then if it's a sin, then it must not be allowed. Now, we know that Romans is true, and if the Bible condemns homosexuality, then it's a sin. Thus, same-sex marriage must not be allowed."

"Obviously you're injecting religion into the issue," Gina responds, as she waves to a friend in the gathering crowd. "But the First Amendment to the Constitution says that the state must not act either to establish a religion or to interfere with religious practices. If the state bars same-sex marriage for your reasons, it acts to establish a religion. So, it must not bar same-sex marriage for your reasons."

Ken opens his mouth to object, but this time it's Gina who's on a roll. "Also," she continues, "our country is based on the principle of equality. If straight couples can get married, and obviously they can, then either same-sex couples can get married or same-sex couples are not equal to straight couples. And if same-sex couples can get married, then our law has to change and other state laws have to change as well. Now, if our country is based on the principle of equality, then same-sex couples are equal to straight couples. Thus, our law has to change."

"Look," says Ken, "marriage has always been between a man and a woman. And if that is so and tradition is worth preserving, then if we allow same-sex marriage, then the very concept of marriage will change and gender roles will switch. Now tradition is worth preserving and gender roles shouldn't switch. Thus, we cannot allow same-sex marriage."

"Ha!" says Gina. "I can see why you don't want gender roles to switch. You can't see yourself in the kitchen preparing meals and washing dishes."

"Well, I don't really relish the idea," Ken admits. "I think God wants us to keep things the way they are. But here's another reason. One of the chief purposes of marriage is raising children, and if that is so, then it's important that the children grow up well adjusted. But if the children are to be well adjusted, then they must have both a male role model and a female role model. If the parents are both men, then the children will have no female role model; if they're both women, then the children will have no male role model. Clearly if the marriage is a same-sex marriage, then the parents are either both men or they are both women. Therefore, the marriage must not be a same-sex marriage."

"Your reasoning is a bit shortsighted," Gina says. "In a same-sex marriage with children, the parents are either both men or they are both women. This much I grant you. But if they are both men, then surely they have close female friends, and if that is so, then the marriage has both male and female role models. If the parents are both women, then surely they have close male friends, and if that is so, then the marriage has both female and male role models. If a marriage has both male and female role models, then the children will be well adjusted. Therefore, in a same-sex marriage with children, the children will be well adjusted. What do you think of that?"

"Well," says Ken, as he scratches his head, "I wonder if those surrogate role models would be as effective as male and female parents. But in either event there is the option of civil unions. Why won't that satisfy you?"

"Civil unions fall short of marriage in too many ways," Gina replies. "They're valid only in the state in which they are performed, and they don't allow the partners either to file a joint federal tax return or to receive Social Security survivor benefits. If they're valid only in the state in which they're performed, then if the couple moves to a different state, then if one partner is hospitalized, the other partner will have no visitation rights. If the partners can't file a joint federal tax return, then they must file as single taxpayers. And if that is so, then they might pay much more in taxes. If the partners don't receive Social Security survivor benefits, then if a partner receiving Social Security benefits dies, then the other will not receive anything as a survivor. Suppose that two partners in a civil union move to a different state, and that one partner, who receives Social Security benefits, is hospitalized and eventually dies. The conclusion is that the other partner will not have either visitation rights while the hospitalized partner is alive or survivor benefits after that partner dies, and the partners might pay much more in taxes. Does that seem like a fair substitute for marriage?"

"Maybe not," Ken says, as he stretches to see above the crowd. "But I still think there's something unnatural about same-sex marriage. Anyway, here are the bride and groom. Let's go inside."

"Good, let's go," says Gina.

6.4   Rules of Replacement II

PREVIEW

Your hike comes to an end on the bank of a river with several Class 3 rapids. Fortunately, before starting out on the hike you had arranged to have your kayak dropped off at this location. Kayaking down the river will pose an even greater—but more exhilarating—challenge than climbing the cliff. Selecting the best route through the rapids requires strategic vision, and negotiating the rocks without capsizing demands skill. You must be constantly aware of where you are and where you want to go. This section of the book supports further practice with this kind of thinking.

The remaining five rules of replacement are as follows:

14. Transposition (Trans):
$(p \supset q) :: (\sim q \supset \sim p)$

15. Material implication (Impl):
$(p \supset q) :: (\sim p \lor q)$

16. Material equivalence (Equiv):
$(p \equiv q) :: [(p \supset q) \cdot (q \supset p)]$
$(p \equiv q) :: [(p \cdot q) \lor (\sim p \cdot \sim q)]$

17. Exportation (Exp):
$[(p \cdot q) \supset r] :: [p \supset (q \supset r)]$

18. Tautology (Taut):
$p :: (p \lor p)$
$p :: (p \cdot p)$

Transposition asserts that the antecedent and consequent of a conditional statement may switch places if and only if tildes are inserted before both or tildes are removed from both. The rule is fairly easy to understand and is easily proved by a truth table.

Material implication is less obvious than transposition, but it can be illustrated by substituting actual statements in place of the letters. For example, the statement "If you bother me, then I'll punch you in the nose" ($B \supset P$) is logically equivalent to "Either you stop bothering me or I'll punch you in the nose" ($\sim B \lor P$). The rule states that a horseshoe may be replaced by a wedge if the left-hand component is negated, and the reverse replacement is allowed if a tilde is deleted from the left-hand component.

Material equivalence has two formulations. The first is the same as the definition of material equivalence given in Section 5.1. The second formulation is easy to remember through recalling the two ways in which $p \equiv q$ may be true. Either p and q are both true or p and q are both false. This, of course, is the meaning of $[(p \cdot q) \vee (\sim p \cdot \sim q)]$.

Exportation is also fairly easy to understand. It asserts that the statement "If we have both p and q, then we have r" is logically equivalent to "If we have p, then if we have q, then we have r." As an illustration of this rule, the statement "If Bob and Sue told the truth, then Jim is guilty" is logically equivalent to "If Bob told the truth, then if Sue told the truth, then Jim is guilty."

Tautology, the last rule introduced in this section, is obvious. Its effect is to eliminate redundancy in disjunctions and conjunctions.

The following proofs illustrate the use of these five rules.

    1. $\sim A$ / $A \supset B$

In this argument the conclusion contains a letter not found in the premise. Obviously, addition must be used to introduce the B. The material implication rule completes the proof:

    1. $\sim A$ / $A \supset B$
    2. $\sim A \vee B$ 1, Add
    3. $A \supset B$ 2, Impl

Here is another example:

    1. $F \supset G$
    2. $F \vee G$ / G

To derive the conclusion of this argument, some method must be found to link the two premises together and eliminate the F. Hypothetical syllogism provides the solution, but first the second premise must be converted into a conditional. Here is the proof:

    1. $F \supset G$
    2. $F \vee G$ / G
    3. $\sim\sim F \vee G$ 2, DN
    4. $\sim F \supset G$ 3, Impl
    5. $\sim F \supset \sim\sim G$ 4, DN
    6. $\sim G \supset F$ 5, Trans
    7. $\sim G \supset G$ 1, 6, HS
    8. $\sim\sim G \vee G$ 7, Impl
    9. $G \vee G$ 8, DN
   10. G 9, Taut

Another example:

    1. $J \supset (K \supset L)$ / $K \supset (J \supset L)$

The conclusion can be obtained by simply rearranging the components of the single premise. Exportation provides the simplest method:

    1. $J \supset (K \supset L)$ / $K \supset (J \supset L)$
    2. $(J \cdot K) \supset L$ 1, Exp
    3. $(K \cdot J) \supset L$ 2, Com
    4. $K \supset (J \supset L)$ 3, Exp

Another example:

    1. $M \supset N$
    2. $M \supset O$ / $M \supset (N \cdot O)$

As with the F and G example, some method must be found to link the two premises together. In this case, however, hypothetical syllogism will not work. The solution lies in setting up a distribution step:

1. $M \supset N$		
2. $M \supset O$		/ $M \supset (N \cdot O)$
3. $\sim M \vee N$	1, Impl	
4. $\sim M \vee O$	2, Impl	
5. $(\sim M \vee N) \cdot (\sim M \vee O)$	3, 4, Conj	
6. $\sim M \vee (N \cdot O)$	5, Dist	
7. $M \supset (N \cdot O)$	6, Impl	

Another example:

1. $P \supset Q$		
2. $R \supset (S \cdot T)$		
3. $\sim R \supset \sim Q$		
4. $S \supset (T \supset P)$		/ $P \equiv R$

The conclusion is a biconditional, and there are only two ways that a biconditional can be obtained from such premises—namely, via the two formulations of the material equivalence rule. The fact that the premises are all conditional statements suggests the first formulation of this rule. Accordingly, we must try to obtain $P \supset R$ and $R \supset P$. Again, the fact that the premises are themselves conditionals suggests hypothetical syllogism to accomplish this. Premises 1 and 3 can be used to set up one hypothetical syllogism; premises 2 and 4 provide the other. Here is the proof:

1. $P \supset Q$		
2. $R \supset (S \cdot T)$		
3. $\sim R \supset \sim Q$		
4. $S \supset (T \supset P)$		/ $P \equiv R$
5. $Q \supset R$	3, Trans	
6. $P \supset R$	1, 5, HS	
7. $(S \cdot T) \supset P$	4, Exp	
8. $R \supset P$	2, 7, HS	
9. $(P \supset R) \cdot (R \supset P)$	6, 8, Conj	
10. $P \equiv R$	9, Equiv	

As we saw in Section 6.3, if it is not readily apparent how the conclusion should be derived, we can use the rules of replacement to deconstruct the conclusion. This will usually provide insight on how best to proceed. Again, this technique is justified because the rules of replacement are two-way rules. As a result, they can be applied in reverse order in the completed proof. Here is an example:

1. $\sim S \supset K$		
2. $S \supset (R \vee M)$		/ $\sim R \supset (\sim M \supset K)$

In deconstructing the conclusion, the form of the conclusion suggests exportation, and the result of this step suggests De Morgan's rule. For further insight, we apply transposition to the latter step. Each step follows from the one preceding it:

$\sim R \supset (\sim M \supset K)$	
$(\sim R \cdot \sim M) \supset K$	Exp
$\sim (R \vee M) \supset K$	DM
$\sim K \supset \sim \sim (R \vee M)$	Trans
$\sim K \supset (R \vee M)$	DN

Now, examining the premises in light of the deconstruction suggests that we begin by setting up a hypothetical syllogism. This will give us the last step in the deconstruction. We can then obtain the conclusion by repeating the deconstruction steps in reverse order. The completed proof is as follows:

1. ~S ⊃ K
2. S ⊃ (R ∨ M)   / ~R ⊃ (~M ⊃ K)
3. ~K ⊃ ~~S   1, Trans
4. ~K ⊃ S   3, DN
5. ~K ⊃ (R ∨ M)   2, 4, HS
6. ~(R ∨ M) ⊃ ~~K   5, Trans
7. ~(R ∨ M) ⊃ K   6, DN
8. (~R • ~M) ⊃ K   7, DM
9. ~R ⊃ (~M ⊃ K)   8, Exp

Here is another example:

1. K ⊃ M
2. L ⊃ M   / (K ∨ L) ⊃ M

In deconstructing the conclusion, the form of the premises suggests that we use some procedure that will combine M separately with K and L. This, in turn, suggests distribution; but before we can use distribution, we must eliminate the horseshoe via material implication. The deconstruction is as follows:

(K ∨ L) ⊃ M
~(K ∨ L) ∨ M   Impl
(~K • ~L) ∨ M   DM
M ∨ (~K • ~L)   Com
(M ∨ ~K) • (M ∨ ~L)   Dist
(~K ∨ M) • (M ∨ ~L)   Com
(~K ∨ M) • (~L ∨ M)   Com
(K ⊃ M) • (~L ∨ M)   Impl
(K ⊃ M) • (L ⊃ M)   Impl

Now, examining the premises in light of the last line of the deconstruction suggests that we begin by joining the premises together via the conjunction rule. The conclusion can then be obtained by reversing the steps of the deconstruction:

1. K ⊃ M
2. L ⊃ M   / (K ∨ L) ⊃ M
3. (K ⊃ M) • (L ⊃ M)   1, 2, Conj
4. (~K ∨ M) • (L ⊃ M)   3, Impl
5. (~K ∨ M) • (~L ∨ M)   4, Impl
6. (M ∨ ~K) • (~L ∨ M)   5, Com
7. (M ∨ ~K) • (M ∨ ~L)   6, Com
8. M ∨ (~K • ~L)   7, Dist
9. (~K • ~L) ∨ M   8, Com
10. ~(K ∨ L) ∨ M   9, DM
11. (K ∨ L) ⊃ M   10, Impl

Note that whenever we use this strategy of working backward from the conclusion, the rules of replacement are the *only* rules we may use. We may not use the rules of implication, because these rules are one-way rules.

This section ends with some strategies that show how the last five rules of replacement can be used together with various other rules.

6

Strategy 17: Material implication can be used to set up hypothetical syllogism:

1. ~A ∨ B
2. ~B ∨ C
3. A ⊃ B   1, Impl
4. B ⊃ C   2, Impl
5. A ⊃ C   3, 4, HS

Strategy 18: Exportation can be used to set up modus ponens:

1. (A • B) ⊃ C
2. A
3. A ⊃ (B ⊃ C)   1, Exp
4. B ⊃ C   2, 3, MP

Strategy 19: Exportation can be used to set up modus tollens:

1. A ⊃ (B ⊃ C)
2. ~C
3. (A • B) ⊃ C   1, Exp
4. ~(A • B)   2, 3, MT

Strategy 20: Addition can be used to set up material implication:

1. A
2. A ∨ ~B   1, Add
3. ~B ∨ A   2, Com
4. B ⊃ A   3, Impl

Strategy 21: Transposition can be used to set up hypothetical syllogism:

1. A ⊃ B
2. ~C ⊃ ~B
3. B ⊃ C   2, Trans
4. A ⊃ C   1, 3, HS

Strategy 22: Transposition can be used to set up constructive dilemma:

1. (A ⊃ B) • (C ⊃ D)
2. ~B ∨ ~D
3. (~B ⊃ ~A) • (C ⊃ D)   1, Trans
4. (~B ⊃ ~A) • (~D ⊃ ~C)   3, Trans
5. ~A ∨ ~C   2, 4, CD

Strategy 23: Constructive dilemma can be used to set up tautology:

1. (A ⊃ C) • (B ⊃ C)
2. A ∨ B
3. C ∨ C   1, 2, CD
4. C   3, Taut

Strategy 24: Material implication can be used to set up tautology:

1. A ⊃ ~A
2. ~A ∨ ~A   1, Impl
3. ~A   2, Taut

Strategy 25: Material implication can be used to set up distribution:

1. $A \supset (B \cdot C)$
2. $\sim A \vee (B \cdot C)$ 1, Impl
3. $(\sim A \vee B) \cdot (\sim A \vee C)$ 2, Dist

EXERCISE 6.4

I. For each of the following lists of premises, derive the indicated conclusion and complete the justification. For tautology, derive a conclusion that is simpler than the premise.

★(1) 1. $H \vee F$
     2. $N \vee \sim S$
     3. $\sim G \vee Q$
     4. _____ ____, Impl

(2) 1. $R \supset (S \supset N)$
    2. $T \supset (U \vee M)$
    3. $K \cdot (L \supset W)$
    4. _____ ____, Exp

(3) 1. $G \equiv R$
    2. $H \supset P$
    3. $\sim F \vee T$
    4. _____ ____, Trans

★(4) 1. $(B \supset N) \cdot (N \supset B)$
     2. $(R \vee F) \cdot (F \vee R)$
     3. $(K \supset C) \vee (C \supset K)$
     4. _____ ____, Equiv

(5) 1. $E \vee \sim E$
    2. $A \vee A$
    3. $G \cdot \sim G$
    4. _____ ____, Taut

(6) 1. $S \vee \sim M$
    2. $\sim N \cdot \sim T$
    3. $\sim L \supset Q$
    4. _____ ____, Trans

★(7) 1. $\sim C \supset \sim F$
     2. $D \vee \sim P$
     3. $\sim R \cdot Q$
     4. _____ ____, Impl

(8) 1. $E \supset (R \cdot Q)$
    2. $(G \cdot N) \supset Z$
    3. $(S \supset M) \supset P$
    4. _____ ____, Exp

(9) 1. $(D \cdot H) \vee (\sim D \cdot \sim H)$
2. $(F \supset J) \cdot (\sim F \supset \sim J)$
3. $(N \vee T) \cdot (\sim N \vee \sim T)$
4. _____ ____, Equiv

★ **(10)** 1. $L \supset (A \supset A)$
2. $K \supset (R \vee \sim R)$
3. $S \supset (G \cdot G)$
4. _____ ____, Taut

(11) 1. $K \cdot (S \vee B)$
2. $\sim F \supset \sim J$
3. $\sim E \vee \sim M$
4. _____ ____, Trans

(12) 1. $H \supset (K \cdot J)$
2. $(N \vee E) \supset B$
3. $C \supset (H \supset A)$
4. _____ ____, Exp

★ **(13)** 1. $(A \supset \sim C) \cdot (C \supset \sim A)$
2. $(W \supset \sim T) \cdot (\sim T \supset W)$
3. $(M \supset \sim E) \cdot (\sim M \supset E)$
4. _____ ____, Equiv

(14) 1. $(\sim K \vee M) \equiv S$
2. $T \vee (F \cdot G)$
3. $R \equiv (N \cdot \sim H)$
4. _____ ____, Impl

(15) 1. $(S \vee S) \supset D$
2. $K \supset (T \cdot \sim T)$
3. $(Q \supset Q) \supset M$
4. _____ ____, Taut

II. In the following symbolized arguments, derive the line needed to obtain the conclusion (last line), and supply the justification for both lines.

★ **(1)** 1. $\sim J \vee M$
2. $M \supset B$
3. _____ ____
4. $J \supset B$ ____

(2) 1. $(J \cdot F) \supset N$
2. J
3. _____ ____
4. $F \supset N$ ____

(3) 1. $C \supset A$
2. $A \supset C$
3. _____ ____
4. $C \equiv A$ ____

★ **(4)** 1. $(G \supset K) \cdot (T \supset K)$
2. $G \vee T$
3. _____ ____
4. K ____

(5) 1. $(G \supset B) \cdot (\sim C \supset \sim H)$
2. $G \vee H$
3. _____ ____
4. $B \vee C$ ____

(6) 1. $J \supset (M \supset Q)$
2. $J \cdot M$
3. _____ ____
4. Q ____

6

★(7) 1. $H \supset (\sim C \vee R)$
2. _____ ___
3. $(H \cdot C) \supset R$ ___

(8) 1. $\sim G \supset \sim T$
2. $G \supset N$
3. _____ ___
4. $T \supset N$ ___

(9) 1. $K \supset (A \supset F)$
2. $\sim F$
3. _____ ___
4. $\sim (K \cdot A)$ ___

(10) 1. $H \supset \sim H$
2. _____ ___
3. $\sim H$ ___

(11) 1. $\sim S$
2. _____ ___
3. $S \supset K$ ___

(12) 1. $M \supset (M \supset D)$
2. _____ ___
3. $M \supset D$ ___

★(13) 1. $(N \supset A) \cdot (\sim N \supset \sim A)$
2. _____ ___
3. $N \equiv A$ ___

(14) 1. $E \cdot R$
2. ___ ___
3. $E \equiv R$ ___

(15) 1. $Q \supset (\sim W \supset \sim G)$
2. _____ ___
3. $(Q \cdot G) \supset W$ ___

III. Use the eighteen rules of inference to derive the conclusions of the following symbolized arguments.

★(1) 1. $(S \cdot K) \supset R$
2. K / $S \supset R$

(2) 1. $T \supset (F \vee F)$
2. $\sim (F \cdot F)$ / $\sim T$

(3) 1. $G \supset E$
2. $H \supset \sim E$ / $G \supset \sim H$

★(4) 1. $S \equiv Q$
2. $\sim S$ / $\sim Q$

(5) 1. $\sim N \vee P$
2. $(N \supset P) \supset T$ / T

(6) 1. $F \supset B$
2. $B \supset (B \supset J)$ / $F \supset J$

★(7) 1. $(B \supset M) \cdot (D \supset M)$
2. $B \vee D$ / M

(8) 1. $Q \supset (F \supset A)$
2. $R \supset (A \supset F)$
3. $Q \cdot R$ / $F \equiv A$

(9) 1. $T \supset (\sim T \vee G)$
2. $\sim G$ / $\sim T$

★(10) 1. $(B \supset G) \cdot (F \supset N)$
2. $\sim (G \cdot N)$ / $\sim (B \cdot F)$

(11) 1. $(J \cdot R) \supset H$
2. $(R \supset H) \supset M$
3. $\sim (P \vee \sim J)$ / $M \cdot \sim P$

(12) 1. T / $S \supset T$

★(13) 1. $K \supset (B \supset {\sim}M)$
     2. $D \supset (K \cdot M)$ / $D \supset {\sim}B$

(14) 1. $(O \supset C) \cdot ({\sim}S \supset {\sim}D)$
     2. $(E \supset D) \cdot ({\sim}E \supset {\sim}C)$ / $O \supset S$

(15) 1. ${\sim}(U \cdot W) \supset X$
     2. $U \supset {\sim}U$ / ${\sim}(U \vee {\sim}X)$

★(16) 1. $T \supset R$
     2. $T \supset {\sim}R$ / ${\sim}T$

(17) 1. $S \vee {\sim}N$
     2. ${\sim}S \vee Q$ / $N \supset Q$

(18) 1. $M \supset (U \supset H)$
     2. $(H \vee {\sim}U) \supset F$ / $M \supset F$

★(19) 1. ${\sim}R \vee P$
     2. $R \vee {\sim}P$ / $R \equiv P$

(20) 1. ${\sim}H \supset B$
     2. ${\sim}H \supset D$
     3. ${\sim}(B \cdot D)$ / H

(21) 1. $J \supset (G \supset L)$ / $G \supset (J \supset L)$

★(22) 1. $S \supset (L \cdot M)$
     2. $M \supset (L \supset R)$ / $S \supset R$

(23) 1. $F \supset (A \cdot K)$
     2. $G \supset ({\sim}A \cdot {\sim}K)$
     3. $F \vee G$ / $A \equiv K$

(24) 1. $(I \supset E) \supset C$
     2. $C \supset {\sim}C$ / I

★(25) 1. $T \supset G$
     2. $S \supset G$ / $(T \vee S) \supset G$

(26) 1. $H \supset U$ / $H \supset (U \vee T)$

(27) 1. $Q \supset (W \cdot D)$ / $Q \supset W$

★(28) 1. $P \supset ({\sim}E \supset B)$
     2. ${\sim}(B \vee E)$ / ${\sim}P$

(29) 1. $(G \supset J) \supset (H \supset Q)$
     2. $J \cdot {\sim}Q$ / ${\sim}H$

(30) 1. $I \vee (N \cdot F)$
     2. $I \supset F$ / F

★(31) 1. $K \equiv R$
     2. $K \supset (R \supset P)$
     3. ${\sim}P$ / ${\sim}R$

6

(32) 1. $C \supset (\sim L \supset Q)$
2. $L \supset \sim C$
3. $\sim Q$ / $\sim C$

(33) 1. $(E \supset A) \cdot (F \supset A)$
2. $E \vee G$
3. $F \vee \sim G$ / A

★ (34) 1. $(F \cdot H) \supset N$
2. $F \vee S$
3. H / $N \vee S$

(35) 1. $T \supset (H \cdot J)$
2. $(H \vee N) \supset T$ / $T \equiv H$

(36) 1. $T \supset \sim(A \supset N)$
2. $T \vee N$ / $T \equiv \sim N$

★ (37) 1. $(D \supset E) \supset (E \supset D)$
2. $(D \equiv E) \supset \sim(G \cdot \sim H)$
3. $E \cdot G$ / $G \cdot H$

(38) 1. $(O \supset R) \supset S$
2. $(P \supset R) \supset \sim S$ / $\sim R$

(39) 1. $(L \vee P) \supset U$
2. $(M \supset U) \supset I$
3. P / I

★ (40) 1. $A \equiv W$
2. $\sim A \vee \sim W$
3. $R \supset A$ / $\sim(W \vee R)$

(41) 1. $(S \vee T) \supset (S \supset \sim T)$
2. $(S \supset \sim T) \supset (T \supset K)$
3. $S \vee T$ / $S \vee K$

(42) 1. $G \equiv M$
2. $G \vee M$
3. $G \supset (M \supset T)$ / T

★ (43) 1. $O \supset (Q \cdot N)$
2. $(N \vee E) \supset S$ / $O \supset S$

(44) 1. $H \equiv I$
2. $H \supset (I \supset F)$
3. $\sim(H \vee I) \supset F$ / F

★ (45) 1. $P \supset A$
2. $Q \supset B$ / $(P \vee Q) \supset (A \vee B)$

IV. Translate the following arguments into symbolic form and then use the eighteen rules of inference to derive the conclusion of each. Use the translation letters in the order in which they are listed.

★**1.** If sports-shoe manufacturers decline to use kangaroo hides in their products, then Australian hunters will cease killing millions of kangaroos yearly. It is not the case that both Australian hunters will cease killing millions of kangaroos yearly and the kangaroo will not be saved from extinction. Therefore, if sports-shoe manufacturers decline to use kangaroo hides in their products, then the kangaroo will be saved from extinction. (D, C, S)

2. If there is a direct correlation between what a nation spends for health care and the health of its citizens, then America has the lowest incidence of disease and the lowest mortality rates of any nation on Earth. But America does not have the lowest mortality rates of any nation on Earth. Therefore, there is not a direct correlation between what a nation spends for health care and the health of its citizens. (C, D, M)

3. It is not the case that strict controls exist on either the manufacture or the sale of handguns. Therefore, if strict controls exist on the sale of handguns, then the use of handguns in the commission of crimes has decreased. (M, S, U)

★4. If birth-control devices are made available in high school clinics, then the incidence of teenage pregnancy will decrease. Therefore, if both birth-control information and birth-control devices are made available in high school clinics, then the incidence of teenage pregnancy will decrease. (D, P, I)

5. If Congress enacts a law that either establishes a religion or prohibits the free exercise of religion, then that law is unconstitutional. Therefore, if Congress enacts a law that establishes a religion, then that law is unconstitutional. (E, P, U)

6. If cigarette smokers are warned of the hazards of smoking and they continue to smoke, then they cannot sue tobacco companies for any resulting lung cancer or emphysema. Cigarette smokers are warned of the hazards of smoking. Therefore, if cigarette smokers continue to smoke, they cannot sue tobacco companies for any resulting lung cancer or emphysema. (W, C, S)

★7. If grade-school children are assigned daily homework, then their achievement level will increase dramatically. But if grade-school children are assigned daily homework, then their love for learning may be dampened. Therefore, if grade-school children are assigned daily homework, then their achievement level will increase dramatically but their love for learning may be dampened. (G, A, L)

8. If a superconducting particle collider is built, then the data yielded will benefit scientists of all nations and it deserves international funding. Either a superconducting particle collider will be built, or the ultimate nature of matter will remain hidden and the data yielded will benefit scientists of all nations. Therefore, the data yielded by a superconducting particle collider will benefit scientists of all nations. (S, D, I, U)

9. If parents are told that their unborn child has Tay–Sachs disease, then if they go ahead with the birth, then they are responsible for their child's pain and suffering. Therefore, if parents are not responsible for their child's pain and suffering, then if they go ahead with the birth, then they were not told that their unborn child had Tay–Sachs disease. (T, G, R)

★10. Vitamin E is an antioxidant and a useless food supplement if and only if it does not reduce heart disease. It is not the case either that vitamin E does not reduce heart disease or is not an antioxidant. Therefore, vitamin E is not a useless food supplement. (A, U, R)

V. The following dialogue contains ten arguments. Translate each into symbolic form and then use the eighteen rules of inference to derive the conclusion of each.

Is This the End?

Brian and Molly are at the memorial service of a mutual friend who had died suddenly the week before. "I'm still shocked to think that Karl is gone," Molly says.

"I know you were quite close to him," Brian says. "But do you think in some sense Karl could still be with us? I mean do you think there could be such a thing as postmortem persistence of consciousness—life after death, as most people say?"

"I wish there were," Molly replies, "and that's what makes death so tragic. As I see it, the mind is totally dependent on the brain, and if that's so, when the brain dies, the mind dies. If the mind dies, then consciousness dies, too. Thus, if the brain dies, then consciousness dies—which means there's no life after death."

"But what makes you think that the mind is totally dependent on the brain?" Brian asks.

"Our day-to-day experience provides lots of evidence," Molly replies. "If you drink alcohol, your mind is affected. If you smoke marijuana, your mind is affected. If your mind is affected by these things, then you have firsthand experience that the mind is dependent on the brain. Thus, if you either smoke marijuana or drink alcohol, then you have firsthand experience that the mind is dependent on the brain."

"So the mind is affected by the brain. Anyone with ordinary sensation knows that," Brian retorts. "If your eye receives a visual stimulus, then that stimulus is sent to the brain and your mind is affected. If your ear receives an auditory stimulus, then your mind is affected. Thus, if either your eye or your ear receives a stimulus, then your mind is affected. But that doesn't prove that the mind is *necessarily* dependent on the brain. And there are lots of reasons for saying that it isn't."

"What reasons are those?" Molly asks.

"Well, we learned about Plato in Introduction to Philosophy," Brian replies. "And Plato held that the mind can conceive ideal objects such as perfect justice and perfect triangularity. Now, if either of these concepts came through the senses, then perfect ideals exist in nature. But no perfect ideals exist in nature. And if the concept of triangularity did not come through the senses, then the mind produced it independently of the brain. But if that is the case or the concept of triangularity is innate, then the mind is not necessarily dependent on the brain. I'll leave the conclusion up to you."

"Very interesting," Molly replies, "but I question whether the mind is really capable of conceiving ideal objects such as perfect justice and perfect triangularity. For me, these things are just words. But there are other reasons for thinking that the mind is *necessarily* dependent on the brain. Consider the visual cortex. The visual cortex is part of the brain. If the visual cortex isn't stimulated, there is no visual sensation. But if visual sensation occurs only if the visual cortex is stimulated, and if the visual cortex is part of the brain, then visual sensation is dependent on the brain. And if that is true and visual

6

sensation is a function of the mind, then the mind is necessarily dependent on the brain. Therefore, if visual sensation is a function of the mind, then the mind is necessarily dependent on the brain."

"Furthermore," Molly continues, "there are many cases where strokes have caused loss of memory, and also loss of speech. But if remembering is a mental function, then if the mind is not necessarily dependent on the brain, then strokes do not cause loss of memory. Therefore, if remembering is a mental function, then the mind is necessarily dependent on the brain."

"It may indeed be the case," Brian replies, "that memory—or at least certain kinds of memory—are dependent on the brain. And the same may be true of sensation. But that doesn't prove that consciousness as such is brain dependent. It seems to me that consciousness as such is a nonmaterial process, and that it can occur only in a nonmaterial entity, such as a soul. And if those two claims are true and the soul is immortal, then consciousness survives the death of the body. Thus, if the soul is immortal, then consciousness survives the death of the body."

"If memory goes with the brain," Molly replies, "then I wonder if the consciousness you speak of is in any way *your* consciousness. But setting that aside, are there any reasons for thinking that the soul is immortal?"

"I think there are," Brian replies. "If the soul is nonmaterial, then it has no parts, and if it has no parts, then it can't come 'a-part'—in other words it can't disintegrate. And if it can't disintegrate, then if nothing can destroy it, then it is immortal. But the soul can be destroyed only if God destroys it, and God does not destroy souls. Therefore, if the soul is nonmaterial, then it is immortal. I think Leibniz invented that argument."

"Fine," Molly says. "But what makes you think that you have a nonmaterial soul in the first place?"

"Well," Brian replies, "according to Descartes, I am essentially either a mind or a body. But if I can doubt that I have a body, then I am not essentially a body. And I can doubt that I have a body. For example I can imagine that I am in *The Matrix,* and that all of my sensations are illusions. If I am essentially a mind, then if the essence of mind is to be nonextended, then I am a nonextended substance. But the essence of mind, being different from the essence of body, is to be nonextended. And if I am a nonextended substance, then I am (or have) a nonmaterial soul. Therefore, I am (or have) a nonmaterial soul."

"Your argument is so abstruse that I don't find it very persuasive," says Molly, as she scratches her head. "I think the evidence is overwhelming that humans are the product of biological evolution, and if that is true and humans have souls, then there is a point in the course of evolution where humans either received or developed a soul. But there is no evidence that humans ever received a soul. Also, there is no evidence that humans ever developed a soul. Therefore, humans do not have souls."

"Wow, that sounds pretty far out," Brian replies. "Well, it looks like the service is ready to start, so we'll have to hang this up. But maybe we can continue it at a later date."

"Maybe we can," Molly replies.

6.5 Conditional Proof

PREVIEW

Returning to our hiking metaphor, suppose, while in the middle of your hike, you come to a fork in the trail. You consult your trail map but find no reference to it. Since the left fork seems to lead off in the direction you want to go, you formulate the assumption that | *this fork is a shortcut that connects with the main trail. You take the left fork and find that you were correct. Then you alter your trail map to show the existence of the fork and the alternate route. Making this alteration resembles conditional proof.*

Conditional proof is a method for deriving a conditional statement (either the conclusion or some intermediate line) that offers the usual advantage of being both shorter and simpler to use than the direct method. Moreover, some arguments have conclusions that cannot be derived by the direct method, so some form of conditional proof must be used on them. Conditional proof may thus be seen as completing the rules of inference. The method consists of assuming the antecedent of the required conditional statement on one line, deriving the consequent on a subsequent line, and then "discharging" this sequence of lines in a conditional statement that exactly replicates the one that was to be obtained.

> **conditional proof:** Assume the antecedent of a needed conditional statement, derive the consequent, and then discharge the indented sequence.

Any argument whose conclusion is a conditional statement is an immediate candidate for conditional proof. Consider the following example:

1. $A \supset (B \cdot C)$
2. $(B \vee D) \supset E$ / $A \supset E$

Using the direct method to derive the conclusion of this argument would require a proof having at least twelve lines, and the precise strategy to be followed in constructing it might not be immediately obvious. Nevertheless, we need only give cursory inspection to the argument to see that the conclusion does indeed follow from the premises. The conclusion states that if we have A, we then have E. Let us suppose, for a moment, that we do have A. We could then derive $B \cdot C$ from the first premise via modus ponens. Simplifying this expression we could derive B, and from this we could get $B \vee D$ via addition. E would then follow from the second premise via modus ponens. In other words, if we assume that we have A, we can get E. But this is exactly what the conclusion says. Thus, we have just proved that the conclusion follows from the premises.

> Conditional proof is usually simpler than direct proof.

The method of conditional proof consists of incorporating this simple thought process into the body of a proof sequence. A conditional proof for this argument requires only eight lines and is substantially simpler than a direct proof:

1. $A \supset (B \cdot C)$
2. $(B \vee D) \supset E$ / $A \supset E$
     3. A ACP
     4. $B \cdot C$ 1, 3, MP
     5. B 4, Simp
     6. $B \vee D$ 5, Add
     7. E 2, 6, MP
8. $A \supset E$ 3–7, CP

6

Lines 3 through 7 are indented to indicate their hypothetical character: They all depend on the assumption introduced in line 3 via ACP (assumption for conditional proof). These lines, which constitute the conditional proof sequence, tell us that if we assume A (line 3), we can derive E (line 7). In line 8 the conditional sequence is discharged in the conditional statement $A \supset E$, which simply reiterates the result of the conditional sequence. Since line 8 is not hypothetical, it is written adjacent to the original margin, under lines 1 and 2. A vertical line is added to the conditional sequence to emphasize the indentation.

The first step in constructing a conditional proof is to decide what should be assumed on the first line of the conditional sequence. While any statement whatsoever *can* be assumed on this line, only the right statement will lead to the desired result. The clue is always provided by the conditional statement to be obtained in the end. The antecedent of this statement is what must be assumed. For example, if the statement to be obtained is $(K \cdot L) \supset M$, then $K \cdot L$ should be assumed on the first line. This line is always indented and tagged with the designation "ACP." Once the initial assumption has been made, the second step is to derive the consequent of the desired conditional statement at the end of the conditional sequence. To do this, we simply apply the ordinary rules of inference to any previous line in the proof (including the assumed line), writing the result directly below the assumed line. The third and final step is to discharge the conditional sequence in a conditional statement. The antecedent of this conditional statement is whatever appears on the first line of the conditional sequence, and the consequent is whatever appears on the last line. For example, if $A \vee B$ is on the first line and $C \cdot D$ is on the last, the sequence is discharged by $(A \vee B) \supset (C \cdot D)$. This discharging line is always written adjacent to the original margin and is tagged with the designation "CP" (conditional proof) together with the numerals indicating the first through the last lines of the sequence.

Conditional proof can also be used to derive a line other than the conclusion of an argument. The following proof, which illustrates this fact, incorporates two conditional sequences one after the other within the scope of a single direct proof:

Conditional proof can be used to derive intermediate lines in a proof.

1. $G \supset (H \cdot I)$		
2. $J \supset (K \cdot L)$		
3. $G \vee J$	/ $H \vee K$	
4. G	ACP	
5. $H \cdot I$	1, 4, MP	
6. H	5, Simp	
7. $G \supset H$	4–6, CP	
8. J	ACP	
9. $K \cdot L$	2, 8, MP	
10. K	9, Simp	
11. $J \supset K$	8–10, CP	
12. $(G \supset H) \cdot (J \supset K)$	7, 11, Conj	
13. $H \vee K$	3, 12, CD	

The first conditional proof sequence gives us $G \supset H$, and the second $J \supset K$. These two lines are then conjoined and used together with line 3 to set up a constructive dilemma, from which the conclusion is derived.

This proof sequence provides a convenient opportunity to introduce an important rule governing conditional proof. The rule states that after a conditional proof sequence has been discharged, no line in the sequence may be used as a justification for a subsequent line in the proof. If, for example, line 5 in the proof just given were used as a justification

6

Gottlob Frege 1848–1925

Pictorial Press Ltd/Alamy

The German mathematician, logician, and philosopher Gottlob Frege (pronounced fray-ga) was born in Wismar, a small town in northern Germany on the Baltic Sea. His parents taught at a private girls' school, which his father had helped to found. Frege attended the local gymnasium, where he studied mathematics, and then the University of Jena, where he studied mathematics, philosophy, and chemistry. After two years he transferred to the University of Göttingen, earning a doctor's degree in mathematics at age twenty-four. He then returned to the University of Jena, where he taught until retiring in 1917. While there he married Margaret Liesburg, who bore him at least two children. The children died young, but years later the couple adopted a son, Alfred.

Frege spent his entire life analyzing the concept of number, developing theories of logic and language, and attempting to reduce arithmetic to logic. In 1879 he published the *Begriffsschrift* ("Concept-Script"), a work written in the tradition of Leibniz that develops a purely formal symbolic language to express any proposition in any area of human discourse. Five years later he published *Die Grundlagen der Arithmetik* ("The Foundations of Arithmetic"), a less technical work containing few symbols that outlined his goal of reducing arithmetic to logic. Then, nine years later he published Volume 1 of *Grundgesetze der Arithmetik* ("Basic Laws of Arithmetic"), which attempted to accomplish the first phase of this reduction.

None of these works were well received, for several reasons: They were ahead of their time, the symbolic notation of the technical works struck readers as bizarre, and they were written in German, whereas most of the new work in logic was being done by English speakers. In fact, the last of these works was so badly reviewed that Frege was forced to publish Volume 2 at his own expense. To make matters worse, in 1902, while Volume 2 was in proof, Frege received a letter from Bertrand Russell that left him "thunderstruck." He was later to remark that it had destroyed his entire life's work.

Basic Law 5 of the *Grundgesetze* provides for the creation of classes of things merely by describing the properties of their members. So Russell invited Frege to create the class of all classes that are not members of themselves, and he then asked whether this very class is a member of itself. If it is a member of itself, then it is one of those classes that are not members of themselves; but if is not a member of itself, then, again, it is one of those classes, and it is a member of itself. The derivation of this contradiction (which has come to be called Russell's paradox) meant that the axioms of the *Grundgesetze* were fatally inconsistent. Frege attempted a last-minute modification of his system, but the change proved unworkable.

Despite this setback, Frege is universally recognized today as one of the most important logicians and philosophers of all time. Single-handedly he developed quantification theory and predicate logic, and his analysis of the concept of number led to a general theory of meaning that introduced the important distinction between *Sinn* ("sense") and *Beduetung* ("reference"). Also, his work on concept clarification initiated the current movement known as analytic philosophy.

for line 9 or line 12, this rule would be violated, and the corresponding inference would be invalid. Once the conditional sequence is discharged, it is sealed off from the remaining part of the proof. The logic behind this rule is easy to understand. The lines in a conditional sequence are hypothetical in that they depend on the assumption stated in the first line. Because no mere assumption can provide any genuine support for anything, neither can any line that depends on such an assumption. When a conditional sequence is discharged, the assumption on which it rests is expressed as the antecedent of a conditional statement. This conditional statement *can* be used to support subsequent lines because it makes no claim that its antecedent is true. The conditional statement merely asserts that *if* its antecedent is true, then its consequent is true, and this, of course, is what has been established by the conditional sequence from which it is obtained.

Just as a conditional sequence can be used within the scope of a direct proof to derive a desired statement, one conditional sequence can be used within the scope of another to derive a desired statement. The following proof provides an example:

1. $L \supset [M \supset (N \lor O)]$
2. $M \supset \sim N$ / $L \supset (\sim M \lor O)$
    3. L ACP
    4. $M \supset (N \lor O)$ 1, 3, MP
        5. M ACP
        6. $N \lor O$ 4, 5, MP
        7. $\sim N$ 2, 5, MP
        8. O 6, 7, DS
    9. $M \supset O$ 5–8, CP
    10. $\sim M \lor O$ 9, Impl
11. $L \supset (\sim M \lor O)$ 3–10, CP

The rule introduced in connection with the previous example applies unchanged to examples of this sort. No line in the sequence 5–8 could be used to support any line subsequent to line 9, and no line in the sequence 3–10 could be used to support any line subsequent to line 11. Lines 3 or 4 could, of course, be used to support any line in the sequence 5–8.

One final reminder regarding conditional proof is that every conditional proof must be discharged. It is absolutely improper to end a proof on an indented line. If this rule is ignored, any conclusion one chooses can be derived from any set of premises. The following invalid proof illustrates this mistake:

1. P / $Q \supset R$
    2. $\sim Q$ ACP
    3. $\sim Q \lor R$ 2, Add
    4. $Q \supset R$ 2, Impl

I. Use conditional proof and the eighteen rules of inference to derive the conclusions of the following symbolized arguments. Having done so, attempt to derive the conclusions without using conditional proof.

★(1) 1. $N \supset O$
    2. $N \supset P$ / $N \supset (O \cdot P)$

(2) 1. $F \supset E$
    2. $(F \cdot E) \supset R$ / $F \supset R$

(3) 1. $G \supset T$
    2. $(T \lor S) \supset K$ / $G \supset K$

★(4) 1. $(G \vee H) \supset (S \cdot T)$
2. $(T \vee U) \supset (C \cdot D)$　　　／ $G \supset C$

(5) 1. $A \supset \sim(A \vee E)$　　　／ $A \supset F$

(6) 1. $J \supset (K \supset L)$
2. $J \supset (M \supset L)$
3. $\sim L$　　　／ $J \supset \sim(K \vee M)$

★(7) 1. $M \vee (N \cdot O)$　　　／ $\sim N \supset M$

(8) 1. $P \supset (Q \vee R)$
2. $(P \supset R) \supset (S \cdot T)$
3. $Q \supset R$　　　／ T

(9) 1. $H \supset (I \supset N)$
2. $(H \supset \sim I) \supset (M \vee N)$
3. $\sim N$　　　／ M

★(10) 1. $C \supset (A \cdot D)$
2. $B \supset (A \cdot E)$　　　／ $(C \vee B) \supset A$

(11) 1. $M \supset (K \supset L)$
2. $(L \vee N) \supset J$　　　／ $M \supset (K \supset J)$

(12) 1. $F \supset (G \cdot H)$　　　／ $(A \supset F) \supset (A \supset H)$

★(13) 1. $R \supset B$
2. $R \supset (B \supset F)$
3. $B \supset (F \supset H)$　　　／ $R \supset H$

(14) 1. $(F \cdot G) \equiv H$
2. $F \supset G$　　　／ $F \equiv H$

(15) 1. $C \supset (D \vee \sim E)$
2. $E \supset (D \supset F)$　　　／ $C \supset (E \supset F)$

★(16) 1. $Q \supset (R \supset S)$
2. $Q \supset (T \supset \sim U)$
3. $U \supset (R \vee T)$　　　／ $Q \supset (U \supset S)$

(17) 1. $N \supset (O \cdot P)$
2. $Q \supset (R \cdot S)$　　　／ $(P \supset Q) \supset (N \supset S)$

(18) 1. $E \supset (F \supset G)$
2. $H \supset (G \supset I)$
3. $(F \supset I) \supset (J \vee \sim H)$　　　／ $(E \cdot H) \supset J$

★(19) 1. $P \supset [(L \vee M) \supset (N \cdot O)]$
2. $(O \vee T) \supset W$　　　／ $P \supset (M \supset W)$

(20) 1. $A \supset [B \supset (C \cdot \sim D)]$
2. $(B \vee E) \supset (D \vee E)$　　　／ $(A \cdot B) \supset (C \cdot E)$

Translate the following arguments into symbolic form, using the letters in the order in which they are listed. Then use conditional proof and the eighteen rules of inference to derive the conclusion of each. Having done so, attempt to derive the conclusion without using conditional proof.

★1. If high-tech products are exported to Russia, then domestic industries will benefit. If the Russians can effectively utilize high-tech products, then their standard of living will improve. Therefore, if high-tech products are exported to Russia and the Russians can effectively utilize them, then their standard of living will improve and domestic industries will benefit. (H, D, U, S)

2. If the police take you into custody, then if they inform you that you have the right to remain silent, then whatever you say will be used against you. If the police inform you that you have the right to remain silent, then if whatever you say will be used against you, then you should not say anything. Therefore, if the police take you into custody, then if they inform you that you have the right to remain silent, then you should not say anything. (P, I, W, S)

3. A doctor must disconnect a dying patient from a respirator if and only if the fact that patients are self-determining implies that the doctor must follow the patient's orders. If a dying patient refuses treatment, then the doctor must disconnect the patient from a respirator and the patient will die peacefully. Patients are self-determining. Therefore, if a dying patient refuses treatment, then the doctor must follow the patient's orders. (D, S, F, R, P)

★4. If jails are overcrowded, then dangerous suspects will be released on their own recognizance. If jails are overcrowded and dangerous suspects are released on their own recognizance, then crime will increase. If no new jails are built and crime increases, then innocent victims will pay the price of increased crime. Therefore, if jails are overcrowded, then if no new jails are built, then innocent victims will pay the price of increased crime. (J, D, C, N, I)

5. If astronauts attempt interplanetary space travel, then heavy shielding will be required to protect them from solar radiation. If massive amounts of either fuel or water are carried, then the spacecraft must be very large. Therefore, if heavy shielding is required to protect the astronauts from solar radiation only if massive amounts of fuel are carried, then if astronauts attempt interplanetary space travel, then the spacecraft must be very large. (A, H, F, W, L)

aplia™
Visit Aplia for section-specific problem sets.

6.6   Indirect Proof

PREVIEW

Let us return to the fork in the trail that we talked about earlier. Suppose you take the left fork but after hiking some distance you reach a dead end. You then alter your trail map showing that the left fork leads to a dead end. This means that the right fork (the non-left fork) is the correct route. Such a procedure resembles indirect proof. In an indirect proof you formulate an assumption inside a proof sequence, and when it leads to a contradiction, you conclude that the assumed statement is false, so its negation is true.

6

Indirect proof is a technique similar to conditional proof that can be used on any argument to derive either the conclusion or some intermediate line leading to the conclusion. It consists of assuming the negation of the statement to be obtained, using this assumption to derive a contradiction, and then concluding that the original assumption is false. This last step, of course, establishes the truth of the statement to be obtained. The following proof sequence uses indirect proof to derive the conclusion:

indirect proof: Assume the negation of the needed statement, derive a contradiction, then discharge the indented sequence.

```
 1. (A ∨ B) ⊃ (C • D)
 2. C ⊃ ~D              / ~A
       3. A             AIP
       4. A ∨ B         3, Add
       5. C • D         1, 4, MP
       6. C             5, Simp
       7. ~D            2, 6, MP
       8. D • C         5, Com
       9. D             8, Simp
      10. D • ~D        7, 9, Conj
11. ~A                  3–10, IP
```

The indirect proof sequence (lines 3–10) begins by assuming the negation of the conclusion. Since the conclusion is a negated statement, it shortens the proof to assume *A* instead of ~ ~*A*. This assumption, which is tagged "AIP" (assumption for indirect proof), leads to a contradiction in line 10. Since any assumption that leads to a contradiction is false, the indirect sequence is discharged (line 11) by asserting the negation of the assumption made in line 3. This line is then tagged with the designation "IP" (indirect proof) together with the numerals indicating the scope of the indirect sequence from which it is obtained.

Indirect proof can be used to derive intermediate lines in a proof.

Indirect proof can also be used to derive an intermediate line leading to the conclusion. Example:

```
 1. E ⊃ [(F ∨ G) ⊃ (H • J)]
 2. E • ~(J ∨ K)            / ~(F ∨ K)
 3. E                       2, Simp
 4. (F ∨ G) ⊃ (H • J)       1, 3, MP
 5. ~(J ∨ K) • E            2, Com
 6. ~(J ∨ K)                5, Simp
 7. ~J • ~K                 6, DM
       8. F                 AIP
       9. F ∨ G             8, Add
      10. H • J             4, 9, MP
      11. J • H             10, Com
      12. J                 11, Simp
      13. ~J                7, Simp
      14. J • ~J            12, 13, Conj
15. ~F                      8–14, IP
16. ~K • ~J                 7, Com
17. ~K                      16, Simp
18. ~F • ~K                 15, 17, Conj
19. ~(F ∨ K)                18, DM
```

Indirect proof can be used to derive the conclusion of any argument.

The indirect proof sequence begins with the assumption of *F* (line 8), leads to a contradiction (line 14), and is discharged (line 15) by asserting the negation of the assumption. One should consider indirect proof whenever a line in a proof appears difficult to obtain.

As with conditional proof, when an indirect proof sequence is discharged, no line in the sequence may be used as a justification for a subsequent line in the proof. In reference to the last proof, this means that none of the lines 8–14 could be used as a justification for any of the lines 16–19. Occasionally, this rule requires certain priorities in the derivation of lines. For example, for the purpose of deriving the contradiction, lines 6 and 7 could have been included as part of the indirect sequence. But this would not have been advisable, because line 7 is needed as a justification for line 16, which lies outside the indirect sequence. If lines 6 and 7 had been included within the indirect sequence, they would have had to be repeated after the sequence had been discharged to allow $\sim K$ to be derived on a line outside the sequence.

Just as a conditional sequence may be constructed within the scope of another conditional sequence, so a conditional sequence may be constructed within the scope of an indirect sequence, and, conversely, an indirect sequence may be constructed within the scope of either a conditional sequence or another indirect sequence. The next example illustrates the use of an indirect sequence within the scope of a conditional sequence:

1.	$L \supset [\sim M \supset (N \bullet O)]$	
2.	$\sim N \bullet P$	$/ L \supset (M \bullet P)$
3.	L	ACP
4.	$\sim M \supset (N \bullet O)$	1, 3, MP
5.	$\sim M$	AIP
6.	$N \bullet O$	4, 5, MP
7.	N	6, Simp
8.	$\sim N$	2, Simp
9.	$N \bullet \sim N$	7, 8, Conj
10.	$\sim \sim M$	5–9, IP
11.	M	10, DN
12.	$P \bullet \sim N$	2, Com
13.	P	12, Simp
14.	$M \bullet P$	11, 13, Conj
15.	$L \supset (M \bullet P)$	3–14, CP

The indirect sequence (lines 5–9) is discharged (line 10) by asserting the negation of the assumption made in line 5. The conditional sequence (lines 3–14) is discharged (line 15) in the conditional statement that has the first line of the sequence as its antecedent and the last line as its consequent.

Indirect proof provides a convenient way for proving the validity of an argument having a tautology for its conclusion. In fact, the only way in which the conclusion of many such arguments can be derived is through either conditional or indirect proof.

For the following argument, indirect proof is the easier of the two:

1.	S	$/ T \vee \sim T$
2.	$\sim (T \vee \sim T)$	AIP
3.	$\sim T \bullet \sim \sim T$	2, DM
4.	$\sim \sim (T \vee \sim T)$	2–3, IP
5.	$T \vee \sim T$	4, DN

Here is another example of an argument having a tautology as its conclusion. In this case, since the conclusion is a conditional statement, conditional proof is the easier alternative:

```
1. S                    / T ⊃ T
  2. T                  ACP
  3. T ∨ T              2, Add
  4. T                  3, Taut
5. T ⊃ T                2–4, CP
```

The similarity of indirect proof to conditional proof may be illustrated by returning to the first example presented in this section. In the proof that follows, conditional proof—not indirect proof—is used to derive the conclusion:

```
1. (A ∨ B) ⊃ (C • D)
2. C ⊃ ~D               / ~A
    3. A                ACP
    4. A ∨ B            3, Add
    5. C • D            1, 4, MP
    6. C                5, Simp
    7. ~D               2, 6, MP
    8. D • C            5, Com
    9. D                8, Simp
   10. D ∨ ~A           9, Add
   11. ~A               7, 10, DS
12. A ⊃ ~A              3–11, CP
13. ~A ∨ ~A             12, Impl
14. ~A                  13, Taut
```

This example illustrates how a conditional proof can be used to derive the conclusion of *any* argument, whether or not the conclusion is a conditional statement. Simply begin by assuming the negation of the conclusion, derive contradictory statements on separate lines, and use these lines to set up a disjunctive syllogism yielding the negation of the assumption as the last line of the conditional sequence. Then, discharge the sequence and use tautology to derive the negation of the assumption outside the sequence.

Conditional proof can be used to derive the conclusion of any argument.

Indirect proof can be viewed as a variety of conditional proof in that it amounts to a modification of the way in which the indented sequence is discharged, resulting in an overall shortening of the proof for many arguments. The indirect proof for the argument just given is repeated as follows, with the requisite changes noted in the margin:

```
1. (A ∨ B) ⊃ (C • D)
2. C ⊃ ~D               / ~A
    3. A                AIP
    4. A ∨ B            3, Add
    5. C • D            1, 4, MP
    6. C                5, Simp
    7. ~D               2, 6, MP
    8. D • C            5, Com
    9. D                8, Simp
   10. D • ~D           7, 9, Conj ⎫ ———— changed
11. ~A                  3–10, IP   ⎭
```

The reminder at the end of the previous section regarding conditional proof pertains to indirect proof as well: It is essential that every indirect proof be discharged. No proof can be ended on an indented line. If this rule is ignored, indirect proof, like conditional proof, can produce any conclusion whatsoever. The following invalid proof illustrates such a mistake:

1.	P	/ Q
2.	Q	AIP
3.	$Q \vee Q$	2, Add
4.	Q	3, Taut

EXERCISE 6.6

I. Use either indirect proof or conditional proof (or both) and the eighteen rules of inference to derive the conclusions of the following symbolized arguments. Having done so, attempt to derive the conclusions without using indirect proof or conditional proof.

★(1) 1. $(S \vee T) \supset {\sim}S$ / ${\sim}S$

(2) 1. $(K \supset K) \supset R$
     2. $(R \vee M) \supset N$ / N

(3) 1. $(C \cdot D) \supset E$
     2. $(D \cdot E) \supset F$ / $(C \cdot D) \supset F$

★(4) 1. $H \supset (L \supset K)$
     2. $L \supset (K \supset {\sim}L)$ / ${\sim}H \vee {\sim}L$

(5) 1. $S \supset (T \vee {\sim}U)$
     2. $U \supset ({\sim}T \vee R)$
     3. $(S \cdot U) \supset {\sim}R$ / ${\sim}S \vee {\sim}U$

(6) 1. ${\sim}A \supset (B \cdot C)$
     2. $D \supset {\sim}C$ / $D \supset A$

★(7) 1. $(E \vee F) \supset (C \cdot D)$
     2. $(D \vee G) \supset H$
     3. $E \vee G$ / H

(8) 1. ${\sim}M \supset (N \cdot O)$
     2. $N \supset P$
     3. $O \supset {\sim}P$ / M

(9) 1. $(R \vee S) \supset T$
     2. $(P \vee Q) \supset T$
     3. $R \vee P$ / T

★(10) 1. K / $S \supset (T \supset S)$

(11) 1. $(A \vee B) \supset C$
     2. $({\sim}A \vee D) \supset E$ / $C \vee E$

(12) 1. $(K \vee L) \supset (M \cdot N)$
     2. $(N \vee O) \supset (P \cdot {\sim}K)$ / ${\sim}K$

★(13) 1. $[C \supset (D \supset C)] \supset E$ $\qquad$ / E

(14) 1. F $\qquad$ / $(G \supset H) \vee (\sim G \supset J)$

(15) 1. $B \supset (K \cdot M)$
$\quad$ 2. $(B \cdot M) \supset (P \equiv \sim P)$ $\qquad$ / $\sim B$

★(16) 1. $(N \vee O) \supset (C \cdot D)$
$\quad$ 2. $(D \vee K) \supset (P \vee \sim C)$
$\quad$ 3. $(P \vee G) \supset \sim(N \cdot D)$ $\qquad$ / $\sim N$

(17) 1. $(R \cdot S) \equiv (G \cdot H)$
$\quad$ 2. $R \supset S$
$\quad$ 3. $H \supset G$ $\qquad$ / $R \equiv H$

(18) 1. $K \supset [(M \vee N) \supset (P \cdot Q)]$
$\quad$ 2. $L \supset [(Q \vee R) \supset (S \cdot \sim N)]$ $\qquad$ / $(K \cdot L) \supset \sim N$

★(19) 1. $A \supset [(N \vee \sim N) \supset (S \vee T)]$
$\quad$ 2. $T \supset \sim(F \vee \sim F)$ $\qquad$ / $A \supset S$

(20) 1. $F \supset [(C \supset C) \supset G]$
$\quad$ 2. $G \supset \{[H \supset (E \supset H)] \supset (K \cdot \sim K)\}$ $\qquad$ / $\sim F$

II. Translate the following arguments into symbolic form, using the letters in the order in which they are listed. Then use indirect proof and the eighteen rules of inference to derive the conclusion of each. Having done so, attempt to derive the conclusion without using indirect proof.

★1. If government deficits continue at their present rate and a recession sets in, then interest on the national debt will become unbearable and the government will default on its loans. If a recession sets in, then the government will not default on its loans. Therefore, either government deficits will not continue at their present rate or a recession will not set in. (C, R, I, D)

2. If either the sea turtle population continues to decrease or rescue efforts are commenced to save the sea turtle from extinction, then nesting sanctuaries will be created and the indiscriminate slaughter of these animals will be halted. If either nesting sanctuaries are created or poachers are arrested, then if the indiscriminate slaughter of these animals is halted, then the sea turtle population will not continue to decrease. Therefore, the sea turtle population will not continue to decrease. (C, R, N, I, P)

3. If asbestos workers sue their employers, then if punitive damages are awarded, then their employers will declare bankruptcy. If asbestos workers sue their employers, then punitive damages will be awarded. If asbestos workers contract asbestosis, then either they will sue their employers or their employers will declare bankruptcy. Therefore, either asbestos workers will not contract asbestosis or their employers will declare bankruptcy. (S, P, B, C)

★4. If astronauts spend long periods in zero gravity only if calcium is resorbed in their bodies, then astronauts on a Mars voyage will arrive with brittle bones. If astronauts attempt a voyage to Mars only if they spend long periods in zero gravity, then astronauts on a Mars voyage will arrive with brittle bones. Therefore, astronauts on a Mars voyage will arrive with brittle bones. (Z, C, B, V)

5. Either deposits should be required on beer and soft-drink containers, or these containers will be discarded along highways and the countryside will look like a dump. If these containers will be discarded either in parks or along highways, then deposits should be required on soft-drink containers. Therefore, deposits should be required on soft-drink containers. (*B, S, H, C, P*)

6.7 Proving Logical Truths

PREVIEW

Let us return to your hike one last time. Suppose that after walking for several hours you find that you are hopelessly lost, and you suspect that you are going in a circle. So, you break a branch off a fallen tree and poke it into the ground beside the trail. After walking another hour, you come upon the same branch. This proves it. Your procedure is a little like proving a tautology. You have proved that if you walk forward from this point you will reach the same point, but this tells you nothing about where you are on the map.

Logical truth (tautology): A statement that is necessarily true.

Both conditional and indirect proof can be used to establish the truth of a logical truth (tautology). Tautological statements can be treated as if they were the conclusions of arguments having no premises. Such a procedure is suggested by the fact that any argument having a tautology for its conclusion is valid regardless of what its premises are. As we saw in the previous section, the proof for such an argument does not use the premises at all but derives the conclusion as the exclusive consequence of either a conditional or an indirect sequence. Using this strategy for logical truths, we write the statement to be proved as if it were the conclusion of an argument, and we indent the first line in the proof and tag it as being the beginning of either a conditional or an indirect sequence. In the end, this sequence is appropriately discharged to yield the desired statement form.

Tautologies are proved using conditional and/or indirect proof.

Tautologies expressed in the form of conditional statements are most easily proved via a conditional sequence. The following example uses two such sequences, one within the scope of the other:

		/ $P \supset (Q \supset P)$
1.	P	ACP
2.	Q	ACP
3.	$P \lor P$	1, Add
4.	P	3, Taut
5.	$Q \supset P$	2–4, CP
6.	$P \supset (Q \supset P)$	1–5, CP

Use conditional proof to derive conditional tautologies.

Notice that line 6 restores the proof to the original margin—line 1 is indented because it introduces the conditional sequence.

Here is a proof of the same statement using an indirect proof. The indirect sequence begins, as usual, with the negation of the statement to be proved:

		/ P ⊃ (Q ⊃ P)
1.	~[P ⊃ (Q ⊃ P)]	AIP
2.	~[~P ∨ (Q ⊃ P)]	1, Impl
3.	~[~P ∨ (~Q ∨ P)]	2, Impl
4.	~~P • ~(~Q ∨ P)	3, DM
5.	P • ~(~Q ∨ P)	4, DN
6.	P • (~~Q • ~P)	5, DM
7.	P • (~P • ~~Q)	6, Com
8.	(P • ~P) • ~~Q	7, Assoc
9.	P • ~P	8, Simp
10.	~~[P ⊃ (Q ⊃ P)]	1–9, IP
11.	P ⊃ (Q ⊃ P)	10, DN

More-complex conditional statements are proved by merely extending the technique used in the first proof. In the following proof, notice how each conditional sequence begins by asserting the antecedent of the conditional statement to be derived:

> Use indirect proof to derive any tautology.

		/ [P ⊃ (Q ⊃ R)] ⊃ [(P ⊃ Q) ⊃ (P ⊃ R)]
1.	P ⊃ (Q ⊃ R)	ACP
2.	P ⊃ Q	ACP
3.	P	ACP
4.	Q ⊃ R	1, 3, MP
5.	Q	2, 3, MP
6.	R	4, 5, MP
7.	P ⊃ R	3–6, CP
8.	(P ⊃ Q) ⊃ (P ⊃ R)	2–7, CP
9.	[P ⊃ (Q ⊃ R)] ⊃ [(P ⊃ Q) ⊃ (P ⊃ R)]	1–8, CP

Tautologies expressed as equivalences are usually proved using two conditional sequences, one after the other. Example:

		/ P ≡ [P • (Q ⊃ P)]
1.	P	ACP
2.	P ∨ ~Q	1, Add
3.	~Q ∨ P	2, Com
4.	Q ⊃ P	3, Impl
5.	P • (Q ⊃ P)	1, 4, Conj
6.	P ⊃ [P • (Q ⊃ P)]	1–5, CP
7.	P • (Q ⊃ P)	ACP
8.	P	7, Simp
9.	[P • (Q ⊃ P)] ⊃ P	7–8, CP
10.	{line 6} • {line 9}	6, 9, Conj
11.	P ≡ [P • (Q ⊃ P)]	10, Equiv

6

Use conditional proof or indirect proof and the eighteen rules of inference to establish the truth of the following tautologies.

★1. $P \supset [(P \supset Q) \supset Q]$

2. $(\sim P \supset Q) \vee (P \supset R)$

3. $P \equiv [P \vee (Q \bullet P)]$

★4. $(P \supset Q) \supset [(P \bullet R) \supset (Q \bullet R)]$

5. $(P \vee \sim Q) \supset [(\sim P \vee R) \supset (Q \supset R)]$

6. $P \equiv [P \bullet (Q \vee \sim Q)]$

★7. $(P \supset Q) \vee (\sim Q \supset P)$

8. $(P \supset Q) \equiv [P \supset (P \bullet Q)]$

9. $[(P \supset Q) \bullet (P \supset R)] \supset [P \supset (Q \bullet R)]$

★10. $[\sim (P \bullet \sim Q) \bullet \sim Q] \supset \sim P$

11. $(P \supset Q) \vee (Q \supset P)$

12. $[P \supset (Q \supset R)] \equiv [Q \supset (P \supset R)]$

★13. $(P \supset Q) \supset [(P \supset \sim Q) \supset \sim P]$

14. $[(P \supset Q) \supset R] \supset [(R \supset \sim R) \supset P]$

15. $(\sim P \vee Q) \supset [(P \vee \sim Q) \supset (P \equiv Q)]$

★16. $\sim [(P \supset \sim P) \bullet (\sim P \supset P)]$

17. $P \supset [(Q \bullet \sim Q) \supset R]$

18. $[(P \bullet Q) \vee R] \supset [(\sim R \vee Q) \supset (P \supset Q)]$

★19. $P \equiv [P \vee (Q \bullet \sim Q)]$

20. $P \supset [Q \equiv (P \supset Q)]$

aplia™

Visit Aplia for section-specific problem sets.

Summary

Natural Deduction in Propositional Logic:
- A step-by-step method for proving the validity of propositional type arguments.
- Shows exactly how the conclusion "comes out" of the premises.
- Consists in applying eighteen rules of inference to the premises and deriving the conclusion as the last line in a sequence of lines.
- Success in using this method requires much practice.

Rules of Inference:
- Rules of implication ("one-way" rules):
  - The premise(s) can be used to derive the conclusion.
  - The conclusion cannot be used to derive the premise(s).

- Rules of replacement ("two-way" rules):
  - Expressed as logical equivalencies.
  - Either side of the equivalence can replace the other.
  - Can be used to "deconstruct" the conclusion for insight into how to derive it.

Conditional Proof:
- A method for deriving a conditional statement.
- Assume the antecedent of the desired conditional on an indented line.
- Derive the consequent of the desired conditional statement.
- Discharge the indented sequence in a conditional statement having the first line of the sequence as the antecedent and the last line as the consequent.
- This method can greatly simplify many proofs.

Indirect Proof:
- A method for deriving any kind of statement.
- Assume the negation of the desired statement (often this is the conclusion) on an indented line.
- Derive a contradiction.
- Any assumption that necessarily leads to a contradiction is false.
- Discharge the indented sequence in a statement consisting of the negation of the first line of the sequence.

Proving Logical Truths (Tautologies):
- Use conditional proof to derive conditionals and biconditionals.
  - Assume the antecedent of the conditional statement on an indented line.
  - Derive the consequent.
  - Discharge the indented sequence in the usual way.
  - Biconditionals require two indented sequences.

- Use indirect proof to derive any logical truth:
  - Assume the negation of the logical truth on an indented line.
  - Derive a contradiction.
  - Discharge the indented sequence in the usual way.

6

Predicate Logic

7.1   Symbols and Translation

PREVIEW

Suppose you are starting up a small business and want to construct a website to promote your product. First, you will assemble the individual web pages. The materials you will use include text, photos, and possibly some video. Constructing an argument in the language of predicate logic is a little like constructing a website. The individual pages are the symbolized premises and conclusion, and the materials you use for constructing them are the symbols introduced in this section of the chapter.

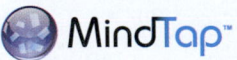 Your personal learning experience—learn anywhere, anytime.

Techniques were developed in earlier chapters for evaluating two basically different kinds of arguments. The chapter on categorical syllogisms dealt with arguments such as the following:

> All student hookups are quickie sexual encounters.
> No quickie sexual encounters are committed relationships.
> Therefore, no student hookups are committed relationships.

In such arguments the fundamental components are *terms*, and the validity of the argument depends on the arrangement of the terms within the premises and conclusion.

The chapter on propositional logic, on the other hand, dealt with arguments such as this:

> If chronic stress is reduced, then relaxation increases and health improves.
> If health improves, then people live longer.
> Therefore, if chronic stress is reduced, then people live longer.

In such arguments the fundamental components are not terms but *statements*. The validity of these arguments depends not on the arrangement of the terms within the statements but on the arrangement of the statements themselves as simple units.

Not all arguments, however, can be assigned to one or the other of these two groups. There is a third type that is a kind of hybrid, sharing features with both categorical syllogisms and propositional arguments. Consider, for example, the following:

> Catherine Zeta-Jones is rich and beautiful.
> If a woman is either rich or famous, she is happy.
> Therefore, Catherine Zeta-Jones is happy.

The validity of this argument depends on both the arrangement of the terms and the arrangement of the statements. Accordingly, neither syllogistic logic nor propositional logic alone is sufficient to establish its validity. What is needed is a third kind of logic that combines the distinctive features of syllogistic logic and propositional logic. This third kind is called **predicate logic**.

The fundamental component in predicate logic is the **predicate**, symbolized by uppercase letters ($A, B, C, \ldots X, Y, Z$), called **predicate symbols**. Here are some examples of bare predicates:

English predicate	Symbolic predicate
___ is a rabbit	R __
___ is gigantic	G __
___ is a doctor	D __
___ is helpless	H __

The blank space immediately following the predicate letter is not part of the predicate; rather, it indicates the place for some lowercase letter that will represent the subject of the statement. Depending on what lowercase letter is used, and on the additional symbolism involved, symbolic predicates may be used to translate three distinct kinds of statements: singular statements, universal statements, and particular statements.

A **singular statement**, you may recall from Section 3.6, is a statement that makes an assertion about a specifically named person, place, thing, or time. Translating a singular statement involves writing a lowercase letter corresponding to the subject of the

predicate logic: A kind of logic in which the fundamental components are predicates.

predicates: Expressions of the form "is a dog," "is an artist," "is red," and so forth.

singular statement: A statement such as "Alice is a pianist."

statement to the immediate right of the uppercase letter corresponding to the predicate. The letters that are allocated to serve as abbreviated names of individuals are the first twenty-three letters of the alphabet (*a, b, c, . . . u, v, w*). These letters are called **individual constants**. Here are some examples of translated statements:

Statement	Symbolic translation
Socrates is mortal.	*Ms*
Tokyo is populous.	*Pt*
The *Sun-Times* is a newspaper.	*Ns*
King Lear is not a fairy tale.	~*Fk*
Berlioz was not a German.	~*Gb*

Compound arrangements of singular statements may be translated by using the familiar connectives of propositional logic. Here are some examples:

Statement	Symbolic translation
If Paris is beautiful, then Andre told the truth.	*Bp* ⊃ *Ta*
Irene is either a doctor or a lawyer.	*Di* ∨ *Li*
Senator Wilkins will be elected only if he campaigns.	*Ew* ⊃ *Cw*
General Motors will prosper if either Nissan is crippled by a strike or Subaru declares bankruptcy.	(*Cn* ∨ *Ds*) ⊃ *Pg*
Indianapolis gets rain if and only if Chicago and Milwaukee get snow.	*Ri* ≡ (*Sc* • *Sm*)

Recall from Chapter 3 that a **universal statement** is a statement that makes an assertion about every member of its subject class. Such statements are either affirmative or negative, depending on whether the statement affirms or denies that the members of the subject class are members of the predicate class. The key to translating universal statements is provided by the Boolean interpretation of these statements (see Section 3.3):

Statement form	Boolean interpretation
All *S* are *P*.	If anything is an *S*, then it is a *P*.
No *S* are *P*.	If anything is an *S*, then it is not a *P*.

According to the Boolean interpretation, universal statements are translated as conditionals. We have a symbol (the horseshoe) to translate conditional statements, so we may use it to translate universal statements. What is still needed, however, is a symbol to indicate that universal statements make an assertion about *every* member of the *S* class. This symbol is called the **universal quantifier**. It is formed by placing a lowercase letter in parentheses, (*x*), and is translated as "for any *x*." The letters that are allocated for forming the universal quantifier are the last three letters of the alphabet (*x, y, z*). These letters are called **individual variables**. They can stand for any item at random in the universe, and they have individual constants as substitution instances.

The horseshoe operator and the universal quantifier are combined to translate universal statements as follows:

Statement form	Symbolic translation	Verbal meaning
All S are P.	$(x)(Sx \supset Px)$	For any x, if x is an S, then x is a P.
No S are P.	$(x)(Sx \supset {\sim}Px)$	For any x, if x is an S, then x is not a P.

Universal statements are usually translated as conditionals.

Because an individual variable can stand for any item at random in the universe, the expression $(x)(Sx \supset Px)$ means "If anything is an S, then it is a P." Also $(x)(Sx \supset {\sim}Px)$ means "If anything is an S, then it is not a P." The fact that these expressions are equivalent to the Boolean interpretation of universal statements may be seen by recalling how the Boolean interpretation is represented by Venn diagrams (see Section 3.3). The Venn diagrams corresponding to the two universal statement forms are as follows:

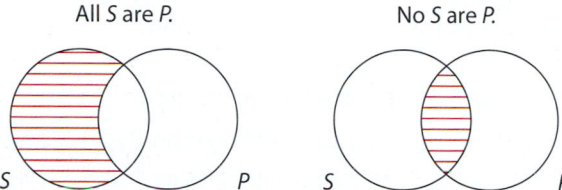

Where shading designates emptiness, the diagram on the left asserts that if anything is in the S circle, it is also in the P circle, and the one on the right asserts that if anything is in the S circle, it is not in the P circle. This is exactly what is asserted by the symbolic expressions just given. These symbolic expressions may therefore be taken as being exactly synonymous with the Boolean interpretation of universal statements.

A possible source of confusion at this point concerns the fact that both S and P in the symbolic expressions are predicates, whereas in the original statement forms S is the subject and P is the predicate. Any problem in this regard vanishes, however, once one understands what happens when universal statements are converted into conditionals. When so converted, S becomes the predicate of the antecedent and P becomes the predicate of the consequent. In other words, in the conditional "If anything is an S, then it is a P," both S and P are predicates. Thus, using predicate symbolism to translate universal statements leads to no difficulties. When translating these statements, the point to remember is simply this: The subject of the original statement is represented by a capital letter in the antecedent, and the predicate by a capital letter in the consequent. Here are some examples:

Statement	Symbolic translation
All skyscrapers are tall.	$(x)(Sx \supset Tx)$
No frogs are birds.	$(x)(Fx \supset {\sim}Bx)$
All ambassadors are statesmen.	$(x)(Ax \supset Sx)$
No diamonds are rubies.	$(x)(Dx \supset {\sim}Rx)$

In these examples, the expressions $Sx \supset Tx$, $Fx \supset {\sim}Bx$, and so on are called statement functions. A **statement function** is the expression that remains when a quantifier is removed from a statement. It is a mere pattern for a statement. It makes no definite assertion about anything in the universe, has no truth value, and cannot be translated as a statement. The variables that occur in statement functions are called **free variables** because they are not bound by any quantifier. In contrast, the variables that occur in statements are called **bound variables**.

7

In using quantifiers to translate statements, we adopt a convention similar to the one adopted for the tilde operator. That is, the quantifier governs only the expression immediately following it. For example, in the statement $(x)(Ax \supset Bx)$ the universal quantifier governs the entire statement function in parentheses—namely, $Ax \supset Bx$. But in the expression $(x)Ax \supset Bx$, the universal quantifier governs only the statement function Ax. The same convention is adopted for the existential quantifier, which will be introduced presently.

Recall from Chapter 3 that a **particular statement** is a statement that makes an assertion about one or more unnamed members of the subject class. As with universal statements, particular statements are either affirmative or negative, depending on whether the statement affirms or denies that members of the subject class are members of the predicate class. Also, as with universal statements, the key to translating particular statements is provided by the Boolean interpretation:

Statement form	Boolean interpretation
Some S are P.	At least one thing is an S and it is also a P.
Some S are not P.	At least one thing is an S and it is not a P.

In other words, particular statements are translated as conjunctions. Since we are already familiar with the symbol for conjunction (the dot), the only additional symbol that we need in order to translate these statements is a symbol for existence. This is provided by the **existential quantifier**, formed by placing a variable to the right of a backward E in parentheses, thus: $(\exists x)$. This symbol is translated "there exists an x such that." The existential quantifier is combined with the dot operator to translate particular statements as follows:

Statement form	Translation	Symbolic verbal meaning
Some S are P.	$(\exists x)(Sx \bullet Px)$	There exists an x such that x is an S and x is a P.
Some S are not P.	$(\exists x)(Sx \bullet {\sim}Px)$	There exists an x such that x is an S and x is not a P.

As in the symbolic expression of universal statements, the letter x is an individual variable, which can stand for any item in the universe. Accordingly, the expression $(\exists x)(Sx \bullet Px)$ means "Something exists that is both an S and a P," and $(\exists x)(Sx \bullet {\sim}Px)$ means "Something exists that is an S and not a P." To see the equivalence of these expressions with the Boolean (and Aristotelian) interpretation of particular statements, it is again useful to recall how these statements are represented by Venn diagrams:

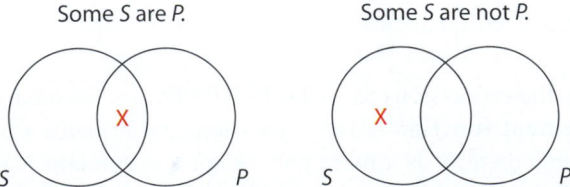

Where the X designates at least one existing item, the diagram on the left asserts that something exists that is both an S and a P, and the one on the right asserts that something exists that is an S and not a P. In other words, these diagrams assert exactly

particular statement:
A statement such as "Some horses are brown" and "Some books are not long."

existential quantifier:
A symbolic expression such as "$(\exists x)$," which means "there exists an x."

Particular statements are usually translated as conjunctions.

7

the same thing as the symbolic expressions just given. These symbolic expressions, therefore, exactly express the Boolean (and Aristotelian) interpretation of particular statements. Here are some examples:

Statement	Symbolic translation
Some men are paupers.	$(\exists x)(Mx \bullet Px)$
Some diseases are not contagious.	$(\exists x)(Dx \bullet \sim Cx)$
Some jobs are boring.	$(\exists x)(Jx \bullet Bx)$
Some vehicles are not motorcycles.	$(\exists x)(Vx \bullet \sim Mx)$

The general rule to follow in translating statements in predicate logic is always to make an effort to understand the meaning of the statement to be translated. If the statement makes an assertion about every member of its subject class, a universal quantifier should be used to translate it; but if it makes an assertion about only one or more members of this class, an existential quantifier should be used.

Many of the principles developed in syllogistic logic (see Section 3.6) may be carried over into predicate logic. Specifically, it should be understood that statements beginning with the words *only* and *none but* are exclusive propositions. When these statements are translated, the term occurring first in the original statement becomes the consequent in the symbolic expression, and the term occurring second becomes the antecedent. One of the few differences in this respect between predicate logic and syllogistic logic concerns singular statements. In syllogistic logic, singular statements are translated as universals, while in predicate logic, as we have seen, they are translated in a unique way. Here are some examples of a variety of statements:

Statement	Symbolic translation
There are happy marriages.	$(\exists x)(Mx \bullet Hx)$
Every pediatrician loses sleep.	$(x)(Px \supset Lx)$
Animals exist.	$(\exists x)Ax$
Unicorns do not exist.	$\sim(\exists x)Ux$ or $(x)\sim Ux$
Anything is conceivable.	$(x)Cx$
Sea lions are mammals.	$(x)(Sx \supset Mx)$
Sea lions live in these caves.	$(\exists x)(Sx \bullet Lx)$
Egomaniacs are not pleasant companions.	$(x)(Ex \supset \sim Px)$
A few egomaniacs did not arrive on time.	$(\exists x)(Ex \bullet \sim Ax)$
Only close friends were invited to the wedding.	$(x)(Ix \supset Cx)$
None but citizens are eligible to vote.	$(x)(Ex \supset Cx)$
It is not the case that every Girl Scout sells cookies.	$\sim(x)(Gx \supset Sx)$ or $(\exists x)(Gx \bullet \sim Sx)$
Not a single psychologist attended the convention.	$\sim(\exists x)(Px \bullet Ax)$ or $(x)(Px \supset \sim Ax)$

As these examples illustrate, the general procedure in translating statements in predicate logic is to render universal statements as conditionals preceded by a universal quantifier, and particular statements as conjunctions preceded by an existential quantifier. However, as the third and fifth examples indicate, there are exceptions to this procedure. A statement that makes an assertion about literally everything in the universe is translated in terms of a single predicate preceded by a universal quantifier, and a statement that asserts that some class of things simply exists is translated in terms of a single predicate preceded by an existential quantifier. The last two examples illustrate that a particular statement is equivalent to a negated universal, and vice versa. The first of these is equivalent to "Some Girl Scouts do not sell cookies" and the second to "No psychologists attended the convention." Actually, any quantified statement can be translated using either a universal or an existential quantifier, provided that one of them is negated. The equivalence of these two forms of expression will be analyzed further in Section 7.3.

More-complex statements may be translated by following the basic rules just presented. Examples:

Statement	Symbolic translation
Only snakes and lizards thrive in the desert.	$(x)[Tx \supset (Sx \lor Lx)]$
Oranges and lemons are citrus fruits.	$(x)[(Ox \lor Lx) \supset Cx]$
Ripe apples are crunchy and delicious.	$(x)[(Rx \cdot Ax) \supset (Cx \cdot Dx)]$
Azaleas bloom if and only if they are fertilized.	$(x)[Ax \supset (Bx \equiv Fx)]$
Peaches are edible unless they are rotten.	$(x)[Px \supset (\sim Rx \supset Ex)]$
	or
	$(x)[Px \supset (Ex \lor Rx)]$
Cats and dogs bite if they are frightened or harassed.	$(x)\{(Cx \lor Dx) \supset [(Fx \lor Hx) \supset Bx]\}$

Notice that the first example is translated in terms of the disjunction $Sx \lor Lx$ even though the English statement reads "snakes *and* lizards." If the translation were rendered as $(x)[Tx \supset (Sx \cdot Lx)]$ it would mean that anything that thrives in the desert is both a snake and a lizard (at the same time). And this is surely *not* what is meant. For the same reason, the second example is translated in terms of the disjunction $Ox \lor Lx$ even though the English reads "oranges *and* lemons." If the statement were translated $(x)[(Ox \cdot Lx) \supset Cx]$, it would mean that anything that is simultaneously an orange and a lemon (and there are none of these) is a citrus fruit. The same principle is used in translating the sixth example, which, incidentally, reads "If anything is a cat or a dog, then if it is frightened or harassed, it bites." The third example employs the conjunction $Rx \cdot Ax$ to translate ripe apples. This, of course, is correct, because such a thing is both ripe and an apple at the same time. The fifth example illustrates the fact that "unless" may be translated as either "if not" or "or."

The operators of propositional logic can be used to form compound arrangements of universal and particular statements, just as they can be used to form compound arrangements of singular statements. Here are some examples:

Statement	Symbolic translation
If Elizabeth is a historian, then some women are historians.	$He \supset (\exists x)(Wx \bullet Hx)$
If some cellists are music directors, then some orchestras are properly led.	$(\exists x)(Cx \bullet Mx) \supset (\exists x)(Ox \bullet Px)$
Either everything is alive or Bergson's theory is not correct.	$(x)Ax \lor {\sim}Cb$
All novels are interesting if and only if some Steinbeck novels are not romances.	$(x)(Nx \supset Ix) \equiv (\exists x)[(Nx \bullet Sx) \bullet {\sim}Rx]$
Green avocados are never purchased unless all the ripe ones are expensive.	$(x)[(Gx \bullet Ax) \supset {\sim}Px] \lor (x)[(Rx \bullet Ax) \supset Ex]$

We have seen that the general procedure is to translate universal statements as conditionals preceded by a universal quantifier, and to translate particular statements as conjunctions preceded by an existential quantifier. Let us see what happens to these translations when they are preceded by the wrong quantifier. Consider the false statement "No cats are animals." This is correctly translated $(x)(Cx \supset {\sim}Ax)$. If, however, it were translated $(\exists x)(Cx \supset {\sim}Ax)$, the symbolic statement would turn out to be true. This may be seen as follows. $(\exists x)(Cx \supset {\sim}Ax)$ is equivalent via material implication to $(\exists x)({\sim}Cx \lor {\sim}Ax)$, which in turn is equivalent via De Morgan's rule to $(\exists x){\sim}(Cx \bullet Ax)$. The latter statement, however, merely asserts that something exists that is not both a cat and an animal—for example, a dog—which is true. Again, consider the true statement "Some cats are animals." This is correctly translated $(\exists x)(Cx \bullet Ax)$. If, however, it were translated $(x)(Cx \bullet Ax)$, the symbolic statement would assert that everything in the universe is both a cat and an animal, which is clearly false. Thus, as these examples illustrate, it is imperative that the two quantifiers not be confused with each other.

One final observation needs to be made. It was mentioned earlier that the letters x, y, and z are reserved for use as variables for translating universal and particular statements. In accord with this convention, the other twenty-three lowercase letters (a, b, c, ... u, v, w) may be used as names for translating singular statements. Thus, for example, "Albert is a scientist" is translated Sa. But a question naturally arises with statements such as "Xerxes was a king." Should this statement be translated Kx? The answer is no. Some other letter, for example the second letter in the name, should be selected instead of x. Maintaining this alphabetical convention will help us avoid mistakes in the next section when we use natural deduction to derive the conclusions of arguments.

EXERCISE 7.1

Translate the following statements into symbolic form. Avoid negation signs preceding quantifiers. The predicate letters are given in parentheses.

★1. Elaine is a chemist. (C)

2. Nancy is not a sales clerk. (S)

3. Neither Wordsworth nor Shelley was Irish. (*I*)

★4. Rachel is either a journalist or a newscaster. (*J, N*)

5. Intel designs a faster chip only if Micron does. (*D*)

6. Belgium and France subsidize the arts only if Austria or Germany expand museum holdings. (*S, E*)

★7. All maples are trees. (*M, T*)

8. Some grapes are sour. (*G, S*)

9. No novels are biographies. (*N, B*)

★10. Some holidays are not relaxing. (*H, R*)

11. If Gertrude is correct, then the Taj Mahal is made of marble. (*C, M*)

12. Gertrude is not correct only if the Taj Mahal is made of granite. (*C, G*)

★13. Tigers exist. (*T*)

14. Anything that leads to violence is wrong. (*L, W*)

15. There are pornographic art works. (*A, P*)

★16. Not every smile is genuine. (*S, G*)

17. Every penguin loves ice. (*P, L*)

18. There is trouble in River City. (*T, R*)

★19. Whoever is a socialite is vain. (*S, V*)

20. Any caring mother is vigilant and nurturing. (*C, M, V, N*)

21. Terrorists are neither rational nor empathic. (*T, R, E*)

★22. Nobody consumed by jealousy is happy. (*C, H*)

23. Everything is imaginable. (*I*)

24. Ghosts do not exist. (*G*)

★25. A thoroughbred is a horse. (*T, H*)

26. A thoroughbred won the race. (*T, W*)

27. Not all mushrooms are edible. (*M, E*)

★28. Not any horse chestnuts are edible. (*H, E*)

29. A few guests arrived late. (*G, A*)

30. None but gentlemen prefer blondes. (*G, P*)

★31. A few cities are neither safe nor beautiful. (*C, S, B*)

32. There are no circular triangles. (*C, T*)

33. Snakes are harmless unless they have fangs. (*S, H, F*)

★34. Some dogs bite if and only if they are teased. (*D, B, T*)

35. An airliner is safe if and only if it is properly maintained. (*A, S, P*)

36. Some companies go bankrupt if sales decline. (C, B, S)

★37. Some children act up only if they are tired. (C, A, T)

38. The only musicians that are available are trombonists. (M, A, T)

39. Only talented musicians perform in the symphony. (T, M, P)

★40. Any well-made car runs smoothly. (W, C, R)

41. Not every foreign car runs smoothly. (F, C, R)

42. A good violin is rare and expensive. (G, V, R, E)

★43. Violins and cellos are stringed instruments. (V, C, S, I)

44. A room with a view is available. (R, V, A)

45. A room with a view is expensive. (R, V, E)

★46. Some French restaurants are exclusive. (F, R, E)

47. Some French cafés are not recommended. (F, C, R)

48. Hurricanes and earthquakes are violent and destructive. (H, E, V, D)

★49. Taylor is guilty if and only if all the witnesses committed perjury. (G, W, C)

50. If any witnesses told the truth, then either Parsons or Harris is guilty. (W, T, G)

51. If all mysteries are interesting, then *Rebecca* is interesting. (M, I)

★52. If there are any interesting mysteries, then *Rebecca* is interesting. (M, I)

53. Skaters and dancers are energetic individuals. (S, D, E, I)

54. Swiss watches are not expensive unless they are made of gold. (S, W, E, M)

★55. If all the buildings in Manhattan are skyscrapers, then the Chrysler building is a skyscraper. (B, M, S)

56. Experienced mechanics are well paid only if all the inexperienced ones are lazy. (E, M, W, L)

57. Balcony seats are never chosen unless all the orchestra seats are taken. (B, S, C, O, T)

★58. Some employees will get raises if and only if some managers are overly generous. (E, R, M, O)

59. The physicists and astronomers at the symposium are listed in the program if they either chair a meeting or read a paper. (P, A, S, L, C, R)

60. If the scientists and technicians are conscientious and exacting, then some of the mission directors will be either pleased or delighted. (S, T, C, E, M, P, D)

7.2   Using the Rules of Inference

PREVIEW

After you have finished constructing your website, you find that you don't like the way certain items are organized on the pages. So, you go back into the site, dismantle the pages, rearrange the items, and then put everything back together again. Using *natural deduction in predicate logic resembles this procedure. First, you dismantle the premises, and you then reorganize the parts to construct the conclusion. Developing a facility with this procedure will sharpen your skills for any task that involves organization.*

The chief reason for using truth-functional operators (the dot, wedge, horseshoe, and so on) in translating statements into the symbolism of predicate logic is to allow for the application of the eighteen rules of inference to derive the conclusion of arguments via natural deduction. Since, however, the first eight of these rules are applicable only to whole lines in an argument, as long as the quantifier is attached to a line, these rules of inference cannot be applied—at least not to the kind of arguments we are about to consider. To provide for their application, four additional rules are required to remove quantifiers at the beginning of a proof sequence and to introduce them, when needed, at the end of the sequence. These four rules are called universal instantiation, universal generalization, existential instantiation, and existential generalization. The first two are used to remove and introduce universal quantifiers, respectively, and the second two to remove and introduce existential quantifiers.

universal instantiation:
Picking an instance for a universal statement.

Let us first consider **universal instantiation**. As an illustration of the need for this rule, consider the following argument:

> All economists are social scientists.
> Paul Krugman is an economist.
> Therefore, Paul Krugman is a social scientist.

This argument, which is clearly valid, is symbolized as follows:

> 1. $(x)(Ex \supset Sx)$
> 2. Ep / Sp

As the argument now stands, none of the first eight rules of inference can be applied; as a result, there is no way in which the two premises can be combined to derive the conclusion. However, if the first premise could be used to derive a line that reads $Ep \supset Sp$, this statement could be combined with the second premise to yield the conclusion via modus ponens. Universal instantiation serves exactly this purpose.

The first premise states that for any item x in the universe, if that item is an E, then it is an S. But since Paul Krugman is himself an item in the universe, the first premise implies that if Paul Krugman is an E, then Paul Krugman is an S. A line stating exactly this can be derived by universal instantiation (UI). In other words, universal instantiation provides us with an *instance* of the universal statement $(x)(Ex \supset Sx)$. In the completed proof, which follows, the p in line 3 is called the **instantial letter**:

> 1. $(x)(Ex \supset Sx)$
> 2. Ep / Sp
> 3. $Ep \supset Sp$ 1, UI
> 4. Sp 2, 3, MP

At this point the question might arise as to why modus ponens is applicable to lines 2 and 3. In Chapter 6 we applied modus ponens to lines of the form $p \supset q$, but are we justified in applying it to a line that reads $Ep \supset Sp$? The answer is yes, because Ep and Sp are simply alternate ways of symbolizing simple statements. As so understood, these symbols do not differ in any material way from the p and q of propositional logic.

We may now give a general definition of instantiation. *Instantiation* is an operation that consists in deleting a quantifier and replacing every variable bound by that quantifier with the same instantial letter. For an example of an operation that violates the rule expressed in this definition, consider line 3 of the foregoing proof. If this line were instantiated as $Ep \supset Sx$, it would not be correct because the x in Sx was not replaced with the instantial letter p.

Let us now consider **universal generalization**. The need for this rule may be illustrated through reference to the following argument:

> All psychiatrists are doctors.
> All doctors are college graduates.
> Therefore, all psychiatrists are college graduates.

universal generalization: Converting a statement function into a universal statement.

This valid argument is symbolized as follows:

1. $(x)(Px \supset Dx)$
2. $(x)(Dx \supset Cx)$ / $(x)(Px \supset Cx)$

Once universal instantiation is applied to the two premises, we will have lines that can be used to set up a hypothetical syllogism. But then we will have to reintroduce a universal quantifier to derive the conclusion as written. This final step is obtained by universal generalization (UG). The justification for such a step lies in the fact that both premises are universal statements. The first states that if *anything* is a P, then it is a D, and the second states that if *anything* is a D, then it is a C. We may therefore conclude that if *anything* is a P, then it is a C. But because of the complete generality of this reasoning process, there is a special way in which we must perform the universal instantiation step. Instead of selecting a *specifically named* instance, as we did in the previous example, we must select a *variable* that can range over every instance in the universe. The variables at our disposal, you may recall from the previous section, are x, y, and z. Let us select y. The completed proof is as follows:

1. $(x)(Px \supset Dx)$
2. $(x)(Dx \supset Cx)$ / $(x)(Px \supset Cx)$
3. $Py \supset Dy$ 1, UI
4. $Dy \supset Cy$ 2, UI
5. $Py \supset Cy$ 3, 4, HS
6. $(x)(Px \supset Cx)$ 5, UG

As noted earlier, the expressions in lines 3, 4, and 5 are called **statement functions**. As such, they are mere patterns for statements; they have no truth value and cannot be translated as statements. Yet if we take certain liberties, we might characterize line 5 as saying "If *it* is a P, then *it* is a C, where "it" designates any item at random in the universe. Line 6 can then be seen as reexpressing this sense of line 5.

statement function: an expression such as $Fx \supset Gx$.

As the two previous examples illustrate, we have two ways of performing universal instantiation. On the one hand, we may instantiate with respect to a *constant*, such as a or b, and on the other, with respect to a *variable*, such as x or y. The exact way in which this operation is to be performed depends on the kind of result intended. If we want

7

some part of a universal statement to match a singular statement on another line, as in the first example, we instantiate with respect to a constant. But if, at the end of the proof, we want to perform universal generalization over some part of the statement we are instantiating, then we *must* instantiate by using a variable. This latter point leads to an important restriction governing universal generalization—namely, that we cannot perform this operation when the instantial letter is a constant. Consider the following *erroneous* proof sequence:

1. *Ta*
2. *(x)Tx*   1, UG (invalid)

If *Ta* means "Albert is a thief," then on the basis of this information, we have concluded (line 2) that everything in the universe is a thief. Clearly, such an inference is invalid. This illustrates the fact that universal generalization can be performed only when the instantial letter (in this case *a*) is a variable.

existential generalization: Converting a symbolic statement about an instance to a particular statement.

Let us now consider **existential generalization**. The need for this operation is illustrated through the following argument:

All tenors are singers.
Andrea Bocelli is a tenor.
Therefore, there is at least one singer.

This argument is symbolized as follows:

1. *(x)(Tx ⊃ Sx)*
2. *Ta*   / *(∃x)Sx*

If we instantiate the first line with respect to *a*, we can obtain *Sa* via modus ponens. But if it is true that Andrea Bocelli is a tenor, then it certainly follows that there is at least one singer (namely, Andrea Bocelli). This last step is accomplished by existential generalization (EG). The proof is as follows:

1. *(x)(Tx ⊃ Sx)*
2. *Ta*   / *(∃x)Sx*
3. *Ta ⊃ Sa*   1, UI
4. *Sa*   2, 3, MP
5. *(∃x)Sx*   4, EG

There are no restrictions on existential generalization, and the operation can be performed when the instantial letter is either a constant (as in the Bocelli example) or a variable. As an instance of the latter, consider the following sequence:

1. *(x)(Px ⊃ Qx)*
2. *(x)Px*   / *(∃x)Qx*
3. *Py ⊃ Qy*   1, UI
4. *Py*   2, UI
5. *Qy*   3, 4, MP
6. *(∃x)Qx*   5, EG

Line 5 states in effect that everything in the universe is a *Q*. From this, the much weaker conclusion follows (line 6) that *something* is a *Q*. If you should wonder how an existential conclusion can be drawn from universal premises, the answer is that predicate logic assumes that at least one thing exists in the universe. Hence, line 2, which asserts that everything in the universe is a *P*, entails that at least one thing is a *P*. Without this assumption, universal instantiation in line 4 would not be possible.

We may now construct a definition of generalization that covers both varieties. *Generalization* in the inclusive sense is an operation that consists in (1) introducing a quantifier immediately prior to a statement, a statement function, or another quantifier, and (2) replacing one or more occurrences of a certain instantial letter in the statement or statement function with the same variable that appears in the quantifier. For universal generalization, *all* occurrences of the instantial letter must be replaced with the variable in the quantifier, and for existential generalization, *at least one* of the instantial letters must be replaced with the variable in the quantifier. Thus, both of the following cases of existential generalization are valid (although the one on the left is by far the more common version):

1. $Fa \cdot Ga$		1. $Fa \cdot Ga$	
2. $(\exists x)(Fx \cdot Gx)$ 1, EG		2. $(\exists x)(Fx \cdot Ga)$ 1, EG	

On the other hand, only one of the following cases of universal generalization is valid:

1. $Fx \supset Gx$		1. $Fx \supset Gx$	
2. $(y)(Fy \supset Gy)$ 1, UG		2. $(y)(Fy \supset Gx)$ 1, UG (invalid)	

The inference on the right is invalid because the *x* in *Gx* was not replaced with the variable in the quantifier (that is, *y*).

Of course, it may happen that the instantial letter is the same as the variable that appears in the quantifier. Thus, the operation "*Gx*, therefore *(x)Gx*" counts as a generalization.

The need for **existential instantiation** can be illustrated through the following argument:

All attorneys are college graduates.
Some attorneys are golfers.
Therefore, some golfers are college graduates.

The symbolic formulation is as follows:

1. $(x)(Ax \supset Cx)$
2. $(\exists x)(Ax \cdot Gx)$ / $(\exists x)(Gx \cdot Cx)$

If both quantifiers can be removed, the conclusion can be derived via simplification, modus ponens, and conjunction. The universal quantifier can be removed by universal instantiation, but to remove the existential quantifier we need existential instantiation. Line 2 states that there is *something* that is both an *A* and a *G*. Existential instantiation consists in giving this something a *name*, for example, "David." We will call this name an "existential name" because it is obtained through existential instantiation. The completed proof is as follows:

1. $(x)(Ax \supset Cx)$
2. $(\exists x)(Ax \cdot Gx)$ / $(\exists x)(Gx \cdot Cx)$
3. $Ad \cdot Gd$ 2, EI
4. $Ad \supset Cd$ 1, UI
5. Ad 3, Simp
6. Cd 4, 5, MP
7. $Gd \cdot Ad$ 3, Com
8. Gd 7, Simp
9. $Gd \cdot Cd$ 6, 8, Conj
10. $(\exists x)(Gx \cdot Cx)$ 9, EG

existential instantiation:
Picking an instance for a particular statement.

7

Examination of this proof reveals an immediate restriction that must be placed on existential instantiation. The name that we have assigned to the particular something in line 2 that is both an *A* and a *G* is a hypothetical name. It would be a mistake to conclude that this something really has that name. Accordingly, we must introduce a restriction that prevents us from ending the proof with some line that includes the letter *d*. If, for example, the proof were ended at line 9, we would be concluding that the something that is a *G* and a *C* really does have the name *d*. This, of course, would not be legitimate, because *d* is an arbitrary name introduced into the proof for mere convenience. To prevent such a mistake, we require that the name selected for existential instantiation not appear to the right of the slanted line adjacent to the last premise that indicates the conclusion to be derived. Since the last line in the proof must be identical to this line, such a restriction prevents us from ending the proof with a line that contains the existential name.

Further examination of this proof indicates another important restriction on existential instantiation. Notice that the line involving existential instantiation is listed before the line involving universal instantiation. There is a reason for this. If the order were reversed, the existential instantiation step would rest on the illicit assumption that the something that is both an *A* and a *G* has the *same* name as the name used in the earlier universal instantiation step. In other words, it would involve the assumption that the something that is both an *A* and a *G* is the very same something named in the line *Ad* ⊃ *Cd*. Of course, no such assumption is legitimate. To keep this mistake from happening, we introduce the restriction that the name introduced by existential instantiation be a new name not occurring earlier in the proof sequence. The following defective proof illustrates what can happen if this restriction is violated:

1.	(∃x)(Fx • Ax)	
2.	(∃x)(Fx • Ox)	/ (∃x)(Ax • Ox)
3.	Fb • Ab	1, EI
4.	Fb • Ob	2, EI (invalid)
5.	Ab • Fb	3, Com
6.	Ab	5, Simp
7.	Ob • Fb	4, Com
8.	Ob	7, Simp
9.	Ab • Ob	6, 8, Conj
10.	(∃x)(Ax • Ox)	9, EG

To see that this proof is indeed defective, let *F* stand for fruits, *A* for apples, and *O* for oranges. The argument that results is:

Some fruits are apples.
Some fruits are oranges.
Therefore, some apples are oranges.

Since the premises are true and the conclusion false, the argument is clearly invalid. The defect in the proof occurs on line 4. This line asserts that the something that is both an *F* and an *O* is the very same something that is both an *F* and an *A*. In other words, the restriction that the name introduced by existential instantiation be a new name not occurring earlier in the proof is violated.

The first restriction on existential instantiation requires that the existential name not occur in the line that indicates the conclusion to be derived, and the second restriction requires that this name be a new name that has not occurred earlier in the proof. These two restrictions can easily be combined into a single restriction that requires that the name introduced by existential instantiation be a new name that has not occurred in *any* previous line, including the line adjacent to the last premise that indicates the conclusion to be derived.

One further restriction that affects all four of these rules of inference requires that the rules be applied only to *whole lines* in a proof. The following sequence illustrates a violation of this restriction:

1. $(x)Px \supset (x)Qx$
2. $Py \supset Qy$ 1, UI (invalid)

In line 2 universal instantiation is applied to both the antecedent and consequent of the first line. To derive line 2 validly, the first line would have to read $(x)(Px \supset Qx)$. With this final restriction in mind, the four new rules of inference, developed on the previous pages, may now be summarized. In the formulation that follows, the symbols $\mathscr{F}x$ and $\mathscr{F}y$ represent any statement function—that is, any symbolic arrangement containing individual variables, such as $Ax \supset Bx$, $Cy \supset (Dy \vee Ey)$, or $Gz \cdot Hz$. The symbol $\mathscr{F}a$ represents any **statement**; that is, any symbolic arrangement containing individual constants (or names), such as $Ac \supset Bc$, $Cm \supset (Dm \vee Em)$, or $Gw \cdot Hw$. And the symbol $\mathscr{F}$ is a predicate variable that represents any predicate such as F, G, or H.*

1. Universal instantiation (UI):

$$\frac{(x)\mathscr{F}x}{\mathscr{F}y} \qquad \frac{(x)\mathscr{F}x}{\mathscr{F}a}$$

2. Universal generalization (UG):

$$\frac{\mathscr{F}y}{(x)\mathscr{F}x} \qquad \text{not allowed:} \quad \frac{\mathscr{F}a}{(x)\mathscr{F}x}$$

3. Existential instantiation (EI):

$$\frac{(\exists x)\mathscr{F}x}{\mathscr{F}a} \qquad \text{not allowed:} \quad \frac{(\exists x)\mathscr{F}x}{\mathscr{F}y}$$

Restriction: The existential name *a* must be a new name that does not appear in any previous line (including the conclusion line).

4. Existential generalization (EG):

$$\frac{\mathscr{F}a}{(\exists x)\mathscr{F}x} \qquad \frac{\mathscr{F}y}{(\exists x)\mathscr{F}x}$$

The *not allowed* version of universal generalization recalls the already familiar fact that generalization is not possible when the instantial letter is a constant. In other words, the mere fact that the individual a is an $\mathscr{F}$ is not sufficient to allow us to conclude that everything in the universe is an $\mathscr{F}$. At present this is the only restriction needed for universal generalization. In Section 7.4, however, an additional restriction will be introduced. The *not allowed* version of existential instantiation merely recalls the fact that this operation is a naming process. Because variables

UG and EI have restrictions.

Some textbooks use Greek letters such as φ (phi) χ (chi) and ψ (psi) in the place of $\mathscr{F}$ to express these and other rules.

7

(x, y, and z) are not names, they cannot be used as instantial letters in existential instantiation.

Let us now investigate some applications of these rules. Consider the following proof:

1. $(x)(Hx \supset Ix)$
2. $(x)(Ix \supset Hx)$ / $(x)(Hx \equiv Ix)$
3. $Hx \supset Ix$ 1, UI
4. $Ix \supset Hx$ 2, UI
5. $(Hx \supset Ix) \cdot (Ix \supset Hx)$ 3, 4, Conj
6. $Hx \equiv Ix$ 5, Equiv
7. $(x)(Hx \equiv Ix)$ 6, UG

Because we want to perform universal generalization on the last line of the proof, we instantiate lines 1 and 2 using a variable, not a constant. Notice that the variable selected for lines 3 and 4 is the same letter that occurs in lines 1 and 2. While a new letter (y or z) *could* have been selected, this is never necessary in such a step. It *is* necessary, however, since we want to combine lines 3 and 4, that the *same* variable be selected in deriving these lines. Another example:

1. $(x)[(Ax \vee Bx) \supset Cx]$
2. $(\exists x)Ax$ / $(\exists x)Cx$
3. Am 2, EI
4. $(Am \vee Bm) \supset Cm$ 1, UI
5. $Am \vee Bm$ 3, Add
6. Cm 4, 5, MP
7. $(\exists x)Cx$ 6, EG

In conformity with the restriction on existential instantiation, the EI step is performed *before* the UI step. The same letter is then selected in the UI step as was used in the EI step. In line 5, Bm is joined disjunctively via addition to Am. This rule applies in predicate logic in basically the same way that it does in propositional logic. Any statement or statement function we choose can be joined disjunctively to a given line.

Another example:

1. $(\exists x)Kx \supset (x)(Lx \supset Mx)$
2. $Kc \cdot Lc$ / Mc
3. Kc 2, Simp
4. $(\exists x)Kx$ 3, EG
5. $(x)(Lx \supset Mx)$ 1, 4, MP
6. $Lc \supset Mc$ 5, UI
7. $Lc \cdot Kc$ 2, Com
8. Lc 7, Simp
9. Mc 6, 8, MP

Since the instantiation (and generalization) rules must be applied to whole lines, it is impossible to instantiate line 1. The only strategy that can be followed is to use some other line to derive the antecedent of this line and then derive the consequent via modus ponens. Once the consequent is derived (line 5), it is instantiated using the same letter that appears in line 2.

7

The next example incorporates all four of the instantiation and generalization rules:

1.	$(x)(Px \supset Qx) \supset (\exists x)(Rx \cdot Sx)$	
2.	$(x)(Px \supset Sx) \cdot (x)(Sx \supset Qx)$	/ $(\exists x)Sx$
3.	$(x)(Px \supset Sx)$	2, Simp
4.	$(x)(Sx \supset Qx) \cdot (x)(Px \supset Sx)$	2, Com
5.	$(x)(Sx \supset Qx)$	4, Simp
6.	$Py \supset Sy$	3, UI
7.	$Sy \supset Qy$	5, UI
8.	$Py \supset Qy$	6, 7, HS
9.	$(x)(Px \supset Qx)$	8, UG
10.	$(\exists x)(Rx \cdot Sx)$	1, 9, MP
11.	$Ra \cdot Sa$	10, EI
12.	$Sa \cdot Ra$	11, Com
13.	Sa	12, Simp
14.	$(\exists x)Sx$	13, EG

As with the previous example, line 1 cannot be instantiated. To instantiate the two conjuncts in line 2, they must first be separated (lines 3 and 5). Because UG is to be used in line 9, lines 3 and 5 are instantiated using a variable. On the other hand, a constant is used to instantiate line 10 because the statement in question is a particular statement.

Another example:

1.	$[(\exists x)Ax \cdot (\exists x)Bx] \supset Cj$	
2.	$(\exists x)(Ax \cdot Dx)$	
3.	$(\exists x)(Bx \cdot Ex)$	/ Cj
4.	$Am \cdot Dm$	2, EI
5.	$Bn \cdot En$	3, EI
6.	Am	4, Simp
7.	Bn	5, Simp
8.	$(\exists x)Ax$	6, EG
9.	$(\exists x)Bx$	7, EG
10.	$(\exists x)Ax \cdot (\exists x)Bx$	8, 9, Conj
11.	Cj	1, 10, MP

When line 2 is instantiated (line 4), a letter other than *j*, which appears in line 1, is selected. Then, when line 3 is instantiated (line 5), another new letter is selected. The conclusion is derived, as in earlier examples, via modus ponens by deriving the antecedent of line 1.

The following examples illustrate *invalid* or *improper* applications of the instantiation and generalization rules:

1.	$Fy \supset Gy$	
2.	$(x)(Fx \supset Gy)$	1, UG	(invalid — every instance of *y* must be replaced with *x*)

1.	$(x)Fx \supset Ga$	
2.	$Fx \supset Ga$	1, UI	(invalid — instantiation can be applied only to whole lines)

1.	$(x)Fx \supset (x)Gx$	
2.	$Fx \supset Gx$	1, UI	(invalid — instantiation can be applied only to whole lines)

1.	Fc	
2.	$(\exists x)Gx$	
3.	Gc	2, EI	(invalid — *c* appears in line 1)

7

1. Fm ⊃ Gm		
2. (x)(Fx ⊃ Gx)	1, UG	(invalid—the instantial letter must be a variable; m is a constant)

1. (∃x)Fx		
2. (∃x)Gx		
3. Fe	1, EI	
4. Ge	2, EI	(invalid—e appears in line 3)

1. Fs • Gs		
2. (∃x)Fx • Gs	1, EG	(improper—generalization can be applied only to whole lines)

1. ~(x)Fx		
2. ~Fy	1, UI	(invalid—lines involving negated quantifiers cannot be instantiated; see Section 7.3)

EXERCISE 7.2

I. Use the eighteen rules of inference to derive the conclusions of the following symbolized arguments. Do not use either conditional proof or indirect proof.

★(1) 1. (x)(Ax ⊃ Bx)
    2. (x)(Bx ⊃ Cx)   / (x)(Ax ⊃ Cx)

(2) 1. (x)(Bx ⊃ Cx)
    2. (∃x)(Ax • Bx)   / (∃x)(Ax • Cx)

(3) 1. (x)(Ax ⊃ Bx)
    2. ~Bm   / (∃x)~Ax

★(4) 1. (x)(Ax ⊃ Bx)
    2. (y)(Ay ∨ ~By)   / (x)(Ax ≡ Bx)

(5) 1. (x)[Ax ⊃ (Bx ∨ Cx)]
    2. Ag • ~Bg   / Cg

(6) 1. (x)[(Ax ∨ Bx) ⊃ Cx]
    2. (∃y)(Ay • Dy)   / (∃y)Cy

★(7) 1. (x)[Jx ⊃ (Kx • Lx)]
    2. (∃y)~Ky   / (∃z)~Jz

(8) 1. (x)[Ax ⊃ (Bx ∨ Cx)]
    2. (∃x)(Ax • ~Cx)   / (∃x)Bx

(9) 1. (x)(Ax ⊃ Bx)
    2. Am • An   / Bm • Bn

★(10) 1. (x)(Ax ⊃ Bx)
    2. Am ∨ An   / Bm ∨ Bn

(11) 1. (x)(Bx ∨ Ax)
    2. (x)(Bx ⊃ Ax)   / (x)Ax

7

(12) 1. $(\exists x)Ax \supset (y)(By \lor \sim Ay)$
   2. An $/ (\exists y)By$

★**(13) 1.** $(x)[(Ax \bullet Bx) \supset Cx]$
   2. $(\exists x)(Bx \bullet \sim Cx)$ $/ (\exists x)\sim Ax$

(14) 1. $(x)(Ax \supset Bx)$
   2. $(x)(Cx \supset Dx)$
   3. $Ae \lor Ce$ $/ (\exists x)(Bx \lor Dx)$

(15) 1. $(\exists x)Ax \supset (x)(Bx \supset Cx)$
   2. $Am \bullet Bm$ $/ Cm$

★**(16) 1.** $(\exists x)Ax \supset (x)Bx$
   2. $(\exists x)Cx \supset (\exists x)Dx$
   3. $An \bullet Cn$ $/ (\exists x)(Bx \bullet Dx)$

(17) 1. $(x)(Ax \bullet Bx)$
   2. $Cr \lor \sim(x)Bx$ $/ (\exists x)(Cx \bullet Ax)$

(18) 1. $(x)[Ax \supset (Bx \equiv Cx)]$
   2. $An \bullet Am$
   3. $Cn \bullet \sim Cm$ $/ Bn \bullet \sim Bm$

★**(19) 1.** $(\exists x)Ax \supset (x)(Cx \supset Bx)$
   2. $(\exists x)(Ax \lor Bx)$
   3. $(x)(Bx \supset Ax)$ $/ (x)(Cx \supset Ax)$

(20) 1. $(\exists x)Ax \supset (x)(Bx \supset Cx)$
   2. $(\exists x)Dx \supset (\exists x)\sim Cx$
   3. $(\exists x)(Ax \bullet Dx)$ $/ (\exists x)\sim Bx$

(21) 1. $(\exists x)(Ax \bullet Bx) \supset (x)(Cx \bullet Dx)$
   2. $(\exists x)Ax \supset (x)(Bx \bullet Cx)$
   3. Ae $/ (\exists x)(Dx \bullet Bx)$

★**(22) 1.** $(x)(Ax \bullet \sim Bx)$
   2. $An \supset [\sim(\exists x)Cx \supset Bc]$
   3. $Am \supset (x)(Cx \supset Dx)$ $/ (\exists x)Dx$

(23) 1. $(x)(Ax \bullet Bx)$
   2. $(x)Ax \supset (Ce \lor \sim Be)$
   3. $(x)Bx \supset [(\exists x)Cx \supset (Dn \lor \sim An)]$ $/ (\exists x)Dx$

(24) 1. $(\exists x)Ax \supset (x)[(Ax \lor Ex) \supset Dx]$
   2. $(\exists x)Dx \supset (x)[Dx \supset (Cx \lor \sim Bx)]$
   3. $An \bullet Bn$ $/ (\exists x)Cx$

★**(25) 1.** $(\exists x)Ax \supset (x)(Ax \supset Bx)$
   2. $(\exists x)Cx \supset (x)\sim(Dx \bullet Bx)$
   3. $(\exists x)(Ax \bullet Cx)$ $/ (\exists x)\sim Dx$

II. Translate the following arguments into symbolic form. Then use the eighteen rules of inference to derive the conclusion of each. Do not use conditional or indirect proof.

★**1.** Oranges are sweet. Also, oranges are fragrant. Therefore, oranges are sweet and fragrant. (O, S, F)

2. Tomatoes are vegetables. Therefore, the tomatoes in the garden are vegetables. (*T, V, G*)

3. Apples and pears grow on trees. Therefore, apples grow on trees. (*A, P, G*)

★4. Carrots are vegetables and peaches are fruit. Furthermore, there are carrots and peaches in the garden. Therefore, there are vegetables and fruit in the garden. (*C, V, P, F, G*)

5. Beans and peas are legumes. There are no legumes in the garden. Therefore, there are no beans in the garden. (*B, P, L, G*)

6. There are some cucumbers in the garden. If there are any cucumbers, there are some pumpkins in the garden. All pumpkins are vegetables. Therefore, there are some vegetables in the garden. (*C, G, P, V*)

★7. All gardeners are industrious people. Furthermore, any person who is industrious is respected. Therefore, since Arthur and Catherine are gardeners, it follows that they are respected. (*G, I, P, R*)

8. Some huckleberries are ripe. Furthermore, some boysenberries are sweet. If there are any huckleberries, then the boysenberries are edible if they are sweet. Therefore, some boysenberries are edible. (*H, R, B, S, E*)

9. If there are any ripe watermelons, then the caretakers performed well. Furthermore, if there are any large watermelons, then whoever performed well will get a bonus. There are some large, ripe watermelons. Therefore, the caretakers will get a bonus. (*R, W, C, P, L, B*)

★10. If the artichokes in the kitchen are ripe, then the guests will be surprised. Furthermore, if the artichokes in the kitchen are flavorful, then the guests will be pleased. The artichokes in the kitchen are ripe and flavorful. Therefore, the guests will be surprised and pleased. (*A, K, R, G, S, F, P*)

III. The following dialogue contains nine arguments. Translate each into symbolic form and then use the eighteen rules of inference to derive the conclusion of each. Some of them are quite challenging.

Where's the Beef?

"Have you decided what to order?" Paul says to Mindy, as he folds his menu and puts it on the table.

"I think I'll have the tofu stir-fry," she replies. "And you?"

"I'll have the rib steak," Paul says. "You know the rib steak is really good here, and so is the pork tenderloin."

"I'm a vegetarian," she says.

"Oh," Paul says. He smiles sheepishly.

Mindy smiles too. "First date," she says.

"Yeah," says Paul. "What made you decide to become a vegetarian?"

"For one thing," Mindy says, "I think a vegetarian diet is healthier. People who eat meat increase their intake of cholesterol and carcinogens. Those who increase their intake of cholesterol run a higher risk of heart attack, and those who increase their intake of carcinogens run a higher risk of cancer.

Anyone who runs a higher risk of heart attack and cancer is less healthy. Thus, people who eat meat are less healthy.

"I might add that if people who eat meat are less healthy, then if parents are responsible, then they will refrain from feeding meat to children. All parents love their children, and if they do, then they are responsible. But if parents refrain from feeding meat to children, then children will grow up to be vegetarians. And if that happens, then nobody will eat meat in the future. Thus, we can look forward to a future where everyone is a vegetarian."

"Well, I won't hold my breath on that," Paul says, as he offers Mindy a slice of bread from the basket on the table. "If children and teenagers fail to eat meat, then they become deficient in zinc. And if children become deficient in zinc, then they risk a weakened immune system. And if that happens, then they are less healthy. Also, if elderly people fail to eat meat, then they become deficient in iron. And if elderly people become deficient in iron, then they risk becoming anemic, and if that happens, they are less healthy. Therefore, if children and elderly people fail to eat meat, then they are less healthy."

Mindy smiles. "That's what zinc tablets and iron supplements are for," she says. Anyway, there are also moral reasons for being a vegetarian. Consider this. Animals are sentient beings—they feel pain, fear, and joy—and they have an interest in preserving their lives. If animals are sentient, then if humans cause animals to suffer, then they act immorally. And if animals have an interest in preserving their lives, then if humans exploit animals, then they act immorally. But if humans kill animals for food, then they cause animals to suffer or they exploit them. Therefore, if humans kill animals for food, then they act immorally."

"I agree with you that animals should not be made to suffer," Paul responds. "But if animals are raised under humane conditions, and some of them are, then they will not be caused to feel pain or distress. And if animals are not caused to feel pain, then we are morally justified in eating them. Thus, we are morally justified in eating some animals."

"I disagree," says Mindy.

"That's because you think that animals have rights," Paul says. "If animals have rights, then they have moral judgment. And if animals have moral judgment, then they respect the rights of other animals. But every animal pursues its own self-interest to the exclusion of other animals, and if that's so, then it does not respect the rights of other animals. Therefore, animals have no moral judgment and they also have no rights."

"Well," Mindy replies, "by that line of reasoning infants and mentally challenged adults have no rights. But everyone recognizes that they do have rights. And if infants have rights, then some people who lack the capacity for moral judgment have rights. But if this is true, then animals have rights, and if they do, then surely they have the right to life. But if animals have the right to life, then if humans are moral, then they must respect that right and they cannot kill animals for food. Thus, if humans are moral, they cannot kill animals for food."

"The question of infants and mentally challenged adults raises an interesting point," Paul says. "I think what it comes down to is this: Something is considered to have rights if and only if it looks human. Infants and mentally challenged adults look human, so they are considered to have rights. But animals do not look human, so they are not considered to have rights."

"That sounds awfully arbitrary," says Mindy. "But I think what it really comes down to is power. Something is considered to have rights if and only if it has as much power as humans. Animals do not have as much power as humans, so animals are not considered to have rights. But that seems terribly wrong to me. It shouldn't be a question of power. Anyway, now that our food has arrived, how's your steak?"

Paul takes a bite. "It's great," he says. "And how's your stir-fry?"

"Great," Mindy says. She laughs. "And so is my conscience."

7.3   Quantifier Negation Rule

PREVIEW

Suppose you want to update your website, but when you try to log in to your account, you find that someone has put a lock on the software program denying you access. A similar situation exists in a symbolized argument when a premise begins with a quantifier preceded by a tilde. The tilde acts like a lock. As long as the lock is there, you cannot apply the instantiation rules to the quantified expression. Learning how to remove these tildes may help you see how to remove obstacles to reasoning in other life pursuits.

The rules of inference developed thus far are not sufficient to derive the conclusion of every argument in predicate logic. For instance, consider the following:

$$\sim(\exists x)(Px \bullet \sim Qx)$$
$$\underline{\sim(x)(\sim Rx \vee Qx)}$$
$$(\exists x)\sim Px$$

Both premises have tildes preceding the quantifiers. As long as they remain, neither statement can be instantiated; and if these statements cannot be instantiated, the conclusion cannot be derived. What is needed is a rule that will allow us to remove the negation signs. This rule, which we will proceed to develop now, is called the quantifier negation rule.

As a basis for developing the quantifier negation rule, consider the following statements:

quantifier negation rule:
A rule for removing or inserting a negation symbol (tilde) preceding a quantifier.

> Everything is beautiful.
> It is not the case that everything is beautiful.
> Something is beautiful.
> It is not the case that something is beautiful.

You should be able to see that these statements are equivalent in meaning to the following statements, respectively:

> It is not the case that something is not beautiful.
> Something is not beautiful.
> It is not the case that everything is not beautiful.
> Everything is not beautiful.

Alfred North Whitehead 1861–1947
Bertrand Russell 1872–1970

Alfred North Whitehead and Bertrand Russell collaborated in writing *Principia Mathematica*, which is generally considered the most important logical endeavor of the twentieth century. It represents an attempt to reduce all of mathematics to logic. Published in three volumes between 1910 and 1913, the manuscript was so huge that it required a "four wheeler" to transport it to the printer. The combined work comprises over 1,900 pages, nearly all of them filled with highly complex and technical notation. The American philosopher Willard Van Orman Quine described the *Principia* as "one of the great intellectual monuments of all time."

Whitehead was born the son of an Anglican minister in Ramsgate, England. He entered Trinity College, Cambridge, with a scholarship in mathematics, and after graduating, he was elected a Fellow of Trinity. While there he published *A Treatise on Universal Algebra*, for which he was elected to the prestigious Royal Society. Whitehead's most distinguished student at Trinity was Bertrand Russell. After Russell graduated he and Whitehead became close friends. At age thirty-one Whitehead married Evelyn Wade, and they had three children, two sons and a daughter.

In 1910 Whitehead left Cambridge for London, where he taught at University College London and later at the Imperial College of Science and Technology. While in London he wrote books in the areas of physics and the philosophy of science. Then in 1924 he was appointed professor of philosophy at Harvard University, where he wrote *Process and Reality*. The book became a cornerstone of what would later be called process philosophy and process theology. Whitehead died at age eighty-six in Cambridge, Massachusetts.

Bertrand Russell, one of the world's best-known intellectuals, was born in Wales to aristocratic parents. Both died

when he was very young, and although they had requested that their son be raised an agnostic, the young Russell was brought up by a staunchly Victorian grandmother who fed him a steady dose of religion. As he grew older he became an atheist (or at best an agnostic) who considered religion little better than superstition. At Trinity College Russell studied mathematics and philosophy and befriended Ludwig Wittgenstein and G. E. Moore, as well as Whitehead. After graduating he was elected fellow of Trinity College and, later, fellow of the Royal Society. He was extremely prolific as a writer, and in 1950 he won the Nobel Prize in literature.

Russell was married four times, engaged in numerous love affairs with prominent women, was imprisoned for six months for opposing conscription in World War I, and was later imprisoned for opposing nuclear weapons. A staunch supporter of birth control, population control, democracy, free trade, and world government, he opposed communism, imperialism, and every form of mind control. He died at age ninety-seven at his home in Wales.

If we generalize these English equivalencies symbolically, we obtain:

$$(x)\mathscr{F}x \quad :: \quad {\sim}(\exists x){\sim}\mathscr{F}x$$
$${\sim}(x)\mathscr{F}x \quad :: \quad (\exists x){\sim}\mathscr{F}x$$
$$(\exists x)\mathscr{F}x \quad :: \quad {\sim}(x){\sim}\mathscr{F}x$$
$${\sim}(\exists x)\mathscr{F}x \quad :: \quad (x){\sim}\mathscr{F}x$$

These four expressions constitute the quantifier negation rule (QN). Since they are stated as logical equivalences, they apply to parts of lines as well as to whole lines. They can be summarized as follows:

7

One type of quantifier can be replaced by the other type if and only if immediately before and after the new quantifier:

1. Tilde operators that were originally present are deleted.

2. Tilde operators that were not originally present are inserted.

To see how the quantifier negation rule is applied, let us return to the argument at the beginning of this section. The proof is as follows:

```
 1.  ~(∃x)(Px • ~Qx)
 2.  ~(x)(~Rx ∨ Qx)        / (∃x)~Px
 3.  (x)~(Px • ~Qx)          1, QN
 4.  (∃x)~(~Rx ∨ Qx)         2, QN
 5.  ~(~Ra ∨ Qa)             4, EI
 6.  ~(Pa • ~Qa)             3, UI
 7.  ~~Ra • ~Qa              5, DM
 8.  ~Pa ∨ ~~Qa              6, DM
 9.  ~Pa ∨ Qa                8, DN
10.  ~Qa • ~~Ra              7, Com
11.  ~Qa                     10, Simp
12.  Qa ∨ ~Pa                9, Com
13.  ~Pa                     11, 12, DS
14.  (∃x)~Px                 13, EG
```

Before either line 1 or line 2 can be instantiated, the tilde operators preceding the quantifiers must be removed. In accordance with the quantifier negation rule, tilde operators are introduced immediately after the new quantifiers in the expressions on lines 3 and 4.

Another example:

```
 1.  (∃x)(Hx • Gx) ⊃ (x)Ix
 2.  ~Im                     / (x)(Hx ⊃ ~Gx)
 3.  (∃x)~Ix                 2, EG
 4.  ~(x)Ix                  3, QN
 5.  ~(∃x)(Hx • Gx)          1, 4, MT
 6.  (x)~(Hx • Gx)           5, QN
 7.  (x)(~Hx ∨ ~Gx)          6, DM
 8.  (x)(Hx ⊃ ~Gx)           7, Impl
```

The statement that *m* is not an *I* (line 2) intuitively implies that not everything is an *I* (line 4); but existential generalization and quantifier negation are needed to get the desired result. Notice that lines 7 and 8 are derived via De Morgan's rule and material implication, even though the quantifier is still attached. Since these rules are rules of replacement, they apply to parts of lines as well as to whole lines. The following example illustrates the same point with respect to the quantifier negation rule:

```
 1.  (∃x)Jx ⊃ ~(∃x)Kx
 2.  (x)~Kx ⊃ (x)~Lx         / (∃x)Jx ⊃ ~(∃x)Lx
 3.  (∃x)Jx ⊃ (x)~Kx         1, QN
 4.  (∃x)Jx ⊃ (x)~Lx         2, 3, HS
 5.  (∃x)Jx ⊃ ~(∃x)Lx        4, QN
```

The quantifier negation rule is applied to only the consequent of line 1, yielding line 3. Similarly, the quantifier negation rule is then applied to only the consequent of line 4, yielding line 5.

I. Use the quantifier negation rule together with the eighteen rules of inference to derive the conclusions of the following symbolized arguments. Do not use either conditional proof or indirect proof.

★(1) 1. $(x)Ax \supset (\exists x)Bx$
   2. $(x)\sim Bx$ / $(\exists x)\sim Ax$

(2) 1. $(\exists x)\sim Ax \lor (\exists x)\sim Bx$
   2. $(x)Bx$ / $\sim(x)Ax$

(3) 1. $\sim(\exists x)Ax$ / $(x)(Ax \supset Bx)$

★(4) 1. $(\exists x)Ax \lor (\exists x)(Bx \cdot Cx)$
   2. $\sim(\exists x)Bx$ / $(\exists x)Ax$

(5) 1. $(x)(Ax \cdot Bx) \lor (x)(Cx \cdot Dx)$
   2. $\sim(x)Dx$ / $(x)Bx$

(6) 1. $(\exists x)\sim Ax \supset (x)(Bx \supset Cx)$
   2. $\sim(x)(Ax \lor Cx)$ / $\sim(x)Bx$

★(7) 1. $(x)(Ax \supset Bx)$
   2. $\sim(x)Cx \lor (x)Ax$
   3. $\sim(x)Bx$ / $(\exists x)\sim Cx$

(8) 1. $(x)Ax \supset (\exists x)\sim Bx$
   2. $\sim(x)Bx \supset (\exists x)\sim Cx$ / $(x)Cx \supset (\exists x)\sim Ax$

(9) 1. $(\exists x)(Ax \lor Bx) \supset (x)Cx$
   2. $(\exists x)\sim Cx$ / $\sim(\exists x)Ax$

★(10) 1. $\sim(\exists x)(Ax \cdot \sim Bx)$
   2. $\sim(\exists x)(Bx \cdot \sim Cx)$ / $(x)(Ax \supset Cx)$

(11) 1. $\sim(\exists x)(Ax \cdot \sim Bx)$
   2. $\sim(\exists x)(Ax \cdot \sim Cx)$ / $(x)[Ax \supset (Bx \cdot Cx)]$

(12) 1. $(x)[(Ax \cdot Bx) \supset Cx]$
   2. $\sim(x)(Ax \supset Cx)$ / $\sim(x)Bx$

★(13) 1. $(x)(Ax \cdot \sim Bx) \supset (\exists x)Cx$
   2. $\sim(\exists x)(Cx \lor Bx)$ / $\sim(x)Ax$

(14) 1. $(\exists x)\sim Ax \supset (x)\sim Bx$
   2. $(\exists x)\sim Ax \supset (\exists x)Bx$
   3. $(x)(Ax \supset Cx)$ / $(x)Cx$

(15) 1. $\sim(\exists x)(Ax \lor Bx)$
   2. $(\exists x)Cx \supset (\exists x)Ax$
   3. $(\exists x)Dx \supset (\exists x)Bx$ / $\sim(\exists x)(Cx \lor Dx)$

★(16) 1. $(\exists x)(Ax \cdot Bx) \supset (x)(Cx \cdot Dx)$
   2. $(x)[(Ax \lor Ex) \cdot (Bx \lor Fx)]$
   3. $\sim(x)Dx$ / $(x)(Ex \lor Fx)$

7

(17) 1. $(\exists x)(Ax \cdot Bx) \vee (\exists x)(Cx \vee Dx)$
    2. $(\exists x)(Ax \vee Cx) \supset (x)Ex$
    3. $\sim En$ / $(\exists x)Dx$

(18) 1. $(\exists x)Ax \supset [(\exists x)Bx \vee (x)Cx]$
    2. $(\exists x)(Ax \cdot \sim Cx)$
    3. $\sim(x)Cx \supset [(x)Fx \supset (x)\sim Bx]$ / $(\exists x)\sim Fx$

★(19) 1. $(\exists x)(Ax \cdot Bx) \supset (x)(Bx \supset Cx)$
    2. $Bn \cdot \sim Cn$ / $\sim(x)Ax$

(20) 1. $(\exists x)Ax \supset \sim(\exists x)(Bx \cdot Ax)$
    2. $\sim(x)Bx \supset \sim(\exists x)(Ex \cdot \sim Bx)$
    3. An / $\sim(x)Ex$

II. Translate the following arguments into symbolic form. Then use the quantifier negation rule and the eighteen rules of inference to derive the conclusion of each. Do not use either conditional proof or indirect proof.

★1. If all the physicians are either hematologists or neurologists, then there are no cardiologists. But Dr. Frank is a cardiologist. Therefore, some physicians are not neurologists. (P, H, N, C)

2. Either Dr. Adams is an internist or all the pathologists are internists. But it is not the case that there are any internists. Therefore, Dr. Adams is not a pathologist. (I, P)

3. If some surgeons are allergists, then some psychiatrists are radiologists. But no psychiatrists are radiologists. Therefore, no surgeons are allergists. (S, A, P, R)

★4. Either some general practitioners are pediatricians or some surgeons are endocrinologists. But it is not the case that there are any endocrinologists. Therefore, there are some pediatricians. (G, P, S, E)

5. All physicians who did not attend medical school are incompetent. It is not the case, however, that some physicians are incompetent. Therefore, all physicians have attended medical school. (P, A, I)

6. It is not the case that some internists are not physicians. Furthermore, it is not the case that some physicians are not doctors of medicine. Therefore, all internists are doctors of medicine. (I, P, D)

★7. All pathologists are specialists and all internists are generalists. Therefore, since it is not the case that some specialists are generalists, it is not the case that some pathologists are internists. (P, S, I, G)

8. If some obstetricians are not gynecologists, then some hematologists are radiologists. But it is not the case that there are any hematologists or gynecologists. Therefore, it is not the case that there are any obstetricians. (O, G, H, R)

9. All poorly trained allergists and dermatologists are untrustworthy specialists. It is not the case, however, that some specialists are untrustworthy. Therefore, it is not the case that some dermatologists are poorly trained. (P, A, D, U, S)

★10. It is not the case that some physicians are either on the golf course or in the hospital. All of the neurologists are physicians in the hospital. Either some physicians are cardiologists or some physicians are neurologists. Therefore, some cardiologists are not on the golf course. (P, G, H, N, C)

7.4 Conditional and Indirect Proof

PREVIEW

Designing a website is likely to be accompanied by various assumptions. You may assume that your customers will find one particular design more appealing than another, or one navigation structure more useful than another. Assumptions can also be made in deriving conclusions in predicate logic. One type of assumption is used in conditional proof, the other in indirect proof. Developing a familiarity with these techniques will sharpen your skills in working with assumptions in other areas of interest.

Many arguments with conclusions that are either difficult or impossible to derive by the conventional method can be handled with ease by using either conditional or indirect proof. The use of these techniques on arguments in predicate logic is basically the same as it is on arguments in propositional logic. Arguments having conclusions expressed in the form of conditional statements or disjunctions (which can be derived from conditional statements) are immediate candidates for conditional proof. For these arguments, the usual strategy is to put the antecedent of the conditional statement to be obtained in the first line of an indented sequence, to derive the consequent as the last line, and to discharge the conditional sequence in a conditional statement that exactly matches the one to be obtained. Here is an example of such a proof:

```
1. (x)(Hx ⊃ Ix)        / (∃x)Hx ⊃ (∃x)Ix
   2. (∃x)Hx           ACP
   3. Ha               2, EI
   4. Ha ⊃ Ia          1, UI
   5. Ia               3, 4, MP
   6. (∃x)Ix           5, EG
7. (∃x)Hx ⊃ (∃x)Ix     2–6, CP
```

In this argument the antecedent of the conclusion is a complete statement consisting of a statement function, *Hx*, preceded by a quantifier. This complete statement is assumed as the first line in the conditional sequence. The instantiation and generalization rules are used within an indented sequence (both conditional and indirect) in basically the same way as they are in a conventional sequence. When the consequent of the conclusion is derived, the conditional sequence is completed, and it is then discharged in a conditional statement having the first line of the sequence as its antecedent and the last line as its consequent.

> For conditional proof, either a statement or a statement function can be assumed on the first line.

The next example differs from the previous one in that the antecedent of the conclusion is a statement function, not a complete statement. With arguments such as this, only the statement function is assumed as the first line in the conditional sequence. The quantifier is added after the sequence is discharged.

```
1. (x)[(Ax ∨ Bx) ⊃ Cx]    / (x)(Ax ⊃ Cx)
   2. Ax                   ACP
   3. Ax ∨ Bx              2, Add
   4. (Ax ∨ Bx) ⊃ Cx       1, UI
   5. Cx                   3, 4, MP
6. Ax ⊃ Cx                 2–5, CP
7. (x)(Ax ⊃ Cx)            6, UG
```

7

These proof techniques require a new restriction on UG.

This example leads to an important restriction on the use of universal generalization. You may recall that the *x* in line 2 of this proof is said to be *free* because it is not bound by any quantifier. (In contrast, the *x*'s in lines 1 and 7 are bound by quantifiers.) The restriction is as follows:

UG: $\dfrac{\mathcal{F}y}{(x)\mathcal{F}x}$ *Restriction*: UG must not be used within the scope of an indented sequence if the instantial variable *y* is free in the first line of that sequence.

The proof just given does not violate this restriction, because UG is not used within the scope of the indented sequence at all. It is used only after the sequence has been discharged, which is perfectly acceptable. If, on the other hand, UG had been applied to line 5 to produce a statement reading (*x*)*Cx*, the restriction would have been violated because the instantial variable *x* is free in the first line of the sequence.

To understand why this restriction is necessary, consider the following *defective* proof:

1.	(x)Rx ⊃ (x)Sx	/ (x)(Rx ⊃ Sx)
2.	Rx	ACP
3.	(x)Rx	2, UG (invalid)
4.	(x)Sx	1, 3, MP
5.	Sx	4, UI
6.	Rx ⊃ Sx	2–5, CP
7.	(x)(Rx ⊃ Sx)	6, UG

If *Rx* means "*x* is a rabbit" and *Sx* means "*x* is a snake," then the premise translates "If everything in the universe is a rabbit, then everything in the universe is a snake." This statement is *true* because the antecedent is false; that is, it is *not* the case that everything in the universe is a rabbit. The conclusion, on the other hand, is *false*, because it asserts that all rabbits are snakes. The argument is therefore invalid. If the restriction on UG had been obeyed, UG could not have been used on line 3 and, as a result, the illicit conclusion could not have been derived.

It is interesting to see what happens when the premise and the conclusion of this defective argument are switched. The proof, which is perfectly legitimate, is as follows:

1.	(x)(Rx ⊃ Sx)	/ (x)Rx ⊃ (x)Sx
2.	(x)Rx	ACP
3.	Rx	2, UI
4.	Rx ⊃ Sx	1, UI
5.	Sx	3, 4, MP
6.	(x)Sx	5, UG
7.	(x)Rx ⊃ (x)Sx	2–6, CP

Notice in this proof that UG *is* used within the scope of a conditional sequence, but the restriction is not violated because the instantial variable *x* is not free in the first line of the sequence.

For indirect proof, either a statement or a statement function can be assumed on the first line.

Let us now consider some examples of *indirect* proof. We begin an indirect sequence by assuming the negation of the statement to be obtained. When a contradiction is derived, the indirect sequence is discharged by asserting the denial of the original assumption. In the examples that follow, the negation of the conclusion is assumed as the first line of the sequence, and the quantifier negation rule is then used to eliminate

7

the tilde. When the resulting statement is then instantiated, a new letter, *m*, is selected that has not appeared anywhere in a previous line. The same letter is then selected for the universal instantiation of line 1:

1. (x)[(Px ⊃ Px) ⊃ (Qx ⊃ Rx)]　　　/ (x)(Qx ⊃ Rx)
　　2. ~(x)(Qx ⊃ Rx)　　　　　　　　AIP
　　3. (∃x)~(Qx ⊃ Rx)　　　　　　　2, QN
　　4. ~(Qm ⊃ Rm)　　　　　　　　　3, EI
　　5. (Pm ⊃ Pm) ⊃ (Qm ⊃ Rm)　　　1, UI
　　6. ~(Pm ⊃ Pm)　　　　　　　　　4, 5, MT
　　7. ~(~Pm ∨ Pm)　　　　　　　　6, Impl
　　8. ~~Pm • ~Pm　　　　　　　　　7, DM
　　9. Pm • ~Pm　　　　　　　　　　8, DN
10. ~~(x)(Qx ⊃ Rx)　　　　　　　　2–9, IP
11. (x)(Qx ⊃ Rx)　　　　　　　　　10, DN

The next example has a particular statement for its conclusion:

1. (∃x)Ax ∨ (∃x)Fx
2. (x)(Ax ⊃ Fx)　　　　　　　　　/ (∃x)Fx
　　3. ~(∃x)Fx　　　　　　　　　　AIP
　　4. (∃x)Fx ∨ (∃x)Ax　　　　　　1, Com
　　5. (∃x)Ax　　　　　　　　　　　3, 4, DS
　　6. Ac　　　　　　　　　　　　　5, EI
　　7. Ac ⊃ Fc　　　　　　　　　　2, UI
　　8. Fc　　　　　　　　　　　　　6, 7, MP
　　9. (x)~Fx　　　　　　　　　　　3, QN
　10. ~Fc　　　　　　　　　　　　　9, UI
　11. Fc • ~Fc　　　　　　　　　　8, 10, Conj
12. ~~(∃x)Fx　　　　　　　　　　　3–11, IP
13. (∃x)Fx　　　　　　　　　　　　12, DN

Since indirect proof sequences are indented, they are subject to the same restriction on universal generalization as are conditional sequences. The following proof, which is similar to the previous one, violates this restriction because the instantial variable *x* is free in the first line of the sequence. The violation (line 4) allows a universal statement to be drawn for the conclusion, whereas only a particular statement is legitimate (as in the prior example):

1. (∃x)Ax ∨ (∃x)Fx
2. (x)(Ax ⊃ Fx)　　　　　　　　　/ (x)Fx
　　3. ~Fx　　　　　　　　　　　　AIP
　　4. (x)~Fx　　　　　　　　　　　3, UG (invalid)
　　5. ~(∃x)Fx　　　　　　　　　　4, QN
　　6. (∃x)Fx ∨ (∃x)Ax　　　　　　1, Com
　　7. (∃x)Ax　　　　　　　　　　　5, 6, DS
　　8. Ac　　　　　　　　　　　　　7, EI
　　9. Ac ⊃ Fc　　　　　　　　　　2, UI
　10. Fc　　　　　　　　　　　　　8, 9, MP
　11. ~Fc　　　　　　　　　　　　　4, UI
　12. Fc • ~Fc　　　　　　　　　　10, 11, Conj

7

13. ~~Fx	3–12, IP
14. Fx	13, DN
15. (x)Fx	14, UG

To see that this argument is indeed invalid, let *Ax* stand for "*x* is an apple" and *Fx* for "*x* is a fruit." The first premise then reads "Either an apple exists or a fruit exists" (which is true), and the second premise reads "All apples are fruits" (which is also true). The conclusion, however, reads "Everything in the universe is a fruit," and this, of course, is false.

As in propositional logic, conditional and indirect sequences in predicate logic may include each other. The following proof uses an indirect sequence within the scope of a conditional sequence.

1.	(x)[(Px ∨ Qx) ⊃ (Rx • Sx)]	/ (∃x)(Px ∨ Sx) ⊃ (∃x)Sx
2.	(∃x)(Px ∨ Sx)	ACP
3.	~(∃x)Sx	AIP
4.	(x)~Sx	3, QN
5.	Pa ∨ Sa	2, EI
6.	~Sa	4, UI
7.	Sa ∨ Pa	5, Com
8.	Pa	6, 7, DS
9.	Pa ∨ Qa	8, Add
10.	(Pa ∨ Qa) ⊃ (Ra • Sa)	1, UI
11.	Ra • Sa	9, 10, MP
12.	Sa • Ra	11, Com
13.	Sa	12, Simp
14.	Sa • ~Sa	6, 13, Conj
15.	~~(∃x)Sx	3–14, IP
16.	(∃x)Sx	15, DN
17.	(∃x)(Px ∨ Sx) ⊃ (∃x)Sx	2–16, CP

The conditional sequence begins, as usual, by assuming the antecedent of the conditional statement to be derived. The objective, then, is to derive the consequent. This is accomplished by the indirect sequence, which begins with the negation of the consequent and ends (line 14) with a contradiction.

EXERCISE 7.4

I. Use either indirect proof or conditional proof to derive the conclusions of the following symbolized arguments.

★(1) 1. (x)(Ax ⊃ Bx)
    2. (x)(Ax ⊃ Cx)   / (x)[Ax ⊃ (Bx • Cx)]

(2) 1. (∃x)Ax ⊃ (∃x)(Bx • Cx)
    2. (∃x)(Cx ∨ Dx) ⊃ (x)Ex   / (x)(Ax ⊃ Ex)

(3) 1. $(\exists x)Ax \supset (\exists x)(Bx \cdot Cx)$
    2. $\sim(\exists x)Cx$ $/ (x)\sim Ax$

★(4) 1. $(x)(Ax \supset Cx)$
    2. $(\exists x)Cx \supset (\exists x)(Bx \cdot Dx)$ $/ (\exists x)Ax \supset (\exists x)Bx$

(5) 1. $(x)(Ax \supset Bx)$
    2. $(x)[(Ax \cdot Bx) \supset Cx]$ $/ (x)(Ax \supset Cx)$

(6) 1. $(\exists x)Ax \supset (x)Bx$
    2. $An \supset \sim Bn$ $/ \sim An$

★(7) 1. $(x)[(Ax \vee Bx) \supset Cx]$
    2. $(x)[(Cx \vee Dx) \supset Ex]$ $/ (x)(Ax \supset Ex)$

(8) 1. $(\exists x)(Ax \vee Bx) \supset \sim(\exists x)Ax$ $/ (x)\sim Ax$

(9) 1. $(x)(Ax \supset Bx)$
    2. $(x)(Cx \supset Dx)$ $/ (\exists x)(Ax \vee Cx) \supset (\exists x)(Bx \vee Dx)$

★(10) 1. $(x)(Ax \supset Bx)$
    2. $Am \vee An$ $/ (\exists x)Bx$

(11) 1. $(x)[(Ax \vee Bx) \supset Cx]$
    2. $(x)[(Cx \vee Dx) \supset \sim Ax]$ $/ (x)\sim Ax$

(12) 1. $(\exists x)Ax \supset (x)(Bx \supset Cx)$
    2. $(\exists x)Dx \supset (x)\sim Cx$ $/ (x)[(Ax \cdot Dx) \supset \sim Bx]$

★(13) 1. $(\exists x)Ax \supset (x)(Bx \supset Cx)$
    2. $(\exists x)Dx \supset (\exists x)Bx$ $/ (\exists x)(Ax \cdot Dx) \supset (\exists x)Cx$

(14) 1. $(\exists x)Ax \vee (\exists x)(Bx \cdot Cx)$
    2. $(x)(Ax \supset Cx)$ $/ (\exists x)Cx$

(15) 1. $(\exists x)Ax \supset (\exists x)(Bx \cdot Cx)$
    2. $(\exists x)Cx \supset (x)(Dx \cdot Ex)$ $/ (x)(Ax \supset Ex)$

★(16) 1. $(x)[(Ax \vee Bx) \supset Cx]$
    2. $(\exists x)(\sim Ax \vee Dx) \supset (x)Ex$ $/ (x)Cx \vee (x)Ex$

(17) 1. $(x)Ax \equiv (\exists x)(Bx \cdot Cx)$
    2. $(x)(Cx \supset Bx)$ $/ (x)Ax \equiv (\exists x)Cx$

(18) 1. $(x)(Ax \equiv Bx)$
    2. $(x)[Ax \supset (Bx \supset Cx)]$
    3. $(\exists x)Ax \vee (\exists x)Bx$ $/ (\exists x)Cx$

★(19) 1. $(x)[Bx \supset (Cx \cdot Dx)]$ $/ (x)(Ax \supset Bx) \supset (x)(Ax \supset Dx)$

(20) 1. $(x)[Ax \supset (Bx \cdot Cx)]$
    2. $(x)[Dx \supset (Ex \cdot Fx)]$ $/ (x)(Cx \supset Dx) \supset (x)(Ax \supset Fx)$

(21) 1. $(\exists x)(Ax \vee Bx)$
    2. $(\exists x)Ax \supset (x)(Cx \supset Bx)$
    3. $(\exists x)Cx$ $/ (\exists x)Bx$

★(22) 1. $(x)Ax \vee (x)Bx$ $/ (x)(Ax \vee Bx)$

7

(23) 1. $(\exists x)(Ax \lor Ex) \supset (x)(Bx \bullet \sim Cx)$
2. $(\exists x)(Bx \lor Fx) \supset (x)(Cx \lor Dx)$ / $(x)(Ax \supset Dx)$

(24) 1. $(x)(Ax \supset Bx)$
2. $\sim(\exists x)Ax \supset (\exists x)(Cx \bullet Dx)$
3. $(\exists x)(Dx \lor Ex) \supset (\exists x)Bx$ / $(\exists x)Bx$

★(25) 1. $(\exists x)Ax \supset (x)(Bx \supset Cx)$
2. $(\exists x)Dx \supset (x)(Ex \supset \sim Bx)$
3. $\sim(\exists x)(Cx \bullet \sim Ex)$ / $(\exists x)(Ax \bullet Dx) \supset \sim(\exists x)Bx$

II. Translate the following arguments into symbolic form. Then use conditional or indirect proof to derive the conclusion of each.

★1. All ambassadors are wealthy. Furthermore, all Republicans are clever. Therefore, all Republican ambassadors are clever and wealthy. (A, W, R, C)

2. All senators are well liked. Also, if there are any well-liked senators, then O'Brien is a voter. Therefore, if there are any senators, then O'Brien is a voter. (S, W, V)

3. If all judges are wise, then some attorneys are rewarded. Furthermore, if there are any judges who are not wise, then some attorneys are rewarded. Therefore, some attorneys are rewarded. (J, W, A, R)

★4. All secretaries and undersecretaries are intelligent and cautious. All those who are cautious or vigilant are restrained and austere. Therefore, all secretaries are austere. (S, U, I, C, V, R, A)

5. All ambassadors are diplomats. Furthermore, all experienced ambassadors are cautious, and all cautious diplomats have foresight. Therefore, all experienced ambassadors have foresight. (A, D, E, C, F)

6. If there are any senators, then some employees are well paid. If there is anyone who is either an employee or a volunteer, then there are some legislative assistants. Either there are some volunteers or there are some senators. Therefore, there are some legislative assistants. (S, E, W, V, L)

★7. If there are any consuls, then all ambassadors are satisfied diplomats. If no consuls are ambassadors, then some diplomats are satisfied. Therefore, some diplomats are satisfied. (C, A, S, D)

8. If there are any voters, then all politicians are astute. If there are any politicians, then whoever is astute is clever. Therefore, if there are any voters, then all politicians are clever. (V, P, A, C)

9. Either no senators are present or no representatives are present. Furthermore, either some senators are present or no women are present. Therefore, none of the representatives who are present are women. (S, P, R, W)

★10. Either some governors are present or some ambassadors are present. If anyone is present, then some ambassadors are clever diplomats. Therefore, some diplomats are clever. (G, P, A, C, D)

aplia™
Visit Aplia for section-specific problem sets.

7

7.5 Proving Invalidity

PREVIEW

Suppose, while updating your website, you replace one entire page with a perfectly good new page. But after making the replacement you find that the site fails to operate properly. You then know that something is wrong with the underlying coding. Similarly, with an argument expressed in predicate logic, if its predicate symbols should be replaced with terms that make its premises true and its conclusion false, then you know that something is wrong with the argument's structure. In other words, the argument is invalid.

In the previous chapter we saw that natural deduction could not be used with any facility to prove invalidity in propositional logic. The same thing can be said about natural deduction in predicate logic. But in predicate logic there is no simple and automatic technique such as truth tables or Venn diagrams to fall back on. Yet, there is one method for proving invalidity that is very intuitive, even though it requires some ingenuity. This is the **counterexample method** for predicate logic. It is essentially identical to the counterexample method introduced in Section 1.5, and it consists in finding a substitution instance of an argument form that has actually true premises and a false conclusion. Of course, such a substitution instance proves the argument form invalid.

counterexample method: Constructing a substitution instance having true premises and false conclusion.

For an illustration of the use of the counterexample method, consider the following invalid symbolized argument:

$(\exists x)(Ax \cdot \sim Bx)$
$(x)(Cx \supset Bx)$ / $(\exists x)(Cx \cdot \sim Ax)$

In creating a substitution instance, beginning with the conclusion is often easiest. The conclusion is translated as "Some *C* are not *A*." Thus, to make this statement false, we need to find an example of a class (for *C*) that is included in another class (for *A*). Cats and animals will serve this purpose. A little ingenuity provides us with the following substitution instance:

Some animals are not mammals.
All cats are mammals.
Therefore, some cats are not animals.

When we produce such a substitution instance, the premises must turn out to be indisputably true in the actual world, and the conclusion indisputably false. Statements involving the names of animal classes are convenient for this purpose, because everyone agrees about cats, dogs, mammals, fish, and so on. Also, several different substitution instances can usually be produced that suffice to prove the argument invalid. Finally, any substitution instance that results in true premises and a true conclusion (or any arrangement other than true premises and false conclusion) proves nothing.

Here is an example of an invalid symbolized argument that includes a singular statement:

$(x)(Ax \supset Bx)$
$\sim Ac$ / $\sim Bc$

7

Kurt Gödel 1906–1978

Alfred Eisenstaedt/Time Life Pictures/Getty Images

Kurt Gödel, generally considered to be the most important logician of the contemporary period, was born in what is today Brno, Czechoslovakia, to a father who managed a textile factory and a mother who was educated and cultured. After excelling at the gymnasium in Brno, Gödel entered the University of Vienna, where he studied mathematics, physics, and philosophy. On completing his undergraduate degree he commenced graduate work in mathematics, earning his doctorate at age twenty-four. Four years later Gödel began teaching at the university as a *Privatdozent*. However, when the Nazis annexed Austria they abolished his teaching position in favor of one that required a political test, and one year later they found him qualified for military service.

In 1940, under threat of being drafted into the German army, Gödel and his wife Adel (whom he had married two years earlier) left for the United States, where he accepted a position at the famous Institute for Advanced Studies, in Princeton, New Jersey. Soon after arriving, he became best of friends with Albert Einstein, with whom he took daily walks. Gödel became a permanent member of the institute in 1946, and five years later he received the first Albert Einstein Award. In 1974 he was awarded the National Medal of Science.

Gödel is most famous for developing incompleteness theorems that relate to the efforts by logicians to reduce arithmetic to logic. Ordinary arithmetic rests on a set of axioms (called the Peano axioms), and for many years logicians thought (or hoped) that all of the theorems of arithmetic could be reduced to those axioms. Such a system would be complete in that every theorem would be linked to the axioms by a logical proof sequence. Quite to the surprise of these logicians, Gödel showed that every axiom system

adequate to support arithmetic contains at least one assertion that is neither provable nor disprovable from the axioms. A second incompleteness theorem showed that the consistency of such a system cannot be proved within the system itself.

As a philosopher Gödel was a Platonic realist and a Leibnizian rationalist. He thought that abstract concepts (such as number and figure) represented objects in an ideal realm that were perfect, changeless, and eternal. As a result he thought that mathematics is a science that describes this ideal realm, and not, as many think, a mere invention of the human mind. Following Leibniz, Gödel conceived the visible world as fundamentally beautiful, perfect, and thoroughly ordered. To complete this perfect world he developed his own ontological argument for the existence of God.

Tragically, from an early age, Gödel was troubled by emotional afflictions, including depression, and as he grew older he suffered from psychotic delusions. In the middle of the winter he would open wide all the windows of his house because he thought that malevolent forces intended to poison him with gas. He also feared they wanted to poison his food, so he ate only his wife's cooking. When Adel became incapacitated from illness, Gödel stopped eating altogether. At age seventy-one he died from malnutrition, at which point his body weighed only sixty-five pounds.

This argument form commits the fallacy of denying the antecedent. Producing a substitution instance is easy:

> All cats are animals.
> Lassie is not a cat.
> Therefore, Lassie is not an animal.

In selecting the name of an individual for the second premise, it is again necessary to pick something that everyone agrees on. Since everyone knows that Lassie is a dog, this name serves our purpose. But if we had selected some other name, such as Trixie or Ajax, this would hardly suffice, because there is no general agreement as to what these names denote.

Here is a slightly more complex example:

(x)[Ax ⊃ (Bx ∨ Cx)]
(x)[Bx ⊃ (Cx • Dx)]   / (x)(Ax ⊃ Dx)

A little ingenuity produces the following substitution instance:

All dogs are either sharks or animals.
All sharks are animals that are fish.
Therefore, all dogs are fish.

The counterexample method is effective with most fairly simple invalid arguments in predicate logic. Since its application depends on the ingenuity of the user, however, it is not particularly well suited for complex arguments.

EXERCISE 7.5

Use the counterexample method to prove that the following symbolized arguments are invalid.

★(1) 1. (x)(Ax ⊃ Bx)
    2. (x)(Ax ⊃ ~Cx)   / (x)(Cx ⊃ Bx)

(2) 1. (∃x)(Ax • Bx)
    2. (x)(Cx ⊃ Ax)   / (∃x)(Cx • Bx)

(3) 1. (x)(Ax ⊃ Bx)
    2. Bc   / Ac

★(4) 1. (∃x)(Ax • Bx)
    2. (∃x)(Ax • Cx)   / (∃x)[Ax • (Bx • Cx)]

(5) 1. (x)[Ax ∨ (Bx ∨ Cx)]   / (x)Ax ∨ [(x)Bx ∨ (x)Cx]

(6) 1. (x)[Ax ⊃ (Bx ∨ Cx)]
    2. (x)[(Bx • Cx) ⊃ Dx]   / (x)(Ax ⊃ Dx)

★(7) 1. (∃x)Ax
    2. (∃x)Bx
    3. (x)(Ax ⊃ ~Cx)   / (∃x)(Bx • ~Cx)

(8) 1. (x)[(Ax ∨ Bx) ⊃ Cx]
    2. (x)[(Cx • Dx) ⊃ Ex]   / (x)(Ax ⊃ Ex)

(9) 1. (x)[(Ax • Bx) ⊃ Cx]
    2. (x)[(Ax • Cx) ⊃ Dx]   / (x)[(Ax • Dx) ⊃ Cx]

★(10) 1. (∃x)(Ax • Bx)
    2. (∃x)(Cx • ~Bx)
    3. (x)(Ax ⊃ Cx)   / (∃x)[(Cx • Bx) • ~Ax]

aplia
Visit Aplia for section-specific problem sets.

7

Summary

Predicate Logic: Combines the use of these symbols:

- The five operators of propositional logic: $\sim$, $\bullet$, $\vee$, $\supset$, $\equiv$
- Symbols for predicates: $G\_$, $H\_$, $K\_$, and so forth.
- Symbols for universal quantifiers: (x), (y), (z)
- Symbols for existential quantifiers: $(\exists x)$, $(\exists y)$, $(\exists z)$
- Symbols for individual variables: x, y, z
- Symbols for individual constants: a, b, c, . . . u, v, w

Statements:

- Singular statements combine predicate symbols with constants: Ga, $Hc \bullet Kc$, and so forth.
- Universal statements are usually translated as conditionals: $(x)(Px \supset Qx)$, and so forth.
- Particular statements are usually translated as conjunctions: $(\exists x)(Px \bullet Qx)$, and so forth.

Using the Rules of Inference (modus ponens, modus tollens, etc.):

- Rules are used in basically the same way as in propositional logic.
- Using the rules usually requires that quantifiers be removed or inserted:
  - Universal instantiation (UI): Removes universal quantifiers.
  - Universal generalization (UG): Introduces universal quantifiers.
  - Existential instantiation (EI): Removes existential quantifiers.
  - Existential generalization (EG): Introduces existential quantifiers.
- Restrictions:
  - For EI, the existential name that is introduced must not appear in any previous line, including the conclusion line.
  - The instantiation and generalization rules can be applied only to whole lines—not parts of lines.

Quantifier Negation Rule:

- Is used to remove or insert tildes preceding quantifiers.
- The instantiation rules cannot be applied if a tilde precedes the quantifier.
- One type of quantifier can be replaced by the other type if and only if immediately before and after the new quantifier:
  - Tildes that were originally there are deleted;
  - Tildes that were not originally there are inserted.

Conditional Proof and Indirect Proof:

- Used in basically the same way as in propositional logic.
- Restriction:
  - UG must not be used within an indented sequence if the instantial variable is free in the first line of that sequence.

Proving Invalidity:

- Counterexample method: Produce a substitution instance of a symbolized argument that has indisputably true premises and an indisputably false conclusion.

Answers to Selected Exercises

Exercise 1.1

I.

1. P: Carbon monoxide molecules happen to be just the right size and shape, and happen to have just the right chemical properties, to fit neatly into cavities within hemoglobin molecules in blood that are normally reserved for oxygen molecules.

   C: Carbon monoxide diminishes the oxygen-carrying capacity of blood.

4. P: When individuals voluntarily abandon property, they forfeit any expectation of privacy in it that they might have had.

   C: A warrantless search and seizure of abandoned property is not unreasonable under the Fourth Amendment.

7. P_1: We need sleep to think clearly, react quickly, and create memories.

   P_2: Studies show that people who are taught mentally challenging tasks do better after a good night's sleep.

   P_3: Other research suggests that sleep is needed for creative problem solving.

   C: It really does matter if you get enough sleep.

10. P_1: Punishment, when speedy and specific, may suppress undesirable behavior.

    P_2: Punishment cannot teach or encourage desirable alternatives.

    C: It is crucial to use positive techniques to model and reinforce appropriate behavior that the person can use in place of the unacceptable response that has to be suppressed.

13. P_1: Private property helps people define themselves.

    P_2: Private property frees people from mundane cares of daily subsistence.

P_3: Private property is finite.

C: No individual should accumulate so much property that others are prevented from accumulating the necessities of life.

16. P_1: The nations of planet earth have acquired nuclear weapons with an explosive power equal to more than a million Hiroshima bombs.

    P_2: Studies suggest that explosion of only half these weapons would produce enough soot, smoke, and dust to blanket the earth, block out the sun, and bring on a nuclear winter that would threaten the survival of the human race.

    C: Radioactive fallout isn't the only concern in the aftermath of nuclear explosions.

19. P_1: Antipoverty programs provide jobs for middle-class professionals in social work, penology, and public health.

    P_2: Such workers' future advancement is tied to the continued growth of bureaucracies dependent on the existence of poverty.

    C: Poverty offers numerous benefits to the nonpoor.

22. P: Take the nurse who alleges that physicians enrich themselves in her hospital through unnecessary surgery; the engineer who discloses safety defects in the braking systems of a fleet of new rapid-transit vehicles; the Defense Department official who alerts Congress to military graft and overspending: All know that they pose a threat to those whom they denounce and that their own careers may be at risk.

    C: The stakes in whistle-blowing are high.

25. P_1: It is generally accepted that by constantly swimming with its mouth open, the shark is simply avoiding suffocation.

    P_2: This assures a continuous flow of oxygen-laden water into the shark's mouth, over its gills, and out through the gill slits.

C: Contrary to the tales of some scuba divers, the toothy, gaping grin on the mouth of an approaching shark is not necessarily anticipatory.

28. P₁: Anyone familiar with our prison system knows that there are some inmates who behave little better than brute beasts.

P₂: If the death penalty had been truly effective as a deterrent, such prisoners would long ago have vanished.

C: The very fact that these prisoners exist is a telling argument against the efficacy of capital punishment as a deterrent.

II.

1. College sports are as much driven by money as are professional sports.
4. Business majors are robbing themselves of the true purpose of collegiate academics, a sacrifice that outweighs the future salary checks.
7. A person cannot reject free will and still insist on criminality and codes of moral behavior.
10. Protecting the environment requires that we limit population growth.

Exercise 1.2

I.

1. Nonargument; explanation.
4. Nonargument; illustration.
7. Argument (conclusion: If stem-cell research is restricted, then people will die prematurely).
10. Nonargument; report.
13. Nonargument; illustration.
16. Nonargument; piece of advice.
19. Argument (conclusion: For organisms at the sea surface, sinking into deep water usually means death).
22. Argument (conclusion: Atoms can combine to form molecules whose properties generally are very different from those of the constituent atoms).
25. Nonargument; explanation.
28. Argument (conclusion: A person never becomes truly self-reliant).
31. This passage could be both an argument and an explanation (conclusion: In areas where rats are a problem, it is very difficult to exterminate them with bait poison).
34. Nonargument; loosely associated statements.

II.

1. Nonargument.
4. Nonargument.
7. Argument (conclusion: Creating a third political party—the independent party—is a good idea).
10. Argument (conclusion: Strong anti-bullying programs are needed to provide a means to report bullying anonymously, to train all school personnel to take reports of bullying seriously, and to offer workshops for children on how to respond to being bullied).

VI.

1. Sufficient: If something is a tiger, then it is an animal.
4. Necessary: If a person has no racket, then he/she cannot play tennis. Or, If a person plays tennis, then he/she has a racket.
7. Sufficient: If leaves burn, then smoke is produced.
10. Necessary: If a person does not utter a falsehood, then he or she does not tell a lie. Or, If a person tells a lie, then he or she utters a falsehood.

Exercise 1.3

I.

1. Deductive (argument based on mathematics; also, conclusion follows necessarily from the premises).
4. Deductive (categorical syllogism; also, conclusion follows necessarily from the premises).
7. Inductive (causal inference; also, conclusion follows only probably from the premise).
10. Inductive (argument from analogy; also, conclusion follows only probably from the premise).
13. Inductive (argument from authority; also, conclusion follows only probably from the premise).
16. Deductive (conclusion follows necessarily from the premise).
19. Inductive (causal inference; also, conclusion follows only probably from the premises).
22. Deductive (conclusion follows necessarily from the premise; this example might also be interpreted as an argument from definition—the definition of "refraction").
25. Inductive (causal inference: The dog's familiarity with the visitor caused the dog to be silent).
28. Inductive (causal inference; also, the word "may" suggests a probabilistic inference).

Exercise 1.4

I.

1. Valid, unsound; false premises, false conclusion.
4. Valid, sound; true premises, true conclusion.
7. Invalid, unsound; true premise, true conclusion.
10. Valid, unsound; false premise, false conclusion.
13. Invalid, unsound; true premises, true conclusion.

II.

1. Strong, cogent; true premise, probably true conclusion.
4. Weak, uncogent; true premise, probably false conclusion.
7. Strong, uncogent; false premise, probably true conclusion.
10. Strong, cogent; true premise, probably true conclusion.
13. Weak, uncogent; true premises, probably false conclusion.

III.

1. Deductive, valid.
4. Deductive, valid.
7. Inductive, weak.
10. Deductive, invalid.
13. Inductive, weak.
16. Deductive, invalid.
19. Inductive, strong.

Exercise 1.5

I.

1. All *G* are *S*.
   <u>All *Q* are *S*.</u>
   All *G* are *Q*.
   All cats are animals. (T)
   <u>All dogs are animals. (T)</u>
   All cats are dogs. (F)
4. No *U* are *P*.
   <u>Some *U* are not *F*.</u>
   Some *F* are not *P*.
   No fish are mammals. (T)
   <u>Some fish are not cats. (T)</u>
   Some cats are not mammals. (F)
7. No *P* are *H*.
   <u>No *C* are *H*.</u>
   No *P* are *C*.
   No dogs are fish. (T)
   <u>No mammals are fish. (T)</u>
   No dogs are mammals. (F)
10. Some *S* are not *O*.
    <u>Some *G* are not *O*.</u>
    Some *S* are not *G*.
    Some dogs are not fish. (T)
    <u>Some animals are not fish. (T)</u>
    Some dogs are not animals. (F)
13. Some *I* are not *E*.
    Some animals are not mammals. (T)

    <u>All *C* are *E*.</u>
    Some *C* are not *I*.
    <u>All cats are mammals. (T)</u>
    Some cats are not animals. (F)

II.

1. If *A* then *E*.
   <u>Not *A*.</u>
   Not *E*.
   If George Washington was assassinated, then George Washington is dead. (T)
   <u>George Washington was not assassinated. (T)</u>
   George Washington is not dead. (F)
4. If *E*, then either *D* or *C*.
   <u>If *D*, then *I*.</u>
   If *E*, then *I*.
   If Tom Cruise is a man, then he is either a mouse or a human. (T)
   <u>If Tom Cruise is a mouse, then he has a tail. (T)</u>
   If Tom Cruise is a man, then he has a tail. (F)
7. All *C* with *L* are either *S* or *I*.
   <u>All *C* are *I*.</u>
   All cats with fur are either mammals or dogs. (T)
   All cats are dogs. (F)
10. All *R* that are *F* are either *L* or *H*.
    <u>All *R* are *H*.</u>
    All *F* are *L*.
    All cats that are mammals are either dogs or animals. (T)
    <u>All cats are animals. (T)</u>
    All mammals are dogs. (F)

Exercise 2.1

1. Formal fallacy.
4. Informal fallacy.
7. Informal fallacy.
10. Formal fallacy.

Exercise 2.2

I.

1. Appeal to pity.
4. Accident.
7. Appeal to force.
10. *Tu quoque* (you, too).
13. Red herring.

16. *Ad hominem* circumstantial.
19. Straw man.
22. Appeal to the people, indirect variety.
25. Missing the point.

Exercise 2.3

I.

1. Hasty generalization (converse accident).
4. Slippery slope.
7. Appeal to ignorance.
10. Appeal to unqualified authority.
13. Weak analogy.

III.

1. Hasty generalization.
4. *Ad hominem* circumstantial.
7. False cause (gambler's fallacy).
10. Straw man.
13. Red herring.
16. Missing the point.
19. Weak analogy.
22. No fallacy.
25. Appeal to ignorance.
28. False cause.

Exercise 2.4

I.

1. False dichotomy.
4. Amphiboly.
7. Begging the question.
10. Equivocation.
13. Composition.
16. Suppressed evidence.
19. Division.
22. Complex question.
25. Begging the question.

III.

1. *Ad hominem* circumstantial.
4. Equivocation.
7. Begging the question.
10. Division.
13. False cause (over-simplified cause).
16. Appeal to unqualified authority.
19. Composition.
22. Weak analogy.
25. Straw man.
28. Accident.
31. Red herring.
34. Amphiboly.
37. False cause (gambler's fallacy).
40. Begging the question.
43. Missing the point or suppressed evidence.
46. Hasty generalization.
49. Composition.

Exercise 2.5

I.

1. Missing the point or begging the question.
4. Composition.
7. No fallacy? Weak analogy?
10. Appeal to unqualified authority. The statement "Only a fool..." involves an *ad hominem* abusive.
13. False cause, suppressed evidence, begging the question. There is little or no evidence of any causal connection between malpractice suits and the decision of some obstetricians to leave the field. An unmentioned factor is the inconvenience of being on call twenty-four hours per day waiting for patients to

2

deliver. There is also little or no evidence of any genuine "law-suit crisis."

16. Begging the question? (Strange argument!)
19. Slippery slope.
22. False cause? No fallacy?
25. False cause.
28. Suppressed evidence? Weak analogy? Begging the question? No fallacy? The Commerce Clause of the U.S. Constitution and pertinent federal legislation prohibit unfair trade practices between states. No equivalent regulations exist for international trade.
31. Appeal to the people (direct variety). Also appeal to pity?
34. Appeal to the people (direct variety)?
37. False dichotomy? No fallacy?
40. Appeal to unqualified authority, slippery slope.
43. Several cases of weak analogy. Also, a possible case of *ad hominem* abusive.
46. Begging the question; straw man.
49. Appeal to unqualified authority. The last paragraph suggests a hasty generalization.
52. Hasty generalization. *Ad hominem* abusive? Also, begging the question or red herring?
55. Weak analogy.
58. Weak analogy? No fallacy?

Exercise 3.1

1. *Quantifier:* some; *subject term:* executive pay packages; *copula:* are; *predicate term:* insults to ordinary workers.
4. *Quantifier:* some; *subject term:* preachers who are intolerant of others' beliefs; *copula:* are not; *predicate term:* television evangelists.
7. *Quantifier:* no; *subject term:* sex education courses that are taught competently; *copula:* are; *predicate term:* programs that are currently eroding public morals.

Exercise 3.2

I.

1. **E** proposition, universal, negative, subject and predicate terms are distributed.
4. **O** proposition, particular, negative, subject term undistributed, predicate term distributed.
7. **I** proposition, particular, affirmative, subject and predicate terms undistributed.

II.

1. No drunk drivers are threats to others on the highway.
4. Some CIA operatives are champions of human rights.

III.

1. Some owners of pit bull terriers are people who can expect expensive lawsuits.
4. No residents of Manhattan are people who can afford to live there.

IV.

1. Some oil spills are not events catastrophic to the environment.
4. All corporate lawyers are people with a social conscience.

Exercise 3.3

I.

1.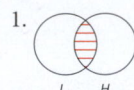

4.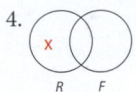

7.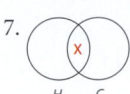

II.

1. Invalid.
4. Valid.
7. Invalid.
10. Valid.
13. Invalid.

Exercise 3.4

I.

1. No non-*B* are *A*. (true)
4. All non-*B* are *A*. (false)
7. Contraposition. (undetermined)
10. Obversion. (false)

II.

1a. All storms intensified by global warming are hurricanes. (not logically equivalent)
2a. No radically egalitarian societies are societies that preserve individual liberties. (logically equivalent)
3a. All physicians eligible to practice are physicians with valid licenses. (logically equivalent)

III.

1. Invalid (illicit conversion).
4. Invalid (illicit contraposition).
7. Valid.
10. Valid.
13. Invalid (illicit conversion).
16. Invalid (illicit contraposition).
19. Valid.

Exercise 3.5

I.

1. (a) False, (b) True, (c) False.
4. (a) Undetermined, (b) True, (c) Undetermined.
7. (a) False, (b) Undetermined, (c) Undetermined.

II.

1. Valid.
4. Invalid (existential fallacy).

7. Invalid (illicit contrary).
10. Invalid (illicit subcontrary).
13. Invalid (existential fallacy).

III.

1. Valid, unsound.
4. Valid, sound.
7. Invalid, unsound (existential fallacy).
10. Invalid, unsound (illicit subcontrary).

IV.

1. All non-*B* are *A*. (true)
4. Some non-*A* are *B*. (undetermined)
7. No non-*A* are *B*. (false)
10. Some non-*A* are not non-*B*. (true)
13. Obversion. (false)
16. Contradiction. (true)
19. Contrary. (undetermined)

V.

1. Valid.
4. Invalid (illicit contraposition).
7. Valid.
10. Invalid (illicit contrary).
13. Invalid (illicit subcontrary).

Exercise 3.6

I.

1. All banks that make too many risky loans are banks that will fail.
4. All substances identical to bromine are substances extractable from seawater.
7. No halogens are chemically inert elements.
10. All ships that fly the Jolly Roger are pirate ships.
13. All bachelors are unmarried men.
16. Some organic silicones are things used as lubricants.
19. Some giant stars are things in the Tarantula Nebula. *Or* All things identical to the Tarantula Nebula are things that contain a giant star.
22. All people who require insulin treatments are diabetics.
25. All cities identical to Berlin are cities that were the setting for the 1936 Olympic Games. *Or* All events identical to the 1936 Olympic Games are events that took place in Berlin.
28. All places there is smoke are places there is fire.
31. All ores identical to pitchblende are radioactive ores.
34. All novels written by John Grisham are novels about lawyers.
37. All times a rainbow occurs are times the sun is shining.
40. Some corporate raiders are people known for their integrity, and some corporate raiders are not people known for their integrity.
43. All people identical to me are people who like strawberries. *Or* All things identical to strawberries are things I like.
46. All places Cynthia wants to travel are places Cynthia travels.

49. No physicists are people who understand the operation of superconductors.
52. All measures that increase efficiency are measures that improve profitability.
55. Some picnics are events entirely free of ants, and some picnics are not events entirely free of ants.
58. Some contestants are people who won prizes.

II.

1. Some figure skating finalists are performers who may win medals.
4. No downhill skiers who suffer from altitude sickness are effective competitors.
7. No matadors are performers who succumb easily to fear.
10. All hungry crocodiles are dangerous animals.

III.

1. No flu vaccines are completely effective medicines. Therefore, some flu vaccines are not completely effective medicines. (valid)
4. All dates that are good dinner companions are dates that do not spend every minute texting. Therefore, all dates that do not spend every minute texting are dates that are not bad dinner companions. (invalid, illicit contrary; obvert premise, contrapose conclusion)
7. No tax cuts are measures that please everyone. Therefore, all tax cuts are measures that please everyone. (invalid, illicit contrary)
10. Some fake artworks are items sold on eBay. Therefore, some items sold on eBay are fake artworks. (valid, convert either the premise or the conclusion)

Exercise 4.1

I.

1. *Major term:* things that produce intense gravity.
   Minor term: extremely dense objects.
   Middle term: neutron stars.
   Mood, figure: **AAA**-3; invalid.
4. *Major term:* good witnesses.
   Minor term: hypnotized people.
   Middle term: people who mix fact with fantasy.
   Mood, figure: **EIO**-1; valid, Boolean.

II.

1. All *B* are *D*.
   <u>No *R* are *D*.</u>
   No *R* are *B*.
   AEE-2
   valid, Boolean
4. No *M* are *F*.
   <u>All *M* are *I*.</u>
   Some *I* are not *F*.
   EAO-3
   invalid, Boolean;
   valid, Aristotelian

4

7. All *P* are *E*.
  All *L* are *P*.
  Some *L* are *E*.
  AAI-1
  invalid
10. Some *O* are not *C*.
  All *S* are *O*.
  Some *S* are *C*.
  OAI-1
  invalid

III.

1. Some *M* are not *P*.
  All *M* are *S*.
  No *S* are *P*.
4. Some *M* are *P*.
  All *S* are *M*.
  No *S* are *P*.
7. All *M* are *P*.
  All *S* are *M*.
  All *S* are *P*.
10. Some *P* are not *M*.
  No *M* are *S*.
  All *S* are *P*.

IV.

1. No dogmatists are scholars who encourage free thinking.
  Some theologians are scholars who encourage free thinking.
  Some theologians are not dogmatists.
4. Some viruses are not things capable of replicating by themselves.
  All viruses are structures that invade cells.
  Some structures that invade cells are not things capable of replicating by themselves.

Exercise 4.2

I.

1. All *C* are *U*.
  Some *U* are *I*.
  Some *I* are *C*.
  AII-4
  invalid

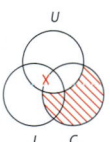

4. All *H* are *D*.
  Some *D* are not *P*.
  Some *P* are not *H*.
  AOO-4
  invalid

7. No *P* are *I*.
  All *F* are *I*.
  No *F* are *P*.
  EAE-2
  valid, Boolean

10. No *C* are *O*.
  Some *D* are not *O*.
  Some *D* are not *C*.
  EOO-2
  invalid

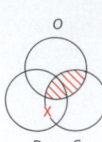

13. No *P* are *W*.
  All *D* are *P*.
  No *D* are *W*.
  EAE-1
  valid, Boolean

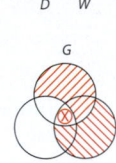

16. All *C* are *G*.
  All *G* are *E*.
  Some *E* are *C*.
  AAI-4
  invalid

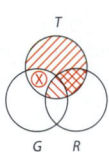

19. No *T* are *R*.
  All *T* are *G*.
  Some *G* are not *R*.
  EAO-3
  invalid, Boolean;
  valid, Aristotelian

II.

1.

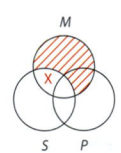

Conclusion: No S are P.

4.

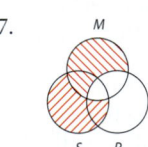

Conclusion: Some S are not P.

7.

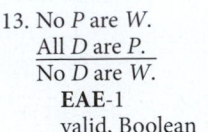

Conclusion: All S are P.

10.

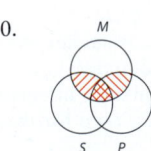

Conclusion: None.

Exercise 4.3

I.

1. All *M* are *P*.
   <u>All *M* are *S*.</u>
   All *S* are *P*.
      invalid;
      illicit minor

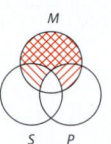

4. All *P* are *M*.
   <u>All *S* are *M*.</u>
   Some *S* are *P*.
      invalid;
      undistributed middle

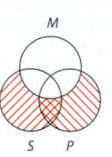

7. No *M* are *P*.
   <u>All *S* are *M*.</u>
   All *S* are *P*.
      invalid;
        drawing affirmative
        conclusion from
        negative premise

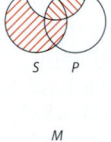

10. Some *M* are *P*.
    <u>All *M* are *S*.</u>
    Some *S* are not *P*.
       invalid;
       illicit major;
       drawing negative
       conclusion from
       affirmative premises

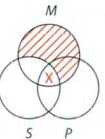

13. All *P* are *M*.
    <u>No *M* are *S*.</u>
    No *S* are *P*.
       valid, Boolean;
       no rules broken

16. No *M* are *P*.
    <u>No *S* are *M*.</u>
    No *S* are *P*.
       invalid;
       exclusive premises

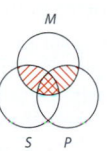

19. All *P* are *M*.
    <u>Some *S* are not *M*.</u>
    Some *S* are not *P*.
       valid, Boolean;
       no rules broken

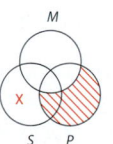

II.

1. Some *N* are *C*.
   <u>Some *C* are *O*.</u>
   Some *O* are *N*.
      invalid;
      undistributed middle

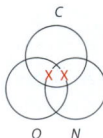

4. Some *C* are not *M*.
   <u>No *C* are *I*.</u>
   Some *I* are not *M*.
      invalid;
      exclusive premises

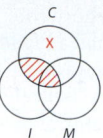

7. No *S* are *V*.
   <u>Some *W* are *V*.</u>
   Some *W* are not *S*.
      valid, Boolean;
      no rules broken

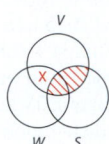

10. All *S* are *M*.
    <u>All *M* are *P*.</u>
    Some *P* are *S*.
       invalid, Boolean;
       valid, Aristotelian;
       existential fallacy,
       Boolean

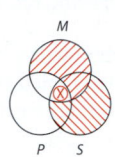

Exercise 4.4

1. Some non-*T* are *M*. (convert, obvert)
   <u>All non-*I* are non-*M*. (contrapose)</u>
   Some *I* are *T*.
   Some *M* are not *T*.
   <u>All *M* are *I*.</u>
   Some *I* are *T*.
      invalid; drawing affirmative conclusion
      from negative premise

4. Some *I* are *C*.
   <u>All *C* are non-*P*.</u>
   Some non-*I* are not *P*. (contrapose)
   Some *I* are *C*.
   <u>All *C* are non-*P*.</u>
   Some non-*P* are not *I*.
      invalid; illicit major

7. All non-*M* are non-*E*. (contrapose)
   <u>Some *P* are not *M*.</u>
   Some *P* are non-*E*. (obvert)
   All *E* are *M*.
   <u>Some *P* are not *M*.</u>
   Some *P* are not *E*.
      valid

10. Some *F* are non-*D*. (obvert)
    <u>No *D* are *V*.</u>
    Some non-*V* are *F*. (convert, obvert)
    Some *F* are not *D*.
    <u>No *D* are *V*.</u>
    Some *F* are not *V*.
       invalid; exclusive premises

Exercise 4.5

1. All scientists who theorize about the nature of time are physicists.
   <u>All people identical to Stephen Hawking are scientists who theorize about the nature of time.</u>
   All people identical to Stephen Hawking are physicists.
      valid

4. All people who wrote the Declaration of Independence are people who had a big impact on civilization.
All people identical to Thomas Jefferson are people who had a big impact on civilization.
All people identical to Thomas Jefferson are people who wrote the Declaration of Independence.
    invalid, undistributed middle

7. Some songs Shania Twain sings are country songs.
All songs Shania Twain wants to sing are songs Shania Twain sings.
Some songs Shania Twain wants to sing are country songs.
    invalid, undistributed middle

10. All TV viewers who receive scrambled signals are viewers with a decoder.
All people who receive digital satellite signals are TV viewers who receive scrambled signals.
All people who receive digital satellite signals are viewers with a decoder.
    valid

13. All diseases carried by recessive genes are diseases that can be inherited by offspring of two carriers.
All diseases identical to cystic fibrosis are diseases carried by recessive genes.
All diseases identical to cystic fibrosis are diseases that can be inherited by offspring of two carriers.
    valid

Exercise 4.6

I.

1. Premise missing: Some police chiefs fix parking tickets.
4. Conclusion missing: A few fraternities have no legitimate role in campus life.
7. Conclusion missing: Some phone calls are not from friends.
10. Premise missing: Whenever there is no military draft, antiwar protests are feeble.
13. Premise missing: No one who thinks that everything is governed by deterministic laws believes in free will.

II.

1. All people who fix parking tickets are people who undermine the evenhanded enforcement of the law.
Some police chiefs are people who fix parking tickets.
Some police chiefs are people who undermine the evenhanded enforcement of the law.
    valid

4. No groups that have dangerous initiation rites are groups that have a legitimate role in campus life.
Some fraternities are groups that have dangerous initiation rites.
Some fraternities are not groups that have a legitimate role in campus life.
    valid

7. All calls from friends are welcome calls.
Some phone calls are not welcome calls.
Some phone calls are not calls from friends.
    valid

10. All times there is no military draft are times antiwar protests are feeble.
All recent years are times there is no military draft.
All recent years are times antiwar protests are feeble.
    valid

13. No people who think that everything is governed by deterministic laws are people who believe in free will.
All mechanistic materialists are people who think everything is governed by deterministic laws.
No mechanistic materialists are people who believe in free will.
    valid

III.

1. No organizations that make alcohol readily available and acceptable are organizations that are serious about fighting alcohol abuse.
All organizations identical to the Defense Department are organizations that make alcohol readily available and acceptable.
No organizations identical to the Defense Department are organizations that are serious about fighting alcohol abuse.

4. All efforts to ban books are efforts that ensure those books will be read.
All efforts by the fundamentalist families in Church Hill, Tennessee, to remove *Macbeth*, etc. from the libraries are efforts to ban books.
All efforts by the fundamentalist families in Church Hill, Tennessee, to remove *Macbeth*, etc. from the libraries are efforts that ensure those books will be read.

7. All policies that promote more college graduates tomorrow are policies that result in higher tax revenues tomorrow.
All policies that offer financial aid to college students today are policies that promote more college graduates tomorrow.
All policies that offer financial aid to college students today are policies that result in higher tax revenues tomorrow.
    and
All policies that result in higher tax revenues tomorrow are good investments in the future.
All policies that offer financial aid to college students today are policies that result in higher tax revenues tomorrow.
All policies that offer financial aid to college students today are good investments in the future.

10. All people who act in ways that decrease their chances of survival are people who will die out through natural selection.
All smokers who continue smoking are people who act in ways that decrease their chances of survival.
All smokers who continue smoking are people who will die out through natural selection.
    and
All people who act in ways that increase their chances of survival are people who will survive through natural selection.
All smokers who quit are people who act in ways that increase their chances of survival.
All smokers who quit are people who will survive through natural selection.

V.

1. All average childless couples are couples who experience higher levels of emotional well-being.
All couples who experience higher levels of emotional well-being are happier couples.
Therefore, all average childless couples are happier couples.

Exercise 4.7

I.

1. All *A* are *B*.
   No *B* are *C*.
   Some *D* are *C*.

   Some *D* are not *A*.
      valid, no rules broken.

4. No *K* are *N*.
   Some *T* are *K*.
   All *T* are *C*.
   Some *C* are *Q*.

   Some *Q* are not *N*.
      invalid—breaks Rule 1: *C* is undistributed in both premises.

7. After contraposing the first premise, obverting the second premise and the conclusion, and rearranging the premises, we have

   No *X* are *W*.
   All *U* are *W*.
   All *V* are *U*.
   All *V* are *Y*.

   No *Y* are *X*.
      invalid—breaks Rule 2: *Y* is distributed in the conclusion but not in the premise.

10. After converting and obverting the second and fourth premises, obverting the third and fifth premises and the conclusion, and rearranging the premises, we have

    All *P* are *Q*.
    All *Q* are *R*.
    All *R* are *S*.
    No *T* are *S*.
    All *T* are *V*.

    No *V* are *P*.
       invalid—breaks Rule 2: *V* is distributed in the conclusion but not in the premise.

II.

1. All things that produce oxygen are things that support human life.
   All rain forests are things that produce oxygen.
   No things that support human life are things that should be destroyed.

   No rain forests are things that should be destroyed.
   After rearranging the premises, we have

   No *S* are *D*.
   All *O* are *S*.
   All *R* are *O*.
   No *R* are *D*.
      valid, no rules broken.

   All *O* are *S*.
   All *R* are *O*.
   No *S* are *D*.
   No *R* are *D*.

4. No brittle things are ductile things.
   All superconductors are ceramics.
   All things that can be pulled into wires are ductile things.
   All ceramics are brittle things.

   No superconductors are things that can be pulled into wires.
   After rearranging the premises, we have

   All *P* are *D*.
   No *B* are *D*.
   All *C* are *B*.
   All *S* are *C*.
   No *S* are *P*.
      valid, no rules broken.

   No *B* are *D*.
   All *S* are *C*.
   All *P* are *D*.
   All *C* are *B*.
   No *S* are *P*.

7. All people who give birth to crack babies are people who
   increase future crime rates.
   Some pregnant women are pregnant crack users.
   All people who increase future crime rates are criminals.
   No pregnant crack users are people who fail to give birth to crack babies.

   Some pregnant women are criminals.
   After obverting the fourth premise and rearranging the premises, we have
   All *I* are *C*.
   All *B* are *I*.
   All *U* are *B*.
   Some *P* are *U*.
   Some *P* are *C*.
      valid, no rules broken.

All *B* are *I*.
Some *P* are *U*.
All *I* are *C*.
No *U* are non-*B*.
Some *P* are *C*.

10. All things that promote skin cancer are things that cause death.
    All things that preserve the ozone layer are things that prevent the release of CFCs.
    No things that resist skin cancer are things that increase UV radiation.
    All things that do not preserve the ozone layer are things that increase UV radiation.
    Some packaging materials are things that release CFCs.
    No things that cause death are things that should be legal.

    Some packaging materials are things that should not be legal.
    After contraposing the second premise, converting and obverting the third
    premise, and obverting the conclusion, we have
    No *C* are *L*.
    All *S* are *C*.
    All *U* are *S*.
    All non-*O* are *U*.
    All *R* are non-*O*.
    Some *M* are *R*.
    Some *M* are not *L*.
       valid, no rules broken.

All *S* are *C*.
All *O* are non-*R*.
No non-*S* are *U*.
All non-*O* are *U*.
Some *M* are *R*.
No *C* are *L*.
Some *M* are non-*L*.

4

III.

1. No ducks are waltzers.
   No officers are non-waltzers.
   All poultry of mine are ducks.

   No poultry of mine are officers.
   After obverting the second premise and rearranging the premises, we have
   All *O* are *W*.
   No *D* are *W*.
   All *P* are *D*.
   No *P* are *O*.
      valid, no rules broken.

No *D* are *W*.
No *O* are non-*W*.
All *P* are *D*.
No *P* are *O*.

4. All hummingbirds are richly colored birds.
   No large birds are birds that live on honey.
   All birds that do not live on honey are birds that are dull in color.
   All hummingbirds are small birds.
   After contraposing the third premise, obverting the conclusion, and
   rearranging the premises, we have
   No *L* are *O*.
   All *R* are *O*.
   All *H* are *R*.
   No *H* are *L*.
      valid, no rules broken.

All *H* are *R*.
No *L* are *O*.
All non-*O* are non-*R*.
All *H* are non-*L*.

7. All books in this library that I do not recommend are books
   that are unhealthy in tone.
   All the bound books are well-written books.
   All the romances are books that are healthy in tone.
   All the unbound books are books in this library that I do not recommend.

   All the romances are well-written books.

All non-*R* are non-*H*.
All *B* are *W*.
All *O* are *H*.
All non-*B* are non-*R*.
All *O* are *W*.

After contraposing the first and fourth premises, we have

All *B* are *W*.
All *R* are *B*.
All *H* are *R*.
All *O* are *H*.
All *O* are *W*.
   valid, no rules broken.

10. All animals that belong to me are animals I trust.   All *A* are *T*.
    All dogs are animals that gnaw bones.   All *D* are *G*.
    All animals I admit to my study are animals that beg when told to do so.   All *S* are *B*.
    All the animals in the yard are animals that belong to me.   All *Y* are *A*.
    All animals I trust are animals I admit into my study.   All *T* are *S*.
    All animals that are willing to beg when told to do so are dogs.   All *B* are *D*.
    All the animals in the yard are animals that gnaw bones.   All *Y* are *G*.
    After rearranging the premises, we have

All *D* are *G*.
All *B* are *D*.
All *S* are *B*.
All *T* are *S*.
All *A* are *T*.
All *Y* are *A*.
All *Y* are *G*.
   valid, no rules broken.

Exercise 5.1

I.

1. ~*C*
4. *H* • *B*
7. *M* ≡ *P*
10. *P* ⊃ *A*
13. *M* • (*E* ∨ *D*)
16. ~*J* • ~*P*
19. ~(*F* ∨ *M*) or ~*F* • ~*M*
22. (*B* ⊃ *C*) ⊃ *R*
25. ~*R* ∨ (*M* ⊃ *P*)
28. (~*P* • ~*C*) ⊃ *M*
31. (*T* • *B*) ∨ (~*Z* • ~*K*)
34. *B* • [*N* ⊃ (*C* ∨ *J*)]
37. *M* ⊃ [*N* ⊃ (*S* • *T*)]
40. ~[(*K* ∨ *S*) • (*C* ∨ *M*)]
43. *I* ≡ *P*
46. ~[(*W* ⊃ *T*) • (*C* ⊃ *K*)]
49. [(*C* • *J*) ≡ *K*] ⊃ ~(*B* ∨ *S*)

II.

1. *R* ∨ *F*
4. ~(*H* ∨ *S*)
7. *S* ⊃ *G*
10. *A* ⊃ (~*N* ⊃ *M*)
13. (*C* • *K*) ≡ *P*
16. [(*T* • *L*) ⊃ *H*] • (*H* ⊃ *I*)
19. (*B* ⊃ *M*) • [(*M* • *I*) ⊃ (*C* • *P*)]

Exercise 5.2

I.

1. Dot.
4. Triple bar.
7. Horseshoe.
10. Wedge.

II.

1. ~ *H*
   Ⓕ T
4. *H* • ~ *N*
   T Ⓕ F T
7. *W* ⊃ *E*
   F Ⓣ F
10. *H* ⊃ (*C* ∨ *E*)
   T Ⓣ T T F
13. ~ (*E* ∨ *F*) ⊃ (*H* • *L*)
   T F F F Ⓣ T T T

III.

1. *A* • *X*
   T Ⓕ F
4. ~ *C* ∨ *Z*
   F T Ⓕ F
7. ~ *X* ⊃ *Z*
   T F Ⓕ F
10. ~ (*A* • ~ *Z*)
   Ⓕ T T T F
13. (*A* • *Y*) ∨ (~ *Z* • *C*)
   T F F Ⓣ T F T T
16. (*C* ≡ ~ *A*) ∨ (*Y* ≡ *Z*)
   T F F T Ⓣ F T F
19. ~ [~ (*X* ⊃ *C*) ≡ ~ (*B* ⊃ *Z*)]
   Ⓣ F F T T F T T F F
22. ~ [(*A* ≡ *X*) ∨ (*Z* ≡ *Y*)] ∨ [(~ *Y* ⊃ *B*) • (*Z* ⊃ *C*)]
   F T F F T F T F Ⓣ T F T T T F T T
25. (*Z* ⊃ *C*) ⊃ {[(~ *X* ⊃ *B*) ⊃ (*C* ⊃ *Y*)] ≡
   F T T Ⓣ T F T T F T F F T
   [(*Z* ⊃ *X*) ⊃ (~ *Y* ⊃ *Z*)]}
   F T F F T F F F

IV.

1. $A \lor P$
   T Ⓣ ?
4. $Q \cdot A$
   ? Ⓡ T
7. $A \supset P$
   T Ⓡ ?
10. $(P \supset A) \equiv (Q \supset B)$
    ? T T Ⓣ ? T T
13. $\sim (Q \cdot Y) \equiv \sim (Q \lor A)$
    T ? F F Ⓕ F ? T T

Exercise 5.3

I.

1. $N \supset (N \supset N)$
```
T [T] T T T
F [T] F T F
```
tautologous

4. $[(E \supset F) \supset F] \supset E$
```
T T T  T T [T] T
T F F  T F [T] T
F T T  T T [F] F
F T F  F F [T] F
```
contingent

7. $[(Z \supset X) \cdot (X \lor Z)] \supset X$
```
T T T T T T T [T] T
T F F F F T T [T] F
F T T T T T F [T] T
F T F F F F F [T] F
```
tautologous

10. $[G \supset (N \supset \sim G)] \cdot [(N \equiv G) \cdot (N \lor G)]$
```
T F T F F T [F] T T T T T T T
T T F T F T [F] F F T F F T T
F T T T T F [F] T F F F T T F
F T F T T F [F] F T F F F F F
```
self-contradictory

13. $[U \cdot (T \lor S)] \equiv [(\sim T \lor \sim U) \cdot (\sim S \lor \sim U)]$
```
T T T T T [F] F T F F T F F T F F T
T T T T F [F] F T F F T F T F T F T
T T F T T [F] F T F F T F F T F F T
T F F F F [F] F T F F T T T F T F T
F F T T T [F] F T T T F T F T T T F
F F T T F [F] F T T T F T T F T T F
F F F T T [F] F T F T T F F T T T F
F F F F F [F] F T F T T F T T T T F
```
self-contradictory

II.

1. $\sim D \lor B$ $\sim (D \cdot \sim B)$
```
F T [T] T    [T] T F F T
F T [F] F    [F] T T T F
T F [T] T    [T] F F F T
T F [T] F    [T] F F T F
```
logically equivalent

4. $R \lor \sim S$ $S \cdot \sim R$
```
T [T] F T    T [F] F T
T [T] T F    F [F] F T
F [F] F T    T [T] T F
F [T] T F    F [F] T F
```
contradictory

7. $(E \supset C) \supset L$ $E \supset (C \supset L)$
```
T T T [T] T    T [T] T T T
T T T [F] F    T [F] T F F
T F F [T] T    T [T] F T T
T F F [T] F    T [T] F T F
F T T [T] T    F [T] T T T
F T T [F] F    F [T] T F F
F T F [T] T    F [T] F T T
F T F [F] F    F [T] F T F
```
consistent

10. $W \equiv (B \cdot T)$ $W \cdot (T \supset \sim B)$
```
T [T] T T T    T [F] T F F T
T [F] T F F    T [T] F T F T
T [F] F F T    T [T] T T T F
T [F] F F F    T [T] F T T F
F [F] T T T    F [F] T F F T
F [T] T F F    F [F] F T F T
F [T] F F T    F [F] T T T F
F [T] F F F    F [F] F T T F
```
inconsistent

13. $H \cdot (K \lor J)$ $(J \cdot H) \lor (H \cdot K)$
```
T [T] T T T    T T T [T] T T T
T [T] T T F    F F T [T] T T T
T [T] F T T    T T T [T] T F F
T [F] F F F    F F T [F] T F F
F [F] T T T    T F F [F] F F T
F [F] T T F    F F F [F] F F T
F [F] F T T    T F F [F] F F F
F [F] F F F    F F F [F] F F F
```
logically equivalent

III.

1. Carlson's prediction is false (self-contradictory).
4. It is possible that both astronomers are correct. If they are, a supernova will not occur within 10 light years of the earth.
7. It is possible that both stockbrokers are correct. If they are, then Datapro will cut back its workforce. We can conclude nothing about Netmark and Compucel.
10. It is possible that Nicole's philosophy makes sense. If it does, then the mind is not identical to the brain, personal freedom exists, and humans are responsible for their actions.

Exercise 5.4

I.

1. $N \supset S$ // $\sim N \supset \sim S$
```
T T T    F T T F T
T F F    F T T T F
F Ⓣ T    T F Ⓕ F T
F T F    T F T T F
```
invalid

4. $D \supset W$ / D // W
```
T  T T   T      T
T  F F   T      F
F  T T   F      T
F  T F   F      F
```
valid

7. Invalid (fails on first line).

10. Valid.

1. Valid.
4. Valid.
7. Invalid (fails on fourth line).
10. Invalid (fails on fourth and sixth lines).
13. Valid.
16. Invalid (fails on third line).
19. Valid.

Exercise 5.5

I.

1. D = True
4. N = Unknown
7. C = True
10. J = Unknown
13. C = True, P = False
16. G = False, K = False
19. L = True
22. H = False, B = False
25. C = Unknown, R = Unknown

II.

Note: Truth values may vary depending on how the problem is done.

1. $B \supset C$ / $\sim C$ // $\sim B$
```
T T F    T F   F T
```
valid

4. $\sim (I \equiv J)$ // $\sim (I \supset J)$
```
T  T F F     F T F F
T  F F T     F F T T
```
invalid

7. $G \supset H$ / $H \supset I$ / $\sim J \supset G$ / $\sim I$ // J
```
T  T T   T T T   T F T T   T T   F
```
valid

10. $(M \lor N) \supset O$ / $O \supset (N \lor P)$ / $M \supset (\sim Q \supset N)$ / $(Q \supset M) \supset \sim P$ // $N \equiv O$
```
T T  T F         T                    T                   T            T F F
      T T   T T F T T   F T       T F F   T F T     F F T
```
invalid

13. $(A \lor B) \supset (C \bullet D)$ / $(X \lor \sim Y) \supset (\sim C \bullet \sim W)$ / $(X \lor Z) \supset (A \bullet E)$ // $\sim X$
```
T T  T F F          T T      T  T F T T F    T T   T  T T T     F T
```
valid

III.

1. $K \equiv (R \lor M)$ / $K \bullet \sim R$ / $M \supset \sim K$
```
T T  F T T    T T T F   T  T F  T
```
inconsistent

4. $(N \lor C) \equiv E$ / $N \supset \sim (C \lor H)$ / $H \supset E$ / $C \supset H$
```
 F T T  T T   F T F  T T T    T T T   T T T
                                      F T T
                                      F T F
```
consistent

7. $S \supset (R \equiv A)$ / $A \supset (W \bullet \sim R)$ / $R \equiv (W \lor T)$ / $S \bullet U$ / $U \supset T$
```
T T  T T F    F T   F F T   T T   T T    T T T    T T T
```
inconsistent

10. $A \lor Z$ / $A \supset (T \cdot F)$ / $Z \supset (M \cdot Q)$ / $Q \supset \sim F$ / $T \supset \sim M$ / $M \supset A$

T T T	(T T F F)	T T T T T	T T T F	F T F T	T T T
T T F	T T T T T	F T F F F	F T F T T T T	F	F T T
						F T F

consistent

Exercise 5.6

I.

1. MT—valid.
4. CD—valid.
7. DD—valid.
10. DA—invalid.
13. DS—valid.
16. AC—invalid.
19. Invalid.

Numbers 7 and 13 must be rewritten as follows:

7. $(E \supset N) \cdot (\sim L \supset \sim K)$
   $\sim N \lor \sim\sim K$
   ———————————
   $\sim E \lor \sim\sim L$

13. $\sim S \lor P$
    $\sim\sim S$
    ———
    P

II.

1. $B \supset G$
   $\sim G$
   ———
   $\sim B$ MT—valid

4. $W \lor \sim M$
   $\sim W$
   ———
   $\sim M$ DS—valid

7. N
   $N \supset B$
   ———
   B MP—valid

10. $(L \supset \sim A) \cdot (C \supset F)$
    $\sim L \cdot \sim C$
    ———————
    $A \cdot \sim F$ invalid

13. $(A \supset E) \cdot (P \supset \sim E)$
    $E \lor \sim E$
    ———————
    $\sim A \lor \sim P$

    rewritten:
    $(A \supset E) \cdot (P \supset \sim E)$
    $\sim E \lor \sim\sim E$
    ——————————
    $\sim A \lor \sim P$ DD—valid

16. $\sim M \supset U$
    U
    ———
    $\sim M$ AC—invalid

19. $S \supset C$
    $I \supset S$
    ———
    $I \supset C$ HS—valid

III.

1. $(S \supset M) \cdot (\sim S \supset F)$
   $S \lor \sim S$
   ———————
   $M \lor F$ CD

Since the second premise is a tautology, it is impossible to escape between the horns. The two available strategies are therefore grasping by the horns and constructing a counterdilemma. If Melinda adequately prepares for the test before the party, then she does not spend the party night studying and she does not fail the test. This would falsify the right-hand conjunct of the first premise, thus falsifying the entire premise. Here is a counterdilemma:

> If Melinda spends the night studying, she will pass the test tomorrow; and if she doesn't spend the night studying, she will go to the party. She will either spend the night studying or not studying. Therefore, she will either pass the test or go to the party.

4. $(C \supset \sim S) \cdot (E \supset S)$
   $S \lor \sim S$
   ———————
   $\sim C \lor \sim E$

   rewritten: $(C \supset \sim S) \cdot (E \supset S)$
                    $\sim\sim S \lor \sim S$
                   ———————
                   $\sim C \lor \sim E$ DD

The second premise is a tautology, so it is impossible to escape between the horns. One could grasp the dilemma by the horns by arguing that corporations could share the cost of neutralizing toxic waste, thus preserving the competitive edge. Here is a constructive counterdilemma:

> If corporations spend money to neutralize their toxic waste, then the environment will be preserved; but if corporations do not spend money to neutralize their toxic waste, then they will remain competitive. Corporations will do one or the other. Therefore, either the environment will be preserved or corporations will remain competitive.

7. $(C \supset L) \cdot (J \supset B)$
   $\sim L \lor \sim B$
   ———————
   $\sim C \lor \sim J$ DD

Here the second premise is not a tautology, so it is possible to escape between the horns. Perhaps students could take a double major in liberal arts and business. One could also grasp the dilemma by the horns by arguing that students could major in a liberal arts field where a job *would* be available upon graduation. Here is a constructive counterdilemma:

> If students major in liberal arts, then they will take courses that are interesting and rewarding; but if they major in business, then they will have a job when they graduate. Students will either major in liberal arts or business. Therefore, either they will take courses that are interesting and rewarding or they will have a job when they graduate.

10. $(P \supset R) \cdot (T \supset E)$
    $P \lor T$
    ———————
    $R \lor E$ CD

The second premise is not a tautology, so it is at least possible to escape between the horns. If we instructed counterterrorist squads to execute terrorists on the spot, we would neither prosecute them nor release them. Can you think of a way to grasp the dilemma by the horns? Here is a counterdilemma:

> If we prosecute suspected terrorists, then we discourage terrorism; but if we release them, then we avoid the risk of retaliation by other terrorists. We must either prosecute or release suspected terrorists. Therefore, either we will discourage terrorism or we will avoid the risk of retaliation by other terrorists.

5

V.

1. If human organs are given first to registered donors, then more people will register as donors. If more people register as donors, then the supply of organs will increase. Therefore, if human organs are given first to registered donors, then the supply of organs will increase. (HS)

4. If group problem solving is important, then we should not emphasize individual testing. Group problem solving is important. Therefore, we should not emphasize individual testing. (MP)

   If we should not emphasize individual testing, then the national math test is a mistake. We should not emphasize individual testing. Therefore, the national math test is a mistake. (MP)

7. If we close the library at Central Juvenile Hall, then delinquents will be deprived of an opportunity to read. If delinquents are deprived of an opportunity to read, then they will not have access to ideas, dreams, and alternative ways of living. Therefore, if we close the library at Central Juvenile Hall, then delinquents will not have access to ideas, dreams, and alternative ways of living. (HS)

   If we close the library at Central Juvenile Hall, then delinquents will not have access to ideas, dreams, and alternative ways of living. Delinquents must have access to ideas, dreams, and alternative ways of living. Therefore, we must not close the library at Central Juvenile Hall. (MT)

10. If viewing adult videos led to violent sex crimes, then there would be over a million violent sex crimes per week. It is not the case that there are over a million violent sex crimes per week. Therefore, viewing adult videos does not lead to violent sex crimes. (MT)

Exercise 6.1

I.

1. $\sim G$	1, 2, MT
4. C	1, 2, DS
7. $F \supset D$	1, 3, HS
10. $G \supset A$	1, 4, HS
13. $\sim\sim C$	1, 3, MT
16. $\sim P$	1, 2, MP
19. $\sim(S \vee C)$	1, 3, MT

II.

1. $\sim B$	
	1, 2, DS
4. $R \supset C$	
	1, 2, HS
7. Q	
	2, 3, MP
10. $\sim A$	
	1, 4, MT
13. $\sim\sim\sim S$	
	3, 4, MT
16. $\sim Z$	
	3, 4, MP
19. $H \vee G$	
	2, 4, MP

III.

(1) 1. $\sim C \supset (A \supset C)$
    2. $\sim C$ $/ \sim A$
    3. $A \supset C$ 1, 2, MP
    4. $\sim A$ 2, 3, MT
(4) 1. $P \supset (G \supset T)$
    2. $Q \supset (T \supset E)$
    3. P

---

    4. Q $/ G \supset E$
    5. $G \supset T$ 1, 3, MP
    6. $T \supset E$ 2, 4, MP
    7. $G \supset E$ 5, 6, HS

(7) 1. $\sim S \supset D$
    2. $\sim S \vee (\sim D \supset K)$
    3. $\sim D$ $/ K$
    4. $\sim\sim S$ 1, 3, MT
    5. $\sim D \supset K$ 2, 4, DS
    6. K 3, 5, MP

(10) 1. $N \supset (J \supset P)$
    2. $(J \supset P) \supset (N \supset J)$
    3. N $/ P$
    4. $J \supset P$ 1, 3, MP
    5. $N \supset J$ 2, 4, MP
    6. $N \supset P$ 4, 5, HS
    7. P 3, 6, MP

(13) 1. $R \supset (G \vee \sim A)$
    2. $(G \vee \sim A) \supset \sim S$
    3. $G \supset S$
    4. R $/ \sim A$
    5. $G \vee \sim A$ 1, 4, MP
    6. $\sim S$ 2, 5, MP
    7. $\sim G$ 3, 6, MT
    8. $\sim A$ 5, 7, DS

(16) 1. $(B \supset \sim M) \supset (T \supset \sim S)$
    2. $B \supset K$
    3. $K \supset \sim M$
    4. $\sim S \supset N$ $/ T \supset N$
    5. $B \supset \sim M$ 2, 3, HS
    6. $T \supset \sim S$ 1, 5, MP
    7. $T \supset N$ 4, 6, HS

(19) 1. $\sim G \supset [G \vee (S \supset G)]$
    2. $(S \vee L) \supset \sim G$
    3. $S \vee L$ $/ L$
    4. $\sim G$ 2, 3, MP
    5. $G \vee (S \supset G)$ 1, 4, MP
    6. $S \supset G$ 4, 5, DS
    7. $\sim S$ 4, 6, MT
    8. L 3, 7, DS

(22) 1. $(C \supset M) \supset (N \supset P)$
    2. $(C \supset N) \supset (N \supset M)$
    3. $(C \supset P) \supset \sim M$
    4. $C \supset N$ $/ \sim C$
    5. $N \supset M$ 2, 4, MP
    6. $C \supset M$ 4, 5, HS
    7. $N \supset P$ 1, 6, MP
    8. $C \supset P$ 4, 7, HS
    9. $\sim M$ 3, 8, MP
    10. $\sim C$ 6, 9, MT

(25) 1. $\sim N \supset [(B \supset D) \supset (N \vee \sim E)]$
    2. $(B \supset E) \supset \sim N$
    3. $B \supset D$
    4. $D \supset E$ $/ \sim D$
    5. $B \supset E$ 3, 4, HS
    6. $\sim N$ 2, 5, MP
    7. $(B \supset D) \supset (N \vee \sim E)$ 1, 6, MP
    8. $N \vee \sim E$ 3, 7, MP
    9. $\sim E$ 6, 8, DS
    10. $\sim D$ 4, 9, MT

6

IV.

(1)
1. $W \supset (P \vee C)$
2. $\sim P$
3. W / C
4. $P \vee C$ 1, 3, MP
5. C 2, 4, DS

(4)
1. $(R \supset L) \supset (L \supset \sim F)$
2. $\sim F \vee (R \supset L)$
3. $\sim \sim F$ / $\sim R$
4. $R \supset L$ 2, 3, DS
5. $L \supset \sim F$ 1, 4, MP
6. $\sim L$ 3, 5, MT
7. $\sim R$ 4, 6, MT

(7)
1. $H \supset (D \equiv A)$
2. $V \vee (R \supset V)$
3. $R \vee H$
4. $\sim V$ / $D \equiv A$
5. $R \supset V$ 2, 4, DS
6. $\sim R$ 4, 5, MT
7. H 3, 6, DS
8. $D \equiv A$ 1, 7, MP

(10)
1. $\sim C \supset [C \vee (J \supset D)]$
2. $C \supset (C \cdot U)$
3. $\sim (C \cdot U)$
4. $\sim D$ / $\sim J$
5. $\sim C$ 2, 3, MT
6. $C \vee (J \supset D)$ 1, 5, MP
7. $J \supset D$ 5, 6, DS
8. $\sim J$ 4, 7, MT

Exercise 6.2

I.

1. B 2
4. $H \vee F$ 1
7. $Q \vee K$ 1
10. $\sim L \vee M$ 1, 2

II.

1. G 2, Simp
      3, Add
4. $T \vee U$ 1, Add
      3, 4, MP
7. $\sim F$ 2, 3, MT
      1, 4, Conj
10. $M \cdot E$ 1, 3, Conj
      2, 4, MP

III.

(1)
1. $\sim M \supset Q$
2. $R \supset \sim T$
3. $\sim M \vee R$ / $Q \vee \sim T$
4. $(\sim M \supset Q) \cdot (R \supset \sim T)$ 1, 2, Conj
5. $Q \vee \sim T$ 3, 4, CD

(4)
1. $(H \vee \sim B) \supset R$
2. $(H \vee \sim M) \supset P$
3. H / $R \cdot P$
4. $H \vee \sim B$ 3, Add
5. R 1, 4, MP
6. $H \vee \sim M$ 3, Add
7. P 2, 6, MP
8. $R \cdot P$ 5, 7, Conj

(7)
1. $(\sim F \vee X) \supset (P \vee T)$
2. $F \supset P$
3. $\sim P$ / T
4. $\sim F$ 2, 3, MT
5. $\sim F \vee X$ 4, Add
6. $P \vee T$ 1, 5, MP
7. T 3, 6, DS

(10)
1. $(D \vee E) \supset (G \cdot H)$
2. $G \supset \sim D$
3. $D \cdot F$ / M
4. D 3, Simp
5. $D \vee E$ 4, Add
6. $G \cdot H$ 1, 5, MP
7. G 6, Simp
8. $\sim D$ 2, 7, MP
9. $D \vee M$ 4, Add
10. M 8, 9, DS

(13)
1. $(C \supset N) \cdot E$
2. $D \vee (N \supset D)$
3. $\sim D$ / $\sim C \vee P$
4. $N \supset D$ 2, 3, DS
5. $\sim N$ 3, 4, MT
6. $C \supset N$ 1, Simp
7. $\sim C$ 5, 6, MT
8. $\sim C \vee P$ 7, Add

(16)
1. $(C \vee \sim G) \supset (\sim P \cdot L)$
2. $(\sim P \cdot C) \supset (C \supset D)$
3. $C \cdot \sim R$ / $D \vee R$
4. C 3, Simp
5. $C \vee \sim G$ 4, Add
6. $\sim P \cdot L$ 1, 5, MP
7. $\sim P$ 6, Simp
8. $\sim P \cdot C$ 4, 7, Conj
9. $C \supset D$ 2, 8 MP
10. D 4, 9, MP
11. $D \vee R$ 10, Add

(19)
1. $(U \cdot \sim \sim P) \supset Q$
2. $\sim O \supset U$
3. $\sim P \supset O$
4. $\sim O \cdot T$ / Q
5. $\sim O$ 4, Simp
6. U 2, 5, MP
7. $\sim \sim P$ 3, 5, MT
8. $U \cdot \sim \sim P$ 6, 7, Conj
9. Q 1, 8, MP

(22)
1. $(\sim K \cdot \sim N) \supset [(\sim P \supset K) \cdot (\sim R \supset G)]$
2. $K \supset N$
3. $\sim N \cdot B$
4. $\sim P \vee \sim R$ / G
5. $\sim N$ 3, Simp
6. $\sim K$ 2, 5, MT
7. $\sim K \cdot \sim N$ 5, 6, Conj

6

8. $(\sim P \supset K) \cdot (\sim R \supset G)$ 1, 7, MP
9. $K \vee G$ 4, 8, CD
10. G 6, 9, DS

(25) 1. $(\sim M \cdot N) \supset [(\sim M \vee H) \supset (K \cdot L)]$
2. $\sim M \cdot (C \supset D)$
3. $\sim N \cdot (F \equiv G)$ $/\ K \cdot \sim N$
4. $\sim M$ 2, Simp
5. $\sim N$ 3, Simp
6. $\sim M \cdot \sim N$ 4, 5, Conj
7. $(\sim M \vee H) \supset (K \cdot L)$ 1, 6, MP
8. $\sim M \vee H$ 4, Add
9. $K \cdot L$ 7, 8, MP
10. K 9, Simp
11. $K \cdot \sim N$ 5, 10, Conj

(28) 1. $(D \supset B) \cdot (C \supset D)$
2. $(B \supset D) \cdot (E \supset C)$
3. $B \vee E$ $/\ D \vee B$
4. $D \vee C$ 2, 3, CD
5. $B \vee D$ 1, 4, CD
6. $B \supset D$ 2, Simp
7. $D \supset B$ 1, Simp
8. $(B \supset D) \cdot (D \supset B)$ 6, 7, Conj
9. $D \vee B$ 5, 8, CD

IV.

(1) 1. $T \supset (Q \cdot F)$
2. $T \cdot C$ $/\ Q \vee O$
3. T 2, Simp
4. $Q \cdot F$ 1, 3, MP
5. Q 4, Simp
6. $Q \vee O$ 5, Add

(4) 1. $M \vee P$
2. $(P \vee S) \supset (R \cdot D)$
3. $\sim M$ $/\ R$
4. P 1, 3, DS
5. $P \vee S$ 4, Add
6. $R \cdot D$ 2, 5, MP
7. R 6, Simp

(7) 1. $(\sim C \vee \sim M) \supset (\sim C \supset T)$
2. $C \vee \sim T$
3. $\sim C$ $/\ B$
4. $\sim C \vee \sim M$ 3, Add
5. $\sim C \supset T$ 1, 4, MP
6. T 3, 5, MP
7. $T \vee B$ 6, Add
8. $\sim T$ 2, 3, DS
9. B 7, 8, DS

(10) 1. $(V \cdot \sim E) \supset (P \supset E)$
2. $V \supset \sim E$
3. $V \cdot I$
4. $\sim E \supset (P \vee J)$ $/\ J \cdot \sim E$
5. V 3, Simp
6. $\sim E$ 2, 5, MP
7. $V \cdot \sim E$ 5, 6, Conj
8. $P \supset E$ 1, 7, MP
9. $\sim P$ 6, 8, MT
10. $P \vee J$ 4, 6, MP
11. J 9, 10, DS
12. $J \cdot \sim E$ 6, 11, Conj

Exercise 6.3

I.

1. $\sim N \cdot \sim G$ 2
4. $A \cdot S$ 3
7. $\sim G \vee \sim\sim Q$ 1
10. $\sim(R \cdot P)$ 1
13. $H \supset \sim(L \vee D)$ 2

II.

1. $C \vee K$ 1, Com
            2, 3, DS
4. $L \cdot (S \cdot F)$ 1, Assoc
            2, Simp
7. $D \cdot (M \vee N)$ 1, Dist
            2, Simp
10. $(D \vee N) \cdot (D \vee H)$ 1, Dist
            2, Simp
13. $M \vee (G \vee T)$ 1, Assoc
            2, 3, DS

III.

(1) 1. $(\sim M \supset P) \cdot (\sim N \supset Q)$
2. $\sim(M \cdot N)$ $/\ P \vee Q$
3. $\sim M \vee \sim N$ 2, DM
4. $P \vee Q$ 1, 3, CD

(4) 1. $\sim(N \cdot T)$
2. T $/\ \sim N$
3. $\sim N \vee \sim T$ 1, DM
4. $\sim T \vee \sim N$ 3, Com
5. $\sim\sim T$ 2, DN
6. $\sim N$ 4, 5, DS

(7) 1. $T \supset (B \vee E)$
2. $\sim E \cdot T$ $/\ B$
3. $T \cdot \sim E$ 2, Com
4. T 3, Simp
5. $B \vee E$ 1, 4 MP
6. $E \vee B$ 5, Com
7. $\sim E$ 2, Simp
8. B 6, 7, DS

(10) 1. $(K \cdot H) \vee (K \cdot L)$
2. $\sim L$ $/\ H$
3. $K \cdot (H \vee L)$ 1, Dist
4. $(H \vee L) \cdot K$ 3, Com
5. $H \vee L$ 4, Simp
6. $L \vee H$ 5, Com
7. H 2, 6, DS

(13) 1. $(E \cdot I) \vee (M \cdot U)$
2. $\sim E$ $/\ \sim(E \vee \sim M)$
3. $\sim E \vee \sim I$ 2, Add
4. $\sim(E \cdot I)$ 3, DM
5. $M \cdot U$ 1, 4, DS
6. M 5, Simp
7. $\sim\sim M$ 6, DN
8. $\sim E \cdot \sim\sim M$ 2, 7, Conj
9. $\sim(E \vee \sim M)$ 8, DM

(16) 1. $(Q \cdot N) \vee (N \cdot T)$
2. $(Q \vee C) \supset \sim N$ $/\ T$
3. $(N \cdot Q) \vee (N \cdot T)$ 1, Com

6

4.	$N \cdot (Q \vee T)$	3, Dist
5.	N	4, Simp
6.	$\sim\sim N$	5, DN
7.	$\sim(Q \vee C)$	2, 6, MT
8.	$\sim Q \cdot \sim C$	7, DM
9.	$\sim Q$	8, Simp
10.	$(Q \vee T) \cdot N$	4, Com
11.	$Q \vee T$	10, Simp
12.	T	9, 11, DS

(19)
1.	$[(I \vee M) \vee G] \supset \sim G$	
2.	$M \vee G$	/ M
3.	$(M \vee G) \vee I$	2, Add
4.	$I \vee (M \vee G)$	3, Com
5.	$(I \vee M) \vee G$	4, Assoc
6.	$\sim G$	1, 5, MP
7.	$G \vee M$	2, Com
8.	M	6, 7, DS

(22)
1.	$S \vee (I \cdot \sim J)$	
2.	$S \supset \sim R$	
3.	$\sim J \supset \sim Q$	/ $\sim(R \cdot Q)$
4.	$(S \vee I) \cdot (S \vee \sim J)$	1, Dist
5.	$(S \vee \sim J) \cdot (S \vee I)$	4, Com
6.	$S \vee \sim J$	5, Simp
7.	$(S \supset \sim R) \cdot (\sim J \supset \sim Q)$	2, 3, Conj
8.	$\sim R \vee \sim Q$	6, 7, CD
9.	$\sim(R \cdot Q)$	8, DM

(25)
1.	$E \vee \sim(D \vee C)$	
2.	$(E \vee \sim D) \supset C$	/ E
3.	$E \vee (\sim D \cdot \sim C)$	1, DM
4.	$(E \vee \sim D) \cdot (E \vee \sim C)$	3, Dist
5.	$E \vee \sim D$	4, Simp
6.	C	2, 5, MP
7.	$(E \vee \sim C) \cdot (E \vee \sim D)$	4, Com
8.	$E \vee \sim C$	7, Simp
9.	$\sim C \vee E$	8, Com
10.	$\sim\sim C$	6, DN
11.	E	9, 10, DS

(28)
1.	$P \vee (I \cdot L)$	
2.	$(P \vee I) \supset \sim(L \vee C)$	
3.	$(P \cdot \sim C) \supset (E \cdot F)$	/ $F \vee D$
4.	$(P \vee I) \cdot (P \vee L)$	1, Dist
5.	$P \vee I$	4, Simp
6.	$\sim(L \vee C)$	2, 5, MP
7.	$\sim L \cdot \sim C$	6, DM
8.	$\sim L$	7, Simp
9.	$(P \vee L) \cdot (P \vee I)$	4, Com
10.	$P \vee L$	9, Simp
11.	$L \vee P$	10, Com
12.	P	8, 11, DS
13.	$\sim C \cdot \sim L$	7, Com
14.	$\sim C$	13, Simp
15.	$P \cdot \sim C$	12, 14, Conj
16.	$E \cdot F$	3, 15, MP
17.	$F \cdot E$	16, Com
18.	F	17, Simp
19.	$F \vee D$	18, Add

(31)
1.	$(\sim R \vee D) \supset \sim(F \cdot G)$	
2.	$(F \cdot R) \supset S$	
3.	$F \cdot \sim S$	/ $\sim(S \vee G)$
4.	$\sim S \cdot F$	3, Com
5.	$\sim S$	4, Simp

6.	$\sim(F \cdot R)$	2, 5, MT
7.	$\sim F \vee \sim R$	6, DM
8.	F	3, Simp
9.	$\sim\sim F$	8, DN
10.	$\sim R$	7, 9, DS
11.	$\sim R \vee D$	10, Add
12.	$\sim(F \cdot G)$	1, 11, MP
13.	$\sim F \vee \sim G$	12, DM
14.	$\sim G$	9, 13, DS
15.	$\sim S \cdot \sim G$	5, 14, Conj
16.	$\sim(S \vee G)$	15, DM

(34)
1.	$(M \cdot N) \vee (O \cdot P)$	
2.	$(N \cdot O) \supset \sim P$	/ N
3.	$[(M \cdot N) \vee O] \cdot [(M \cdot N) \vee P]$	1, Dist
4.	$(M \cdot N) \vee O$	3, Simp
5.	$O \vee (M \cdot N)$	4, Com
6.	$(O \vee M) \cdot (O \vee N)$	5, Dist
7.	$(O \vee N) \cdot (O \vee M)$	6, Com
8.	$O \vee N$	7, Simp
9.	$N \vee O$	8, Com
10.	$\sim P$	2, 9, MP
11.	$[(M \cdot N) \vee P] \cdot [(M \cdot N) \vee O]$	3, Com
12.	$(M \cdot N) \vee P$	11, Simp
13.	$P \vee (M \cdot N)$	12, Com
14.	$M \cdot N$	10, 13, DS
15.	$N \cdot M$	14, Com
16.	N	15, Simp

IV.

(1)
1.	$(S \cdot D) \vee (S \cdot H)$	
2.	$S \supset (I \cdot R)$	/ $S \cdot R$
3.	$S \cdot (D \vee H)$	1, Dist
4.	S	3, Simp
5.	$I \cdot R$	2, 4, MP
6.	$R \cdot I$	5, Com
7.	R	6, Simp
8.	$S \cdot R$	4, 7, Conj

(4)
1.	$G \vee (R \cdot E)$	
2.	$(G \vee E) \supset \sim R$	/ $G \vee M$
3.	$(G \vee R) \cdot (G \vee E)$	1, Dist
4.	$(G \vee E) \cdot (G \vee R)$	3, Com
5.	$G \vee E$	4, Simp
6.	$\sim R$	2, 5, MP
7.	$G \vee R$	3, Simp
8.	$R \vee G$	7, Com
9.	G	6, 8, DS
10.	$G \vee M$	9, Add

(7)
1.	$R \supset (C \vee M)$	
2.	$\sim(I \vee C)$	
3.	$\sim(A \vee M)$	/ $\sim R$
4.	$\sim I \cdot \sim C$	2, DM
5.	$\sim A \cdot \sim M$	3, DM
6.	$\sim C \cdot \sim I$	4, Com
7.	$\sim C$	6, Simp
8.	$\sim M \cdot \sim A$	5, Com
9.	$\sim M$	8, Simp
10.	$\sim C \cdot \sim M$	7, 9, Conj
11.	$\sim(C \vee M)$	10, DM
12.	$\sim R$	1, 11, MT

6

(10) 1. $\sim E \vee (B \bullet P)$
    2. $\sim E \vee (G \bullet W)$
    3. $\sim P \vee \sim W$ / $\sim E$
    4. $(\sim E \vee B) \bullet (\sim E \vee P)$ 1, Dist
    5. $(\sim E \vee P) \bullet (\sim E \vee B)$ 4, Com
    6. $\sim E \vee P$ 5, Simp
    7. $(\sim E \vee G) \bullet (\sim E \vee W)$ 2, Dist
    8. $(\sim E \vee W) \bullet (\sim E \vee G)$ 7, Com
    9. $\sim E \vee W$ 8, Simp
   10. $(\sim E \vee P) \bullet (\sim E \vee W)$ 6, 9, Conj
   11. $\sim E \vee (P \bullet W)$ 10, Dist
   12. $(P \bullet W) \vee \sim E$ 11, Com
   13. $\sim (P \bullet W)$ 3, DM
   14. $\sim E$ 12, 13, DS

Exercise 6.4

I.

  1. $G \supset Q$ 3
  4. $B \equiv N$ 1
  7. $\sim\sim C \vee \sim F$ 1
 10. $S \supset G$ 3
 13. $W \equiv \sim T$ 2

II.

  1. $J \supset M$ 1, Impl
                    2, 3, HS
  4. $K \vee K$ 1, 2, CD
                    3, Taut
  7. $H \supset (C \supset R)$ 1, Impl
                    2, Exp
 10. $\sim H \vee \sim H$ 1, Impl
                    2, Taut
 13. $(N \supset A) \bullet (A \supset N)$ 1, Trans
                    2, Equiv

III.

 (1) 1. $(S \bullet K) \supset R$
    2. K / $S \supset R$
    3. $(K \bullet S) \supset R$ 1, Com
    4. $K \supset (S \supset R)$ 3, Exp
    5. $S \supset R$ 2, 4, MP
 (4) 1. $S \equiv Q$
    2. $\sim S$ / $\sim Q$
    3. $(S \supset Q) \bullet (Q \supset S)$ 1, Equiv
    4. $(Q \supset S) \bullet (S \supset Q)$ 3, Com
    5. $Q \supset S$ 4, Simp
    6. $\sim Q$ 2, 5, MT
 (7) 1. $(B \supset M) \bullet (D \supset M)$
    2. $B \vee D$ / M
    3. $M \vee M$ 1, 2, CD
    4. M 3, Taut
(10) 1. $(B \supset G) \bullet (F \supset N)$
    2. $\sim (G \bullet N)$ / $\sim (B \bullet F)$
    3. $\sim G \vee \sim N$ 2, DM
    4. $(\sim G \supset \sim B) \bullet (F \supset N)$ 1, Trans
    5. $(\sim G \supset \sim B) \bullet (\sim N \supset \sim F)$ 4, Trans
    6. $\sim B \vee \sim F$ 3, 5, CD
    7. $\sim (B \bullet F)$ 6, DM

(13) 1. $K \supset (B \supset \sim M)$
    2. $D \supset (K \bullet M)$ / $D \supset \sim B$
    3. $K \supset (\sim\sim M \supset \sim B)$ 1, Trans
    4. $K \supset (M \supset \sim B)$ 3, DN
    5. $(K \bullet M) \supset \sim B$ 4, Exp
    6. $D \supset \sim B$ 2, 5, HS
(16) 1. $T \supset R$
    2. $T \supset \sim R$ / $\sim T$
    3. $\sim\sim R \supset \sim T$ 2, Trans
    4. $R \supset \sim T$ 3, DN
    5. $T \supset \sim T$ 1, 4, HS
    6. $\sim T \vee \sim T$ 5, Impl
    7. $\sim T$ 6, Taut
(19) 1. $\sim R \vee P$
    2. $R \vee \sim P$ / $R \equiv P$
    3. $R \supset P$ 1, Impl
    4. $\sim P \vee R$ 2, Com
    5. $P \supset R$ 4, Impl
    6. $(R \supset P) \bullet (P \supset R)$ 3, 5, Conj
    7. $R \equiv P$ 6, Equiv
(22) 1. $S \supset (L \bullet M)$
    2. $M \supset (L \supset R)$ / $S \supset R$
    3. $(M \bullet L) \supset R$ 2, Exp
    4. $(L \bullet M) \supset R$ 3, Com
    5. $S \supset R$ 1, 4, HS
(25) 1. $T \supset G$
    2. $S \supset G$ / $(T \vee S) \supset G$
    3. $\sim T \vee G$ 1, Impl
    4. $\sim S \vee G$ 2, Impl
    5. $G \vee \sim T$ 3, Com
    6. $G \vee \sim S$ 4, Com
    7. $(G \vee \sim T) \bullet (G \vee \sim S)$ 5, 6, Conj
    8. $G \vee (\sim T \bullet \sim S)$ 7, Dist
    9. $(\sim T \bullet \sim S) \vee G$ 8, Com
   10. $\sim (T \vee S) \vee G$ 9, DM
   11. $(T \vee S) \supset G$ 10, Impl
(28) 1. $P \supset (\sim E \supset B)$
    2. $\sim (B \vee E)$ / $\sim P$
    3. $\sim (E \vee B)$ 2, Com
    4. $\sim (\sim\sim E \vee B)$ 3, DN
    5. $\sim (\sim E \supset B)$ 4, Impl
    6. $\sim P$ 1, 5, MT
(31) 1. $K \equiv R$
    2. $K \supset (R \supset P)$
    3. $\sim P$ / $\sim R$
    4. $(K \bullet R) \vee (\sim K \bullet \sim R)$ 1, Equiv
    5. $(K \bullet R) \supset P$ 2, Exp
    6. $\sim (K \bullet R)$ 3, 5, MT
    7. $\sim K \bullet \sim R$ 4, 6, DS
    8. $\sim R \bullet \sim K$ 7, Com
    9. $\sim R$ 8, Simp
(34) 1. $(F \bullet H) \supset N$
    2. $F \vee S$
    3. H / $N \vee S$
    4. $(H \bullet F) \supset N$ 1, Com
    5. $H \supset (F \supset N)$ 4, Exp
    6. $F \supset N$ 3, 5, MP
    7. $\sim N \supset \sim F$ 6, Trans
    8. $\sim\sim F \vee S$ 2, DN
    9. $\sim F \supset S$ 8, Impl
   10. $\sim N \supset S$ 7, 9, HS

6

11. $\sim\sim N \lor S$	10, Impl
12. $N \lor S$	11, DN

(37) 1. $(D \supset E) \supset (E \supset D)$

2. $(D \equiv E) \supset \sim(G \bullet \sim H)$

3. $E \bullet G$	$/ G \bullet H$
4. E	3, Simp
5. $E \lor \sim D$	4, Add
6. $\sim D \lor E$	5, Com
7. $D \supset E$	6, Impl
8. $E \supset D$	1, 7, MP
9. $(D \supset E) \bullet (E \supset D)$	7, 8, Conj
10. $D \equiv E$	9, Equiv
11. $\sim(G \bullet \sim H)$	2, 10, MP
12. $\sim G \lor \sim\sim H$	11, DM
13. $\sim G \lor H$	12, DN
14. $G \bullet E$	3, Com
15. G	14, Simp
16. $\sim\sim G$	15, DN
17. H	13, 16, DS
18. $G \bullet H$	15, 17, Conj

(40) 1. $A \equiv W$

2. $\sim A \lor \sim W$

3. $R \supset A$	$/ \sim(W \lor R)$
4. $(A \bullet W) \lor (\sim A \bullet \sim W)$	1, Equiv
5. $\sim(A \bullet W)$	2, DM
6. $\sim A \bullet \sim W$	4, 5, DS
7. $\sim A$	6, Simp
8. $\sim R$	3, 7, MT
9. $\sim W \bullet \sim A$	6, Com
10. $\sim W$	9, Simp
11. $\sim W \bullet \sim R$	8, 10, Conj
12. $\sim(W \lor R)$	11, DM

(43) 1. $O \supset (Q \bullet N)$

2. $(N \lor E) \supset S$

3. $\sim O \lor (Q \bullet N)$	$/ O \supset S$
4. $(\sim O \lor Q) \bullet (\sim O \lor N)$	1, Impl
5. $(\sim O \lor N) \bullet (\sim O \lor Q)$	3, Dist
6. $\sim O \lor N$	4, Com
7. $O \supset N$	5, Simp
8. $\sim(N \lor E) \lor S$	6, Impl
9. $(\sim N \bullet \sim E) \lor S$	2, Impl
10. $S \lor (\sim N \bullet \sim E)$	8, DM
11. $(S \lor \sim N) \bullet (S \lor \sim E)$	9, Com
12. $S \lor \sim N$	10, Dist
13. $\sim N \lor S$	11, Simp
14. $N \supset S$	12, Com
15. $O \supset S$	13, Impl
	7, 14, HS

(45) 1. $P \supset A$

2. $Q \supset B$

3. $\sim P \lor A$	$/ (P \lor Q) \supset (A \lor B)$
4. $\sim Q \lor B$	1, Impl
5. $(\sim P \lor A) \lor B$	2, Impl
6. $(\sim Q \lor B) \lor A$	3, Add
7. $\sim P \lor (A \lor B)$	4, Add
8. $(A \lor B) \lor \sim P$	5, Assoc
9. $\sim Q \lor (B \lor A)$	7, Com
10. $\sim Q \lor (A \lor B)$	6, Assoc
11. $(A \lor B) \lor \sim Q$	9, Com
12. $[(A \lor B) \lor \sim P] \bullet [(A \lor B) \lor \sim Q]$	10, Com
13. $(A \lor B) \lor (\sim P \bullet \sim Q)$	8, 11, Conj
14. $(\sim P \bullet \sim Q) \lor (A \lor B)$	12, Dist
	13, Com

15. $\sim(P \lor Q) \lor (A \lor B)$	14, DM
16. $(P \lor Q) \supset (A \lor B)$	15, Impl

IV.

(1) 1. $D \supset C$

2. $\sim(C \bullet \sim S)$	$/ D \supset S$
3. $\sim C \lor \sim\sim S$	2, DM
4. $C \supset \sim\sim S$	3, Impl
5. $C \supset S$	4, DN
6. $D \supset S$	1, 5, HS

(4) 1. $D \supset P$

2. $\sim D \lor P$	$/ (I \bullet D) \supset P$
3. $(\sim D \lor P) \lor \sim I$	1, Impl
4. $\sim I \lor (\sim D \lor P)$	2, Add
5. $(\sim I \lor \sim D) \lor P$	3, Com
6. $\sim(I \bullet D) \lor P$	4, Assoc
7. $(I \bullet D) \supset P$	5, DM
	6, Impl

(7) 1. $G \supset A$

2. $G \supset L$	$/ G \supset (A \bullet L)$
3. $\sim G \lor A$	1, Impl
4. $\sim G \lor L$	2, Impl
5. $(\sim G \lor A) \bullet (\sim G \lor L)$	3, 4, Conj
6. $\sim G \lor (A \bullet L)$	5, Dist
7. $G \supset (A \bullet L)$	6, Impl

(10) 1. $(A \bullet U) \equiv \sim R$

2. $\sim(\sim R \lor \sim A)$	$/ \sim U$
3. $[(A \bullet U) \supset \sim R] \bullet [\sim R \supset (A \bullet U)]$	1, Equiv
4. $(A \bullet U) \supset \sim R$	3, Simp
5. $\sim\sim R \bullet \sim\sim A$	2, DM
6. $\sim\sim R$	5, Simp
7. $\sim(A \bullet U)$	4, 6, MT
8. $\sim A \lor \sim U$	7, DM
9. $\sim\sim A \bullet \sim\sim R$	5, Com
10. $\sim\sim A$	9, Simp
11. $\sim U$	8, 10, DS

Exercise 6.5

I.

(1) 1. $N \supset O$

2. $N \supset P$	$/ N \supset (O \bullet P)$
3. N	ACP
4. O	1, 3, MP
5. P	2, 3, MP
6. $O \bullet P$	4, 5, Conj
7. $N \supset (O \bullet P)$	3–6, CP

(4) 1. $(G \lor H) \supset (S \bullet T)$

2. $(T \lor U) \supset (C \bullet D)$	$/ G \supset C$
3. G	ACP
4. $G \lor H$	3, Add
5. $S \bullet T$	1, 4, MP
6. $T \bullet S$	5, Com
7. T	6, Simp
8. $T \lor U$	7, Add
9. $C \bullet D$	2, 8, MP
10. C	9, Simp
11. $G \supset C$	3–10, CP

(7) 1. $M \lor (N \bullet O)$ / $\sim N \supset M$

   2. $\sim M$ ACP

   3. $N \bullet O$ 1, 2, DS

   4. N 3, Simp

  5. $\sim M \supset N$ 2–4, CP

  6. $\sim N \supset \sim\sim M$ 5, Trans

  7. $\sim N \supset M$ 6, DN

(10) 1. $C \supset (A \bullet D)$

  2. $B \supset (A \bullet E)$ / $(C \lor B) \supset A$

   3. $C \lor B$ ACP

   4. $[C \supset (A \bullet D)] \bullet [B \supset (A \bullet E)]$ 1, 2, Conj

   5. $(A \bullet D) \lor (A \bullet E)$ 3, 4, CD

   6. $A \bullet (D \lor E)$ 5, Dist

   7. A 6, Simp

  8. $(C \lor B) \supset A$ 3–7, CP

(13) 1. $R \supset B$

  2. $R \supset (B \supset F)$

  3. $B \supset (F \supset H)$ / $R \supset H$

   4. R ACP

   5. B 1, 4, MP

   6. $B \supset F$ 2, 4, MP

   7. F 5, 6, MP

   8. $F \supset H$ 3, 5, MP

   9. H 7, 8, MP

  10. $R \supset H$ 4–9, CP

(16) 1. $Q \supset (R \supset S)$

  2. $Q \supset (T \supset \sim U)$

  3. $U \supset (R \lor T)$ / $Q \supset (U \supset S)$

   4. Q ACP

   5. U ACP

   6. $R \supset S$ 1, 4, MP

   7. $T \supset \sim U$ 2, 4, MP

   8. $\sim\sim U$ 5, DN

   9. $\sim T$ 7, 8, MT

   10. $R \lor T$ 3, 5, MP

   11. $T \lor R$ 10, Com

   12. R 9, 11, DS

   13. S 6, 12, MP

   14. $U \supset S$ 5–13, CP

  15. $Q \supset (U \supset S)$ 4–14, CP

(19) 1. $P \supset [(L \lor M) \supset (N \bullet O)]$

  2. $(O \lor T) \supset W$ / $P \supset (M \supset W)$

   3. P ACP

   4. M ACP

   5. $(L \lor M) \supset (N \bullet O)$ 1, 3, MP

   6. $M \lor L$ 4, Add

   7. $L \lor M$ 6, Com

   8. $N \bullet O$ 5, 7, MP

   9. $O \bullet N$ 8, Com

   10. O 9, Simp

   11. $O \lor T$ 10, Add

   12. W 2, 11, MP

   13. $M \supset W$ 4–12, CP

  14. $P \supset (M \supset W)$ 3–13, CP

II.

(1) 1. $H \supset D$

  2. $U \supset S$ / $(H \bullet U) \supset (S \bullet D)$

   3. $H \bullet U$ ACP

   4. H 3, Simp

   5. D 1, 4, MP

   6. $U \bullet H$ 3, Com

   7. U 6, Simp

   8. S 2, 7, MP

   9. $S \bullet D$ 5, 8, Conj

  10. $(H \bullet U) \supset (S \bullet D)$ 3–9, CP

(4) 1. $J \supset D$

  2. $(J \bullet D) \supset C$

  3. $(N \bullet C) \supset I$ / $J \supset (N \supset I)$

   4. J ACP

   5. N ACP

   6. D 1, 4, MP

   7. $J \bullet D$ 4, 6, Conj

   8. C 2, 7, MP

   9. $N \bullet C$ 5, 8, Conj

   10. I 3, 9, MP

  11. $N \supset I$ 5–10, CP

  12. $J \supset (N \supset I)$ 4–11, CP

Exercise 6.6

I.

(1) 1. $(S \lor T) \supset \sim S$ / $\sim S$

   2. S AIP

   3. $S \lor T$ 2, Add

   4. $\sim S$ 1, 3, MP

   5. $S \bullet \sim S$ 2, 4, Conj

  6. $\sim S$ 2–5, IP

(4) 1. $H \supset (L \supset K)$

  2. $L \supset (K \supset \sim L)$ / $\sim H \lor \sim L$

   3. $H \bullet L$ AIP

   4. H 3, Simp

   5. $L \supset K$ 1, 4, MP

   6. $L \bullet H$ 3, Com

   7. L 6, Simp

   8. $K \supset \sim L$ 2, 7, MP

   9. K 5, 7, MP

   10. $\sim L$ 8, 9, MP

   11. $L \bullet \sim L$ 7, 10, Conj

  12. $\sim (H \bullet L)$ 3–11, IP

  13. $\sim H \lor \sim L$ 12, DM

(7) 1. $(E \lor F) \supset (C \bullet D)$

  2. $(D \lor G) \supset H$

  3. $E \lor G$ / H

   4. $\sim H$ AIP

   5. $\sim (D \lor G)$ 2, 4, MT

   6. $\sim D \bullet \sim G$ 5, DM

   7. $\sim D$ 6, Simp

   8. $\sim D \lor \sim C$ 7, Add

   9. $\sim C \lor \sim D$ 8, Com

   10. $\sim (C \bullet D)$ 9, DM

   11. $\sim (E \lor F)$ 1, 10, MT

   12. $\sim E \bullet \sim F$ 11, DM

   13. $\sim E$ 12, Simp

   14. G 3, 13, DS

   15. $\sim G \bullet \sim D$ 6, Com

6

| 16. ~G   15, Simp
| 17. G • ~G   14, 16, Conj
18. ~~H   4–17, IP
19. H   18, DN
(10) 1. K   / S ⊃ (T ⊃ S)
| 2. S   ACP
| 3. S ∨ ~T   2, Add
| 4. ~T ∨ S   3, Com
| 5. T ⊃ S   4, Impl
6. S ⊃ (T ⊃ S)   2–5, CP
(13) 1. [C ⊃ (D ⊃ C)] ⊃ E   / E
| 2. C   ACP
| 3. C ∨ ~D   2, Add
| 4. ~D ∨ C   3, Com
| 5. D ⊃ C   4, Impl
6. C ⊃ (D ⊃ C)   2–5, CP
7. E   1, 6, MP
(16) 1. (N ∨ O) ⊃ (C • D)
2. (D ∨ K) ⊃ (P ∨ ~C)
3. (P ∨ G) ⊃ ~(N • D)   / ~N
| 4. N   AIP
| 5. N ∨ O   4, Add
| 6. C • D   1, 5, MP
| 7. D • C   6, Com
| 8. D   7, Simp
| 9. D ∨ K   8, Add
| 10. P ∨ ~C   2, 9, MP
| 11. C   6, Simp
| 12. ~C ∨ P   10, Com
| 13. ~~C   11, DN
| 14. P   12, 13, DS
| 15. P ∨ G   14, Add
| 16. ~(N • D)   3, 15, MP
| 17. ~N ∨ ~D   16, DM
| 18. ~~N   4, DN
| 19. ~D   17, 18, DS
| 20. D • ~D   8, 19, Conj
21. ~N   4–20, IP
(19) 1. A ⊃ [(N ∨ ~N) ⊃ (S ∨ T)]
2. T ⊃ ~(F ∨ ~F)   / A ⊃ S
| 3. A • ~S   AIP
| 4. A   3, Simp
| 5. (N ∨ ~N) ⊃ (S ∨ T)   1, 4, MP
| | 6. N   ACP
| | 7. N ∨ N   6, Add
| | 8. N   7, Taut
| 9. N ⊃ N   6–8, CP
| 10. ~N ∨ N   9, Impl
| 11. N ∨ ~N   10, Com
| 12. S ∨ T   5, 11, MP
| 13. ~S • A   3, Com
| 14. ~S   13, Simp
| 15. T   12, 14, DS
| 16. ~(F ∨ ~F)   2, 15, MP
| 17. ~F • ~~F   16, DM
18. ~(A • ~S)   3–17, IP
19. ~A ∨ ~~S   18, DM
20. ~A ∨ S   19, DN
21. A ⊃ S   20, Impl

II.

(1) 1. (C • R) ⊃ (I • D)
2. R ⊃ ~D   / ~C ∨ ~R
| 3. C • R   AIP
| 4. I • D   1, 3, MP
| 5. D • I   4, Com
| 6. D   5, Simp
| 7. R • C   3, Com
| 8. R   7, Simp
| 9. ~D   2, 8, MP
| 10. D • ~D   6, 9, Conj
11. ~(C • R)   3–10, IP
12. ~C ∨ ~R   11, DM
(4) 1. (Z ⊃ C) ⊃ B
2. (V ∨ Z) ⊃ B   / B
| 3. ~B   AIP
| 4. ~(Z ⊃ C)   1, 3, MT
| 5. ~(~Z ∨ C)   4, Impl
| 6. ~~Z • ~C   5, DM
| 7. ~~Z   6, Simp
| 8. ~(V ⊃ Z)   2, 3, MT
| 9. ~(~V ∨ Z)   8, Impl
| 10. ~~V • ~Z   9, DM
| 11. ~Z • ~~V   10, Com
| 12. ~Z   11, Simp
| 13. ~Z • ~~Z   7, 12, Conj
14. ~~B   3–13, IP
15. B   14, DN

Exercise 6.7

(1)   / P ⊃ [(P ⊃ Q) ⊃ Q]
| 1. P   ACP
| | 2. P ⊃ Q   ACP
| | 3. Q   1, 2, MP
| 4. (P ⊃ Q) ⊃ Q   2–3, CP
5. P ⊃ [(P ⊃ Q) ⊃ Q]   1–4, CP
(4)   / (P ⊃ Q) ⊃ [(P • R) ⊃ (Q • R)]
| 1. P ⊃ Q   ACP
| | 2. P • R   ACP
| | 3. P   2, Simp
| | 4. Q   1, 3, MP
| | 5. R • P   2, Com
| | 6. R   5, Simp
| | 7. Q • R   4, 6, Conj
| 8. (P • R) ⊃ (Q • R)   2–7, CP
9. (P ⊃ Q) ⊃ [(P • R) ⊃ (Q • R)]   1–8, CP
(7)   / (P ⊃ Q) ∨ (~Q ⊃ P)
| 1. ~[(P ⊃ Q) ∨ (~Q ⊃ P)]   AIP
| 2. ~(P ⊃ Q) • ~(~Q ⊃ P)   1, DM
| 3. ~(P ⊃ Q)   2, Simp
| 4. ~(~P ∨ Q)   3, Impl
| 5. ~~P • ~Q   4, DM
| 6. P • ~Q   5, DN
| 7. P   6, Simp
| 8. ~(~Q ⊃ P) • ~(P ⊃ Q)   2, Com
| 9. ~(~Q ⊃ P)   8, Simp
| 10. ~(~~Q ∨ P)   9, Impl
| 11. ~(Q ∨ P)   10, DN

6

|12. ~Q • ~P | 11, DM
|13. ~P • ~Q | 12, Com
|14. ~P | 13, Simp
|15. P • ~P | 7, 14, Conj
16. ~~[(P ⊃ Q) ∨ (~Q ⊃ P)] | 1–15, IP
17. (P ⊃ Q) ∨ (~Q ⊃ P) | 16, DN

(10)   / [~(P • ~Q) • ~Q] ⊃ ~P
|1. ~(P • ~Q) • ~Q | ACP
|2. ~(P • ~Q) | 1, Simp
|3. ~P ∨ ~~Q | 2, DM
|4. ~P ∨ Q | 3, DN
|5. ~Q • ~(P • ~Q) | 1, Com
|6. ~Q | 5, Simp
|7. Q ∨ ~P | 4, Com
|8. ~P | 6, 7, DS
9. [~(P • ~Q) • ~Q] ⊃ ~P | 1–8, CP

(13)   / (P ⊃ Q) ⊃ [(P ⊃ ~Q) ⊃ ~P]
|1. P ⊃ Q | ACP
||2. P ⊃ ~Q | ACP
||3. ~~Q ⊃ ~P | 2, Trans
||4. Q ⊃ ~P | 3, DN
||5. P ⊃ ~P | 1, 4, HS
||6. ~P ∨ ~P | 5, Impl
||7. ~P | 6, Taut
|8. (P ⊃ ~Q) ⊃ ~P | 2–7, CP
9. (P ⊃ Q) ⊃ [(P ⊃ ~Q) ⊃ ~P] | 1–8, CP

(16)   / ~[(P ⊃ ~P) • (~P ⊃ P)]
|1. (P ⊃ ~P) • (~P ⊃ P) | AIP
|2. (~P ∨ ~P) • (~P ⊃ P) | 1, Impl
|3. ~P • (~P ⊃ P) | 2, Taut
|4. ~P • (~~P ∨ P) | 3, Impl
|5. ~P • (P ∨ P) | 4, DN
|6. ~P • P | 5, Taut
|7. P • ~P | 6, Com
8. ~[(P ⊃ ~P) • (~P ⊃ P)] | 1–7, IP

(19)   / P ≡ [P ∨ (Q • ~Q)]
|1. P | ACP
|2. P ∨ (Q • ~Q) | 1, Add
3. P ⊃ [P ∨ (Q • ~Q)] | 1–2, CP
|4. P ∨ (Q • ~Q) | ACP
||5. ~P | AIP
||6. Q • ~Q | 4, 5, DS
|7. ~~P | 5–6, IP
|8. P | 7, DN
9. [P ∨ (Q • ~Q)] ⊃ P | 4–8, CP
10. {line 3} • {line 9} | 3, 9, Conj
11. P ≡ [P ∨ (Q • ~Q)] | 10, Equiv

Exercise 7.1

1.   Ce
4.   Jr ∨ Nr
7.   (x)(Mx ⊃ Tx)
10. (∃x)(Hx • ~Rx)
13. (∃x)Tx
16. (∃x)(Sx • ~Gx)
19. (x)(Sx ⊃ Vx)
22. (x)(Cx ⊃ ~Hx)
25. (x)(Tx ⊃ Hx)
28. (x)(Hx ⊃ ~Ex)
31. (∃x)[Cx • ~(Sx ∨ Bx)]

34. (∃x)[Dx • (Bx ≡ Tx)]
37. (∃x)[Cx • (Ax ⊃ Tx)]
40. (x)[(Wx • Cx) ⊃ Rx]
43. (x)[(Vx ∨ Cx) ⊃ (Sx • Ix)]
46. (∃x)[(Fx • Rx) • Ex]
49. Gt ≡ (x)(Wx ⊃ Cx)
52. (∃x)(Ix • Mx) ⊃ Ir
55. (x)[(Bx • Mx) ⊃ Sx] ⊃ Sc
58. (∃x)(Ex • Rx) ≡ (∃x)(Mx • Ox)

Exercise 7.2

I.

(1) 1. (x)(Ax ⊃ Bx)
    2. (x)(Bx ⊃ Cx)   / (x)(Ax ⊃ Cx)
    3. Ax ⊃ Bx | 1, UI
    4. Bx ⊃ Cx | 2, UI
    5. Ax ⊃ Cx | 3, 4, HS
    6. (x)(Ax ⊃ Cx) | 5, UG
(4) 1. (x)(Ax ⊃ Bx)
    2. (y)(Ay ∨ ~By)   / (x)(Ax ≡ Bx)
    3. Ax ⊃ Bx | 1, UI
    4. Ax ∨ ~Bx | 2, UI
    5. ~Bx ∨ Ax | 4, Com
    6. Bx ⊃ Ax | 5, Impl
    7. (Ax ⊃ Bx) • (Bx ⊃ Ax) | 3, 6, Conj
    8. Ax ≡ Bx | 7, Equiv
    9. (x)(Ax ≡ Bx) | 8, UG
(7) 1. (x)[Jx ⊃ (Kx • Lx)]
    2. (∃y)~Ky   / (∃z)~Jz
    3. ~Km | 2, EI
    4. Jm ⊃ (Km • Lm) | 1, UI
    5. ~Km ∨ ~Lm | 3, Add
    6. ~(Km • Lm) | 5, DM
    7. ~Jm | 4, 6, MT
    8. (∃z)~Jz | 7, EG
(10) 1. (x)(Ax ⊃ Bx)
    2. Am ∨ An   / Bm ∨ Bn
    3. Am ⊃ Bm | 1, UI
    4. An ⊃ Bn | 1, UI
    5. (Am ⊃ Bm) • (An ⊃ Bn) | 3, 4, Conj
    6. Bm ∨ Bn | 2, 5, CD
(13) 1. (x)[(Ax • Bx) ⊃ Cx]
    2. (∃x)(Bx • ~Cx)   / (∃x)~Ax
    3. Bm • ~Cm | 2, EI
    4. (Am • Bm) ⊃ Cm | 1, UI
    5. ~Cm • Bm | 3, Com
    6. ~Cm | 5, Simp
    7. ~(Am • Bm) | 4, 6, MT
    8. ~Am ∨ ~Bm | 7, DM
    9. Bm | 3, Simp
    10. ~~Bm | 9, DN
    11. ~Bm ∨ ~Am | 8, Com
    12. ~Am | 10, 11, DS
    13. (∃x)~Ax | 12, EG
(16) 1. (∃x)Ax ⊃ (x)Bx
    2. (∃x)Cx ⊃ (∃x)Dx
    3. An • Cn   / (∃x)(Bx • Dx)
    4. An | 3, Simp
    5. (∃x)Ax | 4, EG

6.	$(x)Bx$	1, 5, MP
7.	$Cn \cdot An$	3, Com
8.	Cn	7, Simp
9.	$(\exists x)Cx$	8, EG
10.	$(\exists x)Dx$	2, 9, MP
11.	Dm	10, EI
12.	Bm	6, UI
13.	$Bm \cdot Dm$	11, 12, Conj
14.	$(\exists x)(Bx \cdot Dx)$	13, EG

(19)
1.	$(\exists x)Ax \supset (x)(Cx \supset Bx)$	
2.	$(\exists x)(Ax \lor Bx)$	
3.	$(x)(Bx \supset Ax)$	$/ (x)(Cx \supset Ax)$
4.	$Am \lor Bm$	2, EI
5.	$Bm \supset Am$	3, UI
6.	$\sim\sim Am \lor Bm$	4, DN
7.	$\sim Am \supset Bm$	6, Impl
8.	$\sim Am \supset Am$	5, 7, HS
9.	$\sim\sim Am \lor Am$	8, Impl
10.	$Am \lor Am$	9, DN
11.	Am	10, Taut
12.	$(\exists x)Ax$	11, EG
13.	$(x)(Cx \supset Bx)$	1, 12, MP
14.	$Cx \supset Bx$	13, UI
15.	$Bx \supset Ax$	3, UI
16.	$Cx \supset Ax$	14, 15, HS
17.	$(x)(Cx \supset Ax)$	16, UG

(22)
1.	$(x)(Ax \cdot \sim Bx)$	
2.	$An \supset [\sim(\exists x)Cx \supset Bc]$	
3.	$Am \supset (x)(Cx \supset Dx)$	$/ (\exists x)Dx$
4.	$An \cdot \sim Bn$	1, UI
5.	An	4, Simp
6.	$\sim(\exists x)Cx \supset Bc$	2, 5, MP
7.	$Am \cdot \sim Bm$	1, UI
8.	Am	7, Simp
9.	$(x)(Cx \supset Dx)$	3, 8, MP
10.	$Ac \cdot \sim Bc$	1, UI
11.	$\sim Bc \cdot Ac$	10, Com
12.	$\sim Bc$	11, Simp
13.	$\sim\sim(\exists x)Cx$	6, 12, MT
14.	$(\exists x)Cx$	13, DN
15.	Cs	14, EI
16.	$Cs \supset Ds$	9, UI
17.	Ds	15, 16, MP
18.	$(\exists x)Dx$	17, EG

(25)
1.	$(\exists x)Ax \supset (x)(Ax \supset Bx)$	
2.	$(\exists x)Cx \supset (x)\sim(Dx \cdot Bx)$	
3.	$(\exists x)(Ax \cdot Cx)$	$/ (\exists x)\sim Dx$
4.	$An \cdot Cn$	3, EI
5.	An	4, Simp
6.	$Cn \cdot An$	4, Com
7.	Cn	6, Simp
8.	$(\exists x)Ax$	5, EG
9.	$(\exists x)Cx$	7, EG
10.	$(x)(Ax \supset Bx)$	1, 8, MP
11.	$An \supset Bn$	10, UI
12.	Bn	5, 11, MP
13.	$(x)\sim(Dx \cdot Bx)$	2, 9, MP
14.	$\sim(Dn \cdot Bn)$	13, UI
15.	$\sim Dn \lor \sim Bn$	14, DM
16.	$\sim Bn \lor \sim Dn$	15, Com
17.	$\sim\sim Bn$	12, DN

18.	$\sim Dn$	16, 17, DS
19.	$(\exists x)\sim Dx$	18, EG

II.

(1)
1.	$(x)(Ox \supset Sx)$	
2.	$(x)(Ox \supset Fx)$	$/ (x)[Ox \supset (Sx \cdot Fx)]$
3.	$Ox \supset Sx$	1, UI
4.	$Ox \supset Fx$	2, UI
5.	$\sim Ox \lor Sx$	3, Impl
6.	$\sim Ox \lor Fx$	4, Impl
7.	$(\sim Ox \lor Sx) \cdot (\sim Ox \lor Fx)$	5, 6, Conj
8.	$\sim Ox \lor (Sx \cdot Fx)$	7, Dist
9.	$Ox \supset (Sx \cdot Fx)$	8, Impl
10.	$(x)[Ox \supset (Sx \cdot Fx)]$	9, UG

(4)
1.	$(x)(Cx \supset Vx) \cdot (x)(Px \supset Fx)$	
2.	$(\exists x)(Cx \cdot Gx) \cdot$	$/ (\exists x)(Vx \cdot Gx) \cdot$
	$(\exists x)(Px \cdot Gx)$	$(\exists x)(Fx \cdot Gx)$
3.	$(\exists x)(Cx \cdot Gx)$	2, Simp
4.	$Cm \cdot Gm$	3, EI
5.	$(\exists x)(Px \cdot Gx) \cdot (\exists x)(Cx \cdot Gx)$	2, Com
6.	$(\exists x)(Px \cdot Gx)$	5, Simp
7.	$Pn \cdot Gn$	6, EI
8.	$(x)(Cx \supset Vx)$	1, Simp
9.	$Cm \supset Vm$	8, UI
10.	Cm	4, Simp
11.	Vm	9, 10, MP
12.	$Gm \cdot Cm$	4, Com
13.	Gm	12, Simp
14.	$Vm \cdot Gm$	11, 13, Conj
15.	$(\exists x)(Vx \cdot Gx)$	14, EG
16.	$(x)(Px \supset Fx) \cdot (x)(Cx \supset Vx)$	1, Com
17.	$(x)(Px \supset Fx)$	16, Simp
18.	$Pn \supset Fn$	17, UI
19.	Pn	7, Simp
20.	Fn	18, 19, MP
21.	$Gn \cdot Pn$	7, Com
22.	Gn	21, Simp
23.	$Fn \cdot Gn$	20, 22, Conj
24.	$(\exists x)(Fx \cdot Gx)$	23, EG
25.	$(\exists x)(Vx \cdot Gx) \cdot$	15, 24, Conj
	$(\exists x)(Fx \cdot Gx)$	

(7)
1.	$(x)[Gx \supset (Ix \cdot Px)]$	
2.	$(x)[(Ix \cdot Px) \supset Rx]$	
3.	$Ga \cdot Gc$	$/ Ra \cdot Rc$
4.	$Gx \supset (Ix \cdot Px)$	1, UI
5.	$(Ix \cdot Px) \supset Rx$	2, UI
6.	$Gx \supset Rx$	4, 5, HS
7.	$(x)(Gx \supset Rx)$	6, UG
8.	$Ga \supset Ra$	7, UI
9.	Ga	3, Simp
10.	Ra	8, 9, MP
11.	$Gc \supset Rc$	7, UI
12.	$Gc \cdot Ga$	3, Com
13.	Gc	12, Simp
14.	Rc	11, 13, MP
15.	$Ra \cdot Rc$	10, 14, Conj

(10)
1.	$(x)[(Ax \cdot Kx) \supset Rx] \supset (x)(Gx \supset Sx)$	
2.	$(x)[(Ax \cdot Kx) \supset Fx] \supset (x)(Gx \supset Px)$	
3.	$(x)[(Ax \cdot Kx) \supset (Rx \cdot Fx)]$	$/ (x)[Gx \supset (Sx \cdot Px)]$

4.	$(Ax \cdot Kx) \supset (Rx \cdot Fx)$	3, UI	
5.	$\sim(Ax \cdot Kx) \vee (Rx \cdot Fx)$	4, Impl	
6.	$[\sim(Ax \cdot Kx) \vee Rx] \cdot$		
	$[\sim(Ax \cdot Kx) \vee Fx]$	5, Dist	
7.	$\sim(Ax \cdot Kx) \vee Rx$	6, Simp	
8.	$[\sim(Ax \cdot Kx) \vee Fx] \cdot$		
	$[\sim(Ax \cdot Kx) \vee Rx]$	6, Com	
9.	$\sim(Ax \cdot Kx) \vee Fx$	8, Simp	
10.	$(Ax \cdot Kx) \supset Rx$	7, Impl	
11.	$(Ax \cdot Kx) \supset Fx$	9, Impl	
12.	$(x)[(Ax \cdot Kx) \supset Rx]$	10, UG	
13.	$(x)[(Ax \cdot Kx) \supset Fx]$	11, UG	
14.	$(x)(Gx \supset Sx)$	1, 12, MP	
15.	$(x)(Gx \supset Px)$	2, 13, MP	
16.	$Gx \supset Sx$	14, UI	
17.	$Gx \supset Px$	15, UI	
18.	$\sim Gx \vee Sx$	16, Impl	
19.	$\sim Gx \vee Px$	17, Impl	
20.	$(\sim Gx \vee Sx) \cdot (\sim Gx \vee Px)$	18, 19, Conj	
21.	$\sim Gx \vee (Sx \cdot Px)$	20, Dist	
22.	$Gx \supset (Sx \cdot Px)$	21, Impl	
23.	$(x)[Gx \supset (Sx \cdot Px)]$	22, UG	

Exercise 7.3

I.

(1) 1.	$(x)Ax \supset (\exists x)Bx$		
2.	$(x)\sim Bx$	/ $(\exists x)\sim Ax$	
3.	$\sim(\exists x)Bx$	2, QN	
4.	$\sim(x)Ax$	1, 3, MT	
5.	$(\exists x)\sim Ax$	4, QN	
(4) 1.	$(\exists x)Ax \vee (\exists x)(Bx \cdot Cx)$		
2.	$\sim(\exists x)Bx$	/ $(\exists x)Ax$	
3.	$(x)\sim Bx$	2, QN	
4.	$\sim Bx$	3, UI	
5.	$\sim Bx \vee \sim Cx$	4, Add	
6.	$\sim(Bx \cdot Cx)$	5, DM	
7.	$(x)\sim(Bx \cdot Cx)$	6, UG	
8.	$\sim(\exists x)(Bx \cdot Cx)$	7, QN	
9.	$(\exists x)(Bx \cdot Cx) \vee (\exists x)Ax$	1, Com	
10.	$(\exists x)Ax$	8, 9, DS	
(7) 1.	$(x)(Ax \supset Bx)$		
2.	$\sim(x)Cx \vee (x)Ax$		
3.	$\sim(x)Bx$	/ $(\exists x)\sim Cx$	
4.	$(\exists x)\sim Bx$	3, QN	
5.	$\sim Bm$	4, EI	
6.	$Am \supset Bm$	1, UI	
7.	$\sim Am$	5, 6, MT	
8.	$(\exists x)\sim Ax$	7, EG	
9.	$\sim(x)Ax$	8, QN	
10.	$(x)Ax \vee \sim(x)Cx$	2, Com	
11.	$\sim(x)Cx$	9, 10, DS	
12.	$(\exists x)\sim Cx$	11, QN	
(10) 1.	$\sim(\exists x)(Ax \cdot \sim Bx)$		
2.	$\sim(\exists x)(Bx \cdot \sim Cx)$	/ $(x)(Ax \supset Cx)$	
3.	$(x)\sim(Ax \cdot \sim Bx)$	1, QN	
4.	$(x)\sim(Bx \cdot \sim Cx)$	2, QN	
5.	$\sim(Ax \cdot \sim Bx)$	3, UI	
6.	$\sim(Bx \cdot \sim Cx)$	4, UI	

7.	$\sim Ax \vee \sim\sim Bx$	5, DM	
8.	$\sim Ax \vee Bx$	7, DN	
9.	$\sim Bx \vee \sim\sim Cx$	6, DM	
10.	$\sim Bx \vee Cx$	9, DN	
11.	$Ax \supset Bx$	8, Impl	
12.	$Bx \supset Cx$	10, Impl	
13.	$Ax \supset Cx$	11, 12, HS	
14.	$(x)(Ax \supset Cx)$	13, UG	
(13) 1.	$(x)(Ax \cdot \sim Bx) \supset (\exists x)Cx$		
2.	$\sim(\exists x)(Cx \vee Bx)$	/ $\sim(x)Ax$	
3.	$(x)\sim(Cx \vee Bx)$	2, QN	
4.	$\sim(Cx \vee Bx)$	3, UI	
5.	$\sim Cx \cdot \sim Bx$	4, DM	
6.	$\sim Cx$	5, Simp	
7.	$(x)\sim Cx$	6, UG	
8.	$\sim(\exists x)Cx$	7, QN	
9.	$\sim(x)(Ax \cdot \sim Bx)$	1, 8, MT	
10.	$(\exists x)\sim(Ax \cdot \sim Bx)$	9, QN	
11.	$\sim(Am \cdot \sim Bm)$	10, EI	
12.	$\sim Am \vee \sim\sim Bm$	11, DM	
13.	$\sim Am \vee Bm$	12, DN	
14.	$\sim Bx \cdot \sim Cx$	5, Com	
15.	$\sim Bx$	14, Simp	
16.	$(x)\sim Bx$	15, UG	
17.	$\sim Bm$	16, UI	
18.	$Bm \vee \sim Am$	13, Com	
19.	$\sim Am$	17, 18, DS	
20.	$(\exists x)\sim Ax$	19, EG	
21.	$\sim(x)Ax$	20, QN	
(16) 1.	$(\exists x)(Ax \cdot Bx) \supset (x)(Cx \cdot Dx)$		
2.	$(x)[(Ax \vee Ex) \cdot (Bx \vee Fx)]$		
3.	$\sim(x)Dx$	/ $(x)(Ex \vee Fx)$	
4.	$(\exists x)\sim Dx$	3, QN	
5.	$\sim Dn$	4, EI	
6.	$\sim Dn \vee \sim Cn$	5, Add	
7.	$\sim Cn \vee \sim Dn$	6, Com	
8.	$\sim(Cn \cdot Dn)$	7, DM	
9.	$(\exists x)\sim(Cx \cdot Dx)$	8, EG	
10.	$\sim(x)(Cx \cdot Dx)$	9, QN	
11.	$\sim(\exists x)(Ax \cdot Bx)$	1, 10, MT	
12.	$(x)\sim(Ax \cdot Bx)$	11, QN	
13.	$\sim(Ax \cdot Bx)$	12, UI	
14	$\sim Ax \vee \sim Bx$	13, DM	
15.	$(Ax \vee Ex) \cdot (Bx \vee Fx)$	2, UI	
16.	$(\sim\sim Ax \vee Ex) \cdot (Bx \vee Fx)$	15, DN	
17.	$(\sim\sim Ax \vee Ex) \cdot (\sim\sim Bx \vee Fx)$	16, DN	
18.	$(\sim Ax \supset Ex) \cdot (\sim\sim Bx \vee Fx)$	17, Impl	
19.	$(\sim Ax \supset Ex) \cdot (\sim Bx \supset Fx)$	18, Impl	
20.	$Ex \vee Fx$	14, 19, CD	
21.	$(x)(Ex \vee Fx)$	20, UG	
(19) 1.	$(\exists x)(Ax \cdot Bx) \supset (x)(Bx \supset Cx)$		
2.	$Bn \cdot \sim Cn$	/ $\sim(x)Ax$	
3.	$(\exists x)(Bx \cdot \sim Cx)$	2, EG	
4.	$(\exists x)(\sim\sim Bx \cdot \sim Cx)$	3, DN	
5.	$(\exists x)\sim(\sim Bx \vee Cx)$	4, DM	
6.	$(\exists x)\sim(Bx \supset Cx)$	5, Impl	
7.	$\sim(x)(Bx \supset Cx)$	6, QN	
8.	$\sim(\exists x)(Ax \cdot Bx)$	1, 7, MT	
9.	$(x)\sim(Ax \cdot Bx)$	8, QN	
10.	$\sim(An \cdot Bn)$	9, UI	
11.	$\sim An \vee \sim Bn$	10, DM	

7

12. $\sim Bn \lor \sim An$	11, Com
13. Bn	2, Simp
14. $\sim\sim Bn$	13, DN
15. $\sim An$	12, 14, DS
16. $(\exists x)\sim Ax$	15, EG
17. $\sim(x)Ax$	16, QN

II.

(1)
1. $(x)[Px \supset (Hx \lor Nx)] \supset \sim(\exists x)Cx$	
2. Cf	/ $(\exists x)(Px \cdot \sim Nx)$
3. $(\exists x)Cx$	2, EG
4. $\sim\sim(\exists x)Cx$	3, DN
5. $\sim(x)[Px \supset (Hx \lor Nx)]$	1, 4, MT
6. $(\exists x)\sim[Px \supset (Hx \lor Nx)]$	5, QN
7. $\sim[Pm \supset (Hm \lor Nm)]$	6, EI
8. $\sim[\sim Pm \lor (Hm \lor Nm)]$	7, Impl
9. $\sim\sim Pm \cdot \sim(Hm \lor Nm)$	8, DM
10. $Pm \cdot \sim(Hm \lor Nm)$	9, DN
11. $Pm \cdot (\sim Hm \cdot \sim Nm)$	10, DM
12. Pm	11, Simp
13. $(Pm \cdot \sim Hm) \cdot \sim Nm$	11, Assoc
14. $\sim Nm \cdot (Pm \cdot \sim Hm)$	13, Com
15. $\sim Nm$	14, Simp
16. $Pm \cdot \sim Nm$	12, 15, Conj
17. $(\exists x)(Px \cdot \sim Nx)$	16, EG

(4)
1. $(\exists x)(Gx \cdot Px) \lor (\exists x)(Sx \cdot Ex)$	
2. $\sim(\exists x)Ex$	/ $(\exists x)Px$
3. $(x)\sim Ex$	2, QN
4. $\sim Ex$	3, UI
5. $\sim Ex \lor \sim Sx$	4, Add
6. $\sim Sx \lor \sim Ex$	5, Com
7. $\sim(Sx \cdot Ex)$	6, DM
8. $(x)\sim(Sx \cdot Ex)$	7, UG
9. $\sim(\exists x)(Sx \cdot Ex)$	8, QN
10. $(\exists x)(Sx \cdot Ex) \lor (\exists x)(Gx \cdot Px)$	1, Com
11. $(\exists x)(Gx \cdot Px)$	9, 10, DS
12. $Gm \cdot Pm$	11, EI
13. $Pm \cdot Gm$	12, Com
14. Pm	13, Simp
15. $(\exists x)Px$	14, EG

(7)
1. $(x)(Px \supset Sx) \cdot (x)(Ix \supset Gx)$	
2. $\sim(\exists x)(Sx \cdot Gx)$	/ $\sim(\exists x)(Px \cdot Ix)$
3. $(x)\sim(Sx \cdot Gx)$	2, QN
4. $\sim(Sx \cdot Gx)$	3, UI
5. $\sim Sx \lor \sim Gx$	4, DM
6. $(x)(Px \supset Sx)$	1, Simp
7. $(x)(Ix \supset Gx) \cdot (x)(Px \supset Sx)$	1, Com
8. $(x)(Ix \supset Gx)$	7, Simp
9. $Px \supset Sx$	6, UI
10. $Ix \supset Gx$	8, UI
11. $\sim Sx \supset \sim Px$	9, Trans
12. $\sim Gx \supset \sim Ix$	10, Trans
13. $(\sim Sx \supset \sim Px) \cdot (\sim Gx \supset \sim Ix)$	11, 12, Conj
14. $\sim Px \lor \sim Ix$	5, 13, CD
15. $\sim(Px \cdot Ix)$	14, DM
16. $(x)\sim(Px \cdot Ix)$	15, UG
17. $\sim(\exists x)(Px \cdot Ix)$	16, QN

(10)
1. $\sim(\exists x)[Px \cdot (Gx \lor Hx)]$	
2. $(x)[Nx \supset (Px \cdot Hx)]$	
3. $(\exists x)(Px \cdot Cx) \lor (\exists x)(Px \cdot Nx)$	/ $(\exists x)(Cx \cdot \sim Gx)$

4. $(x)\sim[Px \cdot (Gx \lor Hx)]$	1, QN
5. $\sim[Px \cdot (Gx \lor Hx)]$	4, UI
6. $\sim Px \lor \sim(Gx \lor Hx)$	5, DM
7. $\sim Px \lor (\sim Gx \cdot \sim Hx)$	6, DM
8. $(\sim Px \lor \sim Gx) \cdot (\sim Px \lor \sim Hx)$	7, Dist
9. $\sim Px \lor \sim Gx$	8, Simp
10. $(\sim Px \lor \sim Hx) \cdot (\sim Px \lor \sim Gx)$	8, Com
11. $\sim Px \lor \sim Hx$	10, Simp
12. $\sim(Px \cdot Hx)$	11, DM
13. $Nx \supset (Px \cdot Hx)$	2, UI
14. $\sim Nx$	12, 13, MT
15. $\sim Nx \lor \sim Px$	14, Add
16. $\sim Px \lor \sim Nx$	15, Com
17. $\sim(Px \cdot Nx)$	16, DM
18. $(x)\sim(Px \cdot Nx)$	17, UG
19. $\sim(\exists x)(Px \cdot Nx)$	18, QN
20. $(\exists x)(Px \cdot Nx) \lor (\exists x)(Px \cdot Cx)$	3, Com
21. $(\exists x)(Px \cdot Cx)$	19, 20, DS
22. $Pm \cdot Cm$	21, EI
23. $(x)(\sim Px \lor \sim Gx)$	9, UG
24. $\sim Pm \lor \sim Gm$	23, UI
25. Pm	22, Simp
26. $\sim\sim Pm$	25, DN
27. $\sim Gm$	24, 26, DS
28. $Cm \cdot Pm$	22, Com
29. Cm	28, Simp
30. $Cm \cdot \sim Gm$	27, 29, Conj
31. $(\exists x)(Cx \cdot \sim Gx)$	30, EG

Exercise 7.4

I.

(1)
1. $(x)(Ax \supset Bx)$	
2. $(x)(Ax \supset Cx)$	/ $(x)[Ax \supset (Bx \cdot Cx)]$
3. Ax	ACP
4. $Ax \supset Bx$	1, UI
5. $Ax \supset Cx$	2, UI
6. Bx	3, 4, MP
7. Cx	3, 5, MP
8. $Bx \cdot Cx$	6, 7, Conj
9. $Ax \supset (Bx \cdot Cx)$	3–8, CP
10. $(x)[Ax \supset (Bx \cdot Cx)]$	9, UG

(4)
1. $(x)(Ax \supset Cx)$	
2. $(\exists x)Cx \supset (\exists x)(Bx \cdot Dx)$	/ $(\exists x)Ax \supset (\exists x)Bx$
3. $(\exists x)Ax$	ACP
4. Am	3, EI
5. $Am \supset Cm$	1, UI
6. Cm	4, 5, MP
7. $(\exists x)Cx$	6, EG
8. $(\exists x)(Bx \cdot Dx)$	2, 7, MP
9. $Bn \cdot Dn$	8, EI
10. Bn	9, Simp
11. $(\exists x)Bx$	10, EG
12. $(\exists x)Ax \supset (\exists x)Bx$	3–11, CP

(7)
1. $(x)[(Ax \lor Bx) \supset Cx]$	
2. $(x)[(Cx \lor Dx) \supset Ex]$	/ $(x)(Ax \supset Ex)$
3. Ax	ACP
4. $(Ax \lor Bx) \supset Cx$	1, UI
5. $(Cx \lor Dx) \supset Ex$	2, UI
6. $Ax \lor Bx$	3, Add

7.	Cx	4, 6, MP
8.	$Cx \lor Dx$	7, Add
9.	Ex	5, 8, MP
10.	$Ax \supset Ex$	3–9, CP
11.	$(x)(Ax \supset Ex)$	10, UG

(10) 1. $(x)(Ax \supset Bx)$
    2. $Am \lor An$ / $(\exists x)Bx$

3.	$\sim(\exists x)Bx$	AIP
4.	$(x)\sim Bx$	3, QN
5.	$Am \supset Bm$	1, UI
6.	$An \supset Bn$	1, UI
7.	$(Am \supset Bm) \cdot (An \supset Bn)$	5, 6, Conj
8.	$Bm \lor Bn$	2, 7, CD
9.	$\sim Bm$	4, UI
10.	Bn	8, 9, DS
11.	$\sim Bn$	4, UI
12.	$Bn \cdot \sim Bn$	10, 11, Conj
13.	$\sim\sim(\exists x)Bx$	3–12, IP
14.	$(\exists x)Bx$	13, DN

(13) 1. $(\exists x)Ax \supset (x)(Bx \supset Cx)$
    2. $(\exists x)Dx \supset (\exists x)Bx$ / $(\exists x)(Ax \cdot Dx) \supset (\exists x)Cx$

3.	$(\exists x)(Ax \cdot Dx)$	ACP
4.	$Am \cdot Dm$	3, EI
5.	Am	4, Simp
6.	$(\exists x)Ax$	5, EG
7.	$(x)(Bx \supset Cx)$	1, 6, MP
8.	$Dm \cdot Am$	4, Com
9.	Dm	8, Simp
10.	$(\exists x)Dx$	9, EG
11.	$(\exists x)Bx$	2, 10, MP
12.	Bn	11, EI
13.	$Bn \supset Cn$	7, UI
14.	Cn	12, 13, MP
15.	$(\exists x)Cx$	14, EG
16.	$(\exists x)(Ax \cdot Dx) \supset (\exists x)Cx$	3–15, CP

(16) 1. $(x)[(Ax \lor Bx) \supset Cx]$
    2. $(\exists x)(\sim Ax \lor Dx) \supset (x)Ex$ / $(x)Cx \lor (x)Ex$

3.	$\sim[(x)Cx \lor (x)Ex]$	AIP
4.	$\sim(x)Cx \cdot \sim(x)Ex$	3, DM
5.	$\sim(x)Cx$	4, Simp
6.	$(\exists x)\sim Cx$	5, QN
7.	$\sim Cm$	6, EI
8.	$(Am \lor Bm) \supset Cm$	1, UI
9.	$\sim(Am \lor Bm)$	7, 8, MT
10.	$\sim Am \cdot \sim Bm$	9, DM
11.	$\sim Am$	10, Simp
12.	$\sim Am \lor Dm$	11, Add
13.	$(\exists x)(\sim Ax \lor Dx)$	12, EG
14.	$(x)Ex$	2, 13, MP
15.	$\sim(x)Ex \cdot \sim(x)Cx$	4, Com
16.	$\sim(x)Ex$	15, Simp
17.	$(x)Ex \cdot \sim(x)Ex$	14, 16, Conj
18.	$\sim\sim[(x)Cx \lor (x)Ex]$	3–17, IP
19.	$(x)Cx \lor (x)Ex$	18, DN

(19) 1. $(x)[Bx \supset (Cx \cdot Dx)]$ / $(x)(Ax \supset Bx) \supset (x)(Ax \supset Dx)$

2.	$(x)(Ax \supset Bx)$	ACP
3.	Ax	ACP
4.	$Ax \supset Bx$	2, UI
5.	Bx	3, 4, MP

6.	$Bx \supset (Cx \cdot Dx)$	1, UI
7.	$Cx \cdot Dx$	5, 6, MP
8.	$Dx \cdot Cx$	7, Com
9.	Dx	8, Simp
10.	$Ax \supset Dx$	3–9, CP
11.	$(x)(Ax \supset Dx)$	10, UG
12.	$(x)(Ax \supset Bx) \supset (x)(Ax \supset Dx)$	2–11, CP

(22) 1. $(x)Ax \lor (x)Bx$ / $(x)(Ax \lor Bx)$

2.	$\sim(x)(Ax \lor Bx)$	AIP
3.	$(\exists x)\sim(Ax \lor Bx)$	2, QN
4.	$(\exists x)(\sim Ax \cdot \sim Bx)$	3, DM
5.	$\sim An \cdot \sim Bn$	4, EI
6.	$\sim An$	5, Simp
7.	$(\exists x)\sim Ax$	6, EG
8.	$\sim(x)Ax$	7, QN
9.	$(x)Bx$	1, 8, DS
10.	Bn	9, UI
11.	$\sim Bn \cdot \sim An$	5, Com
12.	$\sim Bn$	11, Simp
13.	$Bn \cdot \sim Bn$	10, 12, Conj
14.	$\sim\sim(x)(Ax \lor Bx)$	2–13, IP
15.	$(x)(Ax \lor Bx)$	14, DN

(25) 1. $(\exists x)Ax \supset (x)(Bx \supset Cx)$
    2. $(\exists x)Dx \supset (x)(Ex \supset \sim Bx)$
    3. $\sim(\exists x)(Cx \cdot \sim Ex)$ / $(\exists x)(Ax \cdot Dx) \supset \sim(\exists x)Bx$

4.	$(\exists x)(Ax \cdot Dx)$	ACP
5.	$An \cdot Dn$	4, EI
6.	An	5, Simp
7.	$(\exists x)Ax$	6, EG
8.	$(x)(Bx \supset Cx)$	1, 7, MP
9.	$Dn \cdot An$	5, Com
10.	Dn	9, Simp
11.	$(\exists x)Dx$	10, EG
12.	$(x)(Ex \supset \sim Bx)$	2, 11, MP
13.	$(x)\sim(Cx \cdot \sim Ex)$	3, QN
14.	$\sim(Cx \cdot \sim Ex)$	13, UI
15.	$\sim Cx \lor \sim\sim Ex$	14, DM
16.	$\sim Cx \lor Ex$	15, DN
17.	$Cx \supset Ex$	16, Impl
18.	$Bx \supset Cx$	8, UI
19.	$Bx \supset Ex$	17, 18, HS
20.	$Ex \supset \sim Bx$	12, UI
21.	$Bx \supset \sim Bx$	19, 20, HS
22.	$\sim Bx \lor \sim Bx$	21, Impl
23.	$\sim Bx$	22, Taut
24.	$(x)\sim Bx$	23, UG
25.	$\sim(\exists x)Bx$	24, QN
26.	$(\exists x)(Ax \cdot Dx) \supset \sim(\exists x)Bx$	4–25, CP

II.

(1) 1. $(x)(Ax \supset Wx)$
    2. $(x)(Rx \supset Cx)$ / $(x)[(Rx \cdot Ax) \supset (Cx \cdot Wx)]$

3.	$Rx \cdot Ax$	ACP
4.	Rx	3, Simp
5.	$Ax \cdot Rx$	3, Com
6.	Ax	5, Simp
7.	$Ax \supset Wx$	1, UI
8.	$Rx \supset Cx$	2, UI

7

9. Cx	4, 8, MP	
10. Wx	6, 7, MP	
11. $Cx \cdot Wx$	9, 10, Conj	
12. $(Rx \cdot Ax) \supset (Cx \cdot Wx)$	3–11, CP	
13. $(x)[(Rx \cdot Ax) \supset (Cx \cdot Wx)]$	12, UG	

(4) 1. $(x)[(Sx \lor Ux) \supset (Ix \cdot Cx)]$
    2. $(x)[(Cx \lor Vx) \supset (Rx \cdot Ax)]$ / $(x)(Sx \supset Ax)$

3. Sx	ACP	
4. $Sx \lor Ux$	3, Add	
5. $(Sx \lor Ux) \supset (Ix \cdot Cx)$	1, UI	
6. $Ix \cdot Cx$	4, 5, MP	
7. $Cx \cdot Ix$	6, Com	
8. Cx	7, Simp	
9. $Cx \lor Vx$	8, Add	
10. $(Cx \lor Vx) \supset (Rx \cdot Ax)$	2, UI	
11. $Rx \cdot Ax$	9, 10, MP	
12. $Ax \cdot Rx$	11, Com	
13. Ax	12, Simp	
14. $Sx \supset Ax$	3–13, CP	
15. $(x)(Sx \supset Ax)$	14, UG	

(7) 1. $(\exists x)Cx \supset (x)[Ax \supset (Sx \cdot Dx)]$
    2. $(x)(Cx \supset {\sim}Ax) \supset (\exists x)(Dx \cdot Sx)$ / $(\exists x)(Dx \cdot Sx)$

3. ${\sim}(\exists x)(Dx \cdot Sx)$	AIP	
4. ${\sim}(x)(Cx \supset {\sim}Ax)$	2, 3, MT	
5. $(\exists x){\sim}(Cx \supset {\sim}Ax)$	4, QN	
6. ${\sim}(Cm \supset {\sim}Am)$	5, EI	
7. ${\sim}({\sim}Cm \lor {\sim}Am)$	6, Impl	
8. ${\sim}{\sim}Cm \cdot {\sim}{\sim}Am$	7, DM	
9. $Cm \cdot {\sim}{\sim}Am$	8, DN	
10. $Cm \cdot Am$	9, DN	
11. Cm	10, Simp	
12. $(\exists x)Cx$	11, EG	
13. $(x)[Ax \supset (Sx \cdot Dx)]$	1, 12, MP	
14. $Am \supset (Sm \cdot Dm)$	13, UI	
15. $Am \cdot Cm$	10, Com	
16. Am	15, Simp	
17. $Sm \cdot Dm$	14, 16, MP	
18. $Dm \cdot Sm$	17, Com	
19. $(\exists x)(Dx \cdot Sx)$	18, EG	
20. $(\exists x)(Dx \cdot Sx) \cdot$ ${\sim}(\exists x)(Dx \cdot Sx)$	3, 19, Conj	
21. ${\sim}{\sim}(\exists x)(Dx \cdot Sx)$	3–20, IP	
22. $(\exists x)(Dx \cdot Sx)$	21, DN	

(10) 1. $(\exists x)(Gx \cdot Px) \lor (\exists x)(Ax \cdot Px)$
     2. $(\exists x)Px \supset (\exists x)[Ax \cdot (Cx \cdot Dx)]$ / $(\exists x)(Dx \cdot Cx)$

3. ${\sim}(\exists x)Px$	AIP	
4. $(x){\sim}Px$	3, QN	
5. ${\sim}Px$	4, UI	
6. ${\sim}Px \lor {\sim}Gx$	5, Add	
7. ${\sim}Gx \lor {\sim}Px$	6, Com	
8. ${\sim}(Gx \cdot Px)$	7, DM	
9. $(x){\sim}(Gx \cdot Px)$	8, UG	
10. ${\sim}(\exists x)(Gx \cdot Px)$	9, QN	
11. $(\exists x)(Ax \cdot Px)$	1, 10, DS	
12. $Am \cdot Pm$	11, EI	
13. $Pm \cdot Am$	12, Com	
14. Pm	13, Simp	
15. ${\sim}Pm$	4, UI	
16. $Pm \cdot {\sim}Pm$	14, 15, Conj	
17. ${\sim}{\sim}(\exists x)Px$	3–16, IP	
18. $(\exists x)Px$	17, DN	

19. $(\exists x)[Ax \cdot (Cx \cdot Dx)]$	2, 18, MP	
20. $An \cdot (Cn \cdot Dn)$	19, EI	
21. $(Cn \cdot Dn) \cdot An$	20, Com	
22. $Cn \cdot Dn$	21, Simp	
23. $Dn \cdot Cn$	22, Com	
24. $(\exists x)(Dx \cdot Cx)$	23, EG	

Exercise 7.5

I.

1. All cats are animals.
   No cats are dogs.
   ――――――――――
   No dogs are animals.

4. Some mammals are dogs.
   Some mammals write books.
   ――――――――――
   Some mammals are dogs that write books.

7. There are flowers.
   There are dogs.
   No flowers are animals.
   ――――――――――
   Some dogs are not animals.

10. Some mammals are felines.
   Some animals are not felines.
   All mammals are animals.
   ――――――――――
   Some feline animals are not mammals.

7

Glossary/Index

A proposition: A categorical proposition having the form "All *S* are *P*," 143–144

Abelard, Peter, 6, 68

Absorption, 314n

Accident: An informal fallacy that occurs when a general rule is wrongly applied to an atypical specific case, 75–76, 113–114

Ad hominem. See Argument against the person

***Ad hominem* abusive:** A variety of the argument-against-the-person fallacy that occurs when an arguer verbally abuses a second arguer for the purpose of discrediting that person's argument, 73, 123–124

***Ad hominem* circumstantial:** A variety of the argument-against-the-person fallacy that occurs when an arguer cites circumstances that affect a second arguer, for the purpose of discrediting that person's argument, 73

Addition: A valid rule of inference: "*p // p* or *q*," 315–319, 327, 340

Adverbs, translation of, 178–179

Advice. *See* Piece of advice

Affirmative proposition/statement: A proposition/statement that asserts class membership, 143–144, 146

Affirming the consequent: An invalid argument form: "If *p* then *q* / *q* // *p*," 285–286, 289–290, 292–293

Alexander the Great, 14

"All except," "all but," 183

Ambiguity, fallacies of. *See* Fallacies of ambiguity

Ambiguous expression, 101

Ambrose, Alice, 141

Amphiboly: An informal fallacy that occurs when the conclusion of an argument depends on the misinterpretation of a statement that is ambiguous owing to some structural defect, 101, 110–111

Amyntas II, King, 14

Analogy, argument from, 34–35

Antecedent: (1) The component of a conditional statement immediately following the word "if," 21; (2) the component of a conditional statement to the left of the horseshoe, 239

Appeal to fear: A variety of appeal to the people that occurs when an arguer trumps up a fear of something and then uses that fear as a premise for some conclusion, 70

Appeal to force: An informal fallacy that occurs when an arguer threatens a reader or listener for the purpose of getting him or her to accept a conclusion, 67, 123–124

Appeal to ignorance: An informal fallacy that occurs when an arguer uses the fact that nothing has been proved about something, as evidence in support of some conclusion about that thing, 86–88

Appeal to pity: An informal fallacy that occurs when an arguer attempts to evoke pity from a reader or listener for the purpose of getting him or her to accept a conclusion, 68–69, 125

Appeal to snobbery: A variety of the appeal-to-the-people fallacy that occurs when the arguer plays on the reader's or listener's need to feel superior, 71

Appeal to the people: An informal fallacy that occurs when an arguer plays on certain psychological needs for the purpose of getting the reader or listener to accept a conclusion, 69–72, 123

Appeal to tradition: A fallacy that occurs when an arguer cites the fact that something has become a tradition as grounds for a conclusion, 71–72

Appeal to unqualified authority: An informal fallacy that occurs when an arguer cites the testimony of an unqualified authority in support of a conclusion, 85–86, 125

Appeal to vanity: A variety of the appeal-to-the-people fallacy that occurs when an arguer plays on the vanity of the reader or listener, 71

Argument: A group of statements, one or more of which (the premises) are claimed to provide support for, or reasons to believe, one of the others (the conclusion), 2; cogent, 48–50; conditional statements and, 20–23; explanation and, 19–20; form of, 55, 283–293; in science, 35–36; recognition of, 13–23; sound, 44, 49–50 strong, 44–50; valid, 41–44, 50, 54–55. *See also* Deductive argument; Inductive argument

Argument against the person: An informal fallacy that occurs when an arguer verbally attacks the person of a second arguer for the purpose of discrediting his or her argument, 72–75, 122–124

Argument based on mathematics: A deductive argument in which the conclusion depends on some purely arithmetic or geometric computation or measurement, 32

Argument based on signs: An inductive argument that proceeds from the knowledge of a sign to a claim about the thing or situation that the sign symbolizes, 34

Argument form: (1) An arrangement of words and letters such that the uniform substitution of terms or statements in place of the letters results in an argument, 55; (2) an arrangement of statement variables and operators such that the uniform substitution of statements in place of the variables results in an argument, 283–293; invalid, 55–59, 285–286, 288–290; valid, 54–55, 283–287, 290–293

Argument from analogy: An inductive argument that depends on the existence of a similarity between two things or states of affairs, 34–35

Argument from authority: An inductive argument in which the conclusion rests on a statement made by some presumed authority or witness, 34

Argument from compassion, 69

Argument from definition: A deductive argument in which the conclusion is claimed to depend merely on the definition of some word or phrase used in the premise or conclusion, 32

Argument from example: An argument that purports to prove something by giving one or more examples of it, 18–19

Argumentum ad bacculum. See Appeal to force

Argumentum ad hominem. See Argument against the person

Argumentum ad ignorantiam. See Appeal to ignorance

Argumentum ad miserecordiam. See Appeal to pity

Argumentum ad populum. See Appeal to the people

Argumentum ad verecundiam. See Appeal to unqualified authority

Aristotelian sorites, 229n

Aristotelian standpoint/interpretation (traditional standpoint), 148–150, 166, 169–170, 177, 193, 205–207, 213–214; in predicate logic, 368–369; Venn diagrams for, 205–207

Aristotle, 5–6, 14, 31, 36, 48, 65, 142, 148, 210, 244

Associativity: A valid rule of inference that allows for the relocation of parentheses in conjunctions and disjunctions, 324, 327

Avoiding fallacies, 123–127

Axiom of replacement: An axiom that states that logically equivalent expressions may replace one another in a proof sequence, 324

Babbage, Charles, 269

Bandwagon argument: A variety of the appeal-to-the-people fallacy that occurs when the arguer plays on the reader's or listener's need to feel part of a group, 71

"Barbara" syllogism, 6, 193, 204, 221

Barcan formula, 33

Barrow, Harriet, 179

"Because," 3, 20

Begging the question: An informal fallacy that occurs when the arguer creates the illusion

that inadequate premises provide adequate support for the conclusion—by leaving out a key premise, by restating the conclusion as a premise, or by reasoning in a circle, 100, 102–104, 123, 125, 127

Bentham, Jeremy, 179

Biconditional statement (biconditional): A statement having a triple bar as its main operator, 239, 242–243; relating logically equivalent statements, 263; truth-functional definition of, 253

Boethius, 6

Bolzano, Bernard, 6

Boole, George, 6, 149, 200

Boolean standpoint/interpretation (modern standpoint), 148–150, 162–163, 166, 169–170, 177, 193, 199–204, 210–213; in predicate logic, 367–369

"Both . . . not," 245

Bound variable: A variable that is bound by a quantifier, 367

Braces, 243

Brackets, 243

Bryan, William Jennings, 70

Byron, Ada, 269

Carroll, Lewis, 233

Categorical proposition: A proposition that relates two classes (or categories), 139–188; letter names of, 143–144, 146; standard form of, 140

Categorical syllogism: A syllogism in which all three statements are categorical propositions, 32–33, 189–236; exceptive propositions in, 221; figure of, 191–192; form of, 191–192; in ordinary language, 220–221; mood of, 191–192; reconstruction of, from mood and figure, 193–194; reducing the number of terms in, 216–218; rules for, 209–214; standard form of, 190–191; Venn diagrams for, 197–207

Causal inference: An inductive inference that proceeds from knowledge of a cause to a claim about an effect, or from knowledge of an effect to a claim about a cause, 34

Chrysippus, 5–6, 48

Cicero, 48

Circled X, 205–207

Circular reasoning. *See* Begging the question

Class complement, 158

Class statement, 113

Cleanthes, 48

Cogent argument: An inductive argument that is strong, has all true premises, and meets the total evidence requirement, 48–50

Collective predication: An attribute is predicated collectively when it is assigned to a class as a whole, 112–113

Commutativity: A valid rule of inference that provides for the rearrangement of conjunctions and disjunctions, 291–292, 324, 326–328

Complex question: An informal fallacy that occurs when a single question that is really *two* or more questions is asked, and a single

answer is applied to both questions, 100, 104–106, 123

Composition: An informal fallacy that occurs when the conclusion of an argument depends on the erroneous transference of an attribute from the parts of something onto the whole, 102, 111–113

Compound statement: A statement that contains at least one simple statement as a component, 238; truth values of, 250–255

Conclusion: The statement in an argument that the premises are claimed to support or imply, 2–5; tautologous, 270

Conclusion indicator: A word that provides a clue to identifying a conclusion, 3

Conditional proof: A method of proof that consists of assuming the antecedent of a required conditional statement on the first line of an indented sequence, deriving the consequent on a subsequent line, and then discharging the indented sequence in a conditional statement that exactly replicates the one to be obtained, 349–352; in predicate logic, 391–392, 394; incorrect use of, 352; indirect proof and, 357; to prove logical truths, 360–361

Conditional statement (conditional): (1) An "if . . . then" statement, 20–23; (2) a statement having a horseshoe as its main operator, 239, 241–242; comparison of with ordinary language, 256; in propositional logic, 239, 241–242, 252–253; translating into categorical propositions, 181; truth-functional definition of, 252–253. *See also* Corresponding conditional

Conditionally valid: Valid from the Aristotelian standpoint on condition that the subject term of the premise (or premises) denotes actually existing things; conditionally valid inferences, 170, conditionally valid syllogistic forms, 192–193, conditionally valid syllogisms, 206

Conjunct: The component in a conjunctive statement on either side of the main operator, 239

Conjunction: (1) A statement having a dot as its main operator, 239–240; (2) a valid rule of inference: "p / q // p and q," 315–319; comparison of with ordinary language, 255; truth-functional definition of, 251

Conjunctive statement (conjunction): A statement having a dot as its main operator, 239–240

Connectives: Symbols used to connect or negate propositions in propositional logic, 238

Consequent: (1) The component of a conditional statement immediately following the word "then"; the component of a conditional statement that is not the antecedent, 21; (2) the component of a conditional statement to the right of the horseshoe, 239

Consistent statements: Statements for which there is at least one line on their truth tables in which all of them are true, 263–264, 278–280

same truth value on each line under their main operators, 262–263; consistency and, 264

Logically false statement: A statement that is necessarily false, a self-contradictory statement, 262

Logically true statement: A statement that is necessarily true; a tautology, 262; proving, 262, 360–361

Logically undetermined truth value: A condition that exists when a certain statement is not necessarily either true or false, given the truth value of some related statement, 152–153, 157, 162–163, 167–168,

Logicians (biographies): Abelard, 68; Ambrose, 141; Aristotle, 14; Boole, 149; Byron, 269; Chrysippus, 48; De Morgan, 279; Frege, 351; Gödel, 398; Kripke, 217; Leibniz, 244; Marcus, 33; Mill, 179; Ockham, 101; Peirce, 194; Quine, 328; Russell, 387; Venn, 200; Whitehead, 387

Loosely associated statements: Statements that are about the same general subject and that lack an inferential relationship, 16

Ludwig of Bavaria, 101

McCarthy, Joseph, 70

Main operator: The operator (connective) in a compound statement that has as its scope everything else in the statement, 240, 254, 262–264

Major premise: In a categorical syllogism, the premise that contains the major term, 190–191

Major term: In a standard-form categorical syllogism, the predicate of the conclusion, 190–191

Marcus, Ruth Barcan, 33

Marcus, Jules Alexander, 33

Material equivalence: (1) The relation expressed by a truth-functional biconditional, 239, 242–243; comparison with ordinary language, 256; truth-functional definition of, 252–253; (2) a valid rule of inference that allows an equivalence statement to be replaced by a conjunctive statement or a disjunctive statement, 336–338

Material implication: (1) The relation expressed by a truth-functional conditional, 239, 241–242; comparison with ordinary language, 256; truth-functional definition of, 252–253; (2) a valid rule of inference that allows an implication sign to be replaced by a disjunction sign if and only if the antecedent is negated, 336–341

Mental carelessness, 124

Michael of Cesena, 101

Middle term: In a standard-form categorical syllogism, the term that occurs only in the premises, 190–191; of a sorites, 229–230

Milbanke, Annabella, 269

Mill, James, 179

Mill, John Stuart, 6, 179

Minor premise: In a categorical syllogism, the premise that contains the minor term, 190–191

Minor term: In a standard-form categorical syllogism, the subject of the conclusion, 190–191

Missing the point: An informal fallacy that occurs when the premise of an argument entails one particular conclusion but a completely different conclusion is actually drawn, 77–80, 123, 125, 127

Mnemonic device, for distribution, 145–146; for sufficient conditions, necessary conditions, 242

Mob mentality, 69–70

Modal logic: A kind of logic that deals with concepts such as possibility, necessity, belief, and doubt, 5, 7, 217

Modern square of opposition: A diagram that illustrates the necessary relations that prevail between the four kinds of standard-form categorical propositions as interpreted from the Boolean standpoint, 152–153

Modus ponens: A valid argument form/rule of inference: "If *p* then *q* / *p* // *q*," 33, 285, 289–293, 303–309; in predicate logic, 374–375

Modus tollens: A valid argument form/rule of inference: "If *p* then *q* / not *q* // not *p*," 285, 290–293, 303, 305–307

Mood: An attribute of a categorical syllogism that specifies the kind of statements (**A, E, I, O**) that make it up, 191–192

Moore, G. E., 387

Names, existential, 377–378

Natural deduction: A proof procedure by which the conclusion of an argument is derived from the premises through use of rules of inference, 303; in predicate logic, 374–396; in propositional logic, 302–363

Necessary and sufficient condition, 242

Necessary condition: The condition represented by the consequent in a conditional statement, 22–23, 242

Negation: A statement having a tilde as its main operator, 239–240; truth-functional definition of, 251

Negative proposition/statement: A proposition/statement that denies class membership, 143–144, 146

"Neither . . . nor," 245

Newton, Isaac, 244

"No . . . except," 181–182

Non causa pro causa, 90

Non sequitur, 64

Nonarguments, typical kinds of, 15–23

"None but," 181–182; in predicate logic, 369

"None except," 181–182

Nonstandard quantifiers, 180

Nonstandard verbs, translation of, 176–177

"Not both," 245

"Not either," 245

O proposition: A categorical proposition having the form "Some *S* are not *P*," 143–144

Obverse, 159–160, 163

Obversion: An operation that consists of changing the quality of a standard-form categorical proposition and replacing the predicate term with its term complement, 156, 158–160, 163; to reduce the number of terms in a syllogism, 217–218

Ockham, William of, 6, 101

Ockham's razor, 101

"Only," 181; in predicate logic, 369–370

"Only if," 181, 239, 241

Operators: Symbols used to connect simple propositions in propositional logic, 238–240; truth-functional definitions of, 250–253

Opinion: A kind of nonargument composed of statements that express the personal conviction of a speaker or writer without giving any evidence in support of that conviction, 16

Oversimplified cause, 90–91

Parameter: A phrase that, when introduced into a statement, affects the form but not the meaning, 177

Parentheses, 243

Particular proposition/statement: A proposition/statement that makes a claim about one or more (but not all) members of a class, 36, 143–144, 146; in predicate logic, 368–371

Peirce, Benjamin, 194

Peirce, Charles Sanders, 6–7, 149, 194

Peter of Spain, 6

Petitio principii. See Begging the question

Philip of Macedonia, 14

Philo of Magara, 48

Piece of advice: A form of expression that makes a recommendation about some future decision or course of conduct, 16

Plato, 14, 398

Pope John XXII, 101

Post, Emil, 7

Post hoc ergo propter hoc, 90

Predicate: An expression of the form "is a bird," "is a house," and "are fish," 365; distinguished from predicate term, 141

Predicate logic: A kind of logic that combines the symbolism of propositional logic with symbols used to translate predicates, 364–400

Predicate symbol: An uppercase letter used to translate a predicate, 365

Predicate term: In a standard-form categorical proposition, the term that comes immediately after the copula, 140–141

Predicate variable, 379

Predication. *See* Collective predication; Distributive predication

Prediction: An inductive argument that proceeds from knowledge of some event in the relative past to a claim about some other event in the relative future, 34–35

Premise: A statement in an argument that sets forth evidence, 2–5; exclusive, 212; inconsistent, 269–270, 317–318

Premise indicator: A word that provides a clue to identifying a premise, 3–4

Presumption, fallacies of. *See* Fallacies of presumption

Presuppositions, 125–126

A Concise Introduction to Logic, Twelfth Edition
Patrick J. Hurley

Guide to Important Rules & Argument Forms

Traditional Square of Opposition

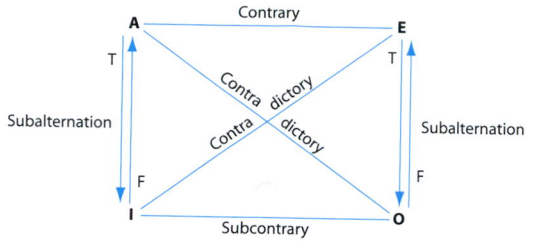

Logically Equivalent Statement Forms

Conversion	*Given statement*	*Converse*
	E: No *S* are *P.*	No *P* are *S.*
	I: Some *S* are *P.*	Some *P* are *S.*
Obversion	*Given statement*	*Obverse*
	A: All *S* are *P.*	No *S* are non-*P.*
	E: No *S* are *P.*	All *S* are non-*P.*
	I: Some *S* are *P.*	Some *S* are not non-*P.*
	O: Some *S* are not *P.*	Some *S* are non-*P.*
Contraposition	*Given statement*	*Contrapositive*
	A: All *S* are *P.*	All non-*P* are non-*S.*
	O: Some *S* are not *P.*	Some non-*P* are not non-*S.*

Valid Syllogistic Forms

Unconditionally Valid Forms

Figure 1	Figure 2	Figure 3	Figure 4
AAA	EAE	IAI	AEE
EAE	AEE	AII	IAI
AII	EIO	OAO	EIO
EIO	AOO	EIO	

Conditionally Valid Forms

Figure 1	Figure 2	Figure 3	Figure 4	Required condition
AAI	AEO		AEO	*S* exist
EAO	EAO			
		AAI	EAO	*M* exist
		EAO		
			AAI	*P* exist

Rules for Categorical Syllogisms

Rule 1:   **The middle term must be distributed at least once.**
Fallacy: Undistributed middle

Rule 2:   **If a term is distributed in the conclusion, then it must be distributed in a premise.**
Fallacy: Illicit major; illicit minor

Rule 3:   **Two negative premises are not allowed.**
Fallacy: Exclusive premises

Rule 4:   **A negative premise requires a negative conclusion, and a negative conclusion requires a negative premise.**
Fallacy: Drawing an affirmative conclusion from a negative premise; drawing a negative conclusion from affirmative premises

Rule 5:   **If both premises are universal, the conclusion cannot be particular.**
Fallacy: Existential fallacy

NOTE: If only Rule 5 is broken, the syllogism is valid from the Aristotelian standpoint if the critical term denotes actually existing things.

Rules of Implication

1. Modus ponens (MP)

$$p \supset q$$
$$\underline{p}$$
$$q$$

2. Modus tollens (MT)

$$p \supset q$$
$$\underline{\sim q}$$
$$\sim p$$

3. Pure hypothetical syllogism (HS)

$$p \supset q$$
$$\underline{q \supset r}$$
$$p \supset r$$

4. Disjunctive syllogism (DS)

$$p \vee q$$
$$\underline{\sim p}$$
$$q$$

5. Constructive dilemma (CD)

$$(p \supset q) \cdot (r \supset s)$$
$$\underline{p \vee r}$$
$$q \vee s$$

6. Simplification (Simp)

$$\underline{p \cdot q}$$
$$p$$

7. Conjunction (Conj)

$$p$$
$$\underline{q}$$
$$p \cdot q$$

8. Addition (Add)

$$\underline{p}$$
$$p \vee q$$

Rules of Replacement

9. De Morgan's rule (DM)

$\sim(p \cdot q) :: (\sim p \vee \sim q)$
$\sim(p \vee q) :: (\sim p \cdot \sim q)$

10. Commutativity (Com)

$(p \vee q) :: (q \vee p)$
$(p \cdot q) :: (q \cdot p)$

11. Associativity (Assoc)

$[p \vee (q \vee r)] :: [(p \vee q) \vee r]$
$[p \cdot (q \cdot r)] :: [(p \cdot q) \cdot r]$

12. Distribution (Dist)

$[p \cdot (q \vee r)] :: [(p \cdot q) \vee (p \cdot r)]$
$[p \vee (q \cdot r)] :: [(p \vee q) \cdot (p \vee r)]$

13. Double negation (DN)

$p :: \sim\sim p$

14. Transposition (Trans)

$(p \supset q) :: (\sim q \supset \sim p)$

15. Material implication (Impl)

$(p \supset q) :: (\sim p \vee q)$

16. Material equivalence (Equiv)

$(p \equiv q) :: [(p \supset q) \cdot (q \supset p)]$
$(p \equiv q) :: [(p \cdot q) \vee (\sim p \cdot \sim q)]$

17. Exportation (Exp)

$[(p \cdot q) \supset r] :: [p \supset (q \supset r)]$

18. Tautology (Taut)

$p :: (p \vee p)$
$p :: (p \cdot p)$

Truth Tables for the Propositional Operators

p	q	$\sim p$	$p \cdot q$	$p \vee q$	$p \supset q$	$p \equiv q$
T	T	F	T	T	T	T
T	F	F	F	T	F	F
F	T	T	F	T	T	F
F	F	T	F	F	T	T

Rules for Removing and Introducing Quantifiers

($a, b, c, \ldots u, v, w$ are individual constants; x, y, z are individual variables)

1. Universal instantiation (UI)

$$\frac{(x)\mathscr{F}x}{\mathscr{F}y} \qquad \frac{(x)\mathscr{F}x}{\mathscr{F}a}$$

2. Universal generalization (UG)

$$\frac{\mathscr{F}y}{(x)\mathscr{F}x} \quad \text{not allowed:} \quad \frac{\mathscr{F}a}{(x)\mathscr{F}x}$$

Restrictions: *(conditional and indirect proof)* (1) UG must not be used within the scope of an indented sequence if the instantial variable y is free in the first line of that sequence.

(overlapping quantifiers) (2) UG must not be used if the instantial variable y is free in any preceding line obtained by EI.

3. Existential instantiation (EI)

$$\frac{(\exists x)\mathscr{F}x}{\mathscr{F}a} \quad \text{not allowed:} \quad \frac{(\exists x)\mathscr{F}x}{\mathscr{F}y}$$

Restriction: The existential name a must be a new name that does not appear in any previous line (including the conclusion line).

4. Existential generalization (EG)

$$\frac{\mathscr{F}a}{(\exists x)\mathscr{F}x} \qquad \frac{\mathscr{F}y}{(\exists x)\mathscr{F}x}$$

Quantifier Negation Rule

$(x)\mathscr{F}x :: \sim(\exists x)\sim\mathscr{F}x$ $(\exists x)\mathscr{F}x :: \sim(x)\sim\mathscr{F}x$
$\sim(x)\mathscr{F}x :: (\exists x)\sim\mathscr{F}x$ $\sim(\exists x)\mathscr{F}x :: (x)\sim\mathscr{F}x$

Conditional Proof

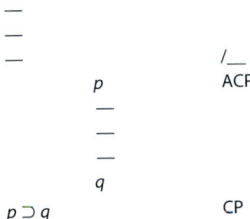

Indirect Proof

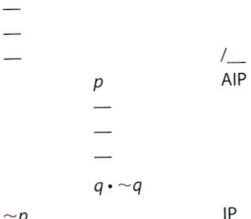

Rules for the Probability Calculus

1. $P(A \text{ or not } A) = 1$
2. $P(A \text{ and not } A) = 0$
3. $P(A \text{ and } B) = P(A) \times P(B)$ (when A and B are independent)
4. $P(A \text{ and } B) = P(A) \times P(B \text{ given } A)$
5. $P(A \text{ or } B) = P(A) + P(B)$ (when A and B are mutually exclusive)
6. $P(A \text{ or } B) = P(A) + P(B) - P(A \text{ and } B)$
7. $P(A) = 1 - P(\text{not } A)$

Identity Rules

1. Prem.
$x = x$

2. $x = y :: y = x$

3. $\mathscr{F}x$
$\underline{x = y}$
$\mathscr{F}y$